VIXENS DISTURBING VINEYARDS:

EMBARRASSMENT AND EMBRACEMENT OF SCRIPTURES

JUDAISM AND JEWISH LIFE

ACADEMIC STUDIES PRESS

VIXENS DISTURBING VINEYARDS:

EMBARRASSMENT AND EMBRACEMENT OF SCRIPTURES:

Festschrift in Honor of Harry Fox (leBeit Yoreh)

Edited by: Tzemah Yoreh, Aubrey Glazer, Justin Jaron Lewis and Miryam Segal

Boston

2010

Library of Congress Cataloging-in-Publication Data

Vixens disturbing vineyards : embarrassment and embracement of Scriptures : festschrift in honor of Harry Fox leBeit Yoreh / edited by Tzemah Yoreh ... [et al.].

p. cm. -- (Judaism and Jewish life)

Includes bibliographical references and index.

ISBN 978-1-934843-41-3 (hardback : alk. paper) 1. Bible. O.T.--Criticism, interpretation, etc., Jewish. 2. Bible. O.T.--Criticism, interpretation, etc. 3. Judaism--Relations. 4. Rabbinical literature--History and criticism. 5. Gentiles in the Old Testament. 6. Gentiles in rabbinical literature. 7. Jewish ethics. 8. Embarrassment. I. Fox, Harry, 1946- II. Yoreh, Tzemah, 1978-

BS1186.V59 2010

221.6--dc22

2010003571

ISBN 978-1-934843-41-3

Book design by Olga Grabovsky

On the cover: *The Vineyard* (detail). Acrylic on canvas. Copyright ©2004 Elyssa Wortzman

Published by Academic Studies Press in 2010

28 Montfern Avenue

Brighton, MA 02135, USA

press@academicstudiespress.com

www.academicstudiespress.com

CONTENTS

ENGLISH CONTRIBUTIONS

TALMUD AND MIDRASH

COMIC INTERLUDE

HEBREW CONTRIBUTIONS

INTRODUCTION

THE EMBARRASSMENT OF EMBARRASSMENT

Harry Fox (leBeit Yoreh), University of Toronto

Of the range of emotions studied primarily by psychologists and occasionally by psychoanalysts and philosophers, embarrassment is usually left on the backburner. It seldom makes it to the indices of entire books devoted to the subject of emotion or the titles of articles written on emotions. Insofar as it warrants mention at all it is usually subsumed under shame as the weaker cousin or synonym; in contemporary speech and writing they are often used interchangeably. As such, embarrassment is viewed as a self-designating emotion one feels when one's face becomes flushed in public situations — the moment may be as benign as an anecdote told before an audience or an introduction that is too flattering. Shame, its next of kin, would then be used to describe the feeling one has when one's face whitens because of some public disclosure of some indiscretion or another.[1] The feeling of humiliation accompanies what we consider to be our own failings and inadequacies. Only insofar as one may feel "ill-at-ease" or "disappointment" is there any overlap between the feelings of "embarrassment" in what follows and the aforementioned common uses of the word. In what follows, embarrassment is an inwardly felt emotion that is outwardly directed. It involves the embarrassment we occasionally feel about the bad behavior or actions taken by others. It is primarily distinguishable

1 See mAvot 3:11; Kallah 1:8; bBerakhot 43b; bKetubot 67b; bSotah 10b; bBaba Metzia 58b, 59a; bSanhedrin 99a, 107a; bMakkot 24a; *Otsar ha-midrashim* (Eisenstein) *Marganita devei Rav*, 356. Variant readings of the citations include whether the problem is to cause your fellow's face to whiten or redden (blush). These two reactions probably adhere to different emotions. Blushing may be a reaction to no more than mild teasing and so seems to be the weaker cousin of shame, whereas the paling of the skin may attend shameful public disclosure or very bad news.

from being ashamed of the actions of others by our accompanying notion of moral superiority. Because it is difficult for us to admit the failings of our children, our friends, our scriptures, we often are anxious not to articulate these feelings. Would we be willing to admit to our own feelings they would be compounded by shame. Insofar as embarrassment is somewhat exterior to us, whereas shame is interior, it contains a rational element. It is this rational element that also provides the bridge which links embarrassment to texts. Indeed such may be our embarrassment with texts that it provides a litmus test as to whether the text in question was/is/will be considered canonical. This is the case because texts which we deem non-canonical, and these are the vast majority of present-day creations, may simply be ignored and sent to the dung heap of history. Ignoring embarrassing texts is the first-line defense in having to deal with whatever is deemed to be their negative import; below I shall provide some examples of this even for scriptures which are already canonical. Obviously, embarrassing texts could historically have become canonical because they were not deemed to be quite so embarrassing at the time they became sacrosanct. Often the process of either ignoring or rewriting the traditional embarrassing text is a process that preceded our received text. Such a venture often allowed texts already considered sacred by a previous generation to remain in circulation and continue to be sacred for subsequent ones. Hence in the scholarly literature one may, for example, on occasion see the word "embarrassment" used in reference to Aristotle's notion of natural slavery. Aristotle's texts, as part of the Western canon, yield such reactions of embarrassment because one asks how someone so wise could ever have held such a view. Yet Aristotle did hold such a view and could have held it because the paradigm shift toward universal notions of human dignity and human rights had not yet occurred. And even after they already existed, a further paradigm shift was required to consider women as a group enfranchised by such ideas. In their turn gender, color, race, sexual orientation, religion, class and more have been used as exclusionary categories to notions of universal rights and dignity. Hence one of the areas in which public apologetics occur in reference to the Hebrew Bible on the part of pulpit rabbis is the treatment of slaves. The standard direction of such feeble attempts is to compare to the condition of workers today, their freedom minimized by descriptive qualifiers such as "as if," "sweatshops," "assembly line," "minimum wages," and others which gloss over the critical differences.

I will now turn briefly to three further examples found in scriptures. One of the most hotly debated and discussed examples in recent times involves the environmentalist debate centering around Genesis 1:28, the verse seen as responsible for creating a Judeo-Christian myth of human dominion over the rest of the universe, including a god-sanctioned right to exploit all natural resources and populate the entire world. As these are considered the primary reasons for the present environmental crises, Christianity and more particularly Judaism have borne the brunt and the sting of such criticism. Those embarrassed and burdened by this verse and the unrelenting critique it unleashes have felt compelled to rise up in defense of Christianity and Judaism, usually by claiming a "misunderstanding," "mistranslation," or "incompleteness" of the true picture available from the tradition.

Yet another biblical verse recently addressed in wide circles in response to the repeated exploitation of rape as a weapon of war directed chiefly against women and girls in such conflicts as Bosnia and Rwanda is Deuteronomy 21:11-14 which describes the so-called beautiful female captive. In this case embarrassment with these scriptures grew over time and accelerated with the widespread rape of Jewish women by Roman soldiers in the aftermath of the rebellions of 66-70 CE and 132-135 CE. Josephus and the rabbis all register various degrees of embarrassment.

The genocidal wars depicted in scripture against the so-called Seven Canaanite Nations became embarrassing with the widespread dispersion of the Jews, whereas the genocidal warfare against the Amalekites did not. Nonetheless reaction to scriptures is on-going and the case of the Amalekites is especially controversial and embarrassing since the genocidal war waged against the Jews by the Germans under Hitler.

The story of David and Bathsheba (2 Samuel, chapters 11-12) has merited an enormous amount of attention. The first level of embarrassment is within the realm of scriptures themselves. Already for the ancient Chronicler who took upon himself to rewrite Israelite history, this account of David provided a text that was too bloody, too violent, too sexually explicit to preserve as an historical record of his ancestors. Hence the event was conveniently lost — the

Chronicler expunged it from his record of events. What did not happen or what may be suppressed, need not embarrass, at least, not any longer. Renaissance painters, on the other hand, found the story titillating as did playwrights. The rabbinic sages of antiquity mitigated the circumstances of the event by providing Bathsheba with a (conditional) writ of divorce in which the conditions were not met and she had sexual congress with David while a divorcée. Such rabbinic niceties as requiring a minimal waiting period of three months between "marriages" or David's encouragement of Uriah to provide him with a conjugal opportunity are merely glossed over and ignored. The sages of antiquity replied to these charges concerning the progenitor of the Messiah with a denial of all culpability: "Whoever says that David sinned is nothing other than mistaken" (bShabbat 56a). Even now such accusations leveled against David continue to receive heated rebuttal from religious members of the Israeli parliament. They severely rebuked the "guilty" party and demanded that she recant her statements. Small wonder that even so tried, tested and seasoned a biblical scholar as James Kugel eloquently reacted to such claims made against David with an insider/outsider dichotomy. In response to charges that David was a "murderer," a "rapist," an "adulterer," and a "sinner," he suggested that Scripture has offered us an object lesson of how not to behave. The embarrassment of scriptures proffers many and various responses. Occasionally one may become embarrassed with the embarrassment of others. This can lead to interesting situations and opportunities.

II

Embarrassment and re-embracement are two moments in the reading, misreading and re-reading of scriptures. By scriptures we mean to include the widest possible assortment of texts that are canonical or classical enough to continue to be read even if their status is non-canonical. Despite what Harold Bloom calls our "belatedness" in this process, every reading community has its way of confronting that moment of embarrassment so as to embrace or reject its implications. These implications are especially strong in religious cultures with a nomian tradition. The variety of experience that constitutes a nomos or behavior of a community is intimately related to its preferred narratives or master narrative. By entering into that very tension between what I call embarrassment and embracement, every strong reader recognizes the anxiety of a narrative's influence upon a community's nomos.

By the embarrassment of Scripture, for example, we could consider the following situation and its re-readings: due to changing mores the rabbinic sages held the opinion that no gentile girl over the age of three can be considered a virgin. The rabbinic sages claim that Rebecca was under the age of three when she was betrothed to Isaac, because they have an interest in providing a legal guarantee that she was a virgin when she married him. In our reading today, we in turn are likely embarrassed by the sages who in order to protect their notion of virginity and its necessity would have the patriarch Isaac marry a mere baby — a clear example of child abuse. We therefore prefer the original Biblical account in which Rebecca seems to be a more mature young woman and is consulted regarding her marriage. This process of embarrassment of embarrassment we call re-embracement. We may in turn be embarrassed by other elements of the story like the use of a veil to hide the face. At the same time, other reading communities may desire to embrace the veil as well, and elements of the text, transformed and transmuted, appear in the traditional Jewish wedding ceremony. Examples abound in all aspects of halakha and aggada through to the contemporary moment.

The nature of embarrassment is that it becomes a catalyst for strong readings or rather (mis)readings, what Bloom calls misprision. We of course are cognizant of those strong readers due to the traces left by them in what remains as a written record. They are simultaneously aware of the overpowering influence the scriptures have had and the difficulty of escaping their embrace to allow for new human creativity — what Bloom calls the anxiety of influence. These inspired readers of the canonical texts caused them to swerve in new directions, leaving the earlier texts to be understood through the pulse of these strong readers. Embarrassment as a catalyst is another stage in the process of what Bloom calls the anxiety of influence. From embarrassment to anxiety to embarrassment to embracement, these inspired readers continue Bloom's insights into the afterlife and inter-relationship of texts and their constant re-readings.

To sum up, already within the briefly told biblical story of David and Bathsheba we have a text replete with difficult gaps, ellipses, silences that speak volumes to the attentive contemporary listener. Collective punishment, allusions to other adjacent texts all add to the chaotic emotions elicited by the scriptural texts especially for the believer or the adherent of the biblical faith for whom the scriptures prove terribly embarrassing. Biblical scholars and adherents have used other terms to express the emotion of embarrassment. These terms — such as troubling or ill-at-ease, or bothersome or disturbing or different or toxic or ambivalent — all hide to some extent the emotion of embarrassment and deflect it toward the rational. The trouble with such terms is that they identify the emotion only vaguely. This is also the case for many apologetic or ethical differences, responses first triggered by embarrassment, that is, an emotion which is partially irrational yet really present. With reactions such as silence or denial available, they do not provide the same catalytic effect as embarrassment which has the benefit of being more motivational, a catalyst for positive behavior or *tikkun olam* (mending the world) because it is less apologetic. Embarrassment creates an incentive and an inducement for change. It is at that point that anxiety takes hold. This anxiety grows from the template of embarrassment as it becomes inextricably linked with the consequent feeling of belatedness. How can one introduce change into one's tradition without taking down the whole house? How can one change that which has been held sacred for so long, had so many martyrs die in defense of its cause? Hence doubt is a nagging feeling that accompanies this embarrassment and anxiety. Could Aristotle, the court historian or the biblical legislator possibly say or mean what we think he says or means? The admission of embarrassment becomes a front-line defense for the matter at hand not to be (mis)used as the warrant to perpetuate such bad behavior that the canonical text not be operational as initially understood. It is also important insofar as it affords an opportunity for theologians to provide strong readings of these texts that cause the canonical, hence sacred, tradition to swerve in new and more benign directions. I hope that this indicates at least some of the usefulness this concept has for canonical texts. Other non-canonical texts that are toxic should be ignored and discarded. Just as embarrassment acted as an initial catalyst to such strong reading and re-reading, so too the occasional embarrassment with embarrassment acts as a secondary catalyst for re-embracement.

Finally, it seems to me, that the idea often serves as a defining line for a dogmatic orthodoxy which refuses to see anything in scriptures as embarrassing for either itself or the sages of the past. This state of the denial of embarrassment indicates a high degree of anxiety for surely this emotion is both unavoidable and recognizable in our contemporary readings and reactions to scriptures. Needless to say retrojecting an emotion onto the sages in the past is somewhat speculative.

III

There is at present a growing group of scholars exploring this concept of embarrassment as a tool in humanities research. The embarrassment of some rabbinic sages with their interpretation of the Noahide laws on abortion, the legal rejection of the opposition and its reintroduction into the modern debate caused by present-day right-to-life views are as well as the desire to repopulate the Jewish people after the Holocaust are explored and exposed by Tirzah Meacham with whom I have exchanged ideas and more for some thirty-eight years. Very close to my heart is the short Hebrew essay written by the youngest contributor to this volume, Yoam Yoreh, on the (Captive) Beautiful Woman. Like the mystic adepts or the yeshiva scholars of modern prewar Europe who would forge a connection between pages of gemara even when a leaf or more had fallen or been removed from their book, she is capable of connecting any text to another. She passionately called this text an example of "toxic Judaism" (I prefer the less general term "toxic texts" since I am not as prone to youthful hyperbole). She is one who knows of her own accord. I am not sure whether the Torah was as happy as the day it was given at Sinai but I am very proud of this vixen. Tanhum Yoreh first learned of the apologetic embarrassment of Jewish and Christian environmentalists in an undergraduate course which I teach. Many years later, when he began his doctoral studies on Judaism and the environment, I urged him to fully explore the tradition histories of Genesis 1:28 and 2:15. His study demonstrates the significance and the usefulness of causing traditions to swerve even when (mis)guided by apologetics.

It is through frequent exchanges with Tzemah Yoreh that I learned just how pervasive embarrassment is in the early redaction history of scriptures.

Though not initially guided in any way by this terminology, his superb philology based on a very disciplined redaction history of the texts involving notions of supplementation, repetition, ellipsis and the like, time and again revealed how embarrassment was amongst the primary motives for interference with the sacred sources by later supplementors. His results will in time revolutionize redaction studies of these canonical texts.

Laliv Clenman chose to address a midrashic attempt to render an embarrassing legal position against intermarriage as authoritative, despite numerous contradictory scriptures. She thus demonstrates how a topic once fluid becomes rigidly fixed.

Shana Husband demonstrates the astonishing power of what an intelligent reading may produce. Reading without prejudice, using what Roland Barthes called naïveté, she demonstrates how following closely notions of time and place indicates that the conflict between Early Christianity as depicted in the New Testament and its contemporaneous Judaism is much wider, more pervasive and deeper than hitherto indicated in recent studies. Boyarin and others have argued for a much slower and later notion of the divergence of two sister religions as opposed to the rapid emergence of a rebellious daughter religion. She does so without relying on the usual toxic texts found in the Gospels of Matthew chapter 23 and John chapter 19.

For one semester Eva Mozarek spent some thirty hours a week preparing midrashic texts in Hebrew for my course, more than all her other courses combined, discovering time and again that she had not prepared "adequately"! A year and a half later, she has produced the exquisite analysis presented here, obviously having overcome all her so-called inadequacies, becoming truly proficient in *aggada*. It is breathtaking to see how much may be contained in a single tradition of the sages when all its facets are revealed so brilliantly.

Ilana Kurshan, who regularly turns law into humorous verse, invites Rav and Shmuel to her kitchen. Much to her embarrassment her computer, literally *deus ex machina,* resolves their conflicts and she invites a friend over.

Aryeh Strakovsky deals with the embarrassment of one *lex talionis* rule in Scripture, its literal meaning and swerved rereading by the sages. His courage in doing the same to allow women into the hallowed halls of the yeshiva institution is exemplary.

Elisha Ancselovits, with whom I shared some lengthy conversations on what the new contemporaneous post post-modern rabbi would need to do and to know, is a bastion of unflagging support for the higher education of men and women in support of a new egalitarianism. His pursuit of a knowledgeable non-gender biased rabbinate is inspirational.

Yaakov Elman has created two new fields of study for others to emulate: the first is the study of Jewish-Iranian cultural connections in the Babylonian Talmud, a field previously relegated to no more than a philological curiosity; the second is fearlessly addressing the need for a new post-Holocaust theology. He has overcome much adversity, remains generous with his time and knowledge, and personally holds a synthesis between the great deeds of Rabbi Jonathan b. Uziel and the conflicting minutiae of Abaye and Rava.

Justin Jaron Lewis, Yiddishist, Storywriter and Raconteur as well as researcher of folktales, demonstrates time and again what a rich and rewarding topic the study of Hasidic stories is. The story in this volume is about the reception history of these stories — especially the ones that tell of miracles. Both within the Hasidic communities in which they originated and among the scholars who have studied them they remain a topic replete with embarrassment and embracement.

On the one hand, we live in an age of ever increasing secularization, including one that emphasizes atheism, and on the other hand, an age of religious fundamentalism. It is therefore of special interest to see how the divide between science and religion plays itself out in a religious thinker with a foot in these both camps. Ira Robinson brings us this topic of embarrassment and embracement in the evolution of a contemporary Jewish theologian with his usual clarity.

What remains of embarrassment in Eliezer Segal's discussion of the rebellious son is Rabbi Akiva's abhorrence of capital punishment. In the debate on "how much Hellenism in Jewish Palestine", the swing continues to be away from Lieberman's minimalism. With this clear example of Platonic influence (perhaps via Philo?) on the early rabbinic sages, Segal contributes mightily to this critique.

Any criticism of Lieberman was once considered so audacious as to make one's reputation (cf. my "As if With a Finger"). Although few dared challenge his constructs in the past, scholarship has finally turned to a more balanced consideration. This we witness in Alon Goshen's reasoned critique of

Lieberman's position on the Song of Songs as a systematically exegeted work. Few bricks remain of that original edifice. I too have benefited from Goshen's clear-headedness by having studies of mine he has graciously edited saved from error — or worse — esotericism.

My studies on Judaism and homosexuality remains in manuscript form. Nonetheless, I am delighted that this study became in part at least, a template for Aubrey Glazer's major contribution to re-viewing the concept of *devekut* in Jewish mysticism. Everything that Glazer touches becomes trans-formed and I daresay that everyone he touches is greatly enriched. He adds great poetry to all our lives.

In our embrace of homosexuality as a normative Jewish response to sexuality, we often forget about heteronormativity and any of its allures and/or pitfalls. Bonna Haberman-Browns deals with both in a deeply moving and nuanced study. Her wellspring bubbles over with living waters drawn from the depths of her spirit.

In our post-Renaissance notions of "progress," it would seem that a straight line of steady progress could be drawn from the Bible to Maimonides on demythologizing Judaism. Along comes Herb Basser and shows that there are a goodly number of bumps and byways in such a road. There is no one outside of my immediate family with whom I have shared more torah. He continues to generously enrich us all.

Hindy Najman is a fresh mind that revives and energizes flagging spirits. She has not only studied, written and rewritten torah but has also (re)written the map of how we do Judaism in Toronto, bringing together community, colleagues and administration in a new harmony.

Eric Lawee's studies on the canonization of Rashi's Bible commentary demonstrate how embarrassment may be used as a vehicle and indicator of this process of sacralization. As a result, one may go on to ask — is it in fact that constant engagement of the Tosafot with Rashi's Talmud commentary that made it the central feature of all Talmudic exegesis to this day? Lawee continues not only to be engaged in serious and important scholarship but to retain a sense of humor despite adversity.

Simcha Fishbane retains a love of learning that is infectious. A tireless organizer, he constantly mobilizes the scholarly community to share his ideas from China to Russia to Israel and North America. His account of how mourning customs become appended to the counting of days between Passover and Shavuot is more thrilling than any NCIS detective investigation.

Yossi Tubi constantly demonstrates the interconnection of Hebrew and Arabic cultures. Such connections often tend to embarrass both participants in the exchange, yet the rich harvest and fruit of cross-fertilization yielded one of the greatest cultures created by humans in the past. His patience knows no bounds; may his scholarship be a foretaste of what peace may one day yield.

Alan Verskin demonstrates just how far discipline wedded to native intelligence may go. He became a master of Hebrew and Arabic because of a desire to read Maimonides in the original languages in which he expressed himself. His dedication is exemplary and the results are fascinating.

Paul Pessach Heger returned to the house of learning at the stage in life when most people retire. In the twenty-three years since then, he has engaged in the process of achieving the goals he set out for himself at that time, namely, to understand how the diverse sectarianism of the Second Temple emerged and merged into a normative rabbinic Judaism. In the process, he has constantly challenged scholarly assumptions and demonstrated how their constructs were often found wanting. I have affected his religion and he in turn has affected my politics. Whereas religion and politics do not usually mix well, we have found a way to exchange ideas on both.

Gyongyi Hegedus is able to take complex and difficult ideas in philosophy and present them comprehensively and with great clarity. I do not know how her translation of Saadya Gaon into Hungarian has fared. It is a commonplace that Hungarians generally are able only to communicate with each other and no one else. Hungarians, however, who learn languages, having once mastered their own, can conquer the world. Hegedus is just such a communicator.

Ed Elkin is my paradigm of *torah* and *derekh eretz*, intelligence and *mentschlikh* humanity. With patience and education he has become a shepherd to an egalitarian congregation that spans three and sometimes four generations, willing to take on green projects, support worthwhile social action and democratize egalitarianism to be inclusive of all people without gender bias, racial bias, sexual orientation bias, age bias or any form of bigotry whatsoever — a remarkable achievement. In this contribution Elkin shows how a vocabulary very much parallel to the one in place in this volume informs a debate on the embarrassing notion of divine election or its pejorative articulation — favoritism. It demonstrates how informed discussion is possible without the terminology developed here. The question to be asked is whether our vocabulary facilitates re-embracement of Jewish values after they have swerved to detoxify their previously constructed meanings.

Miryam Segal brings text to life. There is an angel (and probably also a *dybbuk*) that inhabit her soul which when asked like the prophet Ezekiel. "Shall these dry bones live?" answers in a resounding affirmative. Be it a poem of Bialik, or a *haftara* from Isaiah, you have not understood a fraction of its dramatic effect until you have heard it rendered by Segal. More than others, she has caused the original ideas of embarrassment to swerve in new directions. In the voice of her strong readings, our topic will need to be rethought.

Pearl Elman's contribution to this volume is based on an essay which predates the introduction of the terminology developed in this volume. As such it should be compared and contrasted with the contribution in Hebrew by Yoam Yoreh who wrote her essay after the usage of words like embarrassment and embracement had become a commonplace in the academic discourse of our small circle of scholars. Her article demonstrates that no matter what our approach may be, toxic texts are always identifiable; we are grateful to Elman for setting off the alarm by dealing with such unpleasantries early. In an age when rape during warfare and after battle has become such a commonplace, we must be reminded that the patina and veneer which have made the beautiful captive so fascinating a topic — she is after all, called beautiful — in fact betrays an ugly reality.

Albert Dov Friedberg moves easily between the worlds of finance and learning because for him it is not education which is a means to riches but riches, which are means to education. Friedberg demonstrates that the pivotal figure of all Jewish studies, Maimonides, was constantly motivated by embarrassment with his past heritage, reading and rereading it constantly and causing it to swerve in new directions. We at times need to do the same to Maimonides when his position comes under scrutiny and critique — a process that began during his own lifetime, often initiated by Maimonides himself.

I must admit to being a most reluctant bride. My initial reaction to the idea of producing a *festschrift* in my honor even before I had turned sixty was to treat it as a mean joke. For other than my life sentence, I was unaware of any lurking fatal disease with which I had been afflicted. Why then visit this plague on my being before I had so much as produced a single published article on the subject of embarrassment? My manuscript on the subject is a work in progress and may yet be two or three years away from completion. My own contribution to this volume delayed the appearance of some of the articles submitted in this volume for several years. I am deeply regretful for this since Shmuel Safrai and his daughter Chana Safrai, a pioneer of higher Jewish education for women, could not witness the fruit of their labour. Shmuel was one of my teachers and Chana and I would often exchange ideas. They are sorely missed. May we continue to merit the torah continuing unabated in Ze'ev Safrai's work which he has shared with us. To this list I am most pained to also add Diane Kriger, a human rights advocate, lawyer, and scholar who passed away recently before she could see her own book on slavery. It is her study of slavery, now in press, that alerted me to how very embarrassing this situation is. She lives on in our memories and in her important work. She has shown how making topics taboo in the form of embarrassment glosses over problems and that embracement of the difficulties allows for a productive and necessary confrontation that would otherwise be lacking.

The power of my oral torah over the written is that all the contributors to this volume led by my impetuous prodigal son, prolific post-doctoral and doctoral students and some of my closest friends and esteemed colleagues got my point immediately. Being the strong readers that they are, they have embarrassed me tremendously, for now I must face the anxiety of belatedness in reference to an idea I first presented orally about a decade ago. Even those who believed the idea of embarrassment had already been used in the past by others now acknowledge that they first heard it in conversations with me. Unlike myself, some enthusiasts perform precepts like Abraham on his way to the sacrifice of Isaac and the word embarrassment used in the particular way I have defined it is already in print. Nonetheless, both these and those have used this idea in their own work in a multiplicity of new directions. My path has led to many highways for which I am most grateful and heartened.

JUDAISM AND GENOCIDE: THE EMBARRASSMENT OF JEWISH JIHAD

Harry Fox (leBeit Yoreh), University of Toronto

I

Of the series of studies I have conducted on the theme of the Embarrassment of Scriptures, it is safe to say that none is more embarrassing to me personally than Scripture's treatment of Amalek.[1] As a contemporary Jew, a son of Holocaust survivors and the grandson, great-grandson, nephew and first cousin many times over to its victims, their treatment remains for me one of Scripture's greatest enigmas. Joseph Schachter in his study of Amalek;[2] — although his perspective and attitude differ radically from mine and the one presented in this essay — summarized the problem well:

> [T]his same Jew is confronted with the most explicit Mitzvah which commands him to commit genocide… Theoretically the Halakhic Jew, were he to

1 The topics of genocide, Amalek, and the Canaanite nations all have huge bibliographies, especially in biblical studies. Our references in what follows are merely representative; no attempt has been made to be exhaustive in our citations. The same is true for the traditional literature, again cited very selectively. As a result ooccasionally much material is summarized in but a few words. Furthermore, not all topics of embarrassment concerning Amalek are explored. For example, the problem of bSanhedrin 96b which mentions that the progeny of Amalek learned/taught Torah at Benei Brak; or how is it possible for Esther and Mordecai to benefit from Amalek when given dominion over the house of Haman (Esther 8:1, 2, 7); or how is it that Saul, the greatest sage of his day, would err by not killing Agag? See Daniel Ginsberg, "Concerning the Laws of Wiping Out the Amalek," *Moriah* 29 (1-2) (2008): 145-149 (Hebrew). Many books address these topics and must await another occasion.

2 See Joseph Schachter, *Amalek: A Study of the Rabbinic Model of Ultimate Criminality*, (Jerusalem, 1977), 2.

> be confronted with a bona fide descendent of Amalek, would be dutybound to kill him/her forthwith without the necessity or requirement to obtain a mandate from any rabbinical court. Furthermore the Halakhic archaeologist who uncovered an Amalekite artifact would be required to destroy it.

Schachter even goes on to mention the modern and contemporaneous notion of embarrassment that embraces this topic:[3]

> Amalek as the principle of evil by contrast has suffered a decline in the vast literature created by Anglo-Jewish writers. Surveys of the sermon manuals, apologetics, and Jewish Thought periodicals, would indicate that Amalek has indeed been blotted out. This may very well be because the modern Jew is highly embarrassed with the Mitzvah associated with Amalek. Perhaps Nazism and Hitler have replaced him.

Biblical scriptures record a relatively large number of instances of genocidal activity on the part of the Israelites toward their neighbors and fellow occupiers of the land.[4] Contemporary responses today run the full gamut of 1) embarrassment, 2) apologetics, 3) justification, 4) disbelief, and even 5) glorification. Embarrassment is linked to the Holocaust suffered by the Jewish people in the twentieth century. Apologetics is linked to a study of ancient anthropology — everyone was doing it so why not the Israelites too?[5] Justification is linked to

---

3 Op. cit. p. 18

4 The theme recurs in all accounts of conquest of the land of Israel by the Israelites from its local inhabitants, especially in the five books of the Torah and the book of Joshua. See Pekka Pitkamon, "Memory, Witnesses and Genocide in the Book of Joshua," *JSOT* sup. ser. No. 461, Sheffield (2007): 268-280; Carl S. Ehrlich, "Joshua, Judaism and Genocide," in *Jewish Studies at the Turn of the 20th Century: Proceedings of the 6th EAJS Congress Toledo July 1998, Volume 1: Biblical, Rabbinical, and Medieval Studies*, (Leiden, Boston,Koln: Brill, 1999), 117-124. Mark G. Brett, "Genocide in Deuteronomy: Postcolonial Variations in Mimetic Desire," *Seeing Signals, Reading Signs JSOT* sup. ser. no. 415, Sheffield (2004): 75-89; Rivon Krygier, "Did God Command the Extermination of the Canaanites? The Rabbis' Encounter with Genocide," *Conservative Judaism* 57, 2 (2005): 78-94; Michael Freeman, "Religion, Nationalism and Genocide: Ancient Judaism Revisited," *Archives Européennes de Sociologie*, 35, 2 (1994): 259-282; Eugene Korn, "Moralization in Jewish Law: Genocide, Divine Commands and Rabbinical Reasoning," *Edah* 5, 2 (2006; e-journal).

5 Scott B. Noegel, "Dismemberment, Creation, and Ritual: Images of Divine Violence in the Ancient Near East," in *Belief and Bloodshed: Religion and Violence Across Time and Traditions*,

finding a warrant for genocide in the bad behavior of the intended victims, be they Amalekites, Canaanites, or others.[6] Disbelief is linked to the need to repeat the call for the genocide of Amalek in subsequent historical periods, a sure sign that the policy was largely ignored as it was with respect to the inhabitants of the land. Finally, glorification is the by-product of identifying behavior considered so reprehensible as to render the genocidal reactions heroic. Examples of this include identifying the Amalekites with contemporary enemies of the Jewish people such as the Nazis, or with contemporary enemies of Israel, such as the Palestinians.[7]

ed. James K. Wellman, Jr. (Lanham, MD: Rowman and Littlefield Publishers, 2007). For apologetics related to embarrassment see Avi Sagi, "The Punishment of Amalek in Jewish Tradition: Coping with the Moral Problem," *Harvard Theological Review* 87 (1994): 323-346; my citations are to the fuller Hebrew version in *Multiculturalism in Democratic and Jewish State*, eds. Menachem Mautner, Avi Sagi, Ronen Shamir (Tel Aviv: Tel Aviv University Press, 1998), 477-510; ibid., "The Punishment of Amalek," [Hebrew] *Shdeymot* 2-3 (1995): 64-78; Norman Lamm, "Amalek and the Seven Nations: A Case of Law vs. Morality," in *War and Peace in the Jewish Tradition*, eds. Lawrence Schiffman and Joel B. Wolowelsky (New York: Yeshiva University Press, 2007), 201-238.

6 Devora Ushpizai, "The Background to the Confrontation of Amalek-Israel," [Hebrew] *Shemaatin* 121-122 (1995): 93-100. Concerning Canaanites and warrants in post-Biblical literature see Kattel Berthelot, "'*Ils Jettent au Feu leurs Fils et leurs Filles Pour leurs Dieux,': Une Justification Humaniste du Massacre des Cananéens dans les textes juifs anciens?" Revue Biblique* 112 (2) (2005): 161-191; Robert L. Cohn, "Before Israel: The Canaanites as Other in Biblical Tradition," in *The Other in Jewish Thought and History: Construction of Jewish Culture and Identity*, eds. Lawrence J. Silberstein and Robert L. Cohn (New York and London: New York University Press 1994), 74-90; Rivon Krygier, *op. cit.* (above n. 4) 78-94. Concerning otherness see Trude Dothan and Robert L. Cohn, "The Philistine as Other: Biblical Rhetoric and Archaeological Reality," ibid. *The Other in Jewish Thought* 61-73. Concerning Midianites see Shelomo Gutel, "God's Revenge on Midyan," [Hebrew] *Sinai* 137 (2005-2006): 67-94.

7 In point of fact the biblical Amalek has served as a prototype of other enemies of Israel from antiquity to the present with constant contemporization taking place. This includes Nazis, Germans, Christians, Muslims, Arabs and Palestinians — to name but a few of the identifications available. Concerning the general history of contemporization see Elliott Horwitz, "From the Generation of Moses to the Generation of the Messiah: The Jews Confront 'Amalek' and his Incarnations," [Hebrew] *Zion* 64 (1999): 425-454. On contemporization of Amalek with Germans see Ushpizai, *ibid.* 100, n. 70; David Patterson, *Emil L. Fackenheim: A Jewish Philosopher's Response to the Holocaust* (Syracuse: Syracuse University Press, 2008), 54-55; Gershon Greenberg, "Amaleq during the Shoah: Jewish Orthodox Thought," in *The Path of the Spirit: The Eliezer Schweid Jubilee Volume* (ed. Yehoyada Amir) vol. 2 (*Jerusalem Studies in Jewish Thought* 6) (2005): 891-973 (see especially 891, n. 1 which lists previous bibliography on Amalek); Mordecai Flabinsky, *Amalek shel Torah*, (Israel, 1999; 7th ed.), especially 591-648; Dean Garrett Stoud, "Reading the Old Testament

Rabbinic responses to the same verses run from the subversive to the severely limiting to an acceptance of the biblical parameters. An example of a subversive response would be using the following source in regard to the Seven Canaanite Nations or the Amalekites. The mishna of tractate Yadayim 4:4 (bYoma 54a) records the belief that "Senaharib, the Assyrian king, already conflated all these nations." It follows that the genocidal demands of Scripture bear no contemporaneous force and may therefore be safely ignored. Other rabbinic efforts delimited the import of the law either by gender — only to males — or by location — only in the Land of Israel.[8]

It is in regard to the Amalekites that Robert Cover's claims in his works, "Violence and the Word" and "Nomos and Narrative," possess their most significant resonance when applied to the rabbinic sages.[9] The sages could readily have dismissed the Amalekites and neutralized the plain sense of Scripture by claiming that they, too, have suffered dispersion and no longer constitute a coherent political and ethnic entity.[10] Yet with the Amalekites, as opposed to the Seven Nations, the shadow of the field of pain and death casts an emotion whose memory within scripture does not fade and becomes translated beyond it into the very fabric of the law itself.[11] It is these traces which I shall describe here.

---

in the Third Reich," *Journal of Genocide Research* 4, 2 (2002): 253-268; Mayer Herskovics, *The Lesson of Amalek: A Teaching Guide*, ed. Els Bendheim (Jerusalem, 1997); Joel Schwartz, *Yemei purim kollel zekhirat maase amalek u-mihyato* (Jerusalem, 1999), 138; Rav Ahron Soloveichik, *The Warmth and the Light: Illuminating Approaches to the Weekly Torah Portions* (Genesis Jerusalem Press, 1992), 197-209. Concerning other contemporization see Joseph Stern, *Maimonides on Amalek*, loc. cit. below n. 21, 386, n. 10. Concerning contemporization as Palestinians see Matityahu Glazerson, *The Secret of Philistines and the Disengagement in Stages* (Jerusalem, 2005); Elliott Horowitz, *Reckless Rites: Purim and the Legacy of Jewish Violence* (Princeton and Oxford: Princeton University Press, 2006), 1-20.

8 See Alter Mordecai Fogel, Sefer Yaale BeRosh: On Megilat Esther and Concerns of Purim [Hebrew] (A. M. Fogel: London, 2008).

9 Robert M. Cover, "Violence and the Word," *The Yale Law Journal* 95 (8) (Charles L. Black, Jr. Festschrift; July 1986): 1601-1629; ibid. "Nomos and Narrative," *Harvard Law Review* 97:4 (1983): 4-68.

10 There are indeed some scholars who wish to make such a claim in reference to Maimonides. See below.

11 Although the law remained throughout the Middle Ages, it is not metioned in *Sefer Mitzvot Qatan,* the *Turim* and the *Shulhann Arukh*. See above n. 7, Horowitz, *From the Generation of Moses*, 447, 449.

Scripture provides precious little in the way of cause or due process in allowing us to comprehend the warrant for these genocides. One is left greatly perplexed. The enemy is known but its sins are not enumerated clearly. They are described only vaguely with an emphasis on the enemy's otherness.[12] There almost seems to be a cover-up of the *casus belli*, as if there is little justification other than an agenda of displacement.[13]

II

In the Bible, Amalek is a direct descendent of Abraham in whom all the families of the earth are blessed (Genesis 12:2) and is counted among the offspring God promises will be as numerous as the stars in heaven (Genesis 15:5). The direct line of descent is Abraham, Isaac, Esau, Eliphaz, Amalek. How does the transformation from blessed descendent of Abraham to the Even Shoshan dictionary's definition of Amalek as "an epithet for an evil one who hates Israel" happen? Or consider Ben Yehuda's historical dictionary's definition of Amalek as "evil enemies": how does that occur? During World War II identification of the Germans with Amalek was widespread in rabbinic literature, as documented in Gershon Greenberg's recent study.[14]

12 For some general academic studies of the reception of the law of Amalek, see: Louis H. Feldman, *"Remember Amalek!": Vengeance, Zealotry and Group Destruction in the Bible According to Philo, Pseudo-Philo and Josephus* (Cincinnati: HUC Press, 2004). Concerning Amalek within see Elijah Judah Schochet, *Amalek: The Enemy Within* (Los Angeles, Cedarhunt, Jerusalem: Los Angeles Mimetav Press 1991). On being disturbed by the treatment of Amalek see Gabriel Goldman, *Ze Shalal David: The Destruction of Amalek in the Halakha and Aggada*, (Kefar Adumim, Israel): 1995, 4-7, 17. For Rabbi Z. Y. Kook on Amalek as Germans see ibid. 44 and for Yosef Dov Soloveitchik on Amalek as Arabs, see ibid. 33, 35. Concerning war with Amalek and the Seven Nations see David Schatz, "Introduction" in *War and Peace in the Jewish Tradition*, eds. Lawrence Schiffman and Joel B. Wolowelsky (New York: Yeshiva University Press, 2007), xiii-xxxviii; Shalom Carmi, "The Origin of Nations and the Shadow of Violence: Theological Perspectives in Canaan and Amalek," in *War and Peace*, 163-199; Moshe Sokolow, "'What is this Bleating of Sheep in My Ears': Spoils of War/Wars of Spoil," in *War and Peace*, 133-161.

13 Concerning displacement see Edward W. Said, *Peace and its Discontents: Essays on Palestine in the Middle East Peace Process* (with a preface by Christopher Hitchens; New York: Vintage Books, 1996), cf. Michel Onfray, *In Defense of Atheism: The Case Against Christianity, Judaism and Islam*, tr. Jeremy Leggatt (Toronto: Penguin Canada, 2008), 195.

14 See above n. 7.

Anachronistic updating of this principle today includes identifying Amalek with the Palestinians and, through secondary identification,using it to libel figures such as Sharon or Rabin who were also occasionally vilified in Israel by posters depicting them as Nazis in SS uniforms.[15] Such practices are of course a commonplace in anti-Semitic caricatures of Jews drawn in the Muslim press. The possibility of such easy reversals in Israeli politics from hero to devil incarnate and their use in anti-Semitic caricatures should be a cause of great alarm.

This facile mobility of character assassination is doubly embarrassing: once for the reference to the Holocaust with its phony warrant for genocide perpetrated on the Jewish body; again because the charge against present-day Israel, especially after the Six Day War, is that a peace settlement is still out of reach in part because of an agenda of displacement and West Bank settlement policies. All of the classical extra-biblical sources of the rabbinic sages seem to contain no such concerns whatsoever in accepting the formulation of scripture. One extreme formulation of such an attitude is found in *Pesikta deRav Kahana* (Piska three, section 16, Mandelbaum, 53):

> Rabbi Levi in the name of Rabbi Huna son of Rabbi Hanina: All the while that the seed of Amalek exists in the world — the Name is not complete and the Throne is not complete. Once the seed of Amalek is lost from the world, the Name is complete and the Throne is complete.

Amalek functions as a fatal flaw in the universe, affecting the wholeness of God.

Yet despite this attitude which effectively blames Amalek for all the ills of the universe, one does detect in the literature of the sages a degree of embarrassment about Scripture's lack of justification and its assumptions regarding the Amalekites. These provide for the denigration of Amalekites who are

15 David Golinkin, "Are Jews Still Commanded to Blot Out the Memory of Amalek?" in *Insight Israel, Jewish Law, and the Jewish Calendar* (Jerusalem: Leshon Limudim Ltd. Second Series by David Golinkin, 2003), 59-67; Avi Sagi, *Judaism Between Religion and* Morality (Tel Aviv: Hakibbutz Hameuhad, 1998; Yaaqov Medan, "The Amalek Issue: God's Command and Morality — Can They Go Together," [Hebrew] *Ha-Aher — Bayn Adam le-atzmo Ulezulato* Memorial Volume for Dudi Doitsh (Tel Aviv: Yediot Ahronot, 2001), 367-401. See also above n. 6 and Horowitz, *Reckless Rites*, 3-8.

compared to flies or dogs.[16] In light of Nazi propaganda these depictions are especially embarrassing to the contemporary reader. Yet other midrashic sources emphasize the rapacious nature of the Amalekites who went out of their way to fight the Israelites and encouraged others to take up arms as well.[17] These texts enhance the warrant for genocide and as such betray the embarrassment the sages must have felt about Scripture's failure to provide any meaningful explanation for the extreme measure demanded of the Israelites. Two midrashic sources are of particular interest because they provide justification for mutual enmity, a tit-for-tat of wrongs committed by each party to the other. We find in Pesikta Rabbati piska 13:

> Why did the Holy One Blessed Be see fit to let cruelty be the attribute [or: measure] toward Amalek, saying: *thou shalt blot out the remembrance of Amalek* (Deuteronomy 25:19); and *slay both man and woman, infant and suckling* (I Samuel 15:3)? Because the Holy One Blessed Be said, I am anticipating something which Amalek is otherwise committed to do. It is revealed and known to Me how an Amalekite will decree death for *young and old, little children and women, in one day* (Esther 3:13). Hence, *Slay both man and woman* (I Samuel 15:3), and *thou shalt blot out the remembrance of Amalek,* who therefore will have been made to *eat the fruit of their own way* (Proverbs 1:31).

In Esther Rabbah 7:13 the sages imagine Haman's interior monologue:

> What do you advise me to do? Balaam replied, 'Go and make war on them; for if you make war on them you will prevail against them, for they depend on the merit of their ancestor Abraham, and you also being the descendent of Abraham can participate in the merit of Abraham, forthwith he made war on them. What did that leader of theirs, Moses, do? He had a disciple named Joshua son of Nun who was very cruel and pitiless. Moses said to him, *Choose us some men, and go battle with Amalek* (Exodus 17:9). I do not know if those men whom he chose were sorcerers or great warriors, but what did that Moses

16 See for example, Pesikta deRav Kahana *Piska* 3, 8 (Mandelbaum, 47). Also see, for example, Midrash Tanhuma (Buber) *ki teitzei* 12.

17 See n. 16 Midrash Tanhuma and, for example, Mekhilta deRabbi Ishmael (Horowitz-Rabin) (Jerusalem: Sifrei Shalem 1970), 176-177.

do? He took a staff in his hand, and did something or other with it, and when Amalek attacked them he uttered some incantation or other against them and they became powerless and fell before them, as it says, *And Joshua discomfited Amalek and his people with the edge of the sword* (ibid. 13). They attacked the two mighty kings Sihon and Og, against whom no man could stand, and they managed by unknown means to kill them. The kings of Midian came against them and they managed to kill them also by unknown means: Further, what did the disciple of that Moses do? He led Israel into the land of Canaan and not only did he take their land but he slew thirty-one kings of them and divided their land among the Israelites, and he showed them no pity and those whom he did not want to kill became slaves to him. Sisera and his hosts came against them and they did something or other to the stream of Kishon which swept and carried them away and cast them into the ocean, as it says, *The brook Kishon swept them away* (Judges 5:21). The first king they had was named Saul, and he went and fought against the land of my ancestor Amalek and slew 100,000 horsemen of them on one day, and had no pity on man or woman, on babe or suckling, but killed them all. And then how he treated my ancestor Agag. At first he spared him, but afterwards one of them named Samuel came and cut him in pieces and gave his flesh to be eaten by the fowl of heaven, as it says, *So Samuel hewed Agag in pieces* (I Samuel 15:33); and so he inflicted on him an unnatural death, as you have heard. After this they had a king named David son of Jesse, who destroyed and exterminated all other peoples without pity, as it says, *And David... left neither man nor woman alive* (ibid. 27:9). After him came his son Solomon who erected for Israel a certain building called the Temple. They had certain things in it, and when they made war they used to go into it and do some magic there, and when they came out they used to slay and lay waste without end. As a result of their great prosperity they rebelled against their God, who had grown old, and Nebuchadnezzar came and burnt that Temple of theirs, and carried them off from their land and brought them amongst us. And still they have not changed their vile ways, and although they are in exile among us they mock us and our religion. Now therefore we have come to a unanimous decision and we have cast lots to destroy them and to discover what is an auspicious time for that purpose. Their lot has fallen upon the month of Adar, and the thirteenth day thereof. Now, therefore, when these

> letters reach you, keep yourselves in readiness for that day to destroy all the Jews among you both young and old, children and women on one day, and not to leave of them a remnant or fugitive.

These texts see the conflict between Israel and Amalek as cycles of violence with Jewish culpability as great as that of the Amalekites.

III

Whereas the listing of one precept for Amalek with a brief mention in the introduction to *Halakhot Gedolot* could subsequently have been dismissed by the ritual blotting out of the mention of Haman by noise and merriment at the celebration of the Purim festival, Maimonides' detailed mention of three precepts on Amalek is not so easily ignored. The biblical commandment in Deuteronomy 25:17: "Remember what Amalek did to you on the way upon your leaving Egypt," receives codification by its inclusion in the list of 613 commandments compiled by Maimonides. The 189th positive commandment reads: "to remember what Amalek did to you always as it states: *Remember what Amalek did to you* etc." Maimonides lists this commandment again in his introduction to *Laws of Kings*, "to remember what Amalek did." This commandment to remember is linked in all these locations to a much more pernicious commandment in Deuteronomy 25:19: "Wipe out the memory of Amalek from beneath the heavens — do not forget." Maimonides also lists this as positive commandment 188: "to extirpate Amalek's progeny as it says, *wipe out the memory of Amalek,*" and in the introduction to *Laws of Kings*, "to wipe out the progeny of Amalek." The end of the above verse, "do not forget," is listed under number 59 of the negative commandments: "that the evil deed of Amalek which he did to us should not be erased from our hearts, as it says '*do not forget.*'" And again this is listed in the introduction to the *Laws of Kings*, "not to forget his evil deeds and his ambush of you on the way."

The absolute seriousness of these commandments is highlighted by the way the codes articulate them and the associations they make. In the list of positive commandments, the commandment to destroy Amalek is linked to the utter annihilation of the seven original nations of the Land of Israel. The latter uses the same terminology as the commandment to eradicate an idolatrous city, which is listed as a separate positive commandment. Again, all these are listed in the introduction to the *Laws of Kings*. Moreover, these commandments are deemed operational as they are listed by Maimonides in the details of the *Laws of Kings* as well (1:1; 1:2; 5:1; 5: 4-5; 6:1; 6:4-6). Like Rashi,[18] Maimonides provides graphic detail and, as fanciful as ideologies may be, this one has an afterlife that extends to this day. The appearance of these precepts in the Book of Precepts is troubling enough; the influence of the Islamic Jihad on Maimonides' formulation on warfare has been noted in the scholarship. Indeed, Maimonides provides an entire jihadist agenda in the Laws of Kings.[19] In his *Guide for the Perplexed*, Maimonides goes on to provide a carefully spelled-out justification for listing these precepts, that is, he provides a warrant for genocide.[20]

Stern's strong and sometimes brilliant (mis)reading of Maimonides is a futile attempt to whitewash the clearly genocidal policies codified by Maimonides in his law code, *Mishneh Torah* and *Book of Precepts*. Maimonides goes on to fully articulate a justification for this extreme posture (of which he is fully aware) in his *Guide for the Perplexed*. Stern's decontextualized quotes from the *Guide* obfuscate Maimonides' position which in fact argues that scripture desires to make of Amalek an example in order to deter the bad behavior of other people who would see Amalekite actions as exemplary. This position is

18 See Rashi's commentary to Deuteronomy 25:19, Ecclesiastes 1:10 and elsewhere.

19 On Maimonides' use of force to spread monotheism see Gerald J. Blidstein, "Spreading the Faith as a Goal in the Doctrine of Maimonides," in *Peace and War in Jewish Culture*, ed. Avriel Bar-Levav, (Zalman Shazar Center for Jewish History, Jerusalem and Center for the study of Jewish Culture, University of Haifa: 2006), 85-97 [Hebrew]; ibid., "Holy War in Maimonidean Law," in *Perspectives on Maimonides: Philosophical and Historical Studies*, ed. Joel Kraemer (Oxford: Littman Library of Jewish StudieslLitm, 1991, 209-220; ibid. *Political Concepts in Maimonidean Halakha* [Hebrew], chapter 9 "War and the Relationship to Gentiles" (Ramat Gan: Bar Ilan University Press , 2001, 230-263. Concerning Medieval Islamic Jihad see Joel L. Kraemer, "The Jihad of the Falasifa," *JSAI* 10 (1987): 288-325; ibid., "War, Conquest, and the Treatment of Religious Minorities in Medieval Islam," in *Violence and Defense in the Jewish Experience*, eds. Salo W. Baron and George S. Wise, (Philadelphia: Jewish Publication Society, 1977), 143-159.

20 See Joseph Stern, "Maimonides on Amalek, Self-Corrective Mechanisms, and the War against Idolatry," in *Judaism and Modernity: The Religious Philosophy of David Hartman*, ed. Jonathan W. Malino (Ashgate, 2004), 359-392. Cf. Friedberg (below, n. 28) on Amalek 138-142, especially 21, n. 45 *contra* Stern and 162-166.

consistent with Maimonides' very low opinion of idolaters; in his estimation they are essentially subhuman:

> Such individuals as the furthermost Turks found in the remote North, the Negroes found in the remote South, and those who resemble them among those that are with us in these climes. The status of those is like that of irrational animals. To my mind they do not have the rank of men, but have among the beings a rank lower than the rank of man but higher than the rank of apes. For they have the external shape and lineaments of a man and a faculty of discernment that is superior to that of the apes. (*Guide* iii, 51, 618-619)

Taking the lives of such people is of little consequence as may be seen from the following legal position in *Issurei Biah* 12:10:

> But an Israelite who has sexual relations with a Gentile female, whether she is a minor of three years and a day or a major, whether single or a man's wife, and even if he was a minor of nine years and a day, since he had sexual relations with the Gentile woman deliberately — behold she is killed like an animal because a stumbling block came to Israel through her. And this matter is made explicit in the Torah (Numbers 31:10-18).

Maimonides alludes to the genocide of the Midianites which he also misreads. The last verse (Numbers 31:18) clearly states that "all the female children, that have not known man by lying with him, keep alive for your-selves." Furthermore at the end of chapter 10 of *Hilkhot Avoda Zara* we find the extent of Maimonidean extremism and consistency on this matter:

> ... [H]owever, when the hand of Israel is hard on them we are not allowed to leave any idolaters amongst us. And even one who is only a temporary sojourner or a transient merchant wandering from place to place, he is not to traverse in our land until he accepts the Seven Noahide laws as it is stated: they should not dwell in your land — even for an hour.

The Rabad (loc. cit.) pounces on this formulation in his glosses to *Mishneh Torah*: "This we have neither found nor heard ever." Maimonides' genocidal policy for the Seven Canaanite Nations and Amalek is articulated in his laws relating to kings, *Hilkhot Melakhim* 1:1; 1:2; 5:1 which paraphrase what is found in the *Book of Precepts* as noted above. The same is true for 5:4-5. Stern (368) wishes to argue that the expression (5:4) "and their memory is lost" nullifies or at least neutralizes the effects applies to Amalek (5:5) as well as to the Seven Nations (5:4). In my opinion this is due to his embarrassment with the Maimonidean position on Amalek. Horowitz, *From the Generations of Moses* (pp. 431-432, notes 25-26, 446-447), argues that in contradistinction to his own son R. Abraham, Maimonides made the distinction deliberately as he felt Amalekites probably still existed, perhaps even somewhere in Europe.

There are scholars (e.g., Stern 362) who have wanted to read 6:1-3 "We do not make war on any person in the world until we call for peace ... if they accept the peace and the seven Noahide laws we do not kill them," as if there were no exceptions to its universalistic formulation. Verily, these people must nonetheless serve Israel and pay Israel work taxes as well as monetary taxes and do menial slave labor — but they are not killed. If one would not read onward, it could mean that this must be true for the Seven Nations and Amalek as well. Indeed there are those scholars, as we shall soon see, who wish to read the following laws (6:4-6) not as exceptions but as qualifications, that is, as if 6:4-6 can be read for its opposite implications such that "And if they did not accept peace or accepted peace and did not accept the Seven Laws" (6:4), becomes if they accept these conditions they live. Maimonides, however, after articulating a selective genocide of adult males in the case of non-acceptance (6:4) indicates that these conditions hold only in a voluntary war "with the other nations." Maimonides then continues "... however, the Seven Nations and Amalek *who did not accept peace* [emphasis added] we do not leave even one person [alive] as it is stated... *do not leave even one person alive.* And so it says concerning Amalek: *Wipe out the memory of Amalek.*" The only exception to this is the Hivite people of Givon who were saved because of their subterfuge and the solemn oath of the Israelites even though they also deserved to be killed. The rest refused peace because God had encouraged them to fight. *They are not given a second chance at peace and neither are the Amalekites.* The only groups above about whom Maimonides equivocates are the Amonites and Moabites (6:6) who though they ought not be offered peace — indeed one is forbidden by scripture from doing so — nonetheless if they surrender of their own accord and accept the conditions outlined above "they are accepted."

Sagi attempts to (mis)read Maimonides' *Hilkhot Sanhedrin* 18:6 as saying that David kills the Amalekite sojourner *only* [emphasis added] as a monarchic privilege or temporary decree but under other circumstances would not do so.[21] Once again Maimonides is stating a fact, not a condition or a rule. We do not know that Maimonides would have insisted on such a distinction but it is highly unlikely given that the tradition has already dismissed the import or potential of this source to neutralize the Amalekite laws. This is similar to the dismissal of the Senaharib affect mentioned above. Likewise the tradition that the progeny of Haman taught/learned at Benei Brak is nowhere cited by Maimonides and has likewise generally been dismissed as a source to counter the legal force of genocide. Maimonides is not dealing with Amalek *per se* but the prerogatives of individuals such as David, the king, to act without due process. Amalekites could nonetheless be subject to extirpation by due process. Indeed, for Maimonides, as I read him, they certainly are. Sagi goes on to make a similar argument for *Hilkhot Melakhim* 5:4 [*sic*] which should read 6:4.[22] Sagi followed by Stern[23] (mis)quotes the text by leaving out "however" which opens the law as an exception to the rules preceding it in 6:1-3 as I have just argued. Sagi further cites Rabad's gloss but not its continuation. Rabad wishes to state that Maimonides' text is corrupt because we kill Amalekites even if they do accept peace or the Seven Laws. This, however, is exactly what Maimonides is also saying because no inference may be made from what for him is a statement of fact that "they did not accept peace." Their non-acceptance of peace is the warrant for their genocide as already noted by Blidstein whose own difficulty with 6:5 is resolved because it, too, is a statement of fact and as such justifies the extreme actions taken — disproportionate warfare as a response to terrorism[24]. Terrorism flies in the face of any and all rules of engagement precisely because it has no rules. Its goals are not eventual peace but disruption of any effort at compromise or accommodation. Though it may be true that its total eradication is the only option available, that remains a

21 See n. 15, and see Avi Sagi above n. 5, p. 501.

22 Op. cit. p. 503

23 Op. cit. n. 15, see pp. 386-387, n. 14.

24 Loc. cit. n. 20. See 94-95, n. 36-43. Blidstein (89, n. 16) is uncertain as how to interpret Rabad: is this a suggested textual emendation or a halakhic disagreement?

far cry from the policies advocated by Maimonides. Success is possible by less drastic means, or so one would wish.

Sagi makes yet one more attempt to show that despite all of Maimonides' Amalek rhetoric in which he articulates what seems to be an uncompromising position that justifies that people's annihilation as an example,[25] he in fact allowed them a way out via conversion to Judaism. In *Hilkhot Issurei Biah* 12:17 Maimonides states the following universal rule:

> When each and every idolater converts and accepts upon himself all the precepts of the Torah, and slaves when they are freed, lo they are like Israel in all respects as it is stated: *The congregation — one statute will [govern] you*, and [they] are permitted to enter the congregation of God immediately.

Maimonides concludes the chapter (12:25) with what seems to be an equivalent general statement:

> When Senaharib king of Assyria rose up he conflated all the nations and mixed [them] with each other and exiled them from their places. And these Egyptians in the land of Egypt, they are now a different people. And so are the Edomites in the Field of Edom. And since the foreign nations that are not allowed to [enter] in all of the nations of the world were conflated so they are permitted [to enter therefore] all are permitted. Since all who leave them to convert have a claim that he left the majority, hence when a convert converts at this time in every place whether an Edomite, whether an Egyptian, whether an Amonite, whether a Moabite, whether a Cushite, whether the rest of the nations — both the males and the females are permitted to come into the congregation immediately.

On the basis of an *argumentum ex silentio*, Sagi claims that since the Amalekites are not mentioned anywhere in this section, it follows that they are accepted as proselytes. Hence they need not be eradicated! Sagi is aware of how radical Maimonides' position is made out to be. Schwartz also concludes that once an Amalekite converts, he no longer belongs to the category of Amalekite — though for him it is sufficient for them to accept the Seven Noahide Laws

25 Sagi, 500.

to avoid retribution.[26] This is also the position of Ridbaz and R. Yosef Karo in *Kesef Mishneh* and *Lehem Mishneh* to *Hilkhot Melakhim* 6:4 but cf. Migdal Oz (*Hil. Mel. 6:4*). My resistance to this (mis)reading of Maimonides is not because I do not like it — indeed it is brilliant and mitigates many unseemly matters. It evokes a sigh of relief — if only the Amalekites would convert, I/we are not obligated to murder them. Phew! That was close. But what if they choose not to convert? If a captive refuses adult male circumcision or the minimal Seven Noahide Laws "they are killed immediately" (*Hilkhot Milah* 1:6).[27] Moreover, what of all the sources that mention explicitly that Jews are enjoined *not* to accept proselytes from Amalek, such as Pesikta deRav Kahana 3:16 (Mandelbaum 52)?

> It was repeated in the name of Rabbi Eliezer: The Holy One Blessed Be vowed a solemn oath: my right arm, my right arm, my throne, my throne, that if converts will come from all the nations of the world that I will accept them, and from the seed of Amalek — I will never accept them. Thus did David do…"

The text quotes 2 Samuel 1:13 in which King David kills someone claiming to be the son of an Amalekite proselyte. Moreover this law is brought in the tannaitic sources, Mekhilta (Horowitz-Rabin 187) and Mekhilta deRashbi (Melamed-Epstein 127) on Exodus 17:16, also as a tradition David quotes in the name of Moses. This position was also accepted by medieval exegetes like Ralbag on 2 Samuel 1:14.

Despite the argument outlined by Sagi, Maimonides' silence on Amalek is more likely to be consistent with these traditions than to be opposed to them. Amalek is not mentioned because the conversion of Amalek is unacceptable to David, Moses and God. This position also follows from the way in which Maimonides has structured the architecture of his legal edifice both here and in *Hilkhot Melakhim* chapter 6. Maimonides opens a large umbrella to gather in all elements of the tradition. He opens with a sweeping generalization — a legal position that is universal (12:17). He then sets out conditions that must be met

26 See above n. 6.

27 Blidstein, *Concepts*, p. 232 n. 8 *loc.cit* above n. 20. See also *Hilkhot Melakhim* 8:9 in reference to the captive woman and the discussion of Joseph Dov Solveitchik, *Igrot HaGRID Halavi* (Jerusalem: 2001), 46-49.

for this rule to hold — in this case the convert is to marry an Israelite (12:17). Then Maimonides sets out exceptions (12:17) to these marital rules for foreign nations (12:17-21) and goes on to deal with an even more exceptional case (12:22): "Whoever converts from the Seven Nations is not forbidden by the Torah to enter the congregation." Nonetheless Maimonides continues (12:22) to state that only the Givonites converted, after which he goes on to deal with their special case further (12:23-24). Maimonides does not mention at all that all the other Canaanites of the same Seven Nations were annihilated in battle with Israel. This is not a failure on his part. Here he is dealing with converts and elsewhere, that is, in *Hilkhot Melakhim* he deals with their genocide, for it is the prerogative of kings to conduct that war. Only at the very end (12:25) does Maimonides let us know that his entire edifice is (for the time being) in abeyance as history has intervened so as to make it impossible to keep these laws (cf. *Hilkhot Sota* for a similar structure). *Hilkhot Melakhim* outlined above is also similar in its structure — and this provides some insight into how the entire code is constructed. It follows that Amalek is not an exceptional case as are the Givonites, Amonites, Moabites, etc. — hence they are not mentioned. Neither is Amalek like all the other nations— and I would insist that the entire biblical and tannaitic and amoraic tradition confirms this. They are not mentioned because it would be absurd to discuss people subject to genocide as the subjects of conversion. Nowhere does Maimonides consider the subject of genocide taboo, nor does he shy away from it as we shall soon see. I also believe that it is patently absurd to think that Maimonides was easier on the Amalekites (and against all traditional sources of authority on Amalek) while remaining a conservative traditionalist on Amonites and Moabites and the others. The justification for this genocidal policy — as embarrassing as it is for many of the commentators on *Hilkhot Melakhim* (loc. cit.) as well as modern scholars such as Sagi[28] — is carefully articulated by Maimonides in the third part of his *Guide for the Perplexed.*

> The Book of Judges also includes the commandment to destroy the seed of Amalek, for one particular tribe or nation ought to be punished, just as one particular individual is punished, so that all tribes should be deterred and

28 But cf. contra Sagi, Horowitz, From the Generations of Moses [loc cit n. 7], 446-450.

> should not cooperate in doing evil. For they will say: Lest it be done to me what was done to the sons of such and such a man. Thus even if there should grow up among them a wicked corrupt man who does not care about the wickedness of his soul and does not think of the wickedness of his action, he will not find a helper of his own tribe to help him in the wicked things whose realization he desires. Accordingly it was commanded that Amalek who hastened to use the sword, should be exterminated by the sword. On the other hand, *Amon* and *Moab*, who acted in a vile manner and caused harm by means of a stratagem, were punished only by the prohibition against becoming related to them through marriage, by being considered worthless, and by their friendship being shunned. All these matters belong to the divine estimation of penalties, and so these should not be too great or too small, as He may He be exalted, has made it clear: *According to his wickedness...* (*Guide* iii:41, 566).

If this were not enough, Maimonides returns yet again to the theme of genocide while dealing with the embarrassment of foreign genealogies being included in Scripture.

> The enumeration of the tribes of the children of *Se'ir* and of their individual genealogy is made with a view to *one simple commandment*: for He, may He be exalted, has commanded exterminating only the seed of *Amaleq*. Now *Amaleq was the son of Eliphaz and Timna the sister of Lotan*. He did not command killing the other children of *Esau*.... Accordingly if there had been no explanation concerning these genealogies and their particulars, all of them would have been killed through neglectfulness.... All this was an act of justice on the part of God lest a tribe he killed indiscriminately in the course of the extermination of another tribe. For the *decree* was only directed against the descendants of *Amaleq*, and we have already explained in what way wisdom is manifested therein. (*Guide* iii:50, 614-615).

IV

What was on the legal books was at least written about as if it were actually also carried out in active warfare (Exodus 17: 8-14) and most graphically 1 Samuel 15:30: "Now go and strike at Amalek, and utterly destroy them and all that is his. And do not have mercy on him and you shall kill [all] from man to woman, from toddler to nursing infant, from ox to lamb, from camel to mule." Rashi and others say that the purpose of such total annihilation is that no one would be able to say that this cow, ox, camel came from Amalek. Saul in fact spares some choice cattle, apparently with the intention of sacrificing these on an altar. He also spares the Amalekite King Agag, whom Samuel personally slays. (1 Samuel 15:9;33).

The violence committed by the prophet Samuel was profoundly disturbing to Martin Buber and he wrote about his reaction to reading this section of Scripture.[29]

> I repeated to my partner in dialogue how dreadful it had already been to me when I was a boy to read this as the message of God (and my heart compelled me to read it over again or at least to think about the fact that this was written in the Bible). I told him how already at that time it horrified me to read or to remember how the heathen king went up to the prophet with the words on his lips "Surely the bitterness of death is past," and was hewn to pieces by him. I said to my partner: "I have never been able to believe that this is the message of God. I do not believe it."... "I believe," I replied without reflecting, "that Samuel has misunderstood God."

What Buber admits here is his embarrassment by scripture. His excuse for Samuel's behavior as "misunderstood God" is an attempt on his part to at least salvage God from the text. Given the above record this is no easy task as the attribution of near omnicide is attributed to this God in the biblical flood story in Genesis.

29 See *The Philosophy of Martin Buber*, ed. Paul Arthur Schilpp and Maurice Friedman (London, La Salle, IL: Cambridge University Press, 1967), 31-32. For a citation referring to Buber but without citation see above, n. 11 Feldman, *Remember Amalek*, ix.

V

The ancient traditional literature of the sages by and large has no fixed notion of any limit as to divine commandments. The one exception is Rabbi Simlai, who indicates that there are 613 commandments but — if he provided a list none has survived in any form. Furthermore the two commandments indicated by him as belonging to the list are not free of creating new problems as recently studied by Friedberg.[30] If these are commandments then surely Scripture contains far and away more than 613 of them. For example the word "no" appears over one thousand times from Exodus 12 to Deuteronomy. Compare this number to the 365 negative commandments. The same is true for the normative list of positive commandments.

Given the fact that what is listed or not listed creates a distinct *nomos*, one in which transgression is an offense to public propriety punishable by a legal system, it is evident that Robert Cover's claim in "Nomos and Narrative" is to be taken seriously, namely that "the jurisgenerative principle by which legal meaning proliferates in all communities never exists in isolation from violence" (40). This violence is abundantly clear in the scriptural record demanding by claims of divine decree genocide and ethnocide of the Seven Nations or Canaanites, the Midianites and the Amalekites. One might make the feeble argument that such were the motives of revenge in antiquity (e.g., the Shekhemites), that the motivation for such atrocities needed no further justification, hence no warrant for genocide as apologies for its implementation. This surely cannot be the case for all generations, for all time. What occasion would permit the argument Cover brings in the Mennonite *amicus* brief at Bob Jones University? "Our religious beliefs, however, are very deeply held. When these beliefs collide with the demands of society, our highest allegiance must be toward God, and we must say with the men of God of the past, 'We must obey God rather than men.'"[31] Such strongly held belief motivated Abraham to sacrifice Isaac (Genesis 22:1-12, 19; original story as told in *E: the First*

30 See Albert D. Friedberg, "An Evaluation of Maimonides' Enumeration of the 613 Commandments, with Special Emphasis on the Positive Commandments," Ph.D. Dissertation University of Toronto, 2008, 1-31, especially 19-24.

31 Cover, "Nomos and Narrative," p. 27 and below n. 49.

Book of God),[32] Phineas to spear the Israelite man with the Midianite woman (Numbers 25:6-9), and allowed Samuel to behead the Amalekite King Agag (1 Samuel 15:32-33). Each action is acknowledged by God as a favorable act. True, the rabbinic sages are unhappy with the fact that Phineas did not follow the due process of law in meting out justice.[33] Cover indicates that "[b]ecause in capital punishment the action or *deed* is extreme and irrevocable, there is pressure placed on the *word* — the interpretation that establishes the legal justification for the act" (Cover 1986, 1622). In a footnote Cover elaborates: "This pressure for more certain justification of the death sentence lies behind the development of the 'super due process' position with regard to death penalty cases" (1622, n.50). Nonetheless even "super due process" of law is inadequate. Cover indicates that "[t]o any person endowed with the normal inhibitions against the imposition of pain and death, the deed of capital punishment entails a special measure of reluctance and abhorrence which constitute the gulf that must be bridged between interpretation and action." (1622) But there may be special cases in which such reluctance proves inadequate as a deterrent or antidote to haste, error in judgment, and zealotry or the social need for what Girard calls scapegoating.[34] The reason for this is affirmed by Cover:

> At the same time, the fact that capital punishment constitutes the most plain, the most deliberate, and the most thoughtful manifestation of legal interpretation and violence make the imposition of the sentence an especially powerful test of the faith and commitment of the interpreters. (Cover 1986, 1622)

For Jews the risk is twofold and they must walk through a minefield strewn with what for them constitute two normally friendly and mutually supportive forces: scripture and tradition. Scripture credits explicitly the zealous behavior

32 See Tzemah Yoreh, "The Elohistic Source: Its Structure and Unity," [Hebrew] Ph.D. Dissertation, The Hebrew University, Jerusalem, 2003, 27-45.

33 See ySanhedrin 9:11, 26b and obliquely in bSanhedrin 82a.

34 Rene Girard, *The Scapegoat*, tr. Yvonne Freciero (Baltimore: Johns Hopkins University Press, 1986). See also Walter Burkert, Rene Girard and Jonathan Z. Smith, *Violent Origins: Ritual Killing and Cultural Formation*, ed. Robert G. Hamerton-Kelly (Stanford: Stanford University Press, 1987); Andrew J. McKenna, *Violence and Difference: Girard, Derrida, and Deconstruction* (Urbana and Chicago: University of Illinois Press, 1992); Michael Kirwan, *Discovering Girard*, Lanham, MD: Cowley Publications, 2005), 38-62.

and divine sanction of genocidal action, whereas tradition enhances its warrant, further justifying the unconscionable.

At the Nuremberg Trials the standard mantra of all Nazi prisoners of war in the face of the genocidal atrocities was one of following orders. Obedience is seen as a higher good, proper behaviour, an instance of what Cover calls "the shadow of coercion" (Cover 1983, 40). Scripture and tradition become dangerously powerful when the crucible of normative jurisprudence privileges them as Maimonides did.

The significance of so illustrious a legal philosopher and judge as Maimonides lending his prestige to such legislation marked as the violence of legal acts (cf. Nazi judges) should not be lost on us in light of Cover's opening comments to his important essay "Violence and the Word." (1601)

> Legal interpretation takes place in a field of pain and death. This is true in several senses. Legal interpretive acts signal and occasion the imposition of violence upon others: A judge articulates her understanding of a text, and as a result, somebody loses his freedom, his property, his children, even his life. Interpretations in law also constitute justifications for violence which has already occurred or which is about to occur. When interpreters have finished their work, they frequently leave behind victims whose lives have been torn apart by these organized, social practices of violence. Neither legal interpretation nor the violence it occasions may be properly understood apart from one another.

What to do? The courage of confrontation is resolutely required. Unfortunately, Cover provides us with some guidelines as to what could be at stake in such a process based on past experience in "Nomos and Narrative." (49)

> Whenever a community resists a rule of silence or some other law of the state, it necessarily enters into a secondary hermeneutic — the interpretation of the texts of resistance. For a group to live its law in the face of the predictable employment of violence against it requires a new elaboration of "law" — the development of an understanding of what is right and just in the violent contexts that the group will encounter. The group must understand the normative implications of struggle and the meaning of suffering and must accept responsibility for the results of the confrontations that will ensue.

The most extreme formulation is provided by Cover in a footnote: "This "understanding" may include acceptance of responsibility for shedding blood or for others' shedding of it" (Cover 1983, 49 n. 133).

VI

Tadeusz Borowski in his semi-biographical account of his experiences in Nazi concentration camps, *This Way for the Gas, Ladies and Gentleman*, depicts the following gruesome scenarios of new arrivals:[35]

> Here is a woman — she walks quickly but tries to appear calm. A small child with a pink cherub's face runs after her and, unable to keep up, stretches out his little arms and cries: 'Mama! Mama!' 'Pick up your child, woman!' 'It's not mine, sir, not mine!' she shouts hysterically and runs on, covering her face with her hands. She wants to hide, she wants to reach those who will not ride the trucks, those who will go on foot, those who will stay alive. She is young, healthy, good-looking, she wants to live. But the child runs after her, wailing loudly: 'Mama, mama, don't leave me!' 'It's not mine, not mine, no!' Andrei, a sailor from Sevastopol, grabs hold of her. His eyes are glassy from vodka and the heat. With one powerful blow he knocks her off her feet, then, as she falls, takes her by the hair and pulls her up again. His face twitches with rage.
>
> 'Ah, you bloody Jewess! So you're running from your own child! I'll show you, you whore!' His huge hand chokes her, he lifts her in the air and heaves her on to the truck like a heavy sack of grain.
>
> Here! And take this with you, bitch! And he throws a child at her feet. 'Gut gemacht, good work. That's the way to deal with degenerate mothers,' says the S.S. man standing at the foot of the truck. 'Gut, gut, Russki.'

Without relenting, Borowski continues:

35 Tadeusz Borowski, *This Way for the Gas, Ladies and Gentlemen*, tr. and abridged Barbara Vedder (New York: Penguin Books, 1976 [1959]), 43.

> I go back inside the train; I carry out dead infants; I unload luggage. I touch corpses, but I cannot overcome the mounting, uncontrollable terror. I try to escape from the corpses, but they are everywhere: lined up on the gravel, on the cement edge of the ramp, inside the cattle cars. Babies, hideous naked women, men twisted by convulsions. I run off as far as I can go, but immediately a whip slashes across my back. Out of the corner of my eye I see an S.S. man, swearing profusely. (Borowski 45)

Two final stories from Borowski with which I shall burden you:

> Several other men are carrying a small girl with only one leg. They hold her by the arms and the one leg. Tears are running down her face and she whispers faintly: 'Sir, it hurts, it hurts…"' they throw her on top of the corpses. She will burn alive along with them…".
>
> 'My God, man, I am finished, absolutely finished!' 'So soon? After only two transports?' (Borowski 46)

The second story in this sequence:

> Another whistle, another transport…" Only this time a little girl pushes herself halfway through the small window and, losing her balance, falls out on the gravel. Stunned she lies still for a moment, then stands up and begins walking around in a circle, faster and faster, waving her rigid arms in the air, breathing loudly and spasmodically, whining in a faint voice. Her mind has given way in the inferno inside the train. The whining is hard on the nerves: an S.S. man approaches calmly, his heavy boot strikes between her shoulders. She falls. Holding her down with his foot, he draws his revolver, fires once, then again. She remains face down, kicking the gravel with her feet, until she stiffens. They proceed to unseal the train. (Borowski 47-48)

Perhaps it is easy to see how contemporization of the Amalekite concept would lead to an identification of Amalekites with Germans. Perhaps if one had witnessed terror attacks on civilian populations, as Israel has suffered from Palestinian suicide bombers, one might continue to contemporize the biblical scriptures meant to be true for all time to specify the Palestinians as the neo-

Amalekites. The principle of contemporization first occurs in Scripture itself in the biblical book of Esther. In that book Haman wishes to destroy the Jews as graphically depicted by Esther to Ahasuerus (7:4) "For we have been sold, my people and I, to be destroyed, massacred, and exterminated." Perhaps I would have translated this as "to be destroyed, killed and annihilated." The King James Version has "to be destroyed, to be slain, and to perish." In any case it is clear that the use of "exterminated" in a post-Holocaust Jewish translation like that of the Jewish Publication Society is an attempt to identify Haman as a precursor to or foreshadowing of Hitler. For already in his manifesto *Mein Kampf* Hitler used the imagery of parasites to describe the Jewish people:[36] "The Jew's life as a parasite in the body of other nations and states explains a characteristic which once caused Schopenhauer, as has already been mentioned, to call him the 'great master of lying.'" Hitler's final solution for these perpetually lying parasites was extermination befitting vermin. Zyklon B used to gas Jews was also an effective delousing method for clothing.

The contemporization of the Amalekite concept already occurs implicitly in the choice of Haman's patronym (Esther 3:1), "Haman son of Hammedatha the Agagite." Agag is the Amalekite king slaughtered by Samuel. What is implicit in Scripture is made explicit by Josephus in *Antiquities* (xi 209-214):

> Now wherever Haman, the son of Amadethos who was of Amalekite descent went in to the king, the foreigners and Persians prostrated themselves before him, for Artaxerxes had ordered that he should receive this honour from them. But Mordecai because of his wisdom and his native law would not prostrate himself before any man and Haman, having observed this, inquired from what people he came. And when he learned that he was a Jew, he became indignant and remarked to himself that whereas the free-born Persians prostrated themselves before him, this man, who was a slave, did not see fit to do so. And although he wished to be avenged on Mordecai, he considered it too little to ask that he alone be punished by the king, but decided to *exterminate* his whole nation, for he naturally hated the Jews because his own race, the Amalekites, had been destroyed by them.

36 Adolf Hitler, *Mein Kampf*, tr. Ralph Manheim (Boston: Houghton Mifflin Co., 1971 [1925]), 305.

> Accordingly, he went to the King and brought a charge, saying that there was a certain wicked nation scattered throughout the habitable land ruled by him, which was unfriendly and unsocial and neither had the same religion nor practised the same laws as others, "but both by its customs and practices it is the enemy of your people and of all mankind. If you wish to lay up a store of good deeds with your subjects, you will give orders to destroy this nation root and branch and leave not a remnant of them to be kept either in slavery or in captivity." ... This sum of the money he said he would gladly furnish in order that the kingdom might be rid of this *plague* and have peace. [Emphasis added]

The edict is further reiterated: "Wherefore I order you to destroy all those who are pointed out by Haman, my second father, with their wives and children, without sparing anyone or disobeying my written order by giving more heed to pity then to my instructions." (*Antiquities* xi, 218)

This identification between Haman and the Amalekites is also made by the Aramaic targum. One might ask how any of these identifications makes sense if Agag and all the Amalekites had already been killed by Saul and Samuel. This problem is already solved by Pseudo-Philo's *Biblical Antiquities* (58:2-3):

> And Saul went off and attacked Amalek. And he let Agag, the king of Amalek, live because he said to him, "I will show you hidden treasures."... And God said to Samuel "the king has been corrupted with silver, and he has let the king of Amalek and his wife live. And now let them be, so that Agag may come together with his wife tonight; and you will kill him tomorrow. But his wife they will keep safe until she bears a male child, and she also will die. And he who will be born from her will become a stumbling block for Saul."

Other solutions offered by the midrash link Agag to Haman without explicitly mentioning how this was accomplished before Samuel dismembers him.[37]

Further contemporization is accomplished in several ways. Rashi in his commentary to Isaiah 34:10 concerning a prophecy of great slaughter among the Edomites conflates the prophecy with Exodus 17:16, "The Lord will be at war with Amalek from generation to generation."

37 See *Pirkei deRabbi Eliezer*, chapter 49; *Eliyahu Rabbah*, chapter 18; and parallels.

> *From generation to generation* — from that generation to the last generation. Another matter: This is Moses' curse (Exodus 17) *The Lord will be at war with Amalek from generation to generation* — from the generation of Moses to the generation of Saul. And from there to the generation of Mordecai and from there to the generation of our King Messiah.

Identification is also made between Edom, Esau and Amalek. Rashi on Ecclesiastes (1:10) reflects on the possibility of truly unprecedented events: "An aggadic midrash explicates this in reference to the obliteration of the memory of Amalek and the end of the memory of Edom who is to be obliterated as it says (Ovadiah 1): *They will be no remnant for the house of Esau.*" This constellation of identities allows for the easy identification of Amalek with Christianity, an identification discussed in the scholarship on the topic.[38]

As is evident the lines of traditions mentioned hitherto embraced the biblical verses and breathed new life into them by updating their application. So why if we are still commanded to blot out the memory of Amalek is all this so terribly embarrassing to me and other scholars such as Golinkin who has recently addressed the question?[39] Of the numerous texts one may cite from tradition only one expresses some explicit embarrassment with the genocidal commandment (bYoma 22b):

> Rabbi Mani says... that King Saul argued with God: If the Torah said (Deuteronomy 21:1-9) that if you find an unidentified dead body between two cities, you must bring an *eglah arufah*, a sacrifice as a form of atonement for that one death, how much more so for all of these souls! And if an [Amalekite] sinned, did his animal sin? If adults sinned, did the children sin?

The Talmud does not leave the matter here (Golinkin ends his quotation of the text here) but continues: "A [divine] Echo came forth and said to him (Ecclesiastes 7): *Do not be overly righteous.* And when Saul said to Doag, 'Return and smite the priests,' a divine echo came forth and said to him, 'Do not be overly wicked.'" Genocide commanded by the deity is admissible but not genocide approved by humans alone.

38 See above n. 7, Horowitz, *From the Generation of Moses.*

39 See above n. 15.

What we are dealing with here are what may be called "toxic texts" or "texts of terror." One may argue in favor of the efficacy of targeted assassinations such as the summary disposal of Haman without due process (Esther 7:9-10), or even for pre-emptive strikes such as the posture taken against the gentile enemies of Israel reported in Shushan and the Persian satrapies (Esther 9:12-16). Imagine a different scenario and the above texts will hit home for you. A Bosnian-style roundup of Palestinian children and their grandparents and great-grandparents has just arrived on a crowded bus to a site outside Dimona. They are meant to be counter-hostages to the soldiers taken by Palestinian jihadi terrorists. A group of religious elite soldiers identifies these prisoners as latter-day descendents of Amalek. It even turns out that some carry identity cards indicating their place of birth as Amalekite territory. DNA scans also confirm their status as progeny of ancient Amalekites whose remains were found in a pile of bones dating back to Saul.[40] Do we now become neo-Nazis? Do we affirm Hitler's final solution for the Jews on the neo-Amalekites? I have no doubt that there are some, like Baruch Goldstein,[41] who would answer in the affirmative. Perhaps quite a number of others would also do so as his gravesite is apparently a pilgrimage site. What to do? The answer has been provided by Nancy and tradition (at least as I understand it turned on its head).[42] Nancy requests a radical transformation in which our fascination with religious fanaticism and violence be turned into identification with the victim and transmogrified into art.

40 Mark Y. Stoeckle and Paul D.N. Herbert, "Barcode of Life," *Scientific American* (October 2008): 82-88; Boensri Dickinson, "Your Genome Decoded, While-U-Wait," *Discover* (October 2008): 48. Much speculation concerning so-called Jewish genes exist. Most of the studies are antiquated, poorly controlled and agenda driven. See Paul Wexler, *The Non-Jewish Origins of the Sephardic Jews* (New York:SUNY Press, 1996); Yaakov Kleiman, *DNA and Tradition: The Genetic Link to the Ancient Hebrews* (Englewood, NJ: Devora Publishing, 2004); Hillel Halkin, "Jews and Their DNA," *Commentary* (September 2008): 37-43; *AJS Perspectives:The Jewish Race* (Fall 2007): 8-38.

41 See Horowitz, *Reckless Rites* (above n. 7), 4-12.

42 De Beistegui, Miguel. "Sacrifice Revisited," in *On Jean-Luc Nancy: The Sense of Philosophy*, ed. Darren Shepherd, Simon Sparks and Colin Thomas (London and New York: Routledge, 1997), 162-167 (quoting Jean-Luc Nancy).

It seems tradition also has arrived at such in the form of carnivalesque noisemakers.[43] For in the face of overwhelming attendant, imminent evil and its violent expression, the world must make as much noise as possible. Like the Who in Dr. Seuss' *Horton Hears a Who*, not one shirker should exist as a silent protestor or a so-called innocent bystander. Too much is at risk.

First, the memory of Amalek must remain not because the nation may readily be conflated with other perpetrators of evil but so as to never forget their own behavior and actions. In a poem that serves as a preface to Primo Levi's book *Survival in Auschwitz*, Levi alludes to the *shema* prayer, and insists that the Holocaust, that is, human beings' inhumanity to each other, never be forgotten.[44]

> Meditate that this came about:
> I command these words to you.
> Carve them in your hearts
> At home, in the street.
> Going to bed, rising;
> Repeat them to your children,
> Or may your house fall apart,
> May illness impede you,
> May your children turn their faces from you.

The commandment to annihilate them, to exterminate them, be they Amalekites or Germans or Palestinians, must be eliminated, as has already begun to happen for Amalek. In its place I suggest a new-old *mitzvah,* the stewardship verse from Genesis 2:15 so often quoted as an example of Jewish environmental ethics: "And God took Adam and placed him in the Garden of Eden, to till it and to tend it."

---

43 Brian M. Britt, "Erasing Amalek: Remembering to Forget with Derrida and Biblical Tradition," in *Derrida's Bible: (Reading a Page of Scripture with a Little Help from Derrida)*, ed. Yvonne Sherwood (New York: Palgrave McMillan, 2004), 61-77, especially 71. See also the gloss of Ramah cited by Horowitz, *From the Generation of Moses* (above n. 6), 449 n. 96.

44 Originally published in Italian, the book has been re-printed and translated many times. Levi's first title (translated) was *If this be a Man*.

One of the most significant difficulties in the false identification of the Germans, or even the Nazis, with Amalek is the resultant problematic which this willfully created anachronism provides both for a proper understanding of the past and, more significantly, of the present, including the Holocaust itself. If the Nazis are to be tainted with the ancient stigma of Amalekitism, then in a sense their moral decrepitude is diminished. After all, if their innate nature is due to a genetic defect, it is part of God's DNA distribution with which they are tainted. How then can Amalek behave other than as Amalek and how can they not be enemies of the Jews? The indentification of Germans with Amalekites is understood in two ways: (1) all who embody evil are Amalekites by a process of allegorization of Amalekitism; (2) Germans are a transmigration of Amalekite souls.[45] A corollary of the second idea is that those who were their victims are a transmigration of the souls of the Israelites who sinned in the sin of the golden calf. In other words they suffered from bad karma. The difficulty withthis idea of punishment for transgressions in a previous lifetime is manifold. (1) The cardinal sin of the Israelites in the desert for which they wander for forty years is the sin of fearing to enter the Promised Land. (2) Even if we accept the golden calf incident as the cardinal sin, the number affected is 600,000 men of military age, not six million victims of Nazism. (3) There are important sages such as Rav Sa'adia Gaon who vociferously deny transmigration of souls as a Jewish concept though one could argue that resurrection of the dead is but an extreme form of the idea.[46] (4) A central tenet of Judaism is that one should die for one's own sins. The theological reply attempting to save the above construct would be that those guiltless victims died as atonement for the sins of their brethren with the golden calf. (5) Why were the victims mainly children, women and old people when the participants in the golden calf incident were male

45 This was proposed to me in a conversation with a Hasidic scribe in Jerusalem.

46 Saadiah ben Joseph, *Book of Beliefs and Convictions (Opinions)* Treatise 6 Chapter 8 (for an English translation see the edition of Samuel Rosenblatt, [New Haven: Yale University Press, 1948], 259-263; as well as others). See *Encyclopedia Judaica* s.v. gilgul. See also Mark Verman, "Reincarnation and Theodicy: Traversing Philosophy, Psychology, and Mysticism," in *Be'erot Yitzhak: Studies in Memory of Isadore Twersky*, ed. Jay M. Harris (Cambridge, MA and London: Harvard University Press, 2005), 399-426.

adults? According to the midrash, women did not participate in the sin of the golden calf.[47]

On the other hand, by implying that the ancient Amalekites were as bad as the Nazis we diminish the uniqueness of the Holocaust experience. Though I acknowledge the Armenian Holocaust and the massacres in Rwanda and other acts of evil on a massive scale, no one has ever devised so diabolical a killing system as the Nazis did, a universe wholly committed to the murder primarily of Jews, and secondarily of Roma. My father overpowered and disarmed a German Nazi concentration camp guard on a forced march from Auschwitz in the dying days of the Second World War. He did not kill the Nazi. If Nazis are Amalekites, he is not simply an everyday hero who proves that even Nazis could not turn him into a murderer. He did not do so even when in a court of law it would likely have been considered at least partially justifiable as revenge, or a form of self-defense, or simply dismissed as a common event of the times. Jewishly speaking, he would also have to be considered a sinner for disobeying the commandment to destroy Amalek.[48] As he did to the monarch Saul, Samuel would have torn off my father's ragged concentration camp vestments to tell him that his act of humanity was heinous in the eyes of God who would see that his descendents, that is, myself and my children, my sisters and their progeny, would have our family line extirpated, cut off. Samuel and scripture would have seen his act of sparing the Nazi's life as one of defiance. But despite all he witnessed, my father believed in the due process of law. To this end he gave testimony in the Canadian prosecution of Nazi criminals. The law was sacrosanct, not to be taken lightly and not to be taken Phineaslike into one's own hands in the heat of passion even if this could be given a successful legal defense in a court of law. The Nazis were far, far worse than the ancient Amalekites or any evil predicaments Biblical exhortations could conjure. They defied human

47 See *Pirkei d'R. Eliezer,* chapter 45. See also *Leviticus Rabbah* chapter 2 (Margulies 36, n. 1; Jerusalem: Jewish Theological Seminary of America, 1972).

48 See above n. 11, Goldman 7, who after citing Maimonides states, "This despite the psychlogical difficulty to keep [the Commandment], behold the psychological difficulty in not keeping it is even greater." On page 4 he writes, "the commandment to wipe out the memory of Amalek raises certain difficulties for Israel who are [by nature] compassionate, the children of compassionate ones." [Hebrew]

imagination in their evil conduct. Not all the stories of what constituted their evil deeds have been told, nor will they ever be told in full. Confessional American TV tabloids would have many lifetimes worth of material in describing each scratch in a gas chamber wall or how guards knew all the Jews inside were dead because they no longer heard the sounds of *shema yisrael* or *ani ma'amin* coming from the gassed victims. My informant is David Weiss Halivni who was told this by someone he knew who had been assigned crematoria work.

In my youth I would fantasize about killing Nazis. Cops and robbers, or Indians and Cowboys—the racism of the latter game should be duly noted—were replaced by Jews versus Germans or Nazis.[49] In such play one would have the opportunity to not only "die" but also to "kill". How would I have fared in "real" life?

I do not know, but I do have one related and more recent story to tell. I was walking along the streets of downtown Toronto on Bloor Street at Spadina which is near my Canadian home when I saw a very dark-skinned person dressed in full Nazi regalia with a swastika on his T-shirt mouthing anti-Semitic slogans. My usual reaction would have been to avoid such toxic individuals as there is precious little I, who look very Jewish, could say to him other than offer an immediate target for his venom and hatred. This time I acted differently and confronted the teenager or young man because I felt I could give him something to think about that might turn his testosterone to less hateful pursuits. I asked him if he knew that Hitler had no love for dark-skinned people and that if he successfully had killed all the Jews of the world, he certainly would have turned on the blacks of Europe and elsewhere next. My basis for this is that Hitler was greatly displeased with the

49 See Robert Warrior, "Canaanites, Cowboys, and Indians," *Union Seminary Quarterly Review* (*USQR*) 59 (1-2) (2005): 1-8. On the identification of Native Americans by Christians as Amalek thereby creating the justification to kill them, see Susan Niditch, *War in the Hebrew Bible: A Study in the Ethics of Violence* (New York, Oxford: Oxford University Press, 1993), 3-4. Concerning racism see Sylvester Johnson, "New Israel, New Canaan: The Bible, the People of God, and the American Holocaust," *USQR* 59 (1-2) (2005): 25-39; Jennifer Harvey, "The (Im) moral Origins of White U.S.-American Identity: Native/African/English, Savage/Heathen Christian," *USQR* 59 (1-2) (2005): 79-113. Concerning the reaction to racism see Mary Ann Tolbert, "The Reproduction of Domination," *USQR* 59 (1-2) (2005): 9-14; Randall C. Bailey, "He Didn't Even Tell Us the Worst of It," *USQR* 59 (1-2) (2005): 15-24.

American delegation to the Olympic Games at Berlin in 1936 which included African-Americans who had won medals demonstrating athletic prowess and superiority over white Aryans. Unfortunately, my effort to turn his head around was not successful, at least not immediately, and I, of course, had no way to follow up my efforts to educate this person. My only reward was to be heaped with verbal abuse. Surely one must be vigilant concerning the neo-Nazi party whose main headquarters are in the Milton area of Ontario. I would go further and make it a criminal offense in Canada to display, wear or own Nazi regalia, especially items with swastikas on them, as is the case in Germany today. I, however, would be greatly embarrassed, disappointed, chagrined and would need to vigorously oppose and protest anyone who would consider them as modern day manifestations of the Amalekitism subject to counter-genocidal warfare.

VII

Above and elsewhere I have submitted that the way out of the vicious cycle of violence depicted and hence to some extent envisioned by Cover may be overcome only by a more benign process. The contemporary theological implications are significant. By admitting our embarrassment with Scripture we open up the possibility of neutralization of the embarrassing ideas. We open ourselves up to the possibility that they may no longer be operational in our time and in our place. Such a notion has a venerable history in the internal mechanism and unfolding of Judaism. At some point the concept of commandments that were not followed in our day was integrated into and even influenced the academic curriculum. So, for example, all laws pertaining to the Temple were "temporarily" abrogated because there no longer was a temple. This is very convenient for present-day Jews as it means that we are not required to struggle with Islam over the Temple Mount. According to many rabbinic authorities we should not even visit the Temple Mount — a prohibition transgressed by Ariel Sharon's infamous visit and provocation which helped lauch the intifada as a reaction. Though such a reaction would probably have happened in any case, his visit served as a catalyst. To have a new Temple on the Temple Mount would at worst require the destruction of the present one (cf. Hindu-Muslim strife in India or Taliban-Buddhist conflicts in Afghanistan) or at best a sharing of facilities (cf. Hebron). Happily for Jews and Judaism the third Temple was to be a heavenly one not built by human hands. In such an event I am confident that no one will argue as to who has the rights to worship on the Mount. It is important for religions and nations to develop coping mechanisms consistent with allowing neighbors and even competitors to live in peace if not in harmony. The notion of embarrassment allows for such a process of accommodation. Hence, for example, Christian embarrassment with statements in the Gospel of Matthew or in the Gospel of John concerning the Jews must become, if they are not already, a source of Christian embarrassment. Only at such a point will the attendant anti-Semitism they generated be sufficiently addressed in a positive manner and no longer be used as an excuse to hate Jews or worse.

What is true for Christianity and Christians, Islam and Moslems, is also true for Judaism and Jews. Even where motivated by revenge, we must relegate our murderous memories to the past. They can never again become motivational by false conflation of past and present, nor ever again operational.[50]

Just as we demand that Christians relinquish the hold their holy and sanctified scriptures may still have on them concerning the charge of deicide against the Jews, whatever the contested veracity of such a claim may be, so too must we Jews give up any claims toxic scriptures may still have on us concerning the Seven Nations and the Amalekites. This in turn opens up the possibility of amelioration and forgiveness for wrongs of the past and

---

50 Needless to say genocide is a violation of human rights. See *Genocide and Human Rights: A Philosophical Guide*, ed. John K. Roth (New York: Palgrave Macmillan, 2005). It is more often than not justified as a religious obligation mandated by God as a holy war. See, for example, Gerhard Von Rad, *Holy War in Ancient Israel*, tr. and ed. Marva J. Dawn (Grand Rapids, MI: Eerdmans, 1991); Peter C. Craigie, "The problem of "Holy" War" in *The Problem of War in the Old Testament* (Grand Rapids,MI: Eerdmans, 1978), 45-54; Charles Kimball, *When Religion Becomes Evil* (San Francisco: Harper, 2003), 154-185. This is often built on holy hatred. On anti-Semitism as one such hatred, see Robert Michael, *Holy Hatred: Christianity, Antisemiticism,and the Holocaust* (New York: Palgrave Macmillan, 2006).

even of the present among surviving Amalekites and others.[51] Upon such a foundation may we one day have peace, *pacem in terris, salaam, shalom.*

51 See Arie Nadler and Nurit Shnabel, "Instrumental and Socioemotional Paths to Intergroup Reconciliation and the Needs-Based Model of Socioemotional Reconciliation," in *The Social Psychology of Intergroup Reconciliation*, ed. Arie Nadler, Thomas E. Malloy and Jeffrey D. Fisher (New York: Oxford University Press, 2008), 37; Everett L. Worthington, Jr., *Forgiveness and Reconciliation:Theory and Application* (New York and London: Routledge, 2006), 264; Ervin Staub, "Promoting Reconciliation After Genocide and Mass Killing in Rwanda — And Other Post-conflict Settings: Understanding the Roots of Violence, Healing, Shared History and Genocidal Principles," in *The Social Psychology of Intergroup Reconciliation* (ibid.), 395-422; Marc Gopin, "Judaism and Peacebuilding," in *Religion and Peacebuilding*, ed. Harold Coward and Gordon S. Smith (New York: SUNY Press, 2004), 111-127. (Gopin deals with the Palestinians but the entire volume is relevant to the notion of reconciliation after traumatic events.) See also Henry F. Knight, "Coming to Terms with Amalek," in *Post-Shoah Dialogues* (Lanham, MD: University Press of America 2004), 195-207; Alastair G. Hunter, "(De)nominating Amalek," *Sanctified Aggression JSOT* sup. ser. 400, (2003): 92-108.

BIBLE

A RE-EMBRACEMENT OF JUDGES 19: CHALLENGING PUBLIC-PRIVATE BOUNDARIES

Diane Kriger (of Blessed Memory)

WHICH FOREGROUND?

Judges chapter 19 contains a lurid tale that serves as the prelude to and the pretext for a civil war between Benjamin and the rest of the tribes. Compounding the difficulty in understanding the story, the text contains a number of equivocal and contradictory expressions. To summarize, the story relates that a certain Levite, living in the territory of Efraim, took an אשה פלגש, often translated as "concubine." He is called her בעל , husband. Neither person is named. This woman left him, for reasons that are not entirely clear — the Hebrew is ותזנה עליו — to go to her father in Bet Lehem. The Levite follows her and wins her back, and they start out on their return trip after a prolonged delay — unnecessarily prolonged, it seems — at her father's house. Finding themselves at night in Givah in the territory of Benjamin, they lodge with an Efraimite who offers them shelter in his house. However, the house is beset by a mob of Benjaminites, who demand that the Levite be sent out to them, to be used sexually. The host, protecting his male guest, offers the mob his virgin daughter and the *pilegesh* instead, saying, "Do with them what seems good to you." At this point the Levite seizes the *pilegesh* and leaves her outside. She is repeatedly raped. In the morning the Levite opens (Va-Yiftah) the door, (19:27) va-yiftah daltoth ha-bayith, an ironic echo of another Yiftah (opens, also the Hebrew for Jepthah) and and the doom awaiting another woman at his door — and finds the *pilegesh* lying with her hands on the threshold. In what Bal has called the most uncanny sentence of the book of Judges,[1] the Levite simply says to her: "Get up, let's go." Here he is described as her master, not her husband. When she doesn't respond, he lugs her home on a donkey, cuts her up into twelve pieces and sends the pieces throughout Israel, claiming the Benjaminites wanted to kill him, and thereby laying the foundation for a civil war. The succeeding chapters relate that after some initial victories, the tribe of Benjamin is nearly exterminated, and is allowed to repopulate itself by seizing unmarried women at a feast in Shilo. The last verse of the section, in another ironic echo of the words of the host, states: "In those days there was no king in Israel; each man did what was right in his eyes."

What are we, as modern readers, to make of this violent and bizarre prelude?

One strategy is, of course, to dismiss it, as Wellhuasen did, going so far as to call it an example of the supposed "decadence" of later Hebrew literature.[2] Many modern scholars simply ignore the *pilegesh* and delve into the narrative for the historical details that may be buried in it; quite often, issues surrounding the monarchy are derived from such analyses.[3] As Bal has noted, however, this type of focus puts the story of the *pilegesh* on the margins. She, among others, attempts to bring these margins to the fore by questioning the purpose

---

1 M. Bal, *Death and Dissymmetry: The Politics of Coherence in the Book of Judges* (Chicago: University of Chicago Press, 1988), 188.

2 As noted by R. Boling, Judges, The Anchor Bible 6A (Garden City: Doubleday, 1975), 278, citing earlier opinions of Wellhausen and Moore.

3 See, e.g. J. Fokkelman, "Structural Remarks on Judges 9 and 19," in *Sha'arei Talmon: Studies in the Bible, Qumran, and the Ancient Near East Presented to Shemaryahu Talmon*, 33-45, ed. M. Fishbane and E. Tov (Winona Lake: Eisenbrauns, 1992), 43, who argues that chapters 19-20 are a pro-monarchy polemic; Y. Amit, פרשת פילגש בגבעה כפולמוס סמוי נגד מלכות שאול ואהדיה (שופטים י"ט-כ"א) (Bet Miqrah, 1991-2, Jerusalem), 118, who suggests this is a pro-Davidic polemic, emphasizing the ineffectiveness of the Benjaminite Saul (Saul was from Yavesh Gilad [I Sam 10:26], while David, of the family of Boaz, was related to Naomi's husband of Bet Lehem [Ruth 4: 22]; and R. Boling, Judges, 278, who proposes that this is a post-exilic exhortation to return to a united Israel. One might also argue that this is simply an aetiological narrative, reflecting an attempt by representatives of the youngest brother Benjamin (through the men of Givah) to challenge the authority of the older brother Judah, now the "legal" firstborn, through the medium of the pilegesh of Bet Lehem (in Judah).

of this violent passage and locating it within a particular anthropological or sociological context.[4]

My preference, however, is for a third reading, found in bGitt 6b. This reading addresses chapters 19-21 as a coherent whole — in effect, "embracing" all the elements of the biblical text — and thus does not require us to choose between background and foreground:

> Rav Hisda said: A man should not terrorize [(יטיל אימה יתירה בתוך ביתו) throw excessive fear upon] his household — the husband of the *pilegesh* of *Givah* terrorized her and she caused the fall of [הפילה] thousands of Israelites.[5]

The statement can certainly be taken in a number of ways, particularly given that "she caused the fall of" might be seen as some sort of magical imputation of fault to the *pilegesh*. I believe, however, that the statement also reflects a remarkably modern sensibility: it encourages the reader to challenge the falseness of the boundary between "public" and "private." In drawing attention to what Bal has called the "almost obscene conflation of private and public" in the *pilegesh* story, this Bavli reading acknowledges the danger that violence in the so-called private domain, supposedly the world of the home and of women, will inevitably spill over into the public domain, traditionally the world of men.[6]

The point of the Bavli's statement is that we are meant to be disturbed by the story; to fear the private abuse that cannot be contained behind closed doors. There is certainly evidence in the style of chapter 19 of a deliberate attempt, through various devices, to emphasize its macabre and fearful aspects. Many of these have been discussed by scholars: For instance, the use of darkness as

4 See for example Bal, *Death and Dissymmetry*, who argues that the story reflects the tensions involved in the transition from patrilocal to virilocal marriage (86, 92-3); K. Stone, "Gender and Homosexuality in Judges 19: Subject-Honor, Object-Shame?" JSOT 67 (1995): 87-107, who analyzes the story within an anthropological culture of honor-shame, and argues that men of Givah challenged the honor of the Levite first by the threat of homosexual rape, and then by the rape of his woman as proxy (100).

5 This statement is made within the context of a communication between R. Aviatar and Rav Hisda, third-generation Amoraim, regarding a writ of divorce sent from Babylon to Israel.

6 Bal, *Death and Dissymmetry*, 195, quoting Elaine Scarry, *The Body in Pain: The Making and Unmaking of the World* (New York: Oxford University Press, 1985), 53.

a portent of danger, and as associated with the sexuality of "unusual" women;[7] the anonymity of the participants; the exaggerated, nightmare-like delay of the group's departure from Bethlehem and their consequent failure to reach shelter before dark.[8] Allusions to other biblical crises have been detected: for instance, the knife used by the Levite recalls the knife Abraham carried on his way to sacrifice Isaac;[9] the offer of a woman's sexual services in order to save a male guest from homosexual rape recalls the events at Sodom;[10] and the dismemberment of the woman inciting a civil war against Benjamin is possibly a parody of Saul cutting oxen into twelve pieces to rally the people, this time in defense of Yavesh Gilad.[11] The number of such devices and allusions suggests that they are is not coincidental.

In this list of devices I include the use of two terms that are highly equivocal: *pilegesh*, usually translated as "concubine" (also a notoriously ambiguous term in English), and *va-tizneh 'alav*, a phrase that can be associated with sexual promiscuity. Both are terms strongly suggestive of moral fault. Yet, as Rav Hisda's statement emphasizes, it is not any fault-punishment of the woman that is to provide coherence to the story; we are to avoid such assumptions

7 W. Fields, "The Motif 'Night as Danger' Associated with Three Biblical Destruction Narratives," in *Sha'arei Talmon: Studies in the Bible, Qumran, and the Ancient Near East Presented to Shemaryahu Talmon*, 17-32, ed. M. Fishbane and E. Tov (Winona Lake: Eisenbrauns, 1992), 22, 26 who notes a similar use of darkness with respect to the destruction of Sodom in Genesis 19, and the final plague in Exodus 12:29 ("and it came to pass at midnight"). He describes the association of night and non-regular types of female sexuality as an "allo-motif" running through the Bible.

8 See. e.g., Y. Zakovitch "הדגם הספרותי שלושה-ארבעה במקרא", Ph.D. dissertation, Hebrew University, 1977, 334, 336, who suggests that the impression of a deliberate manipulation of time is created in the narrative by a variation of the "three-four" pattern that he argues is prevalent in the biblical text. The Levite's five-day stay at his father-in-law's has three distinct periods: the first three days, the fourth day, when by the usual three-four pattern one would expect the group to leave, and the fifth day, when the group actually leaves. The description of the fourth day is marked by a lengthening of phrases, and the fifth by a shortening of phrases and feeling of urgency; the effect is thus to create peaks and troughs of tension.

9 J. Unterman, "The Literary Influence of 'The Binding of Isaac' (Genesis 22) on 'The Outrage at Gibeah' (Judges 19)," Hebrew Annual Review 4 (1980): 161-6. On the parallels to the sacrifice of Isaac, see especially 162-3.

10 K. Stone, "Gender and Homosexuality," 100.

11 Y. Amit, פרשת פילגש, 11, 113, on the use of place names and events reminiscent of Saul narratives in 1 Sam 11.

regarding cause and effect and shift our focus to the Levite's behaviour and its implications. I will argue that the very equivocality of *pilegesh* and *va-tizneh alav* support Rav Hisda's reading.

WHY A *PILEGESH*?

This term appears sporadically in the Bible — in some instances associated with named individuals — but its precise meaning is vague. It does not appear in the "legal" passages of the Pentateuch. There are traditions deriving *pilegesh* from a combination of Hebrew words,[12] such as פלג and אשה , in effect meaning "half-wife,"[13] or פילוג and שמוש, with the implication of a woman "used" by different men.[14] These are considered by some scholars to be folk-etymologies

---

12 In fact, it seems likely that pilegesh is a foreign loanword. A computer search of the biblical text confirms that the combination lgsh or lqsh is in fact rare in biblical Hebrew, the only other instance being the description of the prophet Nahum as ha-elqoshi (1: 1). Mandelkern, קונקורדנציה לתנ"ך s.v. פילגש, thought the word was Egyptian; others have posited a Hittite origin, or a Phoenician-Semitic loanword from Greek and Latin. For example, see T. McComiskey, "The Status of the Secondary Wife: Its Development in Ancient Near Eastern Law. A Study and Comprehensive Index," Ph.D. dissertation, Brandeis University, 1965, 91 (Greek); J. Brown, Israel and Hellas, ZAW Supplement 231 (Berlin: Walter de Gruyter, 1995), 70 (Hittite); L. Epstein, "The Institution of Concubinage Among the Jews," PAAJS 6 (1934-5): 153-88, at p. 153 (Phoenicio-Semitic). A summary of earlier speculations on the origin of pilegesh is found in C. Rabin, "The Origin of the Hebrew Word Pilegeš," JJS 25 (1974): 353-64, at p. 353, nn. 2-6. Rabin argued for an Indo-European origin, through the medium of contact with the Philistines (358, 360, 361). S. Levin, "Hebrew {pi(y)legeš}, Greek παλλακη, Latin paelex: The Origin of Intermarriage among the Early Indo-Europeans and Semites," General Linguistics 23 (1983): 191-7, at pp. 192, 194, adds a possible motive for the borrowing of this word: The Philistines (Pelasgians in Greek tradition) had a reputation (as attested in Herodotus, Histories, 6.137ff) for "craving foreign women." The appeal of this practice, particularly for men such as the Levite of Judges 19-20 without a stable residence who might thus find it difficult to attract a wife, led to the incorporation of this type of "intermarriage" into other cultures in contact with the Philistines, although it was subject to much censure.

A further point against a Hebrew origin is the absence in biblical Hebrew of a noun with a similar pattern, although there are proper nouns that seem to have the same form. We may note in particular the Assyrian king's name Tiglat Pileser; as Pileser derives from the Akkadian Apil-ešarra, we may question whether the first element of pilegesh derives from Akkadian apil, "son of" or "descendant of."

13 Mandelkern, s.v. פילגש.

14 Midrash Sekhel Tov on Gen 35: 22.

only, but the assumption behind these ideas is interesting: it seems that the *pilegesh* must be located in relation to wives but as an inferior type.

The one attempt at legal definition in rabbinic literature, found in both the Bavli and the Yerushalmi, maintains this assumption though, not surprisingly, these definitions conflict: In the Yerushalmi (yKet 5:52), Rabbi Meir says the *pilegesh* does not have a *ketubbah*; Rabbi Yehudah says she has a *ketubbah* but no *tena'e ketubbah*. In the Bavli, Rav Yehudah says in the name of Rav that a *pilegesh* has neither *qiddushin* nor a *ketubbah* (b Sanh 21b).[15] In the later view of Maimonides, the *pilegesh* had neither *ketubbah* nor *qiddushin*, she was simply bought. He, however, limited *pilagshim* to kings, and stated that an ordinary person who wished to buy a woman was limited to a Hebrew female slave.[16] The sense again is that the *pilegesh* must be placed on a continuum measured in terms of a marriage relationship, which has "legitimate" wives at one end and female slaves at the other. Thus marriage becomes an ordering principle; according to Pateman,[17] this type of thinking defines women solely in terms of the sexual access one may have to them, and the man or men who can gain such access. By corollary, the man's degree of vested interest in each woman determines the extent to which she and her children are to be maintained and protected.

Certain modern scholars continue this attempt to place the *pilegesh* in relation to wives and slaves. Bal argued that *pilegesh* was a wife in the patrilocal *beena* marriage.[18] Ariel, basing himself on the traditional meaning of "halfwife," argued that such a woman was more than likely to have started life as a slave;[19] Patai suggested that such a woman would have retained her slave status and that

15 E. Ellinson, נישואין שלא כדת משה וישראל (Tel Aviv: Dvir, 1975), 96, has argued that while the pasages are likely not contradictory, at least with respect to the idea that a pilegesh has no qiddushin, there is still no evidence in rabbinic law of any fixed halakhah with respect to the legal status of the pilegesh). For instance, he notes that Rashi to Genesis 25: 6 declares that "wives have a ketubbah, pilagshim do not have a ketubbah." This is taken as an indication that Rashi understood the issue between them to relate only to the ketubbah, and thus assumed both had qiddushin (3).

16 Mishneh Torah, Hilkhot Melakhim 4:4.

17 C. Pateman, *The Sexual Contract* (Stanford: Stanford University Press, 1988), 109-10.

18 Bal, *Death and Dissymmetry*, 85; 92-3.

19 Y. Ariel, "הפילגש ומעמדה ההלכתי במקרא", Megadim 8 (1989), 57-67, at pp. 58, 59.

this is what would distinguish her from a "wife";[20] Neufeld saw no philological difference between *amah*, *shifhah* and *pilegesh*, but argued that the *pilegesh* may have been associated with a greater laxity of morals (and was possibly more akin to a prostitute);[21] Epstein designated concubinage as a specific legal status higher than that of the "slave-wife" but lower than that of the "chief" wife.[22]

There are difficulties with each of these arguments. As has been noted, Bal's definition would not fit all biblical instances of *pilegesh*;[23] further, her argument is based on several older theories that are out of favour.[24] There is only one direct instance in which *pilagshim* are associated in any way with slave terminology: Bilhah is called a *pilegesh* only in Gen 35:22, and is otherwise described as an *amah*, *shifhah*, or *ishah*.[25] Epstein's detailed ranking of female legal statuses would not seem to be supported by the biblical text. While it is possible, or perhaps inevitable, that there were ranks of women within a complex household, this cannot be supported simply by assuming, first, that *pilegesh* means "a female concubine," and second, that all women were to be legally ranked according to a single concept of "marriage." I suggest, for several reasons, that the *pilegesh* is not a legal status and was more likely a topos used for a specific literary purpose.

We must first note that the *pilagshim* in Ezekiel 23:20 are clearly referring to males — ותעגבה על פלגשיהם אשר בשר חמורים בשרם וזרמת סוסים זרמתם — despite the attempts by commentators to turn these *pilagshim* into Chaldeans (LXX) or

20 R. Patai, *Sex and Family in the Bible and the Middle East* (New York: Doubleday, 1959), 41-2.

21 E. Neufeld, *Ancient Hebrew Marriage Laws* (London: Longmans, Green, 1944), 121, 123 (based, for instance, on the Bilhah-Reuven incident of Gen 35: 22). McComisky, "Status," 1, 91, also treated the three terms as synonymous, but seems to have considered them all equivalent to "concubine," which he took to be in essence a "secondary wife."

22 Epstein, "Institution," 154, 156.

23 See, e.g., J.C. Exum, *Fragmented Women* (Valley Forge: Trinity Press, 1993), 177, n. 13.

24 Bal relies on the definition of pilegesh in an older version of Koehler/Baumgartner, which has since been changed. Further, her argument is based on descriptions of beena marriage by J. Morgenstern, ZAW 47(n.s. 6) (1929): 91-100, and ZAW 49 (n.s. 8) (1931): 46-58; these in turn rely on a questionable Bachofen-type assumption of a general "advancement" from matriarchal to patriarchal societies.

25 Elsewhere I have argued that the use of pilegesh in Genesis 35: 22 may have been a later insertion. There is also one indirect association: Avimelekh, who is identified as the son of Gideon's (unnamed) pilegesh, is in one instance called a *ben amah* (Jud 9:18).

explain, as Radak did, that it is appropriate to speak of female lewdness (which is of course a characteristic associated only with *pilagshim*, not wives) using male sexual terms. Interestingly, the English word concubine could also refer to males in Late Middle English.[26] For this reason I suggest that a better translation for *pilegesh* is "consort," as it does not have the gendered connotations that "concubine" now has.

Second, certain *pilagshim* are very noticeably associated with male sexual behaviour that is outside "legitimate" boundaries. In addition to the story in Judges, we may note the assault on Bilhah by Reuven, the one instance in which Bilhah is called a *pilegesh*; the alleged assault on Saul's *pilegesh* by Avner; the assault on David's *pilagshim* by his son Avshalom.[27] The male *pilagshim* in Ezekiel 23:20 are also associated with profligate sexual behaviour.

The point therefore is that *pilagshim*, male or female, are outside the boundaries of "legitimate" marriage. Certain scholars have suggested a succession motif underlying the various biblical instances in which males have or demand intercourse with a female *pilegesh* of their father or military superior;[28] the unsuccessful attempt to assert their superiority explains their disqualification from inheritance.[29] Interestingly, Qumran document 4Q252 also seems to make this connection between a relationship with a female *pilegesh* and later

26 The New Shorter OED, 1993, s.v. "concubine." Rabin, "Origin," 36, suggests that the use of a female term to refer to males may be a later, pejorative development. It is just as reasonable to assume that it is the restriction of the term pilegesh to females that is the later development, as in the English case.

27 Gen 35:22, 2 Sam 3: 7, Sam 16: 21-2.

28 See, e.g., R. Patai, *Sex and Family*, 101, 103, who suggests (based apparently on social anthropology assumptions) that it was customary for the son (after the father's death) to marry all the father's wives and concubines, with the exception of his own mother, "to demonstrate definitely the fact of succession." Y. Zakovitch and A. Shinan, מעשה ראובן ובלהה (Jerusalem: Hebrew University, 1984), 1, note that "sex stories" in general are frequently used in the Bible to justify later events, particularly a loss of status. One might question whether such an offence or attempted offence with a wife — Pharaoh and Sarah, Joseph and Potifar's wife, David and Bat Sheva, as examples — has a different aetiological purpose.

29 Reuven's rape/seduction of Bilhah, disqualifying him from first-born status; Ish Boshet's accusation against Avner leading to Avner's defection to David; Avshalom's public sex with David's pilagshim leading to Avshalom's disqualification from kingship. There is also Adoniyahu's request to Solomon (through Bat Sheva) for Avishag, his father's consort, which leads to his death (I Kgs. 2: 22). This request was understood by Solomon as an explicit threat to his kingship.

loss of status, or worse, reinforces the idea that it is dangerous to deal with such women.[30]

What Judges 19 reinforces, however, is the marginality of such *pilagshim*. The *pilegesh* of Givah, like other female *pilagshim*, is herself vulnerable to danger that would ultimately leave her permanently excluded, permanently on the threshold.[31] The reader is thus forced to question whether there can be any unequivocally defined private domain within which women are to be contained.

THE IMPLICATIONS OF ותזנה עליו

The biblical root זנה has an unusual semantic range: in some cases it describes a sexually promiscuous woman,[32] and in some cases it refers to the behaviour of someone who strays into apostasy;[33] in yet other cases neither of these meanings fits.[34] In the opinion of Bird, the root's primary use is to describe all instances of sexual intercourse outside marriage (נאף being used for adultery), while the instances referring to apostasy are simply attenuated

30 The document in general appears to highlight certain Genesis narratives, to clarify or represent them. Col. iv of this document juxtaposes Timna, the pilegesh of Elifaz, the son of Esau (Gen. 36:12), and Bilhah (though, as noted, she is called the pilegesh of Reuven's father only in Gen. 35:22), with Jaob's blessing regarding Reuven in Gen. 49: 4b. Using a reference to Deut. 25: 19, as well as a pesher-type commentary explaining Gen. 49:4b as a reproof, the text suggest these connections with pilagshim as the reason for the destruction of Amaleq (Esau's descendants) and for Reuven's loss of the rights as firstborn.

31 This association between thresholds and ambiguous status is powerfully suggested by Margaret Atwood in her novel *The Handmaid's Tale* (Toronto: McClelland-Bantam, 1986), a dystopia in which young women are forced to bear children to a male elite whose wives are barren. The Handmaid of the title describes her entry into an elite household in this way: "On our first days we are permitted front doors, but after that we're supposed to use the back. Things haven't settled down, it's too soon, everyone is unsure about our exact status. After a while it will be either all front doors or all back." (13)

32 E.g. in references to Dinah and Tamar in Gen. 34: 31; 38: 15, 24.

33 E.g. in Jer. chap. 3; Ezek. 16 and 23; Hos. 4. In some of the prophetic cases, the references to sexual misbehaviour and apostasy are noticeably intermingled; see, e.g., Jer. 5: 7; Ezek. 23: 3; Hos. 9: 1.

34 E.g. Isa. 1: 21 which seems to refer to general lawlessness.

uses of this primary sexual meaning.[35] Certainly the phrase *va-tizneh alav* in Judges 19:2, if translated as "she played the whore against him," as the KJV has done, or "she sinned with Amaleqites," according to Pseudo-Philo 45: 3, might seem to provide an easy moral hook on which to hang the fate of the *pilegesh*.

Yet very few of the early translators and commentators seized on such an iterpretation. The LXX, for instance, says that she simply *eporeuthei ap' autou...kai apeilthe par autou* "departed...and went away from him"; some Targumim (as well as Rashi) similarly state that she "went out" (נפקת ברא). Josephus states that the *pilegesh* (whom he calls a "wife," *gunei*) and her husband quarreled;[36] the character of the Levite, who is later revealed to be abusive, cowardly and deceitful, would certainly allow for such an interpretation. Two third-generation Amoraim seem to have thought her husband was offended by finding either a hair or a fly in inappropriate places.[37]

Without going into a detailed word study of the biblical root זנה, I would argue that these translations point out that there is no particular reason to assume that *zanah* automatically has a nuance of sexual misconduct when applied to women. One may question whether the attenuated meaning associated with apostasy (the supposed "background" meaning, in effect) is actually reflecting the primary meaning, reflecting the general idea of "turning away." Such a meaning is strongly supported if the Hebrew verb is cognate with the Akkadian *zenu*, translated as "to be angry," often found with the preposition *itti*, "with"; the object of this anger can be either humans or gods.[38] One inter-

35 P.Bird, "Prostitution in the Social World and Religious Rhetoric of Ancient Israel," in *Prostitutes and Courtesans in the Ancient World*, 40-58, ed. C. Faraone and L. McClure (Madison: University of Wisconsin Press, 2006), 42, 44.

36 Ant. V, 142.

37 R. Aviatar and R. Yonatan in bGitt. 6b.

38 CAD, s.v. zenu. In the domain of family law, the verb is notably found in certain Old Babylonian marriage contracts in which more than one wife is acquired. The wives can be described as either sisters or as mistress-slave; in both cases there is often a series of clauses specifying the subservience of one wife to the other. One such clause is: zenisa izenni ("her [the "first" wife's] hatings she [the subservient wife] shall hate....". See, e.g., CT II 44 (in M. Schorr, *Urkunden des Altbabylonischen Zivil- und Prozessrechts* [Leipzig: J.C. Hinrichs, 1913], 10-11); CT 48 48:9-11, in R. Westbrook, *Old Babylonian Marriage Law* [Horn: Ferdinand Berger, 1988], 121, with discussion on p. 109.

esting nuance of the Akkadian verb is its frequent association with *suhhuru* or *taru*, verbs meaning "to turn around" or "to turn back"; the implication is that the act of anger includes, in addition to an emotional separation, a physical turning away from the object of the anger.

Thus perhaps it is the association of the Hebrew *zanah* with "harlotry" that is the attenuated or background meaning, referring to a woman who walked away from those on whom she was dependent (husband, father, *yabam*), and who was presumed to support herself by sex for hire.[39] Perhaps such women lived with other *zonot*, like the women who came to Solomon for judgement (1 Kgs 3: 16); or perhaps they were able to go back to their parents, like the *pilegesh* of Judges 19 and like Raẖav (Josh chapters 2 and 6).

Following the early translators and commentators, *va-tizneh alav* becomes "and she left him" — perhaps "over his objections," much as the phrase לדבר על לבה in Judges 1: 5 suggests that the Levite had the need to speak passionately, to overcome the woman's objections.[40] As with the term *pilegesh*, we are forced to re-examine our assumptions regarding the woman: was she simply a promiscuous gadabout, or did she leave for good reason, fearful of the harm that would later materialize? And if we accept the latter interpretation we must acknowledge that there are not separate spheres of violence. Private abuse does have public consequences.

---

39 It is interesting to note that the meaning of the noun zonah was still being debated by tannaim, though at this stage it seems clear that the word was taken to refer to women engaging in sexual intercourse. According to certain sages it was the character of the woman as freely available that determined her status as a zonah, an idea perhaps closer to the modern concept of a harlot. The sages in mYev. 6: 5 claimed a zonah included a freedwoman and a female convert, who were assumed to have been sexually available before manumission or conversion; R. Akiva (bYev. 61b) argued she was a מופקרת (as I argue elsewhere, the implication here is of a woman claimable by anyone), while R. Eliezer (bTem. 30a, bYev. 61b, 76a, bSanh. 51a) claimed that any unmarried woman who had intercourse with an unmarried man was a zonah if the man had no intention of marrying her. Other opinions seem to relate the zonah to "wasted" intercourse. According to R. Yehudah (mYev. 6: 5) the zonah was an אילונית, incapable of procreation, with whom one had intercourse; R. Matia b. Heresh (yYev. 61b) included a wife suspected of being a sotah. One amoraic opinion in bTem. 29b restricted the term to denoting a woman with whom it was specifically forbidden to have intercourse (Rav); another would include one's wife if she were paid to have relations while she was niddah (Levi).

40 Shekhem spoke similarly to Dinah in Gen. 34: 3: וידבר על לב הנערה.

RE-EMBRACING JUDGES 19

In summary, we may argue that the story of the *pilegesh* of Givah is meant to cause the reader to acknowledge his or her sense of discomfort with the behaviour of the individuals depicted therein. Of interest in this regard are several rabbinic dicta that address the question of embarrassment when the honour of biblical actors is at stake. Mishnah Megillah 4: 10 prohibits the reading, or translation into Aramaic, of certain biblical passages that are thought to demean the honour of various patriarchal figures. This passage is not one of them. The Bavli asks why it is not forbidden in order to protect the honour of Benjamin and the answer is, in essence, it just is not. Nor does the Levite escape censure: a passage in bSanh. 103b, for instance, asserts the Israelites were overcome by the Benjaminites because they considered human honour (i.e the Levite's) over divine honour.[41] Building on these views, we may propose that the real embarrassment would be to simply gloss over such passages of violence in the Bible, leaving them hidden behind a mask of honour or rendered non-immediate through too restricted a focus.

41 Tanhuma Vayeshev 2 similarly contrasts the Israelites' avenging of the human affront in Judges19-21 with their failure to act against Micah's idol in the immediately preceding chapter of Judges.

SHEKHEM AND THE SO-CALLED RAPE OF DINA

Tzemah Yoreh, American Jewish University

What could possibly be embarrassing about the following canonical story in Genesis 34? Shekhem Son of Hamor the Hivite rapes Dina Daughter of Jacob,[1] and after the rape asks to marry her. Following the discussion of terms with Hamor, Jacob and his sons agree to this arrangement but only on the condition that Shekhem, Hamor and the male inhabitants of the city circumcise themselves; Shekhem agrees, and the entire city goes ahead with the circumcision. While the newly circumcised men are recuperating, Simon and Levi kill them all and loot their property. I present Genesis 34 as a continuous account but in fact the episode is replete with difficulties: a) Why does Shekhem think he can convince Dina (or her father) to marry him after he rapes her? b) Who are Dina's avengers? Do they include the sons of Jacob who "spoke untruthfully"or just Simon and Levi? c) Who arranges the marriage, Shekhem or his father? d) How can Shekhem negotiate a marriage when Dina is already in his house — he has already seized Dina, what is there left to give? e) Why is Jacob so opposed to Simon and Levi's act of revenge? After all, Shekhem was guilty of raping his daughter and trying to walk off with all his property.

1 This is the simple explanation despite scholars who claim that there was no rape; cf. Lyn M. Becthel, "What if Dina is not Raped?", JSOT 62,(Sheffield: 1994): 19-36, Suzanne Scholz, "Was it Really Rape in Genesis 34? Biblical Scholarship as a Reflection of Cultural Assumptions," in *Escaping Eden*, (Sheffield: 1998), 182-198.

These difficulties have led to the isolation of two sources in the chapter,[2] the Yahwistic source and the Elohistic source,[3] or the Yahwistic source and the Priestly source,[4] combined by a third editor.[5] The documentary researchers, however, have never quite managed to isolate two complete and continuous narratives in chapter 34, and are obliged to make do with two fragmentary accounts.[6] They make their usual assumption that the editor "tailored" both accounts, preserving the details considered important while combining the two sources. This type of problematic analysis has provided (and still provides) ample ammunition for scholars attacking the documentary hypothesis, and rightly so. In my opinion, the sources of the Pentateuch should not be dismissed on account of such attacks. It is necessary, however, to reanalyze the relationship between the sources of Genesis 34 without any presuppositions. Original, parallel and secondary material must be identified using tools of higher criticism. The documentary paradigm should not be "forced" upon the text.

THE CRITICAL DIVISION

A: THE RAPE

The negative tone of the story towards Jacob's family is set in the first verse of the chapter. Dina, daughter of Jacob, proceeds to "check out the daughters

2 One source with Shekhem, Simon and Levi as protagonists and the second source with Hamor and "the sons of Jacob" as protagonists and cf. John Skinner, *Genesis, A Critical and Exegetical Commentary* (ICC) (Edinburgh: T&T Clark, 1910), 417.

3 Cf. Wellhausen in the appendix to his book: Julius Wellhausen, D*ie Composition des Hexateuchsund der Historischen Buecher des Alten Testaments* (Berlin: G. Reimer, 1899), 314-322.

4 Cf. Augustus Dillmann *Die Genesis: Handbuch zum Alten Testament* (Leipzig: S. Hirzel, 1892), 368-369, and Samuel R. Driver, *The Book of Genesis with Introduction and Notes* (Westminster Commentaries) (London: Methuen, 1904), 302.

5 Cf. Hermann Gunkel, Genesis, tr. M. Biddle (Macon, GA: Mercer University Press, 1977), 362, who attributes sporadic words and the occasional clause to the editor. I agree, however, with Van Seters, who claims that "the use of a hypothetical redactor to solve literary problems seems arbitrary and unacceptable."See John Van Seters, "The Silence of Dina" in *Jacob- Commentaire a Plusiers Voix de Gen 25-36* (Geneva: Labor et Fides, 2001), 239-247.

6 Cf. Robin Parry's criticism in "Source Criticism and Genesis 34," Tyndale Bulletin 51:1 (2000): 121-138.

of the land." This initiative is couched in negative terms (ראה ב-)[7] and is deemed inappropriate by many commentators (e.g. Rashi, Kimchi). In verse 2a, Shekhem, ruler of the land sees Dina, and in 2b he rapes her. Immediately afterwards, however, he talks about his love for her, and in the continuation of the narrative (verses 6-19) Shekhem and Hamor make an offer to Jacob's family concerning a possible marriage. As I asked previously, how can you rape a woman and then attempt to seduce her with sweet words and ask her family's permission to marry her?[8] The rape interrupts narrative continuity, causes logical difficulties and therefore should be viewed as secondary. Verse 2b, however, is not the only time the rape is mentioned: verse 5 ("Now Jacob heard that Shekhem had defiled his daughter Dina"),[9] verse 7 ("because he had committed an outrage in Israel by lying with Jacob's daughter"), verse 13b ("because he had defiled their sister Dina"), verse 26 ("and [they] took Dina out of Shekhem's house"), verse 27b ("and [they] plundered the city, because their sister had been defiled"), and verse 31 ("But they said, 'Should our sister be treated like a whore?'") all speak of Dina's "uncleanliness." If verse 2b and the rape theme are secondary, all subsequent mentions of the rape are very likely secondary as well.

SHEKHEM AND HAMOR

The interactions between the characters of chapter 34 can be divided into three categories: Shekhem as a dominant figure, Hamor as a dominant figure, and Hamor and Shekhem as joint players In verse 4 Shekhem asks his father to arrange the marriage and Hamor acts in accordance with this request in verse 6 and verses 8-10: ("And Hamor the father of Shekhem went out to Jacob

7 When the object of ראה ב- is another individual or group it often carries negative conna\ota-tions. See Ps. 54:9; 112:10; 118:7.

8 One could argue for the plausibility of such a course of action in the ancient Near East. According to the laws of Deuteronomy if a man rapes a young woman he is required to pay her bridal price and marry her. This however, is not the case in Genesis 34. Shekhem is the prince of the region and if he raped a woman belonging to a small group of nomads, he wouldn't need to convince the woman to marry him and enter into elaborate negotiations with her father and her brothers; he would just keep her in his house.

9 The English translation is based upon the NRSV.

to speak with him"; "But Hamor spoke with them, saying, "The heart of my son Shekhem longs for your daughter; please give her to him in marriage…"). In verse 11, however, Hamor ceases to be the dominant figure and Shekhem comes into the picture once again and offers a dowry of his own to Dina's father and brothers. Similarly, verse 19 enumerates the conditions Jacob's sons set upon the "youth" and not upon his father. Shekhem and Hamor are joint players in four other verses: "The sons of Jacob answered Shekhem and his father Hamor deceitfully" (13);"So Hamor and his son Shekhem came to the gate of their city" (20); "And all who went out of the city gate heeded Hamor and his son Shekhem" (24); "They killed Hamor and his son Shekhem with the sword"(26).

Why these categories? Verse 2 ("Shekhem son of Hamor the Hivite, prince of the region, saw her…") implies that Shekhem (and not his father) is the city's ruler. This is again implied by Shekhem's independent offer of monetary incentives (11), and by the description of him as the most honoured member of his father's house (19). If Shekhem is able to make an independent offer, why must his father intervene? Moreover, the rape is alluded to three times during the discourse between Hamor and the Israelites. Since the rape is secondary the whole discourse between Hamor and Jacob's sons is likely secondary as well.[10] The third time the agreement between Hamor and Jacob's sons is repeated, Shekhem and Hamor make it clear to their townsmen that the entire affair is a ploy to part Jacob's sons from their property: "Will not their livestock, their property, and all their animals be ours?"(23) We have already encountered one attempt to mar Shekhem's reputation with a rape. This agreement then, which is presented as a conspiracy to cheat Jacob's sons, seems to be another attempt to slander Shekhem and Hamor, and thus may be part of the same editorial stratum. If the agreement itself is secondary then the section in which Hamor makes the initial offer and is the dominant figure belongs to the editorial stratum as well.

What about the verses which have Shekhem and Hamor acting together? In my opinion, these verses can be subdivided into two categories. The verses in

10 Hamor's offer is also part of Westermann's late version which was inserted into the earlier narrative, and see: Claus Westermann, *Genesis 12-36: A Commentary,* tr. J. J. Scullion (Minneapolis: Fortress Press, 1985), 536.

which the removal of Hamor makes the text more legible, and those in which the reverse occurs, in which the textual integrity is disrupted when the name is taken out. The verses belonging to the first sub-group (where the removal of Hamor makes the text more legible) are probably original since they have Shekhem acting independently of his father (at least after we remove Hamor's name). On the other hand, the verses belonging to the second group (where the removal of Hamor causes the text to be less legible) are redactional since they include Hamor as an active participant in the proceedings (and Hamor is a secondary character).

A: FIRST GROUP

1) Verse 13 ("The sons of Jacob answered Shekhem and his father Hamor deceitfully, because he had defiled their sister Dina.") belongs to the first group (where the removal of Hamor makes the text more legible): Removal of "and his father Hamor" creates a continuity between the first half of the verse and the second half, "because he had defiled their sister Dina," since the second half of the verse is in the singular (the second half of the verse refers to the rape and is an addition in and of itself — the editor, however, who added this half verse, refers to a singular antecedent — Shekhem — "forgetting" that he'd added an additional object at the beginning of the verse — Hamor).

2) Verse 18, "Their words pleased Hamor and Hamor's son Shekhem," belongs to this group as well. When the words "Hamor and Hamor's son" are taken out, textual cohesiveness is improved since verse 19 has Shekhem acting independently of his father.

3) Also belonging to this group is verse 24, "And all who went out of the gate of his city heeded Hamor and his son Shekhem; and every male was circumcised, all who went out of the gate of his city." If you take out the words "Hamor and his son" the text becomes more coherent, since other elements of the verse are in the singular, such as "the gate of his city."

B: SECOND GROUP

1) Verse 20: "So Hamor and his son Shekhem came to the gate of their city and spoke to the men of their city, saying," should be included in the second group, since taking Hamor out of the verse produces textual incoherence.

2) Verse 26 belongs to the second group of verses (where the removal of Hamor causes the text to be less legible) as well, for although eliminating Hamor from the verse is not especially problematic one should not arbitrarily assign parts of verses to an editor/glossator.

Our conclusion from the analysis of the above verses is as follows: Shekhem was the main character according to the original stratum: all verses that have Hamor as a protagonist are secondary; and on every other occasion his name was inserted into the text. In other words Hamor was never mentioned in the original stratum. Thus verse 2 which reads " When Shekhem son of Hamor the Hivite, prince of the region saw her...," originally read "When Shekhem the prince of the region saw her..."

SIMON AND LEVI

The question of who participated in the slaughter must now be addressed. Are all Jacob's sons guilty or just Simon and Levi? Until verse 13, the reader understands that the term "Jacob's sons" refers to all eleven of the patriarch's male progeny — all of Jacob's sons spoke deceitfully. In verse 25, however, the term refers exclusively to Simon and Levi, and only Simon and Levi sack the city: "On the third day, when they were still in pain, two of the sons of Jacob, Simon and Levi, Dina's brothers, took their swords and came against the city unawares, and killed all the males." The term "Jacob's sons" appears once again in verse 27 ("And the other sons of Jacob came upon the slain, and plundered the city, because their sister had been defiled.") and it is unclear whether the reference is to the sons as a group or only to Simon and Levi. How then are we to judge the term?

If Simon and Levi are understood as part of a later editorial stratum the problem is solved.[11] The original story recounted a slaughter in which all of Jacob's sons participated. In order to minimize the number of culpable parties and reduce the guilt, the later redactor restricts the act of pillage, attributes it solely to Simon and Levi and presents it as an act of revenge for a rape that is not part of the original stratum. In its original form, stripped of Simon and Levi, verse 25 reads: "On the third day, when they were still in pain, the sons of Jacob, took their swords and came against the city unawares, and killed all the males." The end result of this addition is Simon and Levi's loss of privilege as second and third sons. Since Reuven had already lost his rights after sleeping with Bilhah, the fourth son Judah inherits the rights of the first born (cf. Judah's role in the Joseph cycle). Jacob's harsh reaction is now understood; his sons took advantage of the weakened condition of the innocent inhabitants of Shekhem and killed them. They did not even have the rape as an excuse because according to the original account Shekhem never touched Dina.

CIRCUMCISION

Finally we must consider the circumcision issue. Let us begin with verse 22. It speaks of circumcision in the following way: "that all males among us be circumcised as they are circumcised." (The Hebrew consists of seven words.) In contrast, verse 17 mentions this same act in one word (using only the infinitive construct of the verb "to circumcise"). One should bear in mind that verse 22 was attributed to a secondary stratum and thus any idea emphasized in this verse is very likely secondary as well. Moreover, the phraseology in this verse is identical to the late Priestly injunction of Gen. 17:10 "All males among you be circumcised."

Identifying the circumcision theme as secondary, however, is highly problematic. Circumcision is central to the plot, for without the handicap of circumcision the brothers would not have been able to subdue an entire city. The key to this dilemma is distinguishing between the two components of the

11 Albert de Pury, "Genese XXXIV et L'histoire," RB 76 (1969): 5-49 and Sigo Lehming, "Zur Ueberlieferung von Gen. 34," ZAW 70 (1958): 228-250, but Westermann (536) claims that they were part of the original narrative.

phrase —"all males" and "be circumcised." Only the phrase "All males among you be circumcised" is Priestly and late, while the verb "to circumcise" on its own is not. This distinction is increased by verse 24 in which the construct "all males" appears in conjunction with an almost synonymous expression "all who went out of the gate of his city." One of the two expressions is superfluous, and it seems likely to be "all males" since "all who went out of the gate of his city" appears beforehand in the verse. Thus when "all males" is mentioned in verse 15 ("All males among you be circumcised"), it is likely an addition, one that, like"be circumcised"in verse 17, stood on its own. Why was it important for the editor to append "all males" in verses 15 and 24? It may be that the editor was trying to emphasize that all the males of Shekhem were part of the plot to appropriate Israelite property (vs. 23) and thus the murder of all males in verse 25 was entirely justified.

THE QUESTION OF SOURCES

I have purposely left the question of sources for the end of this article so that the analyses would be relevant to scholars who do not subscribe to the source model (as I do). Thus far I have used such general terms as the "original account" and "the editorial stratum."If one is a source scholar, however, it is possible to be more specific. There is widespread consensus regarding the presence of the Yahwistic source in Genesis 34 among documentarians (Skinner, Driver, Speiser) and even exegetes who suggest alternative supplementary models (Kuenen, Noth, Van-Seters) attribute much of this text to J.[12] J is either one of two parallel accounts or the original account — depending on the model but is never the redactor. I accept the common theme of these analyses and thus attribute my own "original stratum" to J.[13] Van-Seters makes

12 Cf. Abraham Kuenen, "Dina en Shekhem", Theologisch Tijdschrift. XIV (Leiden: Leiden School of Theology, 1880): 257-281, Martin Noth, *A History of Pentateuchal Traditions*, tr. B.W. Anderson (Englewood Cliffs, New Jersey: Prentice Hall, 1972), 31, Van-Seters in his article, noted above.

13 The best linguistic markers are: the use of נער (Ketib) as a feminine noun (vs. 3), found in Gen. 24 (J); דבק ב (vs. 3) for the connection between man and wife (Gen. 2:24- J); the verbal form אחר (vs. 19) which appears here and in Gen. 24:56 (J); and במרמה (vs. 13) which appears here and in Gen. 26:35(J).

a strong case for a Priestly linguistic signature in the redactional stratum of this chapter,[14] but the "holy war" Van Seters speaks of is not exclusive to the Priestly source and is also found in D.[15] It seems likely that the redactor is Priestly but this analysis is certainly relevant even if the labels discarded are applicable if we speak of a basic source. In order to remain outside the debate regarding P's role in the composition of the Pentateuch, I prefer for now to speak of anonymous authors — so that even scholars who don't accept source criticism or the supplementary paradigm may find it relevant.[16]

DIVISION SUMMARY

The following is a short summary of my division. The first verse presents Dina as the initiator of contact with the group of non-Israelites: "Now Dina the daughter of Leah, whom she had borne to Jacob, went out to visit the women of the region." Verse 2a is original except for the words "the son of Hamor the Hivvite" The second half of verse 2, which mentions the rape for the first time, is attributed to the redactor. The original Yahwistic account continues in verse 3 — Shekhem's seduction of Dina with sweet words (but without physical force). Verses 4-10 are attributed to the secondary stratum of the chapter: verses 4, 6, 8-10 recount the negotiations between Hamor, Shekhem's father and Jacob's sons which is a secondary theme (according to the Yahwist, Shekhem conducts the negotiations without his father), and verses 5 and 7 allude to the rape. The Yahwistic account continues in verses 11-12 with Shekhem's marriage proposal. The first half of verse 13 is Yahwistic except for the addition of "Hamor, Shekhem's father." Verse 13b, which alludes to the rape of Dina, belongs to the redactor. Verses 14-15 and 17 describe Jacob's sons' counteroffer, and are assigned to the Yahwistic author with the exception of the words "to them" (in Hebrew, one word) in verse 14a which allude

14 The most prominent linguistic marker is בהמול לכם כל זכר (vss. 15, 22) which is virtually identcal to the commandment in Genesis 17(P), but note also the root "אחז" in the niphal form (vs. 10), as well as קנין (vs. 23), "טמא" (vss. 5, 13) features prominently in P's legal tradition but is not exclusive to the source.

15 For the extermination of the indigenous population in D, cf. Deut. 20:17.

16 For example, Baruch Schwartz, "The Priestly Account of the Theophany and Lawgiving at Sinai" in *Texts, Temples and Traditions*, ed. M. V. Fox, (Winona Lake: Eisenbrauns, 1996), 103-134.

to the addition of Hamor in verse 13a and "all males" in verse 15. Verse 16, which alludes to Hamor's proposal, is a late addition according to the above analysis. The Yahwist continues his story in verses 18-19, describing Shekhem's fulfillment of his part of the bargain (the redactor probably inserted "Hamor, Shekhem's father"). In verses 21-23, Shekhem and Hamor report the agreement to the inhabitants of their city in a decidedly scheming tone, a theme I have identified as secondary. The Yahwist's story continues in verse 24 with the fulfillment of the conditional circumcision of Shekhem and the inhabitants of his city ("Hamor" and "all males" are inserted once more). Verse 25 — the slaughter of the inhabitants of Shekhem — is also Yahwistic, except for the addition of "Dina's brothers Simon and Levi." Verse 26, which describes the vengeful killing of Shekhem and Hamor and mentions the retrieval of Dina from Shekhem's house, alludes to the rape and is therefore secondary. Verses 27-29, which describe the pillage, are uncomplimentary to Jacob's sons and thus are probably original. Jacob's complaint to his sons (verse 30) is original except for the addition of Simon and Levi. Verse 31 is secondary since it once again alludes to Dina's rape.

THE ISOLATED NARRATIVE

34:1 Now Dina the daughter of Leah, whom she had borne to Jacob, went out to visit the women of the region. 2a When Shekhem, prince of the region, saw her 3 his soul was drawn to Dina daughter of Jacob; he loved the girl, and spoke tenderly to her. 11 Shekhem said to her father and to her brothers, "Let me find favor with you, and whatever you say to me I will give. 12 Put the marriage present and gift as high as you like, and I will give whatever you ask me; only give me the girl to be my wife."13(-) The sons of Jacob answered Shekhem deceitfully, 14 They said "We cannot do this thing, to give our sister to one who is uncircumcised, for that would be a disgrace to us. 15(-) Only on this condition will we consent to you: that you will become circumcised as we are. 17 But if you will not listen to us and be circumcised, then we will take our daughter and be gone." 18(-) Their words pleased Shekhem. 19 And the young man did not delay to do the thing, because he was delighted with Jacob's daughter. Now he was the most honored of all his family. 24(-) And all who went out of the city gate heeded Shekhem; and all who went out of the gate of his city was circumcised. 25(-) On the third day, when they were still in pain, the sons of Jacob took their swords and came against the city unawares, and killed all the males. 27(-) And the sons of Jacob came upon the slain, and plundered the city. 28 They took their flocks and their herds, their donkeys, and whatever was in the city and in the field. 29 All their wealth, all their little ones and their wives, all that was in the houses, they captured and made their prey. 30(-) Then Jacob said, "You have brought trouble on me by making me odious to the inhabitants of the land, the Canaanites and the Perizzites; my numbers are few, and if they gather themselves against me and attack me, I shall be destroyed, both I and my household."

THE LATE REDACTOR'S EMBARRASSMENT:

The Yahwist presents a horrific story: All Shekhem wanted to do was marry Jacob's daughter, a marriage befitting his political stature as "ruler of the land." The "youth" seduces Dina with sweet words and asks the permission of her brothers for her hand in marriage. Her brothers answer him deceitfully and stipulate that before marrying their sister, he and all the inhabitants of his city must circumcise themselves. Shekhem responds enthusiastically and the inhabitants of his city go along with him. While the inhabitants of Shekhem are recovering from their circumcision Jacob's sons take advantage of the situation, loot the city and kill all of the males. It is not surprising, then, that a later redactor felt the need to edit the story and preserve the moral fabric of Israel's progenitors. The editor tries to portray Shekhem and the inhabitants of his city in a negative light, and emphasises the rape of Dina and the plot to take advantage of Jacob's sons. This later source presents the killing of all the males in *Shekhem* as revenge for the rape, and at the same time reduces the number of those participating in the slaughter to two, Simon and Levi, who are then subject to their father's curse (49:5 'Simon and Levi are brothers; weapons of violence are their swords. 6 May I never come into their council; may I not be joined to their company for in their anger they killed men, and at their whim they hamstrung oxen. 7 Cursed be their anger, for it is fierce, and their wrath, for it is cruel! I will divide them in Jacob, and scatter them in Israel.).

Even after this redaction, however, the editor is not able to camouflage the injustices perpetrated in this chapter. The most the editor is able to do is transform indiscriminate murder to collective punishment or a "holy war." The (Priestly) editor's ability to reembrace even this most embarrassing text, sharpening it as a tool to further his own agenda, is a potent example of the textual dynamic of embarrassment and re-embracement portrayed so well by my father and others in this volume and elsewhere. Since J is one of the first Biblical authors, and the Priestly editor one of the first Biblical redactors, this example also reverberates throughout history, creating biblical, rabbinic and modern rereadings as we divest ourselves from our long and bloody history of violence and Genocide.

One must, of course, address this shocking portrayal of Israel's progenitors as murderers and thieves in the original J text. The explanation is actually quite simple and I have already touched on it elsewhere.[17] J is interested in emphasising that throughout their history the Israelite line was deserving of lethal punishment, and that YHWH nevertheless preserved them so that future generations would proclaim YHWH's name knowing that only YHWH's mercy stood between them and certain death.[18] Thus J portrays the sons of Jacob as Jacobeans — Hebrew for sinners. A demonstration of this "theology of mercy" is found elsewhere and will be more fully elaborated upon in forthcoming work.

17 See the forthcoming, Tzemah Yoreh, *E: The First Book of God*, BZAW 402 (Berlin and New York: Walter De Gruyter, 2009) [pagination as of yet, unknown].

18 Cf. Ex. 32:11-14, Numbers 14:11-19.

AN EMBARRASSMENT OF RICHES, A PRIDE OF DEPLETION AND THE AMBIGUITY OF ADDRESS

Miryam Segal, Queens College, City University of New York

I. DISSONANCE

When pretense and appearance strike discordant notes, embarrassment ensues. Or perhaps embarrassment and dissonance are closer still, and the moment one hears that discord is itself the moment of embarrassment. Embarrassment is most often generated by a dissonance between one's proclamation about the kind of person one is — whether actually articulated or presumed — and the evidence presented by something or someone momentarily out of one's control. I am embarrassed when my image of myself is undermined, the coherence of my persona disrupted. Embarrassment is the awkwardness of finding oneself in excess, of not knowing where to put one's arms or finding the blood rushing to one's face. (Awkwardness introduces a spatial rather than sonic metaphor: pretense and appearance as the two legs of one person walking in opposite directions, then reversing course and tripping over each other.) But within that experience of dissonance there is also a concession to some truth or to knowledge that one shares with an audience. (For embarrassment, unlike shame, requires a witness to the discrepancy between pretense and appearance.) Embarrassment of Scripture may arise from a dissonance between the prescriptions or ethical imperatives of a biblical text and the practice or behavior or purported values of its readers. One must be a devoted reader to feel embarrassed. The moment of embarrassment, the need to apologize or reconcile indicates textual loyalty of a certain kind — an unwillingness to let the text be relieved completely of its authority or dignity or of being what one had assumed it to be all along — and a simultaneous wish that it not contradict or offend other loyalties or one's particular notion of what the Bible is. One may be embarrassed by Scripture as one is embarrassed by the behavior of someone with whom one is associated. Scripture is less grand, more fallible than one would like it to be. (Yet in other instances grandiosity, when and if it is noticed, may be just as embarrassing as mundanity — more so if the role of that "Scripture" is to represent docility or modesty or simplicity.) But there is also another embarrassment, for it is not only the reader who may be embarrassed by Scripture as by an obnoxious relation. The work itself may awkwardly acknowledge its own fissures, contradictions and (in the modern era, at least) its concomitant unholiness. Embarrassment of Scripture is visible in the Hebrew Bible itself, in the dissonance and contradiction that is the argument and embarrassed response of successive generations of scribes.

II . EMBARRASSMENT AS REDUNDANCY

One oddity of feelings of embarrassment is that they may be generated by the public revelation of something that, well, everyone already knew. (The fact that one's conception was the result of sexual relations between one's biological parents, until recently a universal truth, may be the cause of no small amount of embarrassment when articulated in public by another.) Embarrassment does not require a true revelation. Something was mentioned that ought not have been — an excess of information.

Harry Fox's embarrassment of Scripture, like the 18th century dramatist Leonor-Jean Christine Soulas Allainval's term and the title of one of his plays, *Embarras des Richesses*, from which Fox's term is adapted, is about redundancy, an unnecessary, unwanted and therefore awkward excess: words strewn on a page, shards of engraved stone tablets at the end of the mountain road down which the first scribe of the Israelites lumbered to find the people embarrassing the Scripture, barring it from entry into their community. The text embarrasses by telling one something one would rather not hear. If the one is a scribe, his response may be to write more. Yet by trying to contain the excess through addition, the scribe may in turn create excess for the ear of another reader or a subsequent scribe. The word embarrassment as we use it, to name that awkward feeling caused by a dissonance, of too much having been said, is a late sense of the word. The term *embarras des richesses* preserves an earlier sense of embarrass as *to bar*. What is the connection between that awkward feeling we call embarrassment and the act of barring, or of barring through excess? Is all embarrassment about excess or redundancy, the rush of an excess of blood to the vessels in the face, a baroque overflow beyond the confines of a Baroque era?

III. THE BARRING OF THE LAW; MOSES' REFUSAL OF EMBARRASMENT

The first dissonance between Scripture and practice in the story of the Israelites sounds in the Pentateuch as soon as there is Scripture, in the narration of its genesis in Exodus 32. God has articulated some of the Law in a direct address to the Israelites standing at the foot of Mount Sinai — including the prohibitions against worshipping other gods and against making idols — before turning to Moses who is on the mountain, to teach him the law in greater detail. The Israelites fret over the absence of their leader and instruct Aaron to make them a god.

> The people saw that Moses tarried coming down the mountain. And the people gathered upon Aaron and said to him, rise and make us a god who will go before us, for this man Moses who brought us up from the Land of Egypt — we do not know what has become of him. (Exodus 32:1)

The word *BoSheSh* (tarry, hesitate, stammer) is related to the root for Hebrew word for shame (B*O*Sh). The word's denotation, however, seems connected to embarrassment more than to shame: hesitation and the double *sh* sound imply a lack of control (something we know plagued Moses), and embarrassment is accompanied by an awkwardness, a hesitation or physical stammer. From the people's perspective Moses is lingering. He has indeed become excessive on the mountain inasmuch as he is needed below.

This is not only the perspective of the needy people. Once Moses has received engraved tablets of law, God informs him of his people's infraction. But Moses does not descend immediately. He listens to God's complaints against the Israelites, then pleads on their behalf, gaining God's assurance that he will not destroy the people and make a great nation of Moses himself (as God had threatened to do). Only then does Moses lumber down the mountain, tablets in hand. He arrives within sight of the people at the foot of the mountain to find that, dancing and singing before a golden calf, they have indeed strayed quickly from the path in which God had instructed them. They have contradicted the newly engraved law or, rather, the law has spoken against them — before the fact.

One possible set of responses to a statute in a legal system that seems wrongheaded, unethical or simply impractical is to rewrite, reinterpret or add caveats. A common intra-biblical means for resolving a difference between law and belief, ethics or conviction was to change by addition. The practice of much of higher biblical criticism is based on an assumption of cumulative editing: When an author encountered something in the tradition that was troubling he would not alter the text through erasure but simply add verses, chapters or as little as a single word or letter. These editorial additions could themselves generate new moments of embarrassment for subsequent scribes and readers. This principle of alteration by addition would also be responsible for the texture of the Hebrew Bible — its bumpiness. Even the tiniest of repairs may leave a seam. Over the course of generations this method of the scribal collective would have generated a Scripture that was excessive, redundant, in contradiction with itself. Excess was the opportunity for greater understanding in medieval Jewish commentaries and in Midrash but it was also a potential source of a more universal embarrassment of Scripture than that generated by any particular scribe. This embarrassment is not attributable to a single verse or word or narrative, but to the palimpsest of the biblical text and the process it seems to imply: evidence of overwriting may preclude divine authorship, for how could a holy text be so messy? How can a multi-authored work be divine? Repairs become flaws.

Another response to a contradiction between one's beliefs or desires and the words of the law is to break the law. The Israelites are unembarrassed; they break the law because they must: their needs are immediate, and Moses is lingering. By undermining their monogamous relationship with the God who led them out of Egypt they bar the Law from entry. When Moses stumbles down the mountain with the tablets in his hands to find that the Israelites have broken the law, have worshipped a graven image, he himself breaks the law in another sense: He shatters the tablets upon which the law against graven images has been engraved, as if he cannot tolerate the difference between the world as it is and as it ought to be.[1] He is angry of course, and his hike down the mountain has fed his anger with time. He may have been shocked by what he saw but he cannot claim to be surprised, for God had told him what the Israelites were doing. He knew they were worshipping another god but brought the tablets with him nonetheless. Moses forced the tablets and the sinning Israelites into the same frame only to break the tablets upon entering that frame, refusing their embarrassment by the people.

When I started to consider moments of embarrassment in the Hebrew Bible, Moses was not the first figure to come to mind. The Moses of Scripture is often encumbered, finds it hard to speak, yet for the most part seems preternaturally un-disposed to embarrassment, unshaken by contradiction, impervious to threats to his persona even once he is in the employ of God. Moses is a prince. I can imagine another Moses, one who first laid the tablets down, able to walk or run down the mountain unencumbered by stone. This other Moses would not be created in the image of the God of his books — quick to anger — but would be more deeply troubled by his people's iniquities. He would certainly be embarrassed, possibly even ashamed by the people's betrayal. Embarrassed because their betrayal of God is also a sign of Moses' failure as a leader, of the difference between his persona as the leader who brought the people out of Egypt in the midst of divine miracles and the fact of his aging body stumbling down the mountain, the impotence of the law in his hands and his mouth. Ashamed because a leader may see his people's failure as his own, as the sign of a contradiction between his principles and his failure to enact them.

1 Marc Shell has written extensively on the relationships between image, money and literature (*The Economy of Literature*, Johns Hopkins University Press, 1978; *Money Language and Thought*, Johns Hopkins University Press, 1993), as well as on Moses and stuttering ("Moses' Tongue," *Common Knowledge* 12.1 [2006], 150-176). I am indebted to him for raising for me the problem of the tablets as a graven image.

I can also imagine the Moses of the Bible as he is so often depicted — quick to anger, exhausted by his duties — living out his pentateuchal life through a slightly different narrative structure. This temperamental Moses is also brought to Nebo to see the Land of Israel and is also barred from entry to the land of Canaan, just as Numbers and Deuteronomy tell the story. But in this alternate narrative Moses is not barred from the land of Israel as punishment for hitting the rock instead of speaking to it, but for the sin of shattering the engraving of God's law.[2] Moses' behavior was puzzling to some rabbinic readers who saw a similarity or a converse relationship between the people's behavior and his own reaction to it. One midrash finds an ulterior motive for Moses to shatter the tablets — a kind of sin for a higher purpose. By shattering the tablets, by "sinning" against God's engraving as the people sinned through an un-Godly golden calf, he hoped to dissuade God from choosing himself, Moses, as a replacement for the people and completely destroying the Israelites. "He saw that Israel had no standing [no future] and so tied his own person to them and broke the tablets and said to the Holy One Blessed Be He, they sinned and I sinned for I broke the tablets. If you forgive them, I will also be forgiven." (Exodus Rabbah 46:1).

But the Moses who would be punished for breaking the tablets — his mistake would have been expressing God's anger instead of acting as intercessor. (The other Moses — the one who would lay the tablets down — this is Moses as intercessor, what Pharaoh asks him to be. He would have spared God's stone tablets, run back and forth between the people and their God trying to make peace. He would not have forced the tablets of the law and the Israelites into the same frame. He would have feared and sought to prevent the embarrassment of the Law by the people and even of a fraction of the people by the Law.) I say that this is the same Moses in a slightly different storyline, but perhaps a Moses punished for shattering the tablets could not have represented his God, would not be the same Moses after all. Moses and the God who accompanies him through four books of the Pentateuch trade off their moments of inflexibility. Each alternates between reasoning and pleading with the other — please kill me now rather than force me to lead them; please let me kill them and

2 As noted below, rabbinic literature considers the possibility that God is angry with Moses for breaking the tablets of Law that He wrote.

make you my nation — yet both are described by a shattering of the tablets if that means a refusal of embarrassment or shame, a refusal to acknowledge a rift between persona and person, and an insistence on the difference between an idol and God. The breaking of the tablets is a displaced destruction of the people themselves who fall victim to Moses' wrath in the next passage (and the murder of a portion of the people serves implicitly as a justification to God for saving the people as a whole). There is yet a third victim of Moses' hand, another engraving that is seen as replacing rather than emanating from God: the golden calf that inspires Moses' dramatics. Rather than reading Moses' reaction as disrespectful, as an error (as the biblical tradition could have done, choosing this story to inspire the barring of Moses from the promised land), it is seen as heroic refusal.

Some interpretations posit that God approved of Moses' actions and even congratulated his prophet for breaking his tablets. One might go a step further and see Moses as one who outdoes God, seizes the moment and clarifies the difference between the God of Israel and other gods. Moses may be reacting in anger, but his reaction both accounts for the very difficulty of iconoclasm that his people are subject too — and reiterates it: When I break the tablets of God I do not break God. When I have you drink the crushed remains of the calf, home of your pseudo-God, on the other hand, there is no remainder.

The breaking of the tablets signals a refusal of embarrassment, an inflexible loyalty to the law full circle to the point of disrespect. A new nation of Israelites is required, one that resembles what God's chosen people ought to be. Moses will start over with another set of tablets and a people the Levites have cleansed of three thousand sinners.[3]

IV. MOSES, THE ROCK AND THE MOUNTAIN (IN THE BIBLE AND IN THE 20TH CENTURY)

Rabbinic literature raises the question of Moses' justification in shattering tablets that were both inscribed with God's law and in God's writing. The biblical scribes, however, do not punish Moses for breaking the tablets. Instead

3 Exodus 32:27.

they punish him for his actions in Kadesh when the people demand water and God tells him to draw some from a rock (Numbers 20) —a story bounded on the near side by Miriam's death and the far side by Aaron's. God punishes him (and Aaron) for not sanctifying God "in the eyes" of the Israelites, barring him from entering the Land of Israel. His death is foretold; he will not lead the people to their ultimate destination.

Moses dies on Mount Nebo after seeing the whole of the land of Canaan. The land he sees from the mountaintop for the first and last time and that he will not enter symbolizes his life's work. In the work of a Hebrew poet of the 20th century, the site of Moses' death becomes the symbol of a productive lack.

The heart is listening. The ear attends:
Is he coming? Will he come?
In every expectation
There is the sorrow of Nebo.

One facing the other —the two shores
Of one river.
Fortress of the decree:
Eternally distant.

Spread the hands. See across the way.
There —no entry.
Each man and his Nebo
Upon the great earth.

In the milieu in which Rahel Bluvshtain lived and in which she wrote this poem, the Jewish settlement in Palestine of the 1910s and 1920s, longing, lack, unfulfilled desire were a central trope, figures for contemporary Zionist life. For this poet, the site of Moses' death becomes a symbol of a productive lack. Nebo is about having something left to desire: From the mountaintop Moses sees the land that he will never see up close, never live upon, in which his people will no longer follow him, in which Joshua will replace him as leader. Through the figure of Moses more generally this poet expresses both an ancient romantic connection to the land and a denial that is constitutive of national Jewish identity.[4]

The poem "From Across" [*mi-Neged*] was published in a volume of the same name, which is how Moses' visual position is described in the Bible — from across the Jordan, looking in. A final volume, entitled *Nebo*, was published posthumously. Like all deaths in life rather than in books, Bluvshtain's had in it something of the arbitrary: she died of tuberculosis at the age of 40. Yet her death seemed to reinforce the most popular trope of her poetry that was so much a part of the myth she became, the trope of Nebo, of not quite achieving the goal of redemption, of inhabiting and working and worshipping the land. This was a central element in the myth that formed around the poet and that helped to make her a symbol of the Labor movement in Palestine and of the Jewish settlement more generally — that she was denied the total fulfillment of her Zionist dream of working the land and contributing to building the nation. (She died in Tel Aviv after having had to leave the agricultural collective at Kineret on account of her illness.) The desire for the Land of Israel, for consummation of Zionist longings is kept alive by denial and loss; fulfillment relieves desire and in this frees one of a need for the object of desire. At the same time as this lesson of her poetry was so completely absorbed, the reading public seemed to refuse the obvious implications of her poems. Dan Miron has written of the consistent misreading of her poem, "I can tell only of myself" [*Rak 'al 'atsmi le-saper yada'ti*], in which she compared herself to an ant — but one that moves steadily towards its goal of reaching the top of a tree.[5] Readers more often saw that she was comparing herself to the smallest of creatures. They neglected the grandiosity of the ant that reaches the very top of the tree, the threats and efforts of the great big monster notwithstanding. Modern Hebrew writing was in many ways the modern scripture, a supplement and replacement of Scripture itself. Bluvshtain's grandness was

4 For a rare appraisal of Rahel Bluvshtain's use of biblical tropes see Tali Asher's study of the poet's use of the figure of Moses, "'Ish u-Nevo lo, 'ishah u-Nevo lah" [A Man and his Nebo, A Woman and her Nebo]. In *ha- Ivriyot ha-hadashot* [*The New Hebrew Women*], edited by Margalit Shiloh et al, 347-367. Tel Aviv: Yad Shazar, 2001.

5 See Dan Miron, *Imahot meyasdot, ahayot horgot* [*Founding Mothers, Stepsisters*]. Tel Aviv: Hakibbutz Hameuhad, 1991.

embarrassing, would have told the lie to her persona as a woman speaking without artifice, a simple voice of the people. Likewise, they refused to see that in marking herself as the one who could not quite acquire what she most wanted, as in the Moses poems, she portrayed herself in larger-than-life terms, as a modern-day Moses who may have failed in part but who had grand ambitions and accomplishments.

The Bible punishes Moses, or has God punish him after the fact, after the story was already written. As Kafka writes of the biblical Abraham, "If [a man] already had everything, and yet was to be raised still higher, then something had to be taken away from him, at least in appearance: this would be logical and no leap."[6] Inasmuch as she was received as a mythical figure, Bluvshtain instructs us by example that to become a myth one must "find a need and fool it."[7] The character of Moses was an important one for her precisely because of the bittersweet trajectory of his career — the very goal of his life's work was denied him, something taken away indeed. A sister story of Moses hitting a rock for water appears in Exodus and all is well. The hint of chiasmus and the force of experience would mitigate against Moses' punishment in the second story. This second tale of water issuing from rock at the behest of Moses' staff, the one for which he is barred from entry to the land, is a bumpy text, one that is embarrassing by virtue of the several hands that have written over and in it. The medieval commentators (and others reading it of a piece) struggle to make sense of the plot. The story has been edited by addition to justify Moses' Nebo, to justify God barring his entry into the land. A later scribe has left the stick that was placed in Moss's hand in an earlier iteration but now has God command him — after the fact — to speak to the rock (rather than strike it as he had been ordered to do in Exodus and here too initially) in view of the people. The later scribe sought an excuse for Moses not to enter the land of Israel, for being replaced by Joshua, and chose this story to supply the sin.[8]

6 Franz Kafka, "Abraham," *Parables and Paradoxes*, ed. Nahum Glazer (Shocken, 1961), cited at greater length below.

7 This is a mantra of Bill Griffith's cartoon character Zippy the Pinhead. I am indebted to Jonathan Jarashow for this citation.

8 Tzemah Yoreh's unpublished work on Moses and the Joshua tradition supports the idea that the two overlapped. In this reading, the Moses tradition was edited so as to be consistent with

What embarrassment, if any, requires this emendation? Why choose this story for the sin?

The latter question can be answered again, perhaps, by Moses' obsessive iconoclasm — more obsessive at times even than God's. How could Moses, breaker of tablets, destroyer of the icon of the calf, how could he speak to a rock as if it were, say, God?! Moses ought to have spoken, ought not to have lost patience, yet, at the same time, how poignant, how in character even, for Moses to be squeamish, to be embarrassed by the thought of speaking to a rock. Moses, address a rock? His entire persona (after correcting for such throwbacks in his character development as the copper snake) is based on his refusal to enliven the inanimate object by prayer, by address.

The Joshua tradition, and one scholar's theory of the overlap of the Joshua and Moses traditions, can help to answer the first question:[9] By changing the instructions to Moses after the fact, by leaving him with stick in hand and re-writing God's words as speaking to the rock, the Pentateuch saves Moses or Joshua from the awkward position of arriving at the front of the class to find that someone else had been called. Joshua and Moses: an embarrassment of riches.

V. EMBARRASSING APOSTROPHE

According to Jonathan Culler's "Apostrophe," scholars of Romanticism have consistently ignored apostrophe although it is ubiquitous in Romantic poetry.[10] They have ignored apostrophe because the trope is inherently embarrassing. He illustrates the embarrassment of apostrophe with an imaginary address to a bus:

> Imagine a man standing on a corner in the rain cursing buses: "Come on, damn you! It's been ten minutes!" If he continues apostrophically when other travelers join him on the corner, he makes a spectacle of himself; his apostrophes

the portrayal of Joshua as the Israelite conqueror of the land of Canaan.

9 See note 8.

10 Jonathan Culler, "Apostrophe," Diacritics 7:4 (Winter 1977): 59-69.

work less to establish an *I-Thou* relation between him and the absent bus than to dramatize or constitute an image of self. (63)

Douglas Kneale is nonplussed by Culler's "deliberately corny apostrophe in 'Apostrophe,'" and accounts for it as a Romantic failure rather than by invoking embarrassment.[11] The apostrophe fails "precisely because it lacks this one prerequisite," an emotional prerequisite: It fails because it is not prompted by passion. (Kneale note 13, p. 159) As for embarrassment, "here too we reach a dead end, for nowhere does Culler explain exactly why apostrophes are necessarily embarrassing; as I suggest, some are, and some aren't." (note 31, p. 161)

Kneale's primary criticism of Culler's and others' writing on apostrophe is that they confuse apostrophe with address and with prosopopeia. Apostrophe is one particular form of address, characterized by a turn away from the initial or presumed addressee to another. Kneale dismisses Culler's particular claims, but chooses not to pursue the possibility that apostrophe has something inherently embarrassing in it, Culler's wrong-footedness notwithstanding. Embedded in this clarification of the term apostrophe, however, one can see the possibility of embarrassment. Apostrophe does not guarantee embarrassment, but it contains a potential confusion that seems suited to generating excess, a redundancy that sets the stage for embarrassment.

I am moved to revisit Culler's notion of apostrophe as embarrassing because when I tried to think of moments in the Hebrew Bible that seem characterized by embarrassment, the story of Hannah and Eli came to mind first — a story that turns on a question of address. The barring of Moses from entry into the land as well as the parable at the end of Kafka's "Abraham" to which I shall turn below also turn on a problematic address. The book of Samuel opens with a diptych. Each of the two stories involve Eli the Priest and a member of Elkanah's family; each is characterized by a dramatic Divine address; each of those addresses is confusing, at least for Eli. The first is the story of Hannah on a pilgrimage with her husband and co-wife to Shiloh where Eli the priest presides. In the manner of biblical matriarchs who precede her, she is the childless but favored of two wives. Eli sees Hannah moving her lips but producing

11 Douglas Kneale, "Romantic Aversions: Apostrophe Reconsidered," *English Literary History* 58:1 (Spring 1991): 141-165.

no sound and scolds her for her drunkenness. By rights, Hannah ought to be embarrassed. Her dignified response is anything but:

> No, my master, I am an obstinate woman; I have not drunk wine or hard drink; for I poured my soul before God.
>
> Do not take your servant for a bad woman, for out of great distress and anger have I spoken until now. (I Samuel 1: 15-16)

Indeed, one wonders whether the initiator of embarrassment is not himself embarrassed at this point. Has he not shown himself to be something less than a wise priest, as ineffective in the role he is meant to fill? Hannah was not muttering drunkenly to herself or to an inanimate object. She was speaking to God, pouring her heart out rather than wine. The Rabbis' attribution of the mode of prayer to Hannah is not fanciful; it is a relatively straightforward understanding of Hannah in contrast to the old priest, as innovative in her use of silence and speech.[12] The story of her son Samuel's initiation as prophet is the proper sequel to this story, in which Hannah's strategy is to vow to return her offspring to God as a servant and Nazirite if God blesses her with a child. The stage is set for Eli to once again demonstrate himself to be someone who simply does not comprehend the workings or hear the sounds of speech between human beings and God. (Politics is also at work here: Eli represents the old-world rituals of animal sacrifice. Inasmuch as his sons will be killed by God on account of their corruption of the priesthood and Samuel will become the new leader, this plot favors the modes of prophecy and prayer.)

Hannah's son, now at Shiloh himself and apprenticed to Eli in fulfillment of his mother's bargain with God, awakens to the call of his name. He rushes to Eli's side, but is sent back to bed immediately:

> He said, I have not called [for you], go to bed. And he went to bed. (I Samuel 3:5)

Eli, the priest in charge of sacrifices to God, misapprehends all address both to and from God.

---

12 See, for example, BT Berakhot 31a-b.

This in itself is embarrassing: the man of God who understands less than the wife of one of the worshippers at his altar; who is unable to mentor properly the novice Samuel, the prophet and future leader of the Israelites; whose shame will be his corrupt sons who steal from God and his worshippers, sons who perhaps concretize something of Eli that is wrong or uncomprehending. Shown up by a woman and a lad. There is wisdom simply in knowing that someone is being addressed, and wisdom in simply knowing who is being addressed.

VI . KAFKA'S "ABRAHAM"

Several themes of this essay seem to converge on Franz Kafka's "Abraham," a riff on the biblical character, and you the reader of this short piece may have heard echoes of it in the preceding pages.[13] "Abraham" also riffs the self-contradictory language of the Bible. Kafka's variations on the biblical Abrahams parody the confusing multivocality that makes the iconoclast Moses heal his people with a copper snake or makes the Abraham who tries to cajole God into saving the people of Sodom and Gomorrah a man willing to raise a knife to slaughter his son. Having briefly introduced Abraham, Kafka's narrative quickly leaves the biblical personage behind in favor of a variant Abraham who does not so much as appear in the Bible. Suddenly Kafka's text is inhabited by a multitude of Abrahams each of whom has a laughing wife, does or does not have a house, or even a son, and who reacts to God's request consistent with his own circumstances. "Abraham" is a haunting interpretation but also a funny one that opens up out of the very texture of the Hebrew Bible — the sharp turns that characters take, the psychological contradictions that modern scholars reconcile through a panoply of authors and that the rabbis made sense of through midrash.

> I could magine another Abraham for myself — he certainly would have never gotten to be a patriarch or even an old-clothes dealer — who was prepared to satisfy the demand for a sacrifice immediately, with the promptness of a waiter, but was unable to bring it off because he could not get away, being

13 For example, see the discussion of Moses above.

> indispensable; the household needed him, there was perpetually something or other to put in order, the house was never ready; for without having his house ready, without having something to fall back on, he could not leave — this the Bible also realized, for it says: "He set his house in order." And, in fact, Abraham possessed everything in plenty to start with; if he had not had a house, where would he have raised his son, and in which rafter would he have stuck the sacrificial knife?
>
> This Abraham — but it's an old story not worth discussing any longer. Especially not the real Abraham; he had everything to start with, was brought up to it from childhood — I can't see the leap. If he already had everything, and yet was to be raised still higher, then something had to be taken away from him, at least in appearance: this would be logical and no leap. It was different for the other Abrahams, who stood in the houses they were building and suddenly had to go up on Mount Moriah; it is possible that they did not even have a son, yet already had to sacrifice him. These are impossibilities, and Sarah was right to laugh. (Kafka 42-43)

An embarrassment of riches must be depleted: this the narrator understands. What about an Abraham who feared embarrassment precisely because he was the sort of person who lacked riches, because he was already depleted? Such an Abraham is the object of Kafka's imaginings for much of this short piece:

> But take another Abraham. One who wanted to perform the sacrifice altogether in the right way and had a correct sense in general of the whole affair, but could not believe that he was the one meant, he, an ugly old man, and the dirty youngster that was his child. True faith is not lacking in him, he has his faith; he would make the sacrifice in the right spirit if only he could believe he was the one meant….
>
> It is as if, at the end of the year, when the best student was solemnly about to receive a prize, the worst student rose in the expectant stillness and came forward from his dirty desk in the last row because he had made a mistake of hearing, and the whole class burst out laughing. And perhaps he had made no

> mistake at all, his name really was called, it having been the teacher's intention to make the rewarding of the best student at the same time a punishment for the worst one. (Kafka 44-45)

This Abraham is not sure he is the Abraham who has been called. Is he not too flawed, too ordinary or mediocre, too inferior, even, to be the Abraham that God is calling, the one spoken of in Scripture? He does not want to be as the student who reveals not so much the truth about himself or his ranking in the class — that was already known, or his classmates would not have laughed — but the exposure of his own fantasy of rank and his momentary delusion of grandeur.

This Abraham does not want to be embarrassed. He does not want to be redundant. He does not want to be Moses come to the other side of the river or the big desk to find that Joshua has already been called to the head of the class. Moses was punished in order to save him the embarrassment of hearing his name called, of being a fly on the wall or, as the rabbinic imagination would have it, of being an ignoramus in the yeshiva of Rabbi Akiba.[14]

This treatment of Abraham, of the doubt that might have plagued Kafka's Abraham, brings together the redundancy of embarrassment with both dissonance and the problem of apostrophe's potential embarrassment. Perhaps after all there is embarrassment in an address that seems to come out of nowhere or turn in the middle of a poem or a speech. For how past this turn, in the midst of this turn or even prior to it, can one ever be sure one is being addressed, whether by a teacher or the Divine? How can Samuel know that God has called him? How can Abraham know? How can Moses be sure the rock will respond? The one who is called is not I. The one I want to be is not the person others see and the way I want to be seen may not be the way that others see me. Embarrassment allows for a crisis of identity on both sides of an address but its result as with an embarrassment of Scripture is not foretold. A refusal of that embarrassment — as the refusal of Hannah — may lead to the vanquishing of the old and corrupt and the establishment of newer, more legitimate governance. Or it may lead to the slaughter of thousands in the quest for a more perfect monotheism. Apostrophe holds a great potential for

14 BT Menahot 29a.

embarrassment, for mishearing or, perhaps, for the sadism of a teacher and no mistake at all. How to refuse embarrassment and walk to the front of the room like Hannah, create a new and for a time perhaps less corruptible form of divine communication? How to refuse embarrassment without the awful consequences of a people cleansed of three thousand sinners?

UNABASHEDLY READING DESIRED OUTCOMES INTO SCRIPTURE

Jewish Reaction to External Encroachment on its Cultural Heritage

Paul Heger

1. INTRODUCTION

Biblical exegesis, from its documented start in the period of Ezra and Nehemiah to the last period of the Second Commonwealth, had a decisive impact on Israel's way of life and far-reaching political and social consequences. I do not consider the first documented reform of Josiah as an exegetical phase, since it was presented as a revelation of a hidden book of laws, and not as a different reading of existing writings. Since we possess original and authentic data only from the Qumran group and none from the Pharisees and Sadducees — the major Judean groups at the end of the Second Temple period — we shall have to rely, at times, on the later rabbinic and historical writings.

This study will elaborate on the circumstances in Judah in the period of Ezra and Nehemiah, and will examine the introduction of reforms founded on assumed or real exegesis of extant sacred writings, as well as the practical application of these reforms in daily life. This study will demonstrate, using some examples, how certain desired outcomes were read into Scripture. We have, to our great dismay, a dark hole when it comes to knowledge of events in Judah from the period of Ezra and Nehemiah and the Hasmonean rebellion, a period of great upheaval in Jewish history, and a decisive time, both religiously and culturally.[1] The study will scrutinize the circumstances after the rebellion with particular emphasis on its repercussion on the attitude toward the laws of the Torah. It will look at the rebellion via the lens of two very different outcomes: on the one hand, an enhanced zeal to follow the Torah rules punctiliously, on the other hand, the recognition of pragmatic considerations in the interpretation of its commands, at least by the intellectual segment of society.

2. THE IMPACT OF SCRIPTURE ON ISRAELITE SOCIETY

2.1. EXEGESIS[2] IN THE PERIOD OF EZRA AND NEHEMIAH.

The period of Ezra and Nehemiah, who were the great reformers of Judaism[3] after the return from Babylonian exile, serves as a watershed moment for the radical change in the Torah's interpretation and practical implementation. There is no doubt in scholarly opinion that the Mosaic Law enjoyed a

1 Some apocryphal writings and non-sectarian literature found in Qumran seem to have been composed before the Hasmonean rebellion, but the extent of their impact on specific Jewish doctrines and theology is a debated issue.

2 I wish to emphasize that we have no data regarding how these new rules were presented to the people — that is, how they were perceived as founded upon Scripture. I would speculate that they were simply presented to the uneducated masses as founded upon the Torah. Although the books of Ezra and Nehemiah record a pattern of teaching and interpreting the law, it is most likely that these teachers did not show how they derived these new rules from the Torah. We are also unaware of the precise text of the Torah that was in their hands at the time. I use the terms "exegesis" and "interpretation," as these are the terms utilized in later periods to describe part of the process of creating new law. I am obviously not stating that Ezra acted according to the method of מדרש יוצר (creative midrash); on the contrary I assume that his decisions were founded upon his understanding of the general intent of the Torah, without specific scriptural support. The term "interpretation" utilized in my exposition should be perceived in its broadest aspect as Ezra's understanding of the Torah's Grundnorm. See also Paul Heger, The Three Biblical Altar Laws, Berlin, 1999, pp. 337 ff. and 407 ff., on the reforms of Ezra and Nehemiah.

3 We read in t. Sanh. 4:7: ראוי היה עזרא שתינתן תורה על ידו אילמלא קידמו משה "Ezra would have been worthy of receiving the Torah [and transmit it to Israel], if he were not anticipated by Moses."
We encounter a remarkable statement in b. Suk. 20a, which supports our thesis regarding the circumstances in Judah before Ezra's arrival, and subsequently at the Maccabean rebellion: כשנשתכחה תורה מישראל עלה עזרא מבבל ויסדה "When the Israelites forgot the Torah, Ezra immigrated from Babylon and restored it.

renaissance, or a new birth rather than a rebirth[4] after this period, which was characterized by strict observance and an enhanced attention to numerous details. Such attentiveness to the performance of the biblical precepts must have induced a spate of interpretive activity of the relatively scant and indeterminate biblical texts. In this period we encounter for the first time a requirement to read the Torah before the people[5] and to interpret it. The emphasis is on interpretation and understanding, as we see from the statement of Ezra's intentions in Ezra 7:10,[6] and the accomplishment of this task in Neh. 8:7-8.[7] It seems to me that what we have here is the first occurrence of ritual reform, or change of existent tradition, founded upon interpretation, rather than upon the discovery of "lost" scripture. I refer to the juxtaposition of the modification carried out by Josiah with respect to the Passover ritual, and Ezra and Nehemiah's similar proceedings regarding the intermarriage prohibition and other halakhic innovations. Josiah founded his decision on Shafan's simple reading of the recently found Book of the Covenant.[8] In contrast, Ezra and Nehemiah

4 When the various parts of scripture were composed, and under what circumstances, is a matter of scholarly debate. .

5 In Deut. 31:10-12 the public reading of the Torah was to be performed only once in seven years: מקץ שבע שנים במעד שנת השמטה בחג הסכות "At the end of every seven years, in the year of debt annulment, during the Feast of Tabernacles." From the texts of Ezra and Nehemiah, one has the impression that it was a permanent institution, with clerics appointed to teach the people God's precepts and make these precepts comprehensible to the masses. During this event, the texts were translated and formulated into practical rules.

6 We read there: כי עזרא הכין לבבו לדרש את תורת ה' "For Ezra had devoted himself to the study of the Law of the Lord." The biblical term דרש has many nuances, but I think that in Ezrah we may interpret it as a blend of two meanings: "to investigate" or "to inquire", as in Deut. 13:15 (v. 14 in KJV): ודרשת וחקרת "inquire, probe and investigate," and as in Exod. 18:15: לדרש אלהים "to seek God's will."

7 We read in v. 7: והלוים מבינים את העם "And the Levites instructed the people," and in v. 8: מפרש ושום שכל ויבינו במקרא "making it clear and elucidating the meaning so that the people could understand." The term פרש does not appear often in the Bible; we may consider it in light of לפרש להם "made clear to them [Lev. 24:12]" and כי לא פרש "it was not clear [Num. 15:34]." The LXX translates the term in the Pentateuch with the verb diakrivnw or sunkrivnw "distinguish," and in Neh. With dievstellen ejn ejpisthvmh kurivou "distinguish in the knowledge of God."

8 We read in II Kings 23:2: ויקרא באזניהם את כל דברי ספר הברית הנמצא בבית ה' "He read in their hearing all the words of the Book of the Covenant, which had been found in the temple of the Lord." And in vv. 21-22: ויצו המלך את כל העם לאמר עשו פסח לה' אלהיכם ככתוב על ספר הברית הזה. כי לא נעשה כפסח הזה מימי השפטים אשר שפטו את ישראל וכל ימי מלכי ישראל ומלכי יהודה "The king gave this order to all the people: celebrate the

did not relate or base their decision on a newly found Book, rather it is emphasized that "they found written in the Law, which the Lord had commanded through Moses."[9] Through their attentive reading, re-reading and interpreting the writings of the existing Law, they understood the divine commands differently than previous generations.[10] One cannot exclude the possibilty that they also somewhat altered the received text on the basis of their perception that this should have been the correct original wording.

Let us examine this important precursor which may have served as a model for the author(s) of Ezra and Nehemiah. In 2 Kgs 22:8 we read: ויאמר חלקיהו הכהן הגדול על שפן הספר ספר התורה מצאתי בבית ה׳ "Hilkiah the high priest said to Shaphan the secretary, 'I have found the Book of the Law in the temple of the Lord.'" "The book", an entire opus, hitherto unknown, containing a great number of new rules, was transmitted to the King, as is subsequently recorded. This results in a renewal of the Passover celebration, 2 Kgs 23:21-22: וַיְצַו הַמֶּלֶךְ את כל העם לאמר עשו פסח ׳לה אֱלֹהֵיכֶם כַּכָּתוּב עַל סֵפֶר הַבְּרִית הַזֶּה כִּי לֹא נַעֲשָׂה כַּפֶּסַח הַזֶּה מִימֵי הַשֹּׁפְטִים אֲשֶׁר שָׁפְטוּ אֶת יִשְׂרָאֵל וְכל יְמֵי מַלְכֵי יִשְׂרָאֵל וּמַלְכֵי יְהוּדָה "The king gave this command to all the people: 'Celebrate the Passover honoring the Lord your God, as it is written in this Book of the Covenant. Not since the days of the judges who led Israel, nor throughout the reigns of the kings of Israel and the kings of Judah, had any such Passover been observed.'"[11] The (re)-institution of allegedly ancient rules given to Moses at Sinai, is the same in both cases. There is, however, a distinction in scope between the two occurrences. In 2 Kgs, an entire book, was unexpectedly discovered, whereas in Nehemiah, a few verses of extant books

---

Passover honoring the the Lord your God, as it is written in this Book of the Covenant. Not since the days of the judges who led Israel, nor throughout the days of the kings of Israel and the kings of Judah, had any such Passover been observed."

9 We read in Nehemiah 8:13-14: וביום השני נאספו ראשי האבות לכל העם הכהנים והלוים אל עזרא הספר ולהשכיל אל דברי התורה. וימצאו כתוב בתורה אשר צוה ה׳ ביד משה אשר ישבו בני ישראל בסכות בחג בחדש השביעי "On the second day of the month the heads of all the families, along with the priests and the Levites, gathered around Ezra the scribe to understand the words of the Law. They found written in the Law, which the Lord had commanded through Moses, that the Israelites were to live in booths during the feast of the seventh month."

10 We read in v. 17: ויעשו כל הקהל השבים מן השבי סכות וישבו בסכות כי לא עשו מימי ישוע בן נון כן בני ישראל עד היום ההוא "The whole company that had returned from exile built booths and lived in them. From the days of Joshua son of Nun, the Israelites had not celebrated it thusly until that day."

11 The parallel texts in 2 Chr 34-35 are essentially identical to 2 Kgs.

were mysteriously found. The discovery of a concealed book, hidden for an obscure motive perhaps, seems reasonable, whereas the sudden unveiling of a few verses in an existing book, in comparison, seems entirely unreasonable, re-enforcing our doubt regarding its provenance.

Theirs was the first documented step on the extensive path of adjusting Israelite halakhah based on a novel interpretation of Scripture, distant from its simple meaning and at times in utter opposition to it, often adding precepts and prohibitions without any scriptural foundation. These additions became one of the main features of Jewish law in its further rabbinic development.[12] Ezra and Nehemiah took advantage of their prestige and the political power granted to them by the Persian court, overcame their probable embarrassment, and formulated ordinances they considered vital under the current circumstances, to ensure the continuity of the Jewish people under the Torah rule. They unabashedly declared that the laws they formulated originated in the Torah. They read into the Torah what they considered to be God's intent.

2. 2. EXTENSION OF SABBATH RESTRICTIONS

We read in Neh 13: 15 בימים ההמה ראיתי ביהודה דרכים גתות בשבת ומביאים הערמות ועמסים על החמרים ואף יין ענבים ותאנים וכל משא ומביאים ירושלם ביום השבת ואעיד ביום מכרם ציד "In those days I saw [some] in Judah treading winepresses on the Sabbath and bringing the grain and loading it on donkeys, together with wine, grapes, figs and all other kinds of loads. And they were bringing all this into Jerusalem on the Sabbath. And I warned them against selling food on that day." The KJV adds the term "some" in its translation, creating some ambiguity as to the referent. But from the context of this verse and vv. 17-21 we must assume that it refers to gentiles,[13]

12 Regarding the later rabbinic interpretation method, see P. Heger, The Pluralistic Halakhah, Berlin, 2003.

13 If they were Jews he would not have solved the problem by shutting the gates of Jerusalem; he would have compelled them, by his authority, to cease working on Sabbath, as he did in other similar occurrences. The traditional commentators do not specify who treaded the winepresses, but b. Shab. 123b cites our verse Neh 13:15 as support for a prohibition against carrying on the Sabbath, emphasizing the term ומביאים "they were bringing." Rashi translates this verse, using the term מזלזלים "they were disrespecting" the Sabbath instead of the term מחללים "desecrate," the correct term for doing work on Sabbath, used by Nehemiah in v. 17. Accordingly, he interprets the

who produced the wine and brought it together with other fruits to sell to the Jerusalemite Jews. The purveyors of farm products are the unspecified gentile inhabitants of Judah, whereas the identity of the purveyors of fish and other goods is spelled out in v 16: והצרים ישבו בה מביאים דאג וכל מכר ומכרים בשבת לבני יהודה ובירושלם "Men from Tyre [a coastal city of fishermen and renowned merchants], who lived in Jerusalem were bringing fish and all kinds of merchandise and selling them to the people of Judah and Jerusalem on the Sabbath." Verse 19 records that Nehemiah ordered them to close the gates of Jerusalem on Friday at sundown, causing complaints by the merchants, who resigned themselves to the new circumstances, and did not show up anymore, as v. 21 narrates. It is evident that he chastised the Jerusalemites for buying on Sabbath, an activity not prohibited in the Torah.[14] It is remarkable that the Rabbis did not consider the prohibition of trading on Sabbath a Torah commandment. It is not included in the thirty-nine works deemed forbidden by the Torah,[15] and it is perceived as a rabbinically instituted rule of a preventive nature.

2. 3. EXTENSION OF THE SUKKOT CELEBRATION

The Sukkot celebration, that is, living in the booths at the Harvest Gathering Holiday instituted by Ezra and Nehemiah, develops in a noteworthy way throughout Scripture.

The earliest mention of this holiday, is in Ex 23:16, where it is referred to as חג האסף "Feast of Ingathering," and it is celebrated at the end of the yearly harvest. There are no indications of its date, (only בצאת השנה "at the end of the year"), its duration, and the nature of its rites. In contrast, the "Mazzah" Feast in Ex 23:15 links the festival to the exodus from Egypt. It lasts for seven days it takes place "in the month of Abib," and its ritual obligations are to eat Mazzah and bring an offering, without indicating a required location; there is no

---

phrase יומת מות מחלליה "anyone who desecrated it [the Sabbath] must be put to death," as: הנוהג בה חול בקדושתה "one who conducts himself on the Sabbath as on a weekday" desecrates its holiness.

14 J. Blenkinsopp, Ezra-Nehemiah, Philadelphia, PA, 1988, Vol. 3 declares that the prohibition of selling on Sabbath was established long beforehand, but Nehemiah extended it to the activity of buying from Gentiles (p. 359).

15 See m. Shab. 7:2 and Paul Heger, The Pluralistc Halakhah, Berlin, 2003, pp. 98-100 and notes 12-13.

allusion to Jerusalem, "the place the Lord will choose." The command of Ex 34:22 referring to the Feast of Ingathering is identical in its lack of definition to that of Ex 23:16, as is the command of the Mazzah feast in v.18 and its complement in 34:23, except for the obligation to bring an offering that is missing.

In Deut 16:13-17, we encounter for the first time[16] the term חג הסכות "Feast of the Booths," its seven days period and its ritual obligation to perform pilgrimage to "the place the Lord will choose [Jerusalem]" and to bring an offering. There is no explanation of the name חג הסכת, its rationale as a post-harvest celebration is still indicated, and there is no association with the Exodus from Egypt and no set date. Only in Lev 23:39-36 do we encounter a comprehensive and detailed description of חג הסכת; the text indicates an exact date, a seven day duration, the addition of a distinct holiday on the eighth day, the designation of the first and eighth days as holidays, upon which work is prohibited, and the obligation of offerings and libations every day of the feast. A stylistic oddity should be noted:, after two concluding verses (37 and 38) summarizing the holidays, vv. 39-43 return to the Feast of the Ingathering.[17] The date and duration are repeated, as well as the rationale as a festival the end of the agricultural season and two hitherto unknown ritual obligations are added: one, the celebration with palm fronds and choice fruits, to thank God for the successful harvest, and two, living in the booths, commemorating the Exodus from Egypt. Here, we observe an amalgamation of two distinct rationales for the ritual obligations of this feast. These verses constitute the only association of the Feast with the Exodus in the Pentateuch and it is evident that the text of Leviticus represents the latest version of the command to observe the holiday of Booths. The holiday started without any fixed date and obligation and attained its final stage in the text of Lev 23. Its association with the Exodus

16 The notion that the P source of the Pentateuch is of a later date than Deuteronomy is the more common scholarly opinion, though there is still some disagreement. Certain scholars contend that the final priestly redaction of the Pentateuch, adds to the Deuteronomy text. The duty of pilgrimage to Jerusalem may have been innovated by king Josiah, in whose period the Book of Deuteronomy "was found in the Temple (2 Kgs 22:8)".

17 Scholars debate the motive of the obvious interjection of vv. 39-43 and the apparent contradiction between the eighth day as a separate holiday and as an element of the Sukkot holiday. Some scholars hypothesize an amalgamation of two previously distinct holidays, one of seven days and one of eight days.

indicates the trend to bolster historical consciousness by propagating the great national myth, the Exodus from Egypt, as a means of emphasizing ethnic superiority and separation from other peoples. I would speculate that the motive for the insertion of the Exodus in the later version of the Ten Commandments, as well as for the justification of the Sabbath in Deut 5:15, may also be perceived as bolstering the connection to the greatest Israelite myth. Though the myth of Exodus seems to be linked to the social awareness of a slave's dire condition, the emphasis on God who "brought you out of there with a mighty hand" seems equally significant.

Moreover, it is strange that the text of Num 29:12-24, listing the great variety of obligatory offerings on this holiday and its exact date, does not mention its name, in contrast to all other holidays whose names, in one way or another, are indicated. We read in Num 29:12: ובחמשה עשר יום לחדש השביעי מקרא קדש יהיה לכם כל מלאכת עבדה לא תעשו וחגתם חג 'לה שבעת ימים "On the fifteenth day of the seventh month, hold a sacred assembly and do no regular work. Celebrate a festival to the Lord for seven days." Vv 13-34 record the offerings for each of the eight days, without any indication of the holiday's name and the obligation of living in the booths. When Passover is mentioned, the name פסח is indicated, as is the obligation to eat Matzah. The next holiday is also mentioned by name יום הבכורים "the Day of the First Fruits" and the offering of "New Grain" is also mentioned. Once again, the Feast of the Booth is a peculiar exception. The texts relating to the other holidays evince a process of development, but the texts relating to the Feast of Booths are markedly different from one another.

We do not know how the holidays developed from primitive agrarian phenomena without fixed dates — dependent on the start or conclusion of some vital farming event determined by the weather conditions — to being sophisticated affairs with fixed dates and elaborate rituals. The general path of such development seems obvious; as societies develop, the institutionalization of customs and rituals occurs, leading to fixed dates, uniformity, and refinement of primitive customs. However, with regard to the Sukkot festival, we encounter an entirely new ideology as the basis for the holiday's novel customs, unrelated to the archaic practices. The ingathering of the harvest, the principal motive for the feast in the other texts, does not appear in the introduction of the holiday (verse 34) and is relegated to a secondary position in verse 39; moreover, we encounter in this verse a new concept תחגו את חג ה' "celebrate the festival of the Lord"; the identical concept appears, in a different literary style in verses 34 and 41. The idea that this festival is a divine festival is stressed three times here; but the idea of a people's festival is also present. In Ex 34:22, with respect to the Feast of Weeks and of Ingathering, the phrase תעשה לך, literally "make a holiday for you," appears. Although it does not appear in Leviticus, in Deut 16:13 or in Num 29:1 and 7, this phrase also appears in the texts delineating the Trumpets Festival and the Day of Atonement. I would suggest that these variations and the triple mention of "the festival of the Lord" in Leviticus 23 (above) indicates that the transition from a people's agrarian festivals to ideologically religiously based holidays was accomplished.

The celebration with choice fruit and palm fronds, possibly an archaic ritual practiced at festivals, is reimagined as part of a divine holiday with a religiously inspired element. A Thanksgiving Festival at the end of the agricultural season is replaced with the ritual commemoration of the Exodus, which embodies two new notions:

a) A political-historical one, celebrating the miraculous founding of the nation and —

b) a religiously-inspired notion, i.e. an emphasis upon the nation's eternal indebtedness to God, and a commitment to worship Him as well as obey His commands in gratitude for freeing them from Egyptian slavery by breaking their yoke (Lev 26:13).

Considering the above, I do not hesitate to venture that Ezra and Nehemiah interjected the text of Lev 23:39-43. The administrative activities of Ezra and Nehemiah, demonstrate their understanding of the political situation, and of the necessary steps for building a small distinct nation in an encroaching environment of culturally related and unrelated nations. They concentrated on securing the required authority [from the Persian government], and employed many practical measures to achieve their goal.

2. 4. EXTENSION OF INTERMARRIAGE PROHIBITIONS —REFLECTIONS

We encounter a host of puzzles and serious variations regarding the issue of intermarriage. We read in Ezra 9:1-2: לא נבדלו העם ישראל והכהנים והלוים מעמי הארצות כתועבתיהם לכנעני החתי הפרזי היבוסי העמני המאבי המצרי והאמרי כי נשאו מבנתיהם להם ולבניהם "The people of Israel, including the priests and the Levites, have not kept themselves separate from the neighboring peoples and their detestable practices, specifically those of the Canaanites, Hittites, Perizzites, Jebusites, Ammonites, Moabites, Egyptians and Amorites. They have taken of their daughters as wives for themselves and their sons,[18] and have polluted the holy race with the peoples around them." In contrast to Neh 13:1 in which it is stated that such ordinance was "unexpectedly" found in the Pentateuch, the Ezra narrative in ch. 9 and 10 does not refer to a distinct scriptural prohibition; the "transgressors" are "only" guilty of "broken faith and increasing the guilt of Israel (Ezra 10:10)." The above cited introductory verse uses a "mixed bag" of nations, inconsistent with any single pentateuchal rule regarding intermarriage. It uses an odd term, כְּתֹעֲבֹתֵיהֶם לַכְּנַעֲנִי-that literally means "as their abominations to the Canaanite," with the preposition כְּ "as/like" and לַ "to," which is

18 Monk Bede, an early medieval scholar (beginning of 8th Century), writes that the early returnees cast aside their Israelite wives — who were exhausted and became unattractive due to their poverty and deprivation on the long journey — and married either beautiful local women, or daughters of powerful rich men. He interpreted Mal 2:11-12 literally, and alleges that the prophet accused the returnees of this transgression. Bede, On Ezra and Nehemiah, translated by Scott DeGregorio, Liverpool, 2006, p.136. Modern scholars also suggest pragmatic incentives as the motive for intermarriage, and the motive of those who opposed intermarriage. Daniel L. Smith-Christopher, "The Mixed Marriage Crisis in Ezra 9-10 and Nehemiah 13: A Study of the Sociology of the Post-Exilic Judean Community," Second Temple Studies, eds. Tamar C. Eskenazi and Kent H. Richards, JSOT Supplement, 1994, pp, 243-265, quotes a scholarly opinion that an actual scarcity of Jewish women among the returning exiles was the motive for the mixed marriages (p. 246). The same author (pp. 258-261) and Blenkinsopp, 1988, Vol. 3 (354/5) suggest that political and economic interests of the clergy and aristocratic Jewish clans were the motive behind intermarriages, particularly with Samaritan leading families, due to their dominating status in Judea. Nehemiah's criticism of intermarriage was an element of his struggle for the establishment of the province's autonomy from their Samaritan oriented political attitude, as Ulrich Kellermann, Nehemiah Quellen und Űberlieferung und Geschichte, Berlin, 1967, states (p. 193). Smith-Christopher quotes scholarly opinions contending that the fear that foreign women could inherit the land may have been a major concern of the post-exilic community, and therefore the community opposed mixed marriages (pp. 244/6).

difficult syntactically.[19] It may, however, allude to the intermarriage prohibition in Deut 7:1-4, which states that intermarriage leads to idolatrous worship and note the expression ככל תועבתם in Deut 20:18.[20] But the Ammonites and Moabites are not enumerated in Deut 7, or in 20:18, as being forbidden to the Israelites. Apart from the difficult term כתעבתיהם, which may hint to the deuteronomic interdiction, Ezra adds an utterly new[21] reason: the prevention of the holy seed intermingling with that of the peoples of the land (9:2), and

19 The translators and commentators offered a great array of solutions for this apparently contorted expression. Rashi and Ibn Ezra ignore the problem altogether, but Mezudat David interprets it as, "they still perform the Canaanite abominations." The LXX translates it with the conjunction ejn "with" and the translator, Albert Pietersma, A new English translation of the Septuagint, Oxford, 2007, does not interpret the phrase literally, and writes: "did not put away from themselves the alien nations of the land, as their uncleanness requires." The KJV interprets it: "have not separated themselves from the peoples of the lands, according to their abominations, those of the Canaanites." The NRSV interprets it: "have not put away from themselves the alien peoples of the land and their pollutions." The NIV interprets it: "have not kept themselves separate from the neighbouring peoples with their detestable practices, like those of the Canaanites." Note the variation among the translations which is an indication of an uncertain text.

20 Juha Pakkala, Ezra the Scribe, BZAW, Berlin, 2004, claims that the source of Ezra 9:2 and 12 is Deut 7:3, relying on the similarities of the text regarding the marriage of foreign daughters to Israelites. He relies on the similarity of words, though Ezra mentions only intermarriage to foreign women, whereas Deuteronomy indicates the marriage of Israelite daughters to foreigners as well; only Ezra 9:14 uses the indeterminate ולהתחתן. I prefer to highlight the motive of the prohibition clearly mentioned in Scripture, rather than focus on a similarity of terms that may be casual.

21 Pakkala, ibid, alleges that the concept זרע קודש "holy seed" may be have been deduced by Ezra from the phrase כי עם קדוש אתה לה "for you are a people holy to the Lord (Deut 7:6)." In my opinion, the term holy which is attached to the word Israel in varied instances in Leviticus and Deuteronomy, does not relate to a mixture of the human seed. Moreover, in Deut 7:6, the phrase is connected to an apodictic command to destroy sacred idolatrous artifacts. If this phrase is connected to the preceding prohibition of intermarriage, its emphasis is not on being tempted to join their idolatrous customs, rather it is a precaution against the pollution of the holy seed. The claim that this motive in vv. 4 and 5 was added later, and that originally v. 6 was the reason behind the prohibition, seems to me unwarranted. It would require considering Deut 20:16-18, a passage that highlights the seductive nature of idolatry, as a later addition as well. In both pericopes the phrase החרם תחרים is used and indicates connection: the temptation to be swayed by idolatrous worship is at the root of both the prohibition of intermarriage and the command to annihilate the seven nations. Whether the relevant text of Deuteronomy existed in its current style prior to Ezra, or whether Ezra and later redactors adapted it, is an issue I will address later in the study.

Nehemiah evokes a “modern,” hitherto unprecedented concept of a national language’s religious significance. Ezra, likely avoided mentioning the deuteronomic reasoning, since there was no danger of idolatry in Judea in his period. Instead, he used an undefined derogative term; he also neglects to mention the interdiction against allowing Ammonites and Moabites into the Israelite community, as indicated in Deut 23:5-7.

Ezra cites an incomplete list of six out of the seven nations of Canaan, who must be annihilated (Deut 20:16), and with whom intermarriage is prohibited (Deut 7:1-3). He likely added the Moabites and Ammonites to conform to the general prohibition forbidding the incorporation of these two peoples into the Israelite community, as written in Deut 23:4: לא יבא עמוני ומואבי בקהל ה' גם דור עשירי לא יבא להם בקהל ה' עד עולם “An Ammonite or Moabite shall not enter into the congregation of the Lord; even unto their tenth generation they shall not enter the congregation of the Lord for ever,” omitting the text’s very different reasoning.[22] In Ezra 10 the effected transgression and the dictate to separate from the women and their offspring refers to נשים נכריות “foreign wives,” a generic term, which encompasses all gentiles, and has no biblical origin. Nehemiah states in 13:1 that the Torah prohibits the absorption of Moabites and Ammonites into the congregation of the Lord, indicating the scriptural motive: their failure to offer hospitality to the Israelites at their passage in the desert and their hiring of Balaam to curse the Israelites. In Neh 13: 23-24, the author specifically stresses the Ashdodian women, who were utterly ignored by Ezra: גם בימים ההם ראיתי את היהודים השיבו נשים אשדודיות עמוניות מואביות ובניהם חצי מדבר אשדודית ואינם מכירים לדבר יהודית וכלשון עם ועם “Moreover, in those days I saw men of Judah who had married women from Ashdod, Ammon and Moab. Half of their children spoke the language of Ashdod or the language of one of the other peoples, and did not know how to speak the language of Judah.” Since the women from Ashdod are not included in any biblical prohibition, he innovates a new motive for their inclusion in the intermarriage prohibition. The addition of Egyptians to the list of nations with whom marriage is forbidden, however, appears only

22 We read there: עַל-דְּבַר אֲשֶׁר לֹא-קִדְּמוּ אֶתְכֶם, בַּלֶּחֶם וּבַמַּיִם, בַּדֶּרֶךְ, בְּצֵאתְכֶם מִמִּצְרָיִם; וַאֲשֶׁר שָׂכַר עָלֶיךָ אֶת-בִּלְעָם בֶּן-בְּעוֹר, מִפְּתוֹר אֲרַם נַהֲרַיִם--לְקַלְלֶךָּ. “For they did not come to meet you with bread and water on your way when you came out of Egypt, and they hired Balaam son of Beor from Pethor in Aram Naharaim to pronounce a curse on you.” Compare Neh 13:2.

once — in Ezra 9:1-2. We observe the lack of consistency in these verses and their relationship to the Torah's prohibitions. Scripture did not add the Ammonites and Moabites to the seven nations in Deut 7:1-3, which stresses the prohibition of intermarriage with the seven nations, a rule that seems redundant since they must be totally exterminated.

The intermarriage topic in the books of Ezra and Nehemiah raises many additional questions. Ezra 9 introduces the subject with the phrase "after these things have been done" without indicating which things he refers to, and whether "these things" have any connection to the issue, as one would expect from this peculiar introduction.[23] We are also unaware of who the שרים "leaders"[24] were who approached Ezra, telling him of the indecent affair. In addition, we do not know the status and function of Shecaniah, the main speaker of the people in Ezra 10:2. W. Th. in der Smitten[25] wonders how, before being told by the officials, Ezra was unaware and seemingly surprised by the intermarriage (Ezra 7:24-26). Lester Grabbe[26] also wonders about Ezra's lack of decisive action, despite his authority to enforce the Torah laws. The narratives in Ezra and Nehemiah evince internal inconsistencies, mainly between one another, and raise the question of whether they relate to the same event or to two different occurrences. The order of events is also unclear. If there were two separate episodes, in one the leader's efforts must have failed,[27] though in both events success is indicated.

The biblical commands regarding the association of Israel with members of other nations, equally demonstrates inconsistencies. We read in Deut 23:5

23 Johanna W. H. Van Wijk-Bos, Ezra, Nehemiah and Esther, Louisville, KY, 1998, suggests after Ezra and company accomplished the commissions entrusted to them, "the time had come for certain people to bring a serious matter to Ezra's attention (p. 40)."

24 The LXX translates it as leaders, the KJV interprets it as princes, and the NRSV quotes it as officials. J. Blenkinsopp, Ezra-Nehemiah, Philadelphia, 1988, translates it a "Leading laymen (p. 174)."

25 Dr. Wilhelm Th. In der Smittem, Esra, Assen, 1973, p. 136.

26 Lester I. Grabbe, Ezra-Nehemiah, London-New York, 1998, p. 142.

27 J. Blenkinsopp, Ezra-Nehemiah, writes that the "measures taken by Ezra against intermarriage were not successful (p. 177)." Jacob L. Wright, Rebuilding Identity, The Nehemiah Memoir and its Earliest Readers, BZAW 348, Berlin, 2005, discusses these problems extensively (pp. 243-257), analyzing different critical scholarly opinions and offers his solution involving various layers and adjustments by redactors.

that the reason for the prohibition against absorbing Moabites into the Israelite God's community is: על דבר אשר לא קדמו אתכם בלחם ובמים בדרך בצאתכם ממצרים ואשר שכר עליך את בלעם בן בעור מפתור ארם נהרים לקללך "For they did not come to meet you with bread and water on your way when you came out of Egypt, and they hired Balaam son of Beor from Pethor Aram Naharaim to pronounce a curse on you." We observe a distinction between the first motive written in the plural, referring to both peoples, and the second motive in the singular, likely referring only to Moab, as recorded in Num chapters 22-24. Hence, the Ammonites are blamed for only one mild misdemeanor. It is important to note that the indictment of Moab could be perceived as justification for eternal enmity. The lack of hospitality, the single accusation against Ammon, does not seem reasonable; hospitality is not an obligation and failing to perform it, should not generate such drastic hostility.

Besides this dilemma, a host of textual issues must be addressed. The Israelites, as it seems, did not enter the territory of Ammon and Moab, following the divine command, as we read in Deut 2:19: וקרבת מול בני עמון אל תצרם ואל תתגר בם כי לא אתן מארץ בני עמון לך ירשה כי לבני לוט נתתיה ירשה "When you come to the Ammonites, do not harass them or provoke them to war, for I will not give you possession of any land belonging to the Ammonites. I have given it as a possession to the descendants of Lot." A similar command, regarding the Moabites is repeated almost verbatim in v. 8. No Israelite request of passage, vis-à-vis Ammon and Moab, is recorded as was the case with with Edom in Num 20:17: נעברה נא בארצך "please let us pass through your country." If the Israelites did not enter their lands, because of the divine command, the inhabitants were obviously not morally obligated to extend them hospitality. Oddly, Deut 2:29 implies that the Moabites sold the Israelites food and drink: אכל בכסף תשברני ואכלתי ומים בכסף תתן לי ושתיתי רק אעברה ברגלי כאשר עשו לי בני עשו הישבים בשעיר והמואבים הישבים בער עד אשר אעבר את הירדן "Sell us food to eat and water to drink for their price in silver. Only let us pass through on foot — as the descendants of Esau, who live in Seir, and the Moabites, who live in Ar, did for us-until we cross the Jordan." Though the divine command to buy food and drink appears only in reference to the Edomites in v. 6, we could assume that the Israelites received the same instruction with respect to the Moabites and Ammonites. The rationale not to provoke hostilities with them, is identical.

God allotted them their land and therefore it must remain theirs. We read in Deut 2:5: אל תתגרו בם כי לא אתן לכם מארצם עד מדרך כף רגל כי ירשה לעשו נתתי את הר שעיר "Do not provoke them to war, for I will not give you any of their land, not even enough to put your foot on. I have given Esau the hill country of Seir as his own." We have cited above the command related to the Moabites, and the identical instructions regarding the Ammonites which end with the rationale: כי לבני לוט נתתיה ירשה "I have given it as a possession to the descendants of Lot" in v. 19. Hence, one may deduce that the identical divine instructions regarding the purchase of food and drink from Edom should also apply to Moab and Ammon.

Whether or not the Israelites crossed the boundary of Moab is ambiguous, because on the one hand we read in Deut 2:18: אתה עבר היום את גבול מואב את ער "You shall cross over Ar, the border of Moab (KJV)," "Today you are to pass by the region of Moab at Ar (NIV)," "Today you are going to cross the boundary of Moab at Ar (NRSV)," and the LXX translates: «you will go beside/alongside today the border of Moab around Seir."[28] The MT seems to indicate that the Israelites did not enter Moab, but passed alongside its border, with the LXX and other translations — except possibly the NRSV. On the other hand, Deut 2:8b records: ונפן ונעבר דרך מדבר מואב "We turned and traveled along the desert road of Moab," from which it seems that they did cross into the territory of Moab. In that case, the emphasis on their crossing of the desert may qualify the event, by stressing that they did not pass through a populated area. It raises the question — where did they purchase food and water, mentioned in Deut 2:29. W. Brueggemann[29] opines that the narrative of Deut 2:9-21 is positive vis-a-vis Moab in contrast with Deut 23:4-7.

The issue of the different attitudes toward the neighbouring nations poses a further dilemma. If their behaviour at the exodus from Egypt was the motive regulating the future relationship of Israel with neighbouring nations, one must wonder about the preferential treatment of Edom. Ammon and Moab are discriminated, at most, for failing to demonstrate friendship and hospitality to the Israelites during their passage, whereas Edom, who

28 Note that the LXX reads this text differently than the MT.

29 Walter Brueggemann, Deuteronomy, Nashville, TN, 2001, p. 228.

threatened them with war, despite the Israelites' plea for brotherly compassion (Num 20:14-21),[30] is preferentially biased. Regardless of our above expressed perplexity, one may deduce from Deut 2:8b that Moab did not object to the Israelites' crossing of their desert territory, in contrast to Edom's opposition. Hence, Moab demonstrated a much friendlier demeanour than Edom and their penalization remains incomprehensible. The assertion in Deut 2:29 that Edom sold supplies to the Israelites is equally problematic. Num 20:21 explicitly states "since Edom refused to let them through their territory: ויט ישראל מעליו "Israel turned away from them."

Deut 2:1 affirms again ונסב את הר שעיר ימים רבים "We circled the hill country of Seir for a long time" There seems to be some inconsistency between the narrative in Num 20:14-21 and that of Deut 2:4-8. In contrast with the resolute and fearless attitude recorded in Num, we read in Deut 2:4: בני עשו הישבים בשעיר ויראו מכם "[You are about to pass through the territory of your brothers], the descendants of Esau who live in Seir. They will be afraid of you." Though the narrative in Numbers relates to Edom, and the narrative in Deuteronomy relates to Esau and Har Seir, both sources undoubtedly refer to the same event, yet it seems they are composed by different authors, a fact which was observed already by Gerhard von Rad. The geographical dilemmas in connection with the narratives regarding the Israelite's wanderings surrounding Edom are discussed by Martin Noth. These irregularities indicate unequivocally that the texts relevant to the narratives and associated commands regarding the prohibition to absorb members of the neighbouring nations were tinkered with at various times. They were transformed based on circumstances,[31] which guided the respective authors in their selection and preference of the different

30 I will only cite a few highlights of the extended narrative: כה אמר אחיך ישראל "This is what your brother Israel says," אעברה נא בארצך לא נעבר בשדה ובכרם ולא נשתה מי באר דרך המלך נלך לא נטה ימין ושמאול "Please let us pass through your country. We will not go through any field or vineyard, or drink water from any well. We will travel along the king's highway and not turn to the right or to the left, and Edom's reaction: לא תעבר — You shall not pass.

31 M. Noth, Numbers, translated from German by James D. Martin, London, 1968, already observed "an inimical attitude on the part of Edom towards Israel," although it is referred to as Israel's brother (p. 150). He also notes the inconsistencies in the text, indicating the amalgamation of two sources (p. 149).
Walter Brueggemann, Deuteronomy, writes that it is quite likely that the exclusion of particular nations reflects the convictions of a certain moment in history (p. 228).

nations. [32] J. Pakkala[33] analyzes this point of view, citing scholarly attempts to reconcile these differences "ranging from [attribution to] pre-Dtn and Urdeteronomium to one of its latest expansion."

The objective of the adjustments was, of course, to ensure the cultural identity of the Jews by avoiding any alien influence.[34] This motive guided the initiators of the "adjustments" to the pentateuchal laws, as is indicated explicitly in Deut 7 and 20, and implicitly in the books of Ezra and Nehemiah. We can only speculate regarding the motives for the biblical discrimination of the members of the various nations.[35] I would presume that the Ammonites and Moabites were the nearest neighbours in distance and language, and therefore constituted the greatest danger of interrelation and evil influence; consequently contact with them was categorically precluded.[36] The Egyptians were more remote both physically and linguistically. I have no reasonable hypothesis regarding the preferential treatment of the Edomites; though they were perceived as genealogically related to the Israelites, the historical and prophetical books are brimming with enmity, military confrontations and expectations of their downfall.[37]

---

32 It is interesting to note the rabbinic homilies and dicta with respect to this issue of intermarriage, which are in opposition to Nehemiah's dictate, and demonstrate the effected changes in the list of the nations, and the application of the law as it refers to males and females. We read in m. Yebam. 8:3 עמוני ומואבי אסורים ואיסורן איסור עולם אבל נקבותיהם מותרות מיד "Male Ammonites and Moabites are eternally prohibited [from being absorbed into the Israelite community], but their females are permitted immediately." Moreover, in m.Yad. 4:4 we read of a male Ammonite who desired to convert to Judaism, and the assembly of the Sages decided to accept him, despite the opposition of Rabban Gamaliel the head of the Sanhedrin, declaring: כבר עלה סנחריב מלך אשור ובלבל את כל האומות "Sennacherib king of Assyria had intermingled all the peoples [via population transfer]."

33 J. Pakkala, 2004, pp. 11-115.

34 The term בדל "to separate/isolate" appears six times in the few verses relating to the intermarriage issue in Ezra and Nehemiah.

35 Gerhard Von Rad, Deuteronomy, A Commentary, translated from German by D. Barton, Philadelphia, 1966, writes: "It is difficult to discover the reason for the preferential treatment of the Edomites and Egyptians" (p. 146).

36 It is plausible that the narrative of the incestuous origin of the Ammonites and Moabites of Gen 19:31-38 was also conceived as deterrent to intermarriage with these nations.

37 Examples include Num 20:14-21; Jud 11:17 together with Moab; 2 Sam 8:14; 1 Kgs 11:14-15, 2 Kgs 8:20, 14:7-10; Isa 11:14, 34:1-17; Jer 39:25, chs. 48-49; Eze chs. 35-36; Ps ch. 137; Lam 4:22.

These records prepare the background for the later references to Edom as one of Israel's ultimate enemies.[38]

All these dilemmas cast a dark shadow over the antiquity of the intermarriage prohibition. One must consider whether the circumstances at the return from Babylon necessitated the promulgation of a new theory of זרע קודש "holy seed," at odds with the Torah's friendly and compassionate attitude towards the גר "the aliens" within Israel.[39] Yet, this is a problem we cannot discuss here.

EXCURSUS:

WHETHER OR NOT THE BIBLICAL PROHIBITION OF INCORPORATING AMMONITES AND MOABITES INTO ISRAELITE COMMUNITY ALSO INCLUDED THE ABSORPTION OF THEIR WOMEN THROUGH MARRIAGE

The assumption that the biblical prohibition against incorporation into the community includes Moabite and Ammonite women is a generally accepted postulate. We encounter in b. Yeb.76b-77a an extended deliberation regarding the contradiction between the biblical prohibition to absorb Ammonites and Moabites into the Israelite Community and the genealogy of King David, who was born from the marriage of Ruth the Moabite and Boaz. The Rabbis, declared that the biblical prohibition relates to males, but not to females; therefore, the marriage with Ruth was legitimate. However, at the same time the Rabbis did not apply the same distinction to Egyptians and bastards, though these groups also appear solely in the masculine. Bastards are excluded from joining the Israelite Community forever, and Egyptians are permitted to join only after three generations.

Scholars, for the most part, did not accept the rabbis' solution and hypothesized that the author or redactor of Ruth, who added verses 17-22 to Ruth 4,

38 The preferential treatment of Edom may be a late addition, following their forced conversion to Judaism (ANT: XIII: 257); b. Sanh. 39 b states that the prophet Obadiah was a converted Edomite.

39 See the Excursus regarding King David's descent from Ruth the Moabite and other biblical narratives dealing with intermarriage.

represented a segment of Israelite society hostile to Ezra's prohibition against intermarriage with gentile women. It is plausible that they opposed Ezra's regulation because of their reluctance to change the existing practice and the necessity to divorce their gentile wives and children. The basis for their opposition may have included the intermarriage of Israelite heroes with gentile women, such as Joseph's marriage to an Egyptian (Gen 41:45), Moses' marriage to a Midianite (Ex 2:21) and a Cushite (Num 12:1) and Solomon's marriage to Pharaoh's daughter, recorded without any hint of censure (1 Kings 3:1). They may have disseminated the book of Ruth, or added the genealogy at its end, to bolster their view. The redactor of Ruth discreetly introduces another gentile woman into David's genealogy, — Tamar the Canaanite. The redactor was not content to begin the genealogy with Obed, son of Boaz, Ruth's husband, but started it with Perez, Judah's and Tamar's son (Gen 38:29) without mentioning them; (he assumed that the readers would be aware of Perez's identity and progenitors). Using this strategem, he bolsters the clout of his argument. [40]

Ezra and Nehemiah discouraged intermarriage by dramaturgic spectacles such as beatings, pulling out of hair, cursing, adjurations of the intermarried men by Nehemiah (Neh 13:25), tearing his clothes, pulling out his hair from head and beard, sitting appalled (Ezra 9:3), praying to God in public before a large crowd of Israelites (10:1), kneeling with his hands spread out (Ezra 9:4), and finally threatening the property confiscation of those who would disobey (10:8). This indicates the strength of the opposition to the imposed prohibition. It is the *opinio communis* that the biblical prohibition to incorporate members of some nations into the Israelite community evidently applied to men and women alike. One should note, however, that due to the inferior status of women versus men in Scripture, and in Israelite society, it is plausible that the marriage of an Israelite man with a gentile woman was considered different than the absorption of a gentile male into the community.

40 See also the opinions of other scholars regarding the apparent inconsistency between the biblical prohibitions and the book of Ruth, as for example: Thomas and Dorothy Thompson, "Some Legal Problems in the Book of Ruth", VT 18, (68), pp. 79-99, B. A. Levine, "In Praise of the Israelite Mishpaha: Legal Themes in the Book of Ruth," pp. 95-106, The Quest for the Kingdom of God: Studies in Honor of G. E. Mendehall, eds. H. B. Huffmon et ali., Winona Lake, IND, 1983, Gillis Gerleman, Ruth, Das Hohelied, Neukirchen, 1965, Jack M. Sasson, Ruth, Baltimore, 1979, p. 232.

Women are not part of עדת ה' "the Lord's people" in Num 27:17 and are not counted among the עדת בני ישראל "the Israelite Community" in the census commanded in Num 1. Nor are the women counted among the Israelites who left Egypt, as we read in Ex 12:37: ויסעו בני ישראל מרעמסס סכתה כשש מאות אלף רגלי הגברים לבד מטף "The Israelites journeyed from Rameses to Succoth. There were about six hundred thousand men on foot, besides." In contrast to the male children below twenty, the women were not even mentioned; they were totally ignored as members of the community. It is quite explicit in Deut 25:5-6: כי ישבו אחים יחדו ומת אחד מהם ובן אין לו לא תהיה אשת המת החוצה לאיש זר יבמה יבא עליה ולקחה לו לאשה ויבמה והיה הבכור אשר תלד יקום על שם אחיו המת ולא ימחה שמו מישראל "If brothers are living together and one of them dies without a son,[41] his widow must not marry outside the family. Her husband's brother shall take her and marry her and fulfill the duty of a brother-in-law to her. The first son she bears shall carry on the name of the dead brother so that his name will not be blotted out from Israel." The main motive of levirate marriage is explicitly stated in Scripture, that is, to ensure that the name of the deceased will continue to be part of the Israelite community. Therefore, according to the plain meaning of Scripture, he must have a son; if the deceased had only a daughter, his name would disappear from the community, and thus his living brother must produce an heir on his behalf. The Arab/Muslim custom — similar to the Jewish practice in many aspects, distinguishes between the marriage of a Muslim male with a non-Muslim female, which is allowed, and the marriage of a Muslim female to a non-Muslim male which is forbidden.

These considerations lead me to hypothesize that the Torah had initially not prohibited the marriage of Israelites with Ammonite, Moabite and Egyptian women. A further oddity in Neh 13:3 may perhaps corroborate: ויהי כשמעם את התורה ויבדילו כל ערב מישראל "When the people heard this law [that no Ammonite or Moabite should ever be admitted into the assembly of God, because they had not met the Israelites with food and water but had hired Balaam to curse

41 The Rabbis interpreted the term בן as "a child" of either gender, see m. Yeb. 2:5, b. Yeb. 22a and b. B. Bat. 109a. Though the LXX interprets the term בן as spevrma "seed," implying, as the Rabbis said, a child regardless of its gender, it does not exclude the simple meaning of the term and its original application. It is plausible that at the time of the Bible's translation into Greek, the original custom had changed and that the LXX translation evinces the later understanding.

them], they excluded from Israel all who were of foreign descent." This is the NIV translation of the undefined term ערב; the LXX translates it as ejpivmikto~ "mixed." It seems that this[42] was accomplished without any opposition or coercion. But in v. 25 (quoted above) we read of the difficulties Nehemiah encountered coercing the Israelites to separate from the Ashdodian, Moabite and Ammonite wives.

We can only speculate that in the first instance the people accepted the command without any challenge, because it referred to men; since it was explicitly prohibited in the Torah,[43] as is stressed in Neh 13:1: ביום ההוא נקרא בספר משה באזני העם ונמצא כתוב בו אשר לא יבוא עמני ומאבי בקהל האלהים עד עולם "On that day the Book of Moses was read aloud in the people's hearing and there it was found written that no Ammonite or Moabite should ever be admitted into the assembly of God." In contrast, in vv. 23-25, when Nehemiah complained about gentile women; גם בי–מים ההם ראיתי את היהודים השיבו נשים אשדודיות עמוניות מואביות "Moreover, in those days I saw men of Judah who had married Ashdodian, Ammonite and Moabite women." he met with strong opposition, since intermarriage to gentile women was not perceived as an unequivocally forbidden. It seems that he also promulgated a general decree to prohibit intermarriage between Israelite men and gentile women of all nations, attempting to apply this prohibition — restricted in the Torah to the seven nations — to all gentiles alike. For the extension of this prohibition, he uses Solomon's entrapment by his gentile wives to indicate the de-

42 The term ערב is in the masculine as Ibn Ezra indicates in his interpretation of Deut 23:2: ויבדילו כל ערב (נחמי יג, ג) הם הזכרים ושם פירשתיו "They excluded from Israel all of mixed [origins] (Neh : 13: 3), these are the males, and there I explained it."

43 Isa 56:3-8: וְאַל-יֹאמַר בֶּן-הַנֵּכָר הַנִּלְוָה אֶל ה' לֵאמֹר הַבְדֵּל יַבְדִּילַנִי ה' מֵעַל עַמּוֹ "Let no foreigner who has bound himself to the Lord say, "The Lord will surely exclude me from his people." The passage appears to encourage proselytism, and seems to contradict the adverse spirit of Deut 23:3-4. Since we do not exactly know when Trito-Isaiah was written, there are many ways in which we can solve this contradiction. It may have been written before the period of Ezra-Nehemiah, and the latter abolished it, due to its unfavourable results. Such possibility would support the thesis that Ezra and Nehemiah inserted the relevant text of Deut, and would absolve the author of Isa 56 from explicitly contradicting Deuteronomy. On the other hand, this inclusionism may represent opposition to the new rules, ignoring the deuteronomic text. There is also a possibility that Isa 56:3-8 was formulated long after the period of Ezra-Nehemiah, since some scholars suggest that some of Trito-Isaiah's material may derive from 375-250 BC. In that case, one may conjecture that the danger of assimilation was not as acute as in Ezra and Nehemiah's era.

vious nature of all foreigners, as recorded in 1Kgs 11:1-10. The text there too, seems somewhat ambiguous.[44]

We read in v. 1 that Solomon: "loved many foreign women besides Pharaoh's daughter Moabites, Ammonites, Edomites, Sidonians and Hittites and in v. 2: "They were from nations about which the Lord had told the Israelites: 'you must not intermarry with them, because they will surely turn your hearts after their gods.'" This is the NIV's interpretation, similar to that of Jewish commentators, but the writer/redactor employs the term בוא "to come, enter" used in Deut 23:4: לא יבא עמוני ומואבי בקהל ה' "No Ammonite or Moabite or any of his descendants may enter the assembly of the Lord," relating to this specific prohibition. The LXX translates the term in both sources with the verb eijseluvsetai-"enter," and Onkelos translates the term in Deuteronomy as ידכי "to be cleansed [and thus enter the Lord's community]"; Onkelos and LXX are definitely not referring to marriage. For this prohibition Deut 7:3: ולא תתחתן בם "do not intermarry with them," the term חתן "to marry" is used. Moreover, the intermarriage prohibition relates only to the Seven Nations, and in the list of Solomon's wives only one of these, the Hittites, appears. Hence, the narrative in 1 Kings, entirely absent in Chronicles, does not conform to the deuteronomic rules; it also contradicts the rabbinic claim that the rule of Deut 23:4, refers solely to males. The novel concept of זרע הקדש, "the holy seed," as a motive for prohibiting intermarriage (Ezra 9:2) with gentile women, also strengthens the distinction between man and woman with respect to the rule; man is the generator of the seed. We encounter this expression in Isa 6:13, but there it refers metaphorically to the seed of plants and does not distinguish between men and women. Moreover, scholars argue that verses 12 and 13 constitute a later addition. In fact, the LXX omits the phrase "holy seed" in its translation.

I only allude to the exceptional confusion of this issue and do not intend, at this juncture, to speculate regarding a solution. It seems likely that there were

44 We observe that Kgs does not criticize Solomon specifically for marrying Hittite women, who should have been annihilated, according to Deut 20:16-18, and alludes solely to the intermarriage prohibition of Deut 7:3-4. One must note that Bat Sheba, Solomon's mother was a Hittite, having married Uriah the Hittite, and thus David too married a Hittite, and had at least one, but probably a group of Hittite mercenaries in his army, thus ignoring the obligation to kill them. This fact adds to the complexity of the intermarriage issue and to the dubious origin of the deuteronomic rule.

many distinct and conflicting attitudes regarding intermarriage in Israelite society at the time of Ezra and Nehemiah, and we have dwelt upon the difficulties these leaders encountered in their attempt to impose their novel interpretation of the biblical rules on the Israelites. They were driven by their conviction that the total separation of this small group of people from the surrounding nations — as well as an emphasis on ethnicity and national language-were absolute prerequisites for the Israelites' cultural and religious survival.

2. 5. EXTENSIONS: INTERPRETATION OR ADDITIONS

Whereas the Rabbis had no opportunity to add to Scripture, Ezra and Nehemiah possibly did, since the text had not yet been fully canonized. It is therefore appropriate to consider whether their possibly novel ordinance was founded upon creative interpretation or upon actual additions to the available texts.

THE NEW SABBATH RULES

I assume that Ezra and Nehemiah interpreted the term חלל [45] in Ex 31:14: מחלליה מות יומת "anyone who desecrated it [the Sabbath] must be put to death," as a reference to treating the Sabbath as a week-day, thereby diminishing its holiness, as Rashi explains: הנוהג בה חול בקדושתה. Though Nehemiah does not explicitly refer to the Torah for the justification of his new rule, as he does regarding the Wood Offering (Neh 10:35), his plea for divine recognition of his virtuous deeds refers to his meticulous execution of the divine will, as expressed in Scripture.

THE NEW SUKKOTH ORDINANCES

The link of the festival of Sukkoth to the Exodus, as argued above, is ethnocentrically motivated — a characteristic of Ezra and Nehemiah's activities. The obvious fact that they allege to have "found it," reveals their "fingerprints" and its possible interjection in the previously existing text. The insertion of Lev 24:39-43 is quite probable, the verses appear following the conclusion in

45 This term appears twice in vv. 17 and 18 in Nehemiah's plea to God.

verses 37 and 38[46] and vv. 39 and 41 repeat most of the ordinances of vv. 34-37.[47] Milgrom[48] and some scholars argue that the two lists of plants in Neh 8:15 and in Lev 23:40 are "irreconcilable." It seems to me that these scholars, who consider the traditions to be "independent" of one another are correct in their assumption. The plants in Leviticus were likely part of a hailing celebration, as was customary at that period (John 12:13) to mark the end of the agricultural season, and the plants in Nehemiah were used for the construction of the booths. Verse 17 states explicitly that these branches will serve "to make booths," and is nestled between two verses, which refer exclusively to the construction of the booths. Leviticus does not specify materials for the construction of the booths, but neither does Nehemiah; the allusion is solely to the types of suitable branches considering that it was a first time event. In fact, verse 18 does not mention that the people brought these types of branches; it just says, "They went and brought." The principle of the ritual of booths had perhaps been instituted, but the exact details were still open to personal choice. A similar lack of clarity is apparent when it comes to the exact definition of the term פרי עץ הדר in Lev 23:40, which likely referred to mean an undefined "splendid" fruit.[49] In ANT. III:245, Josephus, a long time after the redaction of Nehemiah and of Leviticus, describes it as a "peach," whereas in ANT XIII 13:372, he refers to it as a citrus fruit. Evidently, in his period no final definition had been established and universally accepted. As in many instances of unclear biblical ordinance, the Rabbis introduced specificity, in this case, the "Etrog" as the fruit to be used in this ritual.

---

46 Verses 37 and 38 read: אלה מועדי ה׳ אשר תקראו אתם מקראי קדש להקריב אשה לה׳ עלה ומנחה זבח ונסכים דבר יום ביומו מלבד שבתת ה׳ ומלבד מתנותיכם ומלבד כל נדריכם ומלבד כל נדבותיכם אשר תתנו לה׳ "These are the Lord's appointed feasts, which you are to proclaim as sacred assemblies for bringing offerings made to the Lord by fire—the burnt offerings and grain offerings, sacrifices and drink offerings required for each day. These offerings are in addition to those for the Lord's Sabbaths and in addition to your gifts and whatever you have vowed and all the freewill offerings you give to the Lord."

47 J. Milgrom, Leviticus, discusses these verses under the subtitle: "Addendum on the Festival of Booths" (p. 283). M. Noth, Leviticus, translated from German by J. E. Anderson, London, 1965 asserts: "the section vv. 39-43 cannot be taken for anything else than a literary edition" (p. 175).

48 Milgrom, Leviticus, p. 283.

49 Onkelos and traditional commentators follow the rabbinic interpretation of "etrog," as a citrus variety. The LXX, however, interprets it as "a seasonal fruit," the KJV "Boughs of goodly trees," and the NIV as "choice fruit."

As mentioned above, the name Sukkoth appears first in Deuteronomy, which does not necessarily contradict our hypothesis. The date of the final redaction of Deuteronomy is still debated and it may well have been at a later date than Nehemiah's interjection. Zec 14:16-20 which also mentions this holiday by name, is generally not attributed to the prophet Zechariah and may also be late. Even if they're not, there is still no mention in Deuteronomy and in Zechariah of the booths custom. The name Sukkoth does not by itself indicate that there existed a ritual obligation to dwell seven days in booths.[50] The term appears often in Scripture as a temporary shelter for people and animals,[51] and is associated in Isa 1: 8 with the vineyard: כסכה בכרם. These temporary shelters were erected at the time of the ingathering of fruits, and at some point the sobriquet סוכות "booths" was attached to the previous undefined term חג.

The obligation to dwell in booths for seven days appears solely in Lev 23, and was "reinstated" by Nehemiah after a long period of "oblivion." In effect, Ezra 3:4: ויעשו את חג הסכות ככתוב "Then in accordance with what is written, they celebrated the Feast of Tabernacles," confirms this assumption. There is no mention of the booths before the foundation of the Temple (3:10); moreover, Nehemiah 8:14 implies that only when the Temple was already functioning was the law to construct booths found, and v. 17 asserts that no booths were built from Joshua's time until then. Hence, as recorded in Ezra 3:4, no booths were erected by the first returnees at the celebration of the Feast of the Booths, regardless of the name Sukkoth. The name Sukkoth, the command to dwell in booths, and the plant ritual, relates — like the other holidays — to the ancient agricultural aspect of the Feast.[52] At the same time, its association with the Exodus infused it with new religious and historical meaning.[53]

---

50 Jacob Milgrom, Leviticus, A Book of Ritual and Ethics, Minn, MN, 2004, writes that the name Sukkoth "became preferable at the Jerusalem Temple (H) and subsequently became mandatory" (282).

51 For example, in Gen 33:17 as a shelter for animals, as a shelter against the sun in Jonah 4:5, as a shelter for commanders of the army in 1 Kgs 20:12, and for the ark, in times of war, in 2 Sam 11:11. Onkelos and the Targum translate the term as מטליא or מטלן "a structure providing shade," from the root טלל "shade, shadow."

52 See M. Noth, Leviticus, p. 176.

53 Jacob M. Myers, Ezra and Nehemiah (Anchor Bible), Garden City, N. Y. 1965, conjectures that the association between Joshua at the institution of the booth festival serves to link it with the

THE NEW INTERMARRIAGE PROHIBITIONS

As argued above, Nehemiah explains the intermarriage prohibition with the Canaanite nations in an entirely new way. Scripture explicitly prohibits intermarriage with both males and females, of the seven peoples who inhabited the Promised Land (but not members of any other nations); so as to avoid exposure to idolatrous influence (Deut 7:1-4)[54] (20:16-18), and thus they all (men, women and children) must be annihilated. The prohibition against absorbing Ammonites and Moabites into the Israelite community appears in Deut 23:4-5, and Nehemiah correctly cites the deuteronomic motive for this exclusion in 13:2: כי לא קדמו את בני ישראל בלחם ובמים וישכר עליו את בלעם לקללו "because they had not met the Israelites with food and water but had hired Balaam to call a curse down on them." Nehemiah widens the prohibition against absorbing Ammonites and Moabites into the Israelite community to include marriage with their women, as we have seen above, particularly in the Excursus and applies it also to women from Ashdod (13:23) — Philistines — who are not mentioned in any Pentateuchal prohibition.

In contrast with Nehemiah's reasoning in 13:2, cited above, he indicates in 13:26 that another reason to avoid intermarriage is the evil influence of foreign women (thus Deut 7:1, with respect to the seven nations of Canaan); he also hints to their sexual immorality, a reason absent from the legal sections of Pentateuch, but see the narrative of Num 25:1: ויחל העם לזנות אל בנות מואב "the men began to engage sexually with Moabite women." However, his primary reason for forbidding marriage to Ashdodian women is utterly novel without any basis in the Torah. We read in Neh 13:24: ובניהם חצי מדבר אשדודית ואינם מכירים לדבר יהודית "Half of their children spoke the language of Ashdod or the language of one of the other peoples, and did not know how to speak the language of Judah." The significance of the knowledge and use of the national language was never an issue in the Torah, and Nehemiah was careful not to mention a biblical source for it. Moreover, as it seems, the returnees from Babylon exile brought with them a foreign language

wilderness period, and to disassociate it from agricultural festivals (p. 157).

54 The dictum in Deut 7:2 is not so explicit as in Deut 20, in which the term החרם is used; the KJV translates it as: "you shall utterly destroy them, following the LXX translation." The verb used in LXX term means to make them disappear.

and script; Ezra is written partly in Aramaic, and according to the Rabbis Ezra also introduced Aramaic script to Judeans.[55] The above irregularities in Nehemiah's arguments are indicative of the problems associated with this prohibition and its relationship to Pentateuchal laws.

It is remarkable that Nehemiah uses the language issue to justify his prohibition against intermarriage with Ashdodian women; as we know, from the Mesha Stele, the Moabites and the Ammonites spoke a language almost identical to Hebrew.[56] Ezra also initiates a novel taboo, extending the prohibition of intermarriage to נשים נכריות מעמי הארץ "foreign women from the people around us," probably referring to all non Israelite women. We can only imagine the embarrassment they had to overcome to promulgate new laws and regulations, alleging that in this way they followed God's will, and likely also the opposition of influential and erudite segments of society.

This extension of the intermarriage prohibition, as compared to rational deduction from earlier sources, leads me to speculate that Ezra and Nehemiah may have also had "their fingers" in the redaction of Deut 23:4-9. The many irregularities concerning their relationship with the surrounding nations, except Samaria, hint to a tampering with this text. As many scholars assert, I speculate that this entire rule, its rationalization and the additional restrictions in vv 5-9 with respect to other neighboring nations, were added to Deuteronomy or altered, at some point in history, in response to changed circumstances. There seems to be one impediment, however, against the possible attribution of these verses to Ezra and Nehemiah.

We read in Lam 1:10: כי ראתה גוים באו מקדשה אשר צויתה לא יבאו בקהל לך "for she hath seen that the heathen are entered into her sanctuary, concerning whom Thou didst command that they should not enter into Thy congregation." The source of this verse appears to be Deut 23:4, and though scholars doubt that it was written

55 We read in b. Sanh. 21b: חזרה וניתנה להם בימי עזרא בכתב אשורית ולשון ארמי "[the Torah] was once more given to them [the Israelites] at the time of Ezra in Assyrian script and in Aramaic language."

56 See F. Israel in D. Cohen (ed.), Les Langues Chamito-semitiques, Paris, 1988 regarding the similarity between Hebrew and the Ammonite language. See also Walter E. Aufrecht, Ancient Ammon, eds. B. Macdonald and Randall Younker, Leiden, 1999, pp.163-188. In an inscription on a bottle we find inscribed, the name of Amminadab, king of the Ammonites (p. 164). This is a fairly common Israelite name עמינדב.; and see p. 171: "there is a close similarity (if not identity) between the two languages [Hebrew and Ammonite]."

by Jeremiah, it seems likely that it was composed before the return from the Babylonian exile, and thus before Ezra and Nehemiah. I would suggest, therefore, that in this case Ezra and Nehemiah have interpreted the pentateuchal law in a most creative manner. They conflated the rules of Deut 7:1-4 and of Deut 23:4-9, (relating to two different topics) applied the intermarriage prohibition to both sets of laws, and extended it indiscriminately to all gentiles, whether they were mentioned in Scripture or not. The objective of this decision was to ensure the cultural identity of the Jews by avoiding any alien influence, in short, to isolate them from the surrounding cultures.[57] On the other hand, the term לבא בקהל in both Deuteronomy and Lamentations does not categorically serve as evidence, since reading them together is somewhat difficult. The people who entered the Temple, and desecrated it, were likely Babylonians — not the Ammonites or Moabites of Deuteronomy. Deuteronomy forbids incorporation into the congregation, whereas Lamentations refers to entering the Temple. The appearance of this phrase in Lamentations thus does not totally eliminate the possibility that Ezra and Nehemiah tampered with these Deuteronomic verses.[58]

I discussed above, Ezra and Nehemiah imposition of laws using the authority granted to them by the Persian sovereign, threatening those who would disobey them with harsh punishments. This indicates that there was opposition to the newly imposed regulations, and indeed, we observe that intermarriage was particularly common practice in all strata of society.[59] We may assume that both sides had to overcome serious embarrassment and apprehension; the group supporting Ezra and Nehemiah experienced trepidation confronting the aristocracy, but they were constrained by what they felt were were genu-

---

57 Christopher-Smith, 1994, suggests that the returnees were under stress, and Ezra's action was an attempt at consolidation of a threatened minority (p. 256).

58 J. Blenkinsopp. Ezra-Nehemiah, notes the same combination of gentile women in 1Kgs 11:1-2 and Ezra 9:1 and wonders "whether it (I Kings) reflects the situation at the time of Ezra and Nehemiah (p. 175)," which is similar to our hypothesis here,

59 We read in Neh 10:29: ושאר העם הכהנים הלוים השוערים המשררים הנתינים וכל הנבדל מעמי הארצות אל תורת האלהים "The rest of the people—priests, Levites, gatekeepers, singers, temple servants and all who separated themselves from the neighboring peoples for the sake of the Law of God" together with v. 31: ואשר לא נתן בנתינו לעמי הארץ ואת בנתיהם לא נקח לבנינו "We promise not to give our daughters in marriage to the peoples around us or take their daughters for our sons." We read in Neh 13:28 that it was a common habit in the High Priest's family.

ine Torah precepts. Likely as not, their opponents also coped with uneasiness when it came to changing rooted habits and separating from their wives and children based on subjective readings of text.[60] Nonetheless, it is quite likely that the majority of the populace willingly accepted the new rules. Regretfully, we have no statistics regarding attitudes to the new regulations. At any rate, one gains the impression from the Ezra and Nehemiah narratives that they breathed new life and vitality into the withered Judaism practiced in Judah.

3. PURPOSE OF EXEGESIS

Ezra and Nehemiah's innovative laws now had to be introduced into daily life; the people had to be persuaded that these "new" regulations were actually embodied in the Torah. Thus, a legal basis was created for the many reforms: the extension of the Sabbath prohibitions and intermarriage laws discussed above, innovations in the performance of holiday rites (as recorded above), the addition of new offerings[61] not mentioned in the Pentateuch.[62] (Ezra introduced the novel concept that community offerings must be twelve in number,

60 In a recently published book by Yonina Dor, Have the "Foreign Women" really been Expelled? (Hebrew), Jerusalem, 2006, the author postulates (246) that they were not really separated, but that they enacted a "Separation Ceremony" and then the women returned home to be with their husbands. It is beyond the scope of this study to critically analyze this book and dispute its conclusions; I do, however, reject the the attempt to justify biblical commands and narratives that may seem immoral to us, by turning the facts on their heads.

61 We read in Ezra 6:17: וצפירי עזין לחטיא על כל ישראל תרי עשר למנין שבטי ישראל "and, as a sin offering for all Israel, twelve male goats, one for each of the tribes of Israel." In 8:35 we encounter an interesting list of offerings: פרים שנים עשר על כל ישראל אילים תשעים וששה כבשים שבעים ושבעה צפירי חטאת שנים עשר הכל עולה לה' "twelve bulls for all Israel, ninety-six rams, seventy-seven male lambs, and as a sin offering twelve male goats, all a burnt offering to the Lord." All these numbers, except for the lambs, are multiples of twelve; one must assume that these numbers have a symbolic meaning. I cannot speculate as to the reason for the exceptional number of the lambs, which is a multiple of seven or eleven. The Sages were well aware of the odd number of the lambs, and ask in b. Tem. 15b: בשלמא פרים ושעירי' כנגד שנים עשר שבטים אלא כבשים כנגד מי אלא הוראת שעה היתה "It is reasonable that the [number of] oxen and male goats correspond to the twelve tribes, but the [number of] lambs, to what does this correspond? [A.] It was an extraordinary, ad hoc command."

62 The twelve male goats offered by the twelve tribal leaders at the Tabernacle's consecration (Num. 7:2-88) are of an entirely different character than the concept of twelve offerings instituted by Ezra. These were clearly offered by the people as a sin offering "for all of Israel," whereas in Num. these offerings — among many others — were given by the leaders on their own behalf.

corresponding to the twelve tribes of Israel,[63] as emphasized in Ezra 6:17; however, no pentateuchal requirement for twelve sacrifices is recorded for any of the sacrifices including obligatory public offerings, the daily offering,[64] or the communal sin offerings.[65]) Ezra and Nehemiah instituted a financial organization of temple revenues[66] and a systematization of holiday celebrations,[67] as recorded in the books bearing their name. There is no textual evidence, however, regarding their system of interpretation, the body of people who helped them accomplish this task, or the extent of their authority.

We can only speculate about these issues, since we have no sources other than those transmitted to us by the author/redactor of the two books of Ezra and Nehemiah. According to these texts Ezra was a סופר מהיר בתורת משה "ready scribe" (KJV) "a teacher well versed (NIV) in the law of Moses (Ezra 7:6)," who: הכין לבבו לדרש את תורת ה' ולעשות וללמד בישראל חק ומשפט "had prepared his heart to seek — (KJV), had devoted himself to the study of — the law of the Lord

63 S. Talmon, The World of Qumran from within, Leiden, 1989, pp. 41ff. suggests that the twelve offerings were to demonstrate that only the returnees were the genuine Jewish people. The identity of צרי יהודה ובנימן "enemies of Judah and Benjamin" in Ezra 4:1 and עם הארץ "the peoples around them" in v. 4 (translation NIV) indicating the group which the Judeans encountered in Judah at their return, is problematic; the text seems to have been "doctored". The traditional interpretation, that the text refers to the Samaritans, cannot be sustained, since they would not have approached the returnees to build the Temple in Jerusalem, since in their Ten Commandments the imperative is to build the Temple on Mount Gerizim. Their obvious response was to obstruct the building of the Temple in Jerusalem, as is indicated in adjacent texts, See Lester L. Grabbe, Ezra-Nehemiah, London-New York, 1998, p. 137. P. R. Davies, 1990 p. 514, writes that "the ruling classes (which included the writing classes) of this period [of the Second Temple] claimed to have originated in Babylon, where they saw themselves as the remnant of pre-exilic 'Israel.'"

64 See Exod. 29:38-42, and vv. 43-45 which relate the sacrifices to God's presence and His dwelling among the people of Israel.

65 Only one ox is required as a sin offering for a transgression by the Israelite community (Lev. 4:14); on the Day of Atonement, two goats are required, one as a regular sin offering and one as a scapegoat (Lev. 16:15-20).

66 The introduction of the yearly levy of a third of a shekel for the sacrificial celebrations (Neh 10:33), the casting of lots for the continuous supply of wood for the altar (Neh 10:34), and the reorganization of the tithes and other grants for the sustenance of the clerics (Neh 10:36-40) and their equitable distribution (Neh 13:10-13), were instituted in order to ensure the smooth functioning of the Temple ceremonies.

67 Ezra 3:3-10 gives the impression of an organized system of offerings; different numbers of offerings for week days and for holidays, of obligatory public offerings and voluntary individual offerings on fixed dates.

(NIV), and to do it (the law), and to teach in Israel statutes and judgments. (Ezra 7:10)."[68] We do not know the precise definition of the term "scribe"[69] in this instance, we have no indication who taught Ezra and the chain of transmission up to him (and note the chain of transmission in m. Abot 1:1,[70] in which oddly enough Ezra does not appear). Ezra's goal is purportedly to teach the Israelites, but we are unaware of his motivations, unlike Nehemiah (in the first verses of the book).[71]

Ezra's position in the Persian administration is unclear, but we may assume that he held a high office and enjoyed great prestige. Artaxerxes granted him a comprehensive charter for the governing of Judah, management of the legal and religious systems, and an almost limitless authority to impose them. According to Neh 2:1 Nehemiah was Artaxerxes's Cupbearer, we may, however, assume that he was not a regular "butler", but that this was an aristocratic title.[72] It is apparent from their activities, and their display of organizational and political acumen, that they gained great "political science" experience from their functions in the Persian administration.[73] They acquired a broader view of political maneuverings and interactions, an awareness of the significance of language and culture for nation building, and the emphasis upon genealogical uniqueness of the "holy seed." Thus, they correctly identified the essentials for

---

68 For דרש, see note 6. The LXX translates the term as zhtevw, to seek," in Esdras II 7:10, and Esdras I has an entirely different text

69 The LXX does not shed any light on this; Esdras II 7:6 translates the term סופר מהיר as "a swift clerk/secretary/scribe"and Esdras I 8:3: "a clever/well suited clerk." Esdras I 8:7 has an entirely different text: "For Ezra possessed great knowledge, so that he omitted nothing from the law of the Lord or the commandments, but taught all of Israel all the ordinances and judgments."

70 We read there: משה קבל תורה מסיני ומסרה ליהושע ויהושע לזקנים וזקנים לנביאים ונביאים מסרוה לאנשי כנסת הגדולה "Moses received from Sinai, and transmitted it to Joshua, and Joshua [transmitted it] to the Elders, and the Elders to the prophets and the prophets transmitted it to the members of the Great Council."

71 He was sorely distressed when he heard from Hanani the grim situation in Judah and Jerusalem.

72 See for example Tobit 1: 22: "For under Sennacherib, king of Assyria, Ahiqar had been chief cupbearer, keeper of the seal, administrator, and treasurer; and Esarhaddon reappointed him."

73 Onkelos translates שר המשקים "Cup-bearer" in Gen 40:2, as רב שקי, and סריס as רברבן, indicating high rank. In 2 Kgs 18:17-36 רבשקה is a high official and likely the commander of the Assyrian army, which besieged Jerusalem.

ensuring the ability of a small people to resist the pressures of assimilation and the political importance of a thriving capital as the central seat of the administration.[74] In light of all above, one cannot exclude the plausibility that they were confident that their goal concurred with the divine will and intention; it motivated them to read into Scripture their consequential regulations, and presented these views, without embarrassment, as if they were literally written in the Torah.

4. COMPARISON WITH RABBINIC METHODS

The Rabbis, although unable to change the text, nevertheless followed in Ezra and Nehemiah's footsteps, developing a comprehensive exegetical method that often interpreted Torah rules in audacious contradiction to the simple meaning of the biblical text. This exegetical system enabled the Sages, to present their halakhot as preserving the immutable scriptural rules, without going against Deut 13:1: לא תסף עליו ולא תגרע ממנו "do not add to it or take away from it". They altered the practical core of the biblical laws, preserving at the same time its formal validity. Many pragmatic considerations contributed to the evolution and expansion of this method. One of the most well known is their treatment of lex talionis. Though Lev 24:19 commands: ואיש כי יתן מום בעמיתו כאשר עשה כן יעשה לו "If anyone injures his neighbour, whatever he has done must be done to him," the Rabbis interpreted the passage to refer to pecuniary compensation, as we read in m. B. Qam. 8:1 and b. B. Qam. 83b. I suspect that the warning of the sinner by two witnesses before the former carries out the transgression as a condition for corporeal punishment — was developed as a consequence of their embarrassment vis-à-vis the prevalence of capital punishment in Scripture. Practical considerations, probably led to their decision

74 We read in Neh 11:1: וישבו שרי העם בירושלם ושאר העם הפילו גורלות להביא אחד מן העשרה לשבת בירושלם עיר הקדש ותשע הידות בערים "Now the leaders of the people settled in Jerusalem, and the rest of the people cast lots to bring one out of every ten to live in Jerusalem, the holy city, while the remaining nine were to stay in their own towns." The narrative does not tell us who initiated this enterprise; although it was likely the politically minded Nehemiah. Though it is presented in v. 2 as a voluntary enterprise: "The people commended all the men who volunteered to live in Jerusalem," one may doubt the veracity of this claim. If indeed, there were volunteers, there would have been no need to cast a lot unless there were too many volunteers, and that does not seem reasonable; in that period, when agriculture was the main occupation and generator of wealth, people would not be eager to leave their property.

to permit the slaughter of suitable animals outside the Temple area, though Deut 12:21 allows it only at a "far away" place. We read in Sifra Lev, Dibura d'Nedaba 13: ושחטו ושחט אותו ושחט אותו מה תלמוד לומר לפי שנאמר וכי ירחק ממך המקום וזבחת ברחוק מקום אתה זובח ואי אתה זובח בקרוב מקום פרט לחולין שלא ישחטו בעזרה "The term slaughter [is written] three times which indicates the following [limitation] since it is written 'if the place the Lord chooses is too far away' [it teaches us] that you may slaughter at a distant place, and you must not slaughter at a close place, [and that means] that one must not slaughter unconsecrated [animals/birds] in the Temple precinct [but everywhere else is permissible]." Instead of considering what it meant to be "far" from Jerusalem, the Rabbis considered the inverse — what does it mean "not close" — and decided that outside the Temple area "not close"; it seems that in this instance practicality ruled the day. The requirement of a three day walk, as Qumran understood the term רחוק, would mean that one could not slaughter animals in the entirety Judah. Such a rule was considered to be unfeasible and an imposition on the public.[75] To avoid misrepresentation, it should be noted that some laws were interpreted quite strictly. We read in m. Hag. 1:8: היתר נדרים פורחין באויר ואין להם על מה שיסמכו הלכות שבת חגיגות והמעילות הרי הם כהררים התלויין בשערה שהן מקרא מועט והלכות מרובות "The rules of [annulment of the] vows are floating in the air and have no [biblical] support; the halakhoth of the Sabbath, the holiday [offerings] and the unlawful use of sacred property are like mountains suspended by a hair, since many halakhoth are supported by a limited text."

Embarrassment, being a subjective sensation with varying intensities, has different effects on different people.[76] It comes as no surprises that segments of Judean society did not accept many pharisaic/rabbinic rulings based on far-fetched interpretation, as is apparent from apocryphal writings and the Qumran Scrolls.[77] I would speculate, for example that, the prohibition against

75 And compare the Rabbinic maxim: אין גוזרין גזרה על הצבור אלא אם כן רוב צבור יכולין לעמוד בה "One does not issue an edict unless the majority of the public can abide by it (b. B. Qama 79b and others)."

76 For an extensive study on how the rabbis effected changes, and at the same time preserved the formal biblical rule, see P. Heger, The Pluralistic Halakhah, Berlin, 2003, pp. 23 ff.

77 Qumran's view regarding lex talionis, is undocumented, but note a somewhat similar philosophical attitude regarding the requirement to forewarn in CD IX:16:22, in which there is a remarkable difference between the mandatory evidence for financial litigations and transgressions requiring capital punishment. See P. Heger, Cult as the Catalyst for Division, Leiden, 2007, p. 93, note 174. We encounter outstanding differences between rabbinic and Qumran rules

polygamy in Qumran, a community that promoted chastity, was motivated by their embarrassment of a custom they regarded as tantamount to debauchery.[78] The Rabbis view regarding chastity was very different and thus,[79] polygamy did not embarrass them.

5. JEWISH REACTION TO EXTERNAL ENCROACHMENT ON ITS CULTURAL HERITAGE.

5. 1. RESILIENCE OF JEWISH ADHERENCE TO TRADITION

It is embarrassing to observe that the legal and practical interventions effected by Ezra and Nehemiah to enforce the strict observance of the Torah in Judah, and the sweeping separation of the Israelites from the surrounding cultures, were conceived of in Babylon. In contrast, the Israelites who remained in Judah and the first group of returnees at the time of King Cyrus' declaration were somewhat indifferent to these issues and to the cultural/religious segregation of the Israelite nation. As a result, circumstances in the Diaspora created the conditions for the Judaic "Renaissance," and the Diaspora's political and spiritual leaders were its flag bearers. They understood that in order

regarding the rabbinic permission to save a life on Sabbath, rejected by Qumran (see Serekh Damascus Frag. 7:I:7-8, Jub. 50:12, and Heger, Cult, pp. 139 ff) and the prohibition of polygamy by Qumran (see CD V:1-6 and P. Heger, "The Development of Qumran Law — Nistarot, Niglot and the Issue of 'Contemporization,'" published in Rev.Q. 23/2, Nov 2007.

78 The issue of whether all Qumran members were celibate or not, is debatable, but there is certainly a general reluctance to have contact with women. They prohibited polygamy (CD-A IV: 20-V:1), as well as intercourse in Jerusalem, because it pollutes the city's holiness (CD-A XII:1-2), and postponed the age of marriage for males to twenty, when they were capable of discerning between good and evil (1QSa I:9-10). Additionally, they forbade the presence of women in the war camp (1QM VII:3) and used the term זנות as a general reference to evil (4Q436 Frag. I II:1, 4Q397 Frag. 6-13: 12, CD-A VIII:5, 1QS IV:10 and many others). See J. M. Baumgarten, "On the Nature of the Seductress in 4Q184," RevQ 15, 57/58, 1991, pp. 133-143, on this issue.

79 The Rabbis do not proscribe sexual activity; they go as far as establishing the obligatory frequency of sexual intercourse — based on the man's occupation — in fulfillment of Ex 21:10. We read in m. Ket. 5:6: הטיילין בכל יום הפועלים שתים בשבת החמרים אחת בשבת הגמלים אחת לשלשים יום הספנים אחת לששה חדשים "Young men with an effortless occupation [are obliged to have intercourse with their wives] every day, labourers twice weekly, those transporting goods by donkey [short distances] once weekly, those transporting with camels [long distances] once every thirty days and seamen once in six months."

to attain their ultimate goal, they must bring their ideology to Judah, the land of their fathers and the nation's religious center. This I would opine, were Ezra's and Nehemiah's motive for their immigration to Judah. The strong desire to ensure the cultural and religious survival of the Jewish people made them aware of the danger of assimilation, of a minority dispersed among an overwhelming majority, with an utterly different religion and way of life. The Jews in Judah who constituted the majority in their area, may have also cherished the Torah, but were not aware of the danger of assimilation. The idea that the Diaspora assured the survival of the Jewish people as a unique cultural entity is paradoxical and embarrassing.

The aborted Assyrian conquest in the late eight century B.C.E may be compared to the period we are examining. Syncretism persisted in Judah during the entire period of the First Commonwealth until, as it seems,[80] the period of King Hezekiah. The shift towards monotheism, occurred at a dangerous political and spiritual crossroads, namely the Assyrian conquest.[81] Rab' Shakeh, who led the Assyrian army, delivered his speech, in Hebrew, directly to the people; in an attempt to shake the people's belief in God's ability to save them from Assyrian dominion. We do not know exactly how the Assyrian siege and occupation ended, since the narrative in Kings and its account of a miraculous plague is our only source.[82] But, as we may deduce from Hezekiah's religious reform, Rab' Shakeh's mockery of Israel's God had the opposite effect, similar to the maxim of Ex 1:12: וכאשר יענו אתו כן ירבה וכן יפרץ "But the more they were oppressed, the more they multiplied and spread." The book of Kings tells of an idolatrous relapse by Hezekiah's son Manasseh, yet this narrative is not entirely convincing, and is perhaps the invention of the redactor in support of his contention that Israel's sins were primarily the fault of their kings, and that they (the kings) brought about the destruction of the Temple. This statement bears out in 2 Chr 33:1-20's account of

80 This is not the place to consider whether the religious reform was carried out at the time of Hezekiah or Josiah, and note the discrepancy on this issue between the records of Kings and Chronicles.

81 See 2 Kgs 18:17.

82 2 Kgs 19:37 narrates that Sennacherib was killed by his sons, after which Essarhadon, another of his sons succeeded him.

Manasseh's repentance,[83] his ensuing salvation from Assyrian imprisonment and return to his kingship in Jerusalem.

Another significant turning point in Israel's history was the Hellenization of the populace and the Hasmonean revolt which sought to undo this influence, which exhibit a similar, though not identical, dynamic of enigma and embarrassment. The High Priest, together with his clan and cadre of prominent intellectual dignitaries, instigated a process of cultural assimilation. The masses, guided by the lower ranked Hasmonean priests, were responsible for the reversal of this trend. The influence of the lower ranked priests led to a renewal of Jewish adherence to the Torah and its precepts. The danger to the traditional Torah way of life provoked the people to fight for their heritage, and, as is common in such cases, they instituted new and radical protective measures.

5. 2. THE EMPOWERMENT OF THE PRIESTHOOD

The measures instituted and enforced by Nehemiah, greatly empowered the Temple, and its clerics, especially the High Priest and his entourage. Nehemiah's concern for an orderly and dignified[84] Temple cult led to his imposition of a temple tax.[85] He renewed the biblical tithes to the priests and Levites[86] and organized the collection and the storage of the various tithes and donations

83 In m. Sanh. 10:2, Rabbi Judah declares that King Manasseh has a part in the world to come, supporting it by the citation of 2 Chr 33:1-20.

84 Malachi complains that the priests showed contempt for God's name. They defiled the food on the altar by offering blind, crippled and diseased animals (Mal 1:6-8).

85 We read in Neh 10:33-35 (KJV 32-34) "We assume the responsibility for carrying out the commands to give a third of a shekel each year for the service of the house of our God: for the bread set out on the table; for the regular grain offerings and burnt offerings; for the offerings on the Sabbaths, New Moon festivals and appointed feasts; for the holy offerings; for sin offerings to make atonement for Israel; and for all the duties of the house of our God. We the priests, the Levites and the people have cast lots to determine when each of our families is to bring to the house of our God at set times each year a contribution of wood to burn on the altar of the Lord our God, as it is written in the Law."

86 See Neh 10:36-39 (KJV 35-37) the provision to bring each year to the priests: the first fruits of the crops and of every fruit tree, the firstborn sons, the firstborn cattle of herds and of flocks, the first of the ground meal, of grain offerings, of the fruit of all trees, of the new wine and oil, and a tithe for the Levites.

in the Temple's storerooms,[87] thus greatly boosting the priestly status. He[88] appointed them as trustees of the Temple's considerable wealth[89] including all tithes.[90]He delegated the construction of the strategic towers of Jerusalem to them, emphasized their illustrious genealogy, and held them responsible for the redressing the social evils in Judean society. These vast powers had an almost immediate corrupting effect; as one may expect: power corrupts, and absolute power corrupts absolutely.[91]

As it seems, the priests, trustees of the tithes stored in the Temple's warehouses, abused their power and withheld tithes to the Levites, as we find in Neh 13:10: ואדעה כי מניות הלוים לא נתנה ויברחו איש לשדהו הלוים והמשררים עשי המלאכה "I also learned that the portions assigned to the Levites had not been given to them, and that all the Levites and singers responsible for the service had gone back to their own fields." The book of Nehemiah does not tell us exactly what happened, or more specifically who withheld the Levites' share. Was it the priests who controlled the warehouses, or did the people unexpectedly stop bringing the Levite's tithes? Rashi, zealous to defend the priestly reputation, writes that the Israelites failed to meet their obligation, but from the context, one may deduce that the fault lay with the embezzling priests.

We read in Neh 12:44: ויפקדו ביום ההוא אנשים על הנשכות לאוצרות לתרומות לראשית ולמעשרות לכנוס בהם לשדי הערים מנאות התורה לכהנים וללוים כי שמחת יהודה על הכהנים ועל הלוים העמדים "At that

87 See Neh 10:40: כי אל הלשכות יביאו בני ישראל ובני הלוי את תרומת הדגן התירוש והיצהר ושם כלי המקדש והכהנים המשרתים והשוערים והמשררים ולא נעזב את בית אלהינו "The people of Israel, including the Levites, are to bring their contributions of grain, new wine and oil to the storerooms where the articles for the sanctuary are kept and where the ministering priests, the gatekeepers and the singers stay."

88 In this case, Ezra is mentioned specifically.

89 See Ezra 8:24: ואבדילה משרי הכהנים שנים עשר לשרביה חשביה ועמהם מאחיהם עשרה "Then I set apart twelve of the leading priests, together with Sherebiah, Hashabiah and ten of their brothers," and entrusted them with the offerings of silver and gold for the Temple (Ezra 8:25-30).

90 See Neh 10:40: כי אל הלשכות יביאו בני ישראל ובני הלוי את תרומת הדגן התירוש והיצהר ושם כלי המקדש והכהנים המשרתים והשוערים והמשררים "The people of Israel, including the Levites, are to bring their contributions of grain, new wine and oil to the storerooms where the articles for the sanctuary are kept and where the ministering priests, the gatekeepers and the singers stay."

91 Power tends to corrupt, and absolute power corrupts absolutely, wrote Lord Acton in a letter to Bishop Mandell Creighton in 1887. For an extensive study on the desire for power, its tactics and corruption, see David Kipnis, The Powerholders, Chicago, 1981, (2nd edition); David Kipnis, Technology and Power, New York, 1990.

time men were appointed to be in charge of the storerooms for the contributions of first fruits and tithes. They were to bring the portions required by the Law for the priests and the Levites from the fields around the towns into the storerooms, for Judah was pleased (rejoiced according to KJV, eujfrosuvne, merriment in the LXX) with the ministering priests and Levites." — implying that the rejoicing populace fulfilled their obligations. Neh 13:11: ואריבה את הסגנים ואמרה מדוע נעזב בית האלהים "So I rebuked the officials and asked them, 'Why is the house of God neglected?'" also places the blame upon the the Temple officials. Nehemiah's redress also demonstrates that there were enough tithes and that the neglect was due to misappropriation. We read in Neh 13:13: "I put Shelemiah the priest, Zadok the scribe, and a Levite named Pedaiah in charge of the storerooms and made Hanan son of Zaccur, the son of Mattaniah, their assistant, because these men were considered trustworthy. They were made responsible for distributing the supplies (tithes) to their brothers." It is evident that such a committee — consisting of the members of both interested parties, the Priests and the Levites, together with a scribe for recording the distribution of the income, and a trusted, impartial arbiter — would only be necessary if the issue were one of distribution between the Priests and Levites.[92] There is no indication of measures to enforce the contribution of the tithes. In fact, "All Judah brought the tithes of grain, new wine and oil into the storerooms" (vs. 12).The author/redactor of the Book of Nehemiah attempted to avoid an explicit accusation of the priestly abuse of power, but allowed us to "read and re-read between the lines" and conclude for ourselves.

At that time, the High Priest, the leader of this group was the highest religious and political authority in Judah. We are unaware of how this concentration of power occurred and the reasons for it. There is no indication in the Bible as to how this shift to a single leader occured. The Davidic scion[93] still

92 J. Blenkinsopp, 1988, Vol. 3 states that the Levites provided important support for Nehemiah's policies, especially in his conflict with the priests, and thus Nehemiah defended their interests and ensured an equitable distribution of the resources (pp. 355/6).

93 The contenders for the political authority were scions of the Davidic lineage, active at the first period of return, and mentioned in Ezra 1:8, 11; 2:2; 3:8; 4:2, 3; 5:2, 14 and 17 and in 1:1, 12, 14;2: 4, 23; in Zech 4:7, 10 and in Neh 7:7, 12:1 and 47. In some occurrences, the name Zerubbabel appears and in others Sheshbazzar, but it is beyond the scope of this study to examine the relationship between the two.

eminent in the first days of the return, disappeared from the Judean horizon. We may speculate that there were tensions between the political and religious authorities, and that at some point the High Priest emerged predominant. Perhaps Zecharias' prophecy, who mentions two leaders of the people, a priest and a prince, is a hint of the beginning of Priestly ascendance.[94] Reading and re-reading the prophecy, we can detect the tension between the two governing organs, a circumstance the prophet did not approve of, exhorting for a more harmonious collaboration between the two chiefs. The struggle between these two authorities and their followers must have been fierce, but was well concealed from the eyes of future generations, to avoid any denigration to the priestly class I have speculated elsewhere[95] that the cessation of prophecy in Israel may have been the result of the priestly hegemony over all "religious" matters, and the forced exclusion of rival elements.[96] Nehemiah, who enjoyed supreme authority granted to him by the Persian administration, had the power to impose his opinion on the priests, and to redress the Levites' grievance. As it seems,[97] however, this was only temporary and following Nehemiah the High Priests retained or regained their authority, which they abused at times, often most criminally, for their financial benefit and to perpetuate their hegemony.[98] The enormous potential for profit inherent in this office may be de-

---

94 We read in Zech 6:13: ועצת שלום תהיה בין שניהם "And there will be harmony between the two." See also Heger, Altars, 357-360.

95 See Heger, Altars, p. 360.

96 Martin Hengel, Schriftauslegung: im antiken Judentum und im Urchristentum,Tübingen,1994, writes that the priests and Levites argued that God's will and commands were now revealed (in the Pentateuch), and that consequently the function of the prophet was redundant. He also conjectures that the priests perceived the prophets as competitors and were opposed to them (pp. 26-27).

97 Regretfully, there is a void of historical records of the internal events that occurred in Judah in the period between the era of Ezra and Nehemiah and the Hellenic occupation.

98 Remarkably, the Rabbis also complained about the priestly abuse of status. We read in t. Men. 13:21: היה אבא שאול בן בטנית ואבא יוסי בן יוחנן איש ירושלם אומר אוי לי מבית ביתוס אוי לי מאלתן אוי לי מבית קדרוס אוי לי מקולמסן אוי לי מבית אלחנן אוי לי מבית לחישתן אוי לי מבית אלישע אוי לי מאגרופן אוי לי מבית ישמעאל בן פיאבי שהם כהנים גדולים ובניהם גזברין וחתניהן אמרכלין ועבדיהן באין וחובטין עלינו במקלות "Abba Saul ben Batnit (a Tana of the second generation) [in the name of] and Abba Jose ben Johanan, a Jersualemite (before the Temple's destruction) says: Woe is to me from the power, of the House of Boethus... the House of Hanin... the House of Kathrus... the House of Ishmael... the House of Phoebus... High priests, their sons are treasurers their sons-in-law are administrators, and their servants hit the people with

duced from the way in which it was gained, which included bribery,[99] murder, matricide and fratricide.[100]

Hellenization was a cultural process catalyzed in part by these higher-class priests who were undoubtedly the leaders of this movement.[101] It is remarkable that the rebellion against Hellenization was initiated, as it seems, by the provincial priesthood, who were joined in their fight by the commoners.[102] Only the Hasmonean priesthood are mentioned in the books of Maccabees as being active in the cultural renaissance movement. As in the time of Nehemiah the menace to traditional Judaism, this time by Hellenization led to an enhanced zeal for a meticulous re-reading of the Torah, and to a punctilious and stricter interpretation of its precepts.

5. 3. THE RENAISSANCE AND ITS PROBLEMS

One should distinguish between the reformations of Ezra and Nehemiah, and that of the Maccabees. In the period of Ezra and Nehemiah the lax attitude towards Torah rules and the potential that they would be utterly disregarded and eventually fall into oblivion catalyzed a return to punctilious observation of the Torah rules. The Maccabean revolution came as a reaction to Hellenization and also led to a more assiduous attention to the commandments, but also to disagreement regarding their correct interpretation. The re-reading of the Torah by Ezra and Nehemiah helped create new laws, whereas in the Maccabean period, it generated an attentiveness vis-à-vis the existing text in an

sticks." We also read in m. Yoma 3:11: ואלו לגנאי של בית גרמו לא רצו ללמד על מעשה לחם הפנים של בית אבטינס לא רצו ללמד על מעשה הקטורת "And these were remembered with disgrace: the House of Garmu [because] they did not want to teach [priests from other clans how to prepare the] Bread of Presence, the House of Abtinas [because] they did not want to teach [priests from other clans how to prepare the complex] mixture of incense."

99 See II Macc. 4:7-8.

100 See Ant. XI:297-301 and XIII:228, 302-303 and 307-311.

101 See Ant. XII:240-241 and II Macc. 4:10.

102 I disagree with Blenkisopp's assertion that the public reading of the Law and its study by the lay and clerical leadership (Neh 8:13) indicates that the clerical monopoly of legal expertise was broken by the laity (p.291). We observe from the book of Maccabbees that much later, in the Hellenistic period, the priests were the leaders on both sides of the conflict.

attempt to understand the vague or concealed instructions. The disparity between those who hoped for the complete integration of the Jews into Hellenic society, and those who opposed it was too great to allow for a compromise; one group had to be defeated,[103] thus the fierce battles between the Hellenizers and the Maccabees.[104]

The question of the relationship of the Maccabeans to the Pharisee and Sadducee split may be raised. There is no evidence for this particular split in Judean society before the Hasmonean period, a hypothesis confirmed by the overwhelming majority of scholars who connect the emergence of the Pharisees and Sadducees to the Maccabean revolt.[105] A short recapitulation of the circumstances is in order. The temple sacrifices may have been interrupted for only three short years,[106] but it is obvious that Hellenistic influence and neglect of a Judaism based on Torah precepts had begun much earlier. M. Stern[107] observes the influence of Hellenization beginning in 200 B.C. E.,[108] the

---

103 See I Macc. 2:44: "And they gathered an army, and slew the sinners in their wrath, and the wicked men in their indignation: and the rest fled to the nations for safety."

104 We read in I Macc. 2:42-43 that the Assideans, zealous for the law and worship of God joined the Maccabees, and supported them.

105 See A. I. Baumgarten, "Rabbinic Literature as a Source for the History of Jewish Sectarianism in the Second Temple Period," Dead Sea Discoveries, 2/1 (1995), 14-57 who states that the "schism began in the years immediately after the ascent of the fist Hasmonean ruler" (p.54). A. Rofe, ראשית צמיחתן של הכתות בימי בית שני, in מדינת החשמונאים לתולדותיה על רקע התקופה ההלניסטית, pp. 409-418, eds. U. Rappaport, and J. Ronen (Jerusalem, 1993) retrojects the establishment of the sects to the period of Ezra and Nehemiah, and represents the reform as a struggle against the social evils of the ruling and corrupt plutocracy. I think that this split, called "Proto-Sectarianism," by S. Cohen, From the Maccabees to the Mishnah, Philadelphia, 1987, should not be classified as sectarianism. It was ended by Ezra and Nehemiah, and has no direct connection to the later Pharisee — Sadducee split. The issues that provoked dissension in Ezra and Nehemiah's period were totally different than the issues that split the population into sects in the middle of the second century B. C. E. Any affinity between the two movements would be remote, just as the suggested link between the Sadducees and the Karaites is unlikely. The appearance of sects at various periods does not indicate any ideological interdependence.

106 Ant. XII:321, based on the narrative in I Mac. 1:54 (145 in Seleucid chronology, 167 B. C. E.) and 4:52 (148 in Seleucid chronology, 164 B. C. E.).

107 M. Stern, יהדות ויוונות in מדינת החשמונאים לתולדותיה על רקע התקופה ההלניסטית במאות השלישית והשנייה לפנה"ס, pp. 55-74, eds. U. Rappaport, J. Ronen (Jerusalem, 1993), p. 68.

108 More precisely in 198 B. C. E. after the battle of Panias. Israel L. Levin, "המאבק הפוליטי בין הפרושים לצדוקים בתקופה החשמונאית" מחקרים בתולדות ישראל בתקופת הבית השני, pp. 287-309, ed. Daniel Schwarz

period of Seleucid dominion over Judah, when Greek names start appearing in Jewish sources. The Books of Maccabees also attests to an extended period of incubation of Hellenistic culture in Judah and the resulting political power struggles,[109] culminating with the climactic interruption of Israelite sacrificial celebrations and the pollution of the altar in 167 B. C. E..[110]

The Hasmonean passion for the performance of the Torah precepts with punctilious literalness faced an insurmountable obstacle. The protracted interruption of the traditional way of life brought with it a loss of the rules and regulations pertaining to all aspects of life: cult celebrations, public administration and organization, and probably certain laws of individual conduct. Similar to Ezra and Nehemiah the Hasmoneans may have fallen back on stringency and attempted to establish stricter laws than those practiced before Hellenization. As we know from the Book of the Maccabees, a great part of the intellectual elite, the priests — especially those of the Jerusalem who had previously been the bearers of tradition and the teachers of the Torah — turned to Hellenism.[111] The Hasmonean priests, leaders of the uprising, were of provincial origin, and probably not particularly erudite in legal minutiae.[112]

(Jerusalem, 1996), p. 287, assumes that the Hellenization process had already begun in the previous (third) century, and reached its climax with Jason's reform.

109 The Book of Maccabees does not elaborate upon the stages in this process but we read in I Mac. 1:11: "In those days lawless people emerged in Israel." It is apparent from the context (vs. 10) that this occurred at the beginning of Antiochus' reign, that is, in 137 according to Seleucid chronology,175 B. C. E. Such a movement by a great number of people could not have occurred suddenly; we must therefore assume a gradual infiltration of Hellenistic culture, as well as the neglect of traditional practices which reached its climax in 175 B.C.E.

110 145 according to the Seleucid chronology, as it appears in I Mac. 1:54-59.

111 II Mac. 4:13-16.

112 According to the organization of the legal system as delineated in Deut. 17:8-13, only the Jerusalemite priests and clerics had the authority to decide on the correct interpretation and application of the law. In v. 8 we read וקמת ועלית אל המקום אשר יבחר ה' "go to the place the Lord your God will choose [to inquire about judicial matters that are unclear]." The exclusivity of Jerusalem is again emphasized in v.10, where the people are exhorted to obey these decisions: ועשית על פי הדבר אשר יגידו לך מן המקום ההוא "You must act according to the decisions they give you at the place the Lord will choose," and again in v. 12, regarding disobedience. This apparently superfluous repetition of the "chosen place — Jerusalem" is indicative of the exclusivity of Jerusalem as the one and only legal center for the entire country. One must therefore assume that the provincial priests, with no authority to decide on legal matters, did not concern themselves with the study

The new leaders and teachers had to start their activity basically from scratch. Differences of interpretation, contrasting recollections of tradition, and last but not least, personal preferences regarding the issues that that faced them at that time lay at the root of the differences between the Pharisees, Sadducees and Essenes.[113] These exegetical perspectives served as the foundation of the rabbinic legal system, and were the source of the argumentative rhetoric, refined and perfected in Talmudic literature.

---

and interpretation of the Torah, with the possible exception of specific rules which concerned them such as sacrifice.

113 See Y. Sussmann, Tarbiz 59/1 1990, pp. 61-2, who emphasizes that the debate in QMMT refers to the conflicts regarding details of the halakhah, not principles of philosophy and faith. G. J. Brooke, "The Scrolls and the Study of the New Testament," The Dead Sea Scrolls at Fifty, eds. R. Kugler and E. Schuller, Atlanta, GA, pp. 61-76, 1999, 68-9, states: "The Temple Scroll has shown clearly that the disputes at the heart of what distinguished one group from another in the two hundred years before the destruction of the temple in 70 CE. were halakhic in kind rather than doctrinal." See M. Kister, "עיונים במגילת מקצת מעשה תורה ועולמה", Tarbiz 68/3, pp. 317-371, 1999 and particularly n. 41, who cites the dispute between Sussmann and J. M. Baumgarten on this issue, and reconciles the two points of view by stating that at any rate the halakhic dissension was the most significant issue between the groups. In "Some Aspects of Qumranic Halakhah," The Madrid Qumran Congress, Vol. 2, pp. 571-588, 1992b, p. 571, Kister declares: "It is clear from the sects' other writings [i.e. other than MMT] that the conflict between the sect and its opponents was, in essence, a halakhic one." Cf. H. Fox (Lebeit Yoreh), "Introducing Tosefta," Introducing Tosefta: Textual Intratextual and Intertextual Studies, eds. H. Fox and T. Meacham pp. 1-31, New York, N. Y. 1999, p. 12, who asserts: "the author of 4QMMT may emphasize these minutiae of the law but these are secondary to the sociological and social rifts." Religion in the Dead Sea Scrolls, eds. J. J. Collins and R. A. Kugler, Grand Rapids, MI, 2000, p. 4, write that the Temple Scroll constitutes proof of the central importance of halakhic (legal), issues for the people of the Scrolls. See also L. Schiffman, "Utopia and Reality : Political Leadership and Organization in the Dead Sea Scrolls Community," Emanuael, Studies in Hebrew Bible, eds. S. M. Paul & ali, Leiden, 2003b, pp. 415-16. H. K. Harrington, "The Halakhah and Religion of Qumran," Religion in the Dead Sea Scrolls, eds. J. J. Collins and R. A. Kugler, pp. 74-89. 2000, p. 74, writes that early Judaism of all types, whether of the Pharisees, Sadducees, Essenes or others, had to deal first and foremost with biblical law; different interpretations guided and distinguished them. J. VanderKam, 2000, "Apocalyptic Tradition in the Dead Sea Scrolls and the Religion of Qumran," pp. 113-134, Religion in the Dead Sea Scrolls p. 134, writes that from the MMT we can deduce that "the initial break of the group centered around disputes about a series of legal points."

I suggest that the halakhic issues were at the root of the disputes and the theological differences followed later, as a second stage in the developmental process of religiously-founded schisms. A theological (or philosophical) premise constitutes the indispensable justification for a shift of, or a controversy about, the correct ritual procedure; sometimes the theology precedes the change in practice, and at other times succeeds it.

6. CONCLUSION

In conclusion, I hope to have demonstrated the concepts of embarrassment, and the reading and re-reading of Scripture in my analysis of two crucial reformations of Judaic law and theology, — that of Ezra and Nehemiah, and that of the Maccabees — I have contemplated, the amazing vitality of Jewish culture, and its resilience, in the face of dangers to its fundaments. Similar reformations are evident in later periods, such as the Hasidic movement in Western Europe following the 12-13th century Crusades, and the astounding renaissance of vibrant ultra-Orthodox communities after their decimation in the Holocaust, however, these are beyond the scope of this study.

REWRITING AS WHITEWASHING: THE CASE OF REWRITTEN BIBLE[1]

Hindy Najman, University of Toronto

My essay addresses the topic of the "embarrassment of scripture" by way of thinking about scripture, responding to its authoritativeness, and reflecting on related concepts of canon, prophecy, and interpretation.

I begin by briefly introducing this so-called genre of rewritten bible. These are texts that rework earlier biblical narratives; whether they are best thought of as constituting a genre is the subject of this essay. There are many such texts throughout the Second Temple period that rewrite earlier narratives by incorporating the old into the new through supplementation, interpretation, recension and even deletion of earlier material.

There are examples where a text from Genesis or Exodus is retold with very little difference. But, more often than not, the retelling involves what we moderns would call radical reworking. These rewritings can already be found in the texts of the Hebrew Bible: for instance, the Chronicler rewrites large portions of 1-2 Kings in ways that "forget" about David's notorious episode with Bathsheba,[2] and Deuteronomy radically reworks laws included in the Covenant Code of Exodus.[3] This rewriting continues throughout the Second

1 This essay is written in honor of Harry Fox. May his light continue to shine brightly.

2 See discussions by Sara Japhet, *I & II Chronicles: A Commentary* (Louisville: Westminster John Knox Press, 1993) and Gary Knoppers, *I Chronicles* (New York: Doubleday, 2004); see also Steven J. Schweitzer, *Reading Utopia in Chronicles* (University of Notre Dame PhD Dissertation, 2005) passim.

3 See Michael Fishbane, *Biblical Interpretation in Ancient Israel* (Oxford: Clarendon Press, 1988) and Bernard M. Levinson, *Deuteronomy and the Hermeneutics of Legal Innovation* (New York: Oxford University Press, 1997).

Temple period, prior to canonization. The actual status of these texts is unclear. Are these texts meant to be authorized and inspired texts, or are they meant as a kind of early midrash on the already authoritative biblical traditions?

I want to consider the example of the Genesis Apocryphon from Qumran, where the concise account from Genesis 12 is "unpacked" in two important ways. This text, which certainly knows traditions that we have come to call the biblical text of Genesis 12, provides a context for understanding why Abram lied to Pharoah about Sarai being his sister so that he would be spared.

In the Genesis Apocryphon, Abram has a dream in which is he told in a vision of two trees that his life is under threat because of Sarai. Thus, the lie is justified as a response to this dream. Moreover, it puts a description of Sarai's beauty into the mouth of one of Pharoah's advisors — again, fleshing out the text of Genesis. The Genesis Apocryphon text justifies Abram's lie and thematizes Sarai's beauty, which is praised (just as is reported in the Genesis text) in the eyes of the Egyptians.[4] Before turning to a more theoretical discussion about the so-called genre of the rewritten bible I want to consider a second example.[5] A very well known story which is all of one verse long in

4 See the discussion of this in J.L. Kugel, *Traditions of the Bible* (Cambridge, MA: Harvard Unversity Press, 1998), 254-256, 271-273.

5 On the genre of rewritten Bible, see Peter S. Alexander, "Retelling the Old Testament," *It is Written: Scripture Citing Scripture: Essays in Honour of Barnabas Lindars,* SSF, eds D.A. Carson and Hugh G.M. Williamson (Cambridge: Cambridge University Press, 1987), 99-121. For a history of scholarship on the issue, see Moshe J. Bernstein, "'Rewritten Bible': A Generic Category Which Has Outlived its Usefulness?" Textus 22 (2005): 169-196. See also George J. Brooke, "Rewritten Bible," Encyclopedia of the Dead Sea Scrolls (Oxford and New York: Oxford University Press, 2000), 777-80; Steven D. Fraade, "Rewritten Bible and Rabbinic Midrash as Commentary," *Current Trends in the Study of Midrash*, ed. C. Bakhos (Leiden: Brill, 2006), 59-78; Betsy Halpern-Amaru, *Rewriting the Bible: Land and Covenant in Postbiblical Jewish Literature* (Valley Forge: Trinity Press International, 1994); Daniel J. Harrington, "The Bible Rewritten (Narratives)," *Early Judaism and Its Modern Interpreters*, eds Robert A. Kraft and George Nickelsburg (Atlanta: Scholars Press, 1986), 239-47; George Nickelsburg, "The Bible Rewritten and Expanded," *Jewish Writings of the Second Temple Period*, ed. Michael Stone (Assen/Philadelphia: Van Gorcum/Fortress, 1984), 89-156; Emmanuel Tov, "Biblical Texts as Reworked in Some Qumran Manuscripts with Special Attention to 4QRP and 4QparaGen-Exod," *The Community of the Renewed Covenant: The Notre Dame Symposium on the Dead Sea Scrolls*, eds. Eugene Ulrich and James C. VanderKam (Notre Dame: University of Notre Dame Press, 1994), 111-34. See also earlier scholarship by Geza Vermes, who coined the term "Rewritten Bible": *Scripture and Tradition in Judaism: Haggadic Studies* (2nd rev. ed.; StPB 4;

the Hebrew Bible is that of Jacob's son Reuben and his sexual intercourse with Bilhah, Jacob's concubine:

ויהי בשכן ישראל בארץ ההוא וילך ראובן וישכב את בלהה פילגש אביו וישמע ישראל

While Israel lived in that land, Reuben went and lay with Bilhah his father's concubine; and Israel heard of it" (Gen. 35:22, NRSV translation).

The passage in Genesis mentions only that Jacob "heard of it." Nothing is said of Jacob's reaction. Apart from a more extensive "blessing," or rather "critical reproach" of Reuben in Genesis 49, the final testament of Jacob to his sons, we have no further reflection on this episode in the book of Genesis.

However, in the book of Jubilees (ca. Second century BCE) and in the Testaments of the Twelve Patriarchs (ca. Second century CE) we see a much longer account of this event:

And Reuben saw Bilhah, the attendant of Rachel (and) his father's concubine, washing in the water privately, and he desired her. And hiding at night, he entered Bilhah's house at night and found her sleeping in her bed, alone in her house. And he lay with her. And she woke up and looked, and behold, Reuben was lying with her on the bed. And she uncovered the hem of her (skirt) and seized him and screamed and recognized that it was Reuben. And she was ashamed because of him and released her hand from upon him. And he fled. And she lamented greatly concerning this matter. And she did not tell anyone at all. And when Jacob came and sought her, she said to him, "I am not clean for you since I have become polluted for you because Reuben has defiled me and lay with me at night, but I was sleeping and I was unaware until he had uncovered my skirt and lain with me. And Jacob was very angry with Reuben because he had lain with Bilhah, for he had uncovered his father's robe. And therefore Jacob did not draw near her since Reuben had defiled her. And the deed of any man who uncovers his father's robe is very evil because he is despicable before the Lord. Therefore it is written and ordered in the heavenly

Leiden: Brill, 1973; 1st ed. 1961) 10, and by Charles Perrot on the notion of "texte continue": *Pseudo-Philon: Les antiquites bibliques*. Tome II: Introduction litteraire, commentaire et index (SC 230; Paris: Cerf, 1976).

tablets that a man should not lie with his father's wife, and he should not uncover his father's robe because that is defilement... And let them not say, "Reuben had life and forgiveness after he lay with his father's concubine and while she had a husband and while her husband, Jacob, his father, was alive." For the ordinance and judgment and law had not been revealed till then (as) completed for everyone, but in your days (it is) like the law of (appointed) times and days and an eternal law for everlasting generations (Jubilees 33:2-16).[6]

Give heed to the words of Reuben, your father.
Do not devote your attention to a woman's looks,
Nor live with a woman who is already married,
Nor become involved in affairs with women.

For if I had not seen Bilhah bathing in a sheltered place, I would not have fallen into this great lawless act. For so absorbed were my senses by her naked femininity that I was not able to sleep until I had performed this revolting act. While our father, Jacob, had gone off to visit his father, Isaac, and we were at Gader near Ephratha in Bethlehem, Bilhah became drunk and was sound asleep, naked in her bedchamber. So when I came in and saw her nakedness, I performed the impious deed without her being aware of it. Leaving her sleeping soundly, I went out. And immediately a messenger from God revealed it to my father. He came and made lamentation over me, and never again touched her. (T. Reuben, 3:9-15)[7]

The texts make the transgression explicit, but they also figure out how to recover the reputation of Jacob's son, Reuben. The embarrassment and awkwardness over the event is very clear, but the interpretive texts do not

6 From the translation by O.S. Wintermute in James H. Charlesworth, *The Old Testament Pseudo-epigrapha* (Doubleday: New York, 1985) 2.119.

7 From the translation by H. C. Kee in Charlesworth, OTP, 1,783. On the interpretative traditions around Reuben's sin, see James L. Kugel, "Reuben's Sin with Bilhah in the Testament of Reuben," *Pomegranates and Golden Bells: Studies in Biblical, Jewish, and Near Eastern Ritual, Law and Literature in Honor of Jacob Milgrom*, eds. David P. Wright, David N. Freedman, and Avi Hurvitz (Winona Lake, IN: Eisenbrauns, 1995), 525-54; for an alternative view, see Ishay Rosen-Zvi, "Bilhah the Temptress: The Testament of Reuben and the Birth of Sexuality," JQR 96.1 (2006): 65-94.

ignore or delete the narrative; rather, they embellish it by supplementation and interpretation. Of course, we have to leave open the possibility that these traditions are as old as the biblical texts themselves, but it is important to note that they are clearly struggling to explain and to preserve the sense of the text in Genesis. Both Jubilees (written in ca. Second century BCE and contemporaneous with some of the latest texts in the corpus of the Old Testament/Hebrew bible) and the Testament of Reuben (written in ca. 200 CE in an early Christian context)[8] should be understood as preserving much older traditions.[9]

There are many such examples that rewrite earlier biblical texts in order to cover up difficulties and to rework inherited traditions so that they can be received in a new context. New social and political contexts often bring with them different kinds of assumptions that require radical reworking of a past authoritative narrative. Thus, the embarrassment over the past often requires a reworking of that past narrative in order to make reception possible. But how is it possible to rewrite a past authoritative narrative? What would the author's or the audience's concept of a "text" have to be in order for it to be possible to rewrite it?

In order to answer these questions we need to return to the question of the so-called genre of rewritten Bible. What use is it to classify texts such as these? When specific features of the genre are articulated, what is illuminated? How does it clarify what we have come to understand as Torah? As interpretation? As midrash? As intertextual interpretation? And what are the limitations of the genre classification? When certain texts are determined to be "insiders"[10]

8 On the dating and provenance of the Testaments, see the work of Marinus De Jonge, "The Main Issues in the Study of the Testaments of the Twelve Patriarchs" and "The Testaments of the Twelve Patriarchs: Christian and Jewish," *Jewish Eschatology, Early Christian Christology and the Testaments of the Twelve Patriarchs* (Leiden: Brill, 1991), 147-63 and 233-43; *Pseudepigrapha of the Old Testament as part of Christian literature: the Case of the Testaments of the Twelve Patriarchs and the Greek Life of Adam and Eve* (Boston: Brill, 2003).

9 See discussions by James L. Kugel on the preservation of early material in such texts: "The Ladder of Jacob," HTR 88 (1995): 209-27; "Levi's Elevation to the Priesthood in Second Temple Writings," HTR 86 (1993): 1-64; "The Story of Dinah in the Testament of Levi," HTR 85 (1992): 1-34.

10 Such as Jubilees and the Genesis Apocryphon.

while other texts are called "outsiders,"[11] is there a risk that important aspects of the texts in question will be overlooked as a result of such grouping?

It is helpful to reflect broadly on genre classification. Texts are typically classified on the basis of shared features to which some significance is attached. Once a set of texts is said to share some group of designated features — or to overlap significantly with respect to those features — then those texts are said to participate in that genre. To be sure, this classification can help refine our characterization of the significant features. Additionally, classification can bring out otherwise missed commonalities and differences. But classification can also lead to rigid thinking that ignores the wider context in which a text is produced. In such cases the definition of a genre *can obscure more than it illuminates.*

The distinction between genres may be a superficial one, especially if it does not correspond to any distinction made explicitly within the culture producing the texts in question, but is imported from other cultures or eras. For example, tragedy and comedy are explicitly distinguished by the Greeks, while poetry and prose are not explicitly distinguished in the Hebrew Scriptures.[12] Superficial observations that employ imported terms can be accurate and even illuminating, and I see no principled reason always to limit oneself to terms used within the culture under investigation. But there is also a danger that one will start to think in terms that are too rigid, and that darkness will be spread instead of light.

Let us turn now from generalities to the particular case in which we are interested. The genre of rewritten Torah surely has shed much light on texts by helping scholars to differentiate between sectarian instruction (1QS) and narrative exegesis (Jubilees and the Genesis Apocryphon), between prophetic prediction (e.g. Pesher) and legal proscription (e.g. 4QMMT). But it is also important to invoke here an important concern voiced by George Brooke[13]:

> RB texts come in almost as many genres as can be found in the biblical books themselves. Rewritten Bible is a label that is suitable for more than just narrative

11 Such as Pesher Habakkuk, 4Q Reworked Pentateuch, and 4Q158 Pentateuch texts.

12 See James L. Kugel, *The Idea of Biblical Poetry* (New Haven: Yale University Press, 1981), 1-95.

13 Brooke, "Rewritten Bible," EDSS 780.

> retellings of the biblical stories. It is a general umbrella term describing the particular kind of intertextual activity that always gives priority to one text over another.

Here Brooke argues that we must not make our definition of rewritten Torah too specific. Rather we should use it as a high-level term covering all biblical genres, in order to signify what might be called a meta-genre.

But we must also not make our definition of rewritten Torah too general. For the term does not, according to Brooke, signify just *any kind* of intertexuality. Rather it refers to a particular kind of intertextual activity that prioritizes one text over another. The crucial question that arises now is: what does "priority" mean here?

One answer is given by those who think that rewritten Torah is midrashic — notably Geza Vermes,[14] perhaps also Moshe Bernstein.[15] Much later rabbinic interpretive collections from the third century CE and following are called rabbinic midrash. I am not going to try to characterize the variety of kinds of midrashim here, but simply state what the scholars who use the term midrashic in this context understand by midrash: texts that presuppose an authoritative and fixed canon and are understood to be commenting on earlier biblical texts or using existing fixed texts to support a particular position. The question is whether the kind of interpretation and relationship with scripture found in later rabbinic midrashim is already to be found in these early second or first century BCE texts. Calling rewritten Torah midrashic would imply that it already presupposes an authoritative and fixed text which does not aspire to replace or to approximate the authority of Genesis, but rather to explain Genesis. On this

14 Geza Vermes defines "rewritten Bible" as "a narrative that follows Scripture but includes a substantial amount of supplements and interpretive developments"; see *The History of the Jewish People in the Age of Jesus Christ* Vol. 3.1 ,eds. Geza Vermes, F. Millar, and M. Goodman (Edinburgh: T&T Clark, 1986); cf. Geza Vermes, *Scripture and Tradition in Judaism* (Leiden: Brill, 1973), 22-28.

15 Bernstein prefers a "Vermes-like narrowness in the employment of the term, demanding comprehensive or broad scope rewriting of narrative and/or legal material with commentary woven into the fabric implicitly, but perhaps not merely a biblical text with some superimposed exegesis…The result of re-adopting this nomenclature will be the restoration of 'rewritten Bible' to its proper place as a subcategory of biblical interpretation in antiquity, one way of the ancient author's putting forth his reading of the Bible"; Moshe Bernstein, "'Rewritten Bible,'" 195-196.

view, the rewriting can never approach in status or in spirit the biblical text, which is already authorized, inscribed and fixed or even canonized.

It seems to me, however, that this construal of the prioritization involved in rewritten Torah is anachronistic. We cannot speak of proto-midrashic interpretations of canonized texts here because the texts that have been classified as rewritten Torah claim revelatory status for themselves and are often treated in scripture-like ways. We do not know if the concept of scripture was operative in the way it came to be operative in ancient Judaism and Christianity. But many of the interpretive texts, both those included and excluded from the genre of rewritten Bible, explicitly claim their inspiration and ought to be included in what we might call revelatory literature that has authoritative status for the community.

Jubilees, for example, explicitly and repeatedly understands itself to be the second law which builds on an already established authoritative tradition, i.e. the first law. It flows from that first revelation at Sinai and asserts that inspiration pre-dates and post-dates Sinai. The text of Jubilees thus stands in a long line of authoritative texts that read and reread older material and resituate the old in the new. But why would this suggest that the old is replaced, which is what many have assumed?[16] To be sure, the evidence at Qumran suggests that the biblical materials are only some of the authoritative materials from this period.[17] Moreover, the narrative of Jubilees itself struggles to negotiate a difficult and at times troubling first law.[18] This is hardly the stuff of replacement or rendering a prior law redundant! Jubilees and the reception of Jubilees, then, fit in quite elegantly with other literature we know to have been produced in

16 See, for example, Ben Z. Wacholder, "Jubilees as the Super Canon: Torah-Admonition versus Torah-Commandment," *Legal Texts and Legal Issues: Proceedings of the Second Meeting of the International Organization for Qumran Studies*, Cambridge 1995, ed. Moshe Bernstein, Florentino Garcia Martinez, and John Kampen; STDJ 23 (Leiden: Brill, 1997), 195-211.

17 See Eugene C. Ulrich, "The Bible in the Making: the Scriptures Found at Qumran," *The Bible at Qumran: Text, Shape and Interpretation*, ed. P.W. Flint (Grand Rapids, MI: Eerdmans, 2001), 51-66, and James C. VanderKam, "Authoritative Literature in the Dead Sea Scrolls," Dead Sea Discoverie 5/3 (1998): 382-402.

18 See Menachem Kister, "על שני מטבעות לשון בספר היובלים", Tarbiz 70/2 (2001): 289-300; Cana Werman, «'התורה והתעודה' הכתובה על הלוחות» Tarbiz 68/4 (1999): 473-492; English version: "The תורה and the תעודה Engraved on the Tablets," Dead Sea Discoveries 9/1 (2002): 75-103.

the period of late Second Temple Judaism (both biblical and non-biblical; cf. Chronicles, the Genesis Apocryphon, and other works).

Jubilees and other similar works demonstrate repeated and ongoing interpretation of the past and claims of divine and angelic revelation.[19] In light of such claims, we can just as easily include the pesher interpretation of the 70 years of Jeremiah in the book of Daniel (Dan. 9) or later in Qumran pesharim, which offer typological interpretations of earlier prophecies with the claim that the interpretations are authoritative and inspired.[20] Still, this new law or new covenant does not render the old redundant.

For now I want to emphasize that the notion of rewritten Bible is simply misleading. The definition of the genre separates a text like Jubilees from texts with which it shares important features. Similarly, it obscures the deep affinities that the authoritative texts at Qumran have with Second Temple literature more generally.

When considered within a broader context of revelatory literature, we see that Qumran and other interpretive Second Temple literature suggest that revelation was considered to be ongoing and persistent throughout the Second Temple period. To be sure, there may have been perceived interruptions, but accessing divine revelation in exile, from the Babylonian exile onward, continued to be understood as a possibility.

The interpretations do not render the texts they are interpreting redundant, but neither do they defer to a past in such a way that the "here and now" is bereft of the inspiration of that past. Now I am moving on to another conception of rewritten Bible. Another, arguably opposing, presupposition that has often been lurking beneath rewritten Torah is that the old authoritative prophecy/ inspiration/revelation is no longer available. In this construal of rewritten Torah, the work of interpretation defers to a priority of revelation which is now remote and inaccessible.

In this account, prophecy has ceased and is no longer possible, so that the new interpretation could not possibly be revelatory. This position is

19 See Hindy Najman, "Angels at Sinai: Exegesis, Theology and Interpretive Authority," Dead Sea Discoveries 8 (2000): 313-333.

20 Pesher Habakkuk, for example, claims inspiration for the Teacher of Righteousness, "to whom God has made known all the mysteries of his servants, the prophets." (1QpHab col. vii).

uncomfortably close to later rabbinic accounts of a prophecy that ended with Haggai, Zechariah and Malachi, or to some recent accounts of prophecy giving way to scribalism, or the oral to the written. The idea is that the old is already fixed and that the past is irrecoverable.

Why argue that rewritten Bible presupposes a fixed, even canonical text which preserves divine inspiration that can never be recovered?

There are, of course, those famous texts that point to the cessation of prophecy in the Second Temple period. But in fact these have been shown time and again not to be claiming anything like the cessation of divine revelation.[21] Rather, at the very most, they speak of the cessation of the institution of prophecy, but not the cessation of revelation by means of prophets who occupy no institutional office.

What about claims in the Qumran corpus? The scrolls repeatedly claim revelatory status no less than the status of Deuteronomy (as *mishneh torah*) or Habakkuk (as actualized new prophecy in the pesher) and Psalms (in the many new authoritative, inspired songs of Qumran).[22] They speak of their interpreter as being inspired. They speak of participation in angelic conversation in which those at prayer gain access to the divine mysteries and cosmic knowledge. Additionally, self-imposed exile in a number of texts found at Qumran is reimagined as an idyllic wilderness in which the *'osei ha-torah* can find their way back to the covenant,[23] now renewed in the echoes of Jeremiah 31:31, *berit hadashah.*

Actually both positions I discussed above presuppose a closure or an ending in Second Temple Judaism that I want to argue did not occur. On the first

21 See Steve Mason's recent essay, "Josephus and His Twenty-Two Book Canon," *The Canon Debate*, eds. Lee M. McDonald and James A. Sanders (Peabody, MA: Hendrickson, 2002), 110-127. To be sure, Josephus argues that post-biblical prophecy has ceased, but at the same time argues that the rewritten narratives are para-prophetic, or that he is claiming an inspired status for his texts without claiming that they are the stuff of prophecy. Mason accuses readers that charge Josephus with being a liar because he radically alters the biblical texts, of assuming anachronistically post-enlightenment expectations of the distinctions between text and interpretation.

22 For example, the "non-canonical" psalms in the Great Psalms Scroll, 11Qpsalmsa.

23 Cf. James C. VanderKam's discussion on *'osei ha-torah* in *The Dead Sea Scrolls Today* (Grand Rapids, MI: Eerdmans, 1994), 92.

problematic use of the term, the old scripture ended and made way for a new second law or new scripture, new covenant and new texts as replacement. First, scripture is over, and now there is an attempt to write a new scripture. But there is no evidence that the production of scripture ceased. On the contrary, the many texts we have from this period suggest ongoing production. According to the second position, the text of the past and its original inspiration are closed off from the present insofar as prophecy has ceased. Again, however, these texts (Jubilees, Temple Scroll, Pesher Habakkuk, 4Ezra, etc.) continue to claim inspiration. Both of those positions seem to be wrong. The new interpretation does not reject or supersede the first scripture, but neither does it give up the possibility of ongoing inspiration.

I want to argue that there are two senses in which the past text maintains a position of priority.

First, new texts often attach themselves to the already established authority of a founder. This can be seen in many texts said to be rewritings, starting with Deuteronomy, the attribution of Psalms to David, the Song of Songs to Solomon, Jubilees to Moses and 4Ezra to Ezra as well as to Job, Moses and Zechariah. Here the very act of rewriting, which is often also attached to a founder, is part of expanding revelatory or, if you will, divine authority, not a compromising of it. As I have written elsewhere, pseudonymous attribution does not falsely attribute new texts to old figures because these new texts cannot invoke their own authority (a claim that has been made of pseudepigraphy).[24] Rather, the old and remote figures can be channeled in order to establish a new authority. This new claim does not attemt to replace the old authoritative figures and in fact confirms their status.

Second, and by analogy, rewriting the Torah can similarly be said to extend the prophetic status attributed to Moses or Solomon (among others) through a rewriting and reworking of already authorized torah. Here, Rewritten Torah should be considered to be participating in the very same exercise as expanding the discourse attributed to a founder. To be sure, we cannot just group all of these texts together in a single genre. For example, 4Q252 (*Commentary on Genesis A*) should be distinguished from the reworking and harmonization of

24 See Hindy Najman, *Seconding Sinai: The Development of Mosaic Discourse in Second Temple Judaism* (Boston: Brill, 2003), 1-15.

4Q reworked Pentateuch. Still, I want to suggest that expansion and reworking of texts can be said to be part of that ongoing openness of the corpus of authoritative writings and the very possibility of ongoing prophecy that was not compromised by exile (self-imposed or otherwise).

Rewritten Torah is not a genre, but rather a meta-genre where old texts are channeled for the authorization of the new. Or, in other words, new interpretations, laws and liturgical practices are attached to the old by reworking, interpreting and expanding the old.

In two senses, then, the older figure and the older texts have priority inasmuch as they contribute to the authorization of the new on the coattails of the old. But this also means that the new texts are participating in the work of ongoing revelation which does not end, which continues to build upon the old and access new contexts for revelation and inspiration. Interpretation in the world of Second Temple Judaism is part of an ever-expanding corpus of authoritative and revelatory writing.

However, the struggle to incorporate and to interpret continues into the later rabbinic period. Let us return to our example of the story of Reuben and Bilhah. The rabbinic texts reflect a profound struggle with this narrative. An early tannaitic tradition (mMegillah 4:9) emphasizes that the narrative should not be translated for the community: מעשה ראובן נקרא ולא מיתרגם. This is to say it is rendered incomprehensible, insofar as the "translation" is intended to render the text comprehensible and accessible (cf. Nehemiah 8:1-8).

Another interpretation, in b. Shabbat 55b, seeks to vindicate Reuben and his progeny by reinterpreting the episode in the following way:

> אלא מה אני מקיים וישכב את בלהה פילגש אביו מלמד שבלבל מצעו של אביו ומעלה עליו הכתוב כאילו שכב עמה תניא ר"ש בן אלעזר אומר מוצל אותו צדיק מאותו עון ולא בא מעשה זה לידו אפשר עתיד זרעו לעמוד על הר עיבל ולומר ארור שוכב עם אשת אביו ויבא חטא זה לידו אלא מה אני מקיים וישכב את בלהה פילגש אביו עלבון אמו תבע אמר אם אחות אמי היתה צרה לאמי שפחת אחות אמי תהא צרה לאמי עמד ובלבל את מצעה

> Then how do I interpret, and he lay with Bilhah his father's concubine? This teaches that he transposed his father's couch, and the Writ imputes [blame] to him as though he had lain with her. It was taught, Rabbi Simeon ben Eleazar

> said: That righteous man was saved from that sin and that deed did not come to his hand. Is it possible that his seed was destined to stand on Mount Ebal and proclaim, 'Cursed be he that lies with his father's wife,' yet this sin should come to his hand? But how do I interpret, and he lay with Bilhah his father's concubine? He resented his mother's humiliation. Said he, 'If my mother's sister was a rival to my mother, shall the bondmaid of my mother's sister be a rival to my mother?'[Thereupon] he arose and transposed her couch (b. Shabbat 55b).[25]

The rereading suggests that Reuben wanted to prevent his mother from continuing to be humiliated by the handmaiden of his recently deceased aunt Rachel. Thus Reuben flipped the beds around so that after the death of her sister, Leah would no longer suffer humiliation. This symbolic act was considered so transgressive that it was as if Reuben had slept with her! In other words, intention and transgression are exaggerated in order to adequately capture the gravity of his sin, rather than what actually happened. Because how, the text seems to ask, could later generations condemn such an action if their own forefather participated in that very transgression?

Considerable acrobatic interpretation goes into the adjusting of these texts in order to insure that they cohere with the law and custom of their own society. This rewriting can be described as apologetic or as embarrassed. But I think that we can say more about these texts against the backdrop of rewritten bible in general and about the Reuben and Bilhah episode in particular.

If it is possible to write over scripture or produce a new version while leaving an existing scripture intact, then we are not only speaking of later communities struggling to appropriate and transmit texts as divinely inspired; we are catching a glimpse of a process that is continuous with the past tradition of scripture production. Rewriting is about rendering the earlier materials relevant to the present by insisting on the inspiration of the new context, a "face-lift" or complete overhaul of the earlier narrative; or, in other words, writing new scripture.

However, such a claim would have to presuppose that the actual rabbinic project is far more inspired and charismatic that it claims to be. By claiming

25 From the Soncino translation.

that rewritten bible is midrashic we now mean exactly the opposite of what scholars of fifty years ago meant when they suggested that pesher is early midrash.[26] Instead, we suggest that the midrashic project is fluid and inspired and continuous with the inspiration of the biblical prophet, seer and scribe. To say that the text of Jubilees or the Testaments is part of midrash is not to claim that there is a canon and that the interpretation can be separated from that canonical text. Instead, these extra-textual traditions are part of the process of scripture production, a process that is still emerging in the Second Temple period and one that continues through the rabbinic period and beyond.

In conclusion: עשות ספרים הרבה אין קץ; "The making of many books is without limit" (Qohelet 12:12). This line is the prophetic message for the future of the Jewish interpretive imagination as it continues to write and overwrite, as if scripture is overwritten with a new text, as in the case of a palimpsest. These texts are not only about embarrassment, but about the ongoing possibility of revelation in interpretation.[27]

---

26 See, for example, William H. Brownlee, *The Midrash Pesher of Habakkuk* (SBLMS 24; Missoula: Scholars Press, 1979).

27 I am indebted to George Brooke, Steven Fraade, Paul Franks, Robert Kraft and Eva Mroczek for their incisive suggestions and helpful comments.

ESTABLISHING A SACRED CHURCH IN THE NEW TESTAMENT

Shana Husband, University of Toronto

In the New Testament there is a strong tension between the church and the synagogue. By studying the ambiguous relationship between the two, the problems in establishing the church as holy are highlighted. The church becomes holy by imitating Judaism, mimicking its rituals and by invalidating the sanctity of the synagogue and its members. The New Testament writers make the church holy through an act of sacred piracy, by "purloining" the preexisting holiness of the synagogue and transferring it to the church. Ultimately, the authority and sacredness of the church is established through a claim that it derives its holiness directly from God, and then by contrasting this with synagogues and temples on earth that only receive their power from man. In the end, the church in the New Testament sets up a hierarchy where it places itself as the holiest of the holy and moves the synagogues to the bottom.

THE SYNAGOGUE AS HOLY

In order for the new church to oppose the synagogue there must be something about it that is worth opposing. It would not make sense to take so much time and effort to write about something that was meaningless. There are many passages in the New Testament that acknowledge the holiness of the synagogue. Many of the new Christians were once Jewish and they respected the synagogues. Jesus himself was brought up as a Jew. He spoke in the synagogues and participated in the temple festivals.

In the Gospel of Luke there is less tension between the synagogue and church compared to elsewhere in the New Testament (a point that will be addressed below). This provides us with the opportunity to study a few cases where the holiness of the synagogue is emphasized. Luke mentions that Jesus used the synagogues to preach his message and that Jesus was well received at times. Luke also says that Jesus continued preaching throughout Judea proclaiming his message in the synagogues.[1]

Luke writes about a healing that Jesus performed, a healing that was considered worthwhile even though the sick man was the slave of a Centurion. Jews were the ones who convinced Jesus to heal the slave. They did this by saying "He is worthy of having you do this for him, for he loves our people, and it is he who built our synagogue for us."[2] Jesus accompanied the people to the slave and healed him. This shows how the individual who built the synagogue was considered worthy of healing just because of his association with the holy place, even if he was not Jewish himself. This testifies to the sanctity of the synagogue.

The Acts of the Apostles gives the reader some insight into the relationship between Jesus and the temple/synagogue as established holy places. We read that Jesus spent his days with the people and ate together and praised God together in the temple.[3] Peter healed a cripple at the "Beautiful Gate" and then they both entered the Temple together.[4] Then there is mention of John and Peter in Solomon's portico preaching to the Israelites and claiming God's authority through mutual "ancestors" including Abraham, Isaac Jacob and Jesus.[5]

This particular passage shows that even after the death of Jesus his disciples continued to preach in the temple. It also shows that the disciples were spending time with Jews. It is safe to assume that the people in the temple were Jewish and not new Christians because it was considered profane to have non-Jewish people in Jewish holy places. At this point, the developing church considered the temple holy or they would not have been preaching in it.

1 Luke 4:42-44.This and all other translations taken from *The New Revised Standard Version: Catholic Edition* (New York: Oxford University Press, 1999).

2 Luke 7:4-6.

3 Acts 2:46.

4 Acts 3:1-9.

5 Acts 3:11-13.

DISTINGUISHING BETWEEN THE CHURCH AND THE SYNAGOGUE

As Paul and Barnabas traveled to spread the good news and attempted to convert the Jews and the Gentiles, they would go to the synagogues for their audience.[6] Why put in the time and effort in these places if they were unholy? It is very difficult to create a new holy place. The emerging Christian sect could not just set up a new building and declare it holy. One must find a way to confer holiness upon a site and this is not so easy to accomplish.

The usual *modus operandi* is to use a place that is already sacred and then distinguish your new place from that existing place. All the church needed to do was to take the original sacred place and represent it as bad or unholy so as to make the second place appear better in contrast. It is almost like transferring the sanctity of the first holy place to the second holy place because the sanctity of the first has been spoiled. This is not unlike when one of two rival siblings points out to the parent the wrongdoing of the other in an attempt to make the teller of tales seem good by contrast.

The authors of the New Testament create a distinction between themselves and the synagogue by using notions of end-time. They do this by appealing to the nostalgia of Jewish people who long for the messiah that their ancestors prophesized. The prophets predicted that the messiah would come and because he has not come, the timeline continues unabated. The church, however, claims that Jesus is the prophesized messiah and the longing for his arrival has now ended. A new beginning is among them. This end-time/new beginning causes time to become cyclical. A new cycle has started which promises restoration of past successes.

As argued above, the church recognizes the synagogue as holy. Not all the people of the synagogue, however, are interested in the good news that Jesus and his followers deliver. Occasionally they must leave the synagogue when a conversion has been unsuccessful, which was common.[7] When they are outside the synagogue they have no holy place. This creates the need to designate a new holy place, preferably holier than the synagogues.

6 Acts 13:42-43.

7 Acts 13:27, 14:1-2.

THE HEAVENLY CHURCH

As mentioned above, one of the ways in which the church does this is by claiming authority over the heavenly realm and that only those who have faith in Jesus can access it. The church claims that Jesus "…is the mediator of a new covenant, so that those who are called may receive the promised eternal inheritance."[8] Jesus "entered into the Holy Place, not with the blood of goats and calves, but with his own blood."[9] Moses may have been a servant of God but Jesus was the Son of God, i.e. "Jesus is worthy of more glory than Moses."[10]

The New Testament claims that the Mosaic covenant is secondary. Jesus enacted a new covenant, implying that it is better than the old one. The church describes the locus of the covenant, *i.e.* the tabernacle and the separation of the holiest of holies which is sanctified through the sacrificial offering of goats and calves.[11] This "earthly sanctuary" is inferior to the church's holy place. The church's "greater and perfect tent" exists in Heaven. A tent "not made with hands, not of this creation,"[12] a tent sanctified with the blood of Jesus rather than the blood of goats and calves.[13]

Anytime there is a challenge to the church's authority they simply appeal to the authority they have from God, as in the following example:

> But Peter and the apostles answered, 'We must obey God rather than any human authority. The God of our ancestors raised up Jesus, whom you had killed by hanging him on a tree. God exalted him at his right hand as Leader and Saviour, so that he might give repentance to Israel and forgiveness of sins. And we are witnesses to these things, and so is the Holy Spirit whom God has given to those who obey him.'[14]

---

8 Heb 9:15.

9 Heb 9:12.

10 Heb 3:1-6.

11 Heb 9:15-22.

12 Heb 9:11.

13 Heb 9:12.

14 Acts 5:29-32.

The church may malign the temple but will also extol it when that suits its agenda. Jesus and his parents go to the temple to celebrate Passover. Jesus is left behind because each of his parents thinks he is with the other. It takes three days to find him and when they do, he is in the temple participating in discussions with the elders. When Jesus' mother expresses her concern Jesus replies: "Why were you searching for me? Did you not know that I must be in my Father's house?"[15] In each of the four gospels, one finds a passage that may be titled *Jesus Cleanses the Temple.* Each account describes Jesus entering the temple and finding a market set up there. He is outraged that a commercial atmosphere has been brought into "his fathers house."[16] In the hands of the unworthy, the sacred temple is made profane and it is only Jesus who can restore it to its original splendor.

JESUS' CRUCIFIXION AND THE JEWS

This leads us to another way the church implicitly and explicitly attacks the synagogue's sacredness. The New Testament holds the Jews responsible for Jesus' death as evident from the quote above. Less explicit examples are found throughout the gospels. There are two ways that the gospel writers lay blame for Jesus' death on the Jews. When they describe the governor, Pilate, who sentenced Jesus; they never mention that he was Roman. The reader is also led to believe that Pilate was ambivalent about the decision to kill Jesus and it was actually the crowd of Jews that pushed for his death. In Matthew the Jews say: "'Let him be crucified!' Then he asked, 'Why, what evil has he done?' But they shouted all the more, 'Let him be crucified!'"[17] Similar accounts are found in Mark 15:13, Luke 23: 21-23 and John 18:40.

JESUS AND THE SYNAGOGUE ELDERS

When Jesus heals synagogue members, the implication is that the synagogue elders are unable to heal and that Jesus is better and holier than the

15 Luke 2:49.

16 Matt 21: 12-17, Mark 11:15, Luke 19:45-47, John 2:13-22.

17 Matt 27:22-23.

elders. In the gospel of Matthew a synagogue leader "knelt before him (Jesus), saying, 'My daughter has just died; but come and lay your hand on her, and she will live.'"[18] The synagogue leader was chosen for a reason. The writers could have simply said that a man came to Jesus for help, implying the elder's inferiority. This dynamic becomes even clearer when we read it over and over again. The repetition effectively hacks away at the synagogue's prestige without attracting attention, as in Mark 1:23-27, 31:1-5, 5:35-42, Luke 4:31-34, 13:10-13, and in the Acts of the Apostles 3:8.

When Jesus' authority is questioned in the temple, the New Testament gives three accounts regarding the inability of the temple's chief priests, scribes and elders to answer his question.[19] Note similar passages in Matthew 21:23-27, Mark 11:27-33 and Luke 20:1-7.

The church leads the reader into believing that the synagogue elders are corrupt and that Jesus is holy. They refer to the synagogue leaders as hypocrites and accuse them of wanting attention for the sake of self-glorification, e.g., "So whenever you give alms, do not sound a trumpet before you, as the hypocrites do in the synagogues and in the streets, so that they be praised by others";[20] "And whenever you pray, do not be like the hypocrites; for they love to stand and pray in the synagogues and at the street corners, so that they may be seen by others."[21] The second quote states that clandestine prayer is preferable. The reader is taught that praying in secret is good and praying publicly is bad. Synagogue members pray in public so they are bad. In short, the church is good and the synagogue is bad. This may seem like a large step to take based on the two quotes above. These are, however, merely examples drawn from many New Testament passages, such as Matthew 23:6-13, Mark 12:38-40, Luke 20:45-47, John 12:42-43, and the Acts of the Apostles 5:17.

---

18 Matt 9:18.

19 Mark 11:28.

20 Matt 6:2.

21 Matt 6:5.

THE SYNAGOGUE AND DASTARDLY DEEDS

Another way that the church debases the synagogues is to talk about the unholy things that occur in synagogues. There are numerous cases of flogging in the synagogues and the temple. Note the warning in Matthew 10:16 to the missionaries to be careful lest they be flogged in the synagogue. In Matthew 23:34-35, the diatribe is taken even further:

> Therefore I send you prophets, sages, and scribes, some of whom you will kill and crucify, and some of whom you will flog in your synagogues and pursue from town to town, so that upon you may come all the righteous blood shed on earth, from the blood of righteous Abel to the blood of Zechariah son of Barachiah, whom you murdered between the sanctuary and the altar.

Not only do the authors of the gospels attack the synagogue. They also attack the history of the Jewish people as described in the Old Testament as this passage from Matthew does:

> Thus you testify against yourselves that you are descendants of those who murdered the prophets. Fill up then, the measure of your ancestors. You snakes, you brood vipers! How can you escape being sentenced to hell?[22]

The church has thus made an association between the synagogues and hell, the unholiest of unholy places. In his gospel, John talks about the rejection of Jesus in the temple. He goes into great detail depicting as savages those who frequent the temple. According to John they intended to stone Jesus, right in the temple.[23] The temple goers are depicted as barbarians who would desecrate their own holy place with an innocent's blood. These threats were realized upon the apostles, thus "They were convinced by him, and when they had called in the apostles, they had them flogged."[24] Stephen was stoned to death in the temple when he chastised the Jews for not respecting their prophets. He said, "You

22 Matt 23:31-33.

23 John 10:22-39.

24 Acts 5:39-40.

stiff-necked people, uncircumcised in heart and ears, you are forever opposing the Holy Spirit, just as your ancestors used to do."[25]

In Luke, Jesus predicts the persecution of his followers, initiated by the synagogue, and makes a parallel between synagogues and prisons.[26] The most explicit example of this negative rhetoric is in the book of Revelation 2:9: "I know…those who say that they are Jews and are not, but are a synagogue of Satan."

THE SYNAGOGUE AND THE SABBATH

Another way that the church chisels away at the sacredness of the synagogue is by demeaning Judaism's holy days. There are several passages where Jesus heals people from the synagogue on the Sabbath. The debate is always whether is it proper for Jesus to do this because it may be seen as working on the day of rest. In each passage the final conclusion is that it is. Stripping the sacredness from the Sabbath allows the church after the New Testament to set up an alternative day of rest, namely Sunday. Jesus explains that working in the field is permitted on the Sabbath since King David worked in the field when his companions were hungry.[27] Matthew degrades the Sabbath further by alluding to the Temple work that goes on during the Sabbath.[28]

At a dinner for Jesus, hosted by the Pharisees on the Sabbath, Jesus heals a man with dropsy. There is a debate whether this is permitted or not and Jesus silences the table with the following ironic statement: "If one of you has a child or an ox that has fallen into a well. Will you not immediately pull it out on the Sabbath? And they could not reply to this."[29]

BELITTLING LAWS AND TRADITIONS

Entrenched traditions are difficult to portray as unholy, but the church manages to do it anyway:

25 Acts 7:1-51.

26 Luke 21:12.

27 Mark 2:25.

28 Matthew 11:5-6.

29 Luke 14:5-6. See also Matthew 12:1-7, 12:9,Mark 2:23-28, Luke 13:10 and John 5:1-8.

> So the Pharisees and the scribes asked him, "Why do your disciples not live according to the tradition of the elders, but eat with defiled hands?" He said to them, "Isaiah prophesied rightly about you hypocrites, as it is written, 'This people honours me with their lips, but their hearts are far from me….' You abandon the commandment of God and hold to human tradition"…Then he called the crowd again and said to them, "Listen to me, all of you, and understand: there is nothing outside a person that by going in can defile, but the things that come out are what defile."[30]

Note the combination of techniques that the church uses to demean the synagogue. Referring to past scripture establishes Jesus' credibility. The elders look foolish because they are "outquoted" by Jesus. Their venerated traditions are then trumped by a higher authority, God. Lastly, Jesus ends with a neat aphorism; he says that it is not what goes in the mouth that matters, it is what comes out of it. The elders spoke of food but Jesus switches the context to words and is thus portrayed as running rhetorical circles around the synagogue elders.

THE DIASPORA

The first mention of a diaspora by the church is in the Acts of the Apostle: "That day a severe persecution began against the church and in Jerusalem, and all except the apostles were scattered throughout the countryside of Judea and Samaria."[31] The *Salutation* of Peter is addressed: "To the exiles of the Dispersion in Ponyus, Galatia, Cappadocia, Asia, and Bithynia, who have been chosen and destined by God the Father and sanctified by the Spirit to be obedient to Jesus Christ and to be sprinkled with his blood: May grace and peace be yours in abundance."[32] The church attempts to create a holy and chosen people by appealing to the idea of Jewish diaspora and concurrent suffering.

30 Mark 7:5-15.

31 Acts 8:1.

32 Peter 1:1-2.

THE CHURCH'S HOLY HISTORY

As the tension between the church and the synagogue increases, the new sect starts to distinguish itself from the synagogue. Paul, once known as Saul, begins this project. Inspired by a miracle, Paul sets out to spread the good news inspired by the Holy Spirit. In three journeys Paul successfully converts people to the new church in many different places all over the Mediterranean. These places included Caesarea, Tyre, Patara, Cyprus, Rhodes, Cos, Miletus, Ephesus, Thessalonica, Philippi, Troas, Antioch, Iconium, Lystra, Corinth, and Attalia. His legwork helps create a proud and distinct church legend.

Paul originally uses the synagogue as a platform to convert adherents: "The same thing occurred in Iconium, where Paul and Barnabas went into the Jewish Synagogue and spoke in such a way that a great number of both Jews and Greeks became believers. But the unbelieving Jews stirred up the Gentiles and poisoned their minds against the brothers."[33] In Corinth, however, the church moves outside the synagogue because of the resistance that Paul meets within it. This move symbolizes the new religion's purposeful distancing from its predecessor. Paul says:

> "Your blood be on your own heads! I am innocent. From now on I will go to the Gentiles." Then he left the synagogue and went to the house of a man named Titius Justus, a worshipper of God; his house was next door to the synagogue.[34]

The tension between the two institutions originates in the synagogue as well as in the church, as is apparent in this speech from Acts.

> "Fellow—Israelites, help! This is the man who is teaching everyone everywhere against our people, our law, and this place; more than that he has actually brought Greeks into the temple and has defiled this holy place."[35]

This is a rare example that demonstrates the position of the synagogue (from a Christian perspective however) vis-a-vis the church which is gradually gaining more authority and establishing itself.

---

33 Acts 14:1-2.

34 Acts 18:7.

35 Acts 21:28

Paul's travels are not unlike the early wanderings of Jesus. These proselytizing voyages are characteristic of the early church and become a huge part of the collective Christian psyche, a way to maintain unity throughout many different countries. The sacredness of sites around the Mediterranean, of course, does not take away from the holiness of Jerusalem. The problem for the church was that Jerusalem was primarily a Jewish site. The church adapted by creating a history to parallel the Jews, the church's diaspora, and then moved on. Any frustrations that the church may have had because they could not claim Jerusalem were not taken out on the holy place. Instead, they belittled the Jews who they believed were "wicked tenants." Jesus asks what the landowner will do when he returns, and says that the vineyard will be punished with a miserable death, and the vineyard will be left to other tenants "who will give him the produce at the harvest time." Jesus adds "Therefore I tell you, the kingdom of God will be taken away from you and given to a people that produce the fruits of the kingdom."[36]

In the book of Revelation the New Jerusalem is described: "I saw no temple in the city."[37] The church has a grand vision that shows Jerusalem as the holiest of the holy, with only Christians in it and without the temple. It is clear where the church stands. They would prefer everyone, except for Christians, to get out of Jerusalem.

NOSTALGIA FOR THE SYNAGOGUE

Not all of the New Testament subverts the synagogue. When one reads between the lines one detects a nostalgia for the synagogue. This is apparent in a comparison of the gospel of Luke and the other three gospels — of the Lord's Prayer in Luke and the Lord's Prayer in Matthew. In Luke the prayer reads: "Father, hallowed be your name. Your kingdom come..."[38] In Matthew it reads: "Our Father in heaven, hallowed be your name. Your kingdom come..."[39]

36 Matt 21:41, 43.

37 Rev 21:22.

38 Luke 11:2.

39 Matt 6:9-10.

In Luke's version, "heaven" is left out; heaven, the final Christian authority is omitted perhaps because the author of Luke is closer to Christianity's Jewish origins and sees no need to appeal to heaven. This tension between the establishment of the new (Christianity) and respect for the old (Judaism) is a constant theme in New Testament writing.

CONCLUSIONS

By mimicking the history and rituals of the synagogue, the New Testament writers attempt to make the new church holy. They belittle the synagogue and their elders and attack their traditions. At the same time however, the church works very hard to gain the same respect that the synagogue already possesses. They create a hierarchy, one in which God the heavenly father is at the top and access is only granted through faith in Jesus. Heaven trumps Jerusalem as the holiest of holies, and the stations on the apostles' voyages become alternative earthly sites for pilgramage. Through time the church acquires its own distinct sanctity — but births are never easy.

TALMUD AND MIDRASH

"IT WAS NOT ACCORDING TO THE WILL OF THE SAGES": HALAKHIC AND AGGADIC RESPONSES TO PINHAS' KILLING OF ZIMRI AND KOZBI IN NUMBERS 25

Laliv Clenman, Univeristy of Toronto

> And Pinhas, son of Eleazar, son of Aaron the priest, saw, and he rose from within the community and he took a spear in his hand. He came after the Israelite man, to the tent, and he pierced the two of them, the Israelite man and the woman in her belly.

So reads Numbers 25:7-8 as it tells of Pinhas' apparently spontaneous killing of the Israelite man and the Midianite woman who are understood to have been engaged in sexual relations. Pinhas' act is met with a wide range of reactions on the part of the Sages. This article will explore the range of rabbinic responses, both *halakhic* (legal) and *aggadic* (narrative), in the Mishna, Babylonian Talmud and Palestinian Talmud to Pinhas' killing of Zimri and Kozbi in Numbers 25.[1] I will argue that analysis of these rabbinic

1 I would like to thank Tirzah Meacham and Harry Fox for reviewing an early version of this paper, and Sarah Hayday for her careful reading of this article. Of the scholarly literature on the topic, the most interesting and relevant to this study includes: Christine Hayes' article: "Palestinian Rabbinic Attitudes to Intermarriage in Historical and Cultural Context," in *Jewish Culture and Society under the Christian Roman Empire*, ed. Richard Lee Kalmin and Seth Schwartz (Leuven: Peeters Publishers, 2003), 36-38, where she includes analysis of the passage in the Palestinian Talmud (Sanhedrin 27b) dealing with Pinhas' killing of Zimri and Kozbi. Also useful is Martin Hengel's *The Zealots: Investigations into the Jewish Freedom Movement in the Period from Herod I until 70 A.D.*,trans. David Smith (Edinburgh : T. & T. Clark, c1989), originally published in German: *Die Zeloten: Untersuchungen zur Juedischen Freiheitsbewegung*

texts dealing with Pinhas, Zimri and Kozbi reveals conflicting opinions about Pinhas' act and the legal and narrative traditions that came to be related to it. These reactions range from open rejection to ambivalence to justification and glorification of the killing. I will argue that even as they respond in a variety of ways, the sources betray a general rabbinic discomfort around Pinhas' killing and its literary and legal legacy. Rabbinic reception of the canonical textual traditions is ultimately uncomfortable and embarrassed, resulting in a rich literary tradition replete with layers of intertextual interpretations.[2]

Rabbinic tradition is engaging with a series of sources including biblical narrative, early rabbinic laws from the tannaitic era, and a variety of *halakhhic* and *aggadic* midrashic interpretive traditions. The central narrative begins one fine day in the Israelite camp, as the second half of Numbers 25 relates the following tale:[3]

NUMBERS 25:6-15:

ו וְהִנֵּה אִישׁ מִבְּנֵי יִשְׂרָאֵל בָּא, וַיַּקְרֵב אֶל-אֶחָיו אֶת-הַמִּדְיָנִית, לְעֵינֵי מֹשֶׁה, וּלְעֵינֵי כָּל-עֲדַת בְּנֵי-יִשְׂרָאֵל; וְהֵמָּה בֹכִים,
פֶּתַח אֹהֶל מוֹעֵד. ז וַיַּרְא, פִּינְחָס בֶּן-אֶלְעָזָר, בֶּן-אַהֲרֹן, הַכֹּהֵן; וַיָּקָם מִתּוֹךְ הָעֵדָה, וַיִּקַּח רֹמַח בְּיָדוֹ. ח וַיָּבֹא אַחַר אִישׁ-
יִשְׂרָאֵל אֶל-הַקֻּבָּה, וַיִּדְקֹר אֶת-שְׁנֵיהֶם — אֵת אִישׁ יִשְׂרָאֵל, וְאֶת-הָאִשָּׁה אֶל-קֳבָתָהּ; וַתֵּעָצַר הַמַּגֵּפָה מֵעַל בְּנֵי יִשְׂרָאֵל.
ט וַיִּהְיוּ, הַמֵּתִים בַּמַּגֵּפָה — אַרְבָּעָה וְעֶשְׂרִים אָלֶף. י וַיְדַבֵּר יְהוָה, אֶל-מֹשֶׁה לֵּאמֹר. יא פִּינְחָס בֶּן-אֶלְעָזָר בֶּן-אַהֲרֹן

---

in der Zeit von Herodes I bis 70n. Chr. (first ed. 1961, second edition 1976), where he deals with many traditions related to Pinhas and the Zealots. See also Hagith Zlotnick Sivan, "The rape of Cozbi (Numbers XXV)," *Vetus Testamentum*, 51,1 (2001): 69-80, and the recent publication by Paul Steinberg, "Phinehas: hero or vigilante?" *Jewish Bible Quarterly*, 35,2 (2007): 119-126. His article presents a general discussion of Numbers 25, the function of God's punishments in the chapter and in general, as well as Pinhas' role in the context of divine punishment.

2 On these notions of interpretation and anxiety see Harold Bloom, *The Anxiety of Influence:A Theory of Poetry* (New York: Oxford University Press), 1973; 2d ed., 1997 and *A Map of Misreading* (New York: Oxford University Press), 1975.

3 Note that the first section of Numbers 25 speaks of the Israelites and Moabites at Shittim, while the second relates to an encounter between an Israelite man and a Midianite woman. It would appear that the chapter is not cohesive. This has led to a conflation of the two events (the Moabites and the Midianite Kozbi) even within Numbers 25, but has also allowed for the incident involving Kozbi to be dealt with relatively independently in some rabbinic sources. An example of a thorough commentary is Baruch A. Levine, *Numbers 21-36: A New Translation with Introduction and Commentary* (The Anchor Bible, New York: Doubleday, 2000), 279-303.

הַכֹּהֵן, הֵשִׁיב אֶת-חֲמָתִי מֵעַל בְּנֵי-יִשְׂרָאֵל, בְּקַנְאוֹ אֶת-קִנְאָתִי בְּתוֹכָם; וְלֹא-כִלִּיתִי אֶת-בְּנֵי-יִשְׂרָאֵל, בְּקִנְאָתִי. יב לָכֵן,
אֱמֹר: הִנְנִי נֹתֵן לוֹ אֶת-בְּרִיתִי, שָׁלוֹם. יג וְהָיְתָה לּוֹ וּלְזַרְעוֹ אַחֲרָיו, בְּרִית כְּהֻנַּת עוֹלָם — תַּחַת אֲשֶׁר קִנֵּא לֵאלֹהָיו,
וַיְכַפֵּר, עַל-בְּנֵי יִשְׂרָאֵל. יד וְשֵׁם אִישׁ יִשְׂרָאֵל הַמֻּכֶּה, אֲשֶׁר הֻכָּה אֶת-הַמִּדְיָנִית — זִמְרִי, בֶּן-סָלוּא: נְשִׂיא בֵית-אָב,
לַשִּׁמְעֹנִי. טו וְשֵׁם הָאִשָּׁה הַמֻּכָּה הַמִּדְיָנִית, כָּזְבִּי בַת-צוּר: רֹאשׁ אֻמּוֹת בֵּית-אָב בְּמִדְיָן, הוּא.

25:6 And behold, a man of the Israelites came and brought the Midianite woman to his brothers, before the eyes of Moses and the eyes of the whole community of the Israelites. And they were crying at the opening of the tent of meeting. 7 And Pinhas,[4] son of Eleazar, son of Aaron the priest, saw, and he rose from within the community and he took a spear in his hand. 8 He came after the Israelite man, to the tent, and he pierced the two of them, the Israelite man and the woman in her belly.[5] And the plague was kept from the Israelites. 9 And the dead in the plague were 24,000. 10 God spoke to Moses saying: 11 Pinhas, son of Eleazar, son of Aaron the priest turned back my wrath from the Israelites in his being jealous with my jealousy[6] among them. And so I did not destroy the Israelites in my jealousy. 12 Therefore, say: I hereby give him my covenant, of peace.[7] 13 And it will be for him and his descendants after him an eternal priestly covenant, because he was jealous for his God and he atoned for the Israelites. 14 And the name of the Israelite man who was killed, the one who was killed with the Midianite woman was Zimri son of Salu, a chief of

4 Pinhas, with the "h" representing the Hebrew "*chet*" may also be transliterated Phinehas or Phineas.

5 Note the similarity between קֻבָתָהּ and הַקֻּבָּה. The first may be understood as "her belly", though the reading "her tent" is not impossible. Levine, in his translation, prefers "at her *qubbah*-tent" (281), whereas Koehler Baumgartner understand it as "stomach," while noting that it is a possible dittography. My translation follows the rabbinic interpretation of this term as referring either to Kozbi (and/or Zimri's) innards, womb or genitalia. See for example on Numbers 25:8, Targum Onkelos " למעהא " and Targum Neofiti " לגו מעיה" or the variant " בבית תורפה ." S.C. Reif, in his article "What Enraged Phinehas?: A Study of Numbers 25:8," *Journal of Biblical Literature*, Vol. 90, No. 2. (June, 1971): 200-206, suggests that the original meaning of the term was "her shrine," and that the translations that understand innards or womb are midrashic in origin. Milgrom in his commentary (*The JPS Torah Commentary: Numbers*. Philadelphia: Jewish Publication Society, 1990) suggests that this term refers to a marriage canopy (215, n.5).

6 Or zeal, so B.D.B. (*A Hebrew and English Lexicon of the Old Testament*, Oxford, 1975). For consistency with the end of the verse, I prefer translating the word as jealousy.

7 Jewish Publication Society *Tanakh* (Philadelphia: JPS, 1999): "of friendship." Levine prefers: "of fellowship" (281).

> a father's house of the Shimonites. 15 And the name of the woman who was killed, the Midianite woman, was Kozbi daughter of Tsur, who was a head of nations of a father's house in Midian.

This narrative in Numbers 25 lends itself well to midrashic explication in that it is powerful, complex and begs many questions. What are Zimri and Kozbi doing? Why does Pinhas kill them and on what authority? Where is Moses, and why are the people crying? Generally speaking, rabbinic tradition understands that Pinhas killed Zimri and Kozbi precisely because they were engaged in public sexual relations.[8] Moses is perceived as relatively passive or forgetful in comparison with Pinhas' quick, decisive, independent and violent action.[9] The text also poses a number of problems when contextualized within biblical law and narrative and later rabbinic developments. In particular, the vigilante killing of a couple because they are engaged in sexual relations has no obvious basis in biblical law, nor in normative rabbinic law, nor in narratives outside of this context. Important questions are raised regarding the role of divine inspiration, divine law, and individual authority in relation to the rabbinic legal system, rabbinic courts and legal precedent. Problems of lineage and identity also figure prominently, as the sources struggle with the complicated legacy of a variety of conflicting descent patterns and methods for determining identity and the boundaries for permissable relationships. The sources in question here all engage with these problems and their ramifications, simultaneously revealing and attempting to resolve the rabbinic discomfort and embarrassment resulting from this narrative tradition.

Based on a perusal of some rabbinic texts, such as the Mishna and sections of both Talmuds, one might assume that rabbinic law simply made use of this story as a basis or justification for a particular legal rule, namely Mishna Sanhedrin 9:6 and the law of the *boel aramit* or the one who has intercourse

8 Hengel states that Zimri and Kozbi were engaged in adulterous relations (147). I would argue that there is no basis whatsoever for this conclusion. Such an interpretation attempts to explain the violence of the attack through reference to adultery (a capital crime) rather than attempting to explore the case as it is.

9 Where the judicial process itself is critiqued it is perceived as overly deliberative, delayed, hesitant and uncertain, just as Moses is.

with an Aramean woman.[10] One might assume that the inclusion of permission to act as a zealot (or *qana*) and kill an Israelite man who is having sexual relations with an Aramean woman in the Mishna represents a categorical acceptance and integration of Numbers 25 and the law of the *boel aramit* in rabbinic tradition.

Closer study, however, suggests that there is evidence in the literature of a wide range of responses to this story, reflecting the multiplicity inherent in the developing rabbinic tradition, as well as the contradictions and gaps between Numbers 25 and certain rabbinic legal rules. There is evidence for the existence of conflicting opinions regarding Pinhas' act and the legal and narrative traditions that came to be related to it. Many of the *halakhic* and *aggadic* sources also reveal attempts to explore and resolve rabbinic discomfort with the killing,[11] either by ruling against such acts or by creating narratives that engage with problematic aspects of the killing. As Hengel notes rather delicately, "those in rabbinic circles who were concerned with the interpretation of Numbers 25 were confronted with certain difficulties" (168). Beginning with mSanhedrin 9:6 and the law of the *boel aramit*, and turning to sections from the Babylonian and the Palestinian Talmuds respectively, we will tease out these various reactions to this story about Pinhas, Zimri and Kozbi.[12]

The relevant section of Mishna Sanhedrin 9:6 reads as follows:

והבועל ארמית קנאין פוגעין בו...[13]

10 Hayes writes that the zealots of mSanhedrin 9:6, who kill the one who has relations with an Aramean woman, are modelled after Pinhas' act in Numbers 25 (Hayes 36).

11 Hayes describes what she calls rabbinic "anxiety" about the Bible containing "no more" than a partial prohibition of intermarriage. Rabbinic attempts to root related laws in ancient layers, along with a desire to "castigate" those involved thus stem from this anxiety (see Hayes 36). I have noted that this pattern continues into the period of the *Rishonim*.

12 Important parallels include: Targum Pseudo-Jonathan to Numbers 25, which includes a lengthy addition, Bamidbar Rabbah, Parashat Balaq, Pisqa 24-25 and Sifrei Bamidbar (Numbers) Parashat Balaq, Pisqa 131. These versions of the midrashim may be loosely grouped together, while the Palestinian Talmud, as we shall see, includes one particularly important unique tradition.

13 The reception and integration of this law into rabbinic *halakhah* is an interesting case. The rabbinic construction of the development of laws against marriage and sexual relations with Gentile women is highly convoluted and, in my view, evidence of the contradictory, incompatible, inconsistent, unclear and fragmentary state of law and narrative on the issue. The origin of the law of the *boel aramit*, and its relationship to other laws related to intermarriage

> ...And one who has intercourse with an Aramean woman: zealots attack him.

This mishna presents, in its typical style, a clear legal ruling: anyone who has intercourse with an Aramean woman is subject to an unusual kind of vigilante justice:[14] being killed by zealots. A zealot or *qana* has the right to kill a man engaged in such an act.[15] I would suggest that the law regarding one who has intercourse with an Aramean woman was strongly influenced by Numbers 25.[16] Numbers 25 is certainly used in the rabbinic literature to justify the

---

and sexual relations between Jews and Gentiles is, therefore, not at all clear. The rule of the *boel aramit* is generally understood to refer to sexual relations with a Gentile woman, as opposed to "marriage" with a Gentile woman (*zenut* vs. *ishut*). (Note, however, that marriage with a Gentile woman is invalid under rabbinic law, as Gentiles are unable to contract *kiddushin*.) With respect to the law of the *boel aramit*, rabbinic *halakhah* is concerned with the following main questions: is this law biblical in origin, does it refer to marriage-like connections or more cursory sexual relations, and does it apply to acts in private as well as in public? Prohibition of sexual relations is attributed in the literature to various sources, such as the court of Shem, the Hasmonean court and the words of the scribes, often with no connection to the rule of the *boel aramit* (see bSanhedrin 82a). Some later commentators argued that the law of the *boel aramit* applies to both public and private since the Hebrew Bible does not legally distinguish between the two spheres. Others argued that the rule applies only to public acts, with some arguing that private acts are instead punishable by *karet* (excision at the hands of heaven). The lack of immediacy of this divine punishment is understood to have been insufficient by some, and so earthly punishments were devised (see Rabbeinu Nissim to bSanhedrin 82a). In general, the later development of the *halakhah* reveals a preoccupation with a sense of powerlessness in the face of such acts. For references on the later halakhic development, see *Entsiklopediya Talmudit* (Yerushalayim: Yad ha-Rav Hertsog, Mekhon ha-Entsiklopediyah ha-Talmudit, 1984), 16, s.v. *boel aramit*.

14 The sources do not relate to the specificity of the Aramean identity. In rabbinic tradition this particular punishment is usually understood to apply to sexual relations with a Gentile woman in public. This term may be used as representative of Gentile. However, it may also indicate a process of transition from particularized national identities to a generalized Gentile other. This is in accordance with the view that Zimri and Kozbi were engaged in sexual relations either in full view of the whole congregation or in view of (and/or with) Zimri's kinsmen. This limitation of the rule to a public act, however, is not always clear in the sources.

15 It may be argued that the zealot has the right or option to do so but is not commanded to do so, such that this is not considered to be a positive commandment (see bSanhedrin 82a, Maimonides' *Mishneh Torah Issurei Biah* 12:4, and *Entsiklopediya Talmudit*, 15). The consequences of this distinction are important for laws of the *rodef*.

16 It is worth noting that we do find the use of the word jealous ones, or zealots, in both this mishna and Numbers 25:11. These terms describe an intense feeling of zeal or jealousy which

existence of the law of the *boel aramit*, as I will discuss below. In this way, an embarrassing law is rendered acceptable because of its supposed biblical source. The question of the actual origin of this mishna is, however, a more complicated matter. There is evidence that this rule existed in early rabbinic law in connection with Numbers 25, as we shall see in both Talmudim. We also find, however, sources that link the law of the *boel aramit* to other biblical laws, rather than linking it to the tale of Pinhas, such as the laws against Molekh worship, and the *bat el-nekhar*, while still others prefer to attribute bans against sexual relations with Gentile women to post-biblical decrees.[17] In short, there is no consensus as to the origin and development of the law of the *boel aramit*, or regarding its relationship to Numbers 25.

Following mSanhedrin 9:6, one could easily conclude that early rabbinic tradition stood solidly behind Pinhas and carried on this legal tradition as a normative *halakhic* rule. As we turn to the Babylonian and Palestinian Talmuds, however, we find that this rule existed in a context characterized by multiplicity and diversity, wherein the rabbis sometimes seem supportive, often ambivalent and occasionally opposed to Pinhas' killing of Zimri and Kozbi and to the Mishna's law permitting vigilante killings. Hengel sees mSanhedrin as an ancient tradition that was rejected in the Tannaitic period, a conclusion that is far too general.[18]

---

is felt by both God and Pinhas, and apparently also the zealots (or jealous ones) of the Mishna. See also Hengel on zeal (146, 149).

17 The interpretation tradition linking the *boel aramit* to Molekh is sometimes attributed to R. Ishmael (see Midrash Tannaim Devarim 18:9); a variation is found in Sifrei Devarim Pisqa 171, there brought in the name of R. Yehudah. Another scriptural connection is sometimes made to Malakhi 2:11-12 and the *bat el-nekhar*; see for example, bSanhedrin 82a. Other traditions make no scriptural link whatsoever; see for example bSanhedrin 82a where Rav Dimi and Ravin both state that they learned in Israel that the source of the *boel aramit* is a Hasmonean decree. One cause of the confusion here is the lack of clarity regarding the origins and nature of the ban on sexual relations (in public and in private) between Jews and Gentiles. It is clear that rabbinic tradition wants to see such a ban but is not entirely certain how to arrive at it.

18 Hengel argues that rabbinic rejection of this tradition was rooted in the actual negative outcomes of what he calls "Zeal for Law" during the first century CE in terms of political and social instability (177). It is important to note that the zeal of the *qana* is not so much a zeal for law, as it is an intense spontaneous emotion driven by moral compulsion and divine inspiration. Though the zealot is constructed outside of Numbers 25 as one who is adhering to a law, I would

Through an analysis of the Talmudic engagement with both Mishna Sanhedrin 9:6 and Numbers 25, a complex set of reactions is revealed. Beginning with the Babylonian Talmud, we find the following midrash which is *aggadic* in terms of genre but deals with a number of complex and important legal issues in a sophisticated manner.

bSANHEDRIN 82A

'ויאמר משה אל — שפטי ישראל' וגו (במדבר כה:ה). הלך שבטו של שמעון אצל זמרי בן סלוא. אמרו לו: הן דנין דיני נפשות שאתה יושב ושותק? מה עשה? עמד וקיבץ עשרים וארבעה אלף מישראל, והלך אצל כזבי. אמר לה: השמיעי לי! אמרה לו: בת מלך אני, וכן צוה לי אבי: לא תשמעי אלא לגדול שבהם. אמר לה: אף הוא נשיא שבט הוא, ולא עוד אלא שהוא גדול ממנו, שהוא שני לבטן והוא שלישי לבטן. תפשה בבלוריתה, והביאה אצל משה. אמר לו: בן עמרם! זו אסורה או מותרת? ואם תאמר אסורה - בת יתרו מי התירה לך? נתעלמה ממנו הלכה. געו כולם בבכיה, והיינו דכתיב (במדבר כ"ה:ו) "והמה בכים פתח אהל מועד". וכתיב, (במדבר כ"ה:ז) 'וירא פנחס בן אלעזר'. מה ראה? אמר רב: ראה מעשה, ונזכר הלכה. אמר לו: אחי אבי אבא, לא כך לימדתני ברדתך מהר סיני: הבועל את הכותית[19] קנאין פוגעין בו!? אמר לו: קריינא דאיגרתא איהו ליהוי פרוונקא.

"Moses said to the judges of Israel... [let each man kill his men who are tied to Baal Peor]"(Numbers 25:5). The tribe of Shimon went to Zimri ben Salu. They said to him: They are sitting in judgment over capital cases, and you sit and are silent!? He [Zimri] stood and he gathered twenty-four thousand of Israel and went to Kozbi.[20] He said to her: Obey me! She said to him: I am a king's daughter and so has my father commanded me: do not obey any but the greatest among them. He said to her [that] he was also a tribal chief, and not only that but he was greater than him [Moses], for he is second from the belly [i.e. the womb] and he [Moses] is third from the belly. He caught her by

suggest that the zealot in fact eschews the legal context, rules and procedures. The zealot acts on the basis of a direct connection to the divine without regard for the law or its institutions.

19 This terminology is variable due to censorship, and all terms refer generally to a category of Gentile women. Other versions have: *haboel nokhrit.*

20 Twenty-four thousand is also the number killed in the plague. In this way, the midrash explains (and justifies) the large number of Israelites killed because of Zimri and Kozbi's actions. This demonstrates some discomfort on their part with the scale of the casualties, perhaps in relation to the severity of the crime.

> her braid and brought her to Moses.[21] He said to him: Son of Amram! Is she[22] [Kozbi] forbidden or permitted? And if you say forbidden, who permitted you to the daughter of Jethro?[23]
>
> He [Moses] forgot the halakhah [and] they all burst into tears, as it is written: "And they were crying at the opening of the tent of meeting." (Numbers 25:6) And it is written: "And Pinhas ben Eleazar saw." (Numbers 25:7) What did he see? Rav said: He saw the act, and remembered the halakhah. He said to him [Pinhas to Moses]: My brother, of my father's father, did you not teach me thus upon your descent from Mount Sinai: One who has intercourse with the Gentile woman, zealots attack him! He said to him [Moses to Pinhas]: The reader of the letter [i.e. Pinhas] — let *him* be the messenger.[24]

These midrashim brought by the Babylonian Talmud serve a number of purposes. From a narrative perspective, they provide a back story connecting the story of Baal Peor (Numbers 25:1-6) to that of Zimri and Kozbi which follows, as well as filling in the personality and motivations of Zimri, explaining the reason for the community's tears as well as Moses' inaction and Pinhas' lethal zeal. These are not merely narrative flourishes, however, as they represent a process of legal interpretation. The midrash explicitly links the narrative of Numbers 25 to the rule of mSanhedrin 9:6 and more generally to the issue of intermarriage, all the while rewriting the narrative such that Pinhas is acting in accordance with rabbinic law. The midrash constructs a comparison between Zimri and Pinhas' ancestral and political status, as well as between the various characters' connections to intermarriage. Underlying this competition is a legal dialogue regarding the rules and narrative traditions

21 Note that this midrash implies a non-consensual act. Even after he attempts to convince her, he grabs her. Sivan discusses the aspect of sexual violation in more detail with reference to the case of Dinah.

22 Literally, "this one."

23 Jethro was a Midianite priest.

24 Here, Moses indirectly tells Pinhas that he should act in accordance with the Mishnaic law of the *boel aramit*. According to rabbinic tradition, a vigilante may not be instructed to kill and must act spontaneously of his own accord. Therefore, Moses could not be the one to direct Pinhas in his zeal.

regulating intermarriage and for determining the identity of the children of such marriages. This reaches its climax as Zimri dares to challenge Moses himself,[25] asking the seminal question: "Is she forbidden or permitted?" The midrash puts a crucial question in Zimri's mouth: Is a Midianite woman, not specifically prohibited anywhere in the Hebrew Bible, permitted in marriage (or in sexual relations)? And if she is not, how can it be that Moses himself has married Tsipporah, also a Midianite woman?[26]

These midrashim use a variety of techniques to deal with the problem of the legal status of marriage and sexual relations[27] between an Israelite man and a Midianite woman.[28] The apparent contradiction between Moses' marriage and Zimri's connection with Kozbi and the lack of a clear biblical ruling on intermarriage or on Midianites specifically, create a confusing legal situation. The midrash raises these problems of its own accord and seeks to resolve them through the interpretive process the discomfort and embarrassment that they cause. Using the device of "*nitalmah mimenu halakhah*," or "[Moses] forgot the *halakhah* [law]," the midrash attempts to construct this legal tradition as authentic, authoritative and decisive. This phrase suggests that Moses forgot the *halakhah* or more literally, that the *halakhah* disappeared from him. The suggestion is that Moses' apparent inaction in the narrative as it is presented in Numbers 25 as well as in the midrash brought in the Babylonian Talmud, does not indicate that this law (that called for Pinhas to kill Zimri and Kozbi) did not exist at that time, or that there were any problems or contradictions between it and its legal and narrative context, or that it was not part of the revelation. To the contrary, it was explicitly given as part of revelation. The rationale for

25 Compare to Numbers 12 where Moses is challenged for his marriage to a Cushite woman. In that case, rabbinic tradition categorically refuses to understand Miriam's critique as an opposition to Moses' intermarriage and erases the issue of intermarriage from the narrative.

26 See Numbers 12:1.

27 While halakhic tradition usually understands the *boel aramit* to refer only to sexual relations of a non-marital type in public (this is how Rashi understands the situation; see Rashi bSanhedrin 82a to mSanhedrin 9:6), this midrash clearly relates it to the issue of intermarriage.

28 Note the merging of the nationally specific identities of Midianite and Aramean in some rabbinic sources. There appears to be a trend away from the particularized identities of the Hebrew Bible, towards an undifferentiated *other* in the rabbinic sources, though it should be noted, as I have argued elsewhere, that many rabbinic sources maintain such identity categories.

Moses' inaction is that he has forgotten the rule. Pinhas therefore reminds Moses of the rule of the *boel aramit*, and Pinhas is then empowered to act[29] as one of the zealots or *qanaim*[30] mentioned in the Mishna (with careful adherence to the rules that zealots are subject to in rabbinic tradition, namely that they cannot be instructed to kill, but must act of their own spontaneous feeling).

The midrash thus positions the rule of Mishna Sanhedrin 9:6 as a *halakhah* that was known from the time of revelation at Sinai. The *aggadah* (narrative) grounds a *halakhah* (law) in the most authoritative level, despite the fact that there is no record of this rule *per se* in the Hebrew Bible. Each is thus used to justify the other in a circular argument: Pinhas' vigilante killing is supported by the Mishna's law, and the Mishna's law is in turn supported by his killing — evidence of the rule's early origins in divine revelation. In this revised narrative, Moses is supposed to have told Pinhas regarding the rule of the *boel aramit: qanaim pogim bo* (the one who has intercourse with an Aramean woman: zealots attack him) on the occasion of his descent from Mount Sinai. Moses, having forgotten the law, and having been subsequently reminded of it by Pinhas, alludes to the fact that Pinhas may take the role of the zealots or *qanaim* with respect to Zimri.[31] Pinhas, of the priestly line, thus becomes a repository, not only for *halakhic* action, but *halakhic* knowledge, authority and memory.[32] The

29 Technically, Pinhas does not need to consult with anyone, nor should he, in order to act as a *qana* in this situation. This interpretive element, however, is important because it confirms the divine origin of the law, as well as explaining why Moses did not act.

30 Hengel argues that the title Zealot was probably derived directly from that of "Phinehas the Zealot" (Hengel 174).

31 This section follows the halakhic positions on how *qanaim pogim bo* functions. This part of the midrash may be an attempt to accommodate the rabbinic rule that one may not instruct a person to act as a '*qana*.' Indeed, the act of Pinhas in Numbers 25 seems to have been such a spontaneous vigilante reaction. In contrast, the midrash suggests that some discussion and suggestion occurred prior to the act.

32 Note that this midrash, found elsewhere anonymously, is here attributed to Rav. Shmuel, in a midrash brought next in the passage, holds that Pinhas did not consult with Moses before killing Zimri and Kozbi (Sanhedrin 82a) because it was a case of *hilul hashem*, or "desecration of God," requiring immediate action without discussion, even though Moses was his "rav." The understanding of public sexual relations with a Gentile woman as *hilul hashem* could ultimately be the main problem with Zimri's act (from a rabbinic perspective). Understanding Zimri and Kozbi's act as *hilul hashem* neatly avoids the general issue of intermarriage by viewing the act as a far more severe violation.

primary function of this approach is to shore up both the biblical narrative and the rabbinic law, revealing the rabbinic discomfort with both Pinhas' act and mSanhedrin 9:6. Pinhas' act and the rule of the *boel aramit* both need to be supported and justified precisely because, from a rabbinic perspective, each is problematic, lacking in legal authority and potentially unjustifiable.

The midrash is not merely concerned with the formalities of justifying the biblical story and the Mishnaic rule. It expresses a deeper anxiety regarding intermarriage in general. This appears to be a general question about sexual relations/marriage with a Midianite woman (rather than a more specific concern about sexual relations with Gentile women in public). This interpretation is further supported by Zimri's subsequent question, which addresses Moses' own intermarriage. The midrash thus responds to the contradiction between a biblical record that appears to permit (or at least does not explicitly prohibit) marriage between Midianites and Israelites,[33] and a rabbinic rule that calls for the killing of an Israelite who has intercourse with an Aramean woman. It also addresses the internal biblical inconsistency between Moses' apparently accepted marriage to the Midianite Tsipporah[34] and the rejection of Zimri's actions with the Midianite Kozbi.[35] Pinhas, however, kills Zimri and spares Moses, which suggests that *qanaim pogim bo* (zealots attack him) applies only to Zimri and not to Moses, even though Moses himself is married to a Midianite. The midrash does not supply a clear reason for this, be it the distinction between public and private, between marital and non-marital sexual relations or otherwise.[36] In the final analysis, aside from rendering

33 The Midianites are not explicitly forbidden in marriage in the Hebrew Bible. Hayes, "Intermarriage and Impurity in Ancient Jewish Sources," *The Harvard Theological Review* 92:1 (1999):6, offers a concise presentation of prohibition and permission of intermarriage in the Hebrew Bible.

34 See, however, Numbers 12, which may be understood as a rejection of Moses' intermarriage, though it is not received as such in rabbinic tradition.

35 This is not to suggest, of course, that the relationship between Zimri and Kozbi was necessarily the same as that between Moses and Tsipporah, or that the threat posed by Zimri's and Kozbi's actions was an element also found in Moses' union. I would speculate that it may be that Zimri's action involved some political link to the Midianites that had military or social significance, while Moses' marriage to Tsipporah had no such connection.

36 Note that Ginzberg, for example, explains the problem of why the rule of the *boel aramit* does not apply to Moses by claiming that Moses married Tsipporah prior to revelation, and so is exempt from the rule (781, n.791). While there are midrashic traditions that have Moses divorce

Pinhas' actions acceptable, this midrash does not explicitly answer Zimri's question or resolve any of the problems related to it. Rather, the questions are left hanging as the Talmud moves to the next midrash, which constructs a legal framework for Pinhas' actions. With this next midrash, bSanhedrin 82b continues with additional traditions that betray an ambivalence towards Pinhas' act. As in the case of the previous midrash, this source points to a discomfort that lies deeper than the problems of legal contradictions, to a more fundamental embarrassment with Pinhas' action in the narrative. There are clear elements of praise, combined with obvious attempts to deal with their own displeasure with or disapproval of Pinhas' sudden violent vigilanteism. This passage relates some of the details of Pinhas' killing of Zimri and Kozbi through a series of statements attributed to Rabbi Yohanan that list the miracles enacted for Pinhas in that moment (bSanhedrin 82b). These include that Zimri could have separated from Kozbi, but did not.[37] Other miracles include that Zimri could have called for help and did not, that Pinhas attacked Zimri and Kozbi in their genitals, that their bodies did not fall off the spear, that an angel came and lifted the lintel so that Pinhas could pass through the doorway (with them still on the spear) and that an angel came and destroyed the people.

These rabbinic rules and the set of miracles may also serve to restrict the actions of the vigilante, as Christine Hayes has suggested. She argues that this midrash "places a strong burden on would-be zealots."[38] These conditions

---

Tsipporah or stop having sexual relations with her after revelation, in my view it is not at all clear that those midrashim do so because of concerns about intermarriage. Rather, emphasizing Moses' ascetic approach to sexuality seems to be the main purpose. This approach is part of a general valuation of sexual control in the *aggadic* midrashim. My argument is supported by the fact that our midrash does not answer Zimri's question in this way (i.e., it does not say that it is permitted for Moses because his marriage was before revelation).

37 According to rabbinic law, Pinhas must have warned Zimri before killing him; this despite the *sugya*'s discussion of the miracles, which clearly describes Pinhas' deceptions in his effort to approach and kill Zimri by surprise. According to Jewish law, if Zimri had separated from Kozbi, Pinhas would not have been permitted to kill him, and if he had tried Zimri could have killed Pinhas in self-defense (bSanhedrin 82a).

38 Hayes 37. She offers a tantalizing parallel in Roman law; see 38, n. 54, citing Susan Tregiari in *Roman Marriage: Iusti Coniuges from the Time of Cicero to the Time of Ulpian* (Oxford: Clarendon Press 1991), 282, wherein a father was permitted, upon discovery of his daughter engaged in adulterous relations in his house, to kill both the adulterer and his daughter under the condition that he kill them both with the same blow.

would, practically speaking, make it very difficult for a zealot to bring about his punishment without miraculous assistance (though presumably a true zealot would believe that such miraculous assistance would come just as it did for Pinhas). This is part of the rabbinic tradition's deflation of Pinhas, in contrast to his treatment in Jubilees and Second Temple sources, where Hayes finds a valorization of his act combined with an encouragement of similar actions.[39] She further argues (about interpretive traditions related to Lev. 18:21) that the Rabbis had a "general discomfort with zealots and the severity of punishment called for in the text — execution by an extra-legal agency."[40]

One might take this argument a step further by breaking down this discomfort into its constituent elements. First is the severity of the application of capital punishment. Rabbinic traditions are generally uncomfortable with the notion that intermarriage and sexual relations between Jews and non-Jews be punishable by death, and do not tend to understand intermarriage *per se* or sexual relations between Jew and Gentile as falling under the rubric of the capital punishments of Leviticus 25.[41] Hengel argues more generally that the Pharisees were hesitant to impose the death penalty (though this is based on Josephus; see Antiquities 13:294) and argues, following mMakkot 1:10[42] and Finkelstein's "The Pharisees"[43] that this trend only increased through the second century CE.[44] He argues further that mSahnedrin 9:6 became "difficult to justify" because it was "no longer in accordance with the later principles of the law."[45] In terms of broader principles (as opposed to the more specific

39 Hayes 38.

40 Hayes 40, n.58.

41 Notable exceptions are Sifra Aharei Mot and some of the traditions related to the worship of the Molekh. Note that Sifra does not relate to Numbers 25 and the traditions related to Molekh are very diverse in their textual connections, with only some of them referring to Numbers 25.

42 The latter part of the mishna clearly indicates a reluctance on the part of R. Eliezer b. Azariah, R. Tarfon and R. Akiva to enact the death penalty, while Rabban Shimon ben Gamliel argues for the deterrent value of executions.

43 Louis Finkelstein, *The Pharisees: the Sociological Background of their Faith* (Philadelphia: Jewish Publication Society of America, 1962).

44 Hengel 168, n.124.

45 Hengel 168.

limitations placed on vigilante killings) I would argue instead that mSanhedrin 9:6 was never in accordance with general halakhic principles or even with the legal rules and systems relating to intermarriage (or sexual relations between Jews and Gentiles) and continues to exist as a rather irregular rule throughout the development of rabbinic tradition.

The vigilante nature of the killing is yet another source of discomfort.[46] I would argue that the rabbinic legal system is struggling with the canonization of vigilante capital punishment. It is hardly surprising that such an elaborately conceived legal system, or systems, would be uncomfortable with giving the legal stamp of approval to an extra-legal act. Hengel argues along these lines, writing that Pharisaic law attempted to limit the option of vigilante killing to cases where the persons were caught in the act. This is part of a divide that Hengel sees between the Pharisaic courts and the zealots' notions of "due process."[47] In terms of the development of rabbinic tradition, I would suggest that ideological and practical problems are caused by the integration of vigilante justice into the mishnaic and later traditions, a type of justice which circumvents rabbinic legal context, reasoning and procedure.[48] For the vigilante, zealot or *qana*, divine inspiration overrides legal procedures, which, as Hengel points out, were often under foreign control. While such legal courts were limited in their jurisdiction and independence, they may have also been perceived as relatively lenient or unable to implement punishment.[49] The application of a rabbinic legal framework to the zealot laws removes much

46 Paul Steinberg, in his article, "Phinehas: hero or vigilante?" (*Jewish Bible Quarterly*, 35,2 [2007]: 119-126), states briefly that, "The most common reaction to Phinehas' act is discomfort. That is, despite the fact that God is content and the sin expiated, Phinehas acted as a vigilante. Not surprisingly, the rabbis of the Talmud distinctly express such a discomfort." (126) He notes as evidence of this discomfort ySanhedrin 27b, and bSanhedrin 82a. Regarding the latter, however, he writes that "82a states that although God's law finds what Phinehas did acceptable, the rabbis do not follow that law." (126, n.10) In my view, the *sugya* does include a number of halakhic checks and balances on vigilante killings, and demonstrates a discomfort with such killings, but it does not actually reject such killings or the law of the *boel aramit*.

47 Hengel 168-169, n. 125.

48 Hengel argues that after the exile, "law came between the individual and God as the norm of man's relationship to God." (154)

49 Hengel 174, n.147.

of their spontaneity, and mediates the zealot's direct connection to the divine through rabbinic *halakhah*.[50]

Another midrash included in this *sugya* raises the problem of the ambiguity of the rules on intermarriage. Rather than praising Pinhas' action, as the many miracles would have us expect, the community here ridicules Pinhas as a hypocrite, while God must come to his defence. Where Zimri challenged Moses in the earlier midrash above, here the people challenge Pinhas. The *sugya* thus compares Moses, Pinhas and Zimri with respect to their connections to intermarriage.

BABYLONIAN TALMUD 82B

התחילו שבטים מבזין אותו: ראיתם בן פוטי זה, שפיטם אבי אמו עגלים לעבודת כוכבים, והרג נשיא שבט מיש-ראל?! בא הכתוב ויחסו: 'פנחס בן אלעזר בן אהרן הכהן.' (במדבר כה:יא). אמר לו הקדוש ברוך הוא למשה: הקדם לו שלום, שנאמר (במדבר כ"ה:יב) לכן אמר הנני נותן לו את בריתי שלום. וראויה כפרה זו שתהא מכפרת והולכת לעולם.

The tribes began to mock him:[51] Have you seen this son of Puti, whose mother's father fattened calves for idol worship, and he has killed a leader of a tribe of Israel?! Scripture came and relayed to him [his lineage]:[52] Pinhas the son of Eleazar the son of Aaron the Kohen (Numbers 25:11). The Holy One Blessed be He said to Moses: Greet him with peace, as it is said: So He said: I hereby give him my covenant of peace (Numbers 25:12). And this atonement is fit to continue atoning forever.

This exegesis brings up yet another instance of intermarriage involving prominent Israelites. Here, Pinhas' mother is thought to have been a daughter of Putiel (Exodus 6:25).[53] Though there is no specific basis for this in the

50 It should be noted that the rabbinic laws also serve to protect the independence of the zealot from outside instruction or interference, perhaps indicating an ambivalent response to the problem of divine inspiration that nullifies the authority of the rabbinic court and contradicts rabbinic normative law.

51 Or: sneer at him, spurn him, mock him.

52 Note it is Scripture and not the divine *per se* that is the actor here.

53 Following Exodus we have no information as to Putiel's origins, but Exodus Rabbah understands him and Jethro to be one and the same. A question worthy of further inquiry is why the

text, the midrash clearly understands that Pinhas himself descended from an intermarriage with a Midianite.[54] In light of Pinhas' own Midianite heritage, his killing of a leader of an Israelite tribe (himself presumably not of mixed heritage) on account of his having relations with a Midianite woman seems hypocritical indeed. Moreover, according to Mishna Kiddushin 3:12, which rules that the offspring of a union between an Israelite man and a Gentile woman takes the Gentile status of its mother, Pinhas would be deemed a Midianite.[55] Perhaps in response to this legal problem, God himself relates his ancestry according to the male line, going back to Aaron. In this manner, the midrash interprets the biblical text in such a way as to dismiss the challenge of matrilineal descent in favor of the patrilineal transmission of priestly and tribal identity, reaffirming the core pattern of transmitting identity from father to son. The recitation of Pinhas' patrilineal lineage avoids the status of any female ancestors, rendering matrilineal connections irrelevant, and ultimately asserting the integrity of the male line and of patrilineal descent in cases of intermarriage with Gentile women.[56] This position flies in the face of the rule of matriliny in intermarriage, as articulated in mKiddushin 3:12.

Sages construct this genealogy for Pinhas. If it is simply because they do not know who Putiel is, why choose this mixed heritage? I would suggest that the *aggadah* on intermarriage actively engages with legal problems, and may here be deliberately creating a challenge between the traditions of patrilineal and matrilineal descent in cases of intermarriage.

54 Jethro was a Midianite. (I tentatively suggest that there may be a link between this midrash and the principle of *kol haposel pasul*, or "all who declare others unfit are themselves unfit.") Hengel writes that the problem was his "insignificant origin," stemming from his mother's lineage, a daughter of "an idolatrous priest who converted." (156-157, n. 66) I would suggest that Hengel's analysis overlooks the main force behind the midrash and the legal complexities that it raises. Such a construction of conversion stems from a discomfort or embarrassment with intermarriage in the received textual tradition in the aggadic material, as I argue in my dissertation.

55 Through the rule of matrilineal descent, Pinhas would take on the status of his mother. Rabbinic tradition generally superimposes rabbinic conversion over biblical intermarriages, such that the Gentile woman becomes a female convert. If we look at the narrative through this lens, Pinhas is the offspring of a female convert and an Israelite man. Following the the law of *pagum* or "blemished" in mKiddushin 3:12 (wherein descent follows the blemished parent), he would probably take the status of the blemished parent, in this case his convert mother.

56 The *halakhic* argument might also be slightly more specific: accepting the offspring of intermarriages where the father is an Israelite and identifying such offspring according to patrilineal descent, while taking a stand against public sexual relations with Gentile women. A stand against any public sexual relations would be expected.

Turning now to the Palestinian Talmud, we find that its engagement with the narrative of Numbers 25 and with the law of the *boel aramit* is far more limited than that of the Babylonian Talmud. The Palestinian Talmud, while it presents two brief familiar midrashim, is particularly notable for its inclusion of unique material, as well as for the various traditions (the miracles, the challenges to Moses and Pinhas) that are missing.

PALESTINIAN TALMUD SANHEDRIN 27B

הלכה יא

הבועל ארמית: תני רבי ישמעאל: זה שהוא נושה גויה ומוליד בנים מעמיד אויבים ממנה למקום. כתיב: 'וירא פינחס בן אלעזר בן אהרן הכהן' (במדבר כה:ז). מה ראה? ראה את המעשה ונזכר להלכה: 'הבועל ארמית הקנאים פוגעין בהן'. תני שלא כרצון חכמים. ופינחס שלא כרצון חכמים?! אמר רבי יודה בר פזי: ביקשו לנדותו אילולי שקפצה עליו רוח הקודש ואמרה: 'והיתה לו ולזרעו אחריו ברית כהונת עולם' וגו' (במדבר כה:יג).

Law 11:

"One who has intercourse with an Aramean woman": R. Yishmael teaches: This is one who marries a Gentile woman and has children; he raises enemies of the Lord from her. It is written: "And Pinhas the son of Eleazar the son of Aaron the priest saw." (Numbers 25:7) What did he see? He saw the act and remembered the *halakhah*: "One who has intercourse with an Aramean woman, the zealots attack them."[57] It is taught that this is not according to the will of the Sages. But [could it be] that Pinhas did not act according to the will of the Sages!? Rabbi Yudah bar Pazi said: They [would have] sought his punishment,[58] were it not for the holy spirit which leapt upon him and said: "And it will be for him and his descendants after him an eternal priesthood..." (Numbers 25: 13)

The treatment of the *boel aramit (*one who has intercourse with an Aramean woman) in ySanhedrin 27b is interesting in that it combines a number of approaches. The *sugya* first brings a statement in the name of R. Yishmael that

57 Note that all sources seem to assume that the Aramean woman represents all Gentile women. The importance and relevance of particular national or ethnic identities so prevalent in the Hebrew Bible appears to have waned.

58 Probably referring to a ban, removal or excommunication.

the *boel aramit* is one who has children by a Gentile woman. He is considered to be raising enemies of the God. This midrash is then attached to a verse from Numbers 25 and to Pinhas' killing of Zimri and Kozbi. This is a somewhat difficult connection thematically, given that Zimri and Kozbi were killed during the act and so presumably did not have any children at all (though sexual intercourse might more generally be linked to reproduction).[59] It may be that the core midrash links the law of the *boel aramit* to the levitical laws against passing seed over to *Molekh*, rather than to Numbers 25.

Indeed, the verse in Numbers 25 is not connected to R. Yishmael's statement so much as it is to the following midrash, quite similar to one included in bSanhedrin. Here we find an anonymous midrash to Numbers 25:7 that uses the notion of the memory of perhaps the most authoritative moment of divine revelation in order to construct a history of origins for the *boel aramit*. The verse merely states that "Pinhas saw," begging the question of what exactly he saw. The midrash explains that he saw the "act" (i.e. Zimri's sexual relations with Kozbi). Upon seeing the act, the midrash explains, Pinhas remembered the law of the *boel aramit*. This midrash claims that *boel aramit* was an ancient legal tradition, and that upon remembering it, Pinhas decided to take action in accordance with it. Rather than positioning Pinhas as a vigilante acting alone out of a sudden jealous feeling, this midrash paints him as knowledgeable in the legal tradition and zealous in upholding it. This revisionist approach neatly (if artificially) connects Mishna and Bible by understanding the law in mSanhedrin 9:6 as the driving force behind Pinhas'

59 The midrash's use of the term marriage in the case of a union with a Gentile woman is of interest. Hayes offers an interesting interpretation of R. Ishmael's interpretation of the *boel aramit*. She argues that the mention of marriage serves to limit the application of the rule to this specific case and "signals a rabbinic aversion to the notion of zealous assaults on those who engage in casual and nonreproductive intercourse." (36) The rationale for this, according to Hayes, is that what she calls a "moral-religious danger" presented by intermarriage *per se* is not present in non-marital/non-procreative relationships. Note, however, that there does not appear to be any evidence that the paradigmatic case of Zimri and Kozbi is understood to involve marriage. Hayes notes, in relation to rabbinic traditions on Leviticus 18:21 (Molekh), that rabbinic tradition is characterized by a "general discomfort with zealots and the severity of punishment called for in the text — execution by an extra-legal agency." (40, n.58) I would emphasize that it may not be (only) the severity of the punishment (in the case of the *boel aramit*) that disturbed them, but the vigilante nature of the punishment, what Hayes calls an "extra-legal agency." It is hardly surprising that rabbinic tradition would be uncomfortable with extra-legal killings.

action in the biblical story. This particular midrash is unquestioningly approving of Pinhas' act, constructing his spontaneous violent response as normative law. Unlike the similar midrash that appears in bSanhedrin, no attempt is made here to bring Pinhas' act in line with the details of rabbinic law on such matters. In addition, ySanhedrin does not relate to Moses or his supposed forgetfulness, preferring to focus exclusively on Pinhas, suggesting a reluctance to use criticism of Moses in order to solve the legal and narrative conundrum.

The Palestinian Talmud diverges even further from bSanhedrin as it immediately questions the authoritative normativity it has just constructed by quoting an anonymous *baraita*[60] that states that Pinhas' killing of Zimri and Kozbi was in fact against the will of the Sages. Here I understand this very short statement to be originating from the Tannaitic tradition, and to be referring to the rabbis. I therefore suggest that we have an early rabbinic statement[61] recording opposition to Pinhas' act.[62] The Palestinian Talmud has thus positioned, on the one hand, the argument that Pinhas represented and acted according to the normative authoritative law of the Sages, while on the other it positions the argument that his action was not in accordance with the position of the Sages at all. The problem posed by these two contradictory traditions that it has juxtaposed is met with a statement of incredulity and doubt, questioning whether it would even be conceivable for Pinhas to have

60 An extra-mishnaic statement.

61 Or at the very least a statement masquerading as an early rabbinic ruling.

62 Note, however, that Hayes refers to this passage as demonstrating the disapproval of the Amoraim (36) and Hengel understands the Sages to be "the members of the 'Synhedrium' of the time, including Moses" while in n.126 he calls it a protest of the scribes" (169). Though the term *tani* (i.e. repeat, teach) here does not necessarily indicate a statement of tannaitic origin, this cannot be ruled out, and it would not be unreasonable to understand it as such. Hengel also argues that mSanhedrin 9:6 was rejected in the tannaitic period, presumably referring to this source in yTalmud. Hengel also calls the Palestinian Talmud's criticism "hidden", which hardly seems to be the case. In my view this statement clearly refers to a tannaitic, or possibly amoraic rabbinic opposition to Pinhas' act, an open expression of the discomfort and embarrassment reflected in the broader literature. The more interesting question is that if Pinhas' act was rejected (as much as possible) by the Palestinian Sages (or at least some segment thereof), we certainly find no suggestion to that effect in the Mishna, and this tradition is not carried in any other source I have found. It is unfortunate that Tosefta does not offer any readings on this issue. There may be an argument to be made from its silence.

done something against the will of the Sages. Since God himself approves of Pinhas' act in Numbers 25:11,[63] one is led to imagine the Sages in disagreement with God, a difficult position to be sure. Are we to understand from this statement that the Sages disagree with Mishna Sanhedrin 9:6? And if the Sages do disagree with Mishna Sanhedrin 9:6, then who supports it? ySanhedrin resolves the problem arising from these two very different traditions on Pinhas' act by confirming that the Sages did indeed disapprove of Pinhas' act. Futhermore, they would have punished Pinhas on account of it,[64] had not God intervened and promised him the priesthood. This *baraita* is thus accepted as authentic, and the Sages are portrayed as having to put up with an act to which they were fundamentally opposed. Following this tradition, there is something in Pinhas' act that flies in the face of (at least one) rabbinic tradition. His killing of Zimri and Kozbi is unacceptable and opposed by the rabbis. Ultimately, however, this rabbinic tradition that would have seen Pinhas judged and sentenced is trumped by divine intervention.

Despite the fact that the opposition to Pinhas' act is ultimately deflected, it represents a unique record of a clear opposition. This may reflect a difference between the Palestinian and Babylonian traditions, though it should be noted that such a clear legal statement is not recorded in any other extant source. In her analysis, Hayes remarks that Pinhas "is less clearly a hero for this Palestinian authority — indeed he borders on dangerous."[65] Hengel notes that "a completely positive assessment of Phinehas' action (Sifre Numbers and Numbers Rabbah) can be contrasted with a cautiously negative attitude (ySanhedrin) on the one hand and a conciliatory approach (bSanhedrin) on the other."[66] My analysis of the Palestinian Talmud's approach is generally in agreement with Hengel's position though in my view Hengel underestimates the degree of opposition expressed therein. I would argue, however, that the

63 Numbers 25:11: "Pinhas son of Eleazar son of Aaron the priest turned back my wrath from the Israelites in his being jealous with my jealousy among them. And so I did not destroy the Israelites in my jealousy."

64 Probably by a ban, a removal or an excommunication.

65 Hayes 38. Note that our texts are not willing to revoke or argue with Pinhas' heavenly support. Hengel states that confirmation by God is not found in yTalmud, but I disagree (see Hengel 159, n.76). The *sugya* clearly submits to the divine voice in Numbers 25, however reluctantly.

66 Hengel 176-177.

danger that Pinhas poses is acutely felt in both Talmuds, as Hengel seems to suggest. Furthermore, following my analysis, even those sources that Hengel considers to be entirely positive in their approach, are engaging with a level of embarrassment felt throughout rabbinic tradition.[67]

In this analysis, we might further consider how the various sources frame Pinhas' action as well as the law of the *boel aramit*. In bSanhedrin, he reacts to Moses' forgetfulness, while in Numbers Rabbah and Sifrei Numbers, Pinhas acts in the face of deliberation or hesitation on the part of the judicial bodies, and in ySanhedrin he simply sees and acts. The first approach serves to link Pinhas' biblical action to Mishnaic law, emphasizing the importance of rabbinic halakhah. The second method rests upon a mistrust of legal procedure and makes no attempt to find a source for his action in an established legal rule. The last approach in ySanhedrin is perhaps indicative of the absence of any attempt to justify his act. In this vein, Hengel notes that, "Silence was one of the most popular polemical means employed by the rabbis."[68]

The contextualization and re-imagining of the killing within a rabbinic legal framework and the emphasis on the divine approval of his act point to a rabbinic sense of powerlessness and to anxiety around the loss of rabbinic authority in this case. Furthermore, I have suggested that while the glorification

---

67 See Numbers Rabbah 20:25 and the end of Sifrei Numbers, Pisqa 131. These sources' approaches are similar to that of the Babylonian Talmud in that they include an extended discussion of the miracles, and an explanation of why Pinhas acted alone. It is notable that neither understands Moses to have been forgetful, rather they refer to (or imply in the case of Sifrei Numbers) a general hesitation regarding the application of the death penalty to Zimri and Kozbi to which Pinhas presents a quick and decisive solution. This support for circumventing legal procedure, coupled with the end of the Pisqa in Numbers Rabbah that emphasizes the role of vigilante punishment in warding off divine anger, supports Hengel's contention that the approach of these sources is linked to debates regarding the ideology of the Zealot movement. Both sources, however, include the various miracles enacted for Pinhas, and Sifrei Numbers adds the narrative wherein Pinhas' own heritage is questioned, which clearly transmits the rabbinic discomfort with the situation, even as these sources support extra-legal vigilante action. Another important source is Targum Pseudo-Jonathan which has major additions in Numbers 25:6-8 and 25:13. Pseudo-Jonathan is reminiscent of bSanhedrin 82a, though it has elements of the traditions mentioned above (see 25:7 where Pinhas clearly acts in a context of judicial impotence).

68 Hengel 168, n. 127.

(or gorification[69]) of Pinhas' act and the miracles that fall upon him suggest the construction of Pinhas as a hero, the effort expended on creating a heroic framework for his actions and all manner of divine and legal justifications is an expression of an underlying discomfort with the killing. The other *aggadic* midrashim brought by the Babylonian Talmud reveal a host of concerns regarding Pinhas' act and the law of the *boel aramit*. These doubts and anxieties are sometimes left unresolved, and sometimes deflected, a pattern not entirely dissimilar from the Palestinian Talmud. I would suggest that rabbinic tradition is essentially embarrassed by this act, though the Talmuds express this response differently. The textual traditions that they have received are problematic, sources of anxiety and discomfort. They must either accept them by reconfiguring them as best they can, or reject them as best they can. These are two positions that are, therefore, not quite as far apart as they seem. In the final analysis, neither is quite completely successful in its efforts to integrate or repudiate either the law of the *boel aramit* or Pinhas' killing of Zimri and Kozbi.

We may conclude that a wide range of responses to the story of Pinhas, Zimri and Kozbi in Numbers 25 is preserved in the literature. In some cases we find conflicting positions on Pinhas' act and the legal traditions that came to be related to it. Often the *halakhic* and *aggadic* sources reveal attempts to explore and resolve rabbinic problems with the killing, by engaging with contradictions with later rabbinic law and by working through discomfort with various aspects of the biblical story, whether it be its violence or its incompatibility with later legal principles. The reactions to Pinhas' killing range from open disgust to ambivalence to attempts to justify and explain the killing. Through this process, rabbinic embarrassment and discomfort become a catalyst for legal and narrative interpretation. The rabbis are challenging, accepting, rejecting and modifying rules and stories as they struggle with their inheritance and build their legacy.

69 This element of graphic gore may be linked to the understanding of acts such as Pinhas' as sacrificial and expiatory in nature. For a discussion of the act of the zealot as sacrifice see Hengel 159, 175.

EMBARRASSMENT AND RE-EMBRACEMENT OF A MIDRASH ON GENESIS 2:23

Eric Lawee, York University

"Aggadah as a problem, challenge, embarrassment and stimulus from R. Hai Gaon through the 16th century. Discuss." This question, which I was asked to address on my comprehensive exams in graduate school, was almost certainly the formulation of my teacher, Isadore Twersky, who did so much to establish *parshanut 'aggadah* as an area of independent scholarly study.[1] The ways that aggadah might embarrass[2] were multifold. They included recurrent attacks on aggadah over the ages by opponents of rabbinic Judaism, Jewish

1 For example, see his seminal essay, "R. Yeda'yah ha-Penini u-ferusho la-'aggadah," in *Studies in Jewish Religious and Intellectual History*, ed. Raphael Loewe and Siegried Stein (Tuscaloosa, Alabama: University of Alabama Press, 1979), 63-82 (Hebrew Section). Other students of Prof. Twersky followed his lead. Note the title of chapter one of Marc Saperstein, *Decoding the Rabbis: A Thirteenth-Century Commentary on the Aggadah* (Cambridge, Mass.: Harvard University Press, 1980): "The Aggadah: Problem and Challenge." In retrospect, I realize that my own formulation, which spoke of nonlegal rabbinic dicta as "variously… sources of stimulation, contention, and embarrasssment" (*Isaac Abarbanel's Stance Toward Tradition: Defense, Dissent, and Dialogue* [Albany: SUNY Press, 2001], 84), reflected the formulation found on my general exams. As for Professor Twersky's notion of aggadah as potential "embarrassment," it is most likely to be traced to the discussion of the treatment of aggadah by medieval philosophers in Gershom Scholem, *Major Trends in Jewish Mysticism* (New York: Schocken, 1941), 31, where this treatment is said to be, in the main, "embarrassed and fumbling."

2 I have not delved into the literature on embarrassment as a psychological and social phenomenon. For the purposes of this paper, I rest content with a definition of embarrassment as "an uncomfortable, aroused state of mortification, abashment, and chagrin" that human beings experience in a way that lower animals do not. See Rowland S. Miller, *Embarrassment: Poise and Peril in Everyday Life* (New York: The Guilford Press, 1996), 1.

(i.e., Karaite) or otherwise (i.e., Christian in the main).[3] Seen thus, the theme of "embarrassment and re-embracement" with respect to aggadah has as some of its correlates derision (*la'ag*) of and apologism for seemingly strange non-legal rabbinic sayings (to use this as a working definition of aggadah).[4] The other circumstances that could generate aggadic embarrassment were various evolutions in post-rabbinic Jewish thought or historical experience that could lead some Jews to conclude that segments of the classical aggadic corpus were problematic — and possibly even heretical.[5]

The following study addresses the theme of rabbinic midrash as a potential source of embarrassment through a case study of selected interpretations of the startling talmudic observation that, prior to the creation of the first human female, "Adam mated with every beast and animal." The study is dedicated to Harry Fox, an undergraduate mentor who taught me, among many other things, the power of a single example to illumine larger trends.

"ADAM MATED WITH EVERY BEAST": ASHKENAZIC READINGS

Tractate Yevamot ascribes the following insight to R. Eleazar:

> Why does scripture say 'this time bone of my bones and flesh of my flesh' (Gen. 2:23)? It teaches that Adam mated with (*she-ba' 'adam 'al*) every [species of] beast (*behemah*) and animal (*ḥayyah*) but his appetite was not assuaged *(lo' nitqarerah da'ato*) until he mated with Eve.[6]

In his commentary on the Talmud, Rashi clarifies R. Eleazar's exegetical point of departure and more or less leaves it at that: "'this time' — whence it may be inferred that at other times he copulated [with others, i.e., the primor-

3 For examples, see Marc Saperstein, *Decoding the Rabbis: A Thirteenth-Century Commentary on the Aggadah* (Cambridge, Mass.: Harvard University Press, 1980), 1-5.

4 See, e.g., Twersky, "R. Yeda'yah ha-Penini," 82; Jacob Elbaum, *Lehavin divrei hakhamim:mivhar divrei mavo' le-'aggadah ule-midrash mi-shel hakhmei yemei ha-benayim*, Sifriyat Dorot (Jerusalem: Mosad Biyalik, 2000), in the index s.v. "'aggadah, la'ag 'al."

5 See, e.g., my "'Israel Has No Messiah' in Late Medieval Spain," *Journal of Jewish Thought and Philosophy* 5 (1995): 245—79.

6 bYevamot 63a.

dial fauna] but they did not assuage him."[7] Explaining the verse cited by his rabbinic predecessor in his *Commentary on the Torah*, Rashi makes a slightly modified version of R. Eleazar's insight his sole comment on Adam's cry of "this time": "it teaches that Adam mated with every beast and animal but he was not assuaged by them."[8] For their part, a few of Rashi's northern French exegetical successors queried aspects of R. Eleazar's dictum. Like Rashi's handling of R. Eleazar's dictum, however, these queries belied no embarrassment at the idea of the first human being engaging in repeated acts of sexual intercourse with sub-human creatures.[9]

Beginning in the thirteenth century, some Christians tried to change this situation. In 1236, Nicholas Donin submitted a litany of thirty-five ostensibly reprehensible rabbinic dicta to Pope Gregory IX, R. Eleazar's midrash among them.[10] Donin cited the midrash again in the "Talmud trial" held at Paris in 1240. A Latin "confession" has the main Jewish disputant in that event, Yehiel ben Joseph, "conceding" — presumably with deep embarrassment — Adam's coitus with all the beasts while still in paradise.[11] By contrast, the Hebrew version of the trial has Yehiel speaking unabashedly of R. Eleazar's "correct inference" from scripture. As for its substance, it presented no difficulty when understood in terms of the absence of a prohibition on bestiality at this fledging stage in human history.[12]

That Ashkenazic scholars of the Middle Ages remained unperturbed by the idea of Adam's sexual relations with animals occasions little surprise since medieval Franco-German savants typically read nonlegal rabbinic dicta with literal reverence. Indeed, during the controversy over rationalism in the 1230s,

7 Rashi to bYevamot 63a, s.v. "zot ha-pa'am": "mikhlal di-fe'amim '*aḥerim* shimmesh ve-lo' 'alu beda'ato."

8 *Hamishah ḥumshei torah: Rashi ha-shalem*, 6 vols. at present (Jerusalem: Ariel Institutes, 1986-2004), Genesis 1:34. Rashi's reworking of the midrash concludes with the idea that Adam was left unsatisfied "by them (*ba-hem*) [i.e., by the beasts and animals]" while omitting the further observation that Adam's sexual impulse was not assuaged "until he mated with Eve."

9 For elaboration, see my "From Sefarad to Ashkenaz," 397-98. (Note that I wrongly ascribed the tosafist interpretation referenced at 397 n. 20 to Judah ben Eleazar.)

10 Isidore Loeb, "La controverse de 1240 sur le Talmud," *Revue des etudes juives* 3 (1881): 54 (no. 34).

11 Ch. Merchavia, *Ha-talmud bi-re'i ha-naṣrut* (Jerusalem: Mosad Biyalik, 1970), 453.

12 *Vikkuaḥ rabbenu Yeḥi'el mi-pariz*, ed. R. Margoliyot (Lvov, n.d.), 26

spokesmen for Franco-German literalism condemned non-literal interpreters of aggadah as "heretics and deniers of the sages and aggadot." Reliance on Maimonidean precedent in no way pardoned this heresy, they added.[13] The thirteenth century German talmudist Moses Taku championed the literalist position with special fervor.[14] Only at the close of the Middle Ages would "the guiding hermeneutic of Ashkenazic theology" cease to be "loyal to the literal sense... of talmudic aggadah."[15] As will soon be seen, this revolution in Ashkenazic theology and hermeneutics was amply reflected in early modern northern and eastern European Jewish sentiment about R. Eleazar's midrash on Adam's relations with the primordial beasts.

"ADAM MATED WITH EVERY BEAST": SEFARDIC RECONFIGURATIONS

If literalism was the rule in medieval Franco-German midrashic exegesis, things were otherwise in Spain, where non-literal aggadic interpretation was considered valid and, at times, imperative.[16] One spur to non-literal interpretation was the potential for aggadic sayings, literally interpreted, to embarrass Jews "in the eyes of the nations." The late fourteenth-century Spanish aggadic interpreter, Shem Tov ben Shaprut, spoke in his aggadah commentary, *Pardes rimmonim*, of people who scorned the sages by composing books in which "aggadot are anthologized and explained in such a way as to make them seem worthless." Shem Tov's preferred interpretive remedy was to hew closely to the (ostensibly) "traditional teachings" (*de'ot toriyyot*) popularized by Maimonides and ibn Ezra since, being "close to philosophy," they "present the aggadot in a form that allows us to speak of them before the nations."[17] Treating R. Eleazar's exposition on

13 Joseph Shatzmiller, "Li-temunat ha-maḥaloqet ha-rishonah 'al kitvei ha-Rambam," *Zion* 34 (1969): 139.

14 *Ketav tammim* in *'Oṣar neḥmad* 3 (1860): 63-64, 68, 77. On later medieval Ashkenazic literalism in midrashic interpretation, see Joseph M. Davis, "Philosophy, Dogma, and Exegesis in Medieval Ashkenazic Judaism: The Evidence of *Sefer Hadrat Qodesh*," *AJS Review* 18 (1993): 212-13, 216-19.

15 Davis, "Philosophy, Dogma, and Exegesis," 197.

16 See, e.g., Israel M. Ta-Shma, *Ha-sifrut ha-parshanit la-talmud be-'eropah uvi-efon 'afrikah: korot, 'ishim ve-shitot*, 2 vols. (Jerusalem: Magnes Press, 1999-2002), 2:190-201.

17 *Pardes rimmonim* (Sabbioneta, 1554), 1-2.

Genesis 2:23 in *Pardes rimmonim*, Shem Tov suggested that Adam's intercourse with animals was not carnal but cognitive and that his encounter with beasts had occurred in his "intellect" as part of an attempt to discern his proper mate through whom to sire offspring.[18] Whether Shem Tov was wholly convinced that this interpretation of R. Eleazar's midrash reflected its original meaning is hard to say. By all indications he did; hence, he was not embarrassed by the midrash. At any rate, Shem Tov indicated that he was more interested in rescuing rabbinic dicta from scorn than "getting to the bottom" of their original meaning.[19]

Among those who scorned rabbinic sayings in Shem Tov's day were high profile Jewish converts to Christianity. There was Pablo de Santa Maria, archbishop of Burgos from 1415 and a favorite of Benedict XIII and Castile's King Henry III, who criticized midrash as part of his anti-Jewish campaign.[20] There was also Jeronimo de Santa Fe, the former Joshua Lorki, who expressed pained disbelief at Pablo's conversion to Christianity — before himself crossing over to the Christian side.[21] Jeronimo's invocation of nonlegal rabbinic discourse was more complex than Pablo's. He interpreted some rabbinic sayings christologically to support his religious claims while censuring others as blasphemous. He used the first technique of christological interpretation of aggadah to buttress eschatological claims in the first sixty-two sessions of his assault on Judaism at the forced disputation of Tortosa and San Mateo of 1413-1414. The more "traditional" Christian approach of denigration of aggadah was invoked in the concluding sessions of the disputation.

Like Nicholas Donin before him, Jeronimo considered R. Eleazar's homily on Adam and the animals a parade example of the Talmud's odious content.

18 Ibid., 36r. This interpretation of R. Eleazar was presumably aided by the verbal formulation of the original midrash, which spoke of Adam's *da'at* not being assuaged (see above at n. 7). For *da'at* as the translation of "intellect" in some strands of medieval Jewish philosophic terminology, see Gad Fruedenthal, "*Ketav ha-da'at* or *Sefer ha-sekhel ve-ha-muskalot*: The Medieval Hebrew Translations of Al-Farabi's *Risalah fi'l-'akl*. A Study in Text History and in the Evolution of Medieval Hebrew Philosophical Terminology," *The Jewish Quarterly Review* 93 (2002): 29-115 (and esp. 41-50).

19 *Pardes rimmonim*, 2r.

20 Ch. Merchavia, "The Talmud in the Additiones of Paul of Burgos," *Journal of Jewish Studies* 16 (1965): 115-34.

21 Benjamin R. Gampel, "A Letter to a Wayward Teacher: The Transformations of Sephardic Culture in Christian Iberia," in *Cultures of the Jews: A New History*, ed. David Biale (New York: Schocken, 2002), 389—447.

Here was a sacrilegious ascription of iniquity to primordial man in his state of prelapsarian obedience, he explained — one that flagrantly contradicted scripture's attestation that "God saw all the things He had made and found them very good" (Gen. 1:31). Just how the rabbis charged with defending Judaism at San Mateo responded is impossible to say. The Latin account of the disputation, imputing to them a deep embarrassment on this score, has them conceding their inability to explain this and other apparently scandalous rabbinic dicta and lamely advancing the claim that the "learned and good" men who first uttered such comments were able to justify their seemingly bizarre remarks.[22]

In the decades after the disputation of Tortosa, Hispano-Jewish scholars cultivating a new genre, supercommentaries on Rashi's *Commentary on the Torah*, continued to advance the noetic interpretation of R. Eleazar's dictum set forth by Shem Tov ben Shaprut. One such was the Aragonese talmudist Moses ibn Gabbai who, writing in his *'Eved shelomo*, intially raised the possibility that R. Eleazar's comment on "this time" should be "understood according to its *prima facie* meaning (*kifshutah*)." He immediately rejected this possibility, however, on the view (opposed to the one stated by Yehiel ben Joseph at Paris) that already prior to Eve's creation Adam was prohibited from participating in illicit sexual relations like bestiality. Was this bit of halakhic argumentation a fig-leaf (to use an apt image in the current context) to conceal ibn Gabbai's embarrassment about a strange rabbinic saying? There is no evidence to this effect. At any rate, having put to rest the plain sense of Rashi's gloss, ibn Gabbai endorsed the cognitive construal favored by the likes of Shem Tov, arguing that Adam "came with his intellect and investigated the nature and temperament of every domesticated animal and wild animal," only to be disappointed that he did "not find one of them fitting for his temperament." At that point, God solved the problem by creating an ideal mate for Adam, one who would become "bone of his bone and flesh of his flesh."[23]

In contrast to the representatives of the Spanish school studied thus far, Moses ibn Gabbai's son-in-law Aaron Aboulrabi, author of a supercommentary on Rashi, expressed clear embarrassment — or rather outright alarm — at the

22 Antonio Pacios Lopez, *La disputa de Tortosa*, 2 vols. (Madrid-Barcelona, 1957), 2:564, 566-67.

23 *'Eved shelomo*, in Oxford, Bodleian Library, MS Hunt. Don. 25 (film no. 16338 at the Institute for Microfilmed Hebrew Manuscripts in Jerusalem), 12v.

literal sense of Rashi's gloss on "this time." "Heaven forefend," he pronounced, "that a person as perfect as he [Adam] should have intercourse with one not of his species." Aboulrabi justified his denial of a literal reading of Rashi's words in two ways. First, Adam would not have communed sexually with animals because he "as yet had no evil inclination." Second, even should one ascribe Adam's ostensible plan to embrace brutes carnally to his sense of an urgent need to propagate his newly created species, this goal patently could not have been accomplished through a union with creatures "not of his species." Having propounded this denial, Aboulrabi availed himself of the familiar Spanish reading of the midrash, insisting that Adam "investigated with his intellect the dispositions of all living things and did not find among them one fittingly disposed to receive the human form through intercourse except Eve."[24] Whatever their differences, both Moses ibn Gabbai and Aaron Aboulrabi negated the actuality of the carnal relations between Adam and the beasts that R. Eleazar and Rashi had asserted. More of a rationalist than his father-in-law, and more given to expressions of (often very strong) sentiment in his supercommentary, Aboulrabi made no effort to hide his chagrin at the literal purport of R. Eleazar's assertion of a sexual encounter between Adam and the primordial beasts.

EARLY MODERN RE-EMBRACEMENTS OF ADAM'S RELATIONS WITH ANIMALS

Early modern Ashkenazic centers of learning saw a number of religious transformations that were shaped, in considerable measure, by the influx of Sefardic literature into northern and eastern European lands in the fifteenth and sixteenth centuries.[25] Signs of the spiritual upheaval appeared in early modern Ashkenazic interpretations of R. Eleazar's dictum in the form they took in supercommentaries on Rashi's *Commentary on the Torah*. Apart from the stimulus of new Sefardic sensibilities, Ashkenazic writers could feel the need to revisit traditional assumptions about midrash in consequence of virulent attacks on the Talmud made by Christian anti-rabbinic writers.

24 *Perushim le-rashi* (Constantinople, [1525?]), 16v.

25 David B. Ruderman, *Jewish Thought and Scientific Discovery in Early Modern Europe* (New Haven: Yale University Press, 1995), 55-68.

One early indicator of rationalism's arrival in the north — and its conjunction with attempts to fend off Christian anti-Jewish attacks — was *Sefer ha-niṣṣaḥon*. Written by the turn-of-the-fifteenth-century Bohemian rabbi Yom Tov Lipmann Mühlhausen, this work stands as "the most widely known polemical work among Jews and Christians in the late Middle Ages and early modern period."[26] In it, Mühlhausen rebutted Christian critiques of R. Eleazar's midrash spurred by its inclusion in Rashi's *Commentary on the Torah*. Mühlhausen argued that the idiom "*ba' 'al*" in Rashi's midrash need not be understood as "the language of copulation." Rather, Adam's "coming" referred to his peregrinations in the garden in quest of an appropriate partner: "he came out seeking to investigate all the species [to ascertain] whether there was another without a helper." Learning there was not, "he was not assuaged" until being paired with Eve. The midrash could not be taken literally; that approach posed the insurmountable logistical hurdle that "it is impossible for the largest of giants to copulate with a mouse or weasel."[27] As shall appear presently, a century on, this way of defusing an embarrassing midrash was put in the mouth of a Jewish character who appeared in a religious colloquy created by a Christian defender of talmudic literature who nevertheless urged the destruction of Jewish anti-Christian works like Mühlhausen's.

Moving from late medieval to early modern Ashkenazic scholarship, one finds that even conservative scholars could evince embarrassment at the literal understanding of R. Eleazar's midrash. Solomon Luria, a pillar (along with Moses Isserles) of Ashkenazic rabbinic learning, departed from the traditional Ashkenazic interpretation of the midrash even as he admitted Rashi's acceptance of it as evidenced in Rashi's Talmud commentary. Faced with this weighty precedent, Luria gingerly suggested that R. Eleazar had "not necessarily intended" to

26 See most recently Ora Limor and and Israel Jacob Yuval, "Skepticism and Conversion: Jews, Christians, and Doubters in *Sefer Ha-Nizzahon*," *in Hebraica Veritas? Christian Hebraists and the Study of Judaism in Early Modern Europe*, ed. Allison P. Coudert and Jeffrey S. Shoulson (Philadelphia: University of Pennsylvania Press, 2004), 159—80 (160 for the cited characterization). For evidence that "Jewish philosophical and polemical texts... walked hand in hand through the centuries," see Daniel J. Lasker, *Jewish Philosophical Polemics Against Christianity in the Middle Ages*, 2nd ed. (Oxford: The Littman Library of Jewish Civilization, 2007) (see "Introduction to the Second Edition," xxi for the just-cited observation).

27 Photocopy of Theodor Hackspan edition (Altdorf-Nerenberg, 1644), with corrections by Johann Christoph Wagenseil, introduction by Frank Talmage (Jerusalem: Merkaz Dinur, 1984), 14.

speak of Adam's actual sexual intercourse with animals when he spoke of Adam "mounting of" (*ba' 'al*) beasts. Rather, he could have meant that Adam came upon the animals "in thought (*ba' ba-maḥashavah*)."[28] By contrast, Hayyim ben Bezalel of Friedberg, author of a combined Torah commentary and supercommentary on Rashi, insisted that Rashi had understood R. Eleazar in non-literal terms. He also decried the literalist interpretation. "Heaven forefend" that the mating of which Rashi spoke denoted copulation, he intoned. Rather, the encounter had occurred "in thought." So understood, what Rashi meant was that Adam "mated with them [the animals] in thought, seeking among them to see which species might be appropriate for him as a mate."[29] Following the path carved out by Spanish forerunners, Ashkenazic scholars with new sensibilities found a way to re-embrace a problematic midrash.

Hayyim ben Bezalel's younger brother, Judah Loew, the leading Ashkenazic theologian of the later sixteenth century, went furthest along the non-literalist path in his aggadic hermeneutic and interpretation of R. Eleazar. In his Rashi supercommentary *Gur 'aryeh*, Loew rejected a literal understanding of Rashi's gloss on "this time" as emphatically as any Spanish writer before him: "Heaven forefend that he [Adam] came upon them for purposes of cohabitation." His characteristically involved rereading of the midrash explained Adam's attachments with animals as flowing from man's position as the "form of all species" (a principle widespread in Loew's writings); told of Adam's search for a proper female reflecting "form's need for something that is matter to it"; explicated Adam's "intercourse" with beasts as an indication of his problematic entry into the material realm; interpreted Adam's ultimate congress with his human female "partner" as signifying a conjunction with a type of matter appropriate to the first human being in his status as a metaphysical entity guided by higher reason, and so forth. Loew openly admitted that one reason for his prolonged treatment of the subject was "in order to explain the words of the [rabbinic] sages since I have noted that the nations are critical of the sages' words." Though gentile critics had singled out R. Eleazar's dictum as an embarrassment, Loew was sure that the critics had failed to fathom the "profundity"

28 *Yeri'ot shelomo* (Benei Berak: n.p., 1984), 8.

29 *Be'er mayyim ḥayyim*, ed. S. F. Schneebalg, 3 vols. (London: n.p., 1964-1971), 1:9.

of the midrash. Indeed, any fair-minded student would quickly discern that "all gentile scholars are 'less than nothing' [Is. 40:17] as compared to their [the sages'] most casual utterances."[30]

To find R. Eleazar's dictum on Adam and the animals problematic was not necessarily to embrace Loew's allegorizing re-embracement of it. Mordechai Jaffe, a student of Moses Isserles and Solomon Luria, again in a supercommentary on Rashi's *Commentary on the Torah*, began his treatment of Rashi's gloss on Gen. 2:23 with a jibe at Loew's descent "to the depths of pseudophilosophy." Yet Jaffe was far from being a literal interpreter of R. Eleazar's remark. "Obviously," he said, "heaven forefend that the human being fabricated by God's hand and created in the divine image would defile himself with this, engaging in unnatural cohabitation with any animal or beast in actuality. Heaven forefend!" As for the reason for rejecting the midrash's literal meaning so emphatically, it was straightforward: the literal meaning of the midrash was disgusting. Indeed, this was the case to such an extent that, contra Loew, no divine interdict was needed to stop the man "fabricated by God's hand" from lapsing into depraved bestiality. Having pronounced anathema on a literal reading of Rashi's gloss and dismissed Loew's explication of it, perhaps on the grounds that it strayed too far from the literal, Jaffe explained R. Eleazar on the premise that sexual relations between Adam and the beasts were impossible due to their inherent degeneracy. What was meant by the midrash was that Adam came "with his knowledge and intellect to [an understanding of] the nature of every beast and animal." Having realized their inappropriateness for him as a mate, Adam's desire for a mate was eventually assuaged with Eve's creation. Even then, however, he preserved absolutely his celibacy in paradise: "there was no intercourse in actuality, neither with beast nor animal nor even Eve, only [intercourse] in his pure and pristine mind."[31]

30 *Humash gur 'aryeh ha-shalem*, ed. Joshua Hartman, 9 vols. (Jerusalem: Mekhon Yerushalayim, 1989), 1:73-74. Cf. Loew's *Be'er ha-golah*, ed. Joshua Hartmann, 3 vols. (Jerusalem: Mekhon Yerushalayim, 2002), 2:62-64 and, for the anti-Christian animus of Loew's aggadic interpretations, Mordechai Breuer, "Vikkuḥo shel maharal mi-prag 'im ha-noṣṣerim: mabat hadash 'al sefer be'er ha-golah," *Tarbiz* 55 (1985-86): 256-57.

31 *'Oṣar perushim 'al ha-torah*, 2 vols. (Jerusalem: Divrei Hakhamim, 1958), 1:14r.

While Judah Loew and Mordechai Jaffe, each in his own way, re-embraced R. Eleazar's saying in a Sefardic manner, other early modern Ashkenazic sages deemed the costs of such re-embracement too high. Notable among them was the seventeenth-century Polish talmudist and Rashi supercommentator, David ben Samuel Halevi ("Taz"), who proposed a vision of the primeval human condition in which sexual congress between man and beast would have been wholly congenial since all creatures were as yet equally "pleasant" and uncorrupted by sin, all having been created through "the utterance of the Holy One, Blessed be He." This being so, David insisted on taking literally R. Eleazar's affirmation of Adam's extensive sexual activity in paradise with beasts. Writing in a watershed period in Ashkenazic religious history when rationalism found itself in retreat and philosophic study became "marginal and suspect," not least before ever more powerful kabbalistic "incursions,"[32] David resoundingly reaffirmed the literalist Ashkenazic midrashic hermeneutic as practiced in bygone days: "we ought not rend the rabbinic sages' words from their plain sense."[33]

In early modern times, as Christian biblicists with a "Hebraist" bent began to explore the Hebrew Bible in unprecedented ways,[34] Christian anti-Jewish polemicists found occasion to exploit the rabbinic idea transmitted by Rashi that Adam engaged in sexual encounters with the primordial beasts. The advent of printing contributed significantly to the wider diffusion in Christian circles of rabbinic interpretations of this sort, with the innovative "rabbinic Bible" — pioneered in 1516-17 by the press in Venice of the Christian Daniel Bomberg — exercising a major influence. With such diffusion came Christian awareness of some of the stranger elements in the classical-medieval Jewish exegetical inheritance and, at times in the wake of such awareness, Christian

32 Joseph M. Davis, *Yom-Tov Lipmann Heller* (Oxford: Littman Library of Jewish Civilization, 2004), 54; idem, "The Cultural and Intellectual History of Ashkenazic Jews 1500—1750: A Selective Bibliography and Essay," *Year Book of the Leo Baeck Institute* 38 (1993): 349-50.

33 *Divrei david*, ed. C. D. Chavel (Jerusalem: Mosad ha-rav Kuk, 1978), 16.

34 The classic study is Jerome Friedman, *The Most Ancient Testimony: Sixteenth-Century Christian-Hebraica in the Age of Renaissance Nostalgia* (Athens, Ohio: Ohio University Press, 1983). For further bibliography, see Amnon Raz-Krakotzkin, "The Censor as a Mediator: Printing, Censorship and the Shaping of Hebrew Literature," in *The Roman Inquisition, the Index and the Jews: Contexts, Sources and Perspectives*, ed. Stephan Wendehorst (Leiden: Brill, 2004), 37 n.4.

efforts to attack these elements. Several sixteenth-century works, like the anonymous *Li Errori & Impieta Retrouate Nelli Libri Del Thalmud* published around mid-century, and the *Bibliotheca Sancta* of 1566 composed by the Jewish apostate Sixtus of Siena, held up R. Eleazar's midrash on Adam and the animals as a parade example of scandalous rabbinic discourse.[35]

While Christian writers often highlighted Jewish interpretations that in one or another way undermined Christianity, they at times addressed segments of Hebraic tradition that seemed offensive or embarrassing even absent any direct interreligious polemical concern. One early modern Christian response to such elements was to censor problematic passages or books.[36] Various comments made by Rashi that appeared in rabbinic Bibles were "corrected" in the later fifteenth and sixteenth centuries by censors, including apostate Jews. Among them was Rashi's gloss on Adam's relations with the animals.[37] But what sentiments underlay this act of expurgation? Scholars have cited repulsion at Adam's bestiality as one possibility and the fact that Rashi problematically imputed sin to the first human being before the fall as another. They have not included simple "embarrassment" among the list of possible explanations.[38] To be sure, the precise interlacings of offense, embarrassment, and glee at Jewish folly that Christian authorities may have felt in this and similar cases are hard to discern.

Early modern censorship of Hebrew books had a "Hebraist framework"; that is, "censorship was initiated precisely because Christians were reading Jewish literature."[39] It is, therefore, not a complete surprise to learn that the main catalyst for Hebrew study among Christians in the early part of the six-

35 Ch. Merchavia, "Kuntres neged ha-talmud mi-yemei serefat ha-talmud be-'italyah," *Tarbiz* 37 (1967-68): 198.

36 See Amnon Raz-Krakotzkin, "Censorship, Editing, and the Reshaping of Jewish Identity: The Catholic Church and Hebrew Literature in the Sixteenth Century," in *Hebraica Veritas? Christian Hebraists and the Study of Judaism in Early Modern Europe*, ed. Allison P. Coudert and Jeffrey S. Shoulson (Philadelphia: University of Pennsylvania Press, 2004), 125-155 (with a full up-to-date bibliography at 146 n. 2).

37 Michael T. Walton and Phyllis J. Walton, "The Censorship of the Rashi Commentary in the Magna Biblia Rabbinica," *Sixteenth Century Journal* 21 (1990): 385-400. While Rashi's whole comment on "this time" was not expurgated, its key sexual elements were (399).

38 Ibid., 397.

39 Raz-Krakotzkin, "The Censor," 39, 37 (respectively).

teenth century was aware of R. Eleazar's midrash on Adam on the animals.[40] Johannes Reuchlin, Germany's first humanist of European distinction and a famous devotee of "Christian Cabbala," addressed the midrash obliquely in his *De Arte Cabalistica*, a work Heiko Oberman describes as "a real step toward Lessing and the Enlightenment" where the religion of Reuchlin's opponents was "taken seriously and recognized for its germ of truth."[41] This staunch defender of the right of German Jews to preserve their religious writings, the Talmud most notably,[42] indirectly took up the cudgels on behalf of R. Eleazar's midrashic dictum on Adam and the animals when he had Simon, the Jew in his fictional religious colloquy, adduce R. Eleazar's dictum as proof that Adam only felt "the pull of sexual attraction" upon encountering Eve. At the same time, Simon expressed his outraged awareness that the dictum had been grossly misinterpreted in ways far more embarrassing to Jews by "men with warped minds, or rather by the devil incarnate or deadly evil spirits" — though how people could believe such a "malicious lie," Simon could not fathom:

> These perverts try to incite all good Christians to turn against us, though we live blamelessly ... They put false constructions on the words of our rabbis: this passage they interpret as: "Adam then copulated foully with all beasts and liv-

40 Heiko Oberman, "Discovery of Hebrew and Discrimination against the Jews: The *Veritas Hebraica* as Double-Edged Sword in Renaissance and Reformation," in *Germania Illustrata: Essays on Early Modern Germany Presented to Gerald Strauss*, ed. Andrew C. Fix and Susan C. Karant-Nunn (Kirksville, Mo.: Sixteenth Century Journal Publishers, 1992), 30, argues that Wesel Gansfort was not merely a forerunner of Reuchlin but a "watershed in his own right," yet allows that it was Reuchlin's name that sixteenth-century Hebraists revered even if they followed "unknowingly" in Gansfort's footsteps. On Reuchlin's Christian Cabbalah, see Moshe Idel's introduction to the Bison Book edition of Reuchlin's *On the Art of the Kabbalah / De arte cabalistica*, trans. Martin and Sarah Goodman (Lincoln: University of Nebraska Press, 1993). Reuchlin's various "Jewish connections" are studied in the collection of articles in *Reuchlinstel und die Juden*, ed. Arno Herzig and Julius H. Schoeps (Sigmaringen: J. Thorbecke, 1993).

41 *The Roots of Anti-Semitism in the Age of Renaissance and Reformation*, trans. James I. Porter (Philadelphia: Fortress Press, 1981), 27.

42 Johannes Reuchlin, *Recommendation Whether to Confiscate, Destroy and Burn All Jewish Books*, trans. Peter Wortsman (New York: Paulist Press, 2000) with thanks to Stephen Burnett for directing my attention to this source.

> ing creatures" — good God, the audacity of these wretches, and all the more so when egged on by the approval of infantile sophists![43]

To explain the problematic text, Reuchlin's Jew had recourse to its interpretation by Yom Tov Lipmann Mühlhausen in *Sefer ha-niṣṣaḥon*, a work Reuchlin apparently knew, though such awareness has seemingly not been noted hitherto. In the first instance, Simon argued lexically, in the manner of Mühlhausen,[44] but he then added *Sefer ha-niṣṣaḥon* argument that there was every reason for all to reject a literal interpretation of R. Eleazar's words as "impossible" since it was not possible that Adam could have "mingled in sexual manner with bugs, fleas, flies, and grasshoppers." Reuchlin's Simon had gone into such detail regarding the midrash in order to warn his interlocutors of "forgeries like this" and the "wicked, petty slanderers, rats leaving the sinking ship, with no sense of responsibility in this or any other matter," who fabricated them.[45] Though willing to see a small number of Hebrew books confiscated and burned, including *Sefer ha-niṣṣaḥon* anonymous earlier namesake *Niṣṣaḥon (Vetus)*,[46] Reuchlin had his Jewish Simon embrace a challenging statement in the Talmud, a work whose right to exist Reuchlin staunchly defended against Dominicans in his day who sought its confiscation and destruction.[47]

TWENTIETH-CENTURY SNAPSHOTS

Engagement with R. Eleazar's dictum continued into modern times, at times arising suddenly in unexpected places (like the writings of Michael Wyschogrod or Emmanuel Levinas). Having surveyed a number of modern and contemporary reactions elsewhere,[48] I conclude this study with but two of a number of twentieth-century readings not discussed in that earlier survey. One is the interpretation of a recent spiritual leader of the German-Jewish

43 *On the Art of the Kabbalah*, 67.

44 *On the Art of the Kabbalah*, 67. Cf. n. 28 above.

45 *On the Art of the Kabbalah*, 67.

46 *Recommendation*, 34.

47 See Elisheva Carlebach, "Critical Introduction," in *Recommendation*, 15-26.

48 "From Sefarad to Ashkenaz," 422-25.

Orthodox community in Washington Heights, Shimon Schwab (1908-1993). The other is found in the Schottenstein Edition of the Talmud produced in Mesorah Publications' "Artscroll" series.

Shimon Schwab began his exposition of R. Eleazar's dictum by raising a logistical objection that rendered it "utterly incomprehensible": "is it possible to say that Adam mated with elephants and donkeys?"[49] After developing ideas about higher order animals in their primal state that made a humananimal coital bond imaginable, Schwab eventually suggested an alternative: "it is possible that the rabbinic sages spoke allusively (*be-remez*) and that actual intercourse [between Adam and the animals] did not occur." On this view, the "mounting" of which R.Eleazar spoke was to be understood cognitively; that is, Adam "probed to essence of every living creature when bestowing upon them names."[50] Though this traditionalist rabbi finds a way to accommodate R. Eleazar's words literally, one senses his discomfiture with them on grounds that are not purely logistical.

What of the Schottenstein Talmud in comparison to earlier "Artscroll" productions? In a recent edition of Rashi's *Commentary on the Torah*, which translates all of Rashi's comments and provides extended treatments of selected ones in annotations at the bottom of the page, Rashi is translated literally as saying that "Adam had relations with every [species of] animal and beast." An elaborative footnote reports Rashi's comment on the relevant talmudic passage and then summons the two approaches to Rashi's gloss found in the early modern Ashkenazic supercommentary literature, the literalist one of David ben Samuel and the decidedly non-literalist one of Judah Loew of Prague. Because of the traditionalism of those who stand behind the "Artscroll" label, a traditionalism which allows them to accept even bizarre-sounding statements found in traditional Jewish literature at face value, the "Artscroll" edition of the *Commentary* is able to provide a balanced view of the supercommentary

49 That Schwab's objection is logistical emerges more clearly from the continuation of his discussion, though he is less explicit on this score than an earlier writer who had articulated a similar objection, like Yom Tov Muhlhausen.

50 *Ma'ayan bet ha-sho'evah* on Gen. 2:23, reading *pilim* for *pulim* (New York, 1994), 10-11 (with thanks to R. Chaim Rapoport for calling this passage to my attention). A number of earlier interpreters had drawn a connection between R. Eleazar's dictum and Adam's naming of the animals. See my articles cited above, n. 6.

tradition on Rashi's midrashic gloss on "this time,"[51] giving the ostensibly embarrassing literalist approach and its non-literalist alternative a more or less equal hearing. And yet, the Schottenstein Talmud abandons this even-handedness. After citing Rashi's gloss on the relevant talmudic passage, the authors of the annotations to bYevamot introduce Loew's opinion "that unquestionably, our Gemara is not to be understood literally." The final holding regarding the dictum's meaning is then stated:

> When our Gemara states that he [Adam] cohabited with them [the animals]... this means that his mind fathomed them to their depths... Adam realized that none of these creatures corresponded to his essence, and thus none of them could be a companion for him. This was the insight that God was waiting for Adam to attain before He created Eve. When Adam encountered Eve and comprehended her nature in all its profundity, his mind was put at peace, for he had finally found a perfect companion.

Effaced by the corporate Artscroll label are authors whose motives are often hard to read.[52] Were they embarrassed by a literal interpretation of R. Eleazar's dictum on Adam and the animals? Did they fear that their audience might be even if they were not? Did they decide simply that the great Judah Loew knew what R. Eleazar truly intended? As with a number of the authors surveyed above, the answers to such questions are far from clear. What is clear is that, when it comes to strange-sounding rabbinic dicta like R. Eleazar's on Adam and the animals, another dictum applies: "where there's a will, there's a way." Applied to the current case, what this means is that where Jews have been determined or eager to re-embrace problematic aggadot, whether in response to outside attacks or simply in response to their own discomfort, an interpretive way has been found to effect the desired reconciliation between the ever-changing Jewish reader and classical aggadic texts.

51 See my "From Sefarad to Ashkenaz," 424.

52 On this aspect of the Artscroll enterprise, see B. Barry Levy, "Contemporary Jewish Booklore: The Exegetical and Editorial Work of Rabbi Meir Zlotowitz and Rabbi Nosson Scherman (or The Artscroll Phenomenon, 2005)," forthcoming (with thanks to Professor Levy for sharing with me a copy of this essay in advance).

DEUTERONOMY 21:10-14:
THE BEAUTIFUL CAPTIVE WOMAN

Pearl Elman

The biblical text of Deuteronomy 21:10-14 translates as follows:

> When you take the field against your enemies, and the Lord your God delivers them into your power and you take some of them captive, and you see among the captives a beautiful woman and you desire her and would take her to wife, you shall bring her into your house, and she shall trim her hair, pare her nails, and discard her captive's garb. She shall spend a month's time in your house lamenting her father and mother; after that you may come to her and possess her, and she shall be your wife. Then, should you no longer want her, you must release her outright. You must not sell her for money: since you had your will of her, you must not enslave her.

This text deals with the treatment of sexually desirable non-Jewish women who are captured in war. In light of recent events in Bosnia, the system of behaviors this section of Deuteronomy posits is particularly germane.

The three Targumim (Pseudo-Onqelos,[1] Pseudo-Jonathan, Neofiti) to Deuteronomy 21:10-14 are similar, but there are two major additions in Ps.-Jonathan Deuteronomy 21:13. The variations in the rest of the translation are minor and usually seem to reflect the same ideas expressed in different words. Close examination of the texts, however, does reveal a difference in attitude. This paper will examine the minor variations in the Targumim, will address

1 It is common to refer to Targum Onqelos as pseudo-Onqelos because it is unlikely that either Onqelos or Aqilas was the final editor or author. In this essay we will retain the reference as Onqelos. Pseudo will henceforth be abbreviated Ps.

attitudinal differences where applicable, and will consider the major additions within Ps.-Jonathan Deuteronomy 21:13.[2]

The root חשק is used twice in Tanakh to denote sexual desire. The first appearance is in the story of Shekhem and Dina in Genesis 34:8, שכם בני חשקה נפשו בבתכם ("My son Shekhem longs for your daughter"). The second is in Deuteronomy 21:11, וחשקת בה ("and you desire her"). Onqelos uses the root רעי, "to desire, to delight in," to translate the word in both places.[3] Ps.-Jonathan uses ידע for Deuteronomy 21, but opts for the root רעי to translate Genesis 34. Neofiti 1 also uses the root רעי to translate Deuteronomy 21. All are equally explicit and there is no mistaking the intent.

Deuteronomy 20:1 and 21:10 are the only two places in Hebrew Scripture which begin כי תצא למלחמה על איבך ("When you take the field against your enemies"). Onqelos translates this phrase לאגחא קרבא, the fighting attack or war. Ps.-Jonathan and Neofiti have לסדרי קרבה "the battle array or battle lines" (Jastrow 959). Grossfeld translates Onqelos as "to wage war"(62), Drazin as "the battle"(198). Le Deaut translates Ps.-Jonathan (173) and Neofiti (382) as "*sortirez au combat*." Each of the translations is accurate but they are not exactly the same. Battle array or battle lines precede the actual battle, which is an important consideration in Deuteronomy 21:1.

In Deuteronomy 20:1ff, it is obvious from the opening of the following verse, והיה כקרבתם אל המלחמה ("Before you join battle"), that the soldiers have not yet begun to fight and are being addressed by the priest in preparation for battle. In this instance "the battle array" is precise.

In the discussion of captive women in Deuteronomy 21:10, it seems obvious that no captives can be taken if the soldiers are merely in battle array. Nevertheless, the different nuances in Ps.-Jonathan and Neofiti, although perhaps imprecise, are not problematic to the understanding of the text.

It is interesting to note that the King James Version offers a different translation for the same Hebrew word in Deuteronomy 20:1 and 21:10. The former is "When thou goest out to battle against thine enemies" and the latter is "When

2 A longer essay of mine on this topic was published "Deuteronomy 21:10-14: the beautiful captive woman" as *Women in Judaism* 1 (Online Journal, Toronto: 1997) but most of what is contained here in this article was excluded.

3 Marcus Jastrow, 486.

thou goest forth to war against thine enemies." This translation accurately reflects the realities of both situations.

An interesting difference in interpretation occurs in the translation of ועשתה את צפרניה, "and she shall do her nails," in Deuteronomy 21:12. The root עשה does not explain what is meant. The same root is used in 2Samuel 19:25 in which Mephibosheth the son of Saul comes down to meet the king and he has neither dressed (עשה) his feet nor has he done (עשה) his beard. Onqelos uses ספר, meaning to cut.

In bYevamot 48a and in Sifrei Devarim piska 212 there is a discussion as to what "she shall do" means. The discussions are almost identical. Moshe David Herr states that Sifrei in its present form was unknown to either the Bavli or the Yerushalmi. (EJ 11:1518) Herr may be correct, but the appearance of two almost verbatim report of discussions, one in Sifrei and one in bYevamot, makes for interesting speculation.

The discourse develops as follows: R. Eliezer maintains that the captive woman should cut her nails citing the following proof: just as the first part of 21:12 denotes an action, i.e., cutting/shaving her head, which means removal, so does the second part denote an action which means removal, i.e., cutting her nails. R. Akiva disagrees. He states that just as the reason for the act of shaving her head was to make her unattractive, so should she let her nails grow and thereby look unattractive. The Talmud seems to support R. Eliezer's view. It quotes 2Sam. 19:25 and then asks, "What is meant by 'did'? [And answers] — removal."

This difference of opinion is reflected in the Targumim, and later commentators are divided on this as well. Targum Jonathan, who translated עשה in 2Sam. 19:25 (see above) as cut, here displays the influence of the school of Akiva, and translates עשתה as תרבי — she shall let her nails grow. Rashi on this verse, Rambam (*Hil. Melakhim* 8:5) and Torah Temima (280) take the same position. Both Ps.-Jonathan and Neofiti 1 translate it as ותצמי ,"she shall cut." Ramban supports this position. Lekach Tov explains that both positions are correct.[4] She allows her nails to grow for a month in order to be unattractive and then she cuts them in time for her conversion immersion. The Toldot Adam commentary on Sifrei mentions this explanation given in Lekach Tov.[5]

4 Pesikta Zutrata (Venice: 1546),70

5 *Sifrey with Commentary by Toldot Adam* [Hebrew] (Jerusalem: Mosad Harav Kook, 1972) ,232

Onqelos' and Neofiti's translations of Deuteronomy 21:13 are straightforward and faithful to the simple meaning of the text. The biblical text reads:

וְהֵסִירָה אֶת שִׂמְלַת שִׁבְיָהּ מֵעָלֶיהָ וְיָשְׁבָה בְּבֵיתֶךָ וּבָכְתָה אֶת אָבִיהָ וְאֶת אִמָּהּ יֶרַח יָמִים וְאַחַר כֵּן תָּבוֹא אֵלֶיהָ וּבְעַלְתָּהּ וְהָיְתָה לְךָ לְאִשָּׁה:

> And she shall discard her captive garb. She shall spend a month's time in your house lamenting her father and mother; after that you may come to her and possess her, and she shall be your wife.

Onqelos translates the second part as: ובתר כן תיעול לותה ותבעלנה ותהי לך לאנתו. He uses the roots בעל, meaning to have intercourse (Jastrow 182), and עול (Jastrow 1050), or possibly עלל (Jastrow 1083), which correspond to the Hebrew root בוא meaning to come.

In a similar vein as Onqelos, Neofiti translates the second part as: ובתר כדן תיעול לוותה תזדמן לווה ותיסב יתה לך לאתה. The root עול remains the same. The root of תזדמן is זמן and it is in the *itpael* pattern which means "joy and wedlock" (Jastrow 404). The intent is similar in meaning to בעל. Where Onqelos uses בעל and Neofiti uses זמן, Ps.-Jonathan uses תפר meaning to join (Jastrow 1689). The meaning of these roots is the same. It can be seen that both Onqelos and Neofiti 1 are faithful to the biblical text in this part of the translation. Ps.-Jonathan's translation of 21:13 will be addressed later in this paper.

In Deuteronomy 21:14 ושלחה לנפשה "you shall let her go where ever she wants to" is translated by the root פטר in Onqelos meaning to send away, divorce. Neofiti uses ותשלי תה ברשות נפשה "you shall send her away with authority over her own person." Ps.-Jonathan, like Onqelos, uses the root פטר but adds לבלחודה בגיטה "alone by an act of divorce." There seems to be an actual legal divorce in Ps.-Jonathan, while the others merely hint at it. Unlike the different translations of חשק "[to] desire" in Deuteronomy 21:11, all three Targumim use תפצת meaning "[to] desire" in Deuteronomy 21:14.

The last part of 21:14 לא תתעמר בה תחת אשר עניתה is translated as: "you shall not make use of her as a slave" (עמר Jastrow 1091) because you have oppressed/violated her (עני Jastrow 1093-94). The Hebrew word עמר is translated by Onqelos, Ps. Jonathan and Neofiti as תתגר which Miqraot Gedolot explains as לשון סוחר — language that merchants use. The verse would then enjoin one not to treat her as one would treat merchandise. In a society in which slaves are in fact merchandise, all four texts would be issuing the same enjoinder.

What is the nature of the sexual act contemplated in Deuteronomy 21:10-14? The use of עניתה in 21:14 is particularly noteworthy. It is in the translation of this word that an attitudinal difference between the Targumim becomes apparent. In 2Samuel 13:11-14, the story of Amnon and Tamar, the root עני is used twice: אל תענני, "do not violate me," and then ויחזק ממנה ויענה וישכב אתה, "he overpowered her, he violated her, and he had intercourse with her." If we understand וישכב אתה to mean "and he had intercourse with her," from the use of עני in the second phrase we can determine that עני can be considered sexual violence. In this instance, when עני is used together with שכב it seems to imply actual rape.

This seems to be the case as well in Genesis 34:2, the story of Dina and Shekhem. There the text says: ויקח אתה וישכב אתה ויענה "he took her, and he had intercourse with he violated her." The word עני alone would not necessarily mean rape but vulgar or coarse sexual expression. Rape is implied here by the use of שכב and עני together.

Deuteronomy 22:25, 28 use two other words to indicate rape: חזק שכב and תפש שכב. Both imply forced intercourse, i.e. rape, when used together, yet neither of these combinations is used in Deuteronomy 21:14. The word עני is used alone in Lamentations 5:11, Ezekiel 22:10, and Judges 19:25. From the context there, עני seems to imply rape.

It is important to determine what is meant by ועניתה in Deuteronomy 21:14, but this discussion may be putting too fine a point on it. Rape is only one way of exerting sexual violence. Clearly sexual violence is conveyed in most of the quoted instances where עני is used. Although there is no specific mention of rape in Deuteronomy 21:14, the word עניתה implies that her consent (if it were given at all) to intercourse was due to her dire circumstances. The expression עניתה is particularly poignant, and Onqelos and Neofiti recognize what the biblical text is conveying, a point which seems to have been missed by Ps.-Jonathan. Onqelos uses ענה in his translation. Neofiti 1 uses והבת רשותך עלה, "you have exercised your power/authority over her." Ps.-Jonathan considers עני to be only actual intercourse as he uses the words ושמשת עמה. The Bible's sensitivity to the captive's powerlessness is not transmitted by Ps.-Jonathan's translation.

A major change away from the biblical text occurs in Targum Ps.-Jonathan Deuteronomy 21:13. The translation substantially alters the thrust of Deuteronomy 21:13 by the inclusion of a number of phrases which do not appear in the biblical text. Ps.-Jonathan reads as follows:

> ותשני ית כסות שבייתה מנה וטבילנה ותגיירינה בביתך ותבכי על טעוות בית אבה ואמה ותשהי תלת ירחין
> די תדע אין היא מעברה ומן בתר כדין תיעול לוותה ותפרין יתה ותהוי לך לאנתו.

The first verb, to remove, becomes ותשני "she will change" which is not a significant difference. A very important variation occurs after the phrase "she shall change the garment of captivity from upon her." The words וטבילנה ותגיירינה בביתך are inserted. Instead of "she shall remain in your house" we now have "you immerse her (root טבל; Jastrow 517) and you will convert her [to Judaism] (root גיר; Jastrow 263) in your house." The insertion of על טעוות בית...מעברה changes "she shall weep for her mother and father" to "she shall weep about the error [idol worship] of her mother's and her father's house and you will wait three months to know if she is pregnant."

It is impossible to know exactly the source of these additions to Ps.-Jonathan. Midrash Tannaim and Midrash HaGadol both speak of idolatry and about conversion and ritual immersion but the wording is not similar. The three-month wait is also mentioned in Midrash Tannaim, Midrash HaGadol and Tosefta Yevamot 6:7. It can be surmised by these inclusions that Targum Ps.-Jonathan has exhibited a different attitude to the socialization of the captive woman than that exhibited by the simple reading of Deuteronomy 21:13, Onqelos, and Neofiti. Nothing is mentioned in those texts about converting a captive gentile wife. The biblical text merely hints at conversion to Judaism by mentioning that the captive must do/cut/let her hair grow as well as her nails and live for one month with her captor before marriage.

Ps.-Jonathan seems to be later than Onqelos and Neofiti (EJ 4:845ff). The inclusion of the conversion ritual and the polemic against idolatry could reflect the needs of the community for which this Targum was written. As it is impossible to date this part of Ps.-Jonathan with any accuracy, this remains largely conjectural. It would seem that in translating Deuteronomy 20:10-14 Onqelos and Neofiti are generally straightforward and faithful to the biblical text. They differ primarily in nuances of interpretation.

Ps.-Jonathan, however, has added a new dimension to our discussion of the captive woman.

CONVERSION OF THE CAPTIVE WOMAN

If the warrior's desire continued and the captive women remaining in the household became a reality, conversion would be necessary to ensure that there was no theological pollution. Although conversion of this captive woman is not specifically mentioned biblically, many sages address this issue in their commentaries. It is also mentioned in Targum Ps.-Jonathan.

Sifrei Devarim (piska 214) alludes to conversion and seems to treat it as mandatory. Rabbi Akiva states that the ritual of weeping, which biblically is for her parents, is actually for her idols. Considering the captive's plight, it is impossible to know exactly which loss she is mourning. Nevertheless, weeping for her gods certainly indicates that Rabbi Akiva considered them lost to her. Discarding idolatrous ways, however, is not necessarily conversion to Israelite ways.

Midrash HaGadol states that if she does not want to convert after thirty days, she is given twelve months to reconsider (מגלגל אליה, Jastrow 244). If she does not want to convert after that, she accepts upon herself the seven Noahide commandments and is like all resident aliens. If she does not want to accept the seven Noahide commandments after the twelve month period, she is executed. This commentary adds a completely new perspective on the issue of conversion. It would seem that according to Midrash HaGadol, conversion is not mandatory, but neither is heathenism allowed.

In bYevamot 47b-48a there may be a difference of opinion. In the discussion about the male proselyte we find that after his immersion, the proselyte is considered an Israelite in all respects and is allowed to marry the daughter of an Israelite. The anonymous *tanna* claims that the captive is permitted to refuse conversion. Rabbi Simeon ben Elaeazar says that a female slave can be forcibly immersed twice and then her master can marry her. The discussion continues as to whether forced conversion applies to a captive woman. While countering an argument made by Rabba, Rav Papa states that captive women were not obligated to perform the commandments.

There is possibly another opinion in bKiddushin 21b which states that a warrior can only take one captive and that he has the right to marry her. The Bavli does not specify if this means forever or only before she is converted (ליקוחין יש לך בה לך לאשות). The Bavli here does not seem to address the possibility that the warrior may not want to marry her at all as this contravenes the biblical text. It would seem from the context that she has no right to refuse, probably because of her status as a captive. Rashi, in his commentary on bKiddushin 21b (*s.v.* veheveita el tokh beitekha), seems to imply that this is a right to a legal marriage. Therefore, as an Israelite may not marry a pagan but may marry a convert, it would seem she can be converted without her consent.

Like Midrash HaGadol, Rambam states that the captive woman is kept for 30 days.[6] If she refuses to convert at the end of that time, she accepts the seven Noahide laws and becomes a resident alien. She is not forced to convert to Judaism, but if she refuses to accept the seven Noahide laws, she is killed.

According to Ramban (on Deut. 21:12), the captive woman is forced to convert to Judaism (מתגיירת בעל כרחה). Unlike other proselytes, no one asks her if she wants to leave her own faith. But her husband/captor tells her that she must obey the Torah of Israel under duress, and leave her gods. Ramban then goes on to say that even if her conversion was due to fear, her conversion stands. The notes to Ramban quote bYevamot 24b "הלכה כדברי האומר כולם גרים הם" as the source for this ruling.

This section of bYevamot describes a discussion of who should and should not be accepted as converts. Among the categories of converts under discussion are people who converted out of fear. Clearly, the captive woman who is forced to convert fits into this category. At the end of this discussion, the statement quoted above is made: "The *halakha* is in keeping with the one who says all of them are converts."

It would seem that the sages were greatly concerned with the theological threat posed by women who had not converted. The post-biblical sources forbade an Israelite man from marrying a non-Israelite woman. Opinion seems to be divided, however, on the question of the captive woman's options. Some

6 Rambam, Hilkhot Melakhim, 8:7ff 1.

sources say she was converted by force. Others say she could opt to accept the seven Noahide laws. If she exercised the latter option, the Israelite was forbidden to marry her. She then became a resident alien. If she refused even the Noahide laws after staying with the man for a year, she was executed.

If and when the captive woman is no longer desired by her Israelite captor, she is allowed to leave whenever she wants. She is not allowed to be sold for money, and she is not allowed to be treated as merchandise (Deuteronomy 21:14). The reason for this is that he had sexually violated her (עניתה). Sifrei points out that she can go anywhere she wants except back to her idols. There is a difference of opinion among the commentators as to whether she actually needs a writ of divorce (*get*) or is simply allowed to leave. In Sifrei we have the statement that according to Rabbi Yonatan, he sends her away by means of a *get*. If she is sick, he must wait until she is well. Using the hermeneutic rule *qal va-homer* (*a fortiori*), Sifrei states that "this law holds for the daughters of Israel who are wholly and ritually pure." It would seem from this statement that she is accorded the same legal rights as a Jewish wife. This statement does not appear in Midrash HaGadol or in Midrash Tannaim. Sifrei Devarim Finkelstein edition (p. 247, n. 6), and Torah Temima (282, no. 92) explain that this statement does not appear in all Sifrei manuscripts and that Rambam and Ramban did not have access to it.

In *Hilkhot Melakhim* 8:7 Rambam plainly states that he lets her go where she pleases, and makes no mention of the requirement of a writ of divorce. This, however, is problematic for Rambam in the previous passage (8:6). There he mentions that the captor performs *kiddushin* and gives the captive a *ketuba*, i.e., marries her through the methods usually recommended by Jewish law. In that case, however, she would need a writ of divorce in order to part formally with the captor just as any Jewish woman would under normal circumstances in order for her marriage through *kiddushin* to be dissolved. Possibly, it can be understood that Rambam means that if he releases her within three months she requires no *get*.

In his discussion on ושלחה לנפשה ("and he shall send her away for herself "), however, Rambam makes the point that she does not require a *get*. He quotes Sifrei but does not quote the statement mentioned above. It seems that the issue of *get* is tied in with the issue of conversion. If yMakkot 2:6 is followed, then there is no intercourse until after conversion. At that time, as the captive is Jewish, the marriage is binding and a *get* would be necessary to dissolve the union.

If the Bavli is followed, then he can send her away after the first intercourse but before conversion, at which point she is not legally married and does not require a *get*. She must be released but not sold or traded. Clearly, it was understood both biblically and post-biblically that intercourse, even once, was a form of oppressing the captive. Sifrei's commentary on "because you had your will of her" is: אפילו לאחר מעשה יחידי "even after a single act."

Midrash Tannaim explains that the text used to arrive at this conclusion was Genesis 34:2 (the story of Dina and Shekhem mentioned above), ויקח אתה וישכב אתה ויענה, "And he took her and he lay with her and he violated her." The sages derive their understanding of עניתה from its use in this context.

The biblical imperative to release the captive woman is obviously not negotiable, but the interpretation is. That the sages chose to interpret her oppression as intercourse displays sensitivity to the captive's plight. Rape of captive women by soldiers has unfortunately been very prevalent recently in the war in Bosnia. Can Deuteronomy 21:10ff be considered anti-rape legislation for soldiers at war? The answer that eventually emerged from this discourse was, unfortunately, that it does not.

Biblically, it seems that the captive woman, by definition, has no choice but to go home with her captor. He is only allowed to have intercourse with her after a period of thirty days during which time she stays in his house. Clearly, immediate rape is not allowed. It can be understood that biblically we may be looking at anti-rape legislation for soldiers at war.

We see actual anti-rape legislation for soldiers directly after battle in yMakkot 2:6 — no intercourse is allowed with the captive unless all the rituals described in the Bible have been performed. This, however, changes in the Bavli. The Bavli does not understand this section of Deuteronomy in the same way as the Yerushalmi. Rather we see in bKiddushin 21b the general consensus that a soldier is allowed one act of intercourse with the captive, but not on the battlefield. Whether he is allowed to have intercourse with her again before he brings her home is a matter of divided opinion. In allowing the soldier this one act of intercourse, the Bavli undoes biblical anti-rape legislation for soldiers after a battle. The Yerushalmi and the Bavli clearly disagree on this issue. As the Bavli is the authoritative Talmud halakhically, its position stands. Therefore Deuteronomy 24:10ff cannot be understood as anti-rape legislation.

CONCLUSION

In general, Neofiti 1 and Targum Onqelos remained faithful to the biblical text of Deuteronomy 21:10-14. There are several additions in Targum Ps.-Jonathan which do not appear biblically. These additions are related to conversion ritual, and they seem to be alluded to in other *midreshei halakha*. As well, in his translation of certain key words, Targum Ps.-Jonathan does not display the sensitivity of the Bible to the powerlessness of the captive.

Legislating behavior is no guarantee that it will be followed, but it does demonstrate the intention of the legislators. The Yerushalmi clearly was against the rape of captive women by soldiers at war. In light of recent events in Bosnia, it must be appreciated how ethically and morally forward thinking this was. Unfortunately, it did not become embedded in codified *halakhah*.

A PEG TO HANG ON: METAPHOR, ANCESTRAL MERIT AND THE MIDRASHIC RELATIONSHIP OF DAVID AND SOLOMON[1]

Eva Mroczek, University of Toronto

The precursors flood us, and our imaginations can die by drowning in them,
but no imaginative life is possible if such inundation is wholly evaded.

Harold Bloom[2]

שיר חנוכת הבית לדוד –

סברין מימר דוד (אמרן) [אמרו], ואת תולה בדוד, שנאמר (ש"הש ד ד) כמגדל דוד צוארך.

אלא ... שלמה אמרה ותלה אותו בדוד

The song for the dedication of the house, of David: we think David uttered
it, and you "hang" it upon David, as Scripture says:
"Like the tower of David is your neck."
But... Solomon uttered it, and "hung" it upon David.
Midrash Shir ha-Shirim Rabbah[3]

1 This essay is dedicated to my teacher, Professor Harry Fox, whose influence on my development as a reader of texts has been nothing short of transformative. It is an honour to contribute my own attempt to think through some issues connected with, and inspired by, his concept of the embarrassment of scripture. I am grateful to have such a masterful guide to this rich tradition.

2 H. Bloom, *The Anxiety of Influence: A Theory of Poetry* (London and New York: Oxford Unversity Press, 1975), 154.

3 Quotations from rabbinic texts are based on the Global Jewish Database (The Responsa Project), Bar Ilan University (online version: http://www.responsa.co.il/home.en-US.aspx). This search tool has also been crucial in locating many of the texts used in this paper. For

INTRODUCTION

In his now-classic book of 1973, *The Anxiety of Influence,* Harold Bloom meditates upon authorship, biography and priority in the history of poetry. He proposes that the history of poetry since Shakespeare is the history of poetic influence: new poets and poems are formed by their predecessors. But this influence and indebtedness to the past is experienced as anxiety: the newcomer on the scene must carve out his own creative space and get out from under the shadow of his great predecessor in order to become a "strong" poet himself. The relationship between generations of poets is a kind of family saga, where the newcomer's attitude toward his poetic "father" is one of deep ambivalence characterized by indebtedness, continuity, and rebellion all at once.

How is this anxiety, this ambivalence about the burden and blessing of the past, resolved?[4] This question is applicable to much more than the history of modern poetry. I would like to ask it about some much earlier texts, namely rabbinic works that deal with questions of ancestral heritage and scriptural authority. How do these texts understand the history of tradition and the authoritative influence of the texts they meditate upon, (mis)interpret, and weave together into new works?

In this paper I would like to explore some midrashic views on the relationship between the present and the past, the dependence of descendants upon their ancestors, and the link between tradition and its new developments. In what way does the past inform and inspire, or constrain and confound, the present? How do Jewish writers in antiquity understand their own position as

the midrashim to Song of Songs and Qohelet I have also consulted the editions of *Midrash rabbahha-mevoar*, ed. A. Steinberger (Mekhon ha-Midrash ha-mevoar: Jerusalem, 1983-84). English translations are my own, guided partially by the Soncino editions (H. Freedman and Maurice Simon, trans. and ed., *Midrash Rabbah Song of Songs* [London: Soncino Press, 1961], and Freedman and Simon, ed., and A. Cohen, trans., *Midrash Rabbah Ecclesiastes* [London: Soncino Press, 1961]) and Jacob Neusner, *Song of Songs Rabbah: An Analytical Translation* (Atlanta: Scholars Press, 1989). English translations of biblical texts are adapted from the NRSV.

4 For Bloom, this is done through a series of six "revisionary rations," imaginative moves that continue the legacy but also misread, reverse, react against the work of the predecessor. This aspect of Bloom's theory is rich but does not directly shape my questions in this paper.

latecomers on the scene, and how do they imagine the progression of the chain of tradition that they have inherited? I would like to ask these extremely broad questions through a particular example that engages the themes of dependence and merit, authority and authorship, and ambivalent filial relationships: some ancient and rabbinic comments about the relationship between David and Solomon, especially in light of the ambivalent status of Solomon himself in the rabbinic imagination.

SOLOMON AND THE AMBIVALENCE OF TRADITION

If we think of Solomon in terms of Bloom's theory of poetic succession, he never becomes a "strong poet." He never gets out from the shadow of his great father. In fact, as we shall see, both his life's great accomplishments, the building of the Temple and the authorship of three biblical books, are somehow contingent on his predecessor.

I propose to use these author-kings and their relationship as a kind of hub from which we can see a constellation of ideas about the complex dependence of present authority on the ancestral past. In the context of rabbinic ideas about Solomon, these are layered questions. On one level, Solomon is a highly ambivalent figure: he is a great, revered sage, and the divinely inspired author of Proverbs, Qohelet and the Song of Songs; at the same time, he is sinful, hoards women and riches and does not live up to his father David's godly ways.[5] It seems to me that the sinfulness of a biblical author, whose works must nevertheless be held in the highest regard and relied upon as holy scripture, must have been a kind of embarrassment for the later tradition that was heir to these texts, and engendered creative interpretations that attempted to make sense of how such a person could be revered and how his

5 Clearly, the account in the book of Kings hardly paints David in such favourable terms. David's sins, however, are whitewashed already by the Chronicler and in subsequent traditions; a Qumran text calls David "perfect (תמים) in all his paths before God and men" (11Qpsalmsa col 27). While David is exalted, Solomon's character remains suspect. See, however, the Greek (LXX) translation of 1 Kings, 3 Kingdoms, which attempts to smooth over some of the more questionable aspects of Solomon's moral conduct; see e.g. D.W. Gooding, "Problems of Text and Midrash in the Third Book of Reigns," *Textus* 7 (1969): 1-29.

texts could be read as scripture.[6] This anxiety, I suggest, was resolved on a second level, which ascribes the idea of an ambivalent dependence back to Solomon's own status as an heir of his predecessor: his relationship with his righteous father David, which is a relationship of both contrast and continuity. Thus, the later tradition's dependence on the Solomonic heritage is possible because Solomon himself is heir to the Davidic heritage, a filial relationship which is conceived of in a variety of (sometimes contradictory) ways. Here, the ideas of ancestral merit and authorship intersect, and have implications for a general picture of the way the rabbis understood their dependence on both ancestral and textual heritage.

HANGING IT UPON DAVID: TWO WAYS INTO THE QUESTION

In the remainder of this paper I would like to explore these questions of ancestral merit and dependence on the past in light of this ambivalent relationship of the rabbis to Solomon and of Solomon to David. My starting point will be an intriguing passage in the midrash to the Song of Songs, which appears in the context of a long homily on the words שיר השירים אשר לשלמה, which, perhaps protesting a bit too much, establishes Solomon as the divinely inspired author (despite all his faults) of Proverbs, Qohelet and the Song of Songs. Within this passage, we find an intriguing suggestion that Solomon might be responsible for still more writings:

ד"א שיר השירים – ר' איבו ור' יהודה. ר' איבו אמר שיר – חד השירים – תרין הא תלתא. ור' יהודה בר סימן אמר שיר השירים כלה חד. לאלין תרתין אחרניאתא מה את עבד לון [חד] שיר המעלות לשלמה וחד מזמור שיר חנודת הבית לדוד – סברין מימר דוד (אמרן) [אמרו] ואת תולה בדוד שנאמר (ש"הש ד ד) כמגדל דוד צוארך. אלא {מה שיר השירים} שלמה אמרה ותלה אותו בדוד (א י).

Another interpretation: the Song of Songs. Rabbi Aibu and Rabbi Yehudah. Rabbi Aibu said, "Song" is one, "Songs" is two; that makes three. Rabbi Yehudah

6 For this idea I am indebted to conversations with Harry Fox about the concept from which this volume gets its title — the "embarrassment of scripture." In this paper I am thinking about it not in terms of embarrassing aspects of biblical narratives and the failings of biblical heroes, but through the problem of reading and revering texts whose author was not a perfectly exemplary figure.

> ben Simon said, the "Song of Songs" is one; what do you do with the other two? [One] is the "Song of Ascents of Solomon," and one is the "Song for the Dedication of the House, of David." We think that David composed it, and you attribute it to [lit. "hang" it upon] David, as it is said: "Like the tower of David is your neck." For {what is the Song of Songs?}[7] Solomon composed it, and attributed it to [lit. "hung" it upon] David.

The basic sense of this passage seems clear: the song for the dedication of the temple (Psalm 30), which bears the name of David and is thought to be composed by him, was really composed by Solomon. This alone is remarkable, for here it seems that we have a self-conscious admission that something like pseudepigraphic attribution has been recognized by the rabbis, even within the scriptural corpus! It seems that תולה בדוד, then, which I have rendered literally as "hang"it upon David, should be understood in terms of authorial attribution.

But there is an ambiguity to this passage, a double layer of possible meaning:[8] for *what* does one really "hang" upon David — the psalm, or the temple? Perhaps the homilist is simply pointing to an ambiguity in the very title of the psalm: *le-David* does not qualify the song but the house— that is, we should place the semantic division of the psalm heading in a different place: A psalm; a song for the dedication of the house of David. This explanation does not make the passage any less striking; indeed, it does not remove, but *doubles* the interpretive possibilities of this text. For the language of "hanging" — dependence, crediting, naming, association — now applies not only to texts, but also to biography.[9] This is reflected by the analogy chosen to illustrate the

7 It appears that the text is corrupt here; מה שיר השירים does not seem to fit the context here. With the emendations suggested by Steinberger and in the Soncino edition, I take the clause שלמה אמרה ותלה אותו to refer to the שיר חנוכת הבית.

8 See the commentary to this passage in Steinberger's *Midrash rabbah ha-mevoar, shir ha-shirim,* vol. 1, 29.

9 Here I am inspired by the work of Hindy Najman, who has written extensively on the practice of pseudepigraphy in ancient Judaism as a way of authorizing texts through linking them with ideal figures of the past, a practice in which both the text and the authoritative figure are transformed. She writes of pseudepigraphic texts, for example texts attributed to Moses or Ezra, as "discourse tied to a founder" whose name and authority are invoked by future writers. The link between the text and the biography or exemplary qualities of the "ideal

credit given to David for Solomon's work: שנאמר (ש"הש ד ד) כמגדל דוד צוארך, where מגדל דוד is supposed to refer to the Temple named for David.[10] Then the passage returns to textuality: שלמה אמרה ותלה אותו בדוד, "Solomon spoke [composed] it, and 'hung' it [presumably the Psalm for the dedication of the Temple] upon David."

How do we understand this kind of pseudonymous writing and building, this "hanging" of words and deeds onto a past figure? Not only the psalm, but also the great work of Solomon's life, the temple, is transformed into a deed of David and given his name. It seems, then, that there is more to the concept and expression of "hanging" something upon David than can be translated with the simple language of attribution. These expressions must be placed in the context of wider Jewish discourse about David and Solomon, and of ancestral heritage more broadly, the legacies of the great figures of the past.

The interpretive context of this passage shapes the remainder of this paper. I will approach my question in two intertwined ways. I will consider some biblical and rabbinic traditions that shed light on issues of ancestral merit and dependence, and betray an anxiety or ambivalence about the way the present is dependent on the past. Also, I will explore the lexical range of, or semantic network generated by, the word תלה, which is used here in the context of Solomon's work being "hung" upon David, but appears also in other contexts that can help us understand its nuanced, ambivalent meanings and related metaphors. Combining these two methods, I believe, sheds light not only on the way Solomon's relationship with his predecessor is imagined and fills in its thematic and lexical context, but also helps us conceptualize more broadly the complex, ambivalent nature of the present's reliance on ancestral tradition, and the way the themes of authorship, biography and priority are imagined in these texts.

---

figure" is crucial. See H. Najman, *Seconding Sinai: The Development of Mosaic Discourse in Second Temple Judaism* (Leiden: Brill, 2003), and e.g. "How Should We Contextualize Pseudepigrapha? Imitation and Emulation in 4 Ezra," In *Flores Florentino: Dead Sea Scrolls and Other Early Jewish Studies in Honour of Florentino Garcia Martinez* (eds A. Hilhorst, E. Puech, and E.J.C. Tigchelaar; Leiden: Brill, 2007), 529-36.

10 See Steinberger, 28-29, and Freedman, 13, n. 4. 230.

HANGING ON TO DAVID: THE RIGHTEOUS KING AND ANCESTRAL MERIT

> True poetic history is the story of how poets as poets have suffered other poets, just as any true biography is the story of how anyone suffered his own family.
>
> Harold Bloom[11]

I would like to begin by considering the context that is invoked by the Phrase "and he hung it upon David" ותלה אותו בדוד in our midrashic text, in light of other traditions about David. While the text is usually translated by the language of attribution, the concept, as I mentioned above, has a much broader, more nuanced meaning that cannot be reduced to issues of authorship alone. Rather, as in Bloom's work, bibliography and biography are intimately connected, and poetic dependence on one's great predecessors is conceived of as a family saga.[12] For example, this text about David from the midrashic compilation *Yalqut Shimoni* uses the language of "hanging" for the association of figures with a metaphorical "father," understanding David as the founder of a line of good kings:

> כה אמר ה׳ אלהי דוד אביך וכי בנו של דוד היה חזקיה והלא כמה דורות היו בינתם, אלא כל מלך כשר שהיה עומד היה תולה בדוד וכל מלך רשע שהיה עומד היה נתלה בירבעם שנאמר על חטאות ירבעם...

> 'Thus says the Lord, God of your father David.' For Hezekiah was the son of David. There were many generations between them, but every suitable king who arose was "hanging" upon David, and every wicked king who arose was "hung" upon Jeroboam, for it says about the sins of Jeroboam...[13]

In this text, Hezekiah is called the "son of David" because he, like all good kings, "hangs" upon, i.e. is linked to, David, while evil kings "are hung" upon, i.e. linked to, Jeroboam. The language evokes continuity and dependence, a

11 *Anxiety of Influence*, 94.

12 Bloom uses the term "family romance" for the fraught relationship of the newcomer poet with his metaphorical "father."

13 Arthur Hyman, Yitshaq Lerrer, and Yitshaq Shiloni, eds., *Yalqut Shimoni: Bamidbar* (Jerusalem: Mosad ha-Rav Kuk, 1973), 529.

figurative sonship or association, an inheritance of merit: Hezekiah is not literally the "son" of David, but he is David's true heir because of his association with him via righteous qualities. There is perhaps a play on words here. The word בן, which literally means "son," is also used figuratively for groups of people who are associated with some quality or idea; just as, for example, the Qumran community divided people into "sons of light" and "sons of darkness," so here Hezekiah is a "son of David" while the wicked kings would presumably be "sons of Jeroboam." The verbs תולה and נתלה appear to participate in a subtle play on words embedded in their forms: the active form for the good kings and a passive one (*niph'al*) for the bad ones, evoking the image that they are literally hung, strung up as punishment for their wickedness.

David, then, is a kind of paradigmatic good king who founds a line of succession and whose influence seems to stretch down through the generations after him. His righteousness not only connects him to the "good" kings. It seems that David and his legacy for the future can be thought of in the context of the rabbinic notion of זכות אבות, the "merit of the fathers/ancestors." The merit of righteous people in earlier times serves as insurance against the abolition of the covenant in case future generations sin;[14] past generations' merit extends over their descendants, both righteous and wicked. Although in rabbinic literature "the merit of the fathers," זכות אבות, is usually associated with the Patriarchs, it applies just as well to the influence of David's righteousness on God's dealings with his heirs — particularly his wise but morally suspect son Solomon. Already in the book of Kings, Solomon is compared unfavourably with David, but escapes immediate punishment because of his father's merits:

5 וילך שלמה אחרי עשתרת אלהי צדנים ואחרי מלכם שקץ עמנים: 6 ויעש שלמה הרע בעיני יהוה ולא מלא
אחרי יהוה כדוד אביו: 7 אז יבנה שלמה במה לכמוש שקץ מואב בהר אשר על–פני ירושלם ולמלך שקץ בני עמון:
8 וכן עשה לכל–נשיו הנכריות מקטירות ומזבחות לאלהיהן: 9 ויתאנף יהוה בשלמה כי–נטה לבבו מעם יהוה
אלהי ישראל הנראה אליו פעמים: 10 וצוה אליו על–הדבר הזה לבלתי–לכת אחרי אלהים אחרים ולא שמר את
אשר–צוה יהוה: ף 11 ויאמר יהוה לשלמה יען אשר היתה–זאת עמך ולא שמרת בריתי וחקתי אשר צויתי עליך

14 This complex idea is developed in a variety of ways in the rabbinic traditions. For a discussion, see E.E. Urbach, *The Sages: Their Concepts and Beliefs* (Jerusalem: Magnes Press, Hebrew University, 1979), 496ff.

קרע אקרע את–הממלכה מעליך ונתתיה לעבדך: 12 אך–בימיך לא אעשנה למען דוד אביך מיד בנך אקרענה:
13 רק את–כל–הממלכה לא אקרע שבט אחד אתן לבנך למען דוד עבדי ולמען ירושלם אשר בחרת:

> 5 For Solomon followed Astarte the goddess of the Sidonians, and Milcom the abomination of the Ammonites. 6 So Solomon did what was evil in the sight of the Lord, and did not completely follow the Lord, as his father David had done. 7 Then Solomon built a high place for Chemosh the abomination of Moab, and for Molech the abomination of the Ammonites, on the mountain east of Jerusalem. 8 He did the same for all his foreign wives, who offered incense and sacrificed to their gods. 9 Then the Lord was angry with Solomon, because his heart had turned away from the Lord, the God of Israel, who had appeared to him twice, 10. and had commanded him concerning this matter, that he should not follow other gods; but he did not observe what the Lord commanded 11. Therefore the Lord said to Solomon, "Since this has been your mind and you have not kept my covenant and my statutes that I have commanded you, I will surely tear the kingdom from you and give it to your servant. 12 Yet for the sake of your father David I will not do it in your lifetime; I will tear it out of the hand of your son. 13 I will not, however, tear away the entire kingdom; I will give one tribe to your son, for the sake of my servant David and for the sake of Jerusalem, which I have chosen." (1 Kings 11:5-13).

Solomon is not punished למען דוד עבדי , "on account /for the sake of David my servant," whose merit protects his son.

The Book of Kings' way of dealing with Solomon's sinfulness is developed along the same lines in a later tradition, Ben Sira's Praise of the Ancestors. For Ben Sira, Solomon is a great sage who is praised for the great wisdom of his youth and for his songs and proverbs, but is morally corrupt:

> 14 How wise you were when you were young! You overflowed like the Nile with understanding. 15 Your influence spread throughout the earth, and you filled it with proverbs having deep meaning. 16 Your fame reached to far-off islands, and you were loved for your peaceful reign. 17 Your songs, proverbs, and parables, and the answers you gave astounded the nations. 18 In the name of the Lord God, who is called the God of Israel, you gathered gold like tin and amassed silver like lead. 19 But you brought in women to lie at your side, and through your body

> you were brought into subjection. 20 You stained your honor, and defiled your family line, so that you brought wrath upon your children, and they were grieved at your folly, 21 because the sovereignty was divided and a rebel kingdom arose out of Ephraim. 22 But the Lord will never give up his mercy, or cause any of his works to perish; he will never blot out the descendants of his chosen one, or destroy the family line of him who loved him. So he gave a remnant to Jacob, and to David a root from his own family (*Ben Sira* 47:14-22).

Here, God abides with the Davidic line *despite* Solomon's sins and *because* of David's devotion. Like the passage about Hezekiah from *Yalqut Shimoni,* the language evokes sonship and association, but unlike that text, in *Ben Sira* we see a contrast between David and his descendant, who has defiled his great family line. In Kings and *Ben Sira*, then, the two monarchs contrast each other. But there is another dimension in which their relationship is conceived — foundation and completion: David is depicted as the true originator of work that Solomon only executes.[15] Most notably, in Chronicles David is the true founder of the temple although it is actually built by his son. He receives a divinely inspired model for the Temple architecture and its liturgical functioning, and in following this blueprint, he does every Temple-related activity short of actually constructing it.[16] Besides setting up the liturgical music, he also makes all the preparations for construction (1 Chron. 22:14):

> והנה בעניי הכינותי לבית–יהוה זהב ככרים מאה–אלף וכסף אלף אלפים ככרים ולנחשת ולברזל אין משקל כי לרב היה ועצים ואבנים הכינותי ועליהם תוסיף:

> See, in my poverty, I have prepared for the House of YHWH one hundred thousand talents of gold and one million talents of silver, and so much copper and iron it cannot be weighed; I have also prepared wood and stone, and you shall add to them.

15 These various ways in which Solomon both reverses and continues the legacy of David are reminiscent of some of Harold Bloom's six "revisionary ratios" in which poets respond to their predecessors, and which include the moves of completion and reversal; I shall not, however, pursue these similarities at length here.

16 See S. Japhet, *The Ideology of the Book of Chronicles and Its Place in Biblical Thought* (Frankfurt am Main; New York: P. Lang, 1997), 229f.

David, then, is the real founder of the temple, and Solomon's work is completely contingent upon him, his plans, raw materials, and authority. Even as Solomon defiles his family line through his sins, he completes his father's legacy.

DAVID AND SOLOMON: CONTINUITY AND CONTRAST IN *SHIR HA-SHIRIM* AND *QOHELET RABBAH*

> "Be me but not me" is the paradox of the precursor's implicit charge to the ephebe. Less intensely, his poem says to its descendant poem: "Be like me but unlike me." If there were no ways of subverting this double bind, every ephebe would develop into a poetic version of a schizophrenic.
>
> Harold Bloom[17]

The relationship between the righteous David and his heir, then, is a complex one, and includes ideas of both contrast and continuity. Let us see how this ambivalence is imagined even more vividly in the midrashim to two Solomonic works, the Songs of Songs and Qohelet, and how other rabbinic traditions about ancestral merit shed light on these texts.

In the passage from *Ben Sira*, we began to see how Solomon's literary activity is considered together with his objectionable biography. It goes without saying that because Solomon is the putative author of three biblical books, the stark contrast between the righteous David and the wicked Solomon must have been embarrassing. In *Shir ha-shirim Rabbah,* too, the issue of Solomon's acceptability as a divinely inspired author is a major preoccupation of the midrash on the opening verses of the Song of Songs.

The homilists' consideration of Solomon's worthiness and authorship begins as follows:

> אמר רבי יהושע בן לוי בשעה שנמנו וגמרו שלשה מלכים וארבעה הדיוטות אין להם חלק לעולם הבא בקשו לצרף שלמה עמהם יצתה בת קול ואמרה אל תגעו במשיחי אמר רבי יהודה בר סימון ולא עוד אלא שנתיחס ראש לשלשלת יוחסין שנאמר ורחבעם בן שלמה אמר רבי יודן בר סימון ולא עוד אלא ששרתה עליו רוח הקדש ואמר שלשה ספרים הללו משלי שיר השירים וקהלת

17 *The Anxiety of Influence*, 70.

> R. Joshua b. Levi said: When they [the men of the Great Assembly] decided by a majority, three kings and four non-royal personages are to have no share in the world to come, they sought to associate Solomon with them, but a *bat qol* went forth and said, "Do not touch my anointed ones." Said R. Judah b. Simon: And moreover, he was placed at the head of a genealogical tree, as it says, "And Rehoboam the son of Solomon reigned in Judah." Said R. Judah b. Simon: And moreover, the holy spirit rested on him and composed these three works: Proverbs, Song of Songs, and Qohelet.[18]

Although initially condemned by the men of the Great Assembly, Solomon is saved *deus ex machina*—style by a *bat qol*, and divinely inspired to write his three books.

Immediately after this account, the midrash moves on to consider Solomon's relationship with David, seeming to neutralize the stark contrast between David and Solomon in the Book of Kings, and show instead that Solomon was in fact like his father. Beginning with the verse "Instead of your fathers shall be your sons" (Ps. 45:17), the midrash says that a righteous man can beget a wicked man and vice versa, adducing scriptural proofs for each case; the righteous David begat the righteous Solomon, for their lives and deeds parallel one another:

> אבל שלמה מלך בן מלך חכם בן חכם צדיק בן צדיק אווגיטוס בן אווגיטוס. את מוצא כל מה שכתוב בזה כתוב בזה דוד מלך ארבעים שנה וזה מלך ארבעים שנה דוד מלך על ישראל ויהודה ובנו מלך על ישראל ויהודה אביו בנה את היסודות והוא בנה את העליונות אביו מלך מסוף העולם ועד סופו וזה מלך מסוף העולם ועד סופו דוד כתב ספרים ושלמה כתב ספרים דוד אמר שירים ושלמה אמר שירים דוד אמר הבלים ושלמה אמר הבלים דוד אמר דברים ושלמה אמר דברים דוד אמר משלים ושלמה אמר משלים דוד קלס באז ושלמה קלס באז דוד בנה מזבח ושלמה בנה מזבח דוד הקריב קרבן ושלמה הקריב קרבן דוד העלה את הארון ושלמה העלה את הארון.

> ... רבי סימון בשם רבי יונתן דבית גוברין בשם רבי יהושע בן לוי אמר הואיל ואת מקישו מקישו מכל צד מה אביו נמחל לו על כל עונותיו שנאמר (שם יב, יג) 'גם ה' העביר הטאתך לא תמות' אף זה כיוצא בו ולא עוד אלא ששרתה עלו רוח הקדש ואמר שלשה ספרים משלי וקהלת ושיר השירים.

18 See also parallel texts in bSanhedrin 10.

> But Solomon was a king and the son of a king, a wise man and the son of a wise man, a righteous man and the son of a righteous man, a noble and the son of a noble. You find that everything that is written about one is written about the other. David reigned for forty years and he reigned for forty years. David reigned over Israel and Judah and his son reigned over Israel and Judah. His son built the foundations [of the temple] and he built the upper parts. His father reigned from one end of the world to the other, and he reigned from one end of the world to the other. David wrote books and Solomon wrote books. David composed songs and Solomon composed songs. David said "vanities" and Solomon said "vanities." David spoke words and Solomon spoke words. David spoke proverbs and Solomon spoke proverbs. David praised [starting] with "az" and Solomon praised with "az." David built an altar and Solomon built an altar. David offered a sacrifice and Solomon offered a sacrifice. David brought up the ark and Solomon brought up the ark.…Rabbi Simon in the name of Rabbi Yonatan from Beit Gubrin in the name of Rabbi Joshua ben Levi said, If you are comparing, then compare them in every way. His father was forgiven his sons, for it says "And the Lord has forgiven your sins and you will not die"; so with the one who came out [of him]. And what is more, the holy spirit rested upon him and he composed three books, Proverbs, Qohelet and the Song of Songs.

David and Solomon are alike in every aspect of their lives and literary activity, even, as R. Shimon importantly adds, in that their sins were forgiven. *All* that is written of one is written of the other: the midrash adduces scriptural proofs for each of the parallels between the two.

The purpose of setting up such a mirror between David and Solomon seems, in light of the context, to be a justification or authorization of Solomon's authorship of Song of Songs (as well as his other works) through a favourable comparison with David. Perhaps in the background of this move is not only Solomon's life, but more specifically the unclear status of Song of Songs and Qohelet in some rabbinic texts.[19] The comparison with David and his Psalms, both unquestioned in authority and status, legitimizes Solomon and his books: Solomon is his father's son in every way, and continues his legacy, literally

19 See e.g. mYadaim 3 and the issue of which books "defile the hands."

builds upon his foundations. David might be the true founder of the temple and the true paradigm of the righteous king and exemplary biblical author, but Solomon continues his legacy by following his cultic, ethical, and textual paradigm, his תבנית.[20]

This reading is supported by a passage in *Bereshit Rabbah* to Genesis 37:2, where the similar expression כל מה שארע לזה ארע בזה, "everything that happened to one happened to the other," is applied to Jacob and Joseph. There, the midrash seeks to explain why the words אלה תולדות יעקב are followed immediately by the name of Joseph, instead of a mention of Reuben, as ordinary genealogy would dictate. The many parallels between what is written of Jacob and Joseph are written in a style that closely resembles, and may have inspired, our passage about David and Solomon:

> לא היה צריך קרא למימר כן אלא אלה תולדות יעקב ראובן אלא מה תלמוד לומר יוסף אלא שכל מה שארע לזה ארע לזה מה זה נולד מהול אף זה נולד מהול מה זה אמו עקרה אף זה אמו עקרה מה זה אמו ילדה שנים אף זה אמו ילדה שנים...
>
> Should Scripture not have said it this way: these are the generations of Jacob — Reuben? But we are taught that it is Joseph. But everything that happened to one happened to the other. One was born circumcised, and the other was born circumcised; one's mother was childless and the other's mother was childless; one's mother bore two and the other's mother bore two...

The comparison, it seems, serves to legitimize Joseph as his father's true heir, even though the "generations of Jacob" should by rights have begun with Reuben. This is reminiscent of the move in the passage from *Yalqut Shimoni* cited above, in which Hezekiah is called David's son even though several generations separate them; the similarity of their moral conduct means that Hezekiah is associated with David in a kind of metaphorical sonship, just

20 I have written about David's example as a תבנית or paradigm for future generations in "Moses, David and Scribal Revelation: Preservation and Renewal in Second Temple Jewish Textual Traditions," in *The Significance of Sinai* (eds. G. Brooke, H. Najman, and L. Stuckenbruck; Themes in Biblical Narrative; Leiden: Brill, 2008), 91-115. There, I also emphasise the connection between the biography and text production, arguing that David as well as Moses are models for future generations through their identity as *scribes* in the second temple period, an identity that encompasses not only textual activity but a righteous life.

as here Joseph is associated with Jacob as his true heir because of the many parallels in their biographies. We find a similar formula, using the phrase "all that is written about the one is written about the other (כל מה שכתוב בזה כתוב בזה) used to compare the biographies and merits of Moses and Jeremiah; although there was never again a "prophet like Moses," Jeremiah's prophetic greatness is compared — and is indeed comparable — to his.[21]

It seems, then, that the rabbinic interpreters are doing what they can to redeem Solomon, to overcome their embarrassment about what otherwise might seem to be this least admirable of biblical authors, by associating Solomon as closely as possible with his righteous father. But this is not always the way the comparison formula is used. Part of the same text about David and Solomon appears in another midrashic work, the Midrash Rabbah to Qohelet, where it takes on completely different connotations and is embedded in a quite different context. Far from exalting Solomon by comparing him favourably with David, here the passage is sandwiched between two less than flattering passages about Solomon, passages which inflect our text with quite a different meaning. The relevant text begins with exegesis of Solomon's names:

> אגור שאגור בדברי תורה יקה שהיה מקיא בדבריו כספל הזה שמתמלא בשעתו ומתפנה בשעתו כך שלמה למד תורה בשעתה ושכחה בשעתה למואל שנם לאל בלבו ואמר יכול אני להרבות ולא לחטא איתיאל שאמר אתי אל ואוכל בן דוד מלך בן מלך חכם בן חכם צדיק בן צדיק אבגינוס בן אבגינוס. רבי יודן בשם רבי אלכסנדרי השור הזה עד שלא נחתכו גידיו נתלה הוא אפלו בגיד אחר משלו אבל משנחתכו גידיו כמה חבלים וכמה מסמרות צריך לתלות בהן כך עד שלא חטא שלמה היה נתלה בזכות עצמו וכיון שחטא תלו לו בזכות אבותיו הדא הוא דכתיב למען דוד עבדי.(א א)

> [Solomon was called] Agur since he was stored with words of Torah. He was called Jakeh because he discharged words like a bowl that is filled at one time and emptied at another time. Similarly did Solomon learn Torah at one time and forget it another time. He was called Lemuel because he spoke against God in his heart, saying, "I can multiply without sinning." He was called Ittiel because he said, "God is with me," and I can [sin]. Son of David: a king and the son of a king, a wise man and the son of a wise man, a righteous man and the son of a righteous man, a noble and the son of a noble. R. Judah said in the

21 See Midrash Zuta to *Eikha,* Parashah 1.

> name of R. Alexandri: An ox, before its tendons are cut, can be pulled ["hung"] by even one of its tendons; but when they have been cut, how many ropes and nails are needed to pull ["hang"] it! Thus, until Solomon sinned, he was hung upon his own merit, but when he sinned, they hung him by the merit of his fathers, for it is written, "On account of David my son" [1 Kgs 11:11-13]. (Qohelet Rabbah 1,1)

Here, the passage beginning with מלך בן מלך does not achieve the legitimization of Solomon through an equation with David.Quite the contrary: the text is placed between two passages that emphasize Solomon's sin, and how different he was from his father. In this case, the connection between Solomon and David does not mean that Solomon is a worthy successor to his father and continues his legacy; rather, it implies that Solomon can get by *only* because he is his father's son, *only* because of his father's merits. In fact, one translation of this passage in *Qohelet Rabbah* interprets these words about Solomon's ancestry as Solomon's own self-justification: since he can rely on David's merit, he may sin with impunity.[22] Here, Solomon is at once protected and condemned by his relationship with his ancestor.

While the text in *Shir ha-Shirim Rabbah* seemed to neutralize the contrast between David and Solomon that we found in 1 Kings 11 and other early texts, the surrounding context in *Qohelet Rabbah* upholds the contrast, even quoting the formulation "for the sake of David my servant." In a most unflattering image, Solomon is compared to an ox whose tendons have been cut and who cannot walk on its own, but must be pulled along ("hung upon") by many ropes and nails — that is, he has sinned and must be pulled along ("hung upon") בזכות אבותיו, by the merit of his ancestors. Here, the embarrassment of having to revere a sinful biblical author is overcome not through the whitewashing of Solomon, but through exalting the power of David's merit. Solomon is venerated, but only למען דוד, on account of David; his authority is fully dependent on — suspended from — David's own.

---

22 This interpretive move is made in the Soncino translation by Cohen. He places the " son of a king" speech in Solomon's mouth. Solomon says to himself that he may sin with impunity because he can rely on his ancestry, the merit of the fathers, to protect him: "...I can multiply [wives] without sinning. He was called 'Ithiel' because he said, 'God is with me,' and I can do so, *seeing that I am* David's son, a king and a king's son..."(4)

A PEG TO HANG ON: METAPHOR AND ANCESTRAL MERIT

> But nothing is got for nothing, and self-appropriation involves the immense anxieties of indebtedness, for what strong maker desires the realization that he has not created himself?
>
> Harold Bloom[23]

In using the language of dependence and suspension, I want to suggest that this complex idea of the dependence of the present and the past, and the intersection between authorship and ancestry, can be illustrated with a lexical study of the root תלה , literally "to hang," and its associated metaphors. We began with a passage in which Solomon "hung" his text and/or his temple on David, תלה אותה בדוד; we saw also that the righteous and wicked kings are all imagined to be "hanging" upon David or Jeroboam; and we read that Solomon, like an ox with its tendons cut, must "hang" off the merit of his father. Clearly, this word casts a wide semantic net, rich with multilayered meanings related to dependence, contingency, and association.

This language of "hanging" generates particularly evocative images and metaphors related to the concept of the merit of ancestors. The core metaphor is that ancestral merit is something fixed and solid. This is illustrated in the ox pericope in *Qohelet Rabbah* by the image of nails (מסמרות) from which the unworthy can hang, or by which they can be dragged along. We find similar imagery in a passage of the Palestinian Talmud, Tractate Berakhot, in the story of R. Akiva's reaction to the appointment of R. Eleazar as the head of the yeshiva:

> והיה ר"ע יושב ומצטער ואמר לא שהוא בן תורה יותר ממני אלא שהוא בן גדולים יותר ממני אשרי אדם שזכו לו אבותיו אשרי אדם שיש לו יתד במי להיתלות בה וכי מה היתה יתידתו של ראב"ע שהיה דור עשירי לעזרא.

And Rabbi Akiva sat and was upset, and he said, it's not that he is a better Torah student ("son of the Torah") than I, but that he is of greater ancestry ("son of

23 *The Anxiety of Influence*, 5.

> great ones") than I.[24] Happy is the man who has ancestral merit, happy is the man who has a peg on which to hang! And what was the peg of Rabbi Eleazar ben Azariah? He was the tenth generation from Ezra. (yBerakhot 47b)

In this passage Rabbi Akiva bemoans the fact that he has only his Torah learning, while R. Eleazar can also count on the merit of his ancestors — he can grasp onto and "hang" from the reputation or influence of his ancestor Ezra, his solid "peg" or nail יתד. The metaphor of "pegs" for righteous ancestors whose merit extends down the generations is not unique to this text. In Genesis Rabbah, Abraham, Isaac, and Jacob are שלושה יתידות גדולות, "three great pegs," in the world (Gen. R. 43:8).[25]

This image of pegs as a metaphor for solidity and dependability has roots in the biblical tradition. We find it in a prophecy in Isaiah 22:

> 20 והיה ביום ההוא וקראתי לעבדי לאליקים בן–חלקיהו 21 והלבשתיו כתנתך ואבנטך אחזקנו וממשלתך אתן
> בידו והיה לאב ליושב ירושלם ולבית יהודה 22 ונתתי מפתח בית–דוד על–שכמו ופתח ואין סגר וסגר ואין פתח
> 23 ותקעתיו יתד במקום נאמן והיה לכסא כבוד לבית אביו 24 ותלו עליו כל כבוד בית–אביו הצאצאים והצפעות
> כל כלי הקטן מכלי האגנות ועד כל–כלי הנבלים 25 ביום ההוא נאם יהוה צבאות תמוש היתד התקועה במקום נאמן
> ונגדעה ונפלה ונכרת המשא אשר–עליה כי יהוה דבר

> 20 In that day I will summon my servant, Eliakim son of Hilkiah. 21 I will clothe him with your robe and fasten your sash around him and hand your authority over to him. He will be a father to those who live in Jerusalem and to the house of Judah. 22 I will place on his shoulder the key to the house of David; what he opens no one can shut, and what he shuts no one can open. 23 I will drive him like a peg into a firm place; he will be a seat of honor for the house of his father. 24 All the glory of his family will hang on him: its offspring and offshoots — all its lesser vessels, from the bowls to all the jars. 25 In that day, declares the LORD Almighty, the peg driven into the firm place will give way; it will be sheared off and will fall, and the load hanging on it will be cut down. The LORD has spoken.

---

24 Once again, we see a kind of subtle play on the idea of sonship as both a family relationship and an association with a particular idea in the concepts בן גדולים and בן תורה.

25 Elsewhere the three patriarchs are described as three great pillars, or the pillars of the throne (see Urbach, 498).

Here, Eliakim is likened to a tent peg, ensuring a secure place for his family (the sprouts and the leaves and various vessels of the metaphor), just as vessels and other objects in a tent would be hung from a rope firmly anchored in the ground.[26]

Once again, a "peg" is something solid, firmly fixed in place — a righteous ancestor upon whom subsequent generations can "hang."

The word יתד itself connotes fixity and firmness. (Jastrow suggests a possible etymological link with the Aramaic עתד , to "put up" or "fix."[27]) Not only can dependable ancestors be pegs — opinions or rulings can be pegs too, as in יתד היא שלא תמוט, "this is a peg which cannot be dislodged," said in reference to a firm opinion in bGittin 17a. Interestingly, a similar image with different wording appears near the end of Qohelet: דברי חכמים כדרבנות וכמשמרות נטועים בעלי אספות ("The sayings of the wise are like goads, and like nails firmly fixed are the collected sayings." [12:11]). Here, we do not see the word יתד, but the fixity of משמרות (an unusual spelling of מסמרות , nails) firmly hammered in (or "planted") is used of wise men and their collected sayings, once again connecting biography and bibliography — a textual and ancestral heritage. What are firm, fixed, and dependable are not only the righteous lives of one's predecessors, whose influence extends down the generations, but also, and perhaps more concretely, their words.

Thus, with the firmly fixed משמרות, we come once again to the image of Solomon as an ox with its tendons cut, who must be pulled or who "hangs" from nails (here spelled מסמרות), which represent the unwavering merit of his father David. What does it mean, though, to *hang* — to be suspended from one's ancestry? The slaughtered ox that is dragged along evokes an image of complete helplessness and lack of agency; it seems that the failure of Solomon to get by on his own merits is well illustrated. But the semantic range of the word תלה is far wider.[28] In the biblical and rabbinic

26 Benjamin Sommer in his commentary to Isaiah 22:23-24 in the *Jewish Study Bible: Jewish Publication Society Tanakh Translation* (Oxford University Press: New York, 2004), 827.

27 Jastrow's *Dictionary of the Targumim, the Talmud Babli and Yerushalmi, and the Midrashic Literature* (Peabody, Mass.: Hendrickson, 2005), as well as the Bar Ilan Jewish Responsa Database; both served as resources for the following lexical discussions.

28 Helene Cixous reads the layered meanings of another such image, Rembrandt's painting *The Slaughtered Ox*, as "The Passion According to Rembrandt. Mourning and the Transfiguration of the Ox," in "Bathsheba or the interior Bible," tr. C.A.F. MacGillivray, in *Stigmata: Escaping*

texts the word is most often used in its literal sense, to denote simply hanging, often the hanging of people as capital punishment (see the usage in Esther, Lamentations, etc.[29]). But besides this, the language of "hanging" is used in various contexts of dependence or ascription. In bBaba Bathra 109b, we read it once again in the context of dependence, similarity and metaphorical sonship:

> וכי בן מנשה הוא והלא בן משה הוא דכתיב (דברי הימים א כג) בני משה גרשם ואליעזר אלא מתוך שעשה מעשה מנשה תלאו הכתוב במנשה הכא נמי מתוך שעשה מעשה מנשה דאתי מיהודה תלאו הכתוב ביהודה אמר רבי יוחנן משום רבי שמעון בן יוחי מכאן שתולין את הקלקלה במקולקל

> Was he the son of Manasseh? Surely he was the son of Moses, for it is written, "the son of Moses: Gershom, and Eliezer"; but [you must say that] because he acted as Manasseh, the Scriptural text "hung" his descent on Manasseh, [so] also here because he acted as Manasseh who descended from Judah, the Scriptural text "hung" his descent on Judah. R. Johanan said in the name of R. Simeon b. Yohai: From here [one may infer] that corruption is "hung" upon the corrupt.

"Hanging" is used for the connection of similar figures to one another, and of a logical tracing back of corruption to corrupt people. Unlike the "hanging" of sinful descendants upon the merit of their righteous ancestors, as in some other rabbinic texts, here the language of "hanging" connects like with like, in a metaphorical filial relationship.

Another conceptually similar meaning has to do with tracing origins, for credit or blame. One example is in mNiddah 9:3, where a stain on a garment is ascribed to someone who had lent it (הרי זה תולה בה). Other uses of the verb include the idea of dependence or contingency — e.g., a law that is contingent on being in the land of Israel (מצוה שהיא תלויה בארץ). It can also be used to mean that something is in doubt, left undecided — that is, suspended, as a judgment,

---

Texts (Routledge: London and New York, 1998), 3-19, 18. I thank Harry Fox for pointing me to this suggestive text.

29 Interpretive motifs based on this verb are also discussed by James Kugel, *In Potiphar's House: The Interpretive Life of Biblical Texts* (San Francisco: Harper, 1990), 184-9, in the context of the harps hanging on trees in Ps. 137.

e.g. ועל החמורות הוא תולה עד שיבא יוה"כ (Yoma 8.8). The noun תלייה from the same root means suspense or doubt. Finally, in Aramaic usage of the root in the targums, it can mean to be fortified, exalted, lifted up — nearly the opposite connotation from being dragged along like a mutilated ox.

Indeed, the semantic nuances of תלה are comparable to the web of meanings woven from the Latin root *pend* in romance languages. The broad semantic range of the word תלה reflects the ambiguous nature of the present's relationship to the past, to ancestry and to tradition. To return to the text which opened our discussion: to say that Solomon's psalm or Solomon's temple — or both — is hung upon David is much more than simply to say he is given pseudonymous credit for them when they were really the work of someone else. It is a statement rich with the context of biblical and rabbinic ideas about the relationship between David and Solomon, the notion of ancestral merit, and the multivalent, sometimes contradictory metaphors and images associated with it.

CONCLUSION

> What the precursors did has thrown the ephebe into the outward and downward motion of repetition, a repetition that the ephebe soon understands must be both undone and dialectically affirmed, and those simultaneously.
>
> Harold Bloom[30]

The present — here represented by Solomon's life and work — can hang on the past in a variety of senses: in the sense of getting by only on its merit (like the helpless ox pulled along by ropes and nails, and the sinful Solomon spared only for David's sake); of being influenced by and equal to it like a child who resembles his father (like the great king, singer and sage, son of the great king, singer and sage); of tracing itself back to a necessary origin (like Solomon the temple builder completing his father's plans, literally building on

30 *The Anxiety of Influence*, 83

his foundations). Translating the passage about Solomon's work being "hung upon David" in terms of "attribution" or "ascription" suggests too simplistic a move; the hanging of text and temple upon David is not merely to call them by his name, but to claim something more complex about origins, dependence, and influence.

Solomon's relationship to his ancestor condemns, constrains, protects, and exalts him all at once. The great achievements of his life as understood by later readers — the temple and three scriptural wisdom books — are both dependent on his ancestor: the temple he built is the בית דוד, "house of David"; his worthiness to author the Song of Songs and Qohelet must be legitimized at least partly through David's merit. Solomon remains an ambivalent figure who, in his own family drama as it unfolds through biblical interpreters, can never get out from under his father's mighty shadow. In his dependence on the past, is Solomon exalted — is he lifted up — or is he strung up for his sins? I think, rather, that he hangs in the balance. Judgment on his life is swung to and fro like a pendulum by his rabbinic interpreters, but is always, ultimately, suspended.

FROM GLUTTON TO GANGSTER

Eliezer Segal, University of Calgary

Any list of embarrassing or morally troubling passages in the Torah must surely reserve an honored place for the law of the stubborn and rebellious son, as set out in Deuteronomy 21:18-22. According to the unembellished words of the scripture, this son is subjected to death by stoning for transgressions that amount to little more than general defiance and overindulgence. In the law that emerges from the Mishnah and Talmuds, the rabbis' discomfort with the application of this law is implicit in their success at effectively neutralizing it. They make the conditions under which the lad could be executed so absurdly restrictive that they could never occur in real life.

It should be noted that the approach described so far is one that was associated primarily with Rabbi Akiva, who was distinguished by his general antipathy towards the death penalty, and whose school played the key role in shaping the teachings of the Mishnah. Akiva's school applied similar hermeneutic strategies to capital crimes in general—though perhaps not as blatantly as in the case of the rebellious son—in order to turn judicial executions into very uncommon occurrences.[1] Talmudic traditions preserve records of opposition to his approach, with respect to both capital punishment and the elimination of the law of the rebellious son. The view to uphold the spirit of the Torah's original purpose is represented by Rabbi Jonathan who is associated with the rival school of Rabbi Ishmael.[2] The novelty of Rabbi Akiva's

1 mMakkot 1:10.

2 David Hoffmann, *Zur Einleitung in die Halachischen Midraschim*, Jahresbericht des Rabbiner-Seminars zu Berlin (Berlin: M. Driesner, 1988); J. N. Epstein, *Prolegomena ad Litteras Tannaiticas*(Tel Aviv and Jerusalem: The Magnes Press and Dvir, 1957), 570 [Hebrew]; Ch.

approach may be appreciated more clearly when we bear in mind that first century Jewish authorities from outside the official rabbinic circles—Philo of Alexandria[3] and Joseph ben Matthiah[4] —are relatively untroubled by the prospect of executing the disobedient son. To their minds, it was sufficient to argue that the authority of the parents in the family was so vital to the foundations of society that any challenge to that authority had to be resisted with uncompromising severity.[5]

Moshe Halbertal has surveyed with admirable clarity the three different hermeneutical strategies that the rabbis employed in order to deal with, and neutralize, the moral embarrassment of the biblical law: (1) by rendering the law unenforceable; (2) by justifying it as an inscrutable divine decree; and (3) by pointing out the profound divine insight into adolescent behavior that anticipated the delinquent's inevitable descent into a pattern of hardened criminality.[6] My purpose here is neither to repeat Halbertal's discussion, nor to dispute its main arguments. I wish merely to focus on a single hermeneu-

---

Albeck, *Introduction to the Talmud, Bavli and Yerushalmi* (Tel-Aviv: Dvir, 1969), 102, 129-130 [Hebrew]; Gunter Stemberger and Hermann Leberecht Strack, *Introduction to the Talmud and Midrash*, trans. Markus N. A. Bockmuehl, 2nd ed. (Edinburgh: T. & T. Clark, 1996), 247-251. The fact that Rabbi Jonathan's tradition is attested only in the Babylonian Talmud (bSanhedrin 71a) adds some support to the argument originally proposed by I. Halevy [Isaac Halevy, *Dorot harishonim*, reprint ed. (Jerusalem: 1966), 1:678-681, etc.] that the school of Rabbi Ishmael migrated to Babylonia in the wake of the Bar Kokhba revolt. See the discussions in: Jacob Neusner, *A History of the Jews in Babylonia*, 2nd ed., 5 vols. (Leiden: E. J. Brill, 1965-1970), 1:125; Isaiah Gafni, *Jews of Babylonia in the Talmudic Era: A Social and Cultural History*, Monographs in Jewish History (Jerusalem: The Zalman Shazar Center for Jewish History, 1990), 81-86 [Hebrew]. But cf. tNega'im 6:1

3 See sources assembled by Isaac Heinemann, *Philons griechische und judische Bildung*, 2nd ed. (Breslau: M. & H. Marcus, 1932), 231-261; Gerald J. Blidstein, *Honor thy Father and Mother: Filial Responsibility in Jewish Law and Ethics* (New York: Ktav, 1976), 7-8, 161; Adele Reinhartz, "Philo's Exposition of the Law and Social History: Methodological Considerations," in *SBL Annual Meeting Seminar Papers* (Atlanta: Scholars Press, 1993), 19-20; Adele Reinhartz, "Parents and Children: A Philonic Perspective," in *The Jewish Family in Antiquity*, ed. Shaye J. D. Cohen, Brown Judaic Studies (Atlanta: Scholars Press, 1993).

4 E.g., Antiquities 4:24-27.

5 See the discussion in: Moshe Halbertal, *Interpretative Revolutions in the Making* (Jerusalem: Magnes, 1997), 64-67 [Hebrew].

6 Ibid., 46-67.

tical anomaly that relates to the last of his three strategies, and to propose an explanation for that phenomenon.

The Mishnah in the tractate Sanhedrin (8:3) explains that the Torah's "stubborn and rebellious son" is being judged and put to death while still a minor in anticipation of his eventual outcome: "The Torah said that he should die [while still] in a state of innocence, and that he should not [wait to] die in a state of guilt."

A baraita brought in the Jerusalem Talmud (ySanh. 8:3 26b) and other sources explains this Mishnah:[7]

> The Holy One (blessed is he) perceived[8] that this person was destined to deplete his father's property and his mother's property;[9] and he would station himself at the crossroads and rob people and kill souls. And in the end he would forget his learning. Therefore the Torah said: Better that he should die in a state of innocence and he should not die in a state of guilt...[10]

---

7 Sifre to Deuteronomy, 220 [Louis Finkelstein, ed., *Siphre ad Deuteronomium* (New York: Jewish Theological Seminary of America, 1969), p. 253]; David Hoffmann, *Midrash Tana'im 'al Sefer Devarim*, 2 vols. (Tel Aviv: [Makor], 1962), 131; bSanhedrin 72a; Tanhuma Ki Tese 1; Solomon Buber, ed., *Midrash Tanhuma*, reprint ed., 5 vols. (Jerusalem: Wagschal, 1990), 5:33. See Halbertal, *Interpretative Revolutions*, 48-49.

8 *Midrash Tanna'im*: "For it is evident and known before the one who spoke and the universe came into existence, etc." See Halbertal, *Interpretative Revolutions*, 50, n. 15.

9 The fear that profligate young men would squander their inheritances by indulging their desires was a recurring motif in ancient moral and religious preaching, and was of special concern to Augustine; see: Geoffrey Stephen Nathan, *The Family in Late Antiquity: The Rise of Christianity and the Endurance of Tradition* (London and New York: Routledge, 2000), 148.

10 The Palestinian Talmud contains the following discussion (ySanh 8:2): "...He is not guilty until he eats it lightly roasted. If he ate it raw, then he is a dog! If he ate it cooked, he is a [normal] human." The traditional commentators to the passage (e.g., M. Margaliot's *Penei Moshe*) interpreted it in light of the Babylonian Talmud's approach, that a fugitive bandit will not become entrenched in his illicit lifestyle unless he develops a liking for half-roasted meat. This, however, does not appear to be a real concern for the Yerushalmi. The mishnah under discussion is likely describing a mode of eating consistent with the "gluttony" and "drunkenness" mentioned in the Deuteronomy; for that purpose, gluttonous eating is being restricted to a narrow range between normal eating and animalistic habits. Understood this way, the passage should probably be grouped together with all the other ones in which the death penalty is effectively avoided by means of absurdly narrow limitations of the conditions under which it can be applied.

The assumption that the lad's rebelliousness involves committing theft against his parents appears in several of the sources, but it is not clear precisely how the rabbis arrived at that assumption,[11] which is not indicated in any obvious way by the text in Deuteronomy. Nevertheless, the Mishnah (Sanhedrin 8:3) states:

> If he stole from his father's property and ate in his father's domain; or from others and ate in the domain of others, from others and ate in his father's domain—he is not deemed a "rebellious son" until he steals from his father and eats in the domain of others.[12]

Similarly, in a baraita cited in several rabbinic compendia, we read the following:

> ...For this reason it teaches "who will not obey" (Deuteronomy 21:18); "who will not obey" (21:21)—in order to draw a verbal analogy [*gezerah shavah*]: Just as the latter "will not obey" means until he steals from his father and from his mother, so too the former "will not obey" implies: until he steals from his father and from his mother.[13]

11 Maimonides, *Mamrim* 7:2 seems to resign himself to the assertion that the rabbis' interpretations of these laws are based on received tradition, and therefore are not subject to exegetical or logical justification. See Chanoch Albeck, ed., *Shisha Sidrei Mishnah* (Jerusalem, Tel-Aviv:Mosad Bialik, 1958), 4:451.

12 The arbitrary quality of this assumption underlies the discussion by Ch. Albeck in his notes to mSanhedrin 8:3. He cites Rabbi Meir Abulafia who was also puzzled by it and suggested two possible reconstructions of the Mishnah's reasoning. According to the first, the assumption was necessary in order to arrive at the conclusion that the lad would eventually take up the profession of armed banditry. This explanation is, of course, circular, since the banditry scenario is no easier to account for exegetically. Abulafia's second proposal links the law to the Torah's phraseology (21:18) "they chastise him"—which he reads in the common rabbinic sense of punishing by lashes, a penalty that could be inflicted for the crime of theft. Considering how many other transgressions are punished in the same manner, this is hardly persuasive. Nevertheless, following a similar mode of reasoning, Albeck suggests that the rabbis were trying to devise a punishable offense that could have been committed by a young adolescent who was still living under his parents' roof and eating at their table. In that context, stealing food from the parents is a natural and understandable example. (Cf. Halbertal, 55, n. 22.)

13 Hoffmann, *Midrash Tana'im 'al Sefer Devarim*, 130: The editor is in doubt as to whether this passage is part of the original midrash. Finkelstein, ed., *Siphre ad Deuteronomium*, 218, 251-252; bSanhedrin 71a.

While the latter verse (Deuteronomy 21:20) is more informative than the former (21:18) in that it specifies the offenses of gluttony and drunkenness, it makes no mention of larceny.[14] This supposed midrashic proof is, therefore, flawed by the circularity of its reasoning. This incongruity indicates how deeply rooted was the assumption that the path of the rebellious son involved stealing. After the condition that the son must have stolen from his parents was enshrined in the Mishnah, it was simply presupposed by the subsequent amoraic discussions. It still seems odd that the rabbis did not propose more rigorous attempts to justify it by means of midrashic or logical reasoning.

It is conceivable, perhaps, that the sages saw in theft a convenient instance of a punishable offense that could develop out of a minor "eating disorder" of gluttony, and then expand into the capital crime of murderous highway robbery.[15] Nevertheless, the conventions of talmudic argumentation lead us to expect a more explicit statement of the reasoning that produced that conclusion.[16]

14 On these matters see the discussions below.

15 Compare the words of Ps. Plutarch [cited by Emiel Eyben, *Restless Youth in Ancient Rome* (London: Routledge, 1993), 14]:

> But the iniquities of youth are often monstrous and wicked—unlimited gluttony, theft of parents' money, gambling, revels, drinking-bouts, love affairs with young girls, and corruption of married women. The impulses of young men should therefore be kept fettered and restrained by careful supervision. For life's prime is prodigal in its pleasures, restive, and in need of a curb, so that parents who do not take hold of the reins with firm hand at this period of life, are manifestly, by their folly, giving to their sons license for wrongdoing.

16 Cf. *Midrash Tana'im*,131: "'Shall stone him with stones...' (Deuteronomy 21:21)—We have heard the penalty, but we did not hear the admonition. Therefore it teaches: 'You shall not eat any flesh with the blood in it' (Leviticus 19:26) [interpreted as:] You shall not eat in a manner that leads to bloodshed. This is the eating of the rebellious son." bSanhedrin 63a cites this passage in the name of the Rabbi Yose bar Hanina, presumably the tanna of that name. The standard printings of the Talmud ascribe the dictum to the amora Rabbi Yohanan; the syntax of the passage (before emendation), however, suggests that it is the continuation of the baraita. See Raphael Nathan Nata Rabbinovicz, *Variae Lectiones in Mischnam et in Talmud Babylonicum [Dikduke Soferim]*, reprint ed., 2 vols. (New York: M. P. Press, 1976), n. 10. "Rabbi Yose ben Hanina is the author according to the printed editions of the *Sifra* (Qedoshim C. 6:1); the dictum, however, is missing from the Vatican manuscript [Louis Finkelstein, *Sifra: or Torat Kohanim, according to Codex Assemani LXVI.* (New York: Jewish Theological Seminary of America, 1956), 405].

The Tosefta teaches:[17]

> The stubborn and rebellious son, even if he set on his table a feast like that of Solomon in his day, is not judged under the law of the stubborn and rebellious son until he inserts into his mouth the designated amount, or until he eats *in the company of similar people.*

The "company of similar people" presupposes membership in a band of robbers,[18] a detail that is not, as far as I am aware, derivable from the biblical sources. It is the same principle that was stated in the Talmud by the amora Rabbi Abbahu: "He is not culpable until he eats in a company that consists entirely of worthless individuals."[19]

It is not difficult to concoct any number of alternative trajectories that would lead from gluttony and drunkenness to an offense punishable by death.[20] If we bear in mind the number of ritual transgressions that involve death penalties according to biblical law, the crime does not even have to involve murder or manslaughter.[21] At any rate, a survey of the relevant tannaitic sources demonstrates beyond doubt that the glutton-thief-brigand trajectory was regarded

17 tSanhedrin, 11:6 [Moses Samuel Zuckermandel, *Tosefta Based on the Erfurt and Viennna Codices*, reprint ed. (Jerusalem: Wahrmann, 1970), 431-432]. See also: Hoffmann, *Midrash Tana'im 'al Sefer Devarim*, 131. The rabbinic sources treat this stipulation as an inference from the Mishnah's ruling (mSanhedrin 8:2) that the Rebellious Son law would not apply where the lad consumed the food in the context of a society assembled for the purpose of performing a religious precept. I am suggesting that the opposite process is more likely, i.e., that the older traditions spoke of his involvement in a gang, and that the Mishnah was subsequently impelled to clarify that the reference was only to a criminal gang, not to an association that was devoted to virtuous activities.

18 On this problematic expression, cf. Saul Lieberman, *Tosefeth Rishonim*, 4 vols. (Jerusalem: Bamberger & Wahrmann, 1939), 2:160.

19 bSanhedrin 90b. See Halbertal, *Interpretative Revolutions*, 56.

20 For that purpose, drunkenness would probably make a more convenient starting-point than gluttony. Eyben, *Restless Youth* , 107-112 gives us an abundant collection of Roman testimonies about drunken mobs of young hooligans prowling the public thoroughfares in search of hapless victims upon whom to wreak violent acts.

21 Poetic justice might ostensibly prefer that the major offense should be one that is punishable by stoning; the Mishnah (mSanhedrin 7:4-8:5) catalogues some eighteen crimes that fit that definition, including sexual offenses and idolatrous or blasphemous practices to which a wayward youth might be seduced by prospects of fine food or liquor. Murder is not one of them; it is punishable by *hereg*, understood as death by sword (see mSanhedrin 9:1).

by the rabbis as much more than a convenient hypothetical possibility. It is described in substantially identical terms throughout the literature. *Midrash Tana'im* has the following discussion:

> You might have argued: Because this one has consumed his father's property he should die! —You say that the rebellious son will be judged on how he turns out? For it is revealed and known before the creator that one day he will ultimately squander all his father's property; and then he will go around in search of more, but will not find any, as it says (Prov. 30:15) "The leech has two daughters; 'Give, give,' they cry." So he goes out to watch the roads and destroys many lives. For this reason the Torah declared: It is preferable that one life be destroyed, rather than allowing many lives to be destroyed.[22] Rabbi Yose the Galilean said: And because this one ate a tartimar[23] of meat....

In the following passage from Midrash Tanna'im,[24] the authors (if only for rhetorical effect) have to explain why the Torah could not simply have treated the case of the rebellious son as a mere sub-category of robbery:

> The rebellious son should have been subsumed under the general rule, as it states (Leviticus 19:13) "You shall not ...rob him";[25] and nonetheless scripture excludes him from the general rule, both in order to treat him leniently and to

22 Hoffmann, *Midrash Tana'im 'al Sefer Devarim* , 131. The editor observes: "Thus far the words of the Mekhilta. From here onwards are the words of the Sifre."

23 τριτημόριον, *triens*; a third [of an *as* or a gold denar, or a weight]; see: Alexander Kohut, ed. *Aruch Completum* (Tel-Aviv: Shiloh, 1970), 4:78; Marcus Jastrow, *A Dictionary of the Targumim,the Talmud Babli and Yerushalmi, and the Midrashic Literature with an Index of Scriptural Quotations* (New York: Jastrow Publishers, 1967), 552; cf. Michael Sokoloff, *A Dictionary of Jewish Palestinian Aramaic of the Byzantine Period*, Dictionaries of Talmud, Midrash, and Targum (Ramat Gan: Bar-Ilan University Press, 1990), 231.

24 Hoffmann, *Midrash Tana'im 'al Sefer Devarim*, 130.

25 See Hoffmann's comment: "This is because the rebellious son is not liable until he steals etc." At the beginning of its pericope on mSanhedrin 8:3, ySanhedrin brings Sifra Qedoshim Parashah 2:1-2 [Finkelstein, *Sifra Vatican MS*, 397], which deals with the scriptural sources for theft in general, but makes no specific reference to the rebellious son. The Sifra text leads to a conclusion (in par. #5, not included in the Yerushalmi citation) that "If you committed theft, then in the end you will deny it, in the end you will commit perjury, in the end you will swear falsely in my name." Perhaps the source was brought here in the Yerushalmi by virtue of their common motif, of a relatively minor offense leading inevitably to a cardinal transgression.

> treat him more stringently, in that he is subject to lashes at the beginning and he is subject to death. It is for this reason that this passage had to be stated.

Sifre Deuteronomy also presumes that the son is being punished for consuming his father's property.[26]

We see, then, how the postulate that stealing is an essential stage in the son's decline is not being offered as just one of several hypothetical scenarios. On the contrary, the tannaitic texts treat it as an essential stage of the process. Yet we remain unable to trace or reconstruct an exegetical path that can account convincingly for the details of this rabbinic depiction of the rebellious son as a delinquent hedonist sliding towards a life of murderous banditry on the crossroads. This difficulty invites us to seek out alternative explanations for the origin of the phenomenon.

There is one particularly well-known passage in ancient literature that suggests itself as a possible source. I am referring to the section at the beginning of Book IX of Plato's *Republic* in which Socrates provides an account of how the progeny of a "democratic personality" is apt to degenerate within a few generations to a state of moral, social and political tyranny.[27] According to Socrates' scheme, the original democratic personality steered a course midway between the austere frugality of his oligarchic father and the anarchic immorality of the worthless masses. This then produced a disciplined and thrifty character that would restrain him from indulging his extravagant passions. Now, however, the son of the democratic man is also being subjected to temptations from "drones," men who are ruled entirely by their lawless desires and make no attempt to inhibit the perverse urges that, in healthy personalities, would be confined to the realm of dreams.

> Then the bestial and savage part, full of food and drink (ἢ σίτων ἢ μέθης πλησθέν), casts off sleep, and seeks to gratify its own characteristic instincts…

26 Sifre to Deuteronomy, no. 218; *Siphre ad Deuteronomium*, 251.

27 James Adam, *The Republic of Plato: Edited with Critical Notes, Commentary and Appendices*, 2d ed., 2 vols., vol. 2 (Cambridge UK: Cambridge University Press, 1963), 325.

> It will commit any foul murder, and there is no food it refuses to eat. In a word, it does not refrain from anything, no matter how foolish or shameful.[28]

The discipline, however, that this son has inherited from his democratic father is too diluted and weak to offer tangible resistance to the enticements of the mob:

> His father and the rest of his family come to the aid of the appetites.[29]

The healthy parental influences cannot compete with the lure of the selfserving drones. The son is now subjected to the tyranny of his hedonism, especially that of drink.[30]

> Socrates: And hasn't a drunken man, my friend, something of a tyrannical cast of mind too?
> Adeimantus: He has.[31]

The young man is enticed to become a leader of the gang of drones who reinforce his base appetites.

> Socrates: And don't lots of terrible appetites sprout up each day and night beside it, creating needs for all sorts of things?
> Adeimantus: Indeed, they do.
> Socrates: So, any income someone like that has is soon spent.
> Adeimantus: Of course.
> Socrates: And the next thing, surely, is borrowing and expenditure of capital.[32]
> Adeimantus: What else?

---

28 571c-d. Plato, *Republic Translated from the New Standard Greek Text, with Introduction*, trans. C. D. C. Reeve (second ed.; Indianapolis and Cambridge: Hackett, 2004), 270; See the Volume 2 in *Plato: The Republic in Two Volumes*, tr. Paul Shorey, ed. T. E. Page (The Loeb Classical Library; London and Cambridge MA: William Heinemann and Harvard University Press, 1956), 336-337.

29 572e; Reeve, 271-272; Loeb 338-339.

30 See Adam, *Republic*, 324.

31 573b-c (Reeve, 272); Loeb 342-343.

32 See Adam, *Republic*, 326.

> Socrates: And when everything is gone (ταχὺ ἄρα ἀναλίσκονται ἐάν τινες ὦσι πρόσοδοι), won't the violent crowd of appetites that have nested within him inevitably shout in protest? And when people of this sort are driven by the stings of these other appetites, but particularly of Passion itself, which leads all the others as if they were its body-guard, stung to frenzy, don't they look to see who possesses anything that can be taken from him by deceit or force?
> Adeimantus: Certainly.
> Socrates: He must take it from every source, then, or live in great suffering and pain.
> Adeimantus: He must.
> Socrates: And just as the late-coming pleasures within him do better than the older ones and steal away their satisfactions, won't he himself, young as he is, think he deserves to do better than his father and mother? And if he has spent his own share, won't he try to take some of his father's wealth by converting it to his own use?
> Adeimantus: Of course.
> Socrates: And if his parents resist him, won't he first try to steal it and deceive them? (ἂν δὲ δὴ αὐτῷ μὴ ἐπιτρέπωσιν, ἆρ᾽ οὐ τὸ μὲν πρῶτον ἐπιχειροῖ ἂν κλέπτειν καὶ ἀπατᾶν τοὺς γονέας)
> Adeimantus: Certainly.
> Socrates: And if he cannot, won't he next try to seize it by force? (ὁπότε δὲ μὴ δύναιτο, ἁρπάζοι ἂν καὶ βιάζοιτο μετὰ τοῦτο)
> Adeimantus: I suppose so.
> Socrates: And if... the old man and woman stand their ground and put up a fight, would he take care and be reluctant to act like a tyrant?
> Adeimantus: I am not very optimistic about the parents of someone like that![33]

For as long as he can maintain his habits and those of his cronies by deceiving or terrorizing his parents, the aspiring tyrant will continue to do so.

> Socrates: What happens to someone like that when the possessions of his father and mother give out (ὅταν δὴ τὰ πατρὸς καὶ μητρὸς ἐπιλείπῃ τὸν τοιοῦτον)

33 573d-274b (Reeve 273); Loeb 344-347.

> and the swarm of pleasures now inside has grown dense? Won't he first try to break into someone's house or snatch the cloak of someone walking late at night? Next, won't he try to clean out some temple?[34]

As he relinquishes all shreds of moral self-restraint, he is ready to act out all his previously repressed fantasies.

> ...so there is no terrible murder, no food, and no act from which he will refrain (οὔτε τινὸς φόνου δεινοῦ ἀφέξεται οὔτε βρώματος οὔτ' ἔργου).[35]

If his tyrannical ambitions cannot be fulfilled in his native city, he might leave to join a foreign tyrant or serve as a mercenary. Otherwise, he will become the chief of a criminal mob in his native town. By setting his sights on political ambitions, he is capable of becoming a true tyrant, lording it over his fellow citizens. Plato, speaking through Socrates, goes on to describe how miserable the life of this tyrant must be, at the mercy of his insatiable lusts, deprived of real friendship, and in a state of constant paranoia.[36]

Clearly, the decline of Plato's tyrant includes all the elements that were presupposed by the rabbinic narrative, as he follows the inexorable course that begins with enslavement to his physical appetites and culminates in the vocation of a cold-blooded warlord. The inevitability of the transition, as Plato presents it, provides a persuasive foundation for the rabbinic argument that "his beginning is being judged in light of his outcome."[37] The sequence includes all the stations that were mentioned by the rabbinic tradition, including the theft of the parents' belongings, the depletion of their resources, the resort to crime in order to maintain his expensive habits, and his ultimate transformation into a powerful and violent robber baron.

---

34 574c-d (Reeve, 274); Loeb 346-349.

35 574d (Reeve, ibid.); Loeb 348-349.

36 See Kraut, 323-327; Adam, *Republic*, 325.

37 The impression (or illusion) of inevitability is enhanced by the literary implementation of the *Republic*'s dialogic character. After the opening pages in which Socrates conducts real debates with the contrary positions of Polemarchus and Thrasymachus, the work turns into a virtual monologue, as Glaucon and Adeimantus do little more than punctuate Socrates' presentation with periodic words of agreement and admiration, giving the impression that the processes and situations that he is describing must follow from one another with inexorable logic.

As we have seen, the halakhah's insistence that theft of the parents' property is an indispensable condition for the son's indictment cannot be plausibly explained without positing an intermediate tradition in which that element is introduced. While this is not as obvious with respect to the "gluttony" aspects of the crime, I would nonetheless argue that a similar inference is justified to some extent.

The Mishnah specifies that the son, in order to be liable, must have consumed a *tartemar* of meat and drunk half a *log* of wine.[38]

> And though there is no absolute proof, there is an indirect allusion to this, as it is written, "be not among winebibbers; among gluttonous eaters of flesh" (Proverbs 23:20).

Actually, the proof-text from Proverbs appears to be a fully adequate one for substantiating the Mishnah's claim that *zolel* and *sobe* in Deuteronomy refer to eating meat and drinking wine.[39] Therefore, the Mishnah's cautious formulation that this is a mere allusion might well be read in the sense that the law was not originally derived from the analogy with Proverbs 23:20, but entered the oral tradition from a different source; while the exegetical proof-text, persuasive as it may be, was a *post facto* addition devised to lend it added force.

38 mSanhedrin 8:2; see also Sifre to Deuteronomy 219 [Finkelstein, ed., *Siphre ad Deuteronomium*, 252]; bSanhedrin 71a.

39 Some of the traditional commentators to the Mishnah and Talmud were sensitive to this problem, and proposed diverse reasons for why the proof was not accepted as fully satisfactory. See Yom-Tov Lipmann Heller's *Tosefot Yom Tov*, Israel Lipschutz's *Tif 'eret Yisra'el* to the Mishnah, etc. On the meanings of the key Hebrew terms see Francis Brown and others, *A Hebrew and English Lexicon of the Old Testament: Based on the Lexicon of William Gesenius as Translated by Edward Robinson* (Oxford: Clarendon Press, 1977); Halbertal, *Interpretative Revolutions*, 49, 51 (n. 16). The Aramaic Targums to 21:20 insert the words "meat" and "wine"; see Bernard Grossfeld, *The Targum Onqelos to Deuteronomy*, ed. Martin McNamara The Aramaic Bible (Wilmington: M. Glazier, 1988), 65; Ernest G. Clarke, *Targum Pseudo-Jonathan: Deuteronomy*, ed. Martin McNamara, The Aramaic Bible (Collegeville, Minn.: Liturgical Press, 1998), 59; Martin McNamara, *Targum Neofiti: Deuteronomy*, ed. Martin McNamara, The Aramaic Bible (Collegeville, MN: Liturgical Press, 1997), 105. Sifre 218 [Finkelstein, ed., *Siphre ad Deuteronomium*, 251] and *Midrash Tanna'im*, 230, suggest some alternative renderings of *zolel ve-sove*, but neither states explicitly that it alludes to theft. The sentence in Sifre that mentions "because this one consumed his father's property" is missing good witnesses, and Finkelstein suggests plausibly that it really belongs to the "Mekhilta to Deuteronomy" (i.e, the original *Midrash Tanna'im*), though it is not found in Hoffmann's edition.

Given that several of those particulars cannot be derived in any overt way from the biblical texts (even when they are channeled through the creative midrashic hermeneutics), it does not seem extravagant to suggest that the author or authors of this early rabbinic depiction of the rebellious son, with all its exegetical and halakhic ramifications, were reading Deuteronomy through a Platonic subtext.

If this reconstruction is correct—and I entertain no illusions that it is conclusive—then it would require us to posit that at least some of the rabbis were familiar enough with Greek philosophical literature for this passage to come to mind as a useful subtext for illuminating the problematic biblical precept. This, in fact, brings us into some notoriously hazardous historical territory. The question of "how much Greek in Jewish Palestine?" is one that has continued to provoke scholarly debate. As I see it, however, the range of scholarly positions on this question is relatively limited. No serious historian would try to claim that the Palestinian rabbis of late antiquity were isolated from the vibrant Hellenistic culture that existed in the land of Israel. The disagreements relate to the degrees of direct or mediated familiarity that the rabbis had of the respective genres of Greek literature and thought. Some, like Yitzhak Baer, stressed the deep influences of Greek philosophical methods and ideas on fundamental areas of rabbinic discourse, in ways that reflect intimate familiarity with Hellenistic literature.[40] Saul Lieberman argued from the dearth of explicit mentions of Greek authors or philosophical terminology, that the rabbis' familiarity with Greek motifs, though perhaps extensive, must have been indirect, based on informal verbal exchanges.[41] An alternative possibility is

40 Y. F. Baer, *Israel among the Nations* (Jerusalem: Bialik Institute, 1955). Saul Lieberman, "How Much Greek in Jewish Palestine?," in *Biblical and Other Studies*, ed. Alexander Altmann (Cambridge MA: Harvard University Press, 1963), 123-125, refers approvingly to studies by Joel, Bacher, Neumark and Kaminka that demonstrate the penetration of Greek philosophical concepts (particularly Stoic ethics) into rabbinic circles. The oeuvre of E. E. Hallevi is largely devoted to the exhaustive amassing of parallels between rabbinic and Greco-Roman texts in order to underscore the fact that talmudic and midrashic Judaism was thoroughly imbued with the cultural conventions of Hellenistic civilization.

41 Lieberman, "How Much Greek in Jewish Palestine?"

that the rabbinic corpus might have undergone an intentional censorship to remove explicit references to Greek thinkers and doctrines.[42]

To be sure, the annals of ancient history furnish an abundance of stories (whether true or propagandistic) of bands of youths who were rallied to the banners of assorted demagogues or political factions that led to violent action and political revolts. In some of those episodes, the delinquents were patricians who were determined to maintain their privileged lifestyles against democratic reforms; in others, they were destitute plebeians who could be seduced by initial offers of debauchery and hedonistic pleasures.[43] A typical characterization was offered by Pseudo-Sallust:[44]

> Mere youths think it a fine thing to waste their own substance and that of others, to refuse nothing of their own lust and the demands of their fellows, to regard such conduct as evidence of manliness and high spirit...Therefore the headstrong spirit...subverts the established order of things, and is eager for a revolution.[45]

42 Such a situation is supposed by Daniel Boyarin, *Border Lines: The Partition of Judaeo-Christianity*, Divinations (Philadelphia: University of Pennsylvania Press, 2004), to account for his thesis that Philonic Logos-theology was widespread among Palestinian Jews (as reflected in the popular Targums), but absent from all the other variegated works of rabbinic literature. See also: Eliezer Segal, "'The Few Contained the Many': Rabbinic Perspectives on the Miraculous and the Impossible," *Journal of Jewish Studies* 54, no. 2 (2003): 281-282. At any rate, we do possess at least one unimpeachable example of the rabbis' familiarity with a passage in a Platonic dialogue; namely, Aristophanes' myth of the androgynous creation of the first humans, from the Symposium. On the uses of this passage in rabbinic literature, see Daniel Boyarin, *Carnal Israel: Reading Sex in Talmudic Culture* (Berkeley: University of California Press, 1993), 36-44; Eliezer Segal, *From Sermon to Commentary: Expounding the Bible in Talmudic Babylonia*, ed. Stephen Wilson, Studies in Christianity and Judaism (Waterloo, Ont.: Canadian Corporation for Studies in Religion/Corporation Canadienne des Sciences Religieuses by Wilfrid Laurier University Press, 2005), 21-27. Some scholars have argued for the Platonic origin of the rabbinic passages describing the preexistence of the soul and its possession of wisdom that is forgotten at birth. See Yitzhak Baer, "Le-veirurah shel torat aharit ha-yamim bimei ha-bayit ha-sheni," *Zion* 23-24 (1958-1959), Efraim Elimelech Urbach, *The Sages: Their Concepts and Beliefs* (Cambridge, MA: Harvard University Press, 1987), 235-250.

43 Eyben, *Restless Youth*, especially 51-67.

44 Cited by Eyben, 63.

45 Much of the scholarly writing on Jewish banditry in the first and second centuries C.E. has tried to stress its political character, especially its connections to the Zealot resistance

It should be noted as well that though Greek authors offer many rationales for strict enforcement of paternal authority and filial respect—most of which are echoed by Philo and Josephus—the notion of a predictable decline into depravity does not, as far as I am aware, appear elsewhere than in Plato.[46]

Even if Plato was not the actual literary or conceptual source for the rabbinic depiction of the rebellious son, the similarities between the descriptions serve to underscore the degree to which the biblical law was *not* perceived as a source of embarrassment for Jews in the Hellenistic cultural environment. This allows us to appreciate the remarkable "new sensitivity"[47] Rabbi Akiva and his school instilled into rabbinic thinking for the sanctity of human life that would relegate this law to the purely theoretical plane, until most Jews would come to regard the execution of the stubborn and rebellious son as abhorrent, and all but unimaginable.

against Rome. For a balanced presentation that also takes into account the criminal and socio-economic aspects of the phenomenon, see Gedalia Alon, *The Jews in Their Land in the Talmudic Age: 70-640 C.E*, trans. Gershon Levi (Jerusalem: Magnes Press, 1980), 570-575. See also Martin Hengel, *The Zealots: Investigations into the Jewish Freedom Movement in the Period from Herod I until 70 A.D*, trans. David Smith (Edinburgh: T. & T. Clark, 1989), especially 380-404; S. Freyne, "Bandits in Galilee: A Contribution to the Study of Social Conditions in First-Century Palestine," in *Social World of Formative Christianity and Judaism: Essays in Tribute to Howard Clark Kee* ed. Jacob Neusner et al. (Philadelphia: Fortress, 1988), 50-68; Terence L. Donaldson, "Rural Bandits, City Mobs and the Zealots," *JSJ* 21 (1990): 19-40.

46 For a useful survey of the relevant texts, see Peter Balla, *The Child-Parent Relationship in the New Testament and its Environment* (Tubingen: Hendrickson MA, 2005).

47 My use of this expression derives from David Flusser, "A New Sensitivity in Judaism and the Christian Message," *Harvard Theological Review* 61 (1968): 107-127.

WORKS CITED:

Adam, James. *The Republic of Plato: Edited with Critical Notes, Commentary and Appendices*. Vol. 2. 2 vols. 2d ed. Cambridge UK: Cambridge University Press, 1963.

Albeck, Ch. *Introduction to the Talmud, Babli and Yerushalmi*. Tel-Aviv: Dvir, 1969.

________, ed. *Shisha Sidre Mishnah*. Jerusalem, Tel-Aviv: Mosad Bialik, 1958.

Alon, Gedalia. *The Jews in Their Land in the Talmudic Age: 70-640 C.E.* Translated by G. Levi. Jerusalem: Magnes Press, 1980.

Baer, Y. F. *Israel among the Nations*. Jerusalem: Bialik Institute, 1955.

________, "Le-Veirurah Shel Torat Aharit Ha-Yamim Bimei Ha-Bayit Ha-Sheni." *Zion* 23-24 (1958-1959): 3-34, 141-165.

Balla, Peter. *The Child-Parent Relationship in the New Testament and Its Environment*. Tubingen: Hendrickson MA, 2005.

Blidstein, Gerald J. *Honor Thy Father and Mother: Filial Responsibility in Jewish Law and Ethics*. New York: Ktav, 1976.

Boyarin, Daniel. *Carnal Israel: Reading Sex in Talmudic Culture* New Historicism. Berkeley: University of California Press, 1993.

________, *Border Lines: The Partition of Judaeo-Christianity* Divinations. Philadelphia: University of Pennsylvania Press, 2004.

Brown, Francis and others. *A Hebrew and English Lexicon of the Old Testament: Based on the Lexicon of William Gesenius as Translated by Edward Robinson*. Oxford: Clarendon Press, 1977.

Buber, Solomon, ed. *Midrash Tanhuma*. Jerusalem: Wagschal, 1990.

Clarke, Ernest G. *Targum Pseudo-Jonathan: Deuteronomy* The Aramaic Bible, ed. M. McNamara. Collegeville, Minn.: Liturgical Press, 1998.

Donaldson, Terence L. "Rural Bandits, City Mobs and the Zealots." *JSJ* 21 (1990): 19-40.

Epstein, J. N. *Prolegomena Ad Litteras Tannaiticas.* Tel Aviv and Jerusalem: The Magnes Press and Dvir, 1957.

Eyben, Emiel. *Restless Youth in Ancient Rome.* London: Routledge, 1993.

Finkelstein, Louis. *Sifra: Or Torat Kohanim, According to Codex Assemani Lxvi.* New York: Jewish Theological Seminary of America, 1956.

________, ed. *Siphre Ad Deuteronomium.* New York: Jewish Theological Seminary of America, 1969.

Flusser, David. "A New Sensitivity in Judaism and the Christian Message." *Harvard Theological Review* 61 (1968): 107-127.

Freyne, S. "Bandits in Galilee: A Contribution to the Study of Social Conditions in First-Century Palestine." In *Social World of Formative Christianity and Judaism: Essays in Tribute to Howard Clark Kee* ed. J. Neusner and others, 50-68. Philadelphia: Fortress, 1988.

Gafni, Isaiah. *Jews of Babylonia in the Talmudic Era: A Social and Cultural History* Monographs in Jewish History. Jerusalem: The Zalman Shazar Center for Jewish History, 1990.

Grossfeld, Bernard. *The Targum Onqelos to Deuteronomy* The Aramaic Bible, ed. M. McNamara. Wilmington: M. Glazier, 1988.

Halbertal, Moshe. *Interpretative Revolutions in the Making* Jerusalem: Magnes, 1997.

Halevy, Isaac. *Dorot Ha-Rishonim.* reprint ed. Jerusalem, 1966.

Heinemann, Isaac. *Philons Griechische Und Judische Bildung.* 2nd ed. Breslau: M. & H. Marcus, 1932.

Hengel, Martin. *The Zealots: Investigations into the Jewish Freedom Movement in the Period from Herod I until 70 A.D.* Translated by D. Smith. Edinburgh: T. & T. Clark, 1989.

Hoffmann, David. *Midrash Tana'im 'Al Sefer Devarim*. 2 vols. Tel Aviv: [Makor], 1962.

________, *Zur Einleitung in Die Halachischen Midraschim* Jahresbericht Des Rabbiner-Seminars Zu Berlin. Berlin: M. Driesner, 1988.

Jastrow, Marcus. *A Dictionary of the Targumim, the Talmud Babli and Yerushalmi ,and the Midrashic Literature. With an Index of Scriptural Quotations*. New York: Jastrow Publishers, 1967.

Kohut, Alexander, ed. *Aruch Completum*. Tel-Aviv: Shiloh, 1970.

Lieberman, Saul. *Tosefeth Rishonim*. 4 vols. Jerusalem: Bamberger & Wahrmann, 1939.

________, "How Much Greek in Jewish Palestine?" In *Biblical and Other Studies*, ed. A. Altmann, 123-141. Cambridge MA: Harvard University Press, 1963.

McNamara, Martin. *Targum Neofiti: Deuteronomy* The Aramaic Bible, ed. M. McNamara. Collegeville, MN: Liturgical Press, 1997.

Nathan, Geoffrey Stephen. *The Family in Late Antiquity: The Rise of Christianity and the Endurance of Tradition*. London and New York: Routledge, 2000.

Neusner, Jacob. *A History of the Jews in Babylonia*. 5 vols. 2nd ed. Leiden: E. J. Brill, 1965-1970.

Rabbinovicz, Raphael Nathan Nata. *Variae Lectiones in Mischnam Et in Talmud Babylonicum [Dikduke Soferim]*. 2 vols. reprint ed. New York: M. P. Press, 1976.

Reinhartz, Adele. "Parents and Children: A Philonic Perspective." In *The Jewish Family in Antiquity*, ed. S. J. D. Cohen, 61-88. Atlanta: Scholars Press, 1993.

________, "Philo's Exposition of the Law and Social History: Methodological Considerations." In *SBL Annual Meeting Seminar Papers*, 6-21. Atlanta: Scholars Press, 1993.

Segal, Eliezer. "'The Few Contained the Many': Rabbinic Perspectives on the Miraculous and the Impossible" *Journal of Jewish Studies* 54, no. 2: 273-282.

________, *From Sermon to Commentary: Expounding the Bible in Talmudic Babylonia* Studies in Christianity and Judaism, ed. S. Wilson. Waterloo, Ont.: Canadian Corporation for Studies in Religion/Corporation Canadienne des Sciences Religieuses by Wilfrid Laurier University Press, 2005.

Sokoloff, Michael. *A Dictionary of Jewish Palestinian Aramaic of the Byzantine Period* Dictionaries of Talmud, Midrash, and Targum. Ramat Gan: Bar-Ilan University Press, 1990.

Stemberger, Gunter, and Hermann Leberecht Strack. *Introduction to the Talmud and Midrash.* Translated by M. N. A. Bockmuehl. 2nd ed. Edinburgh: T. & T. Clark, 1996.

Urbach, Efraim Elimelech. *The Sages: Their Concepts and Beliefs.* Cambridge, MA: Harvard University Press, 1987.

Zuckermandel, Moses Samuel. *Tosefta Based on the Erfurt and Viennna Codices.* reprint ed. Jerusalem: Wahrmann, 1970.

DID THE TANNAIM INTERPRET THE SONG OF SONGS SYSTEMATICALLY? LIEBERMAN RECONSIDERED

Alon Goshen Gottstein, Beit Morasha

Harry has been a rare and faithful colleague. More significantly, he has been a model. Even though our acquaintance can be traced to our student days at Hebrew University in the 1970s and eighties, we became close over the past decade, when Harry was a regular and faithful participant in the annual conference on rabbinic thought that I organized at Beit Morasha. Harry has presented and published on various topics as a result of this common initiative, but it was Harry the person whom I came to appreciate through these many years, as much and even more than his scholarship. Lecturers come and go, always busy, rarely pausing to listen to what others have labored to prepare. That is how many conferences look, especially the less well-funded ones. Against this habit of the Academy, Harry's curiosity, love of learning and above all humility stand out. I recall on various occasions how Harry would turn to me and say: "there's so much to learn from each other, why don't others realize this. I'm here to learn." And indeed, Harry made it his business to be there for the duration of a conference, year after year, always engaging, contributing, challenging and sharing. A colleague in the fullest sense.

I would like to offer in Harry's honor a piece that brings together two of his interests: rabbinic hermeneutics and interpretation and the Song of Songs and its interpretation. We have tackled these issues together in various contexts, in Israel and in Canada. We have spent considerable energy on issues of periodization within rabbinic literature. The present offering brings together all these concerns by addressing the issue of periodization of rabbinic hermeneutics as it touches upon a favored text, the interpretation of the Song of Songs. This constitutes another stone in the edifice of collaboration that we have built over the years and that I hope we shall continue enjoying for years to come.

Saul Lieberman contributed an important appendix to Gershom Scholem's book on Jewish Gnosticism.[1] In it, Lieberman attempted to corroborate Scholem's claims regarding a rabbinic mystical reading of the Song of Songs, from within rabbinic literature.[2] To this end Lieberman analyzed over one hundred and fifty rabbinic sources in a nine page essay. Lieberman's entire edifice is constructed on the claim that the tannaim interpreted the Song of Songs in a sustained manner. Thus, R. Akiba consistently interpreted the Song with regard to the Sinai event, while R. Eliezer consistently interpreted it with regard to the theophany at the Red Sea. It is only in the amoraic period, according to Lieberman, that the consistency of tannatic interpretations gives way to an eclectic interpretation of the Song. "The Tannaim were consistent in their interpretations, and interpreted the Song of Songs each according to his own system, but the Amoraim interpreted according to the opinions of opposing Tannaim."[3] These claims are significant for the student of midrash, and not only for the student of Jewish mysticism. In the present article I shall discuss the validity of Lieberman's construction of tannaitic exegetical practices, without any reference to the use Lieberman makes of this theory for the reconstruction of ancient Jewish mysticism.[4]

1 S.Lieberman, *Mishnat shir ha-shirim*, Appendix D, in G. Scholem, *Jewish Gnosticism,Merkabah Mysticism, and Talmudic Tradition* (2d ed.; New York: Jewish Theological Seminary of America, 1965), 118-126.

2 The present article is part of a larger study examining the rabbinic interpretation of the Song of Songs. In that study I closely examine both Scholem's and Lieberman's work. The present disagreement with Lieberman is part of a larger rejection of his thesis.

3 Lieberman, 122.

4 I shall limit myself to an examination of this specific thesis that Lieberman presents. I shall thus neither engage in a detailed examination of Lieberman's entire argument, nor discuss other issues that are relevant to rabbinic interpretation of the Song of Songs. I attempt both tasks in

Before proceeding to examine Lieberman's analysis, it is important to realize why this thesis is significant for the unfolding of his argument. Several reasons can be suggested for basing his argument on the claim that the tannaim interpreted the Song of Songs systematically.

1. Lieberman takes as his point of departure R. Akiba's classical saying that the Song of Songs is holier than the rest of Scripture.[5] Lieberman attaches great importance to this statement of R. Akiba, and constructs a hermeneutical theory to account for it. To present the Song as unique calls for some hermeneutical theory in light of which it is read. Lieberman's attempt to present sustained tannaitic readings of the Song enables him to point to the hermeneutical uniqueness, and hence the religious uniqueness, of the Song.

2. Presenting the tannaitic readings as sustained readings allows Lieberman to speak of a variety of ancient midrashic interpretations. These interpretations are said to have existed independently of one another. Thus, one can speak of the existence of a plurality of ancient tannaitic midrashim to the Song of Songs. Once we recognize the existence of various such ancient midrashic compilations, it is easier to conceive of the existence of an ancient mystical midrash to the Song of Songs — the Shi'ur Qomah.

3. Suggesting that the Song is read in a sustained manner allows Lieberman to amplify the import of the Song. The Song is not only interpreted in light of certain events, and with reference to them; it was actually recited on those particular occasions. Thus, according to the understanding that the Song is to be interpreted with respect to the Sinai event, the Song was actually initially recited at Sinai. This enables Lieberman to view the Song as a response to the events at Sinai. Therefore, if we realize that God revealed himself at Sinai, the Song can be presented as a response to the vision of God. The description of the lover in the fifth chapter of the Song can be taken to

---

a study I undertake at present, on the rabbinic interpretation of the Song of Songs. Concerning the specific issue of systematic interpretation, I am not aware of any scholarly discussion on the subject aside from that of Lieberman.

5 Mishna Yadayim 3:5. Lieberman, however, relies on an alternate reading, found in a parallel version. See Lieberman, 118.

be the description of the divine person, seen at Sinai. Thus, the notion of a sustained interpretation enables Lieberman to locate the recitation of the Song at a particular point in time, and to view it as an expression of a particular event. This enables Lieberman to introduce visionary and mystical dimensions into the interpretation of the Song. It is only if the entire Song is made to deliver a consistent message, capturing the events of a particular moment of divine revelation, that the description of the lover in Chapter 5 can be taken to be more than mere metaphor. Only then can it be viewed as a record of the vision of God, as experienced at Sinai or at the Red Sea.

4. Lieberman's key witness, a Yemmenite commentary from the middle ages which may contain earlier materials, can only be understood in light of a theory of consistent interpretation. This witness connects *ma'aseh merkabah* and the Song of Songs without reference to the fifth chapter of the Song, the suggested focus of mystical interpretation of the Song key. In relating the Song of Songs to esoteric lore it addresses only the second verse of the Song of Songs. In order to make sense of this witness, Lieberman must provide a theory of consistent and systematic interpretation of the Song, in light of which even the opening verse of the Song can be made to convey mystical significance.

The notion of a sustained interpretation of the Song thus underlies Lieberman's entire edifice. Lieberman can only draw his far-reaching conclusions concerning the mystical nature of the rabbinic interpretation of the Song of Songs because of his far-reaching statements concerning the sustained and systematic nature of rabbinic interpretation of the Song. Lieberman's suggestion is a great novelty for the student of midrash. If there is any distinguishing feature to rabbinic interpretation it is precisely its unsystematic nature. Rabbis do not interpret books, or even chapters of books. As Yitzhak Heinemann aptly describes rabbinic interpretation, it defies the logos of the text, preferring its smaller components over the logic of the whole.[6] This makes rabbinic interpretation highly eclectic. Each verse, or verse particle, can potentially bear a different meaning, which is unrelated to the neighboring verse. Lieberman's

6 I. Heinemann, *Darkhe ha-Aggada*, Jerusalem, 1954, 137 ff.

claim about the rabbinic interpretation of the Song of Songs is thus highly revolutionary. Following Lieberman, we would be forced to view the Song of Songs as departing from the conventional canons of rabbinic interpretation. It, and perhaps it alone, is subject to sustained and systematic interpretation. This is a very radical claim from the perspective of rabbinic hermeneutics. We can understand what prompted Lieberman to make such a bold claim, but we must ask whether such a radical thesis has really been proven. When we frame the question in terms of the relationship of rabbinic interpretation of the Song of Songs to conventional methods of rabbinic interpretation, the discrepancy between the purported interpretation of the Song and the canons of interpretation operating elsewhere already raises doubt about Lieberman's thesis. How could it be that here alone the rabbis deviate from conventional norms?[7] If indeed this the only deviation, surely some theory ought to be advanced by the tannaim in order to justify such deviation from common practice.[8]

To this, other difficulties should be added. According to Lieberman's presentation, the tannaim interpreted the Song of Songs systematically, while the amoraim interpreted the Song according to the varying opinions of the tannaitic authors. While Lieberman does not place a value judgment upon this, we might reflect on the implications of this presentation to the perception of development within rabbinic literature. Most readers will agree that a sustained interpretation represents a higher hermeneutical accomplishment than a sporadic and ununified interpretation. Tannaitic interpretation would thus be viewed as representing a more developed and elaborate stage of midrashic interpretation, and amoraic literature would represent a regression from this high point of rabbinic interpretation. One measure by which we can assess the plausibility of Lieberman's suggestion is the degree to which it concurs with the

7 Lieberman nowhere discusses the relation between the interpretation of the Song and other contexts of rabbinic interpretation. I assume that had Lieberman considered there to be parallels to such sustained interpretation, he would have said so.

8 It is important to point out that the theoretical discussion concerning where the Song was recited, as found in Song of Songs Rabba 1:2 is of amoraic origin. We lack a tannaitic meta-discussion of how the Song of Songs should be interpreted. In light of the radically unique nature of interpretation of the Song by the tannaim, as propounded by Lieberman, we could expect such a discussion.

common perception of the development of midrashic literature. I do not know of any other evidence that points to a degeneration or decline in the powers of rabbinic interpretation from the tannaitic to the amoraic periods. In fact, the early amoraic period might well be presented as the golden age of rabbinic interpretation as witnessed, for example, by the development of literary forms like the petihta. There is nothing in a perusal of the literature that suggests that it has fallen from marks established by an earlier generation.

If Lieberman's presentation of the midrash of individual tannaitic authorities is correct, the degeneration from the interpretation offered by the tannaim to the kind of eclectic interpretation which characterizes the amoraic sources should be dated earlier than the amoraic period. That the Song of Songs is interpreted eclectically is not only a characterization of the amoraic sources; it characterizes the tannaitic midrashim as well. When we examine the use of the Song by the editors of tannaitic midrashic compilations, we realize that the authors are already eclectic in their use of the verses of the Song.[9] Were we to go along with Lieberman we would have to assume that the corruption of tannaitic interpretation occurred already by the end of the tannaitic period. The evidence of the tannaitic editors might make us reconsider Lieberman's suggestion. As this suggestion is based on an analysis of the relevant tannaitic texts, it is best to turn at this point to an examination of the attributed tannaitic

9 In order to demonstrate this point it is sufficient to point out that verses from the Song are applied by the anonymous commentator in the Mekhilta at times to the Red Sea, and at other times to Sinai. The tannaitic midrash, read as a redacted document representing the views or perspectives of its editors, indicates no awareness of tension between the competing sustained readings of the Song from which it must choose, or to which it must give voice. That is, there are no signs that the editor had several sources or interpretive options to choose from. The criterion by which the Song is applied seems to be strictly hermeneutical suitability. If a verse from the Song, like a verse from anywhere else in Scripture, suits particular hermeneutical needs, it is used. For applications of the Song with regard to Israel's presence and deliverance from Egypt, see Mekhilta Pisha 5; 7; Vayehi 1; Shirta 6. For applications to the Red Sea: Vayehi 2; 6; Shirta 6. For applications to Sinai: Bahodesh 3; 9. Applications to the temple: Shirta 3. With regard to the future redemption: Pisha 14. For other interpretations: Shirta 10. It is obvious that in some instances the midrashic compiler applied the different interpretations offered by individual tannaim to their respective contexts. Compare Bahodesh 3 and Vayehi 2. If, however, Lieberman were right we would have to assume that all interpretations found in the Mekhilta sections commenting upon the exodus were from a different school or source than the commentaries upon the Sinai story. This seems to me a very far-reaching supposition.

sayings, both those brought by Lieberman and others that should be viewed in order to assess his thesis.

Let us first determine the scope of the tannaitic evidence. While Lieberman makes a general statement concerning the nature of the tannaitic interpretation of the Song of Songs, in fact his argument centers on the interpretations of R. Akiba and R. Eliezer, who are said to have interpreted the Song systematically with reference to Sinai and the Red Sea, respectively.[10] It is important to realize that the number of sources upon which Lieberman's theory is based is extremely limited. The entire body of evidence amounts to a dozen sayings in which either R. Akiba or R. Eliezer comment upon verses from the Song of Songs. In such a small body of data any deviance from a theory should spell its end. Let us examine the evidence more closely.

If we begin with reference to the tannaitic midrashim we find one tradition attributed to R. Eliezer[11] and two to R. Akiba.[12] While the opinion of R. Eliezer conforms to the manner in which Lieberman presents him, there is no indication that R. Akiba's view, in both tannaitic witness, conforms to the manner in which the sage is presented by Lieberman.[13] Beyond these, in tannaitic

10 The only other sage to whom Lieberman refers as systematically expounding the Song according to R. Eliezer's line of interpretation is R.Pappias. See Lieberman, 120.

11 Mekhilta Pisha 7.

12 Mekhilta Vayehi 6; Shirta 3.

13 It is significant to note that the text in Shirta 3 is the main witness for the association of the vision of God and the Song of Songs in Lieberman's thesis. This key witness does not conform to the hermeneutical theory that serves as the basis for Lieberman's argument. There is nothing in the interpretation of Exodus 15,2 to suggest that R. Akiba applies this verse to Sinai. For that matter, it is unlikely that the verse is applied to the Red Sea, despite the context of the verse under discussion. We seem to have a verse from the Song of Songs interpreted in the constant present, without reference to any particular past historical moment. (See, however, Sifrei Deut., 343, 398, and Midrash Tannaim, 211. These reworkings of R. Akiba's tradition in anonymous fashion suggest an understanding that relates his teaching to the Red Sea). R. Akiba's discussion with Pappias, in Mekhilta Vaheyi 6, also seems to fly in the face of Lieberman's argument. While R. Akiba rejects Pappias' interpretation of Song 1,9, he does seem to maintain the interpretive context with reference to the Red Sea. This verse, which underlies the hermeneutical theory that the song should be interpreted with regard to the events at the Red Sea, in Song of Songs Rabba 1,2, is interpreted in this very manner by R. Akiba. Two conclusions seem to emerge. First, R. Akiba did not interpret the song in a sustained manner. Second, it is probable that the amoraic theory of interpretation also does not intend a systematic interpretation, but rather presents the scope of possible hermeneutical associations.

sources we find only one source that contrasts R. Akiba's interpretation with that of R. Eliezer.[14] This source indeed reads as Lieberman suggests. While R. Eliezer's opinion in this source is consistent with the other instance found in tannaitic literature, R. Akiba offers an interpretation that diverges from the other two instances he addresses. Lieberman's generalization, based upon this single tannaitic source, seems unfounded.

Tannaitic citations in later literature confirm the picture found in tannaitic literature. Interpretation seems to be diverse, and we cannot nail either sage to a particular theory of consistent interpretation. We find both sages offering interpretations that diverge from the pattern Lieberman attempts to establish. We shall analyze these sources in two categories: traditions in which either sage relates to verses from the Song, and traditions that report a direct controversy between the two sages. In the former category we find two teachings associated with R. Eliezer that conform to Lieberman's theory.[15] We also find in R. Eliezer's name, however, several interpretations of the Song of Songs that are thematically totally independent of the Red Sea context.[16] One tradition of R. Akiba's relates to the death of the just.[17] It, too, is independent of the hermeneutical context assigned by Lieberman. The evidence from amoraic testimonies of tannaitic statements indicates hermeneutical plurality, just as the tannaitic sources do.

Let us now turn to the two explicit controversies between R. Akiba and R. Eliezer, as these are recorded in Song of Songs Rabba. In Song of Songs Rabba 1,7,3 we read:

> Go Thy way forth by the Footsteps of the Flock (Song 1,8).
> R. Eliezer and R. Akiba and the Rabbis gave different explanations of this. R. Eliezer said: From the cakes which the Israelites took with them from Egypt...

14 Mekhilta DeRashbi to Exodus 19:17 (143).

15 Song of Songs Rabba 1:5; 2:2.

16 See Leviticus Rabba 19,1 with parallel in Song of Songs Rabba 5:11 and Qohelet Zuta 5:8. In both contexts, R. Eliezer applies the verses from the Song to torah and its study. In Song of Songs Rabba 7:2, R. Eliezer interprets the verse from the Song with reference to pilgrims at the time of the festival.

17 Genesis Rabba 62:8, with a disputed attribution.

> from this you may know what I shall do to them subsequently, and so it is written, "there shall be provision of corn in the land." (Ps. 72,16)
> R. Akiba said: From the way in which I surrounded them with clouds of glory, as it says, "And the Lord went before them by day...the pillar of cloud departed not by day" (Ex. 13,21-2), you may know what I will do to them subsequently, and so it is written, "And there shall be a pavilion for a shadow in the daytime" (Isa. 4,6).[18]

The structure of the derasha is simple. By noting some past favor God has bestowed upon Israel, we get a glimpse of the eschatological favors God will bestow upon Israel in the future. There is nothing inherent in the proof text to limit the exegete. Thus, any favor bestowed by God might be suitable for this derasha. While R. Eliezer does not seem to relate directly to the Red Sea, one might see his interpretation as still linked to the Exodus, the context in which he reads the Song of Songs. There seems to be no association, however, of R. Akiba with Sinai in this interpretation. R. Akiba points to the clouds of glory as an expression of God's favor with Israel, rather than to Sinai. If we had to identify a pattern of interpretation common to both this controversy and the controversy upon which Lieberman constructs his edifice, it might be that R. Akiba tends toward a more "spiritual" emphasis, preferring Sinai to the Red Sea and the clouds of glory to physical food. This, however, is only a vague description of the direction of his method of interpretation. It certainly does not amount to a system, and by no means conforms to Lieberman's claims.

More radical is the next text, with which Lieberman himself attempted to deal. Lieberman was very sensitive to the fact that his theory could be upset by counter-evidence. He therefore offered a reading of the following controversy, based upon a textual emendation. I believe a straightforward reading of this source eliminates the need for textual emendation. More significantly, it further disproves Lieberman's suggestion. Song of Songs Rabba 1,12,1 reads:

> R. Eliezer and R. Akiba and R.Berekah, too, gave different explanations of this verse. R. Eliezer said: "While the king was at his table": while the supreme King of Kings, the Holy One, blessed be He, was at His table in the firmament, Mount

18 The threefold argument continues with attention to the provision of the manna in the desert.

> Sinai was already sending up pillars of smoke, as it says, "And the mountain was burning with fire" (Deut. 4:11). R. Akiba said: While the supreme King of kings, the Holy One, blessed be He, was yet at His table in the firmament, already "The glory of the Lord abode upon Mount Sinai" (Ex. 24:16).[19]

This text obviously contradicts Lieberman's thesis. R. Eliezer is clearly applying a verse from the Song not only to the Torah, but to the Sinai event itself. In order to deal with this difficulty, Lieberman emends the reading of the text to refer to the manifestation of God in the burning bush.[20] The basis for Lieberman's emendation is a difficulty in interpreting this passage. The passage interprets Song 1:12: "While the king sat at his table, my spikenard sent forth its fragrance." The reference to the first part of the verse is clear in these interpretations, but one does not see in what way the second part of the verse figures in either interpretation. Based on this difficulty, Lieberman emends the text, and then establishes a series of associations by which this difficulty is addressed.[21] Having "saved" R. Eliezer's interpretation, Lieberman still declares R.Akiva's interpretation to be enigmatic. The only significant thing, from his perspective, is that the two sages can be cast in light of the Red Sea/Sinai controversy. Lieberman has to settle for an enigmatic text, and an emended one at that, in order to save his theory. A far simpler reading can be offered.

This controversy appears in a long list of interpretations of the verse. We note a very clear pattern in the controversies collected by the editors of Song of Songs Rabba. The opening comments of R.Meir and R.Yehuda resort to both parts of the verse. They introduce the formula that will be echoed in the following interpretations "while the supreme King of Kings, the Holy One, blessed be He, was at His table in the firmament," while they also address the

19 Song of Songs Rabba 1,12,1.

20 Lieberman, 120. He starts out by raising the possibility, hesitantly, but in the course of his argument this possibility becomes established fact. Aware of the problematic reading he offers, he suggests, in note 12, another way of arriving at the same conclusion, which he himself characterizes as hard-pressed (דוחק).

21 These associations are themselves a stretch of the relevant text, as the scent motif is lacking in any of the texts that Lieberman strings, and must be supplied by him. See Lieberman 120.

latter part of the verse, relating to the sending forth of fragrance.[22] Following this, a long series of interpretations is offered that relate only to the former part of the formula. Various situations are presented, all of which conform to the pattern of "while-so-and-so-was happening," already something else was underway. We have eight different interpretations that resort only to the earlier part of the verse, and not to its latter part. The concluding interpretation once more returns to the interpretation of both parts of the verse. R. Eliezer and R. Akiba's interpretations are thus contextual in ignoring the latter part of the verse. There seems to be a tradition that associates this verse with the Sinai event, and several rabbis relate the verse to the context of Sinai. R. Eliezer is no exception. He interprets the verse in accordance with common convention. What then is the difference between his interpretation and that of R.Akiva? One can point to a different level that each of the sages addresses. For R. Eliezer, that which is prepared while God is in the firmament is the smoky mountain. The stage is thus set, and all wait for God's descent. R. Akiba offers a more radical interpretation. God himself is part of the preparation. His glory has descended onto Mount Sinai. R. Akiba raises the interpretive stakes but does not change the context of interpretation. As in previous cases, we may consider his interpretation to be more spiritual, or as relating to what might be perceived as more charged or intense, in a spiritual sense. We note that a similar kind of controversy is repeated further along in the passage, in the dispute between R. Eliezer ben Yakov and the sages:

> R. Eliezer b. Yakov and the Rabbis, too, gave different explanations.
> R. Eliezer said: While the supreme King of kings, the Holy One, Blessed Be He, was still at His table in the firmament, Michael the great prince had already descended and delivered our father Abraham from the fiery furnace.
> The Rabbis, however, say that God Himself came down and delivered him, as it says, "I am the Lord that brought thee out of Ur of the Chaldees" (Gen. 15:7).

22 Incidentally, R.Meir's interpretation of this verse in the context of Sinai seems to conflict with the hermeneutical theory ascribed to him in Song of Songs Rabba 1:2 according to which the Song should be interpreted with regard to the tabernacle. Once more, the theory of sustained interpretation is disproven.

We see that reference to an agent or to God himself constitutes a legitimate basis for offering a different interpretation. This is the case with R. Akiba's reading as well.[23] The controversy between the two sages makes perfect sense when read in context, and when the structure of the entire passage is taken into account.

What emerges from this reading confirms our thesis. Both sages can apply verses from the Song to different contexts. There is no fixed pattern of interpretation. Rather, there seem to be traditions of interpretation. Some verses tended to be interpreted in the context of the Red Sea, others in the context of Sinai. Hermeneutical appropriateness, rather than a fixed theory of interpretation, determined the pattern of interpretation. There seems to be no basis for Lieberman's claim that the tannaim offered sustained readings of the Song of Songs.[24]

Rabbinic literature places formidable challenges before us. The eclectic and disorganized nature of the literature has invited one attempt after another to impose order, system and method upon it. Lieberman's contribution in his *Mishnat shir ha-shirim* is not only a contribution to the study of Jewish mysticism, but also a valiant, if disorderly, attempt to find order and system within rabbinic writings. The suggestions that each rabbi had a systematic approach to Scripture and that this itself constitutes a feature that distinguishes tannaitic from amoraic literature are two suggestions that go a long way to finding method, continuity and system within rabbinic writings. The suggestions are attractive. Alas, my own reading does not permit me to uphold them.

I would like to conclude with a comment of our common teacher, Professor Yakov Zussman, on Lieberman's essay on the Song of Songs. Having worked through the essay, and having struggled with the substantive and methodological issues discussed above, I more or less complained to Zussman about Lieberman's thesis and what I considered to be its flimsy foundations. Zussman replied, if I might paraphrase him, saying: Yes, but it's still a work of genius. Indeed.

23 Compare also the reading of R.Pinehas in R.Hoshaya's name in the same passage.

24 If anything, we probably find the amoraim moving closer than the tannaim to a sustained reading. The systematic discussion of how the Song should be interpreted, in Song of Songs Rabba 1:2 is an amoraic discussion. R.Yohanan does seem to have interpreted the Song regularly in the context of the Sinai event. See Lieberman, 119, n. 7.

THE HALAKHAH FOLLOWS RAVA... EXCEPT WHEN IT DOESN'T: A MEDITATION ON HALAKHIC DECISION-MAKING[1]

Yaakov Elman, Yeshiva University

Officially, Rabbinic Judaism looks for its ethical standards to its foundational texts, the Bible and the Oral Torah. Since, however, cultural change is all but continuous, and stasis is merely the illusion of the backward glance, the foreshortening of distance or the effect of a paucity of data, halakhic decisors must continually struggle with adapting venerable texts to new situations, and, perhaps as perplexing, with justifying them against new mores. The better documented a tradition is, the easier we can see even conservative institutions changing continuously, that is, with the pace of invention (conceptual, technological or otherwise) or merely the change of generations. Nevertheless, so varied are the talmudic texts themselves, that often both traditions are somehow represented in the Talmud, and the decisors simply chose one that is less problematic within the entire structure of their ethical thought.

Rabbinic halakhic traditions from the talmudic era on are relatively well-documented, at least for the Bavli. On the one hand, we have a halakhic culture that demonstrably values precedent and hierarchy. On the other, as we shall see, when even an authoritative from what may be considered talmudic values becomes unendurable, some medieval halakhic decisors — indeed, the most influential among them — find ways to transcend, circumvent or restate

1 It is my great pleasure to dedicate this article to Harry Fox, a great friend, who nevertheless never allows scholarship to interfere with the search for truth, nor truth with friendship. May we long be blessed with the light of Bet Yoreh! I would also like to thank Dr. Samuel Secunda for his discerning comments and sharp eye.

the now undesirable precedent. We shall examine such a case, where an ordinary rule of halakhic decision-making is circumvented, indeed, reversed by the Rif, Maimonides, and Nahmanides — and in stark contrast to the Ran. Nahmanides' reverence for the Rif is clear, even more so than the Geonim, and has recently been documented.[2] However, *his decision in the Rif's favor even against Rava* represents something more than following precedent. Moreover, though formally following the Rif (and also Rav Ashi and Rav Papa), his rhetoric reveals something of the issues of consistency and fairness that underlay his stance, and allows us a narrow glimpse into not only the means, but perhaps also the motives of this decision. His own discussion is particularly enlightening, since, as expected, neither the Rif nor Maimonides reveal the motives underlying their decision.

Perhaps more subtly but more tellingly, this example will serve to illustrate that when viewing the variations in values within the fabric of foundational Jewish texts, from the Talmud through the medieval commentators, modernist views, if one may use such an anachronistic term, are not the exclusive province of the modern era. In this case, where that paragon of cosmopolitanism, Rava of Mahoza, defended a position with whose ethical stance Nahmanides was far from comfortable,[3] we may learn something of the halakhic dialectic that continues from generation to generation.

This is striking because Rava's influence is not merely the consequence of ubiquity. The Mahozans Rava, Rav Nahman, and Rav Papa are mentioned al-

2 See Moshe Halbertal, *Al Derekh ha-Emet: Ha-Ramban vi-Ytzirato shel Masoret*, Jerusalem: Makhon Shalom Hartman, 2006, pp. 77-116, and, in particular, pp. 99, and especially, p. 111, n. 139.

3 For a description of Rava and his times, see my "Middle Persian Culture and Babylonian Sages: Accommodation and Resistance in the Shaping of Rabbinic Legal Tradition," in Charlotte Elisheva Fonrobert and Martin S. Jaffe, eds., *Cambridge Companion to Rabbinic Literature*, Cambridge UP, 2007, pp. 165-197. For data on Mahozan cosmopolitanism, see my "The Socioeconomics of Babylonian Heresy," *Jewish Law Association Studies* XVII, pp. 80-126 (2007). Scholarship on Nahmanides' halakhic works is growing, and such work, by its very nature, requires a close reading of not only his legal reasoning but also his motivations. See most recently Elitzur Avraham Bar-Asher, "Ha-Meni'im "ha-Semuyim" shel ha-Ramban be-'Quntres Dina de-Garmei,'" *Sidra* 20, and consult the literature cited in p. 57, n. 2; add to it the paper by Shalem Yahalom in *Sidra* 22, cited below (see n. 29), and Moshe Halbertal, *Al Derekh ha-Emet*: (see above, n. 2).

most 7,000 times in the Bavli, but the Pumbeditans, Rabbah, Rav Yosef and Abaye appear some 5,000 times.[4] But Rava, the fourth-century Babylonian amora, is all-but-sovereign in talmudic law, at least as far as the Rishonim are concerned. Formally speaking, in all but six cases we decide in his favor in all his disputes with his contemporary Abaye.[5] Rava's master, Rav Nahman, is also all-but-sovereign in matters of civil law, and the Halakhah follows him in all but a handful of cases.[6] It is clear, moreover, that they were authoritative in their own times, and the Bavli's redactors follow Rava in method, outlook, interest and substance. Careful evaluation of the Bavli will show that it is truly a Mahozan compilation in terms of its interests and general trends.[7] Yet Rava's predominance is puzzling, for in many ways, especially in his insistence on intention as an essential ingredient of talmudic law, it often runs against all the sources.[8] This would seem to have put him at a disadvantage in the cut-and-thrust of debate within a traditional society, where the role of precedence would presumably trump creativity. Moreover, it is clear that the Bavli's redactors held to a formalist and hierarchical conception of law, where tannaitic sources must overrule amoraic opinion. When the facts seemed to contradict this rule, as occasionally they do in the case of the first-generation authority Rav, the redactors suggest that he was the exception that proved the

---

4 R. Yehudah, putative founder of the Pumbedita yeshiva, is not yet a Pumbeditan; note that while a number of exegetical principles and interests bind the three Pumbeditans together, R. Yehudah is much closer to his first-generation masters, Rav and Samuel, than to his successors, see: "Ma'aseh bi-Shtei Ayarot: Mahoza u-Pumbedita KeMayatzgot Shtei Tarbuyot Hilkhatiyyot," *Torah li-Shemah: Mehqarim be-Madaei ha-Yahadut li-khvod Prof. Shamma Yehudah Friedman*, Jerusalem: Bar Ilan UP, in association with Makhon Shechter le-Mada'ei Ha-Yahadut, 2007, pp. 3-38.

5 Why this is the case is a question that deserves investigation in its own right, but will not be discussed here; I hope to take it up on another occasion. See below.

6 I have discussed one of these in my "The Socioeconomics of Babylonian Heresy" (see n. 3 above), pp. 85-86. The reason seems to be that in that case R. Nahman, a highly-acculturated Persian-Jewish aristocrat, had made a decision that, while reflecting the values of his class, had moved too far from settled rabbinic policy, at least in the view of the Geonim.

7 See my paper, "Resh Pesahim Ba-Bavli uvi-Yrushalmi: She'elot ba-Arikhah uve-Hithavvut," to be published in the proceedings of a conference held at Bar Ilan University in June, 2006 (in press).

8 I have discussed some of these cases in my "Hercules Within the Halakhic Tradition: A Response to Ronald Dworkin," *Dinei Yisrael* (in press).

rule, since he was considered to have had the status of a tanna.[9] More often, though, such problems were dealt with by reinterpreting one or both of the relevant sources.

At times that did not suffice, and Rava, put on the defensive, openly and publicly admitted error;[10] or seemingly changed his mind, or so the redactors suggest, either because they had a tradition that he had indeed done so, or perhaps simply because they had two contradictory traditions transmitted in his name.[11] The latter seems more likely, since they assumed that he had changed his mind rather than stating, as they did so often, that two tradents differed as to what a particular authority had said.[12] The alternate explanation, that this was only a way of papering over the existence of contradictory traditions, is less likely, since it is clear that the redactors had little difficulty in admitting to alternate attributions or even substantively different traditions, at least within the study hall.[13] Indeed, it may be that we must abandon some of our presuppositions, or perhaps prejudices, regarding how traditional societies operate, or, and this I think more likely, we must reconsider whether Sasanian Mesopotamia was indeed a traditional society in the conventional sense.[14]

At any rate, while amoraim often disagreed, the question here is the basis of the disagreement, especially when a plain-sense reading of the relevant texts — even within the rabbinic canons of interpretation — supports Abaye's view, as it does in our first case. We must then ask what impelled Rava to depart from that reading, or whether such a reading was normative at all. In the following

9 Eruv 50b, Ket 8a, Git 38b, B.B. 42a, Sanh 83b.

10 See Eruv 104a, B.B. 127a, Mak 8a, 8b, Zev 94a, 94b, Men 12b, 97a, Nid 68a.

11 Ber 27a, Shab 111a, (twice), Eruv 14b, Pes 40a (twice), 117b, R.H. 28a, Bez 18b, Meg 10a, Yev 20b, 37a, 76a, 114b, Ket 11b, Git 55b, 77b, Qid 32b, B.Q. 17b, 67b, B.B. 24a. Shev 18a, Men 7b, 67a, Bek 54b.

12 I raise this as a theoretical possibility, since in the 32 cases of the use of this response in the Bavli, the authority is always a tanna: see Ber 3a (twice), 52a, Shab 50b, Eruv 30a, Pes 95b, Bez 23b, 32a, Tan 4b, 28a, Meg 10b, 23a, Yev 101a, Ket 38b, Ned 11a, Sot 20a, Git 28a, Qid 54b, B.Q. 75b, B.B. 11a, Sanh 84a, Ma 16a, Shev 18a, Zev 36a, 36b, 37a, 52b, Men 88b, 108b (twice), Ar 32b, Meil 9a, Nid 53a.

13 For a discussion of some of this, see my "How Should a Talmudic Intellectual History Be Written? A Response to David Kraemer's *Responses to Suffering in Classical Rabbinic Literature*," in *Jewish Quarterly Review* 88/3-4 (1999), pp. 361-386.

14 See my "Hercules" (see n. 7 above).

we shall examine the consistent Mahozan policy limiting a married woman's right to control her property, the conflicting Pumbeditan view, and the medieval response to this dispute. We hope by this binocular vision to shed light on the processes by which rabbinic decision-making was made.

Our test probe will focus on the case of a childless widow who dies before her levirate marriage can be consummated. The talmudic discussion appears in Ket 80b-81a:

מתני'. שומרת יבם שנפלו לה נכסים, מודים ב"ש וב"ה, שמוכרת ונותנת וקיים.

מתה, מה יעשו בכתובתה [רש"י: בנדוניא שהכניסה לו ושמאתן לו בכתובתה וקיבל עליו אחריותן ורשאי להוציאם] ובנכסים הנכנסין והיוצאין עמה [רש"י: הן נכסי מלוג שאין שמין אותם עליו ואינו רשאי להוציאן אלא משנכנסה לרשותו נכנסין עמה וכשהיא יוצאה יוצאין עמה]?

ב"ש אומרים: יחלקו יורשי הבעל עם יורשי האב, וב"ה אומרי': נכסים [רש"י: דצאן ברזל] - בחזקתן, וכתובה [רש"י: מנה מאתים ותוספת {כתובה}][15] בחזקת יורשי הבעל, נכסים הנכנסים והיוצאים עמה - בחזקת יורשי האב....

כנסה - הרי היא כאשתו לכל דבר, בלבד שתהא כתובתה על נכסי בעלה הראשון.

לא יאמר לה הרי כתובתיך מונחת על השלחן, אלא כל נכסיו אחראין לכתובתה. וכן לא יאמר אדם לאשתו הרי כתובתיך מונחת על השלחן, אלא כל נכסיו אחראין לכתובתה.

גירשה - אין לה אלא כתובה. החזירה - הרי היא ככל הנשים, ואין לה אלא כתובה בלבד.

גמ'. איבעיא להו: שומרת יבם שמתה מי קוברה? יורשי הבעל קברי לה, דקא ירתי כתובה, או דלמא יורשי האב קברי לה, דקא ירתי נכסים הנכנסין והיוצאין עמה?

אמר רב עמרם:[16] תא שמע, דתניא: שומרת יבם שמתה יורשיה יורשי כתובתה חייבין בקבורתה.

אמר אביי, אף אנן נמי תנינא: אלמנה ניזונת מנכסי יתומין, ומעשה ידיה שלהן, ואין חייבין בקבורתה, יורשיה יורשי כתובתה חייבין בקבורתה [=משנה כתובות צה ע"ב], ואיזוהי אלמנה שיש לה שני יורשין? הוי אומר: זו שומרת יבם.

אמר רבא, ולימא: אח אני יורש, אשתו אין אני קובר! [רש"י: כתובה זו שאני יורש אין כאן מנדוניית אביה כלום אלא מאתים ותוספת שכתב לה אחי ואין אני יורש אותה אלא אחי.]

15 Rashi read: וכתובה, referring to another category of property, that is, the basic *ketubah* payment of a 100 or 200 *zuz*. See Ran, at the end of his comments on our passage, whose version did not have the *vav*, and he interprets this sentence differently.

16 Presumably this is the second R. Amram, of the third and fourth generation; see H. Albeck, Mavo la-Talmudim, Tel Aviv: Devir, 1969, pp. 373-374

אמר ליה אביי: משום דבאין עליו משני צדדין, אם אחיו יורש - יקבור את אשתו, אם אינו קובר את אשתו - יתן כתובתה.

אמר ליה[17] , הכי קא אמינא: אח אני יורש, את אשתו אין אני קובר, ואי משום כתובה, לא ניתנה כתובה לגבות מחיים! [רש"י: כל זמן שהבעל חי ואני במקום בעל עומד שהייתי מצפה לכונסה]....

והא בעינן כשתנשאי לאחר תטלי מה שכתוב ליכי וליכא!

אמר רב אשי:[18] **יבם נמי כאחר דמי.**

Mishnah: If a woman awaiting the decision of a levir came into the possession of property, Beth Shammai and Beth Hillel agree that she may sell it or give it away, and that her act is legally valid. If she died, what shall be done with her *ketubah* [in this case, the term refers to her dower property, recorded in the *ketubah*, for which the husband assumes responsibility] and with the property that comes in and goes out with her [=her *melog* property, whose capital remains in her possession, but whose usufruct he may consume, without responsibility for it.]? Beth Shammai ruled: The heirs of her husband are to share it with the heirs of her father [since it is uncertain whether the marital bond with the levir constitutes a tie strong enough to make the levir her heir]. Beth Hillel ruled: The "iron sheep" property [=the property she makes over to the husband on condition that he take responsibility for its value] is to remain with those in whose possession it is, the *ketubah* [=in this case, the statutory sum of one or two hundred *zuz* which is entered into all marriage contracts aside from any property the wife brings with her to the marriage, along with any additional amount the husband pledges] is to remain in the possession of the husband's heirs, and the property which goes in and comes out with her remains in possession of the father's heirs.

If [the levir's] brother left money, land shall be bought with it and [the levir, if he contracted marriage with the widow] shall enjoy its usufruct [as above]. [If the deceased brother left] left produce that was detached from the ground, land shall be bought [out of the proceeds] and [the levir] shall enjoy its usufruct. [If it is still] attached to the ground, the land is to be assessed, Rabbi Meir

17 MS Munich adds: Rava.

18 MS Vatican 113: Rava; MS Vatican 487: Abaye, but it is clear from the comments of the Rishonim that they read it in the same way as printed versions.

said, as to how much it is worth together with the produce and how much it is worth without the produce, and with the difference land shall be bought, and [the levir] shall enjoy its usufruct. The Sages, however, rules: Produce which is [still] attached to the ground belongs to him, but that which is detached from the ground passes into the ownership of him who seizes it first. If he [seized it] first, he acquires ownership; if she [seized] it first, land shall be bought with it and [the levir] shall enjoy its usufruct. If [the levir] married her, she shall be considered his wife in all respects, except that her ketubah remains a lien on her first husband's estate. He cannot say to her: "Behold, your *ketubah* lies on the table," but all his property [inherited from his deceased brother] is pledged to her *ketubah*. So too, a man may not say to his wife: "Behold, your *ketubah* lies on the table," but all his property is pledged to her *ketubah*. If [the levir] divorced her [after consummating the marriage], she is entitled to only her *ketubah*. If he subsequently remarried her, she is [to enjoy the same rights as] all other wives, and is entitled only to her *ketubah*.

Gemara: It was asked: If a woman awaiting the levir's decision died, who is to bury her? Are her husband's heirs to bury her because they inherit her *ketubah*, or is it possibly her father's heirs who must bury her, because they inherit the property that comes in and goes out with her?

Rav Amram replied: Come and hear what was taught: If a woman awaiting the decision of the levir died, [81a] it is the duty of her heirs, even those who inherit her *ketubah*, to bury her.

Abaye said: We have also learned a [similar mishnah]: A widow is to be maintained out of the estate of [her deceased husband's] orphans, and her earnings belong to them. It is not their duty, however, to bury her; it is the duty of her heirs, even those who inherit her *ketubah*, to bury her. Now, what widow is it that has two kinds of heirs, [as the expression "her heirs, even those who inherit her *ketubah*," implies that there is another class of heirs who do not inherit her *ketubah*]? Rather, [that mishnah speaks of] a woman awaiting the levir's decision (a *shomeret yavam*).

> Rava said: But could he [=the levir] not plead: "I am only my brother's heir; it is not my duty to bury his wife"? [That is, he inherits only the *ketubah* and additional property his brother gave along with it, but not any of the woman's original property.]
>
> Abaye said: [Such a claim is invalid,] because he is approached by two alternative demands (lit., "they come to him from two sides"): If he is his brother's heir, he should bury [the] wife [as his brother would have done]; if he does not bury the wife, he should return her ketubah [to her heirs].
>
> [Rava] said: It is this that I mean: [He could claim]: I am only my brother's heir; it is not my duty to bury his wife. And if [I am expected to bury her] because of her *ketubah*, [still] a *ketubah* is not collected during [the husband's] lifetime, [and he, the levir, is still alive]....
>
> But is it not required [that the proviso]: "When you will be married to another man, you will receive what is prescribed for you" [be fulfilled] — and is it not [in the case of a woman awaiting her levir who dies before the *yibbum*]?
>
> Rav Ashi said: A levir is also considered "another man" [and thus that proviso is fulfilled by the appearance of the levir].

The sugya poses the question: What does one do when a levirate widow dies before her levirate marriage is consummated? On the one hand, she is still tied to her dead husband; her *ketubah* is paid out of his estate, even after the new marriage is consummated. On the other, her new husband inherits her *ketubah* should she predecease him. Yet another consideration is the undoubted fact that along with the rabbinic ordinance giving the husband the right to inherit the *ketubah* comes the obligation to pay for her funeral — a not inconsiderable sum, then as now.

Abaye's position is easy to understand and justify, and the logic is clear: since her erstwhile brother-in-law has exercised his right to inherit her *ketubah*, he has also assumed the obligation to bury her. However, Rava's support for the levir's demand — "I inherit [her *ketubah*] from my brother, [but] I will not bury her" — is both paradoxical and intuitively unfair. Below I have attempted to explain it in terms of social needs and rabbinic policy, that is, that Rava's policy, here and elsewhere of giving the husband a greater say in the disposition of the wife's property (as opposed to that of Abaye in a number of disputes) was motivated by the need to encourage bachelors to enter the marriage market in Mahoza.

Here, our focus will be primarily on Nahmanides' view of this particular matter. In any case, the principle is laid down in bKet 47b, as emended by the Bavli:

> חייב במזונותיה וכו'. תנו רבנן: תיקנו מזונותיה תחת מעשה ידיה, וקבורתה תחת כתובתה, לפיכך בעל אוכל פירות. פירות מאן דכר שמייהו? חסורי מחסרא והכי קתני: תיקנו מזונותיה תחת מעשה ידיה, ופירקונה תחת פירות, וקבורתה תחת כתובתה, לפיכך בעל אוכל פירות.

> Our rabbis taught: Maintenance was provided for a wife in return for her handiwork, and her burial in return for her *ketubah*.[19] A husband is, therefore, entitled to usufruct. Usufruct! Who mentioned it?

> A clause is missing, and this is the proper reading: Maintenance was provided for a wife in return for her handiwork, her ransom in return for usufruct, and her burial in return for her *ketubah*; a husband, therefore, is entitled to usufruct.

Thus, Rava's decision runs against strong rabbinic precedent, and the medieval commentators are split over the question of whether to follow the general rule that the Halakhah follows Rava in his disputes with Abaye except for the famous six cases alluded to in the acronym יע"ל קג"ם, or whether this is an exception to that rule. The Ran follows the rule, but the Rif, Maimonides and

19 It should be noted that there are cases in Rome in which married women were buried in their *father's* family tomb; "legal responsibility for burial seems to have depended on whether the woman's father or husband had rights to the dowry," as Beryl Rawson has noted in her article, "The Family in Ancient Rome," in Beryl Rawson, ed., *The Family in Ancient Rome: New Perspectives*, Ithaca: Cornell UP, 1986, p. 20. This observation indicates that the equivalence of the *ketubah* and burial responsibilities was not a rabbinic quirk.

Nahmanides (and the Rashba) depart from it.[20] However, since the Rif and Maimonides do not explain their reasoning, it may have been the Tosafists' comment on bYev 39a, s.v. *af al gav* that smoothed the way for Nahmanides; they explain that when amoraic sages after Rava's time took up the case, they may overrule him. That is, "[this case] is not considered in [the rule of] Y'AL QeGaM[21] since [later] amoraim [=Rav Ashi] discuss it [and disagree with Rava]." And that is the mechanism that Nahmanides adopts here in Ketubot. However, an inspection of the sugya will show that Rav Ashi does not really speak to the central issue of burial. But before pursing this line of investigation we must examine the sugya in more detail.

This passage in the Mishnah cannot be considered apart from another passage which considers a related issue, that is, the respective rights that the deceased husband had in regard to his wife's property *vis-à-vis* that of the wife, and then, of course, the parallel issue in regard to the levir and the widow. The issue is debated in a mishnah parallel to mKet 8:6, that of mYev 4:3, that presents a dispute between Beth Hillel and Beth Shammai as to the disposition of property that a widow waiting for levirate marriage has inherited or obtained in some other way and then dies. Since the prospective levir's relationship to his sister-in-law is unclear, the Houses dispute concerns the question of who has rights to the property.

Both Houses agree that when the widow is still alive but not yet married to the levir, she may dispose of the property as she sees fit. The Bavli at Yev 39b-39a discusses a four-pronged dispute among Ulla and Rabbah, and Abaye and Rava in explaining why the Houses agree in the one case but not in the other.

The dispute between Rava and Abaye hinges on the question of the (original) husband's rights to his wife's property in relation to her own rights. According to Abaye, they have equal rights of disposal, but according to Rava, "his hand is greater than her hand." Thus, when rights to property pass from the dead husband to the tentative possession of the levir, he loses a degree of

20 On the complex relationship of Nahmanides to Maimonides, and his defense (in the Spanish tradition) of the Rif, see Moshe Halbertal, *Al Derekh ha-Emet*6 (see 2 above), pp. 77-83.

21 A mnemonic for the six case in which the halakhah follows Abaye in his disputes with Rava; see bB.M. 22b. Note that the cases discussed here are also exceptions to the usual rule, but they are not part of the acronym.

control — since the levirate marriage has still not been consummated,[22] and thus, according to Abaye, she has the preponderant rights to her property, while according to Rava, the two are now equal. According to Rava, then, the difference between the two cases — that is, the first case in the mishnah when the widow is alive, and the second case, when she has died, inheres in this: the new couple has not yet become "engaged" (she is not yet bound — *zequqah* — to him) in the first case, and thus she still controls the property that came to her *after her husband's death*.[23] In the second case, where she has died, the prospective levirate husband has no more than equal rights to the property, at least according to Beth Hillel, and thus the property remains in its original state as far as the husband's heirs and the wife's heirs are concerned (*be-hezqatan*) — the *ketubah* to the husband's heirs, and her dowry, which was recorded in the *ketubah*, to her family, while Beth Shammai holds that though they had become "engaged," she is still not considered his full wife (*nesu'ah*). If she were, the new husband would be her sole heir, but since her status had been doubtful, the property has to be divided *equally* between the two families. Thus the Houses' dispute.

Now, according to Abaye, the first case relates to property she acquired after her first husband's death but before the levirate marriage, but the second refers to property she acquired while the first husband was still alive. Thus, the Houses agree that she controls the property in the first case, but in the second, she and her first husband shared control of the property, but now the levir has lost one degree, and thus the prospective levirate wife — the widow — shares control with the levir but has the upper hand.

Thus, the basic issue between Rava and Abaye relates to the exact degree of control each spouse has in regard to the wife's property, with Abaye taking the wife's side, or perhaps, the more egalitarian side, so to speak.

Before continuing to the discussions of the medieval commentators, let us consider Rav Ashi's role in this debate. As noted above, he does not comment

22 We leave off the question of whether the levir's declaration of intention to enter the marriage is necessary.

23 Technically, Rava actually holds that there is a state of *ziqqah* for the *yevamah*, while R. Nahman does not; see bYev 30a and compare the redactional (re-)construction of Rava's view at bYev 17b.

on the essential issue: the *yevamah*'s burial. His intervention involves another issue: the question of whether, according to the wording of the *ketubah*, the levir can inherit his sister-in-law's *ketubah* at all, since the *ketubah* stipulates that: "When you marry another [man], you shall take what is written for you," that is, you are not entitled to the *ketubah* unless you are free of your first husband, either by divorce or his death. In this case, since she is still bound to the levir, she has never been permitted to marry "another," and is therefore not entitled to the *ketubah*. If she is not entitled to the *ketubah*, she is thus not entitled to the burial expenses that were ordained in its place.

To this redactional comment Rav Ashi responds that the levir is *also* considered an "other [man]," and *so the wording of the ketubah has been fulfilled*. The upshot of this is that she was entitled to the *ketubah*, and so therefore the levir does inherit it from her, and should therefore be obligated to bury her.

We must at least consider momentarily whether the context of Rav Ashi's remark is likely to have been the debate about burial altogether; after all, it may have been directed to the basic question of whether the levir has any right to the *ketubah* at all, since the woman was never actually entitled to it. The answer to this question is simple: he has the rights of a brother if not a levir. If that is so, the question Rav Ashi could have been considering involves the woman's right to the *ketubah*, and therefore her heirs' rights to it. Could it be that Rav Ashi was considering the status of the *ketubah* between the brother's death and the consummation of the levirate marriage? The answer to this is also clear, since by rabbinic teaching, Deut 25:6, the essential point of levirate marriage is that the estate remain within the agnatic family, this possibility is null. Thus, this redactional comment is the only construction that could have been put upon Rav Ashi's comment.

There is another possibility in regard to burial, though: that Rav Ashi's intervention was intended to support Rava and *not* Abaye, as Nahmanides would have it! The argument could have been: True, the wife may have had some residual right to the *ketubah*, had she lived, but as it is, the levir need not bury her. Rav Ashi's argument could have gone along the lines that the Ritva sets down in trying to justify Rava's argument for the levir: even though the husband would have been obligated to bury her by his right to inherit her *ketubah*, I am not.[24]

This indeed may have been Rav Ashi's intent. *However, from the fact that his comment was placed here by the redactors, it is clear that he has been pressed into service as supporting Abaye.* And thus the redactors signal their approval of *Abaye's* view. We should also note, at this point, that if Shamma Friedman is correct, the very determination that we decide with Abaye only in the six cases of Y'AL QeGaM is itself Geonic, and would therefore not have been in force in Rav Ashi's time at all![25] At any rate, that would mean that discomfort with Rava's attempt to justify the levir's claim of the *ketubah* but disclaim responsibility for his brother's widow's funeral can be traced back to the times of the redactors, that is, the late fifth century, or even before the empowerment of women's civil rights under Sasanian law.[26] Thus, the discomfort manifested by the medieval commentators has a much earlier precedent, so to speak.

Again, in that same redactional period Rav Papa, who studied with both Abaye and Rava, declares that an exact reading of the mishnah accords with *Abaye's* position. Here too then the medieval commentators divide on whether we follow Rav Papa in deciding against Rava, or whether the usual rule holds — and this is the point to which the Tosafists' comment refers. Following Rav Yehudai Gaon, they would decide with Abaye against Rava, while others, such as the Rosh, would go with the general rule favoring Rava. In his extensive discussions on this issue in his novellae,[27] Nahmanides outlines the interpretation of Rashi with particular emphasis on Abaye's view, and then sets forth the views of the Rif and Maimonides who both decide cases according to Abaye's

24 We need not follow the convoluted lines of that argument, since it reduces itself to: that is what the rabbis actually decreed; see *Hiddushei ha-Ritva le-Masekhet Ketubot*, ed. R. Moshe Goldstein, Jerusalem: Mosad Harav Kook, 1982, col. 640.

25 See his: "Le-Talmudam shel Ge'onim: Qeta Qadum shel Talmud im Gilyonot Nusah," *Tarbiz* 51 (5742), pp. 37-48. My hesitation here is due to the possibility that the marginal addition may have been motivated by a prior scribal omission.

26 For a discussion of this, see my "Marriage and Marital Property." The date of Wahrām can now be more precisely established, but my more general dating as after the Black Plague outbreak of 542, is confirmed. I hope to discuss the matter of dating of the jurisconsults of Xusrow I's reign elsewhere.

27 See *Hiddushei ha-Ramban al Masekhtot Yevamot ve-Sotah*, ed. Rabbi Samuel Dickman, Jerusalem: Yad HaRav Herzog, 5747, cols. 130-134; further references will be found in the footnotes,

view. Nahmanides also mentions that Rav Yehudai Gaon agrees with Abaye. With his major authorities all agreed, Nahmanides himself has no need to take sides; the issue had already been decided.

Similarly, in our debate in Ketubot, since Rav Ashi intervenes, seemingly on Abaye's side, the way is open for the commentators to decide against Rava, and, as noted, that is exactly what the Rif, Maimonides and Nahmanides do, while the Ran goes with the usual principle, and decides in accordance with Rava. The question is, however, why depart from the established precedent in favor of Rava against Abaye? What impelled these three supremely influential medieval commentators to depart from precedent? Unfortunately, the codificatory style of Rif and Maimonides' great works does not allow us to plumb the depths of their motives except in the most speculative way. However, Nahmanides has recorded his view, at least in part, in his *novellae* on the Ketubot passage.

והא דאבעיא לן שומרת יבם שמתה מי קוברה, הכי פירושו ודאי קיי"ל דקבורתה תחת כתובתה כלומר תחת מנה ומאתים ונדוניא שכל מי שיהא יורש אותה יקבור ואע"פ שאין יורש שניהם כגון א"א [=אשת איש] שמתה שאין לה עיקר קוברה תחת נדוניתה הואיל ואין אחר יורש ממנה כלום אלא זה אבל שומרת יבם שאחרים יורשים משלה לא תיקנו לה קבורה אפי' תחת נדוניא אלא בעל לוקח הוי, ומשלה דהיינו מה שיורשיה יורשין היא נקברת, או דלמא לעולם היא נקברת מכתובתה, או מן העיקר כגון זו או מן הנדוניא כגון א"א שמתה.

ודייקינן עלה ולימא אח אני יורש בכתובה זו ואי משום שעבודא של כתובה לא נתנה כתובה לגבות מחיים הלכך אחיו הוא דקא ירית לה ולא מדידה, ואע"ג דבעל קבר לה תחת כתובה תחת נדוניתה קאמרינן כדפרש"י ז"ל וטעמא דמינה קא ירית אבל הכא לאו מינה קא ירית כתובה הלכך הו"ל כארוס דלא מחייב למקבר ארוסתו, וא"ת יקברנה תחת נדוניא שהרי הוא חולק בנכסי צאן ברזל שהרי בנכסים אלו מכח אחיו הוא בא שאחיו קוברה מחמתן אע"פ שלא נתנה כתובה לגבות מחיים דבעל, איכא למימר דה"ק **אשתו אין אני קובר לבדי אלא יורשי נדוניתה החולקין עמנו יקברוה עמנו שהרי שניהן שוין בשלה**, ולדברינו שפרשנו ביבמות שנכסי צאן ברזל בחזקת יורשי הבעל[28] ואין ליורשי אשה בהם כלום הא דאמר אביי [צ"ל רבא - י"א] אח אני יורש אשתו אין אני קובר, **ה"ק כי תקינו רבנן קבורה תחת כתובה ה"מ** [=הני מילי] **לבעל דמינה ירית דשויוה רבנן כיורש דידה אבל אחי אין אני ראוי לירש מכ– תובתה כלום כשם שאין אני יורש מלוג שלה** ומה שאני איני פורע לה כתובה משום דלא נתנה כתובה לגבות מחיים לא היא ולא נכסי צאן ברזל שבה דתנאי כתובה ככתובה דמי, ואע"ג דארוסה אית לה מפני שלא זכה הבעל בדברים

28 See *Hiddushei ha-Ramban al Yevamot*, ed. R. Shmuel Dickman, Jerusalem: Makhon ha-Talmud ha-Yisraeli ha-Shalem, 5747, *ad* Yev 38a, s.v. *Nekhasim be-hezqatan*, col. 128-129.

הללו אבל משזכה לא נתנו לגבות אף הם מחיים. **ומסקנא יבם נמי כאחר דמי ובין עיקר ובין צאן ברזל מינה דידה קא ירית דידו כידה הלכך קוברה.**

As for that which was asked [in regard] to who pays the funeral expenses for a woman awaiting levirate marriage [who dies before the marriage can be consummated], this is its interpretation: Certainly we hold that "her burial is in place of her *ketubah*," that is, in return for the *mana* or 200 and her dowry, so that whoever inherits them is responsible for the funeral expenses (lit., "buries her"), and even in the case of a [conventionally] married woman who dies [while still married to her husband] who does not have [possession of] the essential [*ketubah* payment, which she only receives in the case of divorce or her husband's death], he [=the husband] pays her funeral expenses in place of her dowry, since no one else but he inherits anything from her [estate]. But [as for a woman awaiting her levirate marriage], [whose heirs] do inherit [something] from her estate, they [=the Sages] did not legislate for her funeral even in return for the dowry. Rather, the husband is considered as a buyer, and from her own [property], that is, [from] what her heirs inherit [from her] is she buried, or, perhaps, her funeral expenses are always paid from her *ketubah* [from additional money stipulated therein], or from the essential [*ketubah*] as in [the case of] this one or from the dowry as in the case of a married woman who died [while still married to her husband].

And we carefully interpret [as follows]: And let him [=the levir] say: I am inheriting [my] brother's [share of] this *ketubah*, and if [you will claim] that there is a lien on [my brother's property], [I can respond] that a *ketubah* is not collected while [the husband or his heir] is alive, therefore it is his brother from whom he inherits it [=the *ketubah*] and not from her [=the would-be levirate wife]. And [thus] even though [ordinarily] a husband pays for the wife's funeral expenses in place of [his rights to] her dowry, [and] we say, as Rashi has interpreted it, that the reason is that [the husband in the usual case] inherits [the *ketubah*] from his wife, here he does not inherit the *ketubah* from her, and therefore he is like a betrothed groom (*arus*) who is not obligated to pay for his would-be wife's funeral expenses.

And if you will say that he should bury her in return for her dowry, for [after all] he shares in her insured property [lit., "iron sheep property," that is, property for whose value the husband obligates himself at the marriage], for in regard to this property he [=the levir] does come as a representative of his [deceased] brother, for his brother would have buried her because [of his rights] to it even though the *ketubah* is not collected in the husband's lifetime, it could be said that this is what he claims: I will not bury his wife myself [that is, without any share from her family or heirs], but let those who inherit her dowry who [thus] share it with me pay for her funeral expenses along with me, since both of them [that is, both of us] are equal in hers [=her dowry property].

And as to our interpretation in [our *novellae*] in Yevamot, that iron sheep property are in the possession of the husband's heirs, and the wife's heirs have no share in them at all, the statement made by Rava [curr. eds.: Abaye] [that the levir claims]: "I am inheriting my brother, I will not bury his wife": this is what he means: When the rabbis legislated burial in return for the *ketubah*, that was only in regard to a husband who inherits from her [=his wife], where the rabbis made him as her heir, as it were, but [the claim of the levir] that I do not have the right [lit., "am not worthy"] of inheriting her *ketubah* at all, just as I do not inherit her iron sheep property, and the [fact that] I will not pay her *ketubah* [to her family or heirs], that is because a *ketubah* cannot be collected [while the husband] is alive, not it and not the iron sheep property, for the stipulations of the *ketubah* are like the *ketubah* itself. And even though a betrothed woman (*arusah*) has [rights to her property], that is because her husband [that is, her betrothed] has not [yet] acquired the rights to these things, but when he does acquire the rights [upon the marriage], they cannot be collected while [he is still] alive.

[But] the conclusion is the levir is considered as "another" [that is, as though he were another man coming to marry her after she is freed from the levir by *halitzah*, as R. Ashi proposes], and [thus it is considered] as though he inherits either the essential *ketubah* or the iron sheep property from her, for his rights [that that property] are equal to her rights [in it], [and] **therefore he buries her**.

In other words, despite Nahmanides' careful attempts to explain (and thus justify) Rava's strained reasoning in support of the levir's claims to the *ketubah*, and also his support of the levir's contradictory denial of responsibility for payment of the woman's funeral expenses, Nahmanides decides, along with Maimonides, that, indeed, the levir, having accepted his sister-in-law's *ketubah*, must also accept the responsibility for her funeral expenses, thus effectively deciding against Rava and with Abaye — and against the usual rule. He does so by accepting Rav Ashi's argument that the levir is indeed considered "another," but that this was no easy matter is demonstrated by the Ran's insistence on following the usual rule.

וקימא לן כרבא דאביי ורבא הלכה כרבא חוץ מיע"ל קג"ם **ואע"ג דמשמע התם** [=**ביבמות לח ע"ב**] **דהלכתא כאביי מדקתני דיקא נמי כו', מ"מ אנן אכלל סמכי'**. נמצא עכשיו לפי רש"י ז"ל דנכסי צאן ברזל לב"ה יחלוקו יורשי הבעל עם האב, ועיקר כתובה א"נ כל מה שכתב לה הבעל משלו כלן ליורשי הבעל, ונכסים הנכנסים והיוצאים עמה דהי[י]נו נכסי מלוג כלן ליורשי האשה, ודוקא שנפלו לה מן הנשואים אבל נפלו לה מן הארוסין כלן ליורשי האשה דלא עדיף יבם מאחיו, דקיי"ל דאינו יורש אשתו ארוסה, ואפשר לומר דכל שנתאלמנה מן הארוסין מוכרת ונותנת וקיים לכתחלה, ודאמרי' התם [=יבמות שם] רישא שנתאלמנה מן הארוסין, וקיי"ל דזיקת ארוסין עושה ספק אירוסין, דהא לא אשכחן מאן דפליג עליה.

Now, we hold like Rava, since [in disputes between] Abaye and Rava he Halakhah follows Rava, aside from [the cases of] YE'AL Q'GAM, even though it appears from there [=Yev 38b] that the halakhah follows Abaye since it is taught there that an exact interpretation of [the Mishnah will support his view, q.v.], nevertheless we rely on the rule. The result is, according to Rashi z.l., that the wife's "iron sheep property" should be divided between the husband's heirs [and those of] the father, according to Beth Hillel, and the essential *ketubah* or whatever the husband wrote for her of his own [property], all go to the husband's heirs, [while] the property that remains with her (lit., "that enter and leave with her (from the marriage), that is, dowry property [*melog*] — all go to the woman's heirs. And this [that is, the property that returns to the husband] refers specifically [to property] that fell to her during the marriage but [as to property] that fell to her during the betrothal — all go to the woman's heirs, for the levir has no greater privileges than the [first] husband, and we hold that he does not inherit a betrothed woman's property. It is possible to say that as long as she was widowed while betrothed, she may alienate (lit., "she sells and gives as a gift") [her own property] and [the transfer] is valid even *ab initio*, as we said there [in Yev *ibid*], the first part of the Mishnah refers to [a woman] widowed while [still only] betrothed, and we hold that the tie of betrothal creates a doubtful state of marriage [until the marriage is consummated], and we have not found anyone who disputes this.

While the dispute may be explained on purely formal grounds, that is, that the Ran does not consider the later amoraic comments of Rav Papa and Rav Ashi as determinative, indeed, that is the explicit basis of his decision. Nahmanides' comment in regard to a related case, where the fiancé refuses to pay burial costs for his fiancée, a claim which has even stronger legal grounds that the levir's, may shed light on Nahmanides' attitude to these questions. He states in his comments to Ket 53a s.v. *vha de-amrinan*: "has she then been married to be thrown to the dogs?" This would then apply all the more to the case of the levir.

הא דאמרינן זיל קבור או הב לה כתובתה קס"ד דקבורתה תחת עיקר כתובתה תקינו לה וזה שכתב לה מן האירוסין ראוי הוא מן הדין לפרוע לה כתובתה אלא לא יפו חכמים כחה יותר מן הנשואה שאם רצה לקבור יקבור ולא יתן, והיינו דאקשינן עלה טעמא דמת הוא הא מתה היא אין לה כתובה דאי כדקאמרת לעולם דינה לגבות אלא שאם אמר לקבור יפטר בכך, ואסקינן דכל דלא קרינא בה לכשתנשאי לאחר תטלי לית לה עיקר וכי תקינו רבנן קבורה לנשואה תקון ותחת נדונייתה שהוא יורש דההיא ליתא בכלל מדרש לכשתנשאי לאחר תטלי דהא ארוסה אינו יורשה. **וקשיא לי כיון דכי שקיל בעל נדוניא ירושה היא היכי אמרינן קבורתה תחת כתובתה והלא אף נכסי מלוג הוא יורש**, ועוד למ"ד ירושת הבעל תורה היא היאך תקינו להחזירה במקצת. ואיכא למימר דה"ק כיון דכתובתה לבעל אי מדאורייתא אי מדרבנן במה תקבר והלא קרובים כיון דאיהו ירית לה קריא ולא ענו **לה לפיכך תקנו לה קבורה ממנו שלא נשאת ע"מ להשליכה לכלבים**, ולפיכך לא אמרו תחת ירושת נכסי מלוג שתקנו מצוי למצוי אבל נכסי מלוג אינו מצוי כלל כנ"ל.

[In regard to] that which we say: "Go, [either] bury [her, i.e., the *arusah*] or give her *ketubah*, we might think that [since] her burial was ordained [by the Sages] in place of her *ketubah*, and this one [=her fiancé] who wrote [it] for her from [the time of] her betrothal, it is proper for him by law to pay her *ketubah* [even though they were not married before she died], however, [the Sages] did not empower her [to an extent] greater than a married woman, [in which case] if he wishes to bury her (i.e., pay her burial costs) he may do so and not pay [her *ketubah*]. And that is what is queried [in the talmudic passage at Ket 53a]: "The reason [she gets her *ketubah*] is that he has died [first, but] if she dies [before him], she [or rather, her estate] has no [rights to the] *ketubah*." For if it is as [you wish] to say, then [the disposition of] her [case] would really be that he pays, but if he agrees to bury her, he would be free of the obligation with that; [however], we have concluded that as long as we read [the language of the *ketubah*] "when you are wed to another [man], you may take the essential [payment of the *ketubah*]," and when the Rabbis ordained her burial they ordained it for a married woman and instead of her dowry that he inherits. And that [midrash of the *ketubah*] in general does not apply [to a betrothed woman]: "when you are wed to another [man], you may take the essential [payment of the *ketubah*]," for when she is [only at the stage of being] a betrothed woman, he [=the prospective husband] does not inherit her [property if she dies before the marriage].[29] **And [this] is difficult for me, [for] since when the [prospective] husband takes her dowry, this is an inheritance, [and so] how can we state [that the Sages ordained] her burial in place of her *ketubah*, does he not even inherit her *melog* property?** And, furthermore, how can the one who holds that [the rule] that the husband's *ketubah* is of biblical authority, how could [the Sages] ordain that it can be returned in part? It could be said that it may be explained as follows: Since her *ketubah* [goes] to the husband, either by biblical or rabbinic authority, how can she be buried (that is, who pays her funeral expenses), for [as to her] relatives, since he [=the husband] inherits her, she will call and who will answer her (that is, her relatives will not assume the expenses since they do not inherit her), and **therefore they ordained her burial in place of her *ketubah*, for was she married (i.e., betrothed) in order [for her body] to be thrown to the dogs?** And that is why they did not ordain her burial in place of the inheritance of her *melog* property, for [they ordained] a usual occurrence for a usual occurrence (that is, burial for a *ketubah*), but *melog* property is not common at all — so it seems to me.

In other words, the fact that Rav Papa and Rav Ashi seem to have supported a reading of the *ketubah* that opposed Rava's was only a means to ensure the desired end, that is, that the levir's basic moral obligation in accordance with

29 This is an assumption that the sugya later refutes.

the Sages' concern that responsibility for the woman's burial must clearly fall on someone, and that someone would naturally be someone whose relation to her gave him a financial stake in her property. Indeed, Nahmanides would extend the obligation further, even beyond marriage, for the burial of a woman who entered a marital relationship but died before it could be consummated, formally, by means of *huppah* and *qiddushin*, fell to her fiancée.

Nahmanides' rhetoric here is striking. No woman would agree to marry (or be betrothed), were her body "to be thrown to the dogs" if she predeceased her husband or fiancé. In other words, no matter the midrashic implications of the wording of the *ketubah*, it is clear that both the woman's own expectations, and I would add, the expectations of a moral society, would require that the obligation of burial not be shirked by means of some legal sleight of hand. Indeed, this may be seen as Nahmanides' restatement of Rav Hisda's use of Prov 17:13 to characterize the view that a fiancé is not responsible for the burial costs of his fiancée: "One who returns evil for good — evil will not move from his house." If that was said of a betrothed woman, why would a woman already married but now having fallen before her levir lose her burial rights as a married woman?

However, as we have seen, even Rav Papa, Rava's most prominent disciple, had trouble with this decision, and, while Rav Ashi's position on the matter is not clear, the redactors understood him as favoring Abaye's. In the next section we will examine some possible explanations for this.

II

The cases we have examined are not the only ones in which Rava takes the husband's side. I have commented above on one that is parallel to the one regarding the husband's right to control his wife's property: the wife's rights *vis-à-vis* that of the husband. To see the issue in context, we must begin three generations earlier, with a decision of the two great first-generation authorities, Rav and Samuel. In B.B. 51b we have the following.:

רב ושמואל דאמרי תרווייהו: בין שנפלו לה נכסים עד שלא נתארסה, בין שנפלו לה נכסים משנתארסה וניסת - הבעל מוציא מיד הלקוחות.

כמאן? דלא כרבי יהודה ולא כר' חנינא בן עקביא!

אינהו דאמרי כרבותינו; דתניא, רבותינו חזרו ונמנו: בין שנפלו לה עד שלא תתארס, ובין שנפלו לה משנתארסה

וניסת - הבעל מוציא מיד הלקוחות.

> Both Rav and Samuel stated: Whether a woman came into the possession of property before she was betrothed or whether she came into possession of property after she was betrothed, her husband may, [if she sold it] after she married, take it away from the buyers.
> In agreement with whose view [is this] — is it either in agreement with that of Rav Yehudah or that of Rav Hanina b. Akavia?
> They stated [their opinion] in accordance with [that] of our masters, for it was taught: Our masters took a [vote, and decided that] whether a woman was betrothed or whether she came into possession after she was betrothed, her husband may, [if she sold it] after she married, take it away from the buyers.[30]

In other words, the husband had a right to any property the woman owned at the time of betrothal — not to mention any that came into her possession afterwards. This opinion is to be found in the Tosefta (tbKet 8:1) as an integral part of the text which appears in our *mishnah*. Whether the Mishnah's redactor omitted this deliberately, or whether it was missing from the text he had, is not clear, but it is cited both in the Bavli and the Yerushalmi.[31] In the end, then, the majority apparently voted to deny women control of property in her possession before betrothal, thus closing a "loophole" of indeterminate size.

Moreover, the husband's right to inherit his dead wife's property, and the denial of the concomitant right to her, is based on a rabbinic exposition of Num 27:11. It is noteworthy that the Bavli itself, in an extended discussion (bB.B. 111b-113a), takes note of the difficulty of justifying that interpretation of the relevant verses; the wife's exclusion from inheritance is difficult to justify on technical midrashic grounds.[32] Moreover, it is elsewhere reported of Rav that he held that the husband's right to inherit his wife was only a rab-

30 bKet 78b.

31 yKet 8:2 (32a).

32 Indeed, the redactional concerns regarding this issue may have been fueled by the stark contrast between rabbinic teaching and Sasanian law on this matter.

binic enactment (bKet 84a).[33] We must thus look elsewhere for the reason for this exclusion of wives.

It is against that background that we should view the double-edged response to this problem in B.B. 128b:

תלמוד בבלי מסכת בבא בתרא דף קכח עמוד ב

שלח ליה ר׳ אבא לרב יוסף בר חמא: האומר תטול אשתי כאחד מן הבנים - נוטלת כאחד מן הבנים.

אמר רבא: ובנכסים של עכשיו, ובבנים הבאין לאחר מכאן.

> Rabbi Abba sent to Rav Joseph b. Hamma: [As for] whoever says: Let my wife take [a share] as one of [my] sons [inherits], she may take [as share equal] to one of the sons.
>
> Said Rava: [This refers] to property now [in possession but not to property acquired later] and to sons later [that is, if there are sons born after this declaration, she must allow her portion to be diminished to provide them with equal shares].

In other words, Rava sought to limit the husband's ability to provide his wife with a share of the inheritance. If Rav Joseph b. Hama was his father, as is the general consensus, this report acquires an additional poignancy.

The result of such legislation restricting her access and control of her own or her husband's property could not have been satisfying to Babylonian Jewish wives. And, indeed, a careful examination of the Bavli's discussion reveals the tensions both within Babylonian marriages, and within the ranks of the rabbinic elite as it attempted to deal with the psychological and social "fallout" of the inequitable control of wealth that these rabbinic enactments produced. The resulting tensions are brought out in the Bavli's discussion of the question of whether a wife can buy a field from her husband, as in this discussion in B.B. 51a:

ולא לאשה בנכסי בעלה וכו׳. פשיטא, כיון דאית לה מזוני - מזוני הוא דקא אכלה! לא צריכא, דיחד לה ארעא אחריתי למזונה. הא ראיה יש, לימא: לגלויי זוזי הוא דבעי! שמעת מינה: המוכר שדה לאשתו - קנתה, ולא אמרינן לגלויי זוזי הוא דבעי!

33 See Rashi *ad loc.*, s.v. *Rav savar.*

לא, אימא: הא ראיה יש בשטר מתנה.

[Since the *mishnah* says only that the wife has no *hazaqah*], we infer that if she brings proof [such as a deed or witnesses that the field has been sold to her] the sale is valid. But cannot the husband plead against this that he merely desired to see if she had any money? May we then not learn from this [*mishnah*] that if a man sells a field to his wife, she becomes the legal owner, and we do not say that he merely desired to see if she had any money?

No, we infer this [instead]: But if she brings a proof, it is effective in the case of a deed of gift, [though not of a deed of sale since in the case of a gift there is no question of enticing her to reveal hidden resources].[34]

In the ensuing debate as construed and constructed by the Bavli, which covers several generations of sages from both Palestine and Babylonia, the issue is whether such an apparent sale was being used by the husband in order to uncover property due to him, which his wife was hiding from him. Various *baraitot* that lend themselves to such an interpretation are examined. A subsidiary question is whether, even if the wife gains possession of the property, the husband is still entitled to the income in any case. As represented in both Talmuds, Palestinian authorities generally take a more positive view of the husband's motives and the wife's rights. The Bavli itself presents the Palestinians as generally interpreting the husband's motives for selling the field to the wife as intended to strengthen her position as owner. The sugya concludes with the following.

אמר רבא, הלכתא: המוכר שדה לאשתו - לא קנתה, והבעל אוכל פירות; במתנה - קנתה, ואין הבעל אוכל פירות.

תרתי? לא קשיא: כאן במעות טמונין, כאן במעות שאין טמונין, דאמר רב יהודה: מעות טמונין - לא קנתה, מעות שאינן טמונין - קנתה.

Rava said: The law is that if a man sells a field to his wife, she does not become the legal owner, and the husband is entitled to the produce, but if he gives it

34 B.B. 51a.

> to her [as a gift], she becomes the legal owner and the husband is not entitled to the produce.
>
> [Do not the] two [halves of Rava's first statement contradict each other — if she does not acquire ownership, how can the husband have a right to the produce alone]?
>
> There are no contradictions. The one [half] refers to the case where the wife has money hidden away [and he was merely attempting to ferret out this money by offering to sell her the field], the other to the case where she does not have money hidden away, since Rav Judah has decided that [if the wife buys with] money hidden away, she does not acquire [it], [and] if with money not hidden away, she does acquire [it].[35]

Of course, Rava's decision, perhaps intentionally, leaves a loophole: what if the husband wished to ferret out any hidden money, but there was none? In this case, the sale would be deemed valid even though the husband had not intended it. With this possibility in mind, a husband would think twice before risking the sale of a field to his wife, unless he were certain that she was withholding his due from him. Whatever Rava's motives, however, the very consideration given to this question indicates that the Babylonian rabbis recognized that their women did not take this inequitable situation without demur.

Before discussing the wider implications of these data, let us briefly examine some of Nahmanides' discussion on B.B. 51b:

> **ומיהו אין הבעל נאמן לומר משלי גנבה או מציאה הן או ממעשה ידיה קמצה וגוף ופירות שלי, אלא כנכסי מלוג הן לכל דבר גוף שלה ופירות שלו,** לפיכך כתב הרב ר' שמואל ז"ל שאם נתגרשה ואחר כך מתה שיחזיר ליורשיה, שהרי משנתגרשה שוב אין לבעלה בהן רשות לא בפירות ולא בירושה, אבל בעבד שנשתחרר יחזור לבעלים שאם נתנו לו במתנה סתם של רבו הן ואם על תנאי עליו הראיה. ויפה כיוון לפי מה שכתבנו.
>
> ובירושלמי בפ' מציאת האשה מצינו גבי מציאת אשה לבעלה ר"י לא אמר כן אלא כדי שלא תהא אשה מברחת זהובים משל בעלה ואומרת מציאה מצאתי הגע עצמך שנתן לה אחר במתנה קול יוצא במתנה ואין קול יוצא למציאה הגע עצמך שמצאת בעדים זו מפני זו (ולפנינו בירו' כתובות פ"ו ה"ג ל ע"א) — י"א]. ושמעינן מינה מדחשו רבנן למציאה שלא תאמר מציאה מצאתי ותקנו חכמים שתהא מציאתה שלו **אלמא דין הוא שתהא נאמנת ויהיו הנכסים שלה** ויש לבעל בהן פירות וירושה, ומיהו במתנה לא חשו לכך שקול יוצא למתנה ואינה מעיזה פניה לומר

35 B.B. 51b.

שלי הם. ובפרק הכותב (ולפנינו ירו' כתובות ט:ד לב ע"א — י"א) כיוצא בה רבי אמי בשם ר' יוחנן בדין היה שאם מכרה ונתנה שיהא מכרה קיים שבסוף זכה בהן. פי' יורש הוא ולא לוקח ראשון, ולמה אמרו בטל שלא תהא אשה מברחת נכסים משל בעלה ואומרת משלי הן. **אלמא נאמנת היא בכך לומר משלי הן** והוא שיאכל הבעל פירות ויהא יורשה ואם אמרה שאין לבעלה רשות בהן בחייה ובמותה לא כל הימנה.

However, the husband is not [considered] trustworthy to say: "She stole this [property] from me," or "It is [her] finding [and thus belongs to me, according to the enactment of the sages]," or "She withheld (lit, "took a handful") [of this property] from her [own] earnings [which belong to me by virtue of an enactment of the sages, since I support her], and [both] the property [itself] and its usufruct (lit., "fruits") are mine." Rather, it is [considered] as *melog* property in every respect, the [property] itself is hers and the fruits are his [as is the usual case]. Therefore, Rabbi Samuel z.l.[=the Rashbam] wrote that if she became divorced and died after [the divorce] that the [property] be returned to her heirs [and not the husband], for once she is divorced, her [former] husband has no rights to it, not the fruits and not the inheritance, but [as regards] a slave who was manumitted [his property] should be returned to the master, for it was given to him as a gift, generally it [belongs] to his master, and if [the property was given to him] on condition [that the master have no rights to it], the proof is on him [that this was indeed so.]
And in the Yerushalmi, in Chapter Metzi'at ha-Ishah [yKet 6:3 (30a)] we find regarding [the matter] of a wife's findings [belonging] to her husband [that] Rav Yose does not say so [=that is, does not agree with Rav Hagai, who suggested that the reason for the enactment was to prevent arguments between the spouses], but rather that [this was enacted] so that a woman should not purloin money from her husband, saying "I have found something." [Now,] consider [a case] in which someone else gave her a gift, [in which case the property would be hers, and so why not in the case of her findings?] [The difference is that in this case] there is a rumor [that is, general public knowledge] [regarding the gift] but there is no rumor regarding the find. [Well, then,] consider [a case] in which she found [something] in front of witnesses, [should the findings not then be hers, since there is no fear of her dissembling or having purloined?] [But, rather,] one [enactment was made] for the sake of the other, [that is, no distinction was made between these cases, and her finding with witnesses was

treated the same as a case in which there were no witnesses]. **Therefore it is logical that she [be considered] trustworthy, and the property [should be] hers, while the husband receives [the property's] income and inheritance, [since in actuality her lack of trustworthiness even when witnesses can corroborate her claim that she found the property is disregarded only so as not to make subtle distinctions between cases].** However, [in the case of] a gift they were not concerned for that [that is, that she would claim that property she had taken from him was actually a gift from someone else, and therefore belonged to her by right, for] she would not be [so] brazen as to say: "It is mine." And in Chapter ha-Kotev [in our editions, in yKet 9:4 (32a)] [there is] a similar [discussion]: Rabbi Ammi in the name of Rav Yohanan: Logically, if she sold [her property] or gave [her property as a gift] her sale should be valid, for in the end he will take possession of them [despite her claims now], [and] even when he yields the usufruct of her property during her lifetime, he will in the end inherit her, but in the meantime she may sell or give the property to someone else]. Explanation: he is [considered as her] heir and the earlier buyer [of her property] is not [her heir, since basically her husband has a lien on it, so to speak], and why [then] did they say [the transaction] is void? In order that a woman should not purloin property from her husband and say: "It is mine" [even though she does indeed have her own property to which the husband is only entitled to the usufruct in her lifetime]. **Therefore, [her testimony] is accepted in that [she may] say: "It is mine," and he [=the husband] will consume the income (lit., "fruit"), and he would inherit her [in regard to this property as well as her other property], and if she said that her husband has no rights to it in her lifetime and after her death, no one will believe her.**

Thus, here Nahmanides accepts the premise that the rabbis had granted a wife's findings to her husband out of a basic mistrust of the wife, that is, the concern that a woman may attempt to deceive her husband and claim property that rightfully belongs to him; his right to her findings was well established in talmudic tradition. But Nahmanides extracts a grain of consolation, for actually, were it not for the concern of purloining (which may not be true), even where there are witnesses to corroborate her claim that she had found the property (and not purloined it), the husband gets the disputed property. Thus, her lack of trustworthiness on this matter is only a legal construct, and not *inherent* in her. *Thus, the husband's claim that the property was actually stolen from him is also not accepted.*

It is interesting that in order to make this point Nahmanides resorted to the Yerushalmi. This would seem to be because the Bavli's treatment of the issue take's Rav Yosi' view (in the Yerushalmi) that the concern that the wife will purloin some of her husband's property is well-founded, and does not provide purchase for Nahmanides' deduction. This suggests in turn that he was searching for a way to mitigate the somewhat misogynist view of the Bavli's sugya on the matter.

Rav Nahman too, Rava's teacher, who also served as a judge in Mahoza, ruled in the husband's favor in other cases. For example, he ruled that the property a woman brought into the marriage whose use she ceded to the husband, but which he had to return to her upon divorce, need not be preserved in any significant way. Return of a chicken's feathers would be sufficient to absolve the husband from responsibility for the chicken, a goat's skin for the goat, and so on (Ket 79a-b). Thus not only Rava, but the Mahozan school consistently ruled in favor of the husband in the matter of a woman's property in marriage.

Why then did Rava and Rav Nahman take the approach to the question of a woman's property in marriage that they did, when Rav Papa did not? It seems to me that we would do well to address the historian's hoary and often embarrassing question: *cui bono*? Who benefits? Why is it that Rava's view always favors the husband's control of his wife's property?

As noted above, I would suggest that one possibility — aside from misogyny that is not particularly evident either in the statements attributed to Rava (though not perhaps to Rav Nahman, see Meg 14b) — is that his approach was rooted in the social situation of his own time and place, a situation however that has, hardly surprisingly, recurred many times in history. Elsewhere, I have described and justified a portrait of the Mahozan Jewish community: it was Persianized, "up-scale," materialistic, and not overly pious — exactly what one would expect of a suburb of the capital of one of the world's great empires. Rava's decisions in regard to the husband's rights over the wife's property were intended to solve a Mahozan crisis of older bachelors who preferred less expensive alternatives to regular matrimony: temporary marriage *à la Perse*,[36] or taking a concubine, where there was no obligation of a *ketubah*-lien on his property, or, again, recourse to the "red-light" district in neighboring Mabrakta,[37] or even intermarriage, which is always a possibility when acculturation has proceeded to a certain point. It had apparently reached that point in Mahoza, where we find explicit concern for it enunciated by scholars with Mahozan connections, Rav Yitzhak Nappaha (who eventually settled in Babylonia, and is associated with Rav Nahman),[38] Rava, and Rav Papa.[39] It should be noted that not only was polygyny practiced among Babylonian Jews, but it also made levirate marriage easier to practice. It was thus hardly surprising that Rava explicitly ruled that levirate marriage had preference over *halitzah*, the ceremony that would release the bereaved widow (Yev 39b). Thus, for Rava at least, this was not a theoretical question, but one with practical consequence.

Later authorities, who served less cosmopolitan (and perhaps less Persianized) communities, or where women's economic position was stronger, as in the Arab world of the High Middle Ages, followed Abaye's view.

That the rabbis were well aware of this problem may be demonstrated by the redactional use of a tannaitic observation, which appears in tKet 12:3, and the gist of which is quoted in redactional contexts in Yev 113a, Ket 87a,and Git 49b.

כתובת אשה בזיבורית דברי ר' ר' יהודה אומ' משם ר' שמעון מפני מה אמרו כתובת אשה בזיבורית **יתר ממה שהאיש רוצה לישא אשה רוצה לינשא** ועוד בושתה של אשה יתר מן האיש אם כן לא תהא לה כתובה אלא שהאשה יוצאה לרצונה ושלא לרצונה והאיש אינו מוציא אלא לרצונו (תוספתא כתובות יב:ג)

A woman's *ketubah* [is collected] from inferior land, the words of Rabbi. Rabbi Yehudah in the name of Rabbi Shimon: Why did they say that a woman's *ketubah* [is collected] from inferior land? [Because] more than a man wants to

36 See my discussion of this option in "Returnable Gifts in Rabbinic and Sasanian Law," *Irano-Judaica* VI, Jerusalem: Makhon Ben Zvi, 2008, pp. 150-195 (in press), and "Marriage and Marital Property in Rabbinic and Sasanian Law," in C. Hezser, ed., *Rabbinic Law in Its Roman and Near Eastern* Context, Tübingen: Mohr-Siebeck, 2003, pp. 227-276.

37 See Rav Nahman's comment and reaction in Ket 10a.

38 See Albeck, *Mavo la-Talmudim*, pp. 252-253.

39 I hope to go into this issue in the near future.

> marry a woman wants to be married. Moreover, a woman's shame [at being single] is greater than a man. If so, let her not have a *ketubah* [at all]? Rather, [the reason is] that a woman leaves [the marriage] both willingly and unwillingly, but a man divorces only willingly.

The same theme is sounded by a saying quoted in the name of the Palestinian Resh Laqish, which, however, surprisingly contains the Persian phrase *tan dō* as an integral part of its structure: "טב למיתב טן דו מליתב ארמלו" : "It is better [for a woman] to sit as two bodies than as a widow" (Yev 118b, Ket 75a, Qid 7a, 41a, B.Q. 111a).

We have seen that Rava's view "purloining" fits well with his policy regarding the husband's rights to his wife's property. Unfortunately, while we have Abaye's demurrals from Rava's views on the second issue, we do not have his views on the first. Was there also a "singles crisis" in Pumbedita, or did the lesser degree of Persianization prevent that from happening? If our conjecture is correct, that Abaye's more egalitarian view revealed a class bias rather than a geographical predisposition, we are still left with the question of the nature of the Pumbeditan marriage market. Alternately, both factors may have been relevant: both cultural and class considerations played a part in Abaye's view, but Abaye did not see these property transactions as being effective in solving the problem.

As noted, however, Rava's view itself has a history not only within the Mahozan school itself, but also goes back to the great authorities of the first generation of Babylonian amoraim. As we know, it is also rooted in the Mishnah itself. The question then arises as to why I posit that Rava was faced with a particularly "Mahozan" problem of a crisis in the marriage market. My reason is that though tannaitic legislation may reflect the usual demographic fact of the existence of an "oversupply" of marriageable women due to their greater resistance to disease and lesser propensity to violence as adolescents, the existence of alternatives to conventional marriage available to bachelors in Mahoza, as noted above: temporary marriage, concubinage, recourse to prostitutes in Mabrakta, and intermarriage — exacerbated the problem there. As noted above, *hatnut* (i.e., intermarriage) does not appear as a concern until the fourth and fifth amoraic generations, particularly in Mahoza (both because of Abaye's demurrals to Rava's policies, and the absence of Pumbeditan concerns for *hatnut*, and the increase of Mahozan concern beginning with Rava in the fourth generation). This indicates that the tannaitic precedents were not necessarily seen as more than theoretical, a means of explaining earlier rulings rather than precedents on which to base contemporary halakhic policy. Rava's decisions were thus not dictated by the past history of rabbinic legislation on this issue. Note also that he himself does not quote these precedents; they are first cited by the redactors, who, however, as I have shown elsewhere, were particularly influenced by Rava and the Mahozan school.[40] His successors or colleagues — Rav Papa particularly, do not seem to have quoted these precedents, either.

The redactional citation of these tannaitic and supposed Palestinian precedents suggests that they too were concerned with this problem. As I mentioned earlier, the Mahozan influence on the redactors was vast, but we cannot be certain whether their socioeconomic and cultural situation mirrored that of Mahoza. As I have pointed out elsewhere, their attitude to the Persian regime was more negative than Rav Nahman's but may still reflect Rava's view. Again, if an increased rate of intermarriage was a result of high acculturation in Mahoza, as suggested above, an acculturation that reached its high point in the middle of the fourth century, there is no reason to expect that such cultural trends would have changed direction by the middle of the fifth, though the anti-Jewish decrees of the late fifth may well have had an effect.[41] And, of course, when we get to the medieval period, the vastly changed circumstances

40 To be published in a volume published by Bar Ilan UP; see also my "Righteousness as Its Own Reward: An Inquiry into the Theologies of the Stam," *Proceedings of the American Academy for Jewish Research* 57 (1991), 35-67.

41 See my "Middle Persian Culture and Babylonian Sages" (n. 2 above), p. 196. I estimate this period of alienation to stem from 468, when the four hundredth anniversary (as they estimated it) of the destruction of the Temple and messianic expectations motivated some Jews to attack a Zoroastrian fire-temple, with predictable results affecting the wider community; for this disaffection see also the opening passage of A.Z., which treats the Persians on a par with the Romans.
After a thoughtful consideration of the issue, Geoffrey Herman, in his recent dissertation, concludes that, while there may have been tensions between Jews and the Sasanian government, there is no evidence of anti-Jewish persecutions; see his "Rashut ha-Golah be-Bavel bi-Tqufat ha-Talmud," Hebrew University, November, 2005, p. 42. Still, toward the end of the Sasanian period, after 468, there were anti-Jewish persecutions; see Josef Wiesehöfer, *Ancient Persia: from 550 BC to 650 AD,* London: I.B. Tauris, 2001, p. 215.

of Jewish exilic life made these issues irrelevant. The problem was resistance to conversion, not intermarriage.

There is another question to consider. Why did it become a perceived problem in only in the fourth generation, when acculturation had presumably begun long before? It may well have been, but in the main we lack Babylonian Jewish sources for the Parthian period, that is, before 224 CE. Still, we may wonder why more concern was not shown, if not by Rav and Samuel, who of course were not in Mahoza, but at least by Rav Nahman. When the origin of the ban on non-Jewish beer is raised (in A.Z. 31b), Rami b. Hamma suggests that it is because of the fear of intermarriage, while Rav Nahman suggests that it was due to fear of the poisonous effects of snake venom introduced into open containers. Since he was a member of the class that would in large measure have been affected by such a problem, I have no solution to offer at this point.

There is another factor to consider: the relation of Rava's policy to that of the Persian ambient culture. In "Marriage and Marital Property" I showed that Sasanian law was much more "liberal" on women's rights to own, inherit, manage and alienate property, and to testify in court than were the rabbis, and suggested that this was a product of a demographic crisis that occurred in the wake of the Black Plague that reached Byzantium in 542, coupled with the losses of upper-class adult males during the course of the wars of the sixth century. Recent work on dating the Sasanian jurisconsults involved in this change bear out this hypothesis.[42] The question before us now is what the situation was in Sasanian law before 542. The fact that a number of these enactments, in particular the question of women's testimony in court, was the subject of dispute, suggests that the situation before the plague was as we may have expected: women did *not* have these rights. The right of women to testify in court, as evidenced by the Sasanian Lawbook (MHD 98:1-5), is attributed to Wahrām, and he almost certainly lived during the reign of Xusro I (539-571).[43] As for other rights, however, especially those over property, I suspect

42 I hope to provide the details of this work elsewhere; in the meantime, the interested reader may consult Alberto Cantera, *Studien zur Pahlavi-Übersetzung des Avesta* (Iranica 7), Wiesbaden: Harrassowitz, 2007, pp. 207-220.

43 See Maria Macuch, *Rechtskasuistik und Gerichtspraxis zu Beginn des siebenten Jahrhunderts im Iran: Die Rechtssammlung des Farrohmard i Wahrāmān,* Wiesbaden: Harrassowitz, 1993 , pp. 582

that Sasanian women could control their own property to a greater extent than Jewish women under Sasanian law, but I cannot yet prove it. Still, the earliest Sasanian jurisconsult mentioned in the Sasanian Law Book that we can date is Sōšāns, who was roughly a contemporary of Ravina and Rav Ashi, that is, somewhere around the end of the fourth or beginning of the fifth century. This then provides us with a period of overlap during which rabbinic and Sasanian jurisconsults whom we know by name were active.

One more factor, which has already been mentioned, but should perhaps be discussed a bit more: socioeconomic status, or class. The society reflected in the Bavli in general, and that of Mahoza in particular, was a highly materialistic one. It is striking that the well-know mishnah in Avot — "Who is wealthy? He who is satisfied with his portion [in life]" is mentioned only once in the entire Bavli (Tam 32a) — all 1.8 million words of it, and then only in a dialogue with Alexander the Great. When Rava wants to motivate his congregants to respect their wives, he suggests that they will become wealthy thereby (B.M. 50a). The Bavli records several cases in which the potential levirs competed so as to gain their deceased brother's property, and had to be fobbed off with a share by the eldest surviving brother (Ket 81b). It is reported that a younger brother, placed in the care of his older brothers, was slaughtered on the eve of Rosh Hashanah (or perhaps, according to some mss, Passover) in order to increase their share in the father's estate (Ket 102b). Here Rava is again encouraging men to marry by offering them financial inducements. Sasanian law, as Roman law, was directed toward the land-owning classes. As I have noted elsewhere, however, some non-Mahozan rabbis were much more "middle class," so to speak than the Mahozans.[44] Rava's legislation regarding marital property fits the Mahozan context very well, and, as far as we can tell, Abaye's disagreements fit that of Pumbedita.

A word should also be said about the social background of Abaye's view. Clearly feminist egalitarianism had no bearing on his interpretation. I have shown elsewhere that Pumbedita's culture, as represented by Abaye, was much more insular than that of Mahoza, as represented by Rava. Pumbedita was located some hundred kilometers from the capital, and there is reason to believe

(text), 587 (translation) and 591-592 (notes).

44 See "Accommodation and Resistance" (see n. 2 above), p. 191.

that friendships between Jews and non-Jews were unthinkable.[45] Its insularity would have protected it against intermarriage and temporary marriage; and the same may perhaps be said of concubinage. As to prostitution, while the sexual urge is universal, it may be significant that it is the Mahozans who seem particularly concerned with fornication.[46] Nonetheless, it is difficult to conceive of any large, cosmopolitan urban area without the availability of prostitution.

Rava and Abaye differ not only in regard to a wife's property; they differ on a number of other issues where they may be expressing class differences. Thus, Rava rules that the "Hebrew slave" of Exod 21:1-7 is owned bodily by his master (*gufo qanuy*) (Qid 16a), while Abaye, at least according to the redactors of B.Q. 113a-b, holds that the six-year period of servitude is considered as a debt that the slave is working off. Rava's master Rav Nahman, perhaps the most Persianized amora in the Bavli, is reported to have remarked that "a slave is not worth the bread in his belly" (B.M. 64b). And here, too, Rava's position runs counter to the general trend of rabbinic legislation, which treats the Hebrew slave more like a worker than it does a "Canaanite slave," who is considered chattel. It is clear, however, from the redactional framework into which Rava's position is placed that the redactors too had problems with Rava's position, the effects of which they attempted to minimize. Nahmanides in his *novellae* on Qid 16a also attempts to reinterpret Rava's view of *gufo qanuy* more along the lines of the general rabbinic view. This may not have been a theoretical issue, though the redactional view is that the institution of the Hebrew slave was in force only when the jubilee was still counted, and so may not have been in force in Rava's time, though this is far from clear (see Arak 29a, Qid 69a). Still, it is possible that Rava refers to a Hebrew slave *owned by a non-Jew*. Rava's may have intended to warn any Babylonian Jew who was tempted to enter debt-slavery that he could not rely on the usual protection that rabbinic law afforded him, though it is unlikely that the rabbis could have acted in such a case against the authority of the Persian courts. I hope to go into this issue in greater detail elsewhere.

45 See "Socioeconomics" (see n. 2 above) esp. pp. 96-98.

46 Aside from Rav Nahman's aforementioned case in Ket 10a, see also his comment in Ket 101b, Rava in Ket 51b, Rav Papa in Ket 36b, and see also that of Rav Nahman's master, Samuel, in Ket 64b.

Again, in Git 37b Abaye seems to favor Rabban Shimon b. Gamaliel's view that it is "just as it is a mitzvah to redeem a free man [from kidnappers] so too is it a mitzvah to redeem slaves [from such captivity]" while Rava is more concerned that a recalcitrant slave might run away to bandit bands and then claim that he was kidnapped, and so there is no mitzvah to redeem him (*q.v.*).

And yet again in regard to another dispute between them, at least as reconstructed by the redactors in B.Q. 113a-b, we find Abaye taking the more "liberal" position, if we may call it that. While both agree that defrauding a non-Jew infringes on the prohibition against acting in such as way as to cause Profanation of the God's Name, they differ on the extent of such actions, with Rava holding — according to the redactors — that withholding a debt payment from a non-Jew does not fall under that rubric, while Abaye does. According to Rava, only outright robbery would be prohibited. This may also conform to Rava's view on one mode of evading Persian taxes in Ned 62b, though there his less than admiring view of the Persian regime — as opposed to the view of Rav Nachman — may have had something to do with it (see Meg 14a).

Thus, an examination of Rava's views on these matters makes it less likely that his views of women's rights to their properties in marriage were specifically tailored to a particular social crisis, but rather of his version of a particular Mahozan upper-class view of life.

When then did Rava "cross the line" that the medieval commentators had set? Based on these cases, it would seem that this occurred only when Mahozan views could no longer be squared with deeply-held rabbinic views that were implanted in the rabbinic system. Violating the rabbinic enactment that obligated the husband, and his heirs, to pay for his wife's burial expenses is one case. Another is when he blurred the distinction between the Hebrew slave and the Canaanite one. In other cases, Rava's authority held. Another guide for this line-setting may have been "a sense of fairness."

In a sense, however, that begs the question. I have shown elsewhere how Rava's cosmopolitanism allowed him to make distinctions that Abaye did not, as in the case of one who worshipped idols out of fear or love (!), where, since the worshipper had not accepted the idol as his god, he was exempt from the death penalty (Sanh 62b). Or his validation of the testimony of a *mumar lehakh'is*, that is, one who consistently violates biblical prohibitions in order to anger God, as opposed to a *mumar le-te'avon*, one who did so in order to satisfy his appetites. Abaye considered both of them as wicked, and therefore would not accept the testimony of either; Rava understood that the latter was a slave to his appetites and thus could be bribed, while the former was "a man of principle," so to speak (Sanh 27a).[47] How does this Rava square with the one we have unveiled? C. E. Hayes' words may be apropos here:

> I am not suggesting that that the rabbis were hermetically sealed off from events around them or that they worked out the halakhah from first principles, like ivory tower philosophers making no reference to anything outside their philosophical system. The very nature of the tradition the rabbis received — a multivoiced tradition with inherent tensions and inconsistencies — would make such a description impossible. I am, however, arguing against a reductive brand of historical analysis which implicitly paints a portrait of tannaitic rulings as a *de novo* creation of the rabbis in response to pressing social, economic, or national crises.[48]

Here we have examined several cases in which Rava not only goes beyond tannaitic rulings, but where Abaye disputes his rulings. This indicates that amoraim in good standing could disagree on such matters even when there was tannaitic precedent. How are we to understand these rulings? In the course of my analysis I have suggested two possibilities: one a response to a social problem, and so Rava can be understood as legislating; the other possibility is that for reasons that are not yet clear, Rava holds a consistent view of women's property rights vis-à-vis their husbands', the nature of Hebrew slavery, and on the issue of *gezel ha-nokhri*, in contrast to his more cosmopolitan views in other areas.

It may be that in the areas of slave law and marital property, Rava merely reflected the attitudes of upper-class Mahozan society into which he rose from his middle class origins,[49] while Abaye's views were shaped either by

47 See my "Hercules Within the Halakhic Tradition," (see n. 7 above, in press).

48 See Christine Elizabeth Hayes, *Between the Babylonian and Palestinian Talmuds: Accounting for Halakhic Differences in Selected Sugyot from Tractate Avodah Zarah*, New York: Oxford UP, 1977, p. 6.

49 Note his prayer for wealth in M.Q. 28a, and see my comments in "Middle Persian Culture" (see n. 2 above), p. 191.

the Pumbeditan "middle class." While Rav Nahman is criticized in Qid 70a-b for allowing his women to mingle with males from outside the family, Rava himself apparently maintained a *bei nashei*, a "women's section" in what seems to have been his own house (Eruv 68a). It may be that only the upper classes could afford to keep their women within the house and away from more economically useful outside activities. If so, Rava's decisions would reflect that lifestyle.[50] In the next generation, Rav Papa, Rava's chief student, introduced the concept of *revah beta'*, the "profit of the house," as a barrier to the husband's presumed right to sell his rights to his wife's income). In other words, according to Rav Papa, and against Yehudah Mar b. Mereimar, the Sages gave the husband the right of usufruct in order that the household economy would profit and the husband, in turn, would be generous with his wife's allowance — but not that the husband was permitted to sell his rights to that usufruct. Even though both Rav Papa and Yehudah Mar b. Mereimar report their positions in the name of Rava, in the light of all that we have discussed it would seem that Rav Papa's view is in a sense a protest against Rava's one-sided approach to the husband's rights to his wife's property, just as his comment in support of Abaye in Yev 39a. And in this case, too, the issue was decided in Rav Papa's favor, presumably because of his greater authority and reputation as Rava's disciple. What is clear, however, is that the question of the husband's rights to his wife's property remained a live issue in the next generation. I hope to return to this question elsewhere.

But, as Hayes has warned, we must beware of a reductionist approach to these matters. My hope is that within the 1.8 million words of the Bavli we will be able to discern not only class and geographical differences, but also individual ones. What is clear, in any case, is that Rava and Abaye held contrasting views on some basic issues, but were consistent within their own approaches, at least within specific areas. Indeed, it may be that Rava's more "liberal" views and his more "conservative" ones may be dated to different stages of his life, though the consistency of his views in specific areas of law would cast doubt on that possibility. In any case, careful study of Rava's views on other matters may yet yield some clues.

---

50 See M.D. Yudelowitz, *Mahoza: Me-Hayyei ha-Yehudim bi-Zman ha-Talmud*, Jerusalem: Mosad Harav Kook, 5707, p. 24.

RABBINIC MINDSETS WITHIN THE UNIVERSAL MYTHIC STRUCTURES OF SACRED HISTORY: A FEW INTERESTING CASES

Herbert Basser, Queens University

The power of the Hebrew Biblical word expresses story lines and laws writ large. But beginning with the Bible itself and forever afterwards sages detected real or imagined passageways to bring the material to life. They injected, deep into the words of Scripture, the familiar ring of mythic tropes. Indeed, even if it be assumed that the Bible attempted to demythologize its narration of Israel's history, rabbis and others found ways to add mythic elements into the biblical narrative for unknown reasons which we might speculate upon. The rabbis of Bamidbar Rabbah 13:12 compared the words of Scripture to a series of huge, slow-moving crests connected together by smaller, rapid currents and very shallow waves that shuttle between them. These minor currents feed the rise of the coming wave by gaining their thrust from the spent wave just passed. I hope herein to illustrate how the rabbis described these undercurrents they read into the texts as in perfect fit with known mythic structures. My examples are for the most part simple and embarrassingly famous. They form merely the tip of the proverbial iceberg. Much more attention needs to be paid to the question if the Rabbis thought mythically as a matter of course. Perhaps they consciously introduced these themes to enable Jews to identify biblical characters according to the well-understood categories expected of significant national history. So, for example, we read in Gen 1 that God created the world and that early on the earth was empty and void, darkness covering tehom — the deep pits — yet God's wind or spirit hovered over the waters enabling creation. We might recognize here the demythologized theme of Marduk's victory over Tiamat or perhaps we might not. Yet Isaiah utilizes the Near Eastern Motif of slaying the Sea Monster to create the world and to part the Red Sea: 51:9-10:

> Awake, awake, put on strength, O arm of the LORD; Awake as in the days of old, the generations of long ago. Was it not You who cut Rahab in pieces, Who pierced the dragon? Was it not You who dried up the sea, The waters of the great deep; Who made the depths of the sea a pathway for the redeemed to cross over?

But there is no mistaking the story of the building of the Temple — The Temple being a microcosm of the created world. Here the myth emerges in all its power — the rebellious deep (Tehom) is conquered so the Temple/world can be established.

> Talmud Bavli Sukka 53a
>
> Rabbi Yochanan said when David dug up the deep channels to construct the Temple, Tehom rose up and sought to inundate the whole world. …he wrote the divine name on a shard and cast it into Tehom and Tehom sank 16000 garmidi.

We consider today the work of several thinkers who help us understand the roots of mythic structures. We might think of Van Gennep[1] who subdivided rites of passage into three stages — *separation, transition,* and *incorporation* (1908/1960, p. 11) and Victor Turner who classified the rites of transition as "one of ambiguity and paradox, a confusion of all the customary categories" (1987, Turner, V. "Betwixt and between: the liminal period in rites of passage." In L. Mahdi, L., S. Foster and M. Little, M. (Eds.), *Betwixt and between: Patterns of masculine and feminine initiation,* LaSalle, IL: Open Court .p. 7) and Joseph Campbell who named the quest adventure *monomyth* (1949, J. Campbell, reprint 1968. *The hero with a thousand faces.* Princeton, NJ: Princeton University Press. p. 30); as Campbell noted, the mythological adventure of the hero is nothing more than Gennep/Turner's description of the rites of passage

1 Van Gennep, Arnold. *The Rites of Passage* (Translated by Monika B. Vizedom and Gabrielle L. Caffee). Chicago, University of Chicago Press, 1960.

of many pre-modern societies. Campbell himself preferred the terms *separation — initiation — return.* (1949/1968, p. 30).

We begin with Genesis 22:14 where Abraham names the mountain upon which he had taken his son Isaac to be sacrificed: "And Abraham named it 'God saw the place'" —the narrator adds: "Someday it will be called 'God is to be seen on the mountain.'" This translation is as good as any since the text defies clear rendition.

But what does it mean? Enter the myth making connectors who adroitly surf the undercurrent joining the past "saw the place" to the future "is to be seen." The rabbis (Tosefta Berakhot 1:15.) relate that the Temple place was separated out as a site fit for sacrifice from the moment God chose that precise place to be the location for Isaac's binding. "Chose," lexically falls within the range of meanings of Hebrew "yireh": "saw." So far we have found Step 1. Separation.

Now the rabbinic passage continues. This place was laid waste to its foundations by Rome. At this point the mountain began a process of shaking up its foundations until, throughout the course of many years of desolation, it continuously reforms itself. Now we have completed Step 2 — the liminal period of exile and trial where the hero struggles against the forces of destruction seeking the forces of reconstruction. Finally the rabbinic passage concludes: In the future, when it will be formed into a perfect mountain, then God's Presence will alight at the site for all time. We have now seen Step 3: the return or incorporation with future boons to the world.

To recap: Abraham's naming the place of Isaac's sacrifice as the special place God has chosen actively separates the site from all others. It is the Temple space where, as Eliade points out, heaven and earth can merge. Still, it is in no way a mountain of perfection yet. The site then moves into a transitional, liminal period where it lies in ruins as its foundations slowly, chosen and watched by God, evolve until they become reconstituted into not just another mountain but the most perfect of mountains where the divine presence stays in end-time forever. Perhaps the early rabbis saw the mountain as the totem of Israel — God's children — singled out by the Covenant of the sacrifice of Isaac to be chosen and watched over by God, deserted to atone through their suffering a long exile away from native soil until reconstituted into a firm height in which God dwells at the end of days.

In the chaos of exile an immature Israel and a shaken mountain quest for God's presence. In the end a mature people and an unmovable mountain of perfection is made for God to dwell on. On this mountain Israel and God see each other. Indeed God has gone upon a quest also — The myth moves from the place where God saw man to the place where now man sees God there as well. God has also been initiated and in the end returns from his transcendent distance to immanent presence in Israelite society. So seems to me the import of the rabbinic tradition just cited and as confirmed by the following account. The desert mentioned in Dt 32:10 evokes the image of Abraham seeking adventures to restore God to his palacious Temple. Anthropologists refer to the desert as the place where initiation is to happen. In the following piece both Abraham and God are initated together in the desert setting. Sifre piska 313 senses the wave present in "He found him in a desert land" (Dt 32:10) — "He" refers to Abraham who acted like the hero in the story of a king — God — whose troops rebelled against him in the wild and uncivilized territory of the desert. After his own guard abandoned him a knight appeared and promised to restore him to his palaces and throne.

Abraham himself was chosen and separated out at the start of Creation. According to Gen. Rabbah 2:3, the rabbis understood that immediately following the destruction of early humankind in the flood God again set in motion a plan that he had built into nature from the beginning of creation. In this text the appearance of Abraham in history is thought to be analogous to that moment when Creation first appeared from Chaos. The wind of God hovered over the dark watery abyss and then light first appeared (Gen. 1:2). This very wind (*ruah*) itself was also thought to be to that wind which calmed the waters at the close of the flood. So the creation process beginning with separation recurs each time the world begins anew. Abraham is a new light, a new creation after the chaos of the flood.

> "And God brought to pass a wind upon the earth… [to assuage the waters of the flood]" (Gen 8:1). God had said how long must the world be mired in darkness (see Gen. 1:2). May light come! For God had said "Let there be light!" (Gen 1:3). Of course this refers to Abraham. (Gen. Rabbah 2:3).

According to the rabbis, Abraham is the primordial light that illumines the darkness, distinguishing good from evil and truth from falsehood. He is the liminal transition figure whose appearance marks a new beginning of Messianic history both in rabbinic traditions such as Pesikta de Rav Kahanna, and in Matthew 1. He represents the initial phase of the Jewish cultural account of the world's saga, a religious pattern already discerned as mono-mythically universal by Van Gennep and Turner. The Talmud gives Abraham this role as well seeing the generations before Abraham as dark chaos. Talmud Bavli Avodah Zara 9a divides a mythical 6000 year Jewish history into three equal periods. The first is one of Chaos. The second is Israel's clinging to Torah which defeats Chaos and finally leads to the possibility of a messianic hereafter of Bliss, Security and Eternal Life. Tripartite mythic divisions of history replicate the tripartite division of human life and vice versa.

The liminal period of Abaraham's adventure is marked by the rabbis as a test (so Gen 22:1 mentions the word outright). The tester is Satan and the place is the barren mountain upon which Abraham has been summoned to offer his son.

> [From Midrash Yelamdenu to Gen 22]: While Abraham and Isaac his son were going to the sacrifice (Isaac not knowing he was to be offered), Satan came and stood to the right of Isaac. He said to him, ill-fated man, son of an ill-fated woman - think of all the fasts your mother endured so you could be born. Now your old man has lost his mind and is going to slaughter you.... Isaac shuddered since he saw no sacrificial ram and intuited what was about to befall him. His father in response told him: God has "chosen" you. Isaac said — since he has "chosen" me, my soul is His. Still, I worry for my mother "and they walked on together" (Gen 22:7) - one to slaughter and the other to be slaughtered. And Isaac was thirty-seven years old at the time.

Concerning the appearance of Satan before Abraham several texts - Gen. 22:2 and 22:4 - from Midrash Aggada, ed. Buber, read as follows:

> Gen. 22:2: While they were walking Satan came to Abraham. He said to him, Have you lost your mind! The son God bestowed upon you at 100 years of age — can you go to slaughter him? It was really me who fooled you and [speaking

> like God] told you, "take your son, your only one ..." (Gen 22:2). I swear it was God who told me. When Satan saw Abraham was disregarding him he immediately approached Isaac...when he saw he had no effect on Isaac he went to Sarah... when she heard she cried out first and wept and her soul left her from so much agony.

> Gen. 22:4: On the third day (Gen 22:4) - why did it take 3 days when the place was so near? But we learn that Satan came and turned himself into a river to block Abraham. Abraham said: I will go into the river to test its depths; and he almost drowned. He prayed that [God] should save him from the water so he would not drown in them. God rebuked Satan (for abusing his power) and Abraham was suddenly once again on solid ground.

In sum, Mishna Avot 5:5 relates that Abraham was tried with 10 trials and passed them all. These episodes again fit into the second part of the triad scheme of classical myth as delineated by Campbell. The added stories, told by midrashim, to the testing of Abraham in Gen 22 are in line with Turner's model concerning the initiation rites of social groups and especially in proving the worth of the hero.

I will now briefly touch on the mythic additions to the Jacob story in which he wrestles a divine figure. Here we need to appeal to the wrestle/dueling episodes that are found in many myths — where either the figures entwine themselves together sparking great conflict or else they melt and twin together.

When Jacob must flee his brother's wrath after he has usurped this latter's first-born privilege he goes into exile to the home of wily Laban. Here, in the fields and wilds of Laban's domain he is tricked and tricked and finally uses his wits to best Laban. The motif is commonly associated with a mythic construct called the trickster figure. At the end of Jacob's exile, as he enters the land promised to him, he wrestles a supernatural being whose identity is ambiguous. Is this being friend or foe, the embodiment of his God or the embodiment of his foe-twin Esau? Is he good or evil? It is all very chaotic — The rabbis suggest this being is both a foe and yet a double of Jacob — reminding us of Gilgamesh's wrestling with Enkidu. In the end Jacob reconciles with Esau only to go again into an exile in Egypt where he dies. What is remarkable is that the rabbis see the figure that Jacob wrestles as Jacob's double — a trickster figure.

Shir hashrim Rabba 3:3 "And a man wrestled with him" Gen 32:25 — "with him" *imo* can also mean "like him" —the rabbis said the angelic man appeared to him in the guise of the boss of sheep rustlers — *archelistes* — so Jacob had sheep and this other had sheep, he had camels and the other had camels — Jacob said to him "inspect my flocks for your stolen sheep and I will inspect your flocks for my stolen sheep." So the angel inspected Jacob's sheep in the blink of an eye — and suddenly the text now switches from Hebrew to Aramaic signaling a popular gloss to the story telling how Jacob's inspection lasted all night and indeed he found his missing sheep. Finally, the text continues and points out that this angel was the guardian angel of Esau.

My point here is to show that the operative elements in myth which at times are absent from the biblical narrative are not infrequently supplied by the rabbis in their stories which both supplement the narratives and interpret them. Early social scientists, such as Otto Rank [*Myth of the Birth of the Hero* (Johns Hopkins, 2004), p. 47.] have detailed the mythic elements in mythic versions of the births of Moses, Buddha, Sargon, Oedipus, Gilgamesh, Cyrus the Great, Romulus and Hercules. The extra-biblical accounts of the births of Abraham and Moses and even Jesus share common motifs with these stories. Inevitably, there is the theme of dreams or prophecies announcing the birth of a child who will challenge a ruler and his culture. The child then must be concealed as the ruler hunts for the child to slaughter him. The child escapes harm and eventually the dream or prophecy comes true.

In conclusion we need to note that the notion of a universal phenomenologically essentialist schema of myth-telling is a modern construct. Myths, except in the myth of the monomyth as given in text-books, are never generic but always contextually and theologically culture specific.

COUNT YOUR BLESSINGS: JEWISH MOURNING RITUALS DURING THE SPRING SEASON

(*Sefirat Haomer*)

Simcha Fishbane, Touro College

INTRODUCTION

Research into the topic of Jewish customs by scholars and rabbis is not a new phenomenon. Their focus has primarily consisted in listing Jewish customs and rituals, tracing their development and offering the traditional rabbinic elucidation as to their rationale. Only a modest amount of research has been involved in the social scientific study of Jewish customs.[1] This essay seeks to employ social scientific theory to understand the significance and evolution of Jewish mourning customs practiced between the Passover (*Pesach*) and the Feast of Weeks (*Shavuot*) holidays. The period when these mourning customs are practiced is known as *sefirat haomer,* "counting of the sheaf," based upon Leviticus (23:15), "And you shall count from the morrow after the Sabbath, from the day you brought the sheaf of the wave offering; seven full weeks shall they be, counting fifty days to the morrow after the seventh Sabbath; then you shall present a cereal offering of new grain to the Lord." These seven full weeks culminate with the Feast of Weeks holiday.

After the destruction of the Second Temple in Jerusalem, the period of *sefirat haomer* took on a new character of semi-mourning, popularly referred to

1 One of the few works on this topic was published by Nissan Rubin: 1995, 1997, 2004.

as "*avelut sefirat haomer*" ("mourning of the *sefirat haomer*"). It is not clear exactly when the observance of mourning customs began, but it is first recorded in the ninth century by Rabbi Natronai Gaon in a responsum[2] in which he confirms the custom of not marrying or working after sunset during this period. The reason for this semi-mourning practice is to commemorate the death of the students of Rabbi Akiva, who allegedly died during this period.

In order to properly understand the implicit message conveyed through these mourning customs, it is necessary to examine in greater detail the story attributed to Rabbi Akiva and his students. In BT Yebamoth 62b it is reported that twenty-four thousand students of Rabbi Akiva died of diphtheria[3] between Passover and the Feast of Weeks. The Talmud attributes their deaths to their failure to show one another due respect. In other early rabbinic sources the versions differ. For example, in *Midrash Koheleth Raba* 11.6, Rabbi Akiva allegedly declared that he lost twelve thousand students. In *Bereshith Raba* 61.5 it is again stated that a total of twelve thousand pupils died, but in contrast to other sources, the time period of their death is not recorded. *Midrash Tanhuma*, (Haye Sara 6), claims that a total of three hundred students died, with no reference to where or when this tragic event occurred.

The later rabbinic sources that apply this attributed historic event as the basis of the mourning customs during the *sefirat haomer* period primarily depend on the Talmudic version as it appears in BT Yebamoth 62b. To understand this version in context, it is necessary to examine the complete discussion presented in the Talmud. While discussing the obligation to have children, the Talmud mentions that this obligation also refers to a man in his elderly years. The editors of the Talmud then interject a statement attributed to Rabbi Akiva that one should also study Torah in old age, thus turning the discussion to the primary agenda of the rabbis, Torah study. The Talmud then cites the story of Rabbi Akiva and his pupils, "It was said that Rabbi Akiva had twelve thousand pairs of disciples from Gabbatha to Antipatris and all of them died at the same time because they did not treat each other with respect… A Tanna taught that all of them died between Passover and the Feast of Weeks. Rabbi

2 *Shaarei Teshuva*, section 278.

3 The word in the Talmud is *ascara;* the standard translation is diphtheria, but David 1997 p. 146 offers additional translations including using the word to mean soldiers.

Hama b. Abba or it might be said Rabbi Hiyya b. Abin said all of them died a cruel death. What was it? Rabbi Nachman replied diphtheria (or croup)."

While this passage is not quoted in most halakhic discussions of *sefirat haomer* mourning customs, the Talmud also informs its readers, "The world remained desolate until Rabbi Akiva came to our Masters in the south and taught the Torah to them. These were Rabbi Meir, Rabbi Judah, Rabbi Jose, Rabbi Simeon and Rabbi Eleazer b. Shammua and it was they who revived the Torah at that time." It is clear from the related Talmudic story that the message being conveyed is the importance of Torah study even in old age. Torah nearly suffered a fatal blow with the death of Rabbi Akiva's students, but Torah is not permitted to pass away and was immediately revived through the teaching of five well known Talmudic personalities.

Most researchers, scholars and rabbis[4] are in agreement that these twenty-four thousand students of Rabbi Akiva were in reality soldiers of Bar Kochva, who participated in the revolt against the Romans; this was a last attempt to restore the Jerusalem Temple society and Jewish sovereignty. HaCohen (1961, p. 30) shows that the word "students" is used by the early rabbis to also mean "soldiers".[5] Furthermore, Rabbi Akiva was known to be a strong supporter of Bar Kochva and even believed him to be the messiah. It is no surprise then, that he would instruct his students to join the forces in the revolt against the Romans. The students' deaths in such a limited period of time as well as in a small geographical area are understandable if we accept the argument that they were also soldiers who died in a lost revolution. The obvious question, then, is why the editors of the Talmud preferred to present the Rabbi Akiva tragedy and ignore the Bar Kochva story? Was there possibly an underlying embarrassment over this political messianism? To reveal the implicit message and agenda of the rabbis, the social scientific theory of collective memory and counter-memory will be discussed.

---

4 See, for example David 1977, Divir 1964 and Hacohen 1961.

5 HaCohen, 1961 p. 30 offers different proof; texts proving the students of Rabbi Akiva were Bar Kochva's soldiers during the revolution.

THE THEORETICAL FRAMEWORK OF COLLECTIVE MEMORY[6]

Collective memory is defined as the redefinition of a historical event that serves the need to define the community. Maurice Halbwachs (1951) in his classic exploration of collective memory concluded that changes in our knowledge of the past correspond to changing organizational needs and to transformations in the structure of society.[7] Zerubavel (1997, p. 8) further develops this point, writing, "The power of collective memory does not lie in its accurate, or systematic, or sophisticated mapping of the past, but in establishing basic images that articulate and reinforce a particular ideology." All social forces are affected by memory, but our interest is religious behavior. How people remember the events of the past will have a profound impact on how they live and act in their present religious lives.

Historians attempt to report the events of the past; they attempt to reconstruct these events from documents or accounts of witnesses. While it is almost impossible for historians to be objective, they attempt to report those facts they choose to record. World-views, political realities and cultural biases influence their thinking, and thus their recording of history. Collective memory, as presented by the religious leaders (in our case, the rabbis) is not concerned with the factual reliability of the historical event. The event is there to serve the religious agenda. Throughout his work *Zakhor*, Y. H. Yerushalmi (1982) emphasizes that history for the rabbis had no meaning or purpose, and *that historical events were there to serve the halakha*, the work of the rabbis (pp.111-113).

Therefore, the way of presenting an event, a war, a discussion, a meeting or the life of an individual depended on the message the rabbis sought to convey or transmit rather than on historical accuracy. As stated by Rubin and Kossman (1997, p.156) "A society that molds its members in accordance with unequivocal memory patterns does not permit them to examine its history in a critical fashion; it constructs for them a collective memory that transmits a

6 For a more extensive discussion of cultural or collective memory see: Halbachs 1952, 1971, 1980; Schwartz 1982; Rodriguez and Fortier 2007, Rubin 1997a.

7 Referred to in Schwartz 1982.

single incontestable message." Rodriguez and Fortier (2007 p. 108) point out that collective memory "is transcendent in that it remains embedded in, yet distinct from everyday experience. Cultural memory[8] is anchored and does not change over time. These authors further point out (p. 23) that "cultural memory continues to exist because it feeds a basic need for identity, salvation, hope and resistance to annihilation." When all is destroyed or seems to be lost in one's social and religious structure, collective memory can empower and renew the life of a people. Lastly, they argue (p.4) that it is through the collective memory of religious experience that a community can ensure its survival.

Rubin and Kosman (p. 158) also differentiate between societies that are aware of history and those that are ahistorical. While both societies are aware of memory, within the group that values history, memory develops "in a progressive causal line from past to future." In a society unaware of or uninterested in its history, "history perceives time as continuously cyclical, expressing the permanent, the stable, the unchanging." In other words, history comes to a standstill. The past and the present then begin to exist on the same plane and the actions and behavior of the heroes of the past resemble the behavior of the present. Collective memory, in the words of Schwartz (1982, p.108), is anchored and does not change over time.[9] Thomas Cottle (1976, pp. 12-13) refers to this as a spatial as opposed to a linear, conception of time.[10] "It is spatial because it suggests that instead of conceiving time as an unbreakable chain of events, we can use our imagination to lift a past instant out of its place on the continuum of time and drop it into another place."

For the ahistorical group, memory is primarily institutionalized and transmitted through ceremony and ritual rather than chronicle.[11] Rodriguez and Fortier (pp.10-14), Rubin and Kosman, and Schwartz (1982) all agree that a society remembers through commemoration, and with symbols or celebration

8 This term is used to emphasize the theme of "memory culture", a system through which a society ensures and preserves its cultural continuity. These scholars identify two distinct characteristics; (p. 1) "(1) the survival of a historically, politically, and socially marginalized group of people, and (2) the role of spirituality as a form of resistance."

9 Schwartz (1982) presents his study of collective memory through the study of icons in a social framework in which history is part of the society.

10 Quoted in Schwartz 1982, p. 395.

11 See also Yerushalmi 1982, p. 15-18.

through ritual. Commemoration, writes Schwartz (1982, p. 377) "is in this sense a register of sacred history." I suggest that collective memory can also be anchored through a reverse procedure. By this I mean that through the prohibition or restriction of specific rituals, symbols or even daily activities, the same social effect can be achieved. I will show this as we discuss the mourning customs of *sefirat haomer*.

THE TALMUD AS HISTORY

History can be defined as the study of the past, focused on human activity and leading up to the present day. It consists primarily of recording the chronicles of past events. The redactors of the Talmud had no interest in history for the sake of history. Jacob Neusner articulated this point in a keynote address at a May 5, 2007 conference at the Talmud Department of Bar Ilan University;[12] "So far as history claims exactly to spell out events that happened at a particular place and time the day before yesterday, the Talmud and the rest of the rabbinic cannon of late antiquity do not serve. They do not supply reliable historical information about once upon a time." Neusner continues to explain that the stories that allegedly took place cannot be validated or verified, or for that matter, falsified or even invalidated.[13]

Classical rabbinic literature was never intended to be considered as historical documentation.[14] For the rabbis there is no real perception of time; there are no such things as earlier and later periods. Time becomes static and a non-developmental phenomenon. Rubin and Kossman (1977 p. 157) quote Levi-Strauss, who refers to this attitude as "a totemic time view."[15] Following Neusner's[16] understanding of the Talmud, Rubin and Kossman continue to explain that such

12 Received by email 11/14/2007 from Jacob Neusner.

13 Following this pattern of thinking Yerushalmi 1982, p. 18 in his discussion of the Talmud era states, "Historical events of the first order are either not recorded at all, or else they are mentioned in so legendary or fragmentary a way as often to preclude even an elementary retrieval of what occurred."

14 Yerushalmi 1982, p. 18 in his footnotes 19 and 20 elaborates the sources for this argument.

15 Levi-Strauss 1966, 223-34.

16 Neusner 1976, p.110.

a perception of static time takes root and develops in a society such as that of the Babylonian world of the Talmud, lacking a territory and an autonomous political framework. For the world of the rabbis, collective memory which combines contemporary time and past time within a simultaneous existence is that process which shapes society as a remembering community. Alleged historical events or statements salvaged by the rabbis were inserted between the folios of the Talmud if they were relevant to the ongoing religious and communal life of the Jews. In other words, communal memory was created to serve the rabbis' agenda and convey an implicit message to the readers.

THE RABBIS OF LATE ANTIQUITY

The rabbis or sages of Mishnaic and Talmudic eras (approximately from 2nd century CE through 6th century CE) did not receive their authority through their family lineage, but rather had to acquire, legitimize and even create it.[17] During the Second Temple period, the leading social groups of Israel were primarily the priests, the monarchy and members of the aristocracy.[18] Ben-Zion (2006 p.130) argues that the rabbis needed to invent a distant past for themselves to legitimize their authority. They applied what we have termed collective memory to achieve this goal. In other words, the sages "symbolically reconstructed a past" irrelevant to historical accuracy. The sages now assumed the role of guardians to carry on the traditions and fill the functions of their predecessors, the prophets and priests. They, the rabbis, had this exclusive right and their authority was attained through their created lineage. Their power was manifested through their knowledge of the oral and written law. Torah was their scepter, their "*urim* and *tumim*." The priestly caste and the Temple society could not be discredited but instead were ignored in favor of the sages.

17 There is no question that the Taanaim in the Mishnaic period had a greater struggle to realize their authority than did the Amoraim during the Talmudic era. By the time of the redaction of the Talmud, approximately in the 6th century, the rabbis were established as the unequivocal Jewish authority. Tensions then existed between the ruling rabbis in Babylonia and Jerusalem, strife that continued into the period of the *Geonim* (approximately 8th to the 11th centuries).

18 Ben-Zion 2006 chapter 3 offers an in-depth presentation of the sages as a group, their relationships with the priests and the formation of their authority. She offers the reader a wide selection of sources on this topic as well as social scientific theory that can be applied to the discussion.

It is interesting to note that in the opening of the tractate Chapters of the Fathers (mAbot), which lists the chronological sequence of the transmission of the Law, the priests are omitted, allowing the sages a direct relationship to Moses and the prophets,[19] the now unequivocal transmitters of the Law.[20] The priestly caste which through the Biblical period served as the guardians of the Law, the teachers of Torah and judges of Israel, were replaced with prophets and sages.[21] This now provided the rabbis the exclusive possession of and a monopoly on the Torah.[22] The written and oral law was now to become the flag of the rabbis. Its knowledge and teaching would form the basis for their authority and the key to entrance and membership in their elite group. They now controlled both the knowledge as well as the Jewish institutions that embodied this wisdom, including the courts and academies.

BT YEBAMOT 62A

Employing the theoretical and methodological suggestions discussed above, we can now understand the Rabbi Akiva story found in BT Yebamot 62a. Bar Kochva represented a yearning and aspiration to return to the Temple world, and therefore to the priestly milieu. Thus to commemorate or underscore the importance of Bar Kochva's revolt was tantamount to negating the goals of the rabbis. They needed to discredit the priestly society and, instead, to perpetuate the law, the basis of their world. It is argued that in the context of collective memory, exalting tragedies is, as a rule, avoided,[23] creating what Zerubavel

19 See Ben-Zion p.132-133, for elaboration on this issue.

20 Although the Bible attributes this role to the priests and not the prophets, the message conveyed by the rabbis is different. See for example Jer. 18, 18; Deut. 17, 19; Ez. 7, 26. On pp. 144 -145 Ben-Zion clarifies her argument and states: the sages "couldn't possibly identify with the priests as their forerunners, since the group the priests represented was the dominant group [with - HF] whom they compete. Thus by eliminating the priests from the list [in Mishnah Tractate Abot] and placing the prophets instead, they could safeguard the group's own distinct identity as guardians-teachers and judges of the law."

21 For a detailed analysis of the organization of the rabbis as an elite group, their relationship and use of the priestly caste to establish their authority, see Ben-Zion 2006, chapter 5.

22 See also Herr 1979 for a discussion of this topic.

23 For a discussion of this topic see Zerubavel, 1995 p. 8.

(1995, p.8) calls "collective amnesia." I suggest that this was not the case with the rabbis. Throughout the Jewish calendar year, catastrophes are commemorated, and they are very much part of the Jewish nation's collective memory.

The rabbis concern, as discussed above, was the Law, its representatives and its representation. Rabbi Akiva and his students represented the Law, and therefore that is the framework in which their misfortune was presented. They, the pupils of Torah study, their deaths and the reason for their deaths, form only the introduction to the message the rabbis desired to convey. It is the second segment of the story, the part that is often ignored, that is the primary theme for the collective memory of a developing rabbinical society. Neither Torah's written nor oral law can be obliterated. Despite its setbacks, it will always have continuation. Rabbi Akiva educates a new cadre of rabbinic scholars to continue the tradition of Torah and, with that, rabbinic hegemony. The rabbis' approach is what Zerubavel (1995, pp. 10-11) refers to as "countermemory," and can be summarized in Zerubavel's theoretical construct. She explains that "commemorative memory represents the political elite's construction of the past, which serves its special interest and promotes its political agenda. Countermemory challenges this hegemony by offering a divergent commemorative narrative representing the views of marginalized individuals or groups within the society. The commemoration of the past can thus become contested territory in which groups engaging in a political conflict promote competing views of the past in order to gain control over the political center or to legitimize a separate orientation."

THE GEONIM

The political concerns of the *geonim* were different from those of their rabbinical predecessors of the Mishnah and Talmud. Tensions with the priests, mentioned above and the establishment of a counter-authoritative rabbinical elite in their place were by now not an issue. While the rabbis of the Talmud were concerned with the redaction of this massive document, the *geonim* (approximately 589 to 1038) were concerned with teaching the law.[24] The *geonim*

24 See Brody, 1998, pp. 13-16.

basically "canonized" the Talmud. These volumes of rabbinic literature and law served as the basis of the *geonim*'s authority. Just as Mishnah was the authoritative "backbone" for *amoraim*,[25] and scripture for the *tanaim*, so did the Talmud serve as a foundation for the power of the *geonim*. The geonim promulgated and taught the Talmud as the ultimate authority in Judaism. Their teachings were in great demand, especially outside of the Jewish communities of Babylonia where Aramaic, the language of the Talmud, was spoken. Thus, the acclaimed historical content of the Talmud was not to be disputed. In other words, the collective memory of specific historical occurrences found in the Talmud, such as the story in Yebamot 62b of Rabbi Akiva and his students, now became institutionalized and were seen as historical fact.

It is in the geonic responsum[26] that we find the first recorded reference to mourning practices during the *sefirat haomer* period. Natronai b. Hilai Gaon (857) of Sura[27] (others argue that this is attributed to Hai Gaon (986-1038), the last of the *geonim*) wrote, "You asked, why do we not betroth and marry between Passover and the Feast of Weeks? Is it because of a prohibition or not? Know, this is not because of a prohibition referred to, but rather as a result of mourning customs. For our rabbis of blessed memory said that Rabbi Akiva had twelve thousand pairs of students and they all died between Passover and the Feast of Weeks since they did not show respect to each other. Furthermore we learned, they all died a strange death from diphtheria. From that time and onwards it was customary for our forefathers not to marry [during this time frame]. Anyone that did marry was not fined, nor punished, nor whipped. If you ask, as a first preference, we rule not to permit marriages. As to betrothal, if someone wants to betroth between Passover and the Feast of Weeks, he is permitted because the real joy is the marriage ceremony under the canopy."

25 Talmudic rabbis, in contrast to the rabbis of the Mishnah known as Tanaim.

26 See Lewin, 1936 pp. 140-141.

27 Most scholars suggest the question and answer attributed to Natronai Gaon belongs to him (Robert Brody, however, in an email correspondence argued that it was written by Hai Gaon.) Lewin (1936 pp. 140-141), offers a response similar to Natronai Gaon's. Also see Brody 1998, pp. 200-201. Furthermore, Rabbi Yerucham in netiv 12, section 2 and netiv 5 section 4 quotes the prohibitions or customs in the name of Hai Gaon. For the purpose of this paper I accept that the prohibitions are geonic, and which of the two *geonim* in question is not relevant to this paper.

An additional responsum attributed to Rav Hai Gaon[28] states: "The custom not to work from sunset to morning is because the students of Rabbi Akiva all died after sunset and were buried after sunset. During this time the nation refrained from working. Furthermore, it states (Leviticus 23:15): 'seven complete weeks (*shabbatot*),' from the language of 'rest and refrain' as it states (Leviticus 25:8), 'seven weeks of years.' Just as in the sabbatical year working the land is prohibited, so during the period of *sefirat haomer* [work is prohibited]. In other words, after sunset one refrains from working." Although an additional reason is offered, mourning for Rabbi Akiva's students is included as one such explanation.

ROMAN AND FOREIGN INFLUENCES

Silberman (1968) in his discussion of the mourning rites during the *sefira* season surveys these rituals, and attributes the reasons behind them to the influences of Roman culture. Since the Gaon ascribes the mourning customs after the death of Rabbi Akiva's students to his forefathers, he places the rituals in the Roman period. For the Romans, May and the first half of June were considered unlucky for marriages.[29] This behavior, it is argued, is connected to the fear of the dead, of ghosts, and of their powers during these weeks. In addition, this time of year brought on anxieties pertaining to the preparations for the harvest and a concomitant fear for the crops, a crucial worry for an agricultural society. The rationale concerning the fear of the dead can also be traced to early rabbinic sources. In mEduyoth 2:10 there is a discussion between Rabbi Akiva and Rabbi Johanan b. Nuri regarding the length of time that the wicked stay in hell. In contrast to Rabbi Akiva who argues the duration is the entire twelve months, Rabbi Johanan claims it is only the time between Passover and the Feast of Weeks. In bSabbath 129b, we also read of the ominous character of this period of time.

To argue that the Natronai Gaon's statement "from that time on" is historically correct, is subject to question. In a period where factual history held little

28 See Lewin, 136, pp. 141.

29 This custom can be traced to earlier pagan beliefs. For the purpose of this essay it is sufficient to relate this to Roman practices.

interest, and no other recorded texts exist as proof of an event recorded seven centuries after it was said to have occurred, there are grounds for challenging its accuracy. The above argument can be considered seriously only if the term forefathers (*rishonim*) actually refers to the rabbis who lived during the Roman period. I suggest that since there is no way to date these statements, the possibility of a later date must be considered. Moreover, since the Talmud does not refer to any mourning rituals connected to the death of Rabbi Akiva's students, this would suggest a later development.

Two questions should then be considered. Why introduce mourning customs, and why so few? There is a longer list of mourning rituals employed in rabbinic literature (as we shall discuss later). The Talmudic rabbis and the early *geonim* were concerned with establishing their authority throughout the Jewish world. Mary Douglas (1978), in her discussion of grid—group, shows that authority is directly related to adherence to law and ritual. Adherence to both strengthens group boundaries and enables a society to survive. What is important for us is to recognize that authority requires the control and introduction of law and ritual as a means of isolating the group. This, on the other hand, strengthens the authority of its leadership. With the acceptance of the Talmud by the Jewish community as an essential work of rabbinic literature, and in so doing institutionalizing its collective memory of historical statements, the establishment of religious rituals would be expected. Furthermore, without ritual the historical event would be lost. Ritual gives memory both life and purpose. For the Jews of the geonic period the death of Rabbi Akiva's students was a historical reality and called for mourning customs to retain its continuity. Public death rituals and memorials, as Douglas (1978, pp. 29 and 32) shows, feed group consciousness and are "ruthlessly exploited for the group purposes." There is much to realize in valuing the memory of renowned dead. Collective memory, as we pointed out earlier, is concerned with the present. The mourning rituals served to maintain society and leadership long after the Roman religious culture flourished. Even though it was important for the rabbis to associate the mourning rites with the Rabbi Akiva story, hundreds of years after the event occurred they realized the weakness and limitation of mourning it, and the *geonim* thus minimized the mourning customs they had introduced.

Although by the geonic times the mourning rituals were attributed to the death of Rabbi Akiva's students, I believe it was implicitly understood by the rabbis that there was a direct relationship here to Bar Kochva's rebellion. As would become clear to later rabbinical authorities, attributing mourning customs to the Rabbi Akiva incident was problematic. During the period of both Natronai Gaon and Hai Gaon, when the responsum concerning Rabbi Akiva's students first appeared, the fear of the Karaite[30] sect hovered over the *geonim*'s heads. The Karaites emphasized the mourning of the Jerusalem Temple. As a symbol of their mourning in the diaspora, they would not eat meat nor listen to music. A Karaite group known as *Avelei Tzion* (Mourners of Zion) was established. To distinguish their practices from the Karaites, the *geonim* listed the minimum number of mourning rituals practiced, and spoke only of not marrying and not working in the evenings during the proscribed period of time.

REFRAINING FROM WORK

The *geonim* tender two mourning rituals during the *sefira* period, not marrying and not working in the evenings. Marriage celebrations were always frowned upon while in mourning or during periods of danger. Marriage represents a new beginning and the opposite of death, and was also an occasion for great joy, inappropriate while mourning.

Our cultural biases do not permit us to recognize the relationship between discontinuing work and mourning. This custom, however, was not strange to the early rabbinic rabbis. Already in the Mishnah (Taanit 1:4-7)[31] the prohibition of work is established as a means of expressing a community's worries or sorrow, as in a time of drought. The time period devoid of work was to be devoted to communal prayer and religious activities. This would have been highly appropriate to an agricultural society such as that in the time of the Mishnah and Talmud, when such behavior was necessary to combat drought; groups would usually need to work together to plant and harvest, and when strength permitted, evenings would be devoted to social interaction. Planting

30 For a discussion of the Karaites see Brody, 1998 pp. 83-99 and Asaf, 1995 pp. 117-1124.

31 See also Tosefta Taanit 1:5-6 , BT. Taanit 12b-14a, PT. Taanit 1:6.

and reaping represent (as in marriage) beginnings and creation in contrast to death and destruction. Even after the Jewish worker left agriculture, the custom of not working after sunset was still retained as a means to signify mourning for the community.[32]

I would like to suggest that the two prohibitions, of no marriage and no work, represent communal mourning[33] in contrast to individual mourning.[34] Other mourning rites such as not cutting hair, abstinence from marital relations and not wearing new clothes can be considered as individual expressions of mourning.[35] To strengthen the collective memory and, therefore, the authority of the Talmud, communal mourning — in contrast to individual mourning — would feed group consciousness and have greater value. As Mary Douglas (1978, p. 32) points out, in a case when the group is weak, death has no social place and is not something to be celebrated publicly. In the case of a strong group structure, funerals are exploited for group purposes. The rabbis' social organization sought to create and maintain a strong group, and thus group mourning rather than individual mourning customs were adopted to commemorate the death of Rabbi Akiva's students.

THE RISHONIM

In the eleventh century, the center of Jewish scholarship shifted from Babylonia to Israel, North Africa and Europe.[36] Great rabbinic authorities appeared in Spain, Italy, Germany and France. Both this period and the rabbis of this time (that followed the *geonim*) were known as the *rishonim* (until approximately the fifteenth century). The Talmud had been "canonized" in the Jewish world, and served as the primary basis of Jewish thought and law. Not all

32 The custom of not working, although codified in the codes of law, was not accepted and practiced. I shall discuss this topic elsewhere.

33 Even though the individual does not work during the seven-day mourning period (*shiva*), the concept and purpose is different. See Rubin 1997, pp. 108-109 and pp. 182-185..

34 Although the refraining from work is instituted as an individual form of mourning, it is also employed as a communal manifestation of tragedy. See Rubin 1997, pp. 182-186.

35 For a socio-anthropological analysis of rabbinic mourning rituals see Rubin 1997.

36 We will focus primarily upon Europe and the Ashkenazic opinions.

the *rishonim* acknowledged mourning customs during *sefirat haomer*. Many of the greatest rabbis, including Rabbi Yitzchak Alfasi (Spain, 1013-1103), Rabbi Yitzchak ben Abba Mari (Provence, 1122-1193) in his halakhic compendium *Ittur*, Maimonides (Rabbi Moses ben Maimon, Spain, 1135-1204) Rabbi Asher ben Yechiel (Germany and Spain, 1250 -1327)[37] do not discuss mourning customs of *sefirat haomer* in either their legal treatises or their Talmudic commentaries. This is natural, since these customs are not mentioned in the Talmud, and these authorities would have had little reason to include a weak and toothless custom in their writings.

In the compendium[38] of Rabbi Yitzchak ibn Ghiyyat (Spain, 1038-1089) we find the first reference to mourning of *sefirat haomer* in the *rishonim*. He mentions the custom of not marrying during this period of mourning for Rabbi Akiva's students, and concludes "and this was the custom of the *geonim*." He also states that not marrying between Passover and the Feast of Weeks is "the custom in all Israel," thus implying that this practice was accepted and observed throughout the Jewish world. Similar declarations were made by other *rishonim* in different geographical locations. The Baal HaTurim (Rabbi Yaakov Ben Asher, Germany and Spain, 1275-1340) who was well versed in both Ashkenazic and Sephardic cultures, also states in his code of law, *Arbaah Turim*, that "it is customary in all locations not to marry between Passover and the Feast of Weeks." Israeli Rabbi Eshtori HaParchi (1280-1345) in his work *Kaftor Va'Ferach*, follows suit and when discussing the mourning customs for the students of Rabbi Akiva states: "In the entire world of Israel they mourn each year ...."

Although not necessarily attributing the mourning rituals to the *geonim*, other *rishonim* include mourning rites in their writings, and view the rituals as an accepted custom. These include Rabbi Avraham Hayarchi (France and Spain, 1155-1215) in his book *HaManhig*,[39] Rabbi Menachem HaMeiri (Provence, 1249-1306) who cites the *geonim* in his commentary on BT Yebam-

37 Oberlander 2005, p. 532 ff. 9 points out that the custom does not appear in any of the writings from Yemen. He attributes this to their dependency on the laws of Maimonides, who did not include these mourning customs in his code.

38 Mea Shearim p. 109.

39 In the laws of engagement and marriage, paragraph 106.

ot 62a, Rabbi Yehoshua ibn Shulv (Spain, c. 1330[40]), Rabbi Aharon HaKohen of Lunel (Provence and Spain, c. 1325) in his compendium of Jewish law *Orchot Chaim*,[41] Rabbi Avraham Klausner (Spain, 14 century) in his *Sefer HaMinhagim*,[42] Rabbi Yaakov Moelin (Germany, 1365-1427) in his *Minhagei Maharil*,[43] and others.[44]

A closer examination of the rabbinic texts of the period reveals that not all *rishonim* were in agreement with the sweeping statements of their contemporaries. Rabbi Tzidkiyah HaRofei (Itally, 1230-1300), Rabbi David Abudraham (Spain, end of the 13th century) in his book the *Sefer Abudraham*, and others as well stated that only a limited number of Jewish communities observed these mourning rituals. Changes in these mourning customs also appeared in the period of the *rishonim*. The time frame for observing the mourning rituals was reduced, supplementary practices were added and new rationalizations were offered.

NEW TIME FRAME

As discussed above, the mourning practices were attributed to the deaths of Rabbi Akiva's students who allegedly died between Passover and the Feast of Weeks. Rabbi Avraham Hayarchi (France and Spain 1155-1215) in his book *HaManhig* is the first to limit the total number of days to mourn. After he states that it is not the custom to marry between Passover and the Feast of Weeks, he adds: "It is the custom in France and Provence to marry from the 32nd [day of the] *omer* and onwards. I heard in the name of Rabbi Zerachyah from Gerona[45] that discovered written in an old book from Spain that they [the students of Rabbi Akiva] died until half [*pros*] of the Feast of Weeks. What is "half [*pros*]?"

40 See his book of sermons, the sermon for the first day of Passover.

41 Laws of Kiddushin, section 21.

42 Laws of Passover, section 129, letter 9.

43 The Laws between Passover and Shavuot letter 3.

44 For additional *rishonim* (and full bibliographic details) who adhere to this view see Sperber 1989 pp.101-117 and Oberlander 2005, pp. 531-532, Nisin 1973, HaCohen 1961.

45 This is R. Zerachyah Halevi, also known as the Baal Hamaor or the Razah (born in Gerona Spain c. 1125 and died in Provence 1186). He was also known for his interest in old books.

We have learned in a Mishnah, one studies the laws of Passover thirty days prior to Passover. Therefore, half of thirty is fifteen days. [Thus fifteen days] prior to the Feast of Weeks is the 33rd day of the *omer*." Even without an explanation of the Rabbi's logic, his conclusion is still clear: mourning rituals are only required for 33 or 34 days instead of 49 days.[46]

This argument and a philosophy of leniency were readily adopted by many of the *rishonim*. Some argued for thirty three days, and others for thirty four, but that is not the topic of our discussion. Examples of these *rishonim* include Rabbi Menachem HaMeiri (Provence, 1249-1306) who states; "We have received from the *geonim*[47] that on the 33rd day of the *omer* the death halted…" Sperber (1989, p. 103) points out that this tradition was accepted, and was transmitted to Rabbi David Abudraham, and then to Rabbi Shimshon ben Tzaddok (Germany c.1285) in his halakhic compilation the *Tashbetz* (part one, section 178).[48] Other rabbis also discuss the change in the number of days, including Rabbi Meir of Rothenburg (Germany, France 1215-1293), who in his work *Minhagei Dbei Maharam MeRothenburg* introduces a new time period that commences with Rosh Chodesh Iyar (15th day of the *omer*) and lasts until the Feast of Weeks. Rabbi Aharon HaKohen of Lunel (Provence and Spain, c. 1325) in his compendium of Jewish law *Orchot Chaim* also joins his colleagues in limiting the days of mourning. They argued as to whether or not the mourning rituals should include the 33rd day to the *omer*. For the purpose of this study it is not the number or the order of the days that were reduced that is of interest, but the significant change in the period of the mourning observances. Finally, the changes were codified in Rabbi Yaacov Baal HaTurim's code of Jewish law *Arbaah Turim, Orakh Chaim* section 493. No matter what time frame was offered, the reason for mourning was attributed by the *rishonim* to collective memory, i.e. the death of Rabbi Akiva's students.

46 For a discussion of how the days of the omer mourning period is calculated, see Sperber 1989 p. 103 ff. 9.

47 There is no proof from any other source that this refers to the earlier discussed *geonim*.

48 See his book of sermons, the sermon for the first day of Passover.

SUPPLEMENTARY PRACTICES

In addition to refraining from marriage and work as discussed above, we find in the writings of the *rishonim*[49] a prohibition again cutting hair, and donning new clothes.[50] The cutting of hair is mentioned in different *rishonim*. Rabbi Yerucham ben Meshulam (France c. 1280, Spain c. 1350),[51] Rabbi Aharon HaKohen of Lunel (Provence and Spain, c. 1325) in his compendium of Jewish law *Orchot Chaim,*[52] and Rabbi Tzidkiyah HaRofei (Italy, 1230-1300) in his halahkic compendium *Shibolei Haleket*[53] and the *Drashot of Rabbi Yehosua Ibn Shulv* (Spain c. 1330);[54] the latter writes: "The custom is to grow a mustache [hair] until *Atzeret* [Shavuot]. It is also prohibited to marry during this time..." This is also dealt with by Rabbi Yosef ben Moshe (Germany c. 1420 — Bavaria c. 1490) in his work *Leket Yosher,*[55] and others. The law is codified in the *Arbaah Turim, Orakh Chaim* section 493 that states; "The custom in certain locales is not to cut the hair. Some cut their hair after the 33rd day of the *omer* for then it is claimed that they [Rabbi Akiva's students] ceased to die."

The prohibition of the wearing of new clothes is also found in some of the *rishonim*. In the book *Minhag Tov,*[56] compiled by an unknown Italian author (c. 1293) it is written "It is a correct custom not to cut one's hair or to don new clothes or anything else new, to have enjoyment in the bath house or to do one's nails from after Passover to the Feast of Weeks". The *Sefer Hatadir* and the *Leket Yosher*[57] follow suit when it comes to acquiring new articles during the mourning period.

---

49 For a comprehensive list of *rishonim* that refer to these prohibitions see Cohen 1985 pp. 218-219 ff. 7.

50 Bloodletting is also mentioned by individual *rishonim* but was not codified.

51 Section Chava, Netiv 28,2.

52 Section 2, p. 62.

53 Section 235.

54 Sermons for the first day of Passover.

55 Page 97.

56 Page 231

57 Page 97. See Oberlander 2005 pp. 536-537 on the *rishonim*.

In his *Responsa Et Decisiones,* Kupfer (1973, p. 114) quotes a responsum in the name of Rav Sherira Gaon in which he presents the same essentials as those of Rav Hai Gaon discussed above, but adds "and not to make new clothes." Kupfer in footnote 3 states that he found no other source for this statement. Rabbinical adjudicators and scholars have not accepted this statement as authentic and have therefore ignored it.[58] The additional prohibitions mentioned by the *Minhag Tov* were not included by other *rishonim*. In fact the *Leket Yosher*[59] explicitly permits the cutting of one's nails during this period.

As was the case regarding changing the time frame, the majority of the *rishonim* tend to attribute the mourning customs to the death of Rabbi Akiva's students.

ADDITIONAL RATIONALIZATIONS

While none of the *rishonim* rejected the successful institutionalization of the collective memory concerning the episode of Rabbi Akiva and his students, at least three additional reasons were presented for observing *avelut sefirat haomer.*[60] First, the *Shibolei Haleket*[61] quotes, citing his brother Rabbi Binyamin, that mourning is related to the period in which the wicked are judged, and that according to the Talmudic Rabbi Yohanan Ben Nuri, the verdict falls between Passover and the Feast of Weeks. Second, between Passover and the Feast of Weeks there is a period of judgment for the success of the crops. In Israel this was the harvest season.[62] This opinion is expressed first in the writings of Rabbi Yerucham ben Meshulam,[63] and was later adapted by other *rishonim* such as the *Drashot of Rabbi Yehosua Ibn Shulv.* David Shmuel (199, p. 153) quotes a rabbinical authority, arguing that the deaths of Rabbi Akiva's students oc-

58 Oberlander 2005 pp. 535-6 accepts the attribution to Rav Sherira and argues that the Sefer Hatadir was influenced by Rav Sherira's statement to prohibit new clothes.

59 Page 97.

60 See HaCohen 1961 p. 28 who lists these new rationalizations.

61 Book two section 235.

62 This rationale is similar to the Roman behavior discussed above.

63 Toldot Adam, Netiv 5, section 4. Oberlander 2005 pp. 533 ff. 22 argues that this statement from Rabbi Yerucham was possibly copied from the Darashot Rabbi Yehosha Ibn Shulv.

curred because these are days of judgment. Third, during the First Crusade in the spring of 1096, Jewish communities were destroyed and thousands of Jews were slaughtered. Many of these massacred Jews were said to have died by martyrdom (*Kiddush Hashem).* The mourning rituals between Passover and the Feast of Weeks would now also include the memory of these martyrs. Death as an act of *Kiddush Hashem* had become the collective memory of the First Crusade. Other historical realities were marginalized or forgotten. This reason — mourning for the martyrs of the Crusades — is found in a number of sources, including *Sefer Minhag Tov, Sefer Haminhagim d'Be Maharam Merothenburg* (Rabbi Meir of Rothenburg, Germany, c. 1215 — France,1293) , *Sefer Haminhagim LeAvraham Klausner* (Rabbi Avraham Klausner, Austria, 14th century), Minhagei Maharil (Rabbi Yaakov Moelin, Germany, 1365-1427) and *Minhage Isaac Tirna* (Rabbi Isaac Tirna, Czechoslovakia, late 14th — early 15th centuries).[64]

DISCUSSION

I have shown in my essay on *kapparot* that when the rabbis were uncomfortable or frustrated (or, in the words of Harry Fox, "embarrassed") with a specific ritual that had become deeply rooted in the Jewish populace, a new rationalization was presented instead of the eradiction of the behavior. In contrast to *kapparot,* where new grounds for the custom were provided, in the case of *avelut sefirat haomer,* new reasons were added to the original ones.

The rabbis did not want to reject the collective memory found in BT Yebamot 62a. They realized that this was part of an accepted and deeply rooted understanding of the mourning customs. Alternatively, they understood the weakness of the collective memory rationale and found it difficult to require specific mourning practices. I find it most unusual that a minor statement based upon an unconvincing source[65] — a statement by Rabbi Avraham Hayarchi (France and Spain, 1155-1215) — would so readily become the basis for mourning accepted by the *rishonim.* Rabbi Avraham Hayarchi's authoritative statement, al-

64 For a more complete list see Cohen 1985, p.221.

65 Even though he quotes an accepted *rishon*, the Raza, it is based upon an unknown source.

though not persuasive, provided the rabbis with an opportunity to reduce the mourning period without endangering the goals of the collective memory.

When a new memory is introduced it can be either a counter-memory or a complementary memory. In the case of a complementary memory, there is an attempt to offer a new meaning and purpose to the original collective memory. Both memories then become relevant for the present needs of the society, while the original collective memory retains its relationship to its past history. When the complementary memory begins to play a role in the collective mind, parts of the original collective memory may be discarded in order to give full credence to the goals of the new memory.

In the case of the plague that struck Rabbi Akiva's students, the reason for their deaths was downplayed in order to emphasize the death of the martyrs of the First Crusade who died honorably by *Kiddush Hashem*. The deaths of Rabbi Akiva's students were not honorable, whereas the deaths of the martyrs of the First Crusade were admirable and praiseworthy, and relevant to the life of contemporary Jewry in the exile. Within the new collective memories, the loss of life contributes to the survival of the collectivity. Patriotic death becomes a form of sacrifice that is rewarded within the larger context of the nation's history. It becomes a source of inspiration to future generations, and therefore generates a sense of continuity.[66] The collective memory of the past, which is required by the time line of the nation and is necessary for its rebirth, is retained and placed in context as a counter-memory, in this case one tailored for incorporation into the life of the Jew in exile — with all its ramifications.

When a collective memory fades, weakens or even requires reshaping, commemorative behavior must be strengthened. The selected memory must be nurtured. Collective memory is substantiated through its different multiple forms of commemoration such as ritual. Rituals are added and the existing ones are reinforced. Zerubavel (1995, p. 95) explains that "through these commemorative rituals, groups create, articulate, and negotiate their shared memories of particular events."

The performance of commemorative rituals allows participants not only to revive and affirm old memories of the past, but also to modify them. Collective

66 Adapted from Zerubavel, 1985, p. 227.

memory contributes to the formation of a specific social structure and highlights the group's distinct identity. In other words, the collective memory is required to speak to the present needs of the society, thereby unifying and consolidating the social order's goals. In addition, the commemorative memories serve the special interests of society's leadership and promote its agenda. This interest can also include the betterment of the people they, the leadership, represent. This new interpretation limiting the time period of mourning was readily accepted by most *rishonim.* The time of mourning was not discarded but rather modified with attempts at offering new rationalizations. Rooted in Jewish culture, the Rabbis could (or would) not eliminate the entire set of mourning customs, but opted to limit the time period, an action acceptable to the society.

The actions of the *rishonim,* in limiting the time period, and institutionalizing the mourning rituals of *sefirat haomer,* involved halakhic challenges and the need for historical justification. It was hard to justify the declaration of a national period of mourning that was based solely upon the account in Yebamot 62a. A possible solution was therefore sought in a dual collective memory, with additional commemorative rituals. The *sefira* period was now identified as a time of mourning, *avelut sefirat haomer,* rather than simply as a mourning custom attached to a specific event. At the same time, the time period was significantly shortened so that it would not be equated with what is considered as the greatest tragedy of Jewish history, the destruction of the Jerusalem Temple.

THE SEPHARDIC COMMUNITY

I have primarily discussed the customs of the Jews in Europe (*Ashkenazim*). Israel and North African Jews (*Sepharadim*) were influenced, in part, by the *Ashkenazic rishonim.* Sperber (1989, chapter 13) devotes an entire chapter to this issue, listing the approaches of the Sephardic rabbis.[67] He emphasizes that the geographical differences between the two communities presented different approaches to the *avelut sefirat haomer.* While in Europe the ritu-

67 See also HaCohen 1961 for a list of Sephardic rabbinical authorities.

als were influenced by the cataclysms of the First Crusade, in North Africa and Israel the observance of mourning rituals remained closer to the geonic approach. In the Sephardic community, which was at a greater distance from Europe, the leniency was greater.

In his discussion of hair cutting during this period, David Abi Zimra (Spain c.1480- Israel 1574)[68] declares that he cuts his hair all of the month of Nisan, and, in different communities, hair is cut every week in honor of the Sabbath. Stronger language is found in the works of Rabbi Shalom ben Yichya Chavshush Hatemani, in his work *Shoshanat HaMelech;*[69] "If they desire to return to their earlier custom to cut their hair [during *sefirat haomer]* they may return. They do not require annulment [of the vow] even though they and their fathers did not [cut their hair] for many years. They did so because they were coerced into such a performance…" Rabbi Joseph David Azulai (Jerusalem, 1724-1807) writes using biting language; "I saw written by the Rav Bareket and the Maharsh Saar Arye in his Chidushav manuscript and our rabbi and teacher Shlomo Lingo that they 'rejected with both hands' the custom not to marry during the *omer*. In accordance with the law and the truthful path there is no place [for these customs].[70] They write it is a new custom and that the rabbis did not sanction it."

In fact, the mourning practices were adopted but without the same emphasis as in Europe. These mourning customs are codified in Rabbi Caro's *Shulkhan Aruch,* and these rulings became decisive for the behavior of the Sephardic Jews. While the Sephardic approach requires further exploration, we will not deal with it in this essay; suffice it to show some of the basic differences between the two communities.

ACHRONIM

The *achronim,* the leading rabbis and adjudicators, followed immediately after the period of the *rishonim*. Among the first of the *achronim* was Rabbi

68 *Hadashot*, part two, section 687.

69 The Laws of *Sefirat Haomer* section 5) quoted in Sperber 1989, p. 116.

70 It is interesting to note that in other writings, Rabbi Azulai accepts the mourning rituals. See Amar 1990, pp. 36-42, HaCohen 1961 p. 26 and Nisin 1973, p.339 .

Joseph Caro (Spain 1488-Israel 1575). His work, the *Shulkhan Aruch,* became the authoritative halakhic code used to this day to explicate all points of Jewish Law. With the added elucidations of the Rema (Rabbi Moses Isserles, Poland, 1529-1572) in his work "HaMapah," which presented the halakhic view of the Ashkenazic communities, the *Shulkhan Aruch* was accepted by all Jewish factions. The *Shulkhan Arukh,* section 493, commences with rephrasing the words of the *Tur*: "It is the practice (*nohagim*[71]) not to marry a woman between Passover and the Feast of Weeks until *Lag Baomer* (the 33rd day of the *sefirat haomer*) [The reason is] because during that time the pupils of Rabbi Akiva died. However to betroth (*lares vlkadesh*) is in order. [In fact] even [as regards] to marriage, if someone went and performed it, he is not punished [for this]."

The Rema appends to this law a discussion of the time frame. The following two paragraphs discuss refraining from hair cutting and the time frame for it. An additional paragraph states, "It is the practice of the women not to do work from Pesach until *Atzeret* from sunset onwards." No mention is found of any of the complementary collective memories or historical events. Even the Talmudic story of Rabbi Akiva is not cited in its entirety, as it was understood that this account would be universally recognized. Only the essence of the original collective memory was in fact codified. The abridged Talmudic statement was sufficient justification for a period of mourning.

As Eliade (1963, p. 51) points out "the vestiges and the ruins of the old cycle must be completely destroyed." Two collective memories cannot successfully function simultaneously. I would also suggest that the collective memories may play a minor role once rituals are codified as halakhah, for once a ritual is codified, the halakhically observant Jew is interested in the nuances of the law rather than its historical force. In the case of *avelut sefirat haomer,* even though Rabbi Caro employs the language "it is the practice [or customary]" this was now law, and the rabbis' discussions were now concerned with the details of performing the mourning rituals. Issues discussed include: May one purchase or move into a new house during this mourning period? Is one permitted to shave before the Sabbath or cut one's nails? To what extent are music and dance prohibited, and is swimming permitted?

---

71 *Nohagim* is also translated customary, but the translator perceived it more as law than custom as in my discussion.

There were a number of unsuccessful attempts to institute the "martyr" rationalization as the basis for the mourning period.[72] An attempt was made to expand the "martyr" rationalization by including commemoration of the massacres that took place during the Cossack insurrection led by Bogadan Chmielnicki in 1648-1649. Most rabbinical authorities generally stated that we mourn because the students of Rabbi Akiva died.

The methodology of Rabbi Israel Hacohen Kagan (Poland, 1838-1933) as shown in his classic commentary on Rabbi Caro's *Shulkhan Aruch,* the Mishnah Berurah,[73] is representative of the halakhic views of the *achronim.* In his discussions of *avelut sefirat haomer* he pays no heed to the collective memory, and focuses primarily on issues concerned with the details of the mourning prohibitions and the time period. This was the approach and view of many of the *achronim.*

In his nine volume halakhic compendium *Arukh Hashulchan,* Rabbi Yechiel Mechel Halevi Epstein (Russia,1829-1907) voices a view expressing the social reality of his time.[74] He was aware both of his own social reality and of the *Wissenschaft des Judentums* and the ideological and political climate of his time. In his discussion of the laws of *avelut sefirat haomer* (Orach Chaim, section 593, paragraph 1-2) he begins with an insightful summary, stating: "The days between Passover and the Feast of Weeks have been declared for hundreds of years by all of Israel to be days of judgment and mourning. As is reported in BT Yebamot 62a, in this brief time period twelve thousand pairs of rabbinical scholars, students of Rabbi Akiva died. They all died from *Ascara.* Furthermore, we have seen that most of the [terrible] decrees that occurred hundreds of years ago in France and Germany occurred during these days. This is clear through the liturgical poetry (*piyutim*) composed by our forefathers for the Sabbath days between Passover and the Feast of Weeks. They are filled with lamentations and expressions of pain and sorrow. There are additional reasons offered for [mourning during] these days that are days of judgment. Therefore, all of Israel has practiced since the time of the *geonim* not to marry..." Rabbi

72 For a list of achronim that discuss these events see Cohen, 1961 and Cohen, 1985, pp. 217-218 and ff. 2-6.

73 See Fishbane 1991 for a discussion of Rabbi Kagan's approach to law.

74 See Fishbane 2008 for a discussion of Rabbi Epstein's halakhic view and methodology.

Epstein has succeeded in summarizing discussions of hundreds of years of Jewish history succinctly and sensitively.[75]

Yerushalmi (1982, pp. 77-103) correctly argues that the Jews did not in fact study the history of their people until the nineteenth century. Rabbi Epstein, I believe, was cognizant of this new wave of scholarship.

Contemporary studies of halakhic Judaism tend towards thematic studies, such as those by Cohen 1985, David 1997, Oberlander 2005, Sperber 1989. History and its place in halakha play a central role in halakhic Judaism's interpretation and analysis. Without deviating from the halakhic norm, customs and laws are placed in both a legal and a historical context. Thus the story of Rabbi Akiva, the revolt of Bar Kochva, the slaughter of the Jews during the First Crusade and other Jewish tragedies receive a new purpose, while collective memories that served the Jewish nation for many centuries are redefined.

CONCLUDING REMARKS

In conclusion, to express in exaggerated form contemporary acceptance (or what Fox calls "embarrassment" and "re-embracement") of the role of the *avelut sefirat haomer* in Jewish culture, I will share an anecdote related to me by Professor Elazar Hurvitz (Yeshiva University, New York). On a Sabbath during the mourning period of the *sefirat haomer*, a Jew returning from his morning prayers witnessed through an open window a fellow Jew shaving — a Biblical prohibition on the Sabbath — with a razor blade, thus violating a second Biblical prohibition. In a loud voice, the passerby exclaimed repeatedly in anger and despair, "*Omer! Omer! Omer!*"

75 Cohen 1985 p. 220 writes that Rabbi Epstein was wrong to state that it was only from the time of the *geonim* that mourning practices were observed. He argues that, based upon the statements of the geonim, mourning rituals for the deaths of Rabbi Akiva's students date back to the period of Rabbi Akiva. I believe that Cohen was not aware of Rabbi Epstein's sensitivity to Jewish history and his ability to analyze texts in this light.

BIBLIOGRAPHY

Amar, Ruven. *Minhagei HaHida* volume 2, Jerusalem, Machon Mishnat Chachamim, 1990. (Hebrew)

Asaf, Simcha. *Tekufat Hageonim V'Sifruta* Mossad Harav Kook. Israel, 1955, (Hebrew)

Ben-Zion, Sigalit. *A Roadmap to the Heavens. An Anthropological Study of Hegemony among Priests, Sages and Layman.* Boston, Academic Studies Press, 2008.

Brody, Robert. *The Geonim of Babylonia and the Shaping of the Medieval Jewish Culture.* Yale University Press, New Haven and London, 1998.

Brody, Robert. *Reading in Geonic Literature.* Israel, Hakibbutz Hameuchad 1998. (Hebrew)

Cohen, Zvi. *Bein Pesach L'Shavuot.* Jerusalem, 1985. (Hebrew)

Cottle, Thomas. *Perceiving Time.* New York, Wiley 1976.

David, Shmuel. *Ner L'Ezrah.* volume 4, Israel, 1997. (Hebrew)

Divir, Yehudah. *Bar Cochvah HaIsh V'Hamashiach* Kiryah Sepher.

Jerusalem, 1964. (Hebrew)

Douglas, Mary.*Cultural Bias* Royal Anthroplogical Institue of Great Britain and Ireland, London, 1978.

Eliade, Mircea.*Myth and Reality* New York, Harper and Row, 1963.

Fishbane, Simcha. *The Method and Meaning of the Mishnah Berurah* Ketav Publishing, Hoboken, N.J., 1991.

Fishbane Simcha "Voodoo or Judaism; The Ritual of Kapparot" *Proceedings of the fourteenth Annual International Interdisciplinary Conference of Jewish Studies* Moscow, 2007.

Fishbane Simcha *The Boldness of an Halakhist* Academic Studies Press, Boston, 2008.

HaCohen Mordechai "Lag BaOmer" in *Machanayim* volume 56, Israel Defense Forces, 1961, p. 20-21. (Hebrew)

Halbwachs Maurice *The Collective Memory* New York Harper and Row, 1980.

Herr M.D. "Continuum of the Chain of Torah Transmission of the Law," in *Zion* 44, pp. 43-56. (Hebrew)

Kupfer Efraim *Responsa Et Decisiones* Sumptibus Societatis Mekize Nirdamin Jerusalem, 1973. (Hebrew)

Lewin B. editor *Ozar ha-Geoinim,* "Masecheth Yebamoth", volume VII. Jerusalem, 1936. (Hebrew)

Levi-Strauss Claude *The Savage Mind,* Chicago, University of Chicago Press,1966.

Neusner Jacob *Between Time and Eternity: The Essentials of Judaism,* Encino, CA, Dickenson, 1976.

Nisin Yitchak "Arichat Nisuim v'Tisporet Byom Haatzmaut" in Nachum Rockever's *Hilchot Yom Haatzmaut vYom Yerushalyim* Misrad Hadatot, Jerusalem, 1973, pp. 334-340. (Hebrew)

Oberlander Gadalia *Minhag Avotenu B'Yadenu* Mercaz Lehalachah, Monsey New York, 2005. Hebrew)

Ricoeur Paul *Memory, History, Forgetting* The University of Chicago Press, Chicago and London, 2004.

Rodriguez Jeanette and Ted Fortier *Cultural Memory*, Austin, University of Texas Press 2007.

Rubin Nissan *The Beginning of Life; Rites of Birth, Circumcision and Redemption of the First Born in the Talmud and Midrash,* Hakkibutz Hameuchad, Israel, 1975. (Hebrew)

Rubin Nissan *The End of Life; Rites of Burial and Mourning in the Talmud and Midrash* Hakkibutz Hameuchad, Israel, 1977 (Hebrew)

Rubin Nissan and Kosman Admiel "The Clothing of Primordial Adam as a Symbol of Apocalyptic Time in the Midrashic Sources" in *The Harvard Theological Review*, Volume 90, No. 2 April, 1997a, pp.155-174.

Rubin Nissan *The Joy of Life; Rites of Betrothal and Marriage in the Talmud and Midrash* Hakkibutz Hameuchad, Israel, 2004. (Hebrew)

Schwartz Barry "The Social Context of Commemoration: A Study in Collective Memory". *Social Forces* Volume 61:2, December 1982.

Sperber Daniel *Minhagei Yisroel*, volume 1, Mossad Harav Kook, Jerusalem 1989. (Hebrew)

Asilberman Lou H. "The Sefirah Season" in *Hebrew Union College Annual* volume XXII, 1949, Ktav Publishing House, Inc. New York, 1968.

Yerushalmi Yosef Haim *Zakhor* Seattle and London, University of Washington Press, 1982.

Zerubavel Yael *Recovered Roots* Chicago and London, the University of Chicago Press, 1995.

Zuker Moshe "Tiguvat Ltnuat Avlei TZion HaKaraim B'Safrut Harabanit" in *Sefer Hayovel L'Rebbi Chanoch Albeck* Mossad Harav Kook, Jerusalem, 1963, pp. 378-401. (Hebrew)

COMIC INTERLUDE

MAKING FISH FOR SHABBAT (YOMA 75A)

Ilana Kurshan

Friday afternoon, two hours before Shabbat. I am preparing salmon in my little Jerusalem studio, listening to a Daf Yomi shiur on my computer.

I am now in the home stretch of Yoma, the only chapter that has anything to do with Yom Kippur as we observe it today. (The first seven chapters are about the Avodah service in the Temple — the slaughtering of goats, the sprinkling of blood, the donning of gold and white vestments with breastplate and tinkling bells.)

The fish is frozen — I still can't bring myself to buy the scaly slimy creatures that flap around in the big wooden buckets, happily oblivious to their dead relatives hanging to dry just meters above.

I unwrap the fish and run out the door to throw the packaging in the green garbage bin outside the apartment — no fishy smells in my home, thank you very much!

I rinse the soft pink flesh under the tap, but the running water makes it hard to hear the voice coming from the computer, which seems, suddenly, to be talking about fish:

"We remember the fish that we ate in Egypt for free." (Numbers 11:5)

How did we get from the self-denial of Yom Kippur to the subject of fish? On Yom Kippur we are commanded to engage in self-affliction (*t'anu et nafshoeteichem*). The manna we ate in the desert was a form of self-affliction as well (*l'maan anotcha*), since the children of Israel had to have faith in God that new manna would fall every day. Instead of the manna, the Israelites really wanted fish, which is the reason that they complained to Moses about the fish they remembered from Egypt.

But did they really get free fish in Egypt? Weren't they slaves? Rav and Shmuel try to make heads and tails of the verse. While listening to their *machloket*, I slice the salmon fillet in two halves. I sprinkle some oregano and lemon juice on Rav and put him in my tiny little toaster; Shmuel will have to wait on the counter for a while.

Rav says, "Fish means fish." Shmuel says, "Fish means illicit sexual relations." I close the toaster door, but they keep at it.

Rav says, "It says 'the fish that we ate'" — this must be a literal reference to food." Shmuel says, "It says 'for free' — did we really get free food? It must mean the illicit sexual relations that the Israelites were free to engage in before they received the Torah."

Rav defends himself, flapping his half-tail vigorously: "When the Israelites were in Egypt, they used to dip their jugs into the Nile. God would cause a miracle to happen: fish would get swept into the jugs as well, and they would have food to eat."

Shmuel insists that eating is a euphemism for something else. He quotes a verse from Proverbs: "Such is the way of the adulteress. She eats, wipes her mouth, and says, 'I have done no wrong'" (30:20).

Shmuel, what a dirty mind you have, I scold the piece of fish lying limply on the counter. I cover him up with a piece of foil and hope that my neighbors cannot hear.

Rav, modestly browning in the oven, has his come-back prepared. "The daughters of Israel were not adulteresses! They were not loose women! After all, as it says in the Song of Songs: 'A locked garden is my beloved bride'" (4:12).

Shmuel is not so sure. "But it says that when the Israelites were in the desert, they were crying for their families! What do you think that means, 'for their families' (Numbers 11:6)? They were bemoaning the fact that now that they had the Torah, they could not just sleep around with any woman they wanted."

"Bing!" The toaster tells me that Rav is ready to come out. I unwrap Shmuel and rest him gently on the oven tray.

"Ha v'ha havay," says the voice on my computer, making peace between the pieces. The Israelites were crying both because they missed the fish, and because they missed the illicit sexual relations they enjoyed in Egypt.

"Ha v'ha havay," I sigh placatingly, placing the two pieces of fish side-by-side in a pyrex dish. I pick up the phone to call a friend. "Do you want to come over for dinner tonight? I just made fish."

MEDIEVAL INTERPRETATION

EMBARRASSMENT AS A MEANS OF EMBRACING AUTHORIAL INTENT

Elisha S. Ancselovits

In the past, intellectual historical and textual critical Judaic scholarship focused on interpretive creativity as a consequence of new social needs, or more precisely — goals. Harry Fox has added a new explanation for creative interpretations, embarrassment: Sometimes we reinterpret texts not merely because they are authoritative and yet must validate the currently appropriate pedagogic or legal message, but rather because they are our cultural texts and thus psychologically "cannot" mean what they seem to say. This is an important contribution since it allows us to speak more clearly of naive yet sophisticated re-readings instead of attributing misreads to either self-conscious reinterpretation[1] or to a simplistic postmodern claim that every text carries meaning only through the reader's immediate personal projection. According to Professor Fox, the pious sage does read the original text clearly but then via embarrassment comes to discern a new interpretation of what it must mean. We now have a clearer way of understanding misreads prompted by piety without attributing to such interpretation a contemporary suspicion of contempt for facts and texts. Although this contribution is to be warmly welcomed, I will argue in this article that embarrassment is actually the necessary key to recovering original intent in a text, intent which is lost when later generations or different contemporary subcultures limit themselves to reading the words of a given text.[2]

1 See, for example, Menachem Fisch, "Canon, controverse et reforme; une reflexion sur l'autre voix du judaisme talmudique", *Les Cahiers du Judaisme*, 18 (2005): 61-75.

2 I am not denying the poststructuralist and even postmodern insights that we can never completely understand the full valence of another's intent, but I am going to illustrate that we can

I will begin by restating Fox's (and Bloom's) position in the similar words of Susan Sontag (from a different context):

> Interpretation first appears in the culture of late classical antiquity, when the power and credibility of myth had been broken by the "realistic" view of the world introduced by scientific enlightenment. Once the question that haunts post-mythic consciousness — that of the *seemliness* of religious symbols — had been asked, the ancient texts were, in their pristine form, no longer acceptable. Then interpretation was summoned, to reconcile the ancient texts to "modern" demands. Thus, the Stoics, to accord with their view that the gods had to be moral, allegorized away the rude features of Zeus and his boisterous clan in Homer's epics.[3]

Fox's and Sontag's observation accurately describes those cases where the reader finds a gap between the respected text and his or her own (sub)culture's norms. In such cases, the reader misreads the "progressive" view into the older text. There is, however, a more common cause for a gap between the reader and the respected text — that the reader treats the text in too sacred a fashion. The reader forgets that these texts are creative and that...

> There is an essential incongruity of creative and critical thinking, of the effort to hold up insights against words and the effort to hold up words against conceptions. Creative minds are more anxious to save what they sense than to refine... what they say.[4]

The pious reader may thus be erroneously embarrassed by what the text appears to mean when read too literally. (The academic reader may, in fact, relish reading the text too literally in order to achieve relative ease of domina-

move beyond the simplistic claim that inasmuch as each person is not understood, we live in a world of Babel. We actually live in a world in which empathetic interpretation allows us to understand the thrust of each person's communicative action in spite of the fact that we cannot reach the depths of the other's experience.

3 Susan Sontag, "Against Interpretation" (1964).

4 Abraham Joshua Heschel, "Anthropopathy", *The Prophets* (New York: Harper & Row, 1962),53-54.

tion.[5]) In this article I will discuss three types of embarrassment that have led me to interpret authorial intent more accurately than simplistic literal reads. In fact, resolving these embarrassments has led me to the method of utilizing embarrassment to more accurately translate cross-culturally with an awareness that all particular human needs are acknowledged and expressed generically *to some degree* in all cultures.

I will now illustrate how each of these three embarrassments has led me to read a given source more accurately. I will then close with a methodological justification of these conclusions:

1. EMBARRASSMENT OVER AN AUTHORITATIVE SOURCE'S SIMPLISTIC CONCLUSION

The following example is one of embarrassment over the apparently super-rationalist ruling of R. Asher b. Yechiel (*Rosh,* 1250-1327) regarding the *mitzvah* to write or buy a Torah scroll.

The background to this ruling is the position of the first generation Babylonian Amora, Rav, who is reported to have validated but criticized the minimalist practice of those who bought a Torah scroll instead of writing one. He considers one who writes a Torah scroll to be equivalent to one who received the Torah at Sinai; the element of personal involvement in copying a scroll is a religious experience that is lacking in buying a Torah scroll which only provides the buyer with the experience of having bought a personal copy of the book of study. Rav's demanding position is "mainstreamed" a generation later by R. Sheshet who argues that if one corrected even one letter in one's scroll, one has connected religiously with Sinai. In other words, everyone should at least buy a Torah scroll while one should ideally write it or at least be actively (or caringly) involved in correcting it.

5 Cf. Renato Rosaldo, "After Objectivism," in Simon During, ed., *The Cultural Studies Reader*(London and New York: Routledge, 1993), 104-117, and Edward Said, *Orientalism* (Harmondsworth: Penguin, 1985), 3.

מנחות דף ל עמוד א (ועוד השווה\י סנהדרין דף כא עמוד ב):

R. Yeshoshua b. Abba in the name of Rav Gidel in the name of Rav: One who buys a Torah scroll from the market is as one who grabbed a mitzvah from the market; if he himself wrote it , Scripture credits him as if he received [the scroll] at Mount Sinai.	ואמר רב יהושע בר אבא אמר רב גידל אמר רב: הלוקח ספר תורה מן השוק — כחוטף מצוה מן השוק, כתבו — מעלה עליו הכתוב כאילו קיבלו מהר סיני.
Rav Sheshet said: If he corrected even one letter, Scripture credits him for writing [the scroll].	אמר רב ששת: אם הגיה אפילו אות אחת, מעלה עליו כאילו כתבו.

Generations later, with the expansion of the written Torah canon to include rabbinic literature, the acquisition of a (relatively expensive) Torah scroll came at the expense of owning books through which to study all of Torah. The Rosh argued that since the point of acquiring a Torah scroll was to insure that people own a personal copy in order to learn Torah readily, one should better spend one's money on buying cheaper versions of the Torah (*chumashim*), in order to be able to afford to buy the Mishnah, the Gemara, and the (Tosafist) commentaries, too. Torah scrolls could be left to the domain of the synagogue.

הלכות ספר תורה לרא"ש סימן א

And I say that it is definitely a great *mitzvah* to write a Torah scroll… but that was [the case] in the earlier generations when they would write a Torah scroll and learn therein.	ואומר אני דודאי מצוה גדולה היא לכתוב ספר תורה... וזהו בדורות הראשונים שהיו כותבים ספר תורה ולומדים בו.

However, today when we write a Torah scroll and place it in the ark in synagogue in order to read publicly, each Israelite man who can afford to do so is obligated to write the Pentateuch, Mishnah, Gemara, and their commentaries in order that he and his sons may study from them since the mitzvah of writing the Torah is in order to learn therein, as it is written "teach it to the Children of Israel to place it in their mouths" (Deuteronomy 31:19)	אבל האידנא שכותבין ספר תורה ומניחין אותו בבתי כנסיות לקרות בו ברבים מצות עשה היא על כל איש מישראל אשר ידו משגת לכתוב חומשי התורה ומשנה וגמרא ופירושיהם להגות בהן הוא ובניו, כי מצות כתיבת התורה היא ללמוד בה כדכתיב ולמדה את בני ישראל שימה בפיהם.
And via the Gemara and the commentaries, he will understand the *mitzvoth* and laws correctly. Therefore, these are the actual books that one is commanded to write and not sell....	ועל ידי הגמרא והפירושים ידע פירוש המצות והדינים על בוריים לכן הם הם הספרים שאדם מצווה לכתבם וגם לא למכרם...

In other words, the Rosh gave greater weight to each individual learning all of Torah — Written and Oral — than to each individual's religious experience of learning from an actual Torah scroll. Thus, if one interprets the Rosh literally, the Rosh is a simplistic super-rationalist who completely missed the import of Rav's and even Rav Sheshet's positions in having people connect experientially via the scroll itself and not merely via the Torah's content. At this point, one can become embarrassed.

If one who is embarrassed then checks the background practices in the Rosh's community, s/he discovers that the Rosh did not ignore the religious experience of personal connection to an authentic Torah scroll. In the Rosh's reality, each man also regularly points at the open communally acquired Torah scroll during communal readings[6], and every man reads from it least once per year — on the holiday of Simhat Torah[7]. In other words, the Rosh maintains the individual's connection with the holy scroll but prioritizes individual expenditure on maximum Torah content.

6 See the Ashkenazic tradition cited in Bet Yosef OH 143:3.

7 The custom of having every man receive an aliyah to the Torah on the holiday of Simhat Torah is already recorded by Rashi's school and was recorded by the Rosh's teacher in Germany, too. See sources in אברהם יערי, תולדות חג שמחת-תורה, מוסד הרב קוק, תשכ"ד, עמ' 92.

To summarize, we have seen that embarrassment can lead one to read the contextual authorial meaning of an authority's ruling instead of mistakenly focusing on a given ruling.

2. EMBARRASSMENT OVER AN AUTHORITATIVE SOURCE MISREADING ITS OWN PRECEDENT SOURCE(S)

In the previous example I discussed an apparently simplistic ruling — which should have been more inclusive of competing human needs, especially in light of informative precedents — that actually turns out to be inclusive of competing needs. In this example, I turn to halakhic arbiters who explicitly validated their positions by reference to specific precedents and yet appear to have completely distorted the positions of those precedents when evaluated on the basis of grammar and any possible holistic read. I am not referring to a mere interpretive gap between the authorial use of language and the interpreter's new understanding of how the author used language (such as we allegedly find in midrash Halakhah[8]). I am referring to interpretations that do not make sense even by the interpreter's own standards of language use.

The first example revolves around the Tannaitic rule that witnesses' testimony must be oral, i.e. that courts are forbidden to accept written testimony. Witnesses and judges must communicate directly — presumably for reasons such as ascertaining that witnesses are testifying truthfully:

ספרי דברים, פסקא קפה

From their "mouths" and not in writing or via a translator	מפיהם — ולא מפי כתבם... ולא מפי מתורגמן

8 As pointed out by both Saul Lieberman and David Daube who noticed that the Tannaim shared a Roman-Greco understanding of how a text is meant to be read. Their position has been summarized (and unconvincingly dismissed) in Louis H. Feldman, *Jew and Gentile in the Ancient World. Attitudes and Interactions from Alexander to Justinian* (Princeton: Princeton University Press, 1993),31. I will offer a different critique of Lieberman and Daube in the future.

As the Amora Abbaye realized, this general concern for truthful testimony is the basis of the specific Tannaitic rule that a mute individual is invalid as a witness:

תלמוד בבלי מסכת גיטין דף עא ע"א

It is taught: [The Biblical injunction against] "One who did not relate [his testimony]", excludes a mute who cannot speak.	תניא: "אם לא יגיד" (ויקרא פרק ה') — פרט לאלם שאינו יכול להגיד;
Why? Let him relate in writing. …	אמאי? הא יכול להגיד מתוך הכתב!
Abbaye said: …for the Merciful One stated: "From their mouths and not in writing [or via a translator]" [Sifrei Devarim, 188].	אמר... אביי: ...דרחמנא אמר: "מפיהם — ולא מפי כתבם [...ולא מפי מתורגמן]" [ספרי דברים, פסקא קפח].

Embarrassingly, when we turn to mercantile Northern European Jews at the end of the early middle ages, we find the following apparently radical misread by Rabbi Yaakov b. Meir (Rabbeinu Tam). He argued that only a mute person cannot testify in writing but speakers may testify in writing — although as we saw, the reason the Talmudic sages exempted and excluded the mute person from testimony is because testimony must be oral:

תוספות מסכת יבמות דף לא עמוד ב[9]

R"I related that R"T validated the present practice of accepting written testimony…	ואמר ר"י דשמע מר"ת שנוהגין עכשיו ששולחין העדים עדותן בכתב ידם לב"ד...
And regarding the teaching that the Merciful required oral and not written testimony	והא דתניא במי שאחזו (גיטין דף עא)... דרחמנא אמר מפיהם ולא מפי כתבם

9 There is no substantive difference between this version and the parallel version found in three other sources: the end of the first Tosafot on Baba Batra 40a, Rosh and Mordechai on Yebamot 31b.

a mute is unique since he cannot speak... but another may testify in writing...	שאני אלם שאין ראוי להגיד... אבל אחר מועיל כתב ידו כשזוכר העדות

This misread could simply be labeled an example of creatively "nullifying" earlier authoritative legal precedent.[10] However, that labeling does no more than either provide the embarrassment with a new name or project a modernist hubristic assumption of the irrelevance of precedent. A closer, embarrassed, examination, on the other hand, reveals that Rabbeinu Tam's read is a reapplication of the underlying Talmudic concern(s) under changed conditions. At this point, the educated reader might think that I have in mind the fact that economic considerations were already incorporated into those Talmudic laws that do not require judges to ascertain as well as possible that the witnesses are testifying truthfully. As regards Talmudic law, we find that the Tannaim put aside the demand for oral testimony and accepted the evidence of notarized contracts (משנה בבא בתרא פרק י, ספרי במדבר פיסקא קטו) and that the high standards of witness interrogation (משנה סנהדרין ה, א-ב) which should theoretically apply to contract disputes (משנה סנהדרין ד: א) were in fact relaxed in favor of a greater supply of credit (רבי חנינא בסנהדרין לב ע"א). Unfortunately, this awareness of the interplay between economic considerations and the rules of testimony might explain Rabbeinu Tam's general acceptance of written testimony but it does not suffice to explain his embarrassing misread of a Talmudic passage.

Let us turn, instead, to consider three other positions of Rabbeinu Tam in regard to testimony and trials. First, Rabbeinu Tam does not forego the requirement that the judges understand the witnesses' language directly.[11] Second, he allows judges to investigate suspicious testimony.[12] Third, Rabbeinu

10 Some intellectual historians would argue that Rabbeinu Tam simply adjusted the halakhah to contemporary needs, while others would argue that he struggled to find the position in the text through an intentional misread. For a summary of the different historical approaches of Urbach, Katz, and Ta-Shma, see יעקב כ"ץ, "עוד על 'סובלנותו של ר' מנחם מאיר המאירי'," ב- הלכה וקבלה. הוצאת מאגנס, עמ' 308-307 and 186-187 ,150 ,23-28 'ישראל מ' תא-שמע, הלכה, מנהג, ומציאות באשכנז *1100-1350*, עמ .

11 Mishnah Makkot 1:9. Rabbeinu Tam presumably follows all other rishonim in allowing judges to question the witnesses through a more fluent translator (following Rava's practice, cited in Makkot 6b); I have not found any rishon who forbids this.

12 In addition to the evidence that Rabbeinu Tam allowed judges to accept convincing invalid testimony and reject unconvincing valid testimony, both his grandfather (Rashi) and his student-

Tam also requires that the judges publish the basis for their verdict if the defendant did not consent to be judged[13] on the basis of written testimony that he decried as false.

If we look at these three points in combination, we see that Rabbeinu Tam did not simply conclude that a society of traveling merchants must accept written testimony in order to not impede intra-Jewish trade and to not limit economic opportunities. Rather, in addition to addressing the need for written testimony, Rabbeinu Tam also addressed the following two concerns that underlie any society's requirement of oral testimony:

1. Witnesses can lie more easily through written testimony; there are no bodily and vocal cues to indicate that a witness is lying.

2. If written testimony were permitted, the audience would not hear the basis of the judges' decisions and there would be less communal oversight (a concern expressed in the procedural rule that courts do not begin judging monetary cases at night, and do not even continue judging capital cases at night [Mishnah Sanhedrin 4:1]).

Rabbeinu Tam addressed these concerns by stipulating two conditions:

1. Written testimony can be accepted *on the condition that it can be investigated orally, later, if the judges so decide.* This redefinition accepts that judges must have the option of demanding oral testimony if they are not satisfied with the written affidavit, and that witnesses can be trusted only if they know that they might be summoned to back up their testimony under direct interrogation by the judges.

---

nephew (R"I) held that any signed document that had been challenged openly as a forgery must be validated — Tosafot Ketubot 19a sv *modeh and* Tosafot Bava Batra 128b sv *nishba.*

For a claim that the Tosaphists required such investigation of suspicious documents *mi-de'orraita* see תשובות חכמי פרובינציה סימן י. I, however, have been unable to find a primary French or Ashkenazic argument of this position before the responsum of the German sage, R. Avigdor HaKohen — cited in הגהות מרדכי על קדושין, סי' תקס"ט.

13 Rabbeinu Tam's position is cited in Tosafot Bava Metzia 69b sv "ki" and in Rosh Bava Metzia 5:45. Same position in Ashkenaz is attributed to R. Yoel HaLevi (12th century), cited in ראבי"ה תשובות וביאורי סוגיות סימן אלף כ.

2. Written testimony can be accepted *on the condition that the judges' ruling will be defended in writing.* This condition provides the plaintiff with a means to oversee the judges.

In other words, Rabbeinu Tam did not simply conclude that in a society of traveling merchants, non-acceptance of written testimony would block all intra-Jewish trade and thus limit economic opportunities. Instead, Rabbeinu Tam incorporated and rebalanced two Talmudic concerns in tension: the concern to limit false testimony via orality and the concern to have market-efficient testimony in order that people may earn money. He exemplified the approach that changes the form of the law in order to best apply all the original concerns under the changed circumstances.

In the light of my interpretation, we now see how Rabbeinu Tam could have actually read the passage from Gittin 71a carefully. Rabbeinu Tam first limited the requirement for "oral testimony" to "testimony [***that can become***] oral" — i.e. written testimony that retains elements of oral testimony. After he re-contextualized that oral testimony need not be oral in actuality just in potentiality, he then actually read the passage *smoothly* as forbidding any written testimony that does not include that potentiality (i.e. the written testimony of a mute).[14] Here is the new yet smooth read:

<u>תלמוד בבלי מסכת גיטין דף עא ע"א {עם הוספות לאור שיטת ר"ת}</u>

תניא: +ויקרא ה'+ אם לא יגיד — פרט לאלם שאינו יכול להגיד {בפני בית דין אם ידרשו לחקור אותו};

אמאי? הא יכול להגיד מתוך הכתב!

אמר.. אביי: ..שאני עדות, דרחמנא אמר: "מפיהם — ולא מפי כתבם {ולכן עדות כשרה חייבת להיות עדות שאותה ניתן בעתיד לחקור בפה בפני בית דין}

Now we see that Rabbeinu Tam apparently read the Talmud intelligently and incorporated several legal precedents by reading them as commanding

14 This method of reading does not only have historical implications. It also has normative implications. According to our read, one who signs (sign language) would not be considered a mute since the concerns have been addressed, while a technoformalist would argue that the Torah requires speech, "mouth". (For an example of a presentation that both explicates underlying concerns in legal formalist language and formally redefines sign language as speech, see my article on people who are both deaf and mute in *Techumin* 21.)

in their underlying reasons and not their specific forms. In other words, if I am embarrassed because I actually believe Rabbeinu Tam's claim that he accepts Talmudic authority and is trying to read the Talmud seriously[15] and not misread the Talmud, I must reach this conclusion that he read for reasons and was not bound by forms.[16]

Having understood Rabbeinu Tam, we can now also understand the Tannaitic midrash Halakhah that required oral testimony. In truth, the Biblical verse does not require oral testimony; it merely requires the testimony of two or three witnesses:

Deuteronomy 17:6 On the basis of two witnesses or three witnesses, he who is to die shall be put to death; he shall not be put to death on the basis of one witness.	דברים יז, ו עַל פִּי שְׁנַיִם עֵדִים אוֹ שְׁלֹשָׁה עֵדִים יוּמַת הַמֵּת לֹא יוּמַת עַל פִּי עֵד אֶחָד:

The correctness of this translation of the phrase "על פי" as "on the basis of" is supported in two ways. The first support is the common Biblical usage of this phrase to mean "on the basis of."[17] The second support is a parallel version of this verse, which is followed by verses that employ different verbs to

15 Within his methodological assumptions about how it is to be read.

16 I thus incorporate the paradigm shift that Renato Rosaldo introduced into anthropology (Renato Rosaldo, "After Objectivism" in Simon During, ed., *The Cultural Studies Reader* (London: Routledge, 1993),104-117) in replacing detached skepticism with an acceptance that people actually mean to do what they say they are doing — in this case that Halakhicists are actually trying to understand precedents. However, I avoid being drawn into the cluster argument of those contemporary intellectual historians of Halakhah (such as Soloveitchik, Ta Shma and Reiner) who also accept that arbiters are serious about their relationship with precedent texts. These historians argue that we must simplistically accept that the arbiters understood those precedents literally and succeeded in explaining themselves literally. They argue that words can and must first be interpreted based on grammar alone independently of the speaker's connotation, that this is the "peshat". (In the most extreme form of some purely deductive and formal lawyers/rabbis the speaker's connotation is never examined, in similarity to the literary method of New Criticism [see Geoffrey Hartman, *Criticism in the Wilderness* (New Haven: Yale University, 1980),156.])

17 ויקרא פרק כז פסוק ח, במדבר פרק כו פסוק נו, משלי פרק כב פסוק ו, בראשית פרק מג פסוק ז, שמות פרק לד פסוק כז

indicate testimony; there is no exclusive Deuteronomic use of this phrase in order to emphasize oral testimony.[18]

However, although the Pentateuch does not require oral testimony, the Tannaitic interpretation is quite justified. Recall our earlier discussion of the greater veracity of oral testimony. In addition, consider that Deuteronomy recognizes that testimony is a form of power against another party and so raises a demand that a conviction be based upon (על פי) trustworthy testimony. In light of these factors, it is appropriate for a later society with a higher percentage of literate people to consider whether testimony may be written and to conclude that testimony must be oral for the sake of veracity. In other words, the *derasha* is a beautiful word play on the real conceptual source of the law.[19]

Once again, embarrassment — in this case, over Talmudic and Medieval sages' distortion of precedents in the Pentateuch and in the Talmud — has led to a more correct reading of those sages' intent.

3. EMBARRASSMENT OVER ISSUES BEING DEBATED THROUGH IRRELEVANT LEGALISTIC CATEGORIES INSTEAD OF BEING OPENLY OVER THE SUBSTANTIVE ISSUES

Thus far we have seen that embarrassment of an apparently simplistic or solipsistic read of precedents can lead one to interpret an authority more accurately. Now I will turn to a last embarrassment that completed my ability to read Halakhic sources more accurately. This was the embarrassment over weighty Halakhic issues that are clearly debated due to the substantive underlying issues but appear to be discussed in legalistic categories that are unrelated to the substantive issues.

18 <u>דברים פרק יט, טו-טז; יח-כ</u>

לֹא יָקוּם עֵד אֶחָד בְּאִישׁ לְכָל עָוֹן וּלְכָל חַטָּאת בְּכָל חֵטְא אֲשֶׁר יֶחֱטָא עַל פִּי שְׁנֵי עֵדִים אוֹ עַל פִּי שְׁלֹשָׁה עֵדִים יָקוּם דָּבָר:

כִּי יָקוּם עֵד חָמָס בְּאִישׁ לַעֲנוֹת בּוֹ סָרָה... וְדָרְשׁוּ הַשֹּׁפְטִים הֵיטֵב וְהִנֵּה עֵד שֶׁקֶר הָעֵד שֶׁקֶר עָנָה בְאָחִיו וַעֲשִׂיתֶם לוֹ כַּאֲשֶׁר זָמַם לַעֲשׂוֹת לְאָחִיו וּבִעַרְתָּ הָרָע מִקִּרְבֶּךָ וְהַנִּשְׁאָרִים יִשְׁמְעוּ וְיִרָאוּ וְלֹא יֹסִפוּ לַעֲשׂוֹת עוֹד כַּדָּבָר הָרָע הַזֶּה בְּקִרְבֶּךָ:

19 (I will not elaborate in this article on my tentative conclusion that this method of reading actually plays out for all midrashei Halakhah from the school of R. Ishmael.)

In order to discuss this category of embarrassment I must first point out that legal concepts are merely the vocabulary of a specialized language (jargon) for expressing universal human issues. Halakhic legal concepts are not meant to be defined formally in order to then be applied consistently in line with the formal definition. I will start with a simple example in which we see this to be true, a responsum of Rabbi Joseph Chaim ben Elijah al-Chakam, the Ben Ish Hai (Baghdad 1835-1909).

EATING A SMALL QUANTITY OF MATZO

The Ben Ish Hai was asked whether an individual who cannot eat the minimal required amount of matzo due to illness should bother eating it at all. He answered that this ***can*** count as a fulfillment of the mitzvah but only if the sick individual has the proper quantity of matzah that s/he would be prepared to eat — at least if s/he were to suddenly cease to be sick. The Ben Ish Hai accomplished this point by use of the legal principle of חזי לאצטרופי. This is a Talmudic term that is used (T.B. Yoma 74b) to explain why one is considered a sinner even if s/he eats a smaller quantity that could be best described as mere tasting or nibbling. The Ben Ish Hai used this term creatively. He used it to argue that the sick individual must actually have the correct quantity of matzah available even as s/he eats less and must be desirous of eating the larger quantity:

שו"ת רב פעלים חלק ג – או"ח סימן לב

Question: A sick individual was warned by the doctor to not eat matzah nor drink four cups of wine at the seder... but the doctor said that minute amounts would not hurt him. Thus they asked if he must eat the minute amount as... a partial *mitzvah*, or else since he is not eating the required size he has [fulfilled] nothing...	**שאלה.** איש אחד חולה שהזהירו הרופא שלא יאכל מצה ולא ישתה יין של ארבע כוסות בליל פסח... אך שאל את הרופא על מעט מצה דהיינו ערך ב' דרהם או שלש, וכן יין שיעור מועט ואמר הרופא שזה השיעור המועט לא יזיק לו. על כן שואלים הלכו אם מחוייב לאכול שיעור המועט הזה, כי... מכל מקום יש בזה קצת מצוה, או דלמא מאחר שאינו אוכל שיעור שלם אין בידו אפילו מקצת. ...

Answer: In a shiur I delivered… I brought proofs that a commandment cannot be fulfilled partially. However, the proofs apply only when that part cannot be combined [with a future part]. After all, it is well known that one can be liable for a partial violation only when that part can be combined with another — as mentioned in Yoma 74. …	**תשובה.** ...ובדרוש שדרשתי... הבאתי ראיות בס"ד דלא אמרינן חצי שיעור במצוות עשה, אך כל הנך ראיות ליתנהו אלא בהיכא דלא חזי לאצטרופי, אבל בהיכא דחזי לאצטרופי ליכא ראיה מהנך, וכבר ידוע דהא דאמרו חצי שיעור אסור מן התורה הוא משום דחזו לאצטרופי וכנזכר בגמרא דיומא דף ע"ד. ...
Now, in this case, it appears that this [minute amount] is fit to combine since the matzah is immediately before him and he is able to eat (except that the doctor warned him to not do so, but if he ignores the doctor's words he can complete the size of an olive. Furthermore, the doctor may retract on that same night based on this individual's pulse… Thus this is considered capable of combination if the doctor permits or this individual ignores the doctor and completes [the required amount]). Thus because one can validly fulfill a commandment partially when it is fit to be combined, this individual fulfills a partial mitzvah.	והנה נידון השאלה הנזכרת נראה דהוא חזי לאצטרופי דהא המצה היא מצויה לפניו, וגברא מצי למיכל ורק הרופא מזהירו שלא לאכול ואם לא יחוש לדברי הרופא הרי זה אפשר שיאכל וישלים כזית, ועוד אפשר שגם הרופא אם רואהו באותה הלילה דפסח בשעה שאוכל המצה יחזור מדעתו ויתן לו רשות להשלים כזית כי יתחדש לו לפי ראות עיניו בדפק שלו ובמיחוש שלו... ועל כן יש לומר חזי לאצטרופי אם יבא הרופא ויתן רשות, ואם הוא לא יחוש לדברי הרופא וישלים, וכיון דחזי לאצטרופי אפשר דיש חצי שיעור במצוות עשה שיש בידו קצת מצוה.

At first glance the Ben Ish Hai abused or creatively misused the legal concept of חזי לאיצטרופי; when incurring a violation for nibbling food on Yom Kippur, we do not require that one actually have more food available or desire to eat more, so there should be no requirement to have the correct quantity of matzah available or to desire to eat more matzah. However, this misuse actually proves that he is not a formalist bound by the terms but rather a *posek* speaking via the jargon.

Once we stop thinking formally his position makes intuitive sense. As regards eating forbidden foods or eating at all on Yom Kippur, eating any quantity already signals a break with the pedestrian mimetic norm of not ingesting at all. This willingness to violate the pedestrian norm can easily change into a more serious violation of actually eating since all that one need do is enlarge one's quantities. Thus, one is considered a sinner for eating at all. As regards the commandments to eat, however, the process is reversed. The commandment is an experiential one, and any failure to experience a minimally sufficient experience, is actually a failure to place oneself into the required experience. Eating less than the minimally experiential amount raises an indication of a reluctance to participate. Thus, nibbling cannot be sufficient unless it is accompanied with the normal sized piece of matzah — thus letting the sick individual indicate and feel that s/he too is participating although s/he cannot eat their quantity. It is similar to receiving a slice of cake at a party although one cannot eat it as opposed to being served crumbs since that is all that one can eat. Thus, the Ben Ish Hai accurately used the term חזי לאיצטרופי more restrictively in regard to fulfilling a mitzvah.

In short, this responsum is based neither on blind obedience to formal categories nor on ingenious (ab)use of formal language in order to achieve a given *pesak*. The underlying concern of the conclusion is simply expressed clearly via the formal language. I have argued elsewhere that this has been the approach of leading Halakhah scholars throughout the generations.[20] For those scholars, legal language and terms are not concepts manipulated as much as concerns taken into account. In order to actually prove this, I should first cite the majority of the responsa of some of the most skilled formalists and then show how even the responsa that appear to separate between the human concerns and the formal halakhic arguments could be read this way, too — as reflecting the human concerns in formal terms. However, this article is not an attempt to prove the historical accurateness of generally understanding sources and responsa in this manner (which I am writing) as much as an attempt to show that embarrassment can lead to a more accurate read. That being the case, I will intentionally limit myself to a most embarrassing case in which there appears to be **no** connection between the formal language and the underlying concern, and show that the formal language can be read as reflecting the underlying concern.

20 אלישע אנצ'לוביץ, "שימוש נאות בשפה פורמלית לקבלת החלטות הלכתיות," **מעגלים** ה (תשס"ז), עמ' 184-157.

Our test example is a row of responsa by R. Yitzhak Yaakov Weiss, the *Minhat Yitzhak* (b. Poland 1902 — d. Israel 1989), on the question of whether a *mamzer* man can marry a semi-convert wife as a means of having children that are not considered his, who can then be converted and considered kosher converts with no taint of *mamzerut*. Due to the length of these sources, I have translated them freely instead of translating closely.

MAMZER AND SHIFHA CANAANIT

The background to these responsa is the norm that the child of incestuous or adulterous relations is a *mamzer/et*, one who is very limited in his or her choice of marital partners and whose children and descendants remain mamzerim *ad infinitum* (unless their status is forgotten)[21]. In the 2nd century CE, R. Tarphon, offered an alternative deterrent to incest other than mamzerut *ad infinitum*, an alternative that would dissolve continuous *mamzerut* and allow male *mamzerim* to procreate. R. Tarphon posited that a mamzer could choose to degrade himself beyond merely marrying a non-wellborn woman. He could choose, instead, to have children with a slave-woman, children that would not inherit him and would not be his offspring under law. Those slave children would not be Jewish but also not *mamzerim*. Thus the mamzer could subsequently free those children who would be kosher converts (of low stature and not legally his children), and their descendants could move up the social scale:

Mishnah Kiddushin 3:18	**משנה מסכת קידושין פרק ג משנה יג**
R. Tarphon says, *mamzerim* can be purified. How? If a mamzer married a slave, the child is a slave [not Jewish and thus not tainted]. If he frees him, the son is a free born [= a new Jew].	רבי טרפון אומר יכולין ממזרים ליטהר. כיצד? ממזר שנשא שפחה הולד עבד. שחררו נמצא הבן בן חורין.

21 **דברים פרק כג פסוק ג:** לֹא יָבֹא מַמְזֵר בִּקְהַל יְדֹוָד גַּם דּוֹר עֲשִׂירִי לֹא יָבֹא לוֹ בִּקְהַל יְדֹוָד:
שולחן ערוך אבן העזר סימן ד סעיף יח: ישראל שנשא ממזרת, או ממזר שנשא ישראלית, הולד ממזר לעולם.

However, in the 16th century Moslem Ottoman Empire and in the 20th century democratic "western world" leading rabbis debated whether a mamzer can halakhically acquire a slave-woman as a wife in a society that does not allow Jews or anyone at all to acquire slaves. In other words, can a relationship that lacks legal sanction and enforcement of ownership of the woman's person, be viewed Halakhically as personal acquisition of a human? If such acquisition is viewed as invalid, the woman remains a gentile and a Jewish man is forbidden to marry her.

In 1965, R. Mordechai Yaakov Breisch (b. Poland, 1896) argued that in spite of the long running debate, halakhic acquisition is definitely valid regardless of civil law as long as the relevant halakhic issue does not depend on actually, practically, owning another but rather in creating an internal halakhic status. Thus, since the mamzer does not actually wish to own this woman but rather to have her become a "partial-convert", the secular law regarding slavery is irrelevant. Furthermore, even if some halakhahic processes become invalid when they contradict secular law, the invalidation is only *mi-de-rabannan* but not *mi-de-orraita*. Thus, the whole debate over this option, the doubt of its validity, is only a minor *safek de-rabannan* — regarding which doubts we are lenient in cases of need:

שו"ת חלקת יעקב אה"ע סימן כג

As regards the fate of *mamzerim* who cannot marry a kosher Jewess since they will thus both violate the injunction against a *mamzer* entering the congregation of Israel… and increase the number of *mamzerim* in the Jewish people	...על גורלם [של ממזרים] מה לעשות — לינשא עם ישראלים, גם האיש גם האשה יתמידו באיסור של לא יבא ממזר בקהל... וגם ירבו ממזרים בישראל —
If he marries a gentile woman, the children will not be *mamzerim* but he himself will violate a serious sin every time he has sexual relations…	ישא נכרית בגויותה, יהני לבנים הנולדים שלא יהיו ממזרים, אבל הוא עצמו יעבור בכל ביאה על איסור... חמור מאוד, כמבואר ברמב"ם ושו"ע,
…that will be compounded by the Biblical injunction against a marital relationship.	ודרך חתנות יש גם איסור תורה —

Marrying a convert is permitted, but the children will not be purified from *mamzerut.*	ישא גיורת דמותרת לממזר... גם כן לא מהני מידי להבנים לטהרם מממזרות..
If so, what will be the fate of these unfortunate people — who if they will remain unmarried will obviously come to violate serious sins.	ואם כן מה יהיה גורלם של האומללים האלו, ולשבת כך בלי אשה בודאי יבאו לידי עבירות חמורות וכמובן.
Thus, the rabbi asks whether one can permit them to have a [halakhically defined] slave woman when the government does not actually recognize any type of slavery.	ועלה בדעת הרב עצה להתיר להם שפחה וכמבואר ב[שולחן ערוך] אבן העזר סימן ד' סעיף כ. והוא בשאלתו, אם היתר זה מועיל גם בזמן הזה, דלפי דינא דמלכותא ליכא היום במדינות האלו סוג עבד או שפחה...
Answer: The contemporary question is whether the acquisition of a slave is halakhically valid today when the government does not recognize the acquisition of slaves...	**תשובה:..** ב) אכן השאלה בזמן הזה דעל פי דינא דמלכותא לא שייך לקנות היום שפחה או עבד — אי מהני זה לענין דיננו, דאם ישראל יקנה בקנין המועיל מן התורה שפחה, אם קנין זה חל...
And although it is obvious that if a gentile were to convert in a kingdom that forbade conversion he would be a Jew...	ואף דזה פשוט דאם עכו"ם אחד יתגייר במלכות שאסור להתגייר על פי דינא דמלכותא, אפילו הכי דינו כישראל לכל דבר...
We can distinguish between the cases since one acquires slaves for servitude, a monetary issue, so that if the economic transaction is invalid there is no slave as regards the injunction [against marrying gentiles]....	אכן יש לחלק, דבקונה עבד או שפחה העיקר לענין עבודה ושירות, וזה דררא דממון וכיון דלא חל הקנין לענין הממון מטעם דינא דמלכותא, ממילא גם לענין איסור לא חל עליה שם עבד או שפחה. ...
As we have seen that the status of a slave woman who was acquired according to Judaic norms and immersed for slavery — against the law of the land — has been debated	ז) מהאמור רואין אנו דשפחה הקנויה עפ"י דרכי הקנינים והוטבלה לשם עבדות ובקבלת מצות אף נגד דינא דמלכותא עכ"פ במחלוקת שנויה אם דינה כשפחה לענין דין תורה,

And even the position that the law of the land overrides is a rabbinic ruling that leaves the action valid on a "Biblical" level....	ועיין בבית שמואל אע"ז סי' כ"ח סק"ג דעתו דדינא דמלכותא דינא הוא רק דר–בנן דמה"ת לא אמרינן דינא דמלכותא דינא. ...
And one can also argue that inasmuch as the [Jewish man's] intent is not to actually acquire her for servitude but rather in order to remove the injunction in order to marry her... all opinions would allows us to ignore the law of the land, just as we do in regard to conversion...	י) ועוד יש סברא לומר בנידון דידן, כיון דאנן סהדי דאין כוונתו כלל לקנותה לשם עבדות רק להפקיע איסורא בכדי שיוכל לישא אותה... אין מתחשבין כלל עם הדינא דמלכותא לכל השיטות וכמו לעניין גירות..
And we know... how much the rabbis in all generations strove to permit daughters of Israel that they need not remain chained [without real husbands], and even relied on minority opinions...	ומצינו.. כמה חתרו רבנים שבכל דור לה–תיר בנות ישראל שלא ישארו עגונות, וס–מכו כמה פעמים אף על דברי יחידים...
All the more so in our case... since a man's pain is stronger and he may come to commit serious sins...	וכל שכן {הכא}... דצערא דגברא קשה מדאיתתא ושלא יבוא לידי עברות חמו–רות...

This was R. Breisch's conclusion. However, his *mechuten*, R. Yitzhak Yaakov Weiss, argued that although he personally agrees with the view that secular law should have no impact on this area of halakhah, such marriage could not be permitted since the matter is debated and an invalid acquisition would mean that the woman has remained a gentile and is Biblically forbidden to the mamzer. Instead he proposed that the woman first be acquired but then be converted fully as if she were a free gentile converting to Judaism. Thus, if her acquisition was valid, her subsequent conversion will be meaningless since she had not been freed, and the children would be semi-Jews who could be freed without any taint. If, on the other hand, she was not acquired halakhically, she would be a convert, whom a mamzer may marry, but the children would theoretically be Jewish *mamzerim*. However, inasmuch as the correct opinion is that the acquisition is valid, and the children's situation is a situation that has no other solution, the halakhic rules call for not being overly strict when no options exist and for considering the children to be converts allowed to marry most any other Jew.

שו"ת מנחת יצחק חלק ה סימן מז

Regarding the matter of not permitting a *mamzer* to purify his children via a slave woman.	בנדון דאין להתיר בזה"ז שפחה לממזר לטהר בניו.
Answer: regarding the question whether the category of slaves exists today when it is in violation of the law of the land there is a rabbinic debate, and so we must be strict regarding this Biblical injunction [against marrying a gentile woman]…	**..תשובה** ...(ג) והנה בנוגע אם שייך בזה"ז דינא דעבדים ושפחות כנענים, כיון דהוי כנגד דינא דמלכותא, יש בזה פלוגתא דרבוותא... (ד) ...ומ"מ כיון דיש פלוגתא דרבוותא, **ובמידי דאורייתא** כנ"ל [של איסור אשה נכרית לגבר יהודי], בודאי יש לילך לחומרא...
Although if we had the right to decide, I think that the correct view is the one that holds that the law of the land is irrelevant…	(ז) אמנם לענ"ד אם היה לנו הרשות להכריע בין אשלי רברבי הנ"ל, היה נראה להצדיק שיטת הסוברים, דלא אמרינן בזה דד"מ דינא. ...
Accordingly, I suggest the following solution that will allow a mamzer to marry such a woman based on an either-or argument and will permit the children *de facto*…	(י) וכיון דאתאן לזה, אפשר להתחכם בהמצאה נכונה, שלהממזר בעצמו, יהיה מותר לכתחי-לה מטעם ממ"נ, והבנים יהיו מותרים מטעם דיעבד,
To wit, he can consensually acquire the gentile woman to become a [semi-]Jewish slave woman with attendant mitzvah obligations…	והיינו, שיקנה נכרית שברצונה ליכנס לדת יש-ראל, בתורת שפחה, ולהטבילה בקבלת עול מצוות לשם עבדות הכל במבואר (ביו"ד סי' רס"ז),

And afterward she will personally accept all the commandments and immerse as a regular convert in front of a court without her master's permission...	ואח"כ תקבל השפחה בעצמה עול מצוות, ותט-בול לשם גירות, בלא רשות האדון שלה, אבל תעשה הכל כדת וכדין לפני בית דין כמבואר שם (סי' רס"ח).
So if she is actually a slave and acquired by the master the conversion is meaningless, since she could not convert without his permission... But if she is not acquired the conversion is valid.	והנה אם חל עליה שם עבדות, וגופה קנוי להאדון, הגירות אינה כלום, שאי אפשר לה להתגייר בלא רשות אדונה.. ואם אין גופה קנוי להאדון, שוב מהני הגירות שלה,
If so, a mamzer may marry her since she is either a slave woman or a convert.	א"כ הרי הממזר יכול לישא אותה לכתחילה בלי שום חשש, מטעם ממ"נ, דהרי היא אחת מת-רתי, או שפחה או גיורת, ומותר בשתיהם,
As regards the children, if the mother has the status of a slave they may enter the congregation after they have been freed, and if she is a full convert then they may not do so...	ובנוגע להוולדות, אם יש לאמם דין שפחה, מו-תרים לבוא בקהל אחרי השחרור, ואם יש לה דין גיורת, אסורים לבוא בקהל, ותלוי בפלוגתא הנ"ל,
But since the [status of the] children is a *de facto* situation [בדיעבד], and the view that permits [purely legal slavery] is more convincing, we may rely on the lenient view.	אבל כיון דבנוגע לדידהו שוב הוי דיעבד... ומס-תבר טעמייהו דהמתירים, שפיר יש לסמוך על המקילים.

R. Weiss argues his position through six responsa. In the course of these responsa he adds that

- inasmuch as the *mamzer* is not intending to acquire the woman as a slave, relying on the acquisition without additional normal conversion in order to allow non-sinful marriage is *more* problematic since R. Tarfon only permitted this option with an actual slave-woman. Thus regular conversion is necessary for the fallback position that the woman is completely Jewish (a convert) and marriage is permitted.

- since slave-women do not have to accept the Torah as seriously, we must require regular conversions lest we end up creating homes of Jewish men married to women who, for all intents and purposes, did not accept Judaism.

He labels the first argument "halakhic" and the second "policy".

שו"ת מנחת יצחק חלק ה סימן מט

Regarding my respected *mechuten*'s suggestion to acquire the slave woman for cohabitation alone — and not for any work or service, in my opinion that would not be considered an acquisition of a person [halakhically].	(ב) ..מה שהעיר כהד"ג מחותני (באות ט'), לקנות שפחה רק לעבדות דתשמיש המטה, ולא לשם שאר עבדות ושירות, הנה לענ"ד בכהאי גוונא לא הוי קניין הגוף...

שו"ת מנחת יצחק חלק ה סימן נ

The reason that this suggestion [of acquiring slaves] has not been carried out is because the sages were worried halakhically and policy-wise.	דהנה י"ל דטעמא רבה איכא בדבר, מה שנתבטל עצה זו, דבודאי לא נעלם מעיני גדולי הדור שלפנינו, גם ההמצאה שכתבנו, אלא שיש לומר שחששו לב' חששות גדולות, א' מצד ההלכה, וב' מצד מכשול.
Regarding Halakhah, this acquisition of a slave is merely a legal fiction to override a Biblical injunction, and so according to many authorities is forbidden. And although we do sometimes permit legal fictions regarding Biblical matters, we sometimes do not, and so we cannot introduce any new fictions.	מצד ההלכה: דבודאי לא יצאנו בכל זה מידי הערמה, שכל ענין של השפחות בזה, לא נעשה רק להערמה... דאם אין כאן שפחה, יש כאן משום גויה, ונוגע לו לאיסור דאורייתא... ולכמה פוסקים הערמה בדאורייתא אסור.. ואף אמנם... דגם במילי דאורייתא, התירו הערמה, מכל מקום גם יש מקומות שאסרו הערמה... ואם כן כיון שלא ניתן לנו הרשות לדמות מילתא למילתא בזה, אין לנו לחדש ענין של הערמה גם בנדון דידן.

מצד מכשול: בנשואי התערובת... שבאים להתגייר רק לפנים בעוה"ר, אבל מחמת שבודקים אותם כדין תורה, ורובם אי אפשר להם להתקיים בקבלת עול מצות, שמאריכין ומסבירים להם כל הקושיים שיש בזה ופורשים, אבל בהתוודע ששייך עניין עבדים ושפחות בזה"ז, ימצאו בית דין של הדיוטות, שילמדו אותם הערמה, שיקנו אותם לעבדים ושפחות, אשר מצד עיקרא דדינא נשתנה דינם בנוגע לקבלת מצות... ואם כן יש לחוש לעורכי דין, שילמדו תועים בינה, לעשות קניינים של עבדים ושפחות, כדי להקל מעליהן עניין חומר קבלת מצות, הנהוג בגירות, ואח"כ ישחררו אותם, ובשחרורן א"צ כלל לקבלת מצות	Regarding policy, there are people who desire to convert insincerely but are stopped by the serious examination, and they may be advised by lawyers to be acquired as slaves who do not have to accept all the mitzvoth, and then they will be freed by their masters without having accepted all the mitzvoth.

שו"ת מנחת יצחק חלק ה סימן מח

(יא) ולכל זה אנו צריכין אף באם הפסולי קהל [=הממזרים], המה שומרי תורה ומצות, ומדקדקים ליקח שפחה שתקבל עליה עול מצות באמת,	We require this [two-step process] even if the mamzerim are Torah observant and careful to acquire a woman who will truly accept the commandments
דאל"כ עוד שייך בזה, מה שכתב הרדב"ז (ח"ב סי' אלף ש"ס) וז"ל, ותו שאני רואה כל השפחות בזמן הזה, אינם מקבלים מצות כלל מדעתן, ואע"פ שאומרת הן מן השפה ולחוץ וכו' עכ"ל.	because we fear the situation that R. David b. Zimra (d. 1573) faced, of "slaves" who do not truly accept all the commandments.

שו"ת מנחת יצחק חלק ה סימן נב

And although my *mechuten* argued that this legal fiction [of simply acquiring slaves against state law] is no different than conversion [against state law], this actually differs even from conversion motivated by a[n external] reason since such converts truly wish to convert	(א) שם (באות א') העיר מחותני הגאון שליט"א על דברינו בענין הער־מה, הנה לענ"ד בודאי הוי הערמה גמו־רה, ואינו דומה לגירות, דאף דנעשה על פי סיבה, מ"מ רצונם בגירות ממש,
— as opposed to the man who does not truly desire to own a slave woman who is his property forever and who cannot be released without a document of release.	מה שאין כן בשפחות, אין כוונתם שתהיה לו שפחה ממש פשוטו כמשמ־עו, שגופה קנוי לו לצמיתות עולם, לע־בוד בה עבודת עבד, ושאף אם ישלחה ממנו, תהיה נצרכת גט שחרור וכו'.

Until this point, the debate embarrassingly reads as a value-debate over potential converts hidden in an irrelevant formal discussion of whether religio-Judaic acquisition is valid when outlawed by the state in spite of a consensus that conversion is valid (as is halakhic-marriage/marital-acquisition in countries that do not allow men to own their wives sexually). The debate over whether to allow marriage through a simple acquisition process (acquisition with slave conversion) or to require a "double conversion" (both acquisition with slave-conversion and full conversion) lest these homes not be Jewish, seems to be grounded in an unrelated formal debate over the validity of such acquisitions.

However, let us review the formal arguments, then add the policy argument, and then add the *Minhat Yitzhak*'s original solution. We will see that they are all components of one argument. R. Weiss argued formally

- that the *mamzer* cannot marry an acquired "slave" since such acquisition may be invalid — in spite of his own conviction that secular law is irrelevant, and the *Helkat Yaakov*'s argument that such acquisition is at least valid *mi-de-orraita*.

- that legal fictions may not be valid — except that he admits that we accept them as valid (but argues that we don't innovate new ones).

In short, acquisition is not valid because the man is not truly acquiring a person whom he can control through corporeal punishment (or sell to another owner if he can't control her).

The policy argument was that

- such "converts" would not be truly Judaic.

- The policy solution was to have the woman undergo a complete conversion, too.

In other words, the *Minhat Yitzhak*'s seamless argument is as follows: Rabi Tarphon permitted a *mamzer* to "marry" a slave-woman who is only nominally Judaic because he can control her, and so in a society that does not actually provide a man with such control, we require a full convert to Judaism; there is no room to argue fictionally that a man is living with a nominally Judaic slave when he is living with a nominally Judaic yet fully free wife.

R. Breisch, on the other hand, called for a more classic situation of having a mamzer somewhat degraded by marrying a woman who is not a full Jewess although her children will become Jewish. He argued coherently (formally and substantively) that this acquisition is simply a lesser conversion to not-fully-Jewish status and so the State's law is irrelevant. Thus the debate between R. Weiss and R. Breisch is as follows: R. Weiss argued that it is better that this woman undergo an additional full conversion that ensures commitment, since there are still degrading elements of the mamzer both marrying a woman of doubtful Jewish status and having to free his children. R. Breisch argued that it is best to not confuse this lesser conversion with full conversion and full converts, and we can rely on the rabbinic courts to ensure that non-committed converts will not be accepted.

To summarize, embarrassment revealed that the formal language and discussion expressed concerns that are critical to the policy argument. We now realize that the formal language is a specialized language for stating *the actual **direct** human concerns* and for showing that those concerns already exist in the halakhic culture and have even been coined into shorthand phrases. Once again, embarrassment can lead to a more careful and accurate read of authorial intent.

4. EMBARRASSMENT OVER AN AUTHORITATIVE SOURCE'S SELF-CONTRADICTION:

Now that we have understood that formalized language is simply a language of discussion, we are able to overcome one more embarrassment — the embarrassment that people face when a legal text appears to contradict its inner logic. We now realize that there is no requirement of formal logical consistency — as if law is to be treated mathematically, but rather that the legal arbiter's argument makes sense in consistently interpreting the data of life in light of the insights of the sources (as we have seen in all the examples cited in this article). Thus another ruling by R. Asher b. Yechiel will become clear. The background to this ruling is the Talmudic position regarding a Jew who declares that he had converted himself as opposed to having been converted. R. Judah declared that this individual is believed regarding his self — and must reconvert, but is not believed as regards his children. In other words, we do not really care to doubt the status of the children who had been born into a Judaic environment and identify as such:

תלמוד בבלי מסכת יבמות דף מז עמוד א

A man once came to R. Yehuda and told him: I converted myself	מעשה באחד שבא לפני רבי יהודה, ואמר לו: נתגיירתי ביני לבין עצמי,
R. Yehuda said to him: Do you have witnesses? He replied: no. Do you have sons? He replied: yes.	א"ל רבי יהודה: יש לך עדים? אמר ליה: לאו. יש לך בנים? א"ל: הן.
[R. Yehuda] told him: You are believed to invalidate yourself, but not your sons.	א"ל: נאמן אתה לפסול את עצמך, ואי אתה נאמן לפסול את בניך.

The Rosh adds that this man is also not believed to forbid his wife to have relations with him, although he is forbidden to have relations with her, since he has declared himself a gentile:

הרא"ש (סי' לה)

That which he said, "you are believed to invalidate yourself" does not mean that he invalidates a daughter of Israel through relations... for his testimony is worthless even as regards himself in terms of invalidating a daughter of Israel if he has relations with her; it is valid only as regards having forbidden himself, and he is forbidden to have relations with a daughter of Israel.	והא דקאמר שנאמן לפסול את עצמו לא לענין זה שאם בא על בת ישראל פסלה... [ד]אין עדותו כלום ואפילו לענין עצמו ואם בא על בת ישראל לא יפסלנה אלא לענין זה מהני עדותו לעצמו דשוי לנפשיה חתיכה דאיסורא ואסור בבת ישראל

Formally, the Rosh's position is tenuous. A non-Jew cannot be obligated to refrain from marrying or having relations with a Jew. Thus, if the wife is permitted to have relations with the husband then he may have relations with her. After all, if he is actually Jewish there is no problem, and if he is not Jewish he is not obligated to refrain from such relations.

Non-formally, however, the Rosh makes sense. He is clearly arguing that a member of the community who suddenly declares that he was never Jewish is not actually believed in terms of history[22] but must correct his statement of separation from the Torah community. Thus, if this Jewish man sticks to his "new" identity his wife need not divorce him and may maintain a marital relationship with all that it entails when life is shared, especially when women are economically dependent upon their husbands. We as a community, however, are meant to intercede and to force him to rejoin the community by conversion. Thus we tell him: "You the Jew — who claims to not be Jewish — are not counted for prayer quorums, believed regarding testimony and oaths, or entitled to communal rights, until you rejoin the Torah community."[23]

---

22 Or else: The actual history of conversion is substantively irrelevant once a person is part of the Torah community. Only when we are faced with incontrovertible evidence that the proper procedures were never followed, do we need to treat the person as a gentile in order to ensure that Jews do not in the future marry gentiles who have not fully adopted an identity of loyalty to Judaism.

23 As Rav Tzvi Pesach Frank (Kovno and Jerusalem, 1874 — 1960) explained Maimonides' legal summation of that same Talmudic passage: this man is believed only as far as being required

Once again, embarrassment has led us to reread a text as a human, possibly wise but definitely human, discussion of human issues. We have moved from the error of a simplistic read of a legal text to a discovery of authorial intent.

JUSTIFICATION OF THESE CONCLUSIONS

At this point, the reader may respond that although s/he was entertained by these reads, I have not shown that these reads reflect authorial intent as much as simply illustrated the phenomenon of rereading from embarrassment and subsequent embracement. However, all the examples that I have provided are embarrassments that would have existed in the minds of the cited authors and their contemporary readers if we accept these individuals' self-perception that they were serious in their acceptance of precedent authority and were trying to read the precedents seriously and not to misread them. In other words, in order to understand these sources emically, we must[24] conclude that this method is historically accurate. It is the only method that makes best sense of the odd data that has never been explained. It may be unsettling; it is a paradigm shift that abandons etic suspicion and emic loyalty for emic yet critical thought.[25]

---

to undergo another conversion but not as far as actually considering him to not be Jewish.

שו"ת הר צבי יורה דעה סימן רכב ד"ה ומכח זה

שמעיקר הדין גם לגבי עצמו אינו נאמן כלל...

כלומר, מה שהוא נאמן לפסול את עצמו זה אינו אלא לענין טבילה שחייב לטבול

24 The word "must" is possibly a difficult word for adherents of the poststructuralist doctrine of indeterminacy of reference, which suggests that random incompatible interpretations can be made to fit the observed facts equally well. I discuss this problem in an upcoming work where I defend this methodology via various epistemological and psychological perspectives.

25 One might argue that although I am not reading etically in the classic sense, I am yet reading "externally" since I am reading the values/human-needs underlying halakhot instead of simply accepting the formal expositions and arguments actually presented by Halakhah decisors (rishonim through poskim). However we have seen that these same "legalistic" expositions and arguments are often very clear statements of values/human-needs once one knows how to read them correctly.

Note: The debate between the formalists or intellectual-historians and us is actually no more severe than the difference between Mishnah (us) and Sifra (them) interpretations of Leviticus. Sifra connects its positions to the words of Leviticus while Mishnah connects its positions to the underlying concepts. I assume that to an outside observer, both are emic. (For a discussion

One might argue, nonetheless, that I am still making a better case for the subject than the subject could have made for himself.[26] At first glance, this is obviously a misplaced accusation inasmuch as a position worded in *langue x* will inevitably sound silly to members of *langue y*; it is only via translation that people realize the overwhelming commonality of statements and behaviors in different cultures. Thus, "we cannot hope to unravel the… realities of the distant past if we look for simple translations and do not grapple with the deep structures of meaning; and these are", admittedly, "going to be debatable."[27]

Nonetheless, there is an underlying justification for those who are critical of this article's reading strategy. To wit, that I must be charitably misreading the sources since I am interpreting more than the authors' words, and all that one can legitimately interpret are words. After all, any other interpretation would "obviously" be an imposed projection of the interpreter's desired positive or negative evaluation of the source. This critique can be divided into two, a principled critique of my thesis and a pragmatic critique.

The principled critique would emanate from scholars who follow Schleiermacher in understanding thought to be identical with language.[28] The prob-

of each of these Tannaitic works relationship to Leviticus, see Jacob Neusner, *Uniting the Dual Torah: Sifra and the Problem of the Mishnah* (Cambridge University Press, 1990),73-74.)]

26 "Against the background of the debate between explanation and understanding, the formidable question of creativity stands out." (Paul Ricoeur, *Hermeneutics and the Human Sciences: Essays on Language, Action, and Interpretation* (Cambridge: Cambridge University Press, 1981),38.)

27 Wendy Davies, "On Servile Status in the Early Middle Ages" in M. L. Bush ed., *Serfdom and Slavery: Studies in Legal Bondage* (London and New York: Longman, 1996),227. To state this differently, if we are to avoid "violations of the principles of discourse and human interaction, such as the Principle of Charity (cf. Davidson: 1974) and the Principle of Humanity (cf. Grady: 1973)," we cannot simply read in a distanced manner of explanation that allows no more than either pedantic repetition (even if in new terminology) or mere discovery of the writer's errors. We must engage in interpretation, in hermeneutics. Unfortunately for the complacency of the academic Talmudist or Halakhicist, "hermeneutics is forever marked by this double filiation — Romantic and critical, critical and Romantic. The proposal to struggle against misunderstanding in the name of the famous adage 'there is hermeneutics where there is misunderstanding' is critical; the proposal to 'understand an author as well and even better than he understands himself' is Romantic." (Paul Ricoeur, *Hermeneutics and the Human Sciences: Essays on Language, Action, and Interpretation* (Cambridge: Cambridge University Press, 1981),46.)

28 They, like Schleiermacher, do take into account the historical and psychological context of the author but only in order to resolve ambiguities on the linguistic level (since terms and grammar of a given language differ in different cultures and because words are polysemous) and to

lem with this principled critique is that it can be shown to be erroneous when applied indiscriminately to all people.[29] The strongest rebuke to this position comes neither from the sources that I have cited, where traditional Halakhah scholars become clear only when their explanatory words are interpreted last, nor from my personal experience of finding fellow intuitive thinkers whose words are misunderstood because we tend to skip "tedious" intermediary steps.[30] Nor does it come from the fact that even in the purest deductive thought-language, mathematics,[31] the most brilliant mathematicians have been intuitive thinkers who worked out their deductive steps only after they intuited the solutions or formulas. Rather, the rebuke begins with a quote from the master of clear thought and prose, George Orwell, who argued that even "abstractions" can and should be thought of in images instead of in words:

When you think of something abstract you are more inclined to use words from the start, and unless you make a conscious effort to prevent it, the existing dialect will come rushing in and do the job for you, at the expense of blurring or even changing your meaning. Probably it is better to put off using words as long as possible and get one's meaning as clear as one can through pictures and sensations. Afterward one can choose — not simply *accept* — the phrases that will best cover the meaning[32]

---

discern the illocutionary force of the author's statement — as one would miss the whole point of Jonathan Swift's writings if one did not realize that he was a satirist.

29 I will now avoid the parallel error of arguing that all people do not think through words. Some people (not discussed in this article) do eventually grow into adults who think through words instead of actually comprehending the images that underlie these shorthand devices, words. These are the people who use words associatively to build deductive arguments in which they "think they understand... when they do but repeat the words softly, or con them in their mind." (Thomas Hobbes, *Leviathan* Bk. 1, ch. 4 — much before the "later Wittgenstein")

30 "We know things with our lives, and live that knowledge, beyond anything any theory has theorized." (Catherine MacKinnon, "From Practice to Theory, or What is a White Woman Anyway?" in Diane Bell and Renate Klein, eds., *Radically Speaking: Feminism Reclaimed* (North Melbourne, Australia, Spinifex: 1996),46.)

31 See the contrast between mathematical and intuitive thinking described by Blaise Pacal, Pensees (1660), translated by W. F. Trotter online at http://www.4literature.net/Blaise_Pascal/Pensees.

32 George Orwell [Eric Arthur Blair], "Politics and the English Language" (1946) available online at http://www.orwell.ru/library/essays/politics/english/e_polit

It continues with such famous writers as Samuel Butler[33] and Coluccio Salutati[34] along with some scientists[35] having described themselves as thinking in images. It concludes with the fact that findings in neurological sciences show that we think even abstract thoughts independently of words.[36]

Having disposed of the principled critique,[37] the more relevant critique is the pragmatic critique that by not focusing on words first we are more prone to impose readings that are not "real" in the sense that they do not emanate from and may not easily fit the author's explanatory words. This, however, is a critique based on a mistaken assumption; my thesis is that one is engaged in realist style history only if one interprets the subject's positions. When one imposes interpretations of the subject's positions from the subject's explanatory words, one may be dismissed as engaging in word fetishism[38] for "if we merely know that someone holds a certain sentence to be true, we know neither what

33 Citation from Samuel Butler's notebook in footnote 139 to idem, Hudibras (1663) online at http://home13.inet.tele.dk/peraten/hudibras.htm.

34 Coluccio Salutati, "Letter to Brother John of San Miniato" (1401) in Ephraim Emerton, *Humanism and Tyranny: Studies in the Italian Trecento* (1925: reprint, Gloucester, MA: P. Smith, 1964), 314.

35 See Thomas Armstrong, *Multiple Intelligences in the Classroom: Second Edition* (Alexandra, VA: Association for Supervision and Curriculum Development, 2000),114.

36 Murray G. Murphey, *Philosophical Foundations of Historical Knowledge* (Albany: State University of New York Press, 1994),4-9.

37 Actually, to dispose of the principled argument, I must first acknowledge that Gadamer and Ricoeur also accept Schleieremacher's emphasis on text: "Schleiermacher makes this clear: to consider the common language is to forget the writer; whereas to understand an individual author is to forget his language which is merely passed over.... The proper task of hermeneutics is accomplished in this second interpretation. What must be reached is the subjectivity of the one who speaks, the language being forgotten. ...But even then, psychological interpretation... is never *restricted* to establishing an affinity with the author. It implies critical motifs in the activity of comparison.... Elsewhere I argue that this... [requires] shifting the interpretative emphasis from the empathic investigation of hidden subjectivities toward the sense and reference of the work itself." (Paul Ricœur, *Hermeneutics and the Human Sciences: Essays on Language, Action, and Interpretation* (Cambridge University Press, 1981),47.) My response to Gadamer and Ricoeur is that the primary work to be studied should be the "reconstructed" prior-to-text intent of the author and not the text, although I agree that one criterion for an acceptable connotation is that it is capable of being read into the denotation.

38 Unless significant correlation between a subject's positions and explanations has shown that this subject actually thinks in words and expresses his or her reasons brilliantly.

he means by the sentence nor what belief his holding it to be true represents."[39] In other words, I am arguing that in trying to discern the meaning of a person's statement we should not be dealing with the gap "between the statement and the will conveyed through it"[40] but rather with the gap "between the will and the statement by which it is conveyed."[41] Accordingly, the criterion for a non-imposed interpretation of a halakhic legislator's position is that the interpretation must match an inductive[42] read of the legislator's multiple positions.[43]

---

39 Donald Davidson, "On the Very Idea of a Conceptual Scheme," *Proceedings and Addresses of the American Philosophical Association* 47 (1974): 18.

40 Hermeneutics as defined by Daniel Statman and Avi Sagi, *Religion and Morality* (Rodopi, 1995),128. [Hebrew original — 1993]

41 "The fundamental fact here is that we lay down rules, a technique, for a game, and that then when we follow the rules, things do not turn out as we had assumed. That we are therefore as it were entangled in our own rules. This entanglement in our rules... throws light on our concept of *meaning* something. For in those cases things turn out otherwise than we had meant.... That is just what we say when, for example, a contradiction appears: 'I didn't mean it like that.'" (Ludwig Wittgenstein, *Philosophical Investigations*, 1 par.125)

42 More accurately: subductive.

43 There is another school that to the best of my knowledge has not spelled out its theoretical foundation, but in practice can be described in one of two contradictory ways: (1) They go further than Schleiermacher and do not merely argue that thought is identical with *inner* language but also with expressed language. (2) They move beyond Gadamer and Ricoeur's search for the text's challenge (as opposed to its original intent) into New Criticism, etc. or toward a Quinian understanding that no two people see the same thing when looking at a given object (there are no identical stimulus meanings); given that state of affairs, we should realize that we can communicate and interact only via the words and not their infinite meanings: "if we... tak[e] the home language at face value, the relativity is resolved. Reference is then explicated in disquotational paradigms... thus 'rabbit' denotes rabbits, whatever they are, and 'Boston' designates Boston." (W. V. Quine, *Pursuit of Truth* [revised edition: Cambridge, MA: Harvard University Press, 1992], 52.)

Thus this school does not deal with the fact that in human speech *expressed* thoughts are only shorthand for inner language/speech; in their academic work they do not read the individual who says "stop at a red light" to mean "stop at a red *traffic* light"; they would read the person who says "you may drive once you have a license" as requiring only a license issued by the state, even if issued due to bureaucratic error, and not as meaning "you may drive once you have a license [and by implication the experience and skill that are usually required in order to get a license]".

In other words, their approach parallels Franz Brentano's erroneous claim that "it is not true that, in a judgment, there are always several ideas related to one another as subject and predicate. This is certainly the case when I say: 'God is just', though not when I say: 'There is a God.'"

To summarize, I do not tolerate "the deceit of mutual understanding irremediably founded on the empty abstraction of the words," since I have argued elsewhere to accept the general truth of "the multiple personality of everyone corresponding to the possibilities of being found in each of us".[44] Thus, I can

---

(Franz Brentano, *The Origin of the Knowledge of Right and Wrong* [1889], translated by Cecil Hague [1902], par. 20 at http://www.archive.org/details/theoriginofthekn00brenuoft HaH). Brentano is wrong, since the person who claims that G-d exists is implicitly stating that experiences and/or traditions X validate the existence of G-d in spite of experiences and/or traditions Y that apparently negate the existence of G-d.

For an example of this school's writings, see: צבי זוהר ואברהם שגיא, גיור וזהות יהודית, מוסד ביאליק ומכון שלום הרטמן, ירושלים, תשנ"ד.

This school can be understood to be serious and consistent in its word-centric approach. When its members engage in the cultural study of contemporary Halakhic communities they do not discuss "rational functional" explanations for "irrational" and "immoral" behaviors since they understand such behaviors to be the product of dominant myths, ideologies. Similarly, they attempt to battle ideas with ideas while a functionalist would attempt to address the (valid) threats and problems that underpin the expression of problematic ideology-behavior.

A more cynical approach to this school, however, might harp on the fact that its practitioners are heavily involved in scholarship as religious polemic and as such may be reading in this method in order to make it easier to manipulate, limit and dismiss sources. The debate between this academic school and all other academic schools, which have some interest in author's intent, would then be described best via Menachem Fisch's description of two legal-school approaches to the canon (alluded to earlier in the body of this article): "Traditionalists and antitraditionalists both take the halakhic canon with utmost seriousness, but differ sorely as to what taking it seriously amounts. For the former, to do so is to hold the bulk of foregoing halakhic rulings as absolutely binding; for the latter, it is to view it as the object of relentless reexamination. ... A dedicated and conscientious traditionalist will never take advantage of his interpretative freedom in order to stray deliberately from what he takes to be the true spirit of the law. ... On an antitraditionalist showing, [however]... the halakhic authorities... are granted the authority not merely to determine what the law says, but to state what it *should* say, and make it say it... because [they]... find fault in the revelation..!" (from Menachem Fisch, "Canon, controverse et réforme; une réflexion sur l'autre voix du judaïsme talmudique", *Les Cahiers du judaisme*, 18: 61-75, 2005.) I acknowledge that Professor Fisch would not apply this criticism to the scholarship of that school.

44 Luigi Pirandello, "Preface to *Six Characters in Search of an Author*" (1925), translated by Eric Bentley, ed., *Naked Masks: Five Plays by Luigi Pirandello* (New York: Dutton, 1952),367. I suppose that the reason that this desire for mutual recognition does not draw me, as it did Pirandello, to fascism is that (other than sharing the late 20th century disillusionment in illusionary statist solutions) I am not tormented by Pirandello's third torment, "the inherent tragic conflict between life (which is always moving and changing) and form (which fixes it immutable)" [ibid]. As I have explained in the body of the text, I see life as driven by both fixed forms that keep recombining in infinite patterns [thus the ability of mutual understanding] and

share an author's embarrassments, realize that I have been misreading the thrust of the author's explanations, and finally discover a read closer to the authorial intent than would be provided by literalism. Thank you Professor Fox for validating the first step, embarrassment, which allows me to have introduced the second step, discovery of authorial intent.

fixed forms that change in valence even when they seem unchanged in form [thus the need to interpret].

THE DOUBLE PATH: THE TWO LAYERS OF THINKING AND THE TWOFOLD NATURE OF KNOWLEDGE IN THE WORKS OF SAADYA GAON

Gyöngyi Hegedűs, University of Western Ontario

This essay is about two types of thinking. The first type is of a polemic and disputatious nature, whereas the second is rather contemplative. The first one is always directed against an opponent and attempts to demolish his view through the application of a univocal terminology and clear logical argumentation. The second one attempts to treat the very fundamental issues of human thinking and to answer the following question: why is everything the way it is? The first type of thinking serves to attain a goal, i.e., to convince the opponent and to defeat him in debate. The second is the fruit of human curiosity and of the solitary activity of a philosopher.

Saadya Gaon, who belonged to the second generation of Judeo-Arabic theologians, was the creator of the earliest Jewish systematic philosophical and polemic literature of the Middle Ages which survived in length[1] and influenced the religious thought of generations of thinkers after him. He appears to excel in both realms. On the one hand, he composed the first handbook of the Jewish creed based on a rational foundation, and on the other hand, he commented on the earliest and the most debated work of Jewish mysticism, the *Sefer Yezirah* 'Book of Formation'. In this article I will primarily focus

1 The work of Saadya's predecessors, such as Isaac Israeli and Da'ud al-Muqammis, had to be reconstructed from fragments. Thus, although these thinkers historically preceded and influenced Saadya's thought, they subsequently became overshadowed by him in the same way as Saadya's fame was later eclipsed by Maimonides, at least in Europe.

on these two books, which are said to be the most significant philosophical achievement of Saadya, that is *The Book of Beliefs and Convictions* (*kitab al-amanat wa-'l-i`tiqadat*) and his *Commentary on the Sefer Yezirah* (*tafsir sefer yezirah*). The first work is the universal guideline of Jewish rational thought, belonging to the same genre as that of the Muslim rationalists (*kalam*), and the second is the expression of another type of philosophy, less rationalistic and polemical in nature.

Saadya became the Gaon of Sura and thus the intellectual leader of the Jewish diaspora in 928. The death of the caliph in 932 and certain changes in the power structure of the empire lead to Saadya's expulsion. Debarred from office, Saadya devoted himself to scholarship during the ensuing years. It was this period of his life that he composed his *Commentary on the Sefer Yezirah*, in 931, and his *Book of Beliefs and Convictions* in 933. With the arrival of a new caliph in 936, Saadya became reinstated as the Gaon of Sura and in 942 six years after his reinstatement, he passed away.

This is not the place to offer an exhaustive list of Saadya's manifold activities,[2] but it is noteworthy that it is not only in philosophy, grammar and calendrical calculations that his knowledge excelled. He also translated texts into Arabic and commented on most books of the Bible (Genesis, Exodus, Proverbs, Job, etc.). He also composed a prayer book (*Siddur*) and a series of halakhic works. In light of this we have to agree with Maimonides who states that "were it not for Saadya the Torah would have well-nigh disappeared from the midst of Israel, for it was he who made manifest what was obscure therein, made strong what had been weakened, and made it known far and wide by word of mouth and in writing."[3] According to a proverbial saying, between the two Moses' (the prophet and Maimonides), there was no noteworthy man in Israel. Supposing there were someone, it would undoubtedly be Saadya.

2 For a complete enumeration of Saadya's activities and for a characterization of his works see Malter, pp 137-271, and the Encyclopedia Judaica, vol. 14, cc 547-553.

3 *Iggeret Teiman*, quoted in the Encyclopedia Judaica, p 554, and in Malter, p 279.

THE BOOK OF BELIEFS AND CONVICTIONS

The *Book of Beliefs and Convictions*, composed in Baghdad in 933 during the period of Saadya's seclusion, is considered to be his philosophical magnum opus. It is intended to be a general guideline for the knowledge of the Jewish faith on rational bases, a presentation destined for a large public. Its structure follows the order established by the Muslim rationalists, the *mutakallimun*.

It begins with a relatively long introductory part (pp 1-32) of an epistemological nature, which treats notions related to knowledge, such as that of doubt, truth, belief, the sources of knowledge, speculation and revelation. The system of epistemology built up in this chapter appears to be based on two principles: (1) that the object and the subject of human knowledge are clearly distinct, and (2) that the external and the internal sources of knowledge, i.e., the sensible and the intelligible realms, correspond to each other. The outcome of the first statement is that most people are lost in "the ocean of the doubts", given the fact that they fail to recognize what is reliable information and what is not. As a good therapist, Saadya goes back to the very foundations of human knowledge, namely, to the perception of the senses common to all. He states that sense perception serves as a general basis for all cognition, that the data furnished by it are usually correct, and that they refer to an objectively existing world (*haqiqa*). But in itself, sense perception does not provide a sufficient basis for cognition. Thus, it is completed by the immediate knowledge of the intellect implanted by God in the soul. According to Saadya (as in the view of the Muslim rationalists), all other notions of an epistemological nature can be understood as being based on the correspondence or non-correspondence of these two bases. The apparent gaps between them are to be bridged by the procedure of speculation (*nazar*), which is represented as the main instrument by which we arrive at reliable knowledge.

After having established these basic principles as the ways in which to achieve knowledge, Saadya addresses the following topics: that of the creation ex nihilo in the first treatise of the *Book of Beliefs and Convictions* (pp 33-75), that of the divine unity in the 2nd treatise (pp 76-115), that of command and prohibition in the 3rd treatise, that of obedience and rebellion, predestination and divine justice in the 4th treatise, and that of the notions of merits and demerits in the 5th treatise (pp 169-192). The 6th treatise (pp 193-217) is composed of two parts, the first one dealing with the essence of the soul and the second part touching upon the concept of death and on what follows after death. The 7th treatise (pp 218-236) concerns the resurrection of the dead in the physical world, the 8th chapter (pp 237-260) focuses on the topic of redemption, the 9th treatise (pp 261-296) tackles the nature of reward and punishment in the world to come, and the 10th chapter is consecrated to the topic of how it is most proper for man to conduct himself in this world (pp 297-324).

According to the methodology of Saadya, each treatise starts with the establishment of the right view concerning a particular topic, next all other views are refuted, and finally the right view is proven on the basis of Scripture. Saadya's opponents, named or anonymous, are numerous. He appears to draw lines of demarcation by logically proved statements against a wide range of the religious and philosophical ideas of his age.

The full title of the *Book of Beliefs and Convictions* is *Kitab al-Mukhtar fi-'l-Amanat wa-'l-I`tiqadat* (The Select Book of Beliefs and Convictions). It is "select" because the work critically considers a variety of views on each topic it discusses, offering arguments for the preferred view and against the views rejected. It can be considered as the summit of the Jewish rational theology (*kalam*), and also as the prefiguration of the *Guide of the Perplexed* of Maimonides, since it intends to function as a complete handbook regarding the beliefs to be accepted and those to be rejected. With the composition of the *Book of Beliefs and Convictions*, Saadya succeeded to attain a double objective. On the one hand, he found a way to articulate the Jewish creed using the language and the thought system of the Islamic rationalists (*mutakallimun*), and on the other hand, he also found the *kalam*ic solution for the demonstration of those articles of faith which are specific for Rabbanite Judaism (e.g., the impossibility of the abrogation of the law revealed on Mount Sinai, and that of the validity of the oral tradition).

THE SEFER YEZIRAH

The *Sefer Yezirah*, Book of Formation, or Book of Creation, is considered to be the earliest extant Hebrew text of systematic speculative thought. It consists of no more than 1600 words and its solemn and enigmatic style makes it one of the basic texts of Jewish mysticism. It is extant in two versions: a shorter one which appears in most editions as the book itself, and a longer version which is normally printed as an appendix. The text was probably composed between the third and the sixth centuries in Palestine, and according to Gershom Scholem, the author, a devout Jew with leanings toward mysticism, whose aim was speculative and magical rather than ecstatic, endeavored to "Judaize" non-Jewish speculations of a Gnostic character.[4]

The central topic of the *Sefer Yezirah* is a compact discourse on cosmology and cosmogony. It opens with the declaration that God created the world by means of "32 secret paths of wisdom". These 32 paths, defined as the ten numbers (*sefirot*) and the twenty-two elemental letters of the Hebrew alphabet, are represented as the foundation of all creation. The first four *sefirot* are said to emanate from each other, the first one being the "spirit of the Living God" (*ruah elohim hayyim*). The elements of air, water and fire came into existence through the condensation of this first ether-like element. The primal air created by God became engraved by the twenty-two letters and the universe resulted, whereas the primal waters generated the cosmic chaos, and from the primal fire the Throne of Glory and the host of the angels came into being. The remaining six *sefirot* represent the six dimensions of space. The ten *sefirot* constitute a closed unit, since "their end is in their beginning and their beginning in their end" and "they revolve in each other".

All the beings in the three strata of cosmos, in the world, in time, and in man's body, came into existence through the interconnection of the twenty-two letters and by way of the 231 gates, i.e., the combinations of the letters into groups of two. The twenty-two basic letters are divided into three groups by the author of the *Sefer Yezirah*. The first group contains the three matrices (*immot*): the letters *alef*, *mem*, and *sin*. They represent the three basic elements (air, water and fire), the three seasons of the year (summer, winter and the transitional season), and the three parts of the human body (head, torso and stomach). The second group consists of seven "double letters" (*beth*, *gimmel*, *daleth*, *kaf*, *pe*, *res*, *tav*), those consonants which have a hard and soft pronunciation

4 See, for instance, the article of Gershom Scholem in the *Encyclopedia Judaica*, vol. 16, cc 782-788 and on its commentaries, see, for example, Vajda's articles (1947, 1949, 1953, 1954, 1963).

when written with or without a point. Through the medium of the double letters were created the seven planets, the seven heavens, the seven days of the week, and the seven orifices of the human body. The twelve remaining "simple letters" correspond to the twelve signs of the zodiac, the twelve months of the year, and the twelve chief limbs of the human body.

In addition, the author gives a phonetic division of the letters into five groups according to the place of the mouth where they are articulated (gutturals, labials, velars, dentals and sibilants).

SAADYA'S COMMENTARY ON THE SEFER YEZIRAH

The manner in which Saadya comments on the text of the *Sefer Yezirah* is somewhat unlike his commentaries on Biblical books. While interpreting the various books of the Bible, his commentary generally follows the text quite closely, often verse by verse, whereas in the *Commentary on the Sefer Yezirah* he usually composes longer, almost independent treatises commenting on larger portions of the text. For Saadya, the translation of the text into Arabic, or its paraphrase, is part of the Commentary. Thus, he also translates the sometimes quite obscure text of the *Sefer Yezirah* into Arabic, often in a way which renders it fit for his interpretive framework. Moreover, he introduced divisions into the text, dividing it into chapters and paragraphs. The sequence of the chapters of the *Commentary on the Sefer Yezirah* is as follows:[5]

The text opens with a methodological introduction (pp 4-16), in which Saadya states that the *Sefer Yezirah* is a speculative search for the originating principle of all visible beings. He legitimizes philosophy by arguing that it is an activity analogous to the acts of the Creator, and establishes its harmony with the Biblical precepts. In the second part of this chapter he discusses the 'vision' of Abraham as described in the *Sefer Yezirah*. Therein, it is stated that Abraham, the patriarch, was able to arrive at an understanding of how things were created in an illuminative experience. Further, (pp 17-40) he discusses two types of wisdom, one attainable to the perception of the subject, the other

5 In the exposition of the content of the chapters, I have focused on the passages with a philosophical relevance and have ignored the lengthy passages dealing with phonetics, the linguistic explanation of Biblical words, astronomy, etc.

remaining beyond it. In the second part of the chapter, Saadya defines the way in which he thinks Abraham, the patriarch, could have arrived at an understanding of how things were created, namely through its representation in his mind. The following analogy is established as the most fitting way to represent the work of creation: between the symmetry of the numeric system and its starting from the number one, and God's creative activity, equally symmetrical, and also starting from the uniqueness of the Creator. In the second part of the chapter, Saadya demonstrates that the traces of God's creative activity are present in all realms of existence.

The second chapter of the *Commentary on the Sefer Yezirah* (pp 41-58) elaborates upon the 'three propositions': (1) the timelessness of wisdom, (2) the three epistemologically significant faculties of the soul, and (3) the "flash-like" (illuminative) character of knowledge. The last part of the chapter treats the laws according to which letters can be combined with each other, and asserts that the sensible differences between beings result from the differences in the proportionality of the numbers and letters lying at their basis. It also affirms the immanence of the Creator in His creation, which is held to be analogous to the way in which the number one indwells in the whole numeric system.

The third chapter (pp 59-71) treats the excellence of the number one, which, in comparison with the rest of the numbers, renders it suitable to represent the relation between the Creator and His creatures. The multiplication of numbers and the resulting exponential increase is also discussed, and a parallel is drawn between the infinite variability within the numeric system and that of the accidents in the work of creation.

The fourth chapter (pp 72-89) first focuses on the various ways in which letters can be joined together, the description of the way in which God dwells in the world.

Chapters 5-8 (pp 90-101) offer general rules and individual examples of how changes in the proportionality of the elements of which a creature consists results in the transformation of their visible character.

THE TWO PATHS TO KNOWLEDGE: EXTERNALIST FOUNDATIONALISM AND INTERNALIST COHERENTISM

It is always a risky enterprise to explain or to classify the thought of a medieval philosopher by using terms which were coined in the twentieth century. We can neither ignore that more than one thousand years has passed since Saadya composed his books, nor can we forget the differences that exist between the two cultures: that of the religious debates of the tenth century East and that of contemporary 'post-modern' Anglo-Saxon and Continental thought. I, however, shall attempt to compare and to draw certain parallelisms between them, as it is my strong conviction that the above described differences between Saadya's two epistemological approaches can be better understood in light of the categories of externalism-internalism and of foundationalism-coherentism, respectively.

THE QUESTION OF EXTERNALISM/INTERNALISM AND FOUNDATIONALISM/COHERENTISM IN CONTEMPORARY EPISTEMOLOGY

The most generally accepted account of the distinction externalism/internalism treats theories of justification: "a theory of justification is *internalist* if and only if it requires that all of the factors needed for a belief to be epistemologically justified for a given person be *cognitively accessible* to that person, *internal* to his cognitive perspective; and *externalist*, if it allows that at least some of the justifying factors need not be thus accessible, so that they can be *external* to the believer's cognitive perspective, beyond his ken."[6] In a broader sense, however, all the epistemological theories, according to which knowledge can be defined as 'justified true belief',[7] are to be considered as externalist.[8] To

6 Bonjour, p 132.

7 'Justified true belief' is the so called 'tripartite' account of knowledge, which is often completed by a fourth condition, namely, that the addition of further truths should not defeat it (quadripartite account).

8 See Dancy (1985), pp 4-5.

state it otherwise : "the externalist holds that a belief may be fully justified if it has certain properties which we may call truth-effective; to fix ideas...,[and] the internalist claims that justification can only be achieved by appeal to elements that are internal to the agent's perspective".[9]

According to the externalist approach, the process of cognition occurs in four steps: (1) there is a 'fact', (2) this 'fact' causes the belief of the person, (3) the belief is justified, and (4) it is justified because the 'fact' in question is true. The 'internalist' adds a fifth statement to the above described four: (5) the person believes that the fact is true. This fifth step signals an 'internalist turn', and it implies that truth can be defined as an assent or insight of the person, rather than some sort of correspondence between a fixed set of unquestioned 'facts' and a personal belief.

(Foundationalism) Thus the externalist approach is dualistic in nature. It needs a doubtless and totally certain foundation in comparison to which a certain belief can or cannot be justified. In this manner, the complete set of beliefs a person holds can be classified as (a) beliefs which can support others and need no support themselves (foundation), and (b) those needing support from others (superstructure). Coherentism, conversely, has a one-layered structure. It does not treat 'objective facts' external to the mind as a sort of foundation, rather it is based on a finite set of information within the ken of the knower and each single known item entails the whole set.[10] Thus, it is more similar to a flexible framework than to a row of basic statements or perceptions. Euclidean geometry provides a perfect example for classical foundationalism.[11] Therein, each piece of concrete information hinges on a very limited numbers of axioms. Knowledge is of a twofold, hierarchical structure, i.e., each single known item is either a basic unquestionable axiom, or a concrete statement derived from one of the basic axioms by clearly defined logical methods. Without the axioms as basic truths, the system would not stand. Thus, the structure of inferential knowledge is ultimately of an explanatory and deductive nature. Another example of foundationalism is empiricism, where sensory states and

9 Dancy (1992), pp 94-95.

10 Dancy (1985), p 8.

11 See Rescher, p 698.

immediate experience function as a non-inferential base of all knowledge. According to this view, epistemology appears to mean "a research program which sets out to show how it is that our beliefs about the external world... can be justified on a base which is restricted to infallible beliefs about our sensory states".[12] Empiricism in this sense is equal to verificationism and thus it necessarily embodies the foundational assymetries (i.e., knowledge is either immediate, and gained directly from the senses, or it is of a secondary, indirect and logically inferred character).

Coherentism, on the other hand, presupposes a network-model, in which things are viewed as an interlacing network of connections. What determines correctness here is a matter of over-all fit, through which every element of the whole interlocks with some others. In this epistemological framework there are no absolutely fixed pivot-points, and instead of fundamentality, enmeshment (a multiplicity of linkages and the patterns of interconnectedness) plays a decisive role determining what truth is. For instance, grammatical systems, wherein mutual coherence is the arbiter of acceptability, function in this way. According to the view of Rescher,[13] coherentism assumes an entirely inward orientation: it does not seek to compare the truth candidates directly with "the facts" outside the epistemic context; rather, having gathered in as much information about the fact as possible, it seeks to sift the true from the false within this body. In this approach, the validation of an item of knowledge means the rationalization of its inclusion alongside others, based on its interrelationship with the rest. Thus, known items must all be linked together in a connected, mutually supportive way rather than having the form of an inferential structure built upon a bedrock of axioms. The coherentist model operates with the equation "justified" = "systematized". The regulative ideal for the organization of knowledge is systematicity, and the basic epistemological aim does not appear to be the explanation of concrete items in a deductive way, or the judgment about their truth-value, but rather the investigation of how well they fit into a framework.[14]

12 Dancy (1985), p 9.

13 In this characterization of coherentism I have relied on Rescher's article (ibid.), pp 698-705.

14 For Dancy and Rescher the externalist approach implies a foundationalist view, and internalism is connected to coherentism. The classification of Bonjour (p 133) is slightly different. According

EXTERNALISM IN THE BOOK OF BELIEFS AND CONVICTIONS

The *Book of Beliefs and Convictions* very clearly exhibits the characteristics of an externalist epistemological system. In this system, knowledge appears to be based on the correspondence of sense perception and universal intuition. While the intellect has at its disposal all the means to achieve a correct understanding, by itself and based only on its capacities it is totally unable to obtain knowledge. This phenomenon is well illustrated by the model of the elimination of uncertainties in ten steps.[15] There sense perception functions as the 'raw material' of cognition, and it is by and through the classification and the 'digestion' of the jumbled data of the external world that the intellect achieves the act of cognition. The sources of knowledge are clearly divided into external and internal ones, and during the process of the acquisition of knowledge the intellect can by no means avoid the sense data which are external to it.

In the *Book of Beliefs and Convictions* then human knowledge is based upon the meeting and the coincidence of an external and an internal factor. The faculty of sense perception, which provides data from the objective world for the soul, is the external basis of cognition, and the immediate knowledge of the intellect serves as its internal foundation. Thus, without the external factor knowledge could not be generated. In this system sense data (*mahsusat*) and the immediate knowledge of the intellect (*ma`qulat*) function as mirrors for each other. The fact that they are created in such a manner that they fit together and complete each other reflects the perfection of the plan of creation, on the one hand, and Saadya's epistemological optimism on the other hand.[16] The cornerstones of Saadya's epistemology, such as the notions of speculation, conviction, truth and

---

to him, foundationalism may be of an internalist nature, if foundational beliefs pertain to immediately experienced states of mind, that is, that they are reflectively accessible. The view labeled by Dancy and Rescher as externalist foundationalism or empiricism, according to which sense perceptions figure as the bases of all knowledge, is classified by Bonjour as reliabilism (p 133). In my opinion, this difference is more terminological usage than essential.

15 *Book of Beliefs and Convictions*, pp 8-11.

16 Saadya openly states in the *Book of Beliefs and Convictions* that the 'nature of creation' is adjusted to human knowledge: "God created as many bodies as He knew we would be capable of taking cognizance of and holding in our minds and as would suffice to serve us as a proof of His sovereignty" (p 85).

belief, are established to be based on the correspondence of the external and the internal sources of knowledge. If the external part is overlooked, the internal source in itself becomes non-efficient and meaningless.

FOUNDATIONALISM IN THE BOOK OF BELIEFS AND CONVICTIONS

At the beginning of the *Book of Beliefs and Convictions*, Saadya affirms that "(t)he principles of the intellect are based (*kanat qawa`iduha mawdu`a*) on the perception of the senses".[17] This means that the immediate knowledge of the intellect (*ma`qul*), in its entirety, follows the line of the sense data (*mahsus*). In fact, the concepts of the intellect are crystallized around sense data and derived from them. The major difficulty met by the human mind when attempting to conceive such notions as the creation ex nihilo, that of the soul or of God, lies in this, i.e., that humans have never witnessed anything like these concepts by the perception of their senses. Elsewhere in the *Book of Beliefs and Convictions*, while criticizing those who understand the anthropomorphic statements about God in the Bible in a literal sense, Saadya states that "an edifice is always built from the foundation upward, never from the top down".[18] By this he means that the first thing to be assured of is that sense perception reflects objective reality,[19] but it does not mean that all statements made by a language shaped by sense perception must be taken in a univocal material sense. Further proof of the externalist foundationalist approach in the *Book of Beliefs and Convictions* is the explicit affirmation that "all objects of knowledge are comprehended through the mediation of the body".[20]

17 *Book of Beliefs and Convictions*, p 2.

18 *al-bina' innama yubna min al-asas ila fawq laysa yubna min fawq ila asfal (Book of Beliefs and Convictions*, p 97)

19 The same statement is made in the *Commentary on the Sefer Yezirah* about the establishment of the reality of things (*ithbat al-haqa'iq*), namely that "at first we establish that these senses do not bring us but reality, so that this light is light in reality..." (*innama nuqirr awwalan bi-anna hadhihi-'l-hawass la tu'addi ilayna illa haqqan fa-hadha-'n-nur nur `ala-'l-haqiqa,...*) (*Commentary on the Sefer Yezirah*, pp 42-43).

20 *gami` al-ma` lumat innama tu` lam bi-tawassut al-gism* (*Book of Beliefs and Convictions*, p 81).

It would, however, be overly simplistic to label the epistemological system of the *Book of Beliefs and Convictions* as mere empiricism or naïve realism. The ascertainment of the fact that sense perception functions as the bedrock of all knowledge is only the beginning of the process of cognition. Moreover, the 'immediate knowledge of the intellect' or 'universal intuition' implanted in the mind by God and thus unattainable to direct sense perception, is another indispensable condition of all human knowledge.[21] Saadya does not only vehemently criticize those who make objective reality dependent upon their personal views. He also turns against the proponents of the doctrine of the eternity of the world saying that "they believe only in what is subject to the perception of their senses",[22] and that they are unable to see that "there is a science that was first served by the sense of sight and then expressed by the faculty of speech."[23] Elsewhere, he affirms that "the foundation and the axle of the entire book [Scripture] (*qa`ida gami` al-kitab wa-qutbuhu*) is [the fact] that there is nothing that resembles Him [God], and He does not resemble any of His works".[24] At this point a question arises: if God is totally transcendent and unreachable by even the most sophisticated speculation of the intellect based on sense perception, on what basis may we make any statement about Him? The answer to this question is given in treatise 6 of the *Book of Beliefs and Convictions* (About the Soul). There Saadya asserts that the soul's substance is more refined and subtle than that of the heavenly spheres and that "it has such a profound wisdom and subtle understanding by which the world is sustained".[25] Elsewhere he asserts that "it [the soul] goes so far as to know even that which is above heaven and earth by vir-

21 For example, the approbation of truthfulness and the disapproval of mendacity, or the axiom that one and the same object cannot be existent and non-existent at the same time, and the impossibility of contraries.

22 *innahum la yusaddiquna illa bima waqa` `alayhi hissuhum* (*Book of Beliefs and Convictions*, p 65).

23 *hahuna `ilman khadimathu hassat al-basar ibtida'an wa-a` raba `anhu-'l-mantiq (Book of Beliefs and Convictions*, p 67).

24 *Book of Beliefs and Convictions*, p 82.

25 *laha hikma `azima wa-afham galila allati biha qawam ad-dunya* (*Book of Beliefs and Convictions*, p 195).

tue of which they exist, I mean the Creator, exalted and sanctified be He".[26] Thus, the invisible soul also functions as a kind of foundation, even if not in the same manner as sense perception.[27] As noted above, sense perception is the "raw-material" of knowledge. The soul, on the other hand, cannot be conceived as a visible basis near to the senses. Rather, it is a notion of such an exalted nature that in an instinctive and inarticulate way it contains all the knowledge of the world, including the knowledge of the Creator. In light of the fact that in the *Book of Beliefs and Convictions* all knowledge is based on two foundations, that of sense perception and that of the potential omniscience of the human soul, I would argue that the epistemology of the *Book of Beliefs and Convictions* can be classified as a sort of 'double foundationalism'.[28] At first glance it appears to be based on sense perception, but ultimately it is founded on the special substance of the human soul.

26 *hatta balagat ila-'l-ma`rifa bima fawqahuma alladhi bihi yakun qawamuhuma a` ni al-bari' ta` ala wa-taqaddasa* (*Book of Beliefs and Convictions*, p 152).

27 After a perusal of the two books, it can be asserted that Saadya uses the concept of basis or foundation (*asl, asas*), in two senses. In the system of the *Book of Beliefs and Convictions*, in which the process of cognition requires a certain period of time, it means a 'starting point', a 'primary stage', or 'a basis whence knowledge is derived', which, with time and with the refinement of the process, becomes less and less important. In the *Commentary on the Sefer Yezirah*, on the other hand, where knowledge is illuminative, the notion of 'foundation' has no temporal dimension. It is of an ontological nature, sustaining the world from within, and its importance as 'arkhe' does not fade away with the passing of time.

28 The above described 'twofold nature' of knowledge, is also noted by Efros. In his article, he argues that Saadya's epistemology is a confluence of Platonic and Aristotelian theories of knowledge. He asserts that Saadya's notion of the soul, which contains all knowledge, comes from the Platonic tradition, whereas the strong accent on the role and importance of sense perception in the process of cognition can be retraced to Aristotelian and Stoic origins. If the focus is the ultimate historical origins of certain crucial concepts in Saadya's philosophy, and if we understand the 'Aristotelian' and 'Platonic' type of thinking in a broad sense, this statement proves to be true. It, however, does not shed much light on the way in which Saadya's epistemological system coheres, nor does it pay anything but scant attention to the epistemological differences between Saadya's works.

INTERNALISM IN THE COMMENTARY ON THE SEFER YEZIRAH

Prior to addressing the question of what internalism means in the context of the epistemology of the *Commentary on the Sefer Yezirah*, I think it is useful to distinguish between the notions of 'internalism' and of 'internalization'.

In the closing remarks of the *Book of Beliefs and Convictions* ,[29] Saadya asks the reader the following question: "Seest thou not that, in such matters as things seen and heard and food and drink, much better results are achieved with the help of the intention of the heart[30] than without it?" It is fair to ask what the meaning of this "intention of the heart" is in a book of a clearly externalist nature. I would argue that in the present context, it refers to the notion of "internalized faith", that is, the strongest type of conviction. Conviction, as demonstrated above, is based on the coincidence of external objective reality (*haqiqa*) and personal attachment. The perfect believers are those who "attain the truth, are cognizant of it and rejoice in it". Due to their firm belief, they are on a higher rank than those who "attain the truth but are nevertheless in doubt concerning it, being neither fully convinced nor firmly grasping it". Lower yet are those who "for a while follow one system of thought and then abandon it on account of some flaw noticed in it, and in this manner remain unsettled throughout life".[31] That means that the soul, which knows by means of its essence (*`alima li-dhatiha*), once having arrived at the truth must firmly attach itself to it and remain united with it. This process, during which a simple opinion is at first well-articulated, then proven, then believed, and then finally becomes an organic part of the soul, can be referred to as "internalization". The final stage of this process is described by Saadya as follows: "Now when a person has achieved the knowledge of this lofty subject by means of rational speculation (*nazar*) and the proof of the miracles and marvels [mentioned in the Holy Writ], his soul believes it as certain and it is mingled with his spirit and becomes an inmate of its innermost recesses…(*ayqanat bihi nafsuhu wa-*

29 *Book of Beliefs and Convictions*, p 324.

30 Intention of the heart: in the Arabic text: *qasd al-qulub*. Rosenblatt translates it as "concentration of the mind" (p 408), which is not a literal translation.

31 See *Book of Beliefs and Convictions*, pp 4-5.

mazaga ruhuhu wa-sara laha fi khuduriha mawgudan)".[32] This "internalization", however, is "externalist" in nature insofar as speculation is dependent upon 'objective facts' in the first instance.

"Internalism", on the other hand, implies that the process of cognition has little recourse to "objective facts", but from the outset is based on introspection. The theory of the *Commentary on the Sefer Yezirah* proceeds in this way. When the text of the *Sefer Yezirah* states that everything is created by the ten numbers and the twenty-two letters, Saadya is aware of the fact that there is no way to demonstrate this statement in objective reality. He even refutes the opinion of those who seek perceptible proofs for this statement. For example, some hold "that the form of most constellations and the parts of the body appear to be similar to those of the letters referred to by the author of the book [*Sefer Yezirah*]".[33] In response, Saadya argues that as each being is created by the whole set of thirty-two (ten numbers and twenty-two letters), we cannot make a direct comparison between the visible forms and those intuited by the mind. Thereby, he rejects the very foundation of externalism, namely, that perceptible facts serve as bases for the concepts of the intellect.[34]

Numbers and letters, the basic building blocks of both creation and of the understanding of the intellect, are from their very nature, unattainable to the senses. Therefore, as opposed to seeking visible proofs, Saadya adopts the "internalist" solution. He asserts that as the human intellect is analogous to that of the divine, the best way for us to conceive of the work of the creation is to represent it by the basic elements of our understanding (i.e., numbers and letters). Analogy (*muqabala*) appears to be a way to conceive of things rather than a visible evidence (*dalil*) *per se*. Thus, to support the validity of the text of the *Sefer Yezirah*, Saadya makes use of an "internalist" solution, and so relies exclusively on elements internal to the agent's perspective.

32 *Book of Beliefs and Convictions*, p 112.

33 *surat akthar al-kawakib wa-'l-a'da' 'ala surat al-huruf allati nasabaha ilayha sahib hadha-'l-kitab* (*Commentary on the Sefer Yezirah*, p 89).

34 In the *Commentary on the Sefer Yezirah* Saadya accepts the testimony of the senses as a valid general source of knowledge, but in the case of the present statement, namely, that the world is created by numbers and letters, the direct use of perceptible facts as proof (*istidlal*) is clearly excluded.

COHERENTISM IN THE COMMENTARY ON THE SEFER YEZIRAH

As discussed earlier, coherentism presupposes (1) an inward orientation, (2) a network-model, and (3) systematicity.

(1) The *Commentary on the Sefer Yezirah* has a tendency to view the work of creation from an inward orientation, as established above.

(2) The network-model is provided by the text of the *Sefer Yezirah* itself. The text no doubt represented a challenge to Saadya, as it is not to comment on it in the rational "*mutakallim* style" which, again, is based on sense perception and on the immediate knowledge of the intellect. Thus, in order to bring the text of the *Sefer Yezirah* nearer to the understanding, he resorted to a style, more internalist and coherentist in nature, that of the "gnosticizing philosophers"[35] of Islam.

(3) Numbers and letters, the basic elements of creation as posited by the text of the *Sefer Yezirah*, from their very essence do not have a meaning or an independent existence in themselves. Letters always occur in words, and numbers are conceived as the "dividing principles between the substances and the parts".[36] Thus, they construct the creatures, material and immaterial, by their interconnection or by their "network". In the two "supplementary propositions" (*al-qawlani al-lahiqani*) of the *Commentary on the Sefer Yezirah* Saadya illustrates the order of creation as follows: "each time the numbers reach ten they return and recur for ever, endlessly for us…, and in the same way, the letters are repeated endlessly, they follow in succession, and they are interconnected endlessly as it appears to us".[37] Their proces-

35 Like that of the Sincere Brethren (*Ikhwan as-Safa'*).

36 *biha tanfasil al-gawahir wa-'l-agza'* (*Commentary on the Sefer Yezirah*, p 12).

37 *al-a`dad kullama balagat ila 'yud'* [10] *ta`ud wa-tatakarrar abadan bila nihaya `indana,…, kadhalika fi-'l-huruf innaha tatakarrar abadan wa-tataradaf wa-tata`aqad bila nihaya* (*Commentary on the Sefer Yezirah*, p 44-45).

sion is similar to that of the angels or to a "wind-storm (*sufa*) in the air".[38] The ontology of the *Commentary on the Sefer Yezirah* is based on systemic relations between elements which have no independent existence. Higher numbers are conceived of as systems subsisting by the mutual sustenance of lower numbers. For instance, the number seven is to be conceived as of two groups of three opposing one another and one [person] who judges between them. The number sixteen is similar to sixteen persons in a war: four kill, and four revive, four are revived and four are killed, and the sixteen stay together as long as they fight. Thus, numbers in Saadya's representation do not have independent substances behind them. They figure as temporary constructions, finite for the Creator and infinite for humans. They all are derived from the One, and if the One disappears, all numbers lose existence. In the work of creation, each creature is connected to the rest, since everything is created by the ten numbers and the twenty two letters (*al-kull-bi-'l-kull*).[39] Space itself, created by the six permutations of the three letters in God's name, is founded on interconnection: "the six directions of the world [:] higher and lower, East and West, and South and North are joined together by the power [of God's name]".[40] Finally, the statement that "each two are separated by a third balancing between them"[41] makes univocally clear that the deep-structure of all creatures is based on interconnection. Thus, sensual perception of facts and objects as sharply distinct is only a superficial impression. In reality, existence has a homogeneous structure wherein the parts are intertwined and form systems which stand in analogy with each other.

38 ibid.

39 See *Commentary on the Sefer Yezirah*, p 70.

40 '*Waw*' [6] *gihat al-`alam [:] al-`uluw wa-'s-sufl wa-'s-sarq wa-'l-garb wa-'l-ganub wa-'s-simal marbuta bi-'l-qudra ba` dan ma` ba` d* (*Commentary on the Sefer Yezirah*, p 87).

41 *kull* '*beth*' [2] *la yatafarraqani illa bi-thalith ya`dil baynahuma* (*Commentary on the Sefer Yezirah*, p 34). Saadya offers examples from various systems, from the field of cosmology: the air balancing between heaven and earth, from the human sphere: the pointer of the scale (*lisan al-mizan*) balancing between the scale-pans, and from law: the existence of a third member of the law court judging in financial cases and thus balancing between the two.

In light of this system, Saadya's definition of wisdom in the *Commentary on the Sefer Yezirah*, as the "arrangement of the things according to their grades and their evaluation according to their range",[42] appears to be the "internalist-coherentist" equivalent of his definition of wisdom in the *Book of Beliefs and Convictions*: "wisdom consists in knowing things as they are in their real observable character, not as someone would desire or like them to be".[43] "Arranging things according to their grades" reflects an ontology wherein things are already arranged into systems[44] and human intelligence, analogous to the divine one, has to "reproduce" the "original" system of the creation on a theoretical, epistemological level. The distinction between the "real observable character", on the one hand, and "the desired character", on the other hand, in the definition of the *Book of Beliefs and Convictions* presupposes an ontology wherein the observation of the senses figures as the "external foundation" to human knowledge.

Ultimately, after having attempted to characterize Saadya's epistemology in the *Book of Beliefs and Convictions* as externalist foundationalism and his theory of knowledge in the *Commentary on the Sefer Yezirah* as internalist coherentism, a last question remains to be answered: do these two frameworks really stand to each other in sharp contradiction? Is it a meaningful question to ask whether the world was created ex nihilo *or* created out of numbers and letters?[45] Or, are these two frameworks simply different approaches to the same problem of creation, examined from different angles and expressed with different terminologies? I would argue for the latter opinion, relying on two authorities: one being a contemporary epistemologist and the other Saadya Gaon himself.

In a recent article,[46] Dancy claims that the long dispute among contemporary epistemologists regarding the preference for *either* externalism *or* internalism is

42 *Commentary on the Sefer Yezirah*, p 43.

43 *Book of Beliefs and Convictions*, p 206.

44 In fact, in the *Commentary on the Sefer Yezirah* Saadya states at various times that "things are arranged in systems and in order (*ʿala nizam wa-tartib*)" (e.g. *Commentary on the Sefer Yezirah*, p 18).

45 For Saadya the alternative of creation *from* letters and numbers is one step short of the theory of the creation ex nihilo. Since the creation ex nihilo is a theory based on speculation, Saadya attempts to offer its visual representation by the creation from numbers and letters.

46 Dancy (1992)

basically meaningless. A trait common to both positions is the assertion that if the belief is justified, the believer is and *vice-versa.*[47] The difference between the two positions appears to be that internalism is agent-centered, whereas externalism appears to be act-centered.[48] Thus, one and the same phenomenon can have either an externalist or an internalist account without excluding the other. That appears to be the case for Saadya. Creation is examined by him from two aspects: as an 'objective' fact in time, clearly provable by "scientific" evidence as in the *Book of Beliefs and Convictions*, and as a phenomenon which functions according to certain laws as in the *Commentary on the Sefer Yezirah.* The two aspects place the agent in different positions of course: the externalist approach of the *Book of Beliefs and Convictions* places him in the position of the objective "observer", whereas according to the internalist stance, he acknowledges that he himself contains the entirety of the laws which direct the whole creation.

CONCLUSION: SAADYA'S AIM IN THE TWO BOOKS

Truth and lie, doubt and certainty, conviction and faith, based on the correspondence, or on the difference between the perception of the senses and the immediate knowledge of the intellect, are of pivotal importance in the epistemology of the *Book of Beliefs and Convictions*, while totally absent in the *Commentary on the Sefer Yezirah.* This difference can be explained by the difference in Saadya's aims with the composition of the two works: whereas the *Book of Beliefs and Convictions* is intended to function as a guide for the perplexed reader, the *Commentary on the Sefer Yezirah* offers an insight into the divine work of creation.

It is a commonplace that Saadya appears to be a continuously argumentative philosopher. Indeed, the tendentiousness underlying the composition of his books may be more easily delineated by finding the ideas against which he wrote rather than searching for direct indications of his intentions. Both books can be conceived as enterprises against two phenomena which are epistemological in nature: the *Book of Beliefs and Convictions* intends to fight against

47 ibid. p 95.

48 ibid. p 97

doubt, hesitation and uncertainty, while the *Commentary on the Sefer Yezirah* tries to deprive the *Sefer Yezirah* of its literal understanding.

On the whole, the *Book of Beliefs and Convictions* is a long and well articulated response to the challenges caused by the uncertainties and doubts faced by the person belonging to the Jewish community of the 10th century Arabic Caliphate. In the introductory part of the book,[49] Saadya remarks with sorrow that "some of these uncertainties so intrigue some persons that in their fancy and belief they become established truths". The opposite of doubt is certainty (*tahaqquq*) and for Saadya it is equivalent to rationally established firm belief. Saadya intends to dispel doubts through a demonstration of the correct method of thinking, which he holds is the only remedy. The notion of belief functions in Saadya as a purely epistemological category. It can be translated as 'truth internalized by the soul as strong conviction'. Doubt or uncertainty, on the other hand, are either partly 'digested' truth, or completely or incompletely internalized untruth.

In the *Book of Beliefs and Convictions* Saadya treats doubt and uncertainty as negative phenomena, as the illness of the human mind, and he attempts to unveil their causes with the care of an accurate physician. The issue of the causes emerges on three levels:

(1) On an individual psychological level, namely, if one suffers from doubts, why does one not engage in speculation about religious doctrines? (2) On the level of the thinking process in general, i.e., what sort of factors may possibly result in a confusion of the thinking process which alone is enabled to dissolve the uncertainties? And finally (3) on the most general existential level: If God is good, and a work of creation is a result of His bounty and His grace, and if truth is so evident, then how can uncertainty and doubt exist at all?

(1) Saadya's response to the first, rather formal, question is the mere enumeration of external situational causes on the one hand, for example, a persuasive speech of the godless or animosity amongst monotheists, and weaknesses of character on the other hand, such as too much concern for bodily appetites or laziness.[50]

49 *Book of Beliefs and Convictions*, p 4.

50 *Book of Beliefs and Convictions*, pp 29-30.

(2) On the level of cognition, confusion may arise both in the realm of sensation (*mahsusat*) and in that of the intelligible notions (*ma`qulat*). It is at this point that Saadya establishes the first golden rule of his didactic system: "The concepts of the intellect are based (*kanat qawa`iduha mawdu`a*) on the perception of the senses".[51] In light of this statement, Saadya's whole epistemological system was often labeled as empirical rationalism, or even as naïve empiricism. I would argue that the situation is much more complex than that.

We constantly have to keep in mind that the *Book of Beliefs and Convictions* is a didactically constructed guideline for people "sunk in the ocean of doubts", and that this statement of Saadya, although it is of crucial importance, represents but one half of his opinion. The other half of the truth (i. e. that the soul knows by its essence, and that sensation is of pivotal importance because of the help it can provide to the soul for strengthening its belief) is told much later, in treatise 6. Moreover, I would like to argue that Saadya, proceeding step by step, using explanatory methods which are "near and not far" (*qariba wa-laysa ba`ida*) from the abilities of human comprehension, develops the entirety of his epistemological system gradually, starting from the least problematic aspect of cognition which is shared by the whole of the human species and even by animals: sensation.

In the field of sensation, the first cause of confusion is "that the seeker is not sufficiently acquainted with the object of his search"; the second is that "he [the seeker] takes his task lightly and falls short in the thoroughness and persistency of his quest".[52] The first cause is of interest here, as the second one, impatience, falls rather more neatly into the category of individual psychological problems discussed in the previous point. The first cause appears to imply that the seeker must have some previous knowledge concerning the object of his search. If, though, the process of cognition starts from sensation, it needs to be asked where this previous knowledge comes from.[53] In the realm of the

51 *Book of Beliefs and Convictions*, p 2.

52 ibid.

53 The concrete example Saadya gives for this first cause of confusion does not leave any doubt about the required existence of a previous knowledge in the process of cognition. The example goes as follows: "If a person were to seek Reuben, the son of Jacob, he could be in doubt about him for only one of two reasons: either because he does not know him well, so that the latter

concepts of the intellect, the second cause of confusion is impatience. Thus, it is similar to the second (psychological) cause in the realm of sensation.[54] The third cause refers to that knowledge which precedes sensation,[55] and the second cause[56] touches upon the knowledge of the intellect which, although it requires sense data, in its totality cannot be derived directly from sensation.

(3) On the existential level, i.e., why is there any doubt and uncertainty at all, Saadya's answer is based on the fact of the createdness *per se*: "Their very being created entities (*kawnuhum makhluqin*) necessitates their uncertainties and illusions."[57] Immediately after this statement he refers to the design of creation (*rasm al-khaliqa*), whereby humans require a span of time for each act they perform. Cognition then, being one of the human acts, requires time too, as does understanding. On this level, doubt and uncertainty do not represent the opposite of firm conviction, but are rather the starting point of the way of cognition leading to it.

In the *Commentary on the Sefer Yezirah* doubt and uncertainty do not present any danger. The enemy Saadya wages war against here is 'interpretation in the material sense' (*tagsim*), or 'univocal understanding' (*tahdid*). Commenting on the text of the *Sefer Yezirah*, his methods and intentions are in complete opposition to those in the *Book of Beliefs and Convictions*. In the latter book he attempts to establish univocal definitions and terms by use of the terminology of the *kalam*. Conversely, in the *Commentary on the Sefer Yezirah* Saadya intends to persuade the reader not to understand the text of the *Sefer Yezirah* in the literal sense, but rather to take it as epitome (*talkhis*), as metaphorical expression (*ta'bir*), or as a mere allusion (*talwih*).

---

might be standing before him without being recognized by him, or he might see someone else and think he is Reuben,..." (ibid.) Thus, without the previous knowledge of the person the whole search process appears to be senseless.

54 "...he takes the quickest and easiest course so that he jumps at the conclusion before having completed the task of reasoning about it." (*Book of Beliefs and Convictions*, p 3).

55 "...the seeker does not know what he is seeking" (ibid.)

56 "...the seeker of intellectual knowledge is unacquainted with the methods of inference (*istidlal*), so that he declares a valid proof (*dalil*) to be no proof and, conversely, he declares what is no proof to be a valid proof...." (ibid.)

57 *Book of Beliefs and Convictions*, p 7.

The creation of the world is a unique divine act, and as such it was unwitnessed. Being unwitnessed and totally unattainable to the senses, the models of cognition elaborated in the *Book of Beliefs and Convictions* which rely upon sense perception are not able to reach its essence. Nor can it be described by a precise and univocal vocabulary. Thus, all that can be said about the work of creation must be understood in a figurative sense (*magaz*). Whereas in the process of cognition based upon sense perception the conceived reality (thanks to the reliability of the senses) coincides with objective reality, in the case of 'unique' phenomena, such as God, the soul or creation, sense perception is totally useless, as the aforementioned phenomena are beyond its reach.

In the *Book of Beliefs and Convictions*, Saadya establishes and proves the fact of creation ex nihilo, but he does not pose the 'how' question, since it escapes all concrete demonstrability. The question as to how or according to what "method" the world was created is answered by the text of the *Sefer Yezirah*, with the condition that the text be taken in the metaphorical sense due to the subtle nature of the object. As Saadya states it: "We can arrive at this only by our thoughts (*fi fikrina*) but we cannot arrive at the understanding of its reality (*wa-laysa nasil ila fi `lihi haqiqan*)".[58] Or, as he states it elsewhere: "When we say that He pressed, filtered, etc., we do not mean that He fabricated (*sana `a*) the things by parts (*ab `adan*), one part after the other. We only intend an introduction (*tawti'a*) and facilitation (*taqdir*) for our understanding, that is, how we can fathom [creation]. Ultimately, we retrace everything to [the statement] that He created it all at one time (*daf`a wahida*)".[59] This procedure of explaining divine acts, otherwise unattainable by the senses, through their 'translation' into the terminology of temporal activities (occurring step by step), is referred to as *taqrib* 'approximation, bringing close (to the human understanding)'.

The intentions underlying the composition of his two books are organically interwoven with the nature of the audience Saadya addressed in his works. The public addressed by the *Book of Beliefs and Convictions* is ultimately the educated members of the Jewish community who had doubts or who were exposed to critique. It is supposed to help the reader both to fight his own

58 *Commentary on the Sefer Yezirah*, p 99.

59 *Commentary on the Sefer Yezirah*, p 85.

uncertainty and to refute opponents. The *Commentary on the Sefer Yezirah*, on the other hand, is intended for a small group of readers, who, considering the text of the *Sefer Yezirah* as an accurate description of the creation, a book revealed to Abraham the patriarch, took it in the literal sense. By commenting on the text, Saadya attempts to exclude it from the realm of discursive understanding, thereby placing it in the domain of metaphorical representation of an event escaping argumentative demonstration.

Thus, in a conclusive way, we may notice that not only Medieval authors in general, but even one and the same thinker may occasionally have the possibility to articulate a certain content (e.g. the creation of the world, eschatology, or exegetical questions) in more than one register, depending on the nature of the situation, on the character of his audience and on his intention. In this sense both Jewish and Muslim thinkers had the capacity to treat religious topics either in an extensive or in an intensive way; i.e. either to rely on obvious sources of human cognition, like the perception of the senses, or to take a more adventurous path and to attempt to offer a kind of allegorical description of God or at least of His works. The history of (medieval) thought abounds in debates between diverse theological schools and worldviews. The exegetical polyvalence of Biblical and Qur'anic texts renders it possible for the authors to express diverse views and to construct diverse philosophical models based on the same verses. After a careful examination, however, in many cases the apparent differences can be reduced to a difference of aspects without invalidating the other view. While analyzing medieval Islamic and Jewish thought-structures it becomes clear that very often we find a strong resemblance between Jewish and Islamic thinkers belonging to the same school, while they stand in sharp contradiction with another school of the same religion.[60] Thus, although this simultaneous use of two different tones may result in apparent contradictions between two texts for the superficial reader, in fact it is only the expression of an "epistemological polyphony" so characteristic of Medieval thought.

60 For example the language and terminology of Jewish and Islamic Neo-Platonists are extremely similar, while both groups were marginalized and silenced by the mainstream Jewish or Muslim orthodoxy. The problem of Jewish and Islamic *kalam* appears to be more complex. Concerning questions as the *creation ex nihilo*, or of God's "undescribability" they offer the same solutions. Conversely, even if they use the same terminology, they differ on questions of the criteria of prophecy, the non-abrogation of Mosaic law etc.

EMBARRASSMENT AS A CREATIVE FORCE IN MAIMONIDES' META-HALAKHIC ENUMERATION OF THE 613 COMMANDMENTS

Albert Dov Friedberg, University of Toronto

Maimonides' Enumeration of the 613 Commandments is an attempt to divide the totality of material constituting the legal portion of the Torah into separate units based on common sense taxonomic principles and rabbinic indications. This division, or individuation, presupposes a broad categorization of the legal material. Maimonides confirms this approach in Rule 7 of his methodology but yet goes on to include in his enumeration certain laws that appear to be only details of much broader laws. For example, positive commandments # 175, #178 and #179 do not meet the criteria of broad laws as they appear to be details of the overall commandments to set up courts and/or to dispense justice. At the same time, their designation does not enjoy specific rabbinic support. While generally individuations are undertaken by legal philosophers to allow for exposition of the legal order, I suggest in this paper that Maimonides may have had other reasons to justify the decision to individuate these three partly related commandments.

Maimonides opens the Introduction to the Code of Law with a verse from Ps (119:7): *Then I would not be ashamed when I regard all Your commandments.* What was the source of his putative embarrassment? In a letter to his close disciple, Joseph ben R. Judah,[1] Maimonides explains that he had undertaken to write the Code for two reasons. First, for himself, as a reference book to consult when he faced pressing legal matters, particularly as he grew older. Second, in his zeal for the glory of God, "in seeing a nation bereft of

1 *Iggerot ha-RaMBaM*, ed.Y. Shailat, vol. 1, p.301.

a truly comprehensive book [*diwan*] of law, and bereft of correct and clear [theological] notions. Therefore I have done what I did, only for the sake of Heaven." Maimonides was not reacting to the impiety of his coreligionists; there is no good reason to believe that the Jews of Cairo and its environs were less punctilious in the observance of the commandments and the study of the Torah than any other Jewish community at the time or in the recent past. Nor does Maimonides appear to complain about the people being so ignorant of the law that he felt impelled to write a Code of Law. What Maimonides does complain about is that the "nation is bereft of a comprehensive book of law, and bereft of correct and clear [theological] notions." Maimonides is embarrassed for and about his people and he wants to act "for the sake of Heaven." What is it all about?

I submit that just possibly Maimonides may have felt a strong sense of embarrassment in front of his royal court colleagues, judges, medics and state administrators. Systematic and comprehensive works of jurisprudence as well as elaborate theological disquisitions circulated widely among the upper strata of Muslim society. By contrast, God's "chosen people" appeared to be intellectually barren. In Maimonides's mind the lack of a *diwan* constituted a *hillul ha-shem*, a profanation of the Name, because the world was likely to ridicule a god that was worshipped by such an intellectually impoverished nation.

Maimonides finds no better way to describe the extraordinary zeal that drove him to undertake the writing of the Code of Law than to quote verbatim the prophet Elijah (Kings I:19:10). The latter, in a fit of zealousness, had exclaimed, *I am moved by zeal for the Lord, the God of Hosts,* in response to the Israelites having forsaken God's covenant, torn down His altars and killed His prophets. The Israelites of Elijah's time, too, had caused God's name to be profaned among the nations. Then and now, God's honor was at stake.

As Kramer has pointed out, Maimonides was immersed in the cultural and intellectual life of Cairo, maintaining close relations with some of the city's most prominent men. He notes, for example, that Abu Imran Musa ibn Maymun al-Qurtubi (as Maimonides was called in Cairo) became a friend and protégé of al-Qadi al-Fadil al-Baysani, Saladin's adviser, chancellor and chief administrator, and perhaps the most powerful political figure in Cairo. In gratitude, Maimonides wrote a treatise *On Poisons and Antidotes* and dedicated it to the Qadi with an extremely generous and laudatory encomium. Through him, Maimonides no doubt became familiar with the workings of the Muslim courts.[2]

Maimonides was not only part of this vibrant cultural milieu, but went so far as to assimilate many linguistic elements of the surrounding milieu into his rulings.[3] Cross-cultural influence can be detected, for instance, in Maimonides' use of Islamic legal terminology, especially in the area of procedural law. Writing with respect to Maimonides' use of the technical terminology of Islamic law in the realm of procedure, Bloomberg says:

> Maimonides' writings are replete with this vocabulary, although, to be sure, he does not always employ Muslim technical terms in precisely the same manner as do the Muslim legal writers. Thus, the parties to a lawsuit are called *khasmān*, as in Muslim law, and the action at law itself is called by the Muslim term *dawā*. In addition, witnesses are called *shuhūd* (singular: *shāhid*), the plaintiff is called *al-muddaī*, the defendant is referred to as *al-muddaā alayhi*, and the object claimed in the action is referred to as *al-muddaa bihī*.
>
> In regard to evidence in particular, the presence of Muslim terminology is striking. Virtually the entire technical vocabulary of Islamic law's system of proof appears in Maimonides. The oral testimony of witnesses — the proof *par excellence* — is termed *bayyina*. An acknowledgement is termed *iqrār*, while a denial is termed *inkār*.
>
> The judicial oath is called *yamīn*, and its refusal is called *nukūl*. A formal legal document, in addition, is termed *wathīqa*.
>
> ...In addition to the very presence of so much of the Muslim technical terminology in Maimonides, that which is most significant is the fact that, in virtually all cases, it can be demonstrated that Maimonides is working with an

2 Kraemer, Joel, "Maimonides' Intellectual Milieu in Cairo," *Maimonide: philosophe et savant (1138-1204)*, eds. Tony Levy and Roshdi Rashid (Leiven: Peeters, 2004).

3 See Libson, Gideon, "Parallels Between Maimonides and Islamic Law," *The Thought of Moses Maimonides: Philosophical and Legal Studies (La Pensée de Maïmonide: études philosophiques et halakhiques)* ed. Ira Robinson et al. (Lewiston, NY: Edwin Mellen Press, 1990). For parallels between Maimonides and the Shāfi'ī school, see Libson, Gideon, "A Guarantee to Present the Debtor: Shmuel ben Hofni's Treatise on Surety, the Responsa of the Geonim, Maimonides and Analogous Muslim Legal Literature," *Shenaton ha-Mishpat ha-Ivry* 13 (1987) and Libson, Gideon, "Surety for Liability in Geonic Literature, Maimonides and Muslim Law [Hebrew]," *Mehqere Talmud*, eds. Y. Sussman and D. Rosenthal, vol. 1 (Jerusalem: 1990).

established usage of Judeo-Arabic legal writing as reflected both in theoretical legal writings and responsa and in court documents from the Genizah.[4]

Given his proximity to the Egyptian administrative and judicial authorities, it would not surprise if Maimonides was anxious to demonstrate that, at the very least, Mosaic laws held their own against Islamic laws.[5] Procedural law was one area where Maimonides may have felt the particular sting of his colleagues, especially given the emergent sophistication of the Islamic courts.[6] Maimonides' appreciation for the progressive aspects of procedural law in the Islamic courts and the embarrassment that these may have caused him if they were found not to be part of the essence of the Mosaic law may have led him to individuate, consciously or unconsciously, the claims of abiding by majority opinion (positive commandment 175), the duty to testify in court when in possession of evidence (positive commandment 178) and the duty to thoroughly examine the testimony of witnesses (positive commandment 179).

This thesis may also explain a longer-than-usual and seemingly out-of-place discourse that Maimonides makes in connection with negative commandment #290. As Maimonides notes in his introduction, the *Sefer ha-Mitsvot*'s glosses on the individual commandments are intended to be concise and to convey only some of the most basic information, such as proof of the claim and a description of the commandment. Deviations from this programmatic statement, as when they contain a rationale, are extremely unusual and tend to reveal in my opinion a heightened sensitivity to the particular subject matter.

4 Bloomberg, Jon Irving, "Arabic Legal Terms in Maimonides," (Ph.D. dissertation: Yale University, 1980), p. 63.

5 Twersky noted, but perhaps not emphatically enough, this competitive aspect: "Codes of law were common in the Islamic world, and inasmuch as Maimonides was generally aware of the surrounding tendencies, this could have provided stimulus." Twersky, *Introduction to the Code of Maimonides* , p. 77. Cf. Fox, "Maimonides on Aging," p. 352, who asks whether the impetus to write the *Guide* came from the Islamic court philosophers who challenged Maimonides "to a demonstration of the inherent logic and theosophical rigor of the Judaic faith."

6 On the progressive nature of Islamic procedural law, see for example, Ziadeh, Faraht J., "Adab al-Qadi and the Protection of Rights at Court," *Studies in Islamic and Judaic Traditions: Papers Presented at the Institute of Islamic-Judaic Studies*, eds. William M. Brinner and Stephen D. Ricks, Brown Judaic Studies (Atlanta: Scholars Press, 1986). On the development of Islamic law in general, see Schacht, *The Origins of Muslim Jurisprudence*, and Schacht, Joseph, *An Introduction to Islamic Law* (Oxford: Oxford University Press, 1982).

This is clearly the case with negative commandment #290 — the claim that the Torah forbade the court from carrying out a sentence in a capital case on the basis of a strong presumption — and it may have been directed as much to his coreligionists as to his colleagues. The discourse reflects the best tradition of courtroom justice. The lengthy passage, only part of which we quote here, parallels some of the concerns expressed in positive commandment #179:

> If we do not give judgment even on the basis of a very strong presumption, the worst that can happen is that the sinner will be acquitted; but if we punish on the strength of presumptions and suppositions, it may be that once we shall put to death an innocent person; and it is better and more satisfactory to acquit a thousand guilty persons than to put once a single innocent man to death.

It should be understood that the enumeration of the commandments was devoid of any halakhic force or consequence. The enumeration was simply a meta-halakhic exercise that consisted in dividing the whole of the Torah into broad and independent commandments, positive and negative ones, each containing a large number of details, stipulations and conditions. In at least two instances, the positive commandments to abide by majority opinion and to thoroughly examine witnesses, Maimonides seems to have exceeded his own requirements. Both commandments appear to be stipulations of the greater themes of having to set up functioning courts and/or to dispense justice. In another instance, Maimonides goes to great lengths to demonstrate that there exists a positive duty to testify in court when in possession of evidence when in fact all we see in the scriptural and rabbinic sources, as I have shown elsewhere, is that there is a threat of punishment for withholding evidence.

Maimonides made it clear that he was embarrassed at the intellectually and culturally impoverished state of affairs of his people and that this feeling impelled him to write a comprehensive Code of Law. I submit that this very feeling led him also to individuate, consciously or unconsciously, a triad of procedural law related commandments which, strictly speaking, did not belong in the methodologically rigorous enumeration of the commandments.

TEACHING PHILOSOPHY TO THE MULTITUDE: AN INTRODUCTION TO THE EDUCATIONAL THEORY OF NISSIM BEN MOSHE OF MARSEILLES[1]

Alan Verskin, Princeton University

It is often claimed that medieval Jewish philosophy is unashamedly elitist. In contrast to Socrates who had been content to discuss philosophy with whomever he met, both freemen and slaves, the medieval philosophers shunned contact with the ignorant multitude. The Jewish philosopher Moses Maimonides (d. 1204) is often seen as personifying this trend. According to him, human beings achieve salvation in accordance with the measure in which they succeed in channeling the emanation of the divine intellect, an activity which requires considerable intellectual ability and expertise. "As for the ignorant and disobedient," he says,

> their state is despicable proportionately to the lack of this emanation, and they have been relegated to the rank of the individuals of all other species of animals: 'He is like the beasts that speak not.'[2] For this reason, it is a light thing to kill them, and has been even enjoined because of its utility.[3]

1 This paper is dedicated to Harry Fox to whom I am very grateful for having initiated me in the mysteries of the *Guide of the Perplexed* during my senior year of college. His close-readings of the *Guide* have continued to influence the way I read the works of Maimonides and his successors. I would also like to thank James Robinson and my father, Milton Verskin, for having commented upon previous versions of this paper.

2 *Psalms* 49: 13 and 21.

3 Moses Maimonides, *The Guide of the Perplexed*, tr. S. Pines (Chicago: University of Chicago Press, 1963), 3: 18, 475.

Maimonides' writings, however, contain the seeds of ideas which have the effect of somewhat negating the severity of this elitism. These ideas were noticed and elaborated upon by many of his philosophical successors. In this paper, I outline how one of his disciples, the fourteenth-century Averroist, Nissim ben Moshe of Marseilles,[4] developed a program of philosophical education which sought to include the enlightenment of the masses.

Not much is known of Nissim ben Moshe's life. Between 1315 and 1330, he produced his only known work which is variously called *Ma'aseh Nissim*, *Sefer ha-Nissim*, or *'Iqqarei ha-Dat*.[5] The work is a philosophical commentary on the Pentateuch which is preceded by a lengthy, fourteen-chapter introduction. Here, Nissim presents with great clarity many of the central problems of medieval philosophy and outlines his understanding of the relation between reason and scripture, and his theory of scriptural interpretation. Since Nissim's ideas represent a creative synthesis of the works of his predecessors, before discussing his own solutions to these problems, I shall outline the philosophical background against which he wrote.

Medieval philosophers in the Aristotelian tradition are faced with the problem that the God in which they believe is very different from the God of scripture. The God of these philosophers is entirely unchanging, expressing neither desires nor emotions. He does not intervene in any of the affairs of the world and stands in relation to it only as the first cause, as the unmoved mover. In contrast, the God of scripture is a moral person who cares for the world that he has created and intervenes in its affairs. The central problem of medieval philosophy was that of arbitrating between these two conflicting views of the nature of God. A common way of explaining the contradiction was to understand scriptural dogma as being expressed for a political purpose, rather than for the purpose of conveying metaphysical truth. For example, since the God of the philosophers does not feel anger, some claimed that all scriptural references to his anger were expressed in order to frighten the masses into obedience, not

4 For a bibliography of the scholarly literature on Nissim, see Howard Kreisel, "Some Observations on *Ma'aseh Nissim* by R. Nissim of Marseilles," *Perspectives on Jewish Thought and Mysticism* (Amsterdam: Harwood Academic Publishers, 1998), 201 ff.

5 Nissim ben Moshe of Marseilles, *Ma'aseh Nissim*, ed. Howard Kreisel (Jerusalem: Mekitse Nirdamim, 2000), 1 ff.

for the purpose of describing an attribute of God's nature. By appreciating the social usefulness of the biblical text, the philosopher was able to overcome his embarrassment over its naïve theology and was able to re-embrace it as a text of practical wisdom.[6] This line of thinking can be traced back to Plato.[7] To maintain order in society, he says, it is often necessary for the lawgiver to depart from what is strictly true. Averroes (d. 1198), the great Muslim Aristotelian philosopher, explains the matter thus in his commentary on Plato's *Republic*:

> Lying tales are necessary for the education of the citizens. There is no lawgiver who does not employ fictitious tales, because this is necessary for the masses if they are to attain happiness.[8]

The presence of what Averroes calls "lying tales" in scripture raises two main issues. First, is the philosopher allowed to teach philosophy if doing so involves the denial of the truth of such "tales" — their allegorical interpretation being regarded as tantamount to a denial? Second, how is one to know whether all of scripture is to be read as "lying tales," or whether there are indeed parts of scripture which contain philosophical truths?

Averroes' answers to these questions are premised on his belief that societal stability and the safety of the philosophers depends upon these "lying tales" not being unmasked to the multitude for what they are. Teaching the true relationship of philosophy and religion to the multitude is therefore out of the question. If a member of the multitude asks about this relationship, he must be told only that the two are compatible and nothing more. For this reason, Averroes simply and unequivocally prohibits the public teaching of philosophical interpretations of scripture because it creates an easy bridge between philosophy and religion.[9] Since he clearly wishes to be seen as adhering to this ruling, he himself employs a recondite and elusive mode of expression when dealing with such subjects with

6 It was Harry Fox who first showed me how this model of embarrassment and re-embracement could be a powerful model for understanding the exegetical strategies of Maimonides and other medieval Jewish philosophers.

7 For example, see Plato, *The Republic*, 389b — c and 414b — 415d.

8 Averroes, *Commentary on Plato's Republic*, ed. and tr. E. I. J. Rosenthal (Cambridge: Cambridge University Press, 1956), 6.

9 Averroes, *The Decisive Treatise*, ed. and tr. C. Butterworth (Salt Lake City: Brigham Young University Press, 2002), 26-27.

the result that it is quite difficult to interpret his views.[10] As I have mentioned, he makes clear in his commentary on Plato's *Republic* that he believes that scripture contains at least some politically necessary falsehoods. He does not, however, make clear whether it might also contain metaphysical truths in addition to these falsehoods. A hint regarding his view is contained in his *Epitome of Aristotle's Parva Naturalia*. The multitude, Averroes claims, believes that "true dreams," soothsaying (*kahānah*), and revelation (*waḥy*), are distinct phenomena. True dreams, they believe, come from angels, soothsaying from the jinn, and revelation from God either directly or through an intermediary. Averroes, however, says that revelation is in fact a phenomenon of the same nature as dreams, and dreams, he says, "cannot possibly deal with any of the theoretical things."[11] Rather, it is *exclusively* through philosophical training and study that human beings can come to knowledge of metaphysical truths. Even if one were to assume hypothetically that metaphysical knowledge could be acquired through revelation, it would have no privileged status, for it "would be superfluous, inasmuch as man has already acquired it in a more perfect manner."[12] Thus it seems that, for Averroes, scripture contains no metaphysical truths, but only those "lying tales" necessary for the felicity of the multitude. This extreme view is one from which he seems to distance himself in his other writings,[13] but it is one which became very important for later Jewish Averroists.[14]

10 For Averroes, the truths of philosophy are to be expressed only in works dealing with pure philosophy which contain no parts dealing with revelation. The multitude are to be banned from reading these books, but since such works are so abstruse and philosophical training is required in order to understand them, there is little danger that they will fall into their hands and cause them harm. See *Decisive Treatise*, 21-22 and 27. Cf. Averroes, *Tahafut al-Tahafut (Incoherence of the Incoherence)*, tr. S. Van Den Bergh (E. J. W. Gibb Memorial Trust, 1954) 1: 215-216.

11 Averroes, *Compendia Librorum Aristotelis qui Parva Naturalia Vocantur*, tr. Moshe Ibn Tibbon (d. 1283) and ed. H. Blumberg (Cambridge: Mediaeval Academy of America, 1954), 44-48. English Translation: *Averroes' Epitome of Parva Naturalia*, tr. H. Blumberg (Cambridge: Mediaeval Academy of America, 1961), 40-43.

12 Ibid. 51-52.

13 There is some debate as to what position Averroes actually takes on this matter. See Herbert Davidson, *Alfarabi, Avicenna and Averroes* (Oxford: Oxford University Press, 1992), 340-351 and Richard C. Taylor, "Davidson on al-Farabi, Avicenna and Averroes: A Critical Review," *Journal of Neoplatonic Studies* 5 (1996), 92-4 and 100-2.

14 For a general overview of the phenomenon of Jewish Averroism, see Georges Vajda, "A propos de l'Averroisme Juif," *Sefarad* 12 (1952), 3-29 and Steven Harvey, "On the Nature

Although Maimonides agrees with Averroes that there are parts of scripture which contradict reason, he nonetheless presents a paradigm in which truth may be found therein.[15] Scripture, he says, is a document which is of benefit both to the elite and to the multitude. It makes itself understandable to the multitude by speaking in a manner that they can understand even if such popular language sometimes does not reflect the subtleties of true belief.[16] Scripture does not, however, abandon the elite. In order to accommodate both audiences, scripture resembles "a well-constructed parable" which possesses both an external and an internal meaning. In his *Guide of the Perplexed*, Maimonides describes his theory thus:

> The Sage has said: *A word fitly spoken is like apples of gold in settings of silver* [Prov. 25:11]... The Sage accordingly said that a saying uttered with a view to two meanings is like an apple of gold overlaid with silver filigree-work having very small holes. Now see how marvelously this dictum describes a well-constructed parable. For he says that in a saying that has two meanings — he means an external and an internal one — the external meaning ought to be as beautiful as silver, while its internal meaning ought to be more beautiful than the external one, the internal being in comparison to the external as gold is to silver. Its external meaning also ought to contain in it something that indicates to someone considering it what is to be found in its internal meaning, as happens in the case of an apple of gold overlaid with silver filigree-work having very small holes. When looked at from a distance or with imperfect attention, it is deemed to be an apple of silver; but when a keen-sighted observer looks at it with full attention, its interior becomes clear to him and he knows that it is of gold. The parables of the prophets, peace be on them, are similar.[17]

and Extent of Jewish Averroism: Renan's *Averroès et l'averroïsme* Revisited." *Jewish Studies Quarterly* 7 (2000), 100-119.

15 For an engaging examination of Maimonides' exegetical strategy, see Sarah Klein-Braslavy, *Perush ha-Rambam le-sipur beri'at ha-'olam* (Jerusalem: Ha-Hevrah le-Heker ha-Mikra, 1987).

16 This, he says, is the meaning of the dictum of the sages, "the Torah speaks in the language of the sons of man." See Maimonides, *The Guide of the Perplexed*, 1: 26, 56. For the dictum of the sages, see, for example, *Babylonian Talmud Yevamot* 71a.

17 Ibid., 1: Introduction, 11-12.

Thus, according to Maimonides, both the external and the internal meanings of scripture have a valuable function. Although the internal meaning is more valuable than the external, the latter should not be merely discarded as worthless dross. On the contrary, Maimonides indicates that the external meaning is carefully crafted and fulfills a useful social purpose.

Should the internal meaning of scripture be conveyed to the multitude or should they merely be taught its external meaning? Maimonides says that the answer depends upon the purpose for which the external meaning is conveyed. If it is conveyed to express a "necessary belief," that is, a belief which is philosophically false but which is vital for the political welfare of the community, the internal meaning must not be conveyed.[18] Such beliefs perform the essential function of playing upon the multitude's fear of punishment or hope of reward in order to secure their obedience to the law. One of the examples which Maimonides gives of such beliefs is scripture's description of God's violent anger against those who disobey his commandments.

In certain cases, scriptural passages which allegorically conceal deeply recondite metaphysical matters must also not be taught to the multitude and should be discussed only by the philosophical elite. Such matters include, for example, the meaning of the "Account of the Beginning," and the "Account of the Chariot" described in chapter one of Ezekiel.[19] However, in contrast to Averroes, Maimonides does believe that there are some philosophical interpretations of scripture which should be conveyed to the multitude. For example, it is obligatory to explain to the multitude the internal meaning of those scriptural passages which suggest God's corporeality. This is because, for Maimonides, divine law is not solely directed towards maintaining social stability but is also directed towards the intellectual improvement of the citizenry.[20] It is therefore not only right, but also obligatory, that the philosopher attend to some aspects of the multitude's philosophical education.

Many post-Maimonidean Jewish philosophers in Provence tend to reject Maimonides' claim that scripture contains philosophical truth. Following

18 Ibid., 3: 28, 512.

19 Ibid., 1: Introduction, 6.

20 Ibid., 2:40, 384.

Averroes, such philosophers believe that it is exclusively through philosophical training and study that human beings can come to knowledge of philosophical truths — and some of them claim that Maimonides himself secretly shared their opinion.[21] On the other hand, many of these philosophers reject Averroes' contention that philosophy should be strictly withheld from the multitude. As they see it, Maimonides was correct in his belief that some philosophical education is good for the multitude — but they have differing views as to exactly what the multitude should be taught.

Samuel ben Judah Ibn Tibbon (d. 1232), who was perhaps the greatest of the Jewish Provençal philosophers, is typical of this trend. He rejects Maimonides' conception of scripture as a "well-constructed parable," arguing instead that there are some biblical passages which have neither a true surface meaning nor a philosophical- allegorical meaning. This is not a defect in scripture. Scripture is not a document which is intended to benefit the elite by teaching metaphysics to them. Rather, the beliefs which it conveys are "intended only to be of advantage to the multitude."[22] Thus, according to Ibn Tibbon, scripture only expresses what Maimonides called "necessary beliefs." Philosophical truths are not to be found in scripture at all, not even beneath the surface. The elite among the ancient Hebrews, he claims, knew philosophical truths, but these were never put into writing and were passed from generation to generation exclusively by word of mouth. Ibn Tibbon, however, does not wish these truths to remain the exclusive property of the elite. Rather, he envisions an historical process of transmission of knowledge, beginning with Moses, which results in an ever-expanding circle of philosophers as the multitude gradually becomes more enlightened over the generations. At the time of Moses, he says, the multitude was heavily influenced by ancient Sabaean idolatrous beliefs and was therefore unable to conceptualize the existence of a non-corporeal entity. Moses thus had to limit himself to establishing only God's unity, but not His incorporeality. In the time of David and Solomon, however, the belief in God's

21 On this matter, see Aviezer Ravitzky, "Secrets of the Guide to the Perplexed: Between the Thirteenth and Twentieth Centuries" in *Studies in Maimonides*, ed. I. Twersky (Cambridge: Harvard University Press, 1990), 159-207.

22 Solomon Ibn Tibbon, *Ma'amar Yiqqavu ha-Mayim*, ed. M. L. Bisliches (Pressburg: Anton Edlen von Schmidt, 1837), 132.

incorporeality and his relation to all existents had become widespread. Under such circumstances, a greater enlightenment of the multitude was possible and therefore Solomon revealed truths not revealed by Moses because "there was no further need of concealment."[23] According to Ibn Tibbon, further progress of this sort was evident in his own time, a fact which he felt made it right for him to reveal some of the philosophical secrets which Maimonides had thought best to keep hidden.

How did Ibn Tibbon think that the multitude should be taught philosophy? Since his major works are scriptural commentaries in which he conveys philosophical ideas, one can perhaps deduce that this is the manner in which he thought such truths are best conveyed.[24] These commentaries never compromise his view that no philosophical truths exist in scripture, even beneath its surface. Rather, he uses the genre of scriptural commentary simply because it is a useful forum for expounding his ideas to the broadest possible audience. He justifies his highly inventive and perhaps even disingenuous use of scriptural commentary by saying that "it is better to force [the meaning of] a phrase than to force reality."[25] In other words, for Ibn Tibbon, the importance of promulgating philosophy far outweighs the need for accuracy in scriptural interpretation.[26]

I come now to Nissim ben Moshe of Marseilles. Nissim further develops Ibn Tibbon's synthesis of Averroes' ideas on prophecy and Maimonides' ideas on educating the multitude. Drawing upon Averroes' *Epitome of Parva Naturalia*, Nissim endorses the view that prophets cannot attain metaphysical knowledge through their prophecy. He criticizes Maimonides' opinion that the prophet can attain metaphysical knowledge:

---

23 Ibid., 174.

24 Samuel Ibn Tibbon's son-in-law and student, Jacob ben Abba Mari Anatoli, employs Ibn Tibbon's methodology in his work *Malmad ha-Talmidim*. The work begins as a series of philosophical commentaries on the weekly Torah portions. See Jacob Anatoli, *Sefer Malmad ha-Talmidim* (Lyck: Mekitse nirdamim, 1866).

25 Ibid., 17.

26 This issue is discussed by Aviezer Ravitzky, "Samuel Ibn Tibbon and the Esoteric Character of the Guide of the Perplexed," *A.J.S. Review* 6 (1981), 113-4. For a different view, see J. Robinson, *Samuel Ibn Tibbon's "Commentary on Ecclesiastes"* (Ph.D. thesis, Harvard University, 2002), 58 ff.

> In my opinion, it is impossible for ideas... that a human being can conceive through speculation and logic to come to him in a vision or dream of prophecy because, if this were possible, speculative thought... would be superfluous... Philosophical investigation would be in vain because the long path is useless once there is another shorter and better path.[27]

Thus, according to Nissim, prophecy, and therefore scripture, which is a product of prophecy, is a phenomenon entirely devoid of philosophical truth.

How then is one to interpret scripture? Is there a way in which one can engage in philosophical exegesis if the content of revelation is not philosophical? Nissim argues that one can engage in philosophical exegesis because, although the content of the Torah is directed to the multitude, that content is presented for the purpose of creating the kind of society which fosters those individuals who have the ability to become philosophers.[28] Nissim, however, unlike Maimonides and Averroes, does not think that this kind of society can be created simply by instilling in the multitude the fear of the violence of God against those who disobey the law. Rather, he thinks that it is also necessary to foster a respect for reason among them. Indeed, he even offers a cautious criticism of Maimonides' contention that one can secure the obedience of the multitude by teaching them pious falsehoods or "necessary truths" regarding the workings of divine justice. If the multitude, he says, are taught that divine reward and punishment will be immediately administered in response to their deeds, "when this does not happen as they imagine, they attribute wrongdoing to God."[29] Thus Nissim thinks that teaching false beliefs about divine justice may very well produce the opposite of the intended effect. A person who observes the commandments out of a belief in an entirely plastic universe shaped only by constant and unfathomable divine intervention could find that the gulf between his expectations and reality undermines his faith in God. Instead, Nissim suggests that the multitude be taught a naturalistic

27 *Ma'aseh Nissim*, Ch. 12, 166.

28 Ibid., Ch. 11, 149 and Ch. 4, 69-70. On the political function of the law in general, see Ch. 3, 66-68.

29 Ibid., Ch. 9, 114.

conception of reward and punishment, that is, they should be taught about the natural evils which result from vice and the natural goods which result from virtue. Although believing in God's violent anger at sinners no doubt provides a dramatic motivation for obedience, Nissim claims that a person who is taught to behave ethically because of the natural consequences of his actions will have a more consistent and dependable source of motivation. A person who believes in naturalistic reward and punishment, he concludes, will be better able to maintain his faith in the face of the vicissitudes of fortune. He will not be led to deny the laws of right and wrong because of a feeling that God neglects their enforcement. Lest his view seem impious, Nissim claims that the rabbis also agree with him in this matter. Citing a passage from the Talmud, he indicates that the rabbis do not teach that reward and punishment is effected by a divine bending of the laws of nature dependent upon the vagaries of human action. On the contrary, Nissim argues,

> [The Sages] of blessed memory indicated that nature's activity is not suspended or changed for the sinner, for they said: 'Suppose a person stole a measure of wheat and sowed it in the ground; it is right that it should not grow, but the world pursues its natural course'[30]

In this passage, Nissim argues, the sages indicate that the obedience of the multitude must be secured without an appeal to a false system of divine justice but through an honest discussion of the natural consequences of human action.

Nissim does not, however, insist that a naturalistic understanding of reward and punishment be forced upon the multitude. If the philosopher feels that, in view of the circumstances prevailing at any particular time and place, it is better for the multitude to understand reward and punishment according to the literal meaning of scripture, he would be justified in teaching them accordingly. The teacher of philosophy must be very sensitive to the needs of his audience so as not to harm them and his society. When, whether and to whom rational explanations are to be given is therefore something which must be decided pragmatically. He writes:

30 Ibid., Ch. 10, 121 and *Babylonian Talmud, Avodah Zarah* 54b.

> The intention of every intelligent person and [likewise] our intention is to reconcile religion with philosophy,[31] insofar as is possible... By saying, 'insofar as is possible,' I mean insofar as is possible from the perspective of religion *qua* religion, for this is not possible from a general perspective. Because religion is given to all — sage and fool, children and women — it is necessary that it speak with each person in a way which is appropriate and useful to him.[32]

The philosopher should therefore be aware that since religion is intended to be of universal benefit, he must vary his teaching to suit the needs of each student.[33]

For Nissim, however, there are still certain falsehoods, or "necessary beliefs," which must be taught to the multitude. Maimonides had said that the "necessary beliefs" which ought to be taught to the multitude were those which played upon its members' fears of punishment or hopes of reward in order to lead them to more meticulous observance of the commandments. Nissim, on the other hand, thinks that "necessary beliefs" are primarily those falsehoods which must be conveyed in order to secure the safety of philosophy itself. According to him, the most important of such falsehoods is the belief that religion is rational and that it is therefore in complete harmony with philosophy. This belief, although Nissim considers it to be false, must be taught in order to instill in the multitude a belief in the piety of the philosophers which in turn would inspire a respect both for them and for their philosophy. This respect is necessary for the physical safety of the philosophers as well as for creating the conditions which facilitate the emergence of new philosophers from the ranks of the multitude. Nissim, like Ibn Tibbon, therefore praises those theologians who attempt to advance interpretations of scripture in harmony with the conclusions of reason, even if these interpretations are, as he puts it, "far-fetched."[34]

---

31 Literally, "that which the intellect indicates."

32 Ibid., Ch. 9, 112.

33 Nissim adds that without an understanding of natural law, a person is unable to understand the relative importance of the commandments and will often "perform the less significant commandments and abandon the valuable ones" [*Ma'aseh Nissim*, Ch. 10, 121]. He thus argues that philosophers actually fulfill the commandments better than non-philosophers as a result of their knowledge of the ultimate intention of the Law. In support of this, he quotes the sages: "The ignorant one is not pious" [*Mishnah Avot* 2, 5].

34 *Ma'aseh Nissim, Commentary on Genesis*, 222.

With this in mind, Nissim says that a rational explanation should be given for religious precepts wherever possible. If this cannot be done, religion is to be defended at all costs because it is vital for the stability of society without which the philosophical life cannot exist. "We are thus obligated," Nissim says, "to use dialectics to save and maintain [religious] opinions, and to refute anyone who comes to dispute them."[35] In *Chapter 4*, Nissim explains what he means by such "dialectics" in a novel adaptation of the Muslim philosopher Abū Nasr al-Fārābī's (d. 950) description of the methodologies of five different groups of dialectical theologians.[36] The first group believes that religious opinions cannot be examined because the human intellect is too weak to apprehend them. The second group searches for "various sensible and intelligible things" which can be used in support of their religion. In the event that there is a conflict between reason and religion, they offer a rationalistic interpretation, however "remote" it may be from the meaning of the religious text. The third group defends religion by finding that which is absurd in religions other than their own and, when a follower of another religion comes to dispute with them, they confront him with the absurdities of his own religion. The fourth group does not believe that sufficient arguments exist to bolster the opinions of its religion but nevertheless tries to shame or coerce people into adopting its beliefs. Finally, the fifth group uses any manner of argumentation even if it embodies falsehood or sophistry. Unlike al-Fārābī, Nissim does not regard the approaches of these groups as being mutually exclusive. In a manner reminiscent of Averroes,[37] Nissim suggests that all of these theological methods are to be used in order to reinforce belief in the Law and thereby ensure political stability. Nissim, however, says that, where possible, the second method is to be preferred — one must strive, even when one knows that one's interpretation is forced, to nonetheless provide rational explanations of scripture.

35 Ibid., Ch. 4, 70.

36 Ibid., 70-71. Nissim quotes from Kalonymus ben Kalonymus ben Me'ir's (b. 1286) translation of al-Fārābī's *Enumeration of the Sciences*. See al-Fārābī, *'Classificazione delle scienze' di Al-Fārābī nella tradizione ebraica: edizione critica e traduzione annota della versione ebraica di Qalonymos ben Qalonymos ben Me'ir*, ed. Mauro Zonta (Torino: Silvio Zamorani, 1992), 115a-116a.

37 E.g., *The Decisive Treatise*, 27-29 and *Incoherence of the Incoherence*, 428-429, 454, 527.

Nissim's approach is illustrated in his discussion of Maimonides' "Thirteen Principles of Faith," all of which, he says, must be believed by the multitude.[38] Wherever possible, he says, the philosopher is to teach the multitude that these principles are in harmony with reason. When they are not in harmony with reason, a number of different approaches must be adopted, depending upon which principles are involved. The majority can be justified with arguments which have the appearance of rationality, but which are in fact specious. Thus, for example, Nissim justifies the rationality of belief in the messiah thus:

> As Aristotle said, in eternal things, what is possible is also necessary.[39] Since Israel is an eternal nation that will never come to an end…, the restoration of government and freedom to Israel as of old is in the category of the possible, not the impossible. It is [therefore] necessary that this possibility come into existence at some point in time.[40]

Nissim clearly views the argument as entirely specious, but provides it as an example of the kind of sophistry which is to be used to protect the philosophers by persuading the multitude of their piety.

Nissim accords a special position to three of Maimonides' "Thirteen Principles": the resurrection of the dead,[41] creation *ex nihilo*, and the uniqueness of Mosaic prophecy.[42] These principles, although completely unsupported by reason, are the very basis of the Torah's moral authority. The importance of the multitude's belief in them is such that the philosopher should not risk teaching pseudo-philosophical explanations of them which might later be exposed

38 Nissim's discussion of the "thirteen principles" is contained in a section exclusively devoted to their analysis as well as in another section on "the promises of the Torah." My analysis draws on both of these sections. See Ma'aseh Nissim, Ch. 10, 118 ff. and Ch. 11, 148 ff.

39 Aristotle, *De Generatione et Corruptione*, 337b-338a.

40 *Ma'aseh Nissim*, Ch. 11, 156

41 This principle is dealt with in *Ma'aseh Nissim*, Ch. 11, 156-157, Ch. 10, 133 and Ch. 4, 74-77.

42 Nissim's understanding of Mosaic prophecy has been discussed by a number of scholars, see Collete Sirat, "The Political Ideas of Nissim Ben Moses of Marseilles," *Jerusalem Studies in Jewish Thought* 9 (1990), 61ff. and Howard Kreisel, "Philosophical-Allegorical Interpretation of the Torah in the Middle Ages: Ma'aseh Nissim by R. Nissim of Marseilles," in Hebrew, in *Me'ah She'arim: Studies in Medieval Jewish Spiritual life in Memory of Isadore Twersky* (Jerusalem: The Hebrew University Magnes Press, 2001), 305.

for what they are. Rather, these principles must be taught to the multitude without philosophical explanation. If a member of the multitude asks whether they are compatible with reason, the philosopher must answer that they can only be learned through revelation since they lie beyond the grasp of reason. Although the philosopher knows that these principles are false, he must nonetheless teach them both in order to protect the philosophers by persuading the multitude of their piety and to prevent the multitude from falling into heresy. Nissim therefore criticizes both Ibn Ezra and Ibn Tibbon for teaching allegorical interpretations of the doctrine of creation *ex nihilo*:

> The opinion of Ibn Ezra and Rabbi Samuel Ibn Tibbon is far-fetched[43] because it is necessary for Moses and for every founder of religion to... introduce a belief in temporal creation and not to deny it. This is because with belief in the eternity of the world all miracles are denied[44] and religion becomes a *nomos* given by free human choice and not a divine religion... According to these two exegetes, Moses speaks to us at the beginning of our Torah in the manner of the silent sensible ones, meaning that his words will be understood in two ways: the multitude will understand what they necessarily need, that is, belief in the temporal creation of all existents other than [God]... and the intelligent will understand the opposite...[45]

Two principles of faith, Nissim says, fall into a special, discretionary category. These are the belief that the Torah is from heaven, and the belief in divine reward and punishment. The philosopher is permitted to offer allegorical interpretations of scriptural passages which deal with such issues if he thinks that they will be well-received by his audience. If, on the other hand, he thinks that such explanations might damage their faith, he is obliged to teach such matters in accordance with the literal meaning of scripture.[46] He cautions the philosopher that there is no religious obligation which forces the multitude to adopt philosophical views. Quoting the *Mekhilta*, he says, "concerning the

43 What is "far-fetched," of course, is not their opinion that the universe is eternal, but their belief that this opinion is expressed in scripture.

44 Cf. *Guide of the Perplexed*, 2: 25, 329-330.

45 *Ma'aseh Nissim, Commentary on Genesis*, 222.

46 Ibid., Ch. 10, 118 and 137.

revealed things, each one made a covenant, but each did not make a covenant concerning the secret things."[47] Therefore, the multitude, if it so desires, is entitled to persist in its non-philosophical beliefs.

At least since Plato, philosophers have been concerned with establishing the conditions necessary for the emergence of new philosophers. For Averroes, this meant no more than freeing the philosopher from the threat of violence. He showed no interest in developing an educational program to spread philosophical ideas among the multitude and thus encouraging the emergence of new philosophers from among them. Maimonides, on the other hand, felt that creating a society friendly towards philosophers also involved bringing the beliefs of the multitude more into line with those of the philosophers. His system of education, however, did not involve much more than instituting a more philosophical understanding of God's unity and incorporeality. The intellectual gap between the philosopher and the multitude was thus still firmly maintained. Provençal philosophers, like Ibn Tibbon and Nissim of Marseilles, significantly broadened the scope of the multitude's philosophical education. Philosophical doctrines were to become an important part of the multitude's educational curriculum. They did not, however, view their work as a break with Maimonides, but as a further development of his thought.

By way of summarizing their attitude, I quote Moses ben Joshua of Narbonne, a fourteenth century Jewish philosopher, whose understanding of Maimonides' teaching on the education of the multitude is, I think, typical of many Provençal Jewish philosophers during this period:

> [Maimonides] briefly hints at what we reveal to you at length, for times naturally change and so do people, and so we can now widen the small holes of the filigree-work with more truths than it was possible to do in the past, for accepted convention is no longer at loggerheads with intellectual truth as much as it was in the past. This is due first and foremost to Maimonides.[48]

---

47 Ibid., Ch. 9, 115-116.

48 Moses of Narbonne, *Bi'ur le-sefer moreh nevukhim* in *Sheloshah qadmone mefarshe ha-moreh* (Jerusalem: n.p., 1960), 2: 19. Quoted in Aviezer Ravitzky, "Secrets of the Guide to the Perplexed," 167.

There is no doubt that there were indeed many elitist aspects of medieval Jewish philosophy. The philosophers were profoundly aware of a great gap between their understanding and that of the average person and consequently did feel a certain sense of superiority. On the other hand, there seems to have been a genuine desire on the part of many of these philosophers to bridge this gap by introducing philosophy into ever broader public discourse. Nissim's distinction was to have served as a creative and eloquent representative of this trend towards greater inclusiveness and the universalization of philosophical education.

MODERN

RABBI NATAN SLIFKIN ON SCIENCE AND TORAH: THE EVOLUTION OF A SEARCH FOR TRUTH

Ira Robinson, Concordia University

From medieval times onward, Jews have confronted the task of attempting to reconcile their understanding of the Judaic tradition and the teachings of science. The major issue they faced was the apparent discrepancy between Torah as it presents itself and the realities of nature as interpreted by science and philosophy in various eras. Nearly always, as is the case in Maimonides' *Guide of the Perplexed*, this perceived conflict resulted in re-reading, re-interpreting, and re-presenting the Hebrew Bible and the statements attributed to the rabbis of late antiquity. This process has resulted in some of the most significant controversies in the history of Judaism.[1]

In contemporary times, major issues like the origins and age of the universe, and the origins and development of life on earth have proven to be areas of controversy among those Jews, particularly the Orthodox, who take seriously the truth claims of traditional Judaism.[2] While there are some Jews who have attempted to avoid a direct confrontation, others have attempted, in numerous ways, to engage in a dialogue between Torah and science. One contemporary Orthodox Jew in particular, Rabbi Natan Slifkin, has written prolifically on these issues in the past decade. His eight books in this area include:

1 See Noah J. Efron, *Judaism and Science: a Historical Introduction* (Westport, Greenwood Press, 2007), p. 75ff. Cf. Daniel Jeremy Silver, *Maimonidean Criticism and the Maimonidean Controversy* (Leiden, Brill, 1965).

2 Cf. Ira Robinson, "'Practically I Am a Fundamentalist': Twentieth Century Orthodox Jews Contend With Evolution and Its Implications", in Geoffrey Cantor and Marc Swetlitz, eds., *Jewish Tradition and the Challenge of Darwinism* (Chicago, University of Chicago Press, 2006), pp. 71-88.

- *Seasons of life: the reflection of the Jewish year in the natural world* [3]
- *In Noah's Footsteps: Biblical Perspectives of the Zoo*[4]
- *The science of Torah: the reflection of Torah in the laws of science, the creation of the universe and the development of life*[5]
- *Nature's song: an elucidation of Perek shirah, the ancient text that lists the philosophical and ethical lessons of the natural world*[6]
- *Mysterious creatures: intriguing Torah enigmas of natural and unnatural history*[7]
- *The Camel, the hare, & the hyrax: a study of the laws of animals with one kosher sign in light of modern zoology*[8]
- *Man and Beast: Our Relationships with Animals in Jewish Law and Thought*[9]
- *The Challenge of Creation: Judaism's Encounter With Science, Cosmology and Creation*[10]

Slifkin's attempt to understand the classical sources of Judaism while remaining true to his conception of scientific truth has caused considerable controversy within the Haredi (ultra-Orthodox) community in both Israel and the United States. This controversy has resulted in a number of prominent Haredi rabbinic figures denouncing his writings and banning them as heretical.[11]

3 Southfield, MI, Targum Press, 1998.

4 Jerusalem, Jerusalem Biblical Zoo, 2000.

5 Southfield, MI, Targum Press, 2001.

6 Southfield, MI, Targum Press, 2001.

7 Southfield, MI, Zoo Torah in conjunction with Targum/Feldheim, 2003.

8 Southfield, MI, Zoo Torah in conjunction with Targum/Feldheim, 2004.

9 Brooklyn, Zoo Torah, 2006.

10 Brooklyn, Zoo Torah/ Yashar Books, 2006.

11 The most comprehensive source for the documents concerning the controversy may be found at Rabbi Slifkin's website, www.zootorah.com in the section headed "Controversy". The

The Slifkin controversy has received considerable press coverage, which will not be reviewed in detail in this article.[12] The major task of this article, rather, will be something that neither the polemic nor the press coverage does — a systematic analysis of Slifkin's publications in order to examine the development of his thought on these issues. His writings will be examined against the background of earlier and contemporary Jewish attempts to understand the implications of scientific thought with respect to the Hebrew Bible and Rabbinic literature.

Rabbi Natan (Nosson)[13] Slifkin was born in Manchester, England in 1975. His father, Michael, was a scientist and an Orthodox Jew.[14] His parents sent him to Yeshivas Shaarei Torah, an Orthodox Jewish school in England, while encouraging his curiosity about the animal world, and his reading in scientific matters. He describes his adolescence in the following way:

> [G]rowing up in modern day England I was also exposed to a large amount of science, art, and popular culture...I had...absorbed certain values and attitudes that were at odds with the attitudes and values in the Torah.[15]

This exposure and these attitudes accompanied him when, in his late teens, Slifkin, like many of his Orthodox peers, went to Israel for a period of study in Midrash Shmuel and Mir Yeshivot, academies of traditional rabbinic learning.[16] Again like many of his peers, he was encouraged by his rabbinic mentors to extend his stay in the yeshiva, and in Israel, indefinitely. He, however,

---

controversy, which is tangential to the subject of this article, exposes some important fault lines within contemporary Orthodoxy and deserves separate study.

12 Among others, see Alex Mindlin, "Religion and Natural History Clash Among the Ultra-Orthodox", *New York Times* March 22, 2005; Stephen I. Weiss, "Orthodox Rabbis Launch Book Ban", *Forward* March 28, 2005; Jennie Rothenberg, "The Heresy of Nosson Slifkin", *Moment* (October, 2005) http://www.jennierothenberg.com/clippings/slifkin.html

13 In an email to the author dated May 15, 2007, Rabbi Slifkin stated that he had always been known as Natan and had adapted Nosson in order to be more acceptable in [Ashkenazic] Haredi circles, but after having been charged with heresy by these circles he no longer cared to go by the name "Nosson".

14 On Slifkin's parents, see *Mysterious Creatures*, p. 12.

15 *Second Focus*, p. 17.

16 On this phenomenon, see William B. Helmreich, *The World of the Yeshiva: An Intimate Portrait of Orthodox Jewry* (New Haven, Yale University Press, 1982).

did not thereby stop his reading of popular science periodicals such as *Scientific American* and *National Geographic* and books, especially on subjects of particular interest to him, including zoology. He was a young man in search of truth, which he and his fellow students understood could be gained through the study of Torah. Furthermore, he was a young man with a talent for writing. At the age of twenty-one, still a yeshiva student, he published his first book, entitled *Lying for Truth: Understanding Yaakov's Deception of Yitzchak.*[17] It is about the contradiction between the biblical patriarch Jacob's apparent deception of his father through his impersonation of his older brother, Esau, and his status as a righteous founder of the people of Israel. He was obviously spurred in his investigations by his desire to discern the truth of the matter through a detailed examination of classical rabbinic exegesis of the topic.

This first book was closely followed by a series of two volumes, entitled *Focus*[18] and *Second Focus*,[19] which dealt with issues related to the weekly synagogue Torah readings. They were originally distributed on a weekly basis and later collected in book form. These studies were likewise spurred, in the words of one of the book's letters of rabbinic approbation, by "a genuine search for truth". It is in *Focus* that Rabbi Slifkin first engages in print the themes that would characterize so much of his later work: the cognitive dissonance between the two intellectual worlds that had shaped him, the yeshiva and science, which seem to say radically incompatible things about such issues as the age of the universe and the origin of species. As he put it, "honesty is the only tool against this problem."[20] It was clear to him at this point that there was no essential barrier between his belief in the Torah and the attaining of scientific truth. As he stated:

> The idea that a religious person is dogmatic and totally unscientific may be true for the religions of the world...but it is not true for the Torah Jew. Gemara is a classic guide to intellectual honesty and objectivity.[21]

17 Southfield, MI, Targum Press, 1996.

18 Co-authored with Yehuda Leib Brea. (Southfield, MI, Targum Press, Yeshivas Midrash Shmuel, 1997).

19 Southfield, MI, Targum Press, 1999.

20 *Focus*, p. 163.

21 *Focus*, p. 165. Cf. the statement of philosopher Menachem Fisch that the Talmud reflects "views of human knowledge, learning and intellectual accomplishment [that] bear a striking

In this first attempt to confront the scientific doctrine of evolution from his Torah perspective, he expressed a relatively conventional Orthodox dismissal of evolution as "a wonderfully tempting release from the shackles of morality".[22] By *Second Focus*, however, he would begin creating his own, idiosyncratic approach to the problem. Somewhat apologetically, he began citing non-Jews or non-Orthodox Jews, rather than Orthodox rabbis alone.[23] As well, he defended the integrity of the scientific enterprise, stating that "the development of science represents the incredible victory of monotheism", a stance that also characterizes his later work.[24] Evolution is approached non-dismissively and with some empathy, since he claimed that, though the theory is false, some form of evolution is compatible with Torah as he understood it:

> There are many Torah sources for limited scale evolution...Micro-evolution does take place; but the mistake that evolutionists make was to extrapolate from micro-evolution to macro-evolution. Things adapt, but they do not totally change. The same is true of the Torah. It adapts...to different conditions.[25]

The idea that the universe is some fifteen billion years old is stated, and if it is not explicitly advocated, it is also not expressly condemned.[26]

By the late 1990s, Rabbi Slifkin had emerged as a figure of some note in Israel's growing Anglophone Orthodox circles. He was particularly known for his attempts to teach his fellow Jews about nature and its relationship to Torah. He became known as the "Zoo rabbi" because of his guided tours of the Jerusalem zoo, his lectures in Orthodox educational institutions catering to students from abroad, his website "zootorah", and his books on various aspects of science and Torah.[27]

---

resemblance" to those that characterize much of modern science. Fisch further writes that "Torah study as it was largely conceived by the Talmudic sages is, in principle, like science, a continuing, open-ended inquiry." Cited in Efron, *Judaism and Science*, p. 42.

22 *Focus*, p. 197.

23 *Second Focus*, p. 19

24 *Second Focus*, p. 52. Cf. *Nature's Song*, p. 127.

25 *Second Focus*, pp. 111-112.

26 *Second Focus*, p. 157.

27 For information on Rabbi Slifkin's books and educational activities, see his website zootorah.com

It is in the books that he began publishing in 1998 that he began confronting more directly some of the cognitive dissonance that exists between a scientific understanding of nature and various statements in Judaic sources. Thus in *Nature's Song* (1998), he discussed a bird mentioned in the poem he was explicating. Without explicitly stating that *Perek Shirah*, a traditional, though not quite canonical source, was wrong, he nonetheless stated:

> Modern Science has no evidence or theory to support the notion that birds spend the winter at the bottom of lakes, despite popular belief in the middle ages in such a phenomenon... Other contenders [for the identity of this particular bird] would be the... penguins. However it is difficult to state that *Perek Shirah* refers to a creature that was unknown until so recently.[28]

Rabbi Slifkin really entered into the thick of things when he published his *Science and Torah* in 2001. There, for the first time, we see a systematic approach to the problematic issues of science and Judaism from the perspective that, properly understood, science can be a basis for religious belief,[29] and that the much-discussed conflict between science and religion is not cut and dried. As he put it:

> Some Jewish writers assume that in a debate between atheist scientists and religious thinkers, one must side fully with the latter. This is a tragic error.[30]

Rabbi Slifkin began with the basic assumption that "there has to be order in the universe, governed by a system of natural law", because, following an essentially kabbalistic position, he asserted that "the universe is a physical manifestation of Torah...Torah is an ordered and structured work...take this spiritual structure, unfold it in the spiritual dimension, and the result is a structured universe".[31] This assumption by Rabbi Slifkin is significant. He does not opt for the idea of a universe that is the result of an arbitrary divine will, but rather the result of an observable and predictable natural law. As a direct result of this assumption, he is unable to simply dismiss what contemporary

28 *Nature's Song*, p. 256.

29 *Science of Torah*, p. 13, cf. p. 49.

30 *Science of Torah*, p. 13. Cf. pp. 162, 195.

31 *Science of Torah*, p. 68. Cf. pp. 214-215.

science has to say about such things as the age of the universe and evolution. He must, therefore, examine these propositions on their merits. Concerning the age of the universe, he stated:

> scientific evidence for an old universe is…so vast and overwhelming that it is rather unwise to simply wave it away (and the effects on Jewish outreach efforts are disastrous).[32]

Of course this understanding necessitates a non-literal interpretation of the Torah's creation narrative. But Slifkin, like Maimonides before him, has no problem with such a non-literal interpretation "where there are overwhelming grounds for accepting such an understanding."[33] At the same time, Slifkin is impatient with Orthodox attempts to discredit the scientific evidence:

> The physical evidence contained in the world must reflect truth. If one is afraid of what scientists may discover, then one is clearly not fully aware that everything discoverable was created by God. Conversely, if one is convinced that God wrote the Torah and created the world then one should fear no scientific research.[34]
>
> In other words, "God is not out to deceive us".[35]

With respect to the evolution of species, Slifkin begins by saying that "it is perfectly possible to accept the scientists' view of the age of the universe and to reject evolution."[36] The view he advocates, however, is hardly a rejection:

> From a secular point of view it is certainly most reasonable to assume that they [creatures] developed—somehow—from the already existing creatures. But it would be a mistake to think that this is solely a secular argument. Even from a religious perspective there are strong grounds for arguing that it is most reasonable that God created new creatures, somehow, from the already existing

32 *Science of Torah*. p. 90. Cf. *Mysterious Creatures*, p. 14.

33 *Science of Torah*, p. 102.

34 *Science of Torah*, p. 111.

35 *Science of Torah*, p. 139.

36 *Science of Torah*, p. 89.

creatures, rather than zapping them into existence out of thin air, as making them from already existing creatures is much more within the realm of natural law. God chooses to work within a system of natural law—not because He has to but because He wants to.[37]

In sum, "one who chooses to accept a scientific explanation for the origin of life is therefore not going against the Torah."[38] He asserts that it is possible for one species to change into another according to classical Torah sources.[39] Finally, Slifkin reveals his personal opinion that "new creatures most likely developed by some process of *derech eretz*, natural law, rather than through an open miracle."[40] It would be simply wrong to state that God cannot, and will not work through evolutionary processes.[41] Slifkin thus defines himself as what he calls a "religious Darwinist",[42] asserting that "secular Darwinist inferences" may indeed contradict religion, but that "the actual theory itself does not".[43]

Thus Jews who "accept that science works",[44] and look to a God "who works through a system of natural law", have a choice not to align themselves with "creationists" who, in looking "for God in miraculous events are committing a grave error."[45]

In his next book, *Mysterious Creatures*, Rabbi Slifkin took an even closer look at the ways in which science was understood in the contemporary Orthodox community. The key issue concerned the scientific knowledge, or lack thereof, of Torah sages—ancient, medieval, and modern. Did their Torah knowledge by definition give them a similarly perfect knowledge of the

37 *Science of Torah*, p. 153, cf. p. 168.

38 *Science of Torah*, p. 164.

39 *Science of Torah*, p. 167.

40 *Science of Torah*, p. 168.

41 *Science of Torah*, p. 195, cf. p. 206.

42 *Science of Torah*, p. 212.

43 *Science of Torah*, p. 212. Cf. *Man and Beast*, p. 90.

44 *Science of Torah*, p. 226

45 Slifkin, "Science Wars" www.torah.org/features/secondlook/sciencewars.html On the attitude of Orthodox Jews toward creationists, see Robinson, "'Practically I am a Fundamentalist': Twentieth Century Orthodox Jews Contend With Evolution and Its Implications", pp. 77-78.

natural world, or did it not? It is Rabbi Slifkin's opinion that, in "the opinions of Ramban and others...even the greatest Torah sages did not necessarily know everything about the natural world." This point of view, however, "is not known or not taught [by the Orthodox]".[46]

The topic of *Mysterious Creatures* is the animals described by Torah sources "whose existence contemporary science denies".[47] This brings the conflict to a head in a way that the previous book did not. It is one thing to interpret a given biblical passage literally or non-literally. It is another thing entirely to argue that Torah sages could have been mistaken in their description of the natural world. Slifkin asserted that this was an issue that "many teachers of Torah are afraid to confront", and thus those within the Orthodox community seeking authoritative answers to their questions "often have no one to turn to for advice", possibly receiving "the impression that Torah Judaism is afraid of honest intellectual investigation."[48] Slifkin enters this minefield with the attitude that:

> The Sages of the Talmud were spiritual giants, whose greatness we cannot fathom. Yet this does not preclude a rational and reasonable discussion of conflicts between sages and scientists.[49]

In evaluating this area, Rabbi Slifkin describes five possible approaches to this conflict :

1. The sages have a perfect, or at least a superior knowledge of nature.

2. Both sages and scientists are correct because nature has changed since Talmudic times.

3. The statements of the sages are misunderstood.

4. The sages spoke metaphorically.

46 *Mysterious Creatures*, dedication.

47 *Mysterious Creatures*, p. 14.

48 Ibid.

49 *Mysterious Creatures*, p. 15.

5. The sages knew no more about nature than others in their time and place.[50]

Rabbi Slifkin rejects the first possibility. In some ways, however, all other possibilities are utilized by him. He thus refuses to believe that the statement of the sages to the effect that babies born in the eighth month of gestation are less likely to survive than those born in the seventh month, or those concerning the size of eggs and olives, were mistaken. For, as he states: "It is clear that such a change [in nature] has happened since the phenomenon is so easy to measure that it is inconceivable that any mistake was made"— though this certainty is somewhat mitigated in a footnote which states that "Historical/Archaeological research in this area would be most valuable."[51]

The previous solution, however, is clearly not Slifkin's preference. Misunderstanding of what the sages said, and the resort to metaphorical language on the grounds "that a literal understanding is too improbable to be true,"[52] are given their due. In the end, though, Rabbi Slifkin is forced to admit that in some cases "since in ancient times there was little information on hand about the natural world, it was not ridiculous [for the sages] to believe in bizarre creatures."[53]

Rabbi Slifkin is quite aware that his evaluation left him open to charges of disrespect for the sages, and he hastened to disarm potential critics by claiming that his position of skeptic is different from that of a scoffer in that "a scoffer draws negative inferences" from an assertion that the sages are not infallible whereas "a skeptic can remain respectful".[54]

Most illustrative of Rabbi Slifkin's manner of analysis is his treatment of the sages' assertion that lice generate spontaneously, which contemporary science asserts to be untrue.[55] Some contemporary Orthodox Jews, including Orthodox scientist Herman Branover, have attempted to avoid the consequences of this problem by asserting that :

50 *Mysterious Creatures*, p. 19.

51 *Mysterious Creatures*, p. 25.

52 *Mysterious Creatures*, p. 32.

53 *Mysterious Creatures*, p. 53.

54 *Mysterious Creatures*, pp. 53-54, cf. p. 231.

55 *Mysterious Creatures*, p. 193, cf. p. 232.

> the sages were not speaking about the lice with which we are familiar...but instead about a particular species of lice that is currently unknown to us, or extinct.[56]

While not ridiculing this view, Rabbi Slifkin dismisses it on logical grounds. Since this assertion of the sages has a contemporary halakhic relevance (lice can be killed on the Sabbath on account of their spontaneous generation whereas other insects cannot) if the sages did indeed refer to a species of lice now extinct or unknown, "then at what point did this ruling become entirely misunderstood and misapplied to ordinary lice?"[57] Rabbi Slifkin also plays the respectful skeptic in his treatment of the modern popular halakhic commentary, *Mishnah Berurah*, written by Rabbi Israel Meir ha-Kohen (Hafets Hayyim). This commentary, according to Rabbin Slifkin, though written at the turn of the twentieth century, continues to state that lice are born through spontaneous generation because its author was a) unaware of the advances of scientific knowledge in this matter, b) he disagreed with the scientific consensus, c) he did not consider it relevant to his halakhic analysis, or d) he had his own, unstated reasons for avoiding the topic.[58]

In his 2004 book, *The Camel, the Hare and the Hyrax*, Rabbi Slifkin addressed what he characterized as a "rare example of the Torah making potentially verifiable scientific statements about the world",[59] namely that the camel, hare and hyrax are animals that "chew their cud" but do not have "split hooves". This statement was taken by some Jews as proving the authenticity of the Torah, since, it is claimed, no other creatures in all the world possess this particular combination. The only problem is, as Rabbi Slifkin states, "simply speaking, the hyrax and the hare do not bring up the cud."[60]

Orthodox attempts to solve this conundrum include approaches we have already met, namely, that the Torah spoke of animals either unknown today or extinct, in order to attempt to preserve their view of the "extraordinary zoo-

56 *Mysterious Creatures*, p. 197.

57 *Mysterious Creatures*, p. 199.

58 *Mysterious Creatures* p. 205.

59 *The Camel, the Hare and the Hyrax*, p. 23.

60 *The Camel, the Hare and the Hyrax*, p. 88.

logical knowledge of the Torah."[61] This is, as Rabbi Slifkin concludes, "highly problematic, to say the least".[62] What remains, then, is for Rabbi Slifkin to posit that whereas:

> the Sages of the Talmud were of extraordinarily great spiritual stature…[and whereas] we should therefore be very wary of attributing any deficiency in their words. Nonetheless…there are numerous statements in the Talmud… pronounced by the Sages according to the scientific knowledge of their day and are subject to being disputed and falsified."[63]

Rabbi Slifkin himself attempts to solve this conundrum by taking that the Torah's term *ma'aleh gerah*, usually translated as "bringing up the cud" has in fact a somewhat broader meaning,[64] but is ultimately forced to conclude that "the Torah is neither proved nor disproved by the camel, the hare and the hyrax."[65]

His latest book, *The Challenge of Creation*, was published in 2006, in the wake of the furor over the banning of his books. It covers much the same areas as his previous *Science of Torah*.[66] Some of the differences between the two books are therefore instructive. The later book is much more up front with its ideological underpinnings. Echoing Maimonides' introduction to his *Guide of the Perplexed*, he states:

> This book…is written for those who are committed to the tenets of Judaism but also respect the modern scientific enterprise…While firmly within the framework of authentic, Orthodox Judaism, [it] is not the method of choice in many segments of the ultra-Orthodox community, [which] may dispute the validity of the modern scientific enterprise…Such people are not the intended audience of this book, and they are advised not to read it.[67]

61 *The Camel, the Hare and the Hyrax*, pp. 88, 90.

62 *The Camel, the Hare and the Hyrax*, p. 91.

63 *The Camel, the Hare and the Hyrax*, p. 209.

64 *The Camel, the Hare and the Hyrax*, p. 223.

65 *The Camel, the Hare and the Hyrax*, p. 231.

66 Rabbi Slifkin has also completed a reworking of his *Mysterious Creatures*, which he has entitled *Sacred Monsters: Mysterious and Mythical Creatures of Scripture, Talmud and Midrash*. This book was not yet available at the time this article was written.

67 *Challenge of Creation*, "About", cf., p. 89.

Having thus attempted to restrict his audience by eliminating those who would most strenuously object to his stance, Rabbi Slifkin addresses once again Orthodox Jews who, he asserts, "are…often suffering from a quiet feeling of unease that Judaism is afraid or incapable of dealing with these topics", whose Judaic "teachers have rebuffed those who asked about dinosaurs and evolution", and whose schools preface government-mandated courses in science "by informing the students that everything which they are about to learn is false."[68]

His response rejects the mysticism that constituted a significant part of his earlier book, and fully embraces a Maimonidean rationalism.[69] He states that he leaves the integrity of Torah uncompromised, though some questions will remain unanswered. These unanswered questions, though, "should not cause a person to abandon his belief in God or Torah."[70] The alternative, "closing off rational inquiry" also poses its danger to Judaism.[71]

In the aftermath of the Haredi condemnation of his work, Rabbi Slifkin began distancing himself, with fewer holds barred, from the perspectives of the Jewish Orthodox who deny the validity of science. They are characterized as a "particular group" with a "narrow perspective".[72] They include Lubavitchers who "still maintain the earlier belief that the earth is at the center of the universe, purporting to base themselves on Einstein's Theory of Relativity."[73] He decries the situation in which he asserts that "many Torah scholars *privately* endorse" his approaches but "will not do so publicly due to the inability of much of the general public to accept it."[74]

Rabbi Slifkin is also stronger in his assertion that Torah can and must be reinterpreted to conform with science.[75] Whereas previously he had justified such a reinterpretation on the basis of the presence of "overwhelming [scien-

68 *Challenge of Creation*, p. 17.

69 *Challenge of Creation*, p. 22.

70 *Challenge of Creation*, pp. 90-91.*Challenge of Creation*

71 *Challenge of Creation*, p. 93

72 *Challenge of Creation*, p. 96.

73 *Challenge of Creation*, p. 127.

74 *Challenge of Creation*, p. 132.

75 *Challenge of Creation*, p. 130.

tific] grounds" for it,[76] now he would proceed with such a reinterpretation even in the absence of internal justifications from the tradition.[77] He is more forceful than previously in his criticism of those Jews who believe that the earth is only *apparently* billions of years old:

> The idea that God deliberately creates false testimony has disturbing implications... One has to rely on God's truthfulness if religion is to function... If God went to enormous lengths to convince us that the world is billions of years old, who are we to disagree?[78]

Finally, he clearly describes the account of creation in the Book of Genesis as not a scientific account, but rather a "theological cosmology".[79]

Clearly the thought of Rabbi Natan Slifkin has undergone a profound evolution. What remains constant in his writing, from its beginning to the present, is his search for the truth. This search has led him to cross an ideological line within contemporary Jewish Orthodoxy between those who live in an intellectual universe in which the greatest sages of the Talmud—then and now—are infallible in all things, and are prepared to engage in extended mental gymnastics to maintain this position, and those who are able to admit the realities of science and adjust their understanding of Torah accordingly.

76 *Science of Torah*, p. 102.

77 *Challenge of Creation*, p. 130.

78 *Challenge of Creation*, p. 167.

79 *Challenge of Creation*, p. 186, cf. p. 344.

MAPPING ALTERNATE TEXTS OF GENDER DIFFERENCE

Bonna Devora Haberman, Hebrew University

The Apollonian male body is a sleek, angular, erect figure. Solid, polished, even monumental, he is as sculpted from stone, his musculature gleaming.[1] This male icon represents the sovereignty of humanity, both the measure, and power. His transcendent essence justifies the privilege of male perspective and authority in culture. The definitive subject, his subjectivity is universal; he stands for humanity. His form occupies and defines the domains of idea, ethic, spirit and theory; his interests dominate the transactions of global society, religion, economy, politics, and art. His relation to the material is willful and controlled; his body is intact and impervious. The phallus is the ubiquitous symbol of his supreme potency and dominion.

In a live interview on an American public radio broadcast, Massachusetts inmate Elizabeth described her recent experience under "eyeball" surveillance at a Boston area prison.[2] Stripped of every garment of clothing, she was restrained at four points, two arms and two legs pinned to the floor of a completely bare cell containing only a plastic mattress. The room had a glass wall where a male guard was stationed to keep watch 24 hours per day. Having recently miscarried a pregnancy, Elizabeth was hemorrhaging heavily, yet the staff denied her sanitary supplies. Feeling utterly humiliated and degraded by her bleeding under male scrutiny, she managed to push the mattress up against the glass to create a sense of privacy. She was reprimanded for obscuring the guard's view.

---

1 Apollo Belvedere is one of the most famous examples of ancient statuary, Greek fifth century B. C. E., white marble, Vatican City, Vatican Museums.

2 NPR broadcast on Friday, October 16, 1998.

The cultural configuration of body not only expresses prevailing conceptions of knowledge, meaning, ethics, aesthetics and power — it is a determinant cause and fortifier of them.[3] Subtle and overt mechanisms in society produce and perform the gendered body. In turn, maintenance of the culturally regulated body is instrumental to the proper function of the body of society. Elizabeth's mortifying testimony of abuse at the hands of a public institution at the heart of a democratic society underlines how systemic power enforces male-gendered discipline of women. While pinned down, Elizabeth's uncontrolled bloody discharge transgresses her bodily boundary. The material of life/death and danger defiles the striving for/to order, to imprison. The male voyeur represents male power and authority; he bears witness to the institutional degradation of a woman and her integrity. The contrast between the Apollonian male body as ideal concept and autonomous subject, and Elizabeth's oozing body as oppressed object renders the moral problematic of gendered embodiment explicit. Gender différence imputes relations of power.[4] The enactment of gender in society drives cultural systems of human oppression and suffering. Paula M. Cooey contends that "the history of idealizing the female body in ways that efface women's subjectivity as women, and the voyeurism correlative with this effacement, require drastic measures."[5]

Gender différence derives from and is informed by literary, philosophic, social, psychological, political and religious ideas. These cultural modes institute and enforce the *opposition* of two differently-sexed bodies and the accompanying difference in male and female being. Among the mechanisms that generate "body," religion operates sometimes discreetly but pervasively and powerfully. According to Judith Butler's deconstruction, undetermined by biology, the engendering of body is sustained through persistent recitation, or reinscription.[6] Myths, doctrines, texts, rituals, imagery, canon, taboos and

3 Michel Foucault's work on prisons and the power to punish influences the current discussion. See *Discipline and Punish: The Birth of the Prison* (Transl. Alan Sheridan; New York: Pantheon, 1978).

4 Foucauldian *différence,* ie, the social construction of difference.

5 *Religious Imagination and the Body. A Feminist Analysis* (New York/Oxford: Oxford UP, 1994), 84.

6 Judith Butler, *Gender Trouble. Feminism and the Subversion of Identity* (London: Routeledge, 1990); and *Bodies that Matter: On the Discursive Limits of "Sex"* (London: Routledge, 1993).

stigmas contribute toward configuring conscious and unconscious, personal and societal mappings of the body. Religious traditions infuse bodies with identity and meaning, and mediate, even constitute experience and behavior. Jonathan Smith, a contemporary historian of religions, comments about the relation between religion, space, and power in society.

> Religion is the quest, within the bounds of the human, historical condition, for the power to manipulate and negotiate one's "situation" so as to have "space" to meaningfully dwell... What we study when we study religion is the variety of attempts to map, construct and inhabit such positions of power through the use of myths, rituals and experiences of transformation.[7]

Here I use a metaphor of "mapping" to chart contiguous and overlapping bodies in biblical and rabbinic texts.[8] These maps demonstrate alternative configurations of the body and being with particular attention to gender, perhaps a foundation for the *drastic measures* that Paula Cooey advocates.

Relentlessly performing gender analysis upon their professor-fathers, French feminists have recorded the problematic body mappings of difference that dominate western culture;[9] they have scrutinized the ideology of the female body as material territory, as abject and grotesque.[10] The unveiling of androcentric structure construes religious texts themselves as latently misogynist. Though fully identifying with the liberationist agenda of feminist interpretation, and also inquiring about deep textual-religious causes of misogyny, I depart from the psychoanalytic essentialism of much of the argument.[11]

7 Jonathan Z. Smith, *Map Is Not Territory* (Leiden, Netherlands: E. J. Brill, 1978), 291.

8 Paula Cooey discusses "mapping" as interactions of site and sign in conceptualization of body. *Religious Imagination and the Body*, 90. See also Fredric Jameson, "Cognitive mapping," in *Marxism and the Interpretation of Culture*, eds. Cary Nelson and Lawrence Grossberg (Urbana: U of Illinois Press, 1988), 347-360; and a critique by Steven Best and Douglas Kellner, *Postmodern Theory: Critical Interrogations* (New York: Guilford Press, 1991), 188-192.

9 Jane Gallop is particularly cogent about this phenomenon. *The Daughter's Seduction. Feminism and Psychoanalysis* (Ithaka: Cornell U.P., 1982).

10 "*Body* [is] the symbolic connection between *woman* and *property*....""" Paula M. Cooey, *Religious Imagination*, 23.

11 My analysis is premised upon work of the *Questions feministes* group of French materialist feminists which undermines sex as *un fait de nature*, by contrast with *Psych(analyse) et Po (litique)* who celebrate the *féminine* as an essential category of experience.

Often the analysis and counter-analysis objectify "woman," *féminité*, disconnecting theory from *les femmes*, live female embodied subjects and agents. Here I sketch an interpretive line of Jewish textuality about the body through primary sources that map male-female body postures. Read against the grain of gender assumptions, these texts suggest alternate mappings to traditional androcentric Western paradigms. The intention is to destabilize the imputed gender difference of the human body. Without a doubt, I have selected these texts carefully; many counter examples may be found both within and outside Jewish tradition. This is an exploratory "mapping" of intersecting and contiguous textual bodies, and of sites where bodies overlap with sacred space and, potentially, with sacred living in community.

AMBIGU(N)ITY

The complexity of the biblical genealogy of the body is expressed by the two versions of Genesis. The second (so-called "J") version of creation and the Garden of Eden has overbearingly configured gender throughout the dominion of Western influence. Blaming Eve for the "fall of humanity" embarrasses, to use Harry Fox's term, and offends contemporary sensibilities. Rabbinic Judaism does not often advocate the doctrine of original sin, nor does it hold women culpable for "falling." Leviticus Rabbah perfunctorily dismisses the mistakes in the Garden of the second creation story and promises future forgiveness,

> ...On the third (day) S/He assembled Adam's dust, in the fourth S/He kneaded it, in the fifth S/He shaped him, in the sixth S/He made him into a lifeless body, in the seventh S/He breathed a soul into him, in the eighth S/He brought him into the Garden of Eden, in the ninth s/he was commanded [against eating of the fruit of the Tree of Knowledge], in the tenth s/he transgressed, in the eleventh s/he was judged, in the twelfth s/he was pardoned. "This" said the Holy One, blessed be S/He, to Adam, "will be a sign to your children. As you stood in judgment before Me this day and came out with a free pardon, so will your children in the future stand in judgment before Me on this day and come out from my presence with a free pardon."[12]

12 *Lev. Rabbah*, Emor, 29.1.

I exercise the prerogative of the "free pardon" bestowed upon Adam by this text, and, I impute, also upon Eve, to focus on the first account that locates humanity within the larger setting of Creation, in the image of the Creator.

> And God said, "Let us make Adam (human), in our image, according to our likeness..." So God created the Adam (the human) in His/Her image, in the image of God S/He created (Adam), male and female S/He created them. (Gen. 1:26-27)

The ambiguity of sex and plural identity is evident in these early verses of the Torah. God and human alike are grammatically characterized as both singular and plural. Insofar as human is *like* God, and this is surely the emphasis of these verses, argues Rachel Adler,[13] both God and human have dual sexuality. This view is reiterated later in the lineage of Adam.

> On the day that S/He created Adam, in the likeness of God S/He made him/her. Male and female S/He created them; S/He blessed them and called their name Adam on the day S/He created them (Gen. 5:1-2).

These verses from the first biblical version of the creation of humanity suggest that both male and female are aspects of the divine image. By referring to "Adam," the human, alternately as singular and plural, the text is ambiguous about his/her identity. While male and female seem to be embodied in the primordial being as two definable aspects, s/he is nevertheless a unified oneness, "Adam." The extent to which these sexualities are two, or blended sexualities along a continuum is unstated. Female and male are certainly not opposed in the text; they are not opposites, but rather a dynamic imbuing one being. This multiple aspect of unity may be read reflexively back to God as the source from whom the image is derived. God's singular identity is composite, comprised at the very least of male and female difference. Female and male-sexed being is, therefore, one of the ways in which humanity is *like* God.

An eloquent midrash in the *Sifra* expresses the priority of the ethical injunction implicit in the creation of Adam in the divine likeness — male and female S/He created them.

13 *Engendering Judaism* (Philadelphia: JPS, 1998), 118.

> "And you shall love your neighbor as yourself" (Lev. 19:17). Rabbi Akiva said: this is the great principle of the Torah. Ben Azzai said: "this is the book of the generations of Adam, when God created the human being, God made Adam in the likeness of God" is an even greater principle.[14]

While the "golden rule" is an inspiring ethical standard, this midrash suggests that there is a prior principle. Caring for one's fellow human being depends upon each person's self-conception; what we wish to have done to us is a function of how society constructs human dignity. Self-perception is extensively influenced by gender. Insofar as each perceives her/himself as a creature who resembles the difference contained within the divine, whose dignity is honored and uplifted, so also we recognize the worthiness of others. From the first biblical creation narrative and its claim of shared human lineage derived from Adam and ultimately from the divine Creator, Ben Azzai advocates for a doctrine of human caring.[15] This midrash argues that the complex identity that comprises primordial Adam — male and female — is the root for loving others.

EMBRACE

A story in the Talmud elaborates about God's likeness. In order to protect the community from becoming exposed to impurity, Rabbi Bana'ah used to mark out the dimensions of caves where there were dead bodies. When he came to the cave of Avraham, he found Eliezer, the servant of Avraham, standing at the entrance.

> Rabbi Bana'ah said to him, "What is Avraham doing?"
> He replied, "He is sleeping in the arms of Sara, and she is looking fondly at his head."
> He said: "go and tell him that Bana'ah is standing at the entrance."
> Avraham said to him, "Let him enter; it is well known that there is no passion in this world."

14 *Sifra on Leviticus*, Isaac H. Weiss, ed. (Vienna: n.p. 1862) 89b.

15 See Monica Jyotsna Melanchthon, "The Grace of God and the *Equality* of Human Persons," *Dialog: A Journal of Theology*, Spring2003, Vol. 42 Issue 1, 8-19.

> So he went in, surveyed the cave, and came out again. When he came to the cave of Adam, a voice came from heaven saying, "You have beheld the likeness of my likeness, but my likeness itself you may not see."
> Having surveyed from the outside only, Rabbi Bana'ah said, "I discerned his two heels, and they were like two orbs of the sun."[16]

In this legend, Rabbi Bana'ah beholds the likeness of God's likeness in Avraham's cave, for Avraham is created in the image of Adam, and Adam in turn is created in God's image. Avraham is engulfed in a caring but sexually passion-less embrace of Sara. This image of the intertwined bodies of man and woman, male and female, without sexual arousal recalls the original Adam of Genesis 1. Indeed the text acknowledges that what Rabbi Bana'ah beholds is the likeness of Adam. The two united forms embody Adam's image: Avraham and Sara together, in a primordial Garden of Eden state prior to the taste of mortality. Together, their bodies figure the divine unified male and female in whose image Adam is created. The description of Adam's own body as *luminescence*, "two orbs of the sun," reinforces the connection with the first creation account. In the second chapter, dust and earth are the raw materials for the human being, whereas light is the primary substance from which creation emanates in Genesis 1.

The inclusion of Sara in the Avraham cave episode is not demanded by the midrashic context. Other biblical ancestors are also interred in the Cave of Machpelah, but they are not mentioned. Sara's presence effects the fulfillment of the image of the united male and female, resembling the original composite Adam. Avraham speaks from his passive prone position, while Sara looks on and embraces him. Death here is alluded to not by total lifelessness, but by the absence of sexual passion which "does not exist in this world," according to the story. Avraham and Sara have melded into the primordial condition of Adam whereby difference operates at such a low register that even a position of contiguity, a total embrace of overlapping bodies, does not generate *eros*. Alternately, the embrace might represent an extended or eternal moment of fulfillment. When union is achieved and desire abates, difference is obfuscated.

16 TB Baba Bathra 58a.

This rabbinic legend echoes the early creation moment of male and female embodied co-existence.

PROSTRATION

A midrashic text about Yitzchak and Rivka describes a different milieu for the proximity of male and female. While fruitfulness is part of the divine promise to Avraham and his descendants, Yitzchak, Avraham and Sara's inheritor, has no offspring in his monogamous relationship with Rivka. The Torah reports that Yitzchak pleads for a child, "in the presence of his woman [Rivka]" (Gen. 25:21). Perhaps one of the narrative purposes of barrenness in the early generations of Genesis is to elicit the responses of the characters to a desperate desire. In the same pulse as the prayer, God immediately accepts the petition; Rivka conceives. The midrash explains the special efficacy of the plea by interpreting the meaning of the phrase "in the presence of his woman [Rivka]":

> Yitzchak prostrates himself here and says, "Sovereign of the universe, all of the children you will give me will be from that righteous woman." Rivka similarly prostrates herself there and says, "All of the children whom you will give me will be from that righteous man."[17]

Whereas the biblical text attributes the prayer only to Yitzchak, the midrash embellishes. In the same way as Yitzchak, Rivka prostrates herself; she prays a parallel prayer. The sages celebrate Yitzchak and Rivka as the uniquely monogamous couple among the patriarchs and matriarchs.[18] Here the midrash depicts them in utter humility, brought low by the experience of barrenness. They plead with God on the basis of their respect for worthiness — each for the other. The two halves of the text map upon one another with perfect symmetry. Both figures flatten themselves in prostration and devotion. The midrash portrays both as embodied spiritual subjects, sharing with their Creator their profound longing for a child. The absence of paternalism, inequality, subordination is notable. They are ungendered except by the requisite Hebrew

17 *Genesis Rabba*, Toldot 63:5.

18 See the Netziv, Rabbi Naftali Zvi Yehudah Berlin (1817-1893), *Ha'emek Davar* on the above verse.

grammatical forms. Their matching prayers mutually engage one another. At the moment when Yitzchak refers and possibly gestures toward Rivka as a righteous being, she is present with him in the space, appealing to God on the grounds of *his* merit. Concurrently, Rivka refers and probably gestures toward Yitzchak as a righteous being, present with her in the space as he appeals to God on the grounds of *her* merit. Their mutual references are a sign of the reciprocity of their connection. The prayers figure mutual interpenetration: she enters his prayer; he enters her prayer. This verbal interfusion of prayers and intentions is a symbolic cause or ground for conceiving their child. Rivka and Yitzchak enact the aspect of the divine image that unifies male and female, invoking the Creation blessing of the first chapter of Genesis, "Be fruitful and multiply."[19] Immediately, the prayer elicits (pro)creative power, for the combined force of the conjoined petition is irresistible to the divine *qua* creator.

FACE TO FACE

A biblical source depicts the bi-fold aspects of the divine within the sacred domain of the Tabernacle where the two cherubs are enclosed.

> 18 And you shall make two cherubim of gold; of beaten work shall you make them, at the two ends of the ark-cover. 19 And make one cherub at the one end, and one cherub at the other end; of one piece with the ark-cover shall you make the cherubim of the two ends thereof. 20 And the cherubim shall spread out their wings on high, screening the ark-cover with their wings, with their faces one to another; toward the ark-cover shall the faces of the cherubim be. 21 And you shall put the ark-cover above upon the ark; and in the ark you shall put the testimony that I shall give you. 22 And there I will meet with you, and I will speak with you from above the ark-cover, from between the two cherubim which are upon the ark of the testimony, of all things which I will give you as commandment to the children of Israel.[20]

19 Genesis 1:28.

20 Exodus 25.

Inside the Tabernacle, the divine throne rested upon the wings of the cherubs while the *Shekhina* hovered over it.[21] The embodied imagery of cherubs within the sacred enclosure of the biblical Tabernacle is uniquely egalitarian. While signifiers of the union of male and female within the godhead, or the people of Israel with God, the material, forms, positions and movements of the two cherubs are undifferentiated by sex or gender.[22] If they are male and female lovers, the biblical text depicts them in identical bodies, with mutual affinity and enthusiasm. According to the narrative in Genesis, cherubs are more reliable and obedient than humans; they support divine order on earth. Cherubs are charged to guard the Tree of Life from further transgression by man and woman after the expulsion from the Garden of Eden.[23] In a prophetic vision, the cherubs are mythic beings who escape the gendered constructs of human culture. Ezekiel describes human forms, faces and hands, ungendered beings who populate the sacred chariot.[24] In these biblical materials, cherubs are human-like mediators between God and human temptations and the presumed corruptions of human desire.

IMMODEST CHERUBS

Each of the texts I have discussed above conceives embodied interaction as the occasion for reciprocal engagement. On the surface, this embodiment appears to be asexual — there is no mention or even allusion to different male and female sexuality; no gender roles are thereby determined. By contrast with the biblical text about the Tabernacle, the Talmud debates the relative postures of the pair, attributing to them volition and desire to face one another when Israel is obedient, and to turn away from one another when Israel disobeys the will of God.[25] Kabalistic elaborations of this episode describe the choreography of the cherubs, male and female, representing the unification and separation of the female and male aspects of the divine in response to human

21 Numbers Rabbah 4:13.

22 Exodus 25:18-20.

23 Genesis 3:24.

24 Ezekiel 1:5-28.

25 TB BB 99a.

behavior.[26] In mystical literatures, the inter-relationships of male and female aspects of the divine are obvious and pervasive. The Zoharic legend of supernal adornment, wedding and union of bride and groom, however, reflects and re-inscribes the gendered human counterparts. The woman is passive while the male "students" bedeck, perfume, and beautify her — objectify her.[27] The following rabbinic passages elaborate the sighting of the intertwined bodies of the cherubs by Jewish pilgrims when they arrive at the Jerusalem Temple differently.[28]

> Rabbi Katina said, "When the Israelites would ascend (to the Holy Temple) on the Festival, (the priest) would roll up the curtain (*parochet*) for them, and display for them the cherubs, who were joined together." The priest would then tell them, "Behold, the beloved feelings for you on the part of the Omnipresent are like the beloved feelings of a male for a female."[29]

Charged with erotic imagery, the passage alludes to the intercourse of God with the Jewish people. Rabbi Nahman relieves concern expressed in the text about the exposed embrace and the implicit immodesty of the woman. The cherubs are equally demonstrative and active, yet the male redactor is singly concerned with the exposure of the woman. Dispelling concern, the text produces an explanation of the female cherub's bold sexuality.

> That may be compared to a bride: As long as she is in her father's house, she is modest before her spouse, but when she comes to her father-in-law's house, she is no longer reserved in regard to him."[30]

Particular interest in the female cherub's immodesty has a number of possible explanations. Might the female body inappropriately arouse the presumed male voyeur? Yet the text does not distinguish her sexuality *qua* cherub from that of the male. Alternately, perhaps the Talmud is bothered not so much by

26 Abraham ben Eliezer ha-Levi, *Sefer Masoret ha-Hokhmah*, printed by Gershom Scholem in *Kiryat Sefer*, 7(1930): 451.

27 *Zohar*, Introduction, I:8a.

28 BB 99a; Yoma 54a.

29 Yoma 54a.

30 Yoma 54a.

the fact *that* she is exposed, but by *what* the exposure reveals — the demeanor and activity of the female cherub. Whereas in her own father's house, she was required to respect the gendered expectations of modesty, in her father-in-law's house, that is, in the Temple, she is able to caress her lover freely without gendered inhibition. She is publicly revealed to be an equal partner to an embracing union.

ALIGNMENT

In each of these textual sources, male and female are aligned with one another symmetrically. The male and female form part of one identity; they enact a union of different elements. The absence of any manifestation of gendered power is remarkable. The texts demonstrate the possibility of a contiguous, overlapping map of male and female bodies. The source and cause of these mappings is attributed to the divine being, whose oneness comprises sex difference, yet is neither rupturing nor oppressive.

This paper begins with the contrast between the celestial Apollonian male and Elizabeth confined in her cell at four points. The cultural mapping of sexuality onto a gendered power-grid creates oppressive relationships between the sexual identities of male and female people. Indeed gender-based oppression in the basic dyad of human relationship is a root of other oppressions in society — class, race, disability *et cetera*. Monique Wittig has articulated the problematic obsession with sexual difference. "For there is no sex. There is but sex that is oppressed and sex that oppresses."[31] The textual examples I have brought here demonstrate the possibility of a dignified and mutual connection between males and females even while their sexual identity is intact. Rivka and Yitzchak work collaboratively toward conception without mastery of one sex over the other. These texts perform a refined choreography of mutual embrace between male and female. This pattern is both subtly erotic and affirms male and female integrity and wholeness without re-inscribing sexual difference-based oppression. Luce Irigaray describes a realm of intimacy that is flowing with the interchange of partners delighting in and supporting one-another.

31 "The category of sex," in *Sex in Question: French Materialist Feminism*, Diana Leonard and Lisa Adkins eds. (Exeter, GB: Taylor & Francis, 1996), 25.

> Before orality comes to be, touch is already in existence. No nourishment can compensate for the grace or work of touching. Touch makes it possible to wait, to gather strength, so that the other will return to caress and reshape, from within and from without, a flesh that is given back to itself in the gesture of love. The most subtly necessary guardian of my life is the other's flesh.[32]

There is not even a hint of superiority or oppression in this passage that articulates love unfettered by discourse.

In conclusion, the texts I have selected here map private, intimate, even concealed territories: pre-Garden space; a burial cave; a prayer chamber; and a conjugal couch. They describe a sublime, intertwined embrace of two subjects, an embodied replica of the divine unity in the presence of *différance*. From these texts we distill a paradigm of differently gendered male-female relationships wherein the integrity and subjectivity of each is radically preserved, while mutual combination and intersection are honored, even exalted. Considering the massive scale of gender-based oppressions in humanity, the current work proposes an alternative. Our challenge is to transcribe and perform these texts privately and publicly — in place of gendered maps of power and domination.

32 Luce Irigaray, *An Ethics of Sexual Difference*, Carolyn Burke and Gillian C. Gill trans. (Ithaka: Cornell U.P., 1993) 187.

HOW CAN THEY BE BETTER THAN US? EMBARRASSMENT AND LEGISLATION[1]

Tirzah Meacham, University of Toronto

Rabbinic literature exhibits a high level of chauvinism when relating to other groups. Attributing moral inferiority to the Other was a commonplace: adultery, rape, incest, sodomy, and bestiality in the sexual realm, as well as a host of other crimes such as murder, mutilation, and theft. The automatic talmudic response to non-Jews was to assume that they were idol worshipers, making any wine in an open vessel unfit if a non-Jewish garrison had passed through; and guilty of sexual sins, assuming that any Jewish woman who had been taken captive by Gentiles had been raped unless a complicated system of testimony was able to contradict that; and promiscuous so that any Gentile girl who converts to Judaism after the age of three years and a day is assumed to be a non-virgin.

According to rabbinic literature all human beings prior to the giving of the Torah at Sinai were considered children of Noah, *benei Noah*, that is, descendents of Noah after the flood.[2] Once Abraham accepted monotheism, his offspring or at least those who became Israel were separated and identi-

---

1 I dedicate this article this article to Harry Fox who has encouraged me in my academic pursuits, been my most severe critic, provided me the greatest encouragement, and fathered our children. His fierce intellectual honesty is a model for all scholars. We have shared great joys and deep sorrows in our first thirty seven years together — many connected to our children. Throughout those years he has nurtured our love and never allowed us to stray from our commitment to continual growth. And he has consistently made me laugh. May he and I together be blessed to see the fruits of our children and grandchildren.

2 Many of the background references found below are taken from *Encyclopedia Talmudit sv ben Noah* (henceforth *ET*) found on The Responsa Project CD version 15+. According to mNedarim 3:11 one who vows not to have benefit from a *ben Noah* is allowed to benefit from Israel but prohibited to benefit from the rest of the nations of the world.

fied through his line.[3] At Sinai Israel became a nation separate from the rest of humanity because they accepted the obligation to adhere to the laws of the Torah but until then the children of Israel, too, were considered *benei Noah*. Sinaitic revelation strengthened the dichotomy between Israel and the children of Noah. This is, of course, an anachronistic description of Israel's relationship to other nations.

Other peoples, too, had basic laws and legal systems. The rabbinic sages, probably in the tannaitic era, enumerated a set of laws which they considered universally applicable, even to Israel prior to the revelation, what some might call a natural law of sorts. These laws were then considered binding on all other nations (*benei Noah*) and came to be known as the seven mitzvot of *benei Noah*, or the Noahide laws. Whether Noahide law is identical to natural law is a question which will be addressed to some degree below. The way in which Noahide law functions in rabbinic literature seems to be quite similar to the way Romans used a version of Roman law to adjudicate issues among non-Roman citizens or between non-Roman citizens and Romans.[4] Natural law is, nonetheless, a human construct. We designate practices that help ensure a reasonably peaceful and constructive continuation of society, and call those practices natural law. The element of universality is considered to be a basic part of natural law but individual societies will embody their particularistic preferences in their own legal systems. We can see that Christian and Jewish incest/adultery laws differ in detail but are much closer together than Zoroastrian laws in the same area. Similarly, in a religious world what constitutes blasphemy will differ according to the deity/deities one worships. Atheism was not part of *homo religiosus*' theological possibilities though today if we were to construct a system of natural law it is likely that blasphemy would no longer be part of it. Or possibly a redefinition of blasphemy in a secular manner would be substituted, that is, lack of belief in the establishment of the courts and legal system would constitute a transgression. Identifying idol worship as

3 The discussion in bNedarim 31a excludes Ishmael and Esau and their offspring from the Abrahamic line.

4 See David Novak, *Natural Law in Judaism*, Cambridge: Cambridge University Press, 1998, p. 140-150. Bernard S. Jackson, "The Jewish View of Natural Law," *Journal of Jewish studies*, 52 (1), Spring 2001, 136-145, reviews Novak's presentation of the issue.

a Noahide prohibition clearly privileges monotheism, an opinion which can hardly be considered universal in antiquity when the law was formulated. It may have identified a particularistic (Jewish) willingness to have economic and some level of social interaction with non-idol worshipers but it did not describe religious practices current at its inception.

Prior to Sinai the Noahide laws were binding on everyone even those destined to become Israel.[5] For Jews Torah law superseded Noahide law because it created a far more comprehensive legal system particularly as it came to be interpreted by the sages. Talmudic sages developed the idea that a law binding *benei Noah* remained in effect on Israel if it were reiterated at the revelation.[6] The reverse of this would be that if the revelation contained opinions to the contrary, Israel was bound to follow the Oral Torah. Here the thorny issue of whether oral law constitutes a part of Sinaitic revelation arises. The Sages assume a simultaneous revelation of the dual Torah.

This paper will examine how the prohibition against homicide came to include, for certain rabbinic sages, feticide or abortion for *benei Noah.* This anomalous situation, a prohibition for *benei Noah* which is permitted for Israel, created a dialectic of embarrassment. Those sages who did not accept this minority opinion still had to deal with the principle that anything forbidden to a non-Jew could not be permitted to a Jew (bSanhedrin 59a) because if the prohibition demonstrated theological superiority, Israel should also be included in the prohibition. The act of necessity, cutting up a fetus prior to or during birth to save the mother's life, stands in direct contradiction to the midrash attributed to Rabbi Yishmael which makes abortion a capital crime for *benei Noah.* The talmudic sources on abortion are generally in contradiction to Rabbi Yishmael's position. When the actual abortion debate of the 20th century became a central theological discussion, the inconsistency of the sources and the discomfort of the medieval commentaries became full-blown

5 This can be seen when rabbinical literature anachronistically attributes to the patriarchs the keeping of a variety of *mitzvot*, including refusal to worship idols. See, for example, Theodore-Albeck, *Bereishit Rabbah* (2nd edition), Jerusalem: Wahrmann Books, 1965, vol. 1 *paresha* 38, p. 361-364; *Otzar HaMidrashim* (Eisenstein) Avraham Avinu p. 8, and the reference to the incident in bAvoda Zara 3a.

6 See the discussion on this topic in bSanhedrin 59ab.

embarrassment. We will see the response of some of the current deeply embarrassed writers and examine what they left out in their arguments (and will express our own embarrassment over their position).

The seven Noahide laws were considered the foundation of a basic law-abiding society. Some claim that those who kept the Noahide laws were those who were God-fearing (*yirei shamayim*) and with whom it was suitable for Jews to interact. Presumably those who did not abide by these basic laws were subject to adjudication from the courts which the various nations established. Maimonides refers to those who accept the Noahide laws as "among the righteous of the peoples of the world and they have a place in the world to come" (*Hil. Melakhim* 8:11) but if they do not fulfill the commandments voluntarily, they are not considered "*ger toshav,*" the alien resident, nor of the righteous of the nations of the world nor of their sages. It should be noted that a variety of terms were in use in biblical and rabbinic literature to designate peoples other than Israel, for example, *ger, ger toshav, ger tzedeq, yirei shamayim* and *benei Noah*. It is clear that these definitions did not remain stable in these very different eras when Israel had hegemony over their land or when they were subject to foreign rule.[7]

Tosefta Avoda Zara 8:4 and bSanhedrin 56ab have the same basic list of Noahide laws in a slightly different order. The laws include: 1) establishment of laws and courts,[8] 2) blasphemy, 3) idol worship, 4) sexual transgressions, 5) homicide, 6) theft, and 7) eating a limb from a living animal. Other attempts are made to include blood from a living animal, castration, sorcery (including divination, enchanters, wizardry, necromancy, witchcraft, etc.) and "mixtures"

7 See the discussion of Terence Callahan, "The Background of the Apostolic Decree (At 15:20, 29; 21:25)," *Catholic Biblical Quarterly* 55, (2) (1993) 284-297 and of David Novak, *The Image of the Non-Jew in Judaism: An Historical and Constructive Study of the Noahide Laws,* Lampeter, Dyfed, Wales: The Edwin Mellen Press, 1983, 14-28. Novak concludes, probably correctly, that "[t]he concept of the seven Noahide laws appears to be a theological-juridical theory rather than a functioning body of laws administered by Jews or Gentiles actually living under their suzerainty at any time in history."

8 This is the only positive commandment as the remaining laws are prohibitions. Some scholars, like David Novak, *Halakha in a Theological Dimension*, Chico, California: Scholars Press, 1985 p. 89 describe this as the prohibition of anarchy. In *The Image* (54-55), however, he translates Nachmanides on Genesis 34:13 as "adjudication" and Maimonides (*Hilkhot Melakhim* 9:14) as "the obligation to install judges and legal authorities and to judge according to the six commandments and to warn the people," implying a positive commandment.

where animals of different species are made to work together.[9] The list of seven mentioned above became the official, if disputed, list. The discussion in bSanhedrin 56b attempts to derive these commandments from Genesis 2:16: וַיְצַו ה' אֱלֹהִים עַל הָאָדָם לֵאמֹר מִכֹּל עֵץ הַגָּן אָכֹל תֹּאכֵל: "The Lord God commanded concerning the human saying: From every tree in the garden you may surely eat." Each word or phrase of this verse is considered to be the source of one of the seven laws. According to the order of the Hebrew verse we have the following derivations: וַיְצַו "Commanded" — these are the laws [and courts]; ה' [tetragramaton] "The Lord — this is blasphemy; אֱלֹהִים "God" — this is idol worship; עַל הָאָדָם "Concerning the human" — this is homicide; לֵאמֹר "Saying" — these are sexual transgressions; מִכֹּל עֵץ הַגָּן "From every tree in the garden" — this is theft; אָכֹל תֹּאכֵל "You shall surely eat" — this is a limb from a living animal. Each derivation is followed by another verse which connects the midrashic exposition to the desired law. Although this verse is addressed to "the human"/Adam, the progenitor of the human race, the verse dealing with proof for homicide is addressed to Noah — the post-flood progenitor of the human race. This address contributes to the sense of universality of laws. The talmudic sages attempted to derive these precepts from biblical statements by God either to Adam or to Noah, that is, those human beings who flourished prior to the revelation given to Abraham which led to the eventual formation of the Jewish people at the Sinaitic revelation. Maimonides sees this as a chronological progression: Adam who had six commandments, Noah to whom a seventh (*eiver min ha-hai*) was added, Abraham to whom circumcision was added and who prayed in the morning, Isaac who tithed and prayed in the afternoon, Jacob who did not eat the *gid ha-nashe* and who prayed in the

9 bHullin 92ab claims that there are thirty commandments for *benei Noah* but does not give a list of the thirty but refers to not providing a *ketuba* in the event of a homosexual relationship, not weighing out publicly the flesh from a human corpse for consumption, and respecting the Torah. Rashi (loc. cit.) thus assumes that homosexual relations are permitted to *benei Noah* as is cannibalism though he brings an alternate commentary that the reference is to the meat of dead animals which were not slaughtered properly. yAvoda Zara 2:1, 40c brings a midrash on Zekharia 11:12 "Then I said to them, 'If you are satisfied, pay me my wages; if not, do not.' So they weighed out my wages, thirty shekels of silver" referring to the thirty mitzvot that *benei Noah* will take upon themselves in the future and be rewarded for fulfilling them. Aaron Greenbaum, "Thirty Mitzvot of *Benei Noah* according to Rav Shmuel ben Hofni Gaon," *Sinai* 72 (1-7), 1973, 204-221 brings a list of thirty mitzvot from a *geniza* fragment according to which Rav Shmuel ben Hofni enumerated them presumably as a commentary on bHullin 92a.

evening, the Israelites in Egypt had yet more commandments and finally Moses received the entire Torah (Rambam *Hil. Melakhim* 9:1).

The talmudic discussion continues on Sanhedrin 57a:

> Rabbi Yaaqov bar Aha found written in an aggadic book of the House of Rav: A *ben Noah* is executed with one judge, one witness and without warning on the testimony of a man but not on a woman, even a relative. In the name of Rabbi Yishmael they said: Also because of embryos/fetuses. From where do we have these things? Rav Yehuda says: Scripture says (Genesis 9:5) *But your blood of your souls I shall seek* — even by one judge; *from the hand of every living* — even without warning; *I shall seek it from the hand of the person* — even one witness; *from the hand of a man* — not the hand of a woman; *his brother* — even a relative. In the name of Rabbi Yishmael they said: this is also the case concerning embryos/fetuses. What is the reason of Rabbi Yishmael? For it is written (Genesis 9:6) *One who spills the blood of the human in the human, his blood shall be spilled...* Who is the person inside a person? I would say this is the embryo/fetus in its mother's uterus. The first sage, is the sage from the house of Manasheh who said: All the executions for *benei Noah* are by strangulation...

The verse which is considered to be a prooftext to midrash attributed to Rabbi Yishmael which includes an embryo/fetus in the prohibition of homicide is Genesis 9:6: "One who spills the blood of the human, by a human his blood shall be spilled because in the image of God [he] created/made the human," שֹׁפֵךְ דַּם הָאָדָם בָּאָדָם דָּמוֹ יִשָּׁפֵךְ כִּי בְּצֶלֶם אֱלֹהִים עָשָׂה אֶת הָאָדָם.

This exegetical exercise attributed to Rabbi Yishmael can only be classified as bizarre midrash for several reasons: 1) the verse is from Genesis, the book of foundational myths and not generally considered a source of law; 2) the reading tradition of the *ta'amim* separate the phrases "the blood of the human" and "by a human"; and 3) the distortion of the simple meaning of the text, the phrase "by/through a human" (באדם) is understood to mean "in a human", that is, a person which is inside a person, an embryo or fetus in its mother's uterus. According to this midrash, feticide — abortion is prohibited to *benei Noah*. The sages, on the other hand, interpret this to mean capital punishment through a human court by strangulation where no blood is lost. In bSanhedrin 57a Rav Yosef or alternatively, the house of Rav derives capital punishment for three commandments of *benei Noah*: sexual transgressions, murder and blasphemy. Another talmudic tradition states that for four transgressions *benei Noah* are executed, adding idol worship or alternatively theft. Yet another tradition states that for all seven they are executed. Underlying the verse position is a definite theological conflict which the rabbinic sages phrased in terms of liability to capital punishment, a fantasy, because they did not have this political power at this period in history.

It seems quite clear that the midrash attributed to Rabbi Yishmael reflects a reaction of other, non-Jewish groups to a current practice. The midrash is, after all, relating to *benei Noah* and does not reflect the Jewish view. Scholars of the ancient world such as Michael Gorman, John Riddle, and Konstantinos Kapparis[10] have demonstrated that contraceptives and abortifacients were readily available in this period. Determining the efficacy of the drugs and distinguishing between contraceptives and abortifacients is much more difficult. The additional problematic of their safety to the woman may have been addressed in what has been incorrectly called the Hippocratic Oath which prohibited providing an abortion. Recipes for oral drugs, pessaries, barrier methods, externally applied poultices and creams, and directions for surgical abortion are found in Egyptian papyri and Greek and Roman medical texts. References to oral drugs (*kos 'iqarin*) are found in mShabbat 14:3 and bShabbat 110ab as a treatment for jaundice and abnormal uterine bleeding but with the potential to cause sterility; and *sama de'aqarta* in bYevamot 65b as a permanent sterilizing potion, pessaries/barrier methods (*mokh*) in the famous *baraita* in tNiddah 2:6 and the parallels in bYevamot 12b; 100b; bKetubot 39a; and bNedarim 35b; and surgical methods (*hotkhin et ha'ubar*) in mOhalot 7:6 and mNiddah 3:5 (*mehutakh*) all without prohibition though there may be some conditions.

Other talmudic attempts at extending the laws applying to *benei Noah* include a prohibition about castration (bSanhedrin 56b) and a prohibition about divorce for "other nations" (yQiddushin 1:1, 58c). Julius Cassanus was among the ascetic

10 Michael J. Gorman, *Abortion and the Early Church: Christian, Jewish and Pagan Attitudes and the Greco-Roman World*, Downers Grove, Illinois: InterVarsity Press, 1982, especially Chapter 1; John M. Riddle, *Contraception and Abortion from the Ancient World to the Renaissance*, Cambridge,MA: Harvard University Press, 1992, especially Chapter 2; Konstantinos Kapparis, *Abortion in the Ancient World*, London: Duckworth Academic Press, 2002 especially pp. 7-32

Gnostics in the second century who encouraged castration as a means of ending birth and corruption.[11] This generated Christian condemnation of castration which bSanhedrin 56b may have been reflecting. Divorce is seen negatively in the New Testament and perhaps yQiddushin reflects that Christian belief. Abortion was condemned by early Christianity, possibly on a basis of the Septuagint. According to Noonan who considers the *Letter of Barnabas* 19.5 to be an early second century document, it directly prohibits abortion. This was also the case in the *Apocalypse of Peter* and the *Apocalypse of Paul.* Tertullian (*Apology* 9.8) and Cyprian (*Epistles* 52.2) vehemently condemn abortion in the third century.[12] Another practice prohibited and punishable by death to *benei Noah* according to yQiddushin 1:1, 58c was "unnatural intercourse" (*biah shelo kedarka*), practices that were also prohibited by the early church.[13] There is also the possibility of Jewish reaction to Roman practices which during the first century B.C.E. and the first century C.E. apparently had a high rate of abortion and some level of *patria potestas* was still practiced.[14] There are many other extensions or limitations on what is permitted to *benei Noah* in talmudic literature and the connection to Christianity, Gnosticism, Manichaeism and other religious sects as well as to parallel legal systems in the land of Israel, for example, Roman law and in Babylonia, for example, Zoroastrian law is worthy of examination. Medical texts are a source of instruction in reference to contraception and abortion as well as sometimes expressing attitudes toward the practices.

THE ABORTION CORPUS

The abortion corpus begins in the Bible Exodus 21:22:

11 See John T. Noonan, Jr., *Contraception: A History of Its Treatment by the Catholic Theologians and Canonists*, Cambridge, MA: The Belknap Press of Harvard University Press, 1986 (enlarged edition), especially pp. 56-106.

12 Noonan, ibid., 86-88 and notes 33-36.

13 Noonan, ibid. 34-36 (*coitus interruptus*); 56-106 (emphasizing intercourse for procreation); 162-164 (prohibition of oral and anal intercourse and prohibition of vaginal intercourse if the woman is astride the man).

14 Noonan, ibid. 85; Gorman, ibid. 24-32; Riddle, ibid. 62-65, 76-85.

> If men strive and strike a pregnant woman and her products of conception go out, if there is no *ason* the man shall surely be punished [monetarily] according to what the husband of the woman and the judges determine. But if there is an *ason* (a tragedy), life for life shall be given.

According to this biblical text, a person who inadvertently causes a spontaneous abortion or miscarriage is subject to a monetary fine to the woman's husband for loss of his offspring. If, however, the pregnant woman dies as a result of the men's fight, they are liable for her death. The monetary fine for loss of the embryo/fetus demonstrates that the embryo/fetus does not have the legal status of a human being prior to birth. The Septuagint, however, interprets the word *ason* differently, that is, based on stage of gestation and formation of the fetus. It is probably derived from the Aramaic root אסי, connected with health and wholeness. According to that tradition once the formation of the fetus has reached a particular stage of development at which human characteristics are obvious, causing a miscarriage is considered murder. Prior to that stage, there is merely a monetary penalty.[15] That tradition, of course, became the basis of the Christian/Catholic position on abortion. Subsequently there was disagreement concerning what stage of gestation constituted formation: quickening, four months, eighty days, forty days or at conception. Ensoulment, when the vitalizing element entered the human matter, became an issue closely connected with formation.

Mekhilta deR. Yishmael on these verses gives the standard rabbinic stance that monetary compensation is all that is required if the woman does not die.

> And if men strive ... But Scripture comes to teach you that the compensation for injuries to a wife is to be paid to her husband, and compensation for her fetuses also belongs to the husband; and that one who incurred the penalty of death is exempt from making monetary compensation.... What then is the

15 See the extended discussion by David M. Feldman, *Birth Control in Jewish Law: Marital Relations, Contraception, and Abortion as set forth in the Classic Texts of Jewish Law*, New York: New York University Press, 1968 republished in Israel (third edition — with Epilogue) 1995, 251-275. Michael J. Gorman, *Abortion and the Early Church: Christian*, 33-45 has a shorter and less accurate discussion on the Jewish position. The clearest and most far-reaching discussion is by Daniel Schiff, *Abortion in Judaism*, Cambridge: Cambridge University Press, 2002, especially 12-26.

> purpose of saying: *And if men strive together*? Because it says: *And he that smite anybody mortally* (Leviticus 24:17), which I might understand to mean even if he kills a child born after only eight months of pregnancy.[16] Therefore it says: *And if men strive together*, thereby telling us that one is not guilty of death unless he kills a viable child.... *And yet no harm follow*. To the woman. *He shall surely be fined*. For the fetuses. You interpreted that way but perhaps [it means] *no harm follow* (*velo yiheye ason*) to the fetuses, *he shall surely be fined* for the woman? Scripture says: *But if any harm follow, t[hen you shall give life for life* (Ex. 21:23)]. Therefore when Scripture says: *And yet no harm follow*,[it must mean,] to the woman; *he shall surely be fined*, for the fetuses. But may it mean, no harm follow to the woman or to the fetuses? But if you should interpret it in this manner — then he [the husband] would have to pay for the services of a midwife! Hence when the Scripture says: *no harm follow*, [it must mean,] to the woman; *he shall surely be fined*, for the fetuses. (*Mekhilta deRabbi Ishmael, Mishpatim-Neziqin, paresha* 8)[17]

Mekhilta deRashbi[18] specifically excludes a fetus from the term *ish* for any liability for murder. "*And there is no harm* I understand there is no harm to the woman or [perhaps] there is no harm to the fetuses? The text says, *one who strikes a person* (*ish*) excludes fetuses." These texts constitute what is considered the normative position of the land of Israel concerning the status of the embryo/fetus. The opinion attributed to Rabbi Yishmael is a minority opinion. We would expect to find his opinion in *Mekhilta deR. Yishmael* but perhaps the silence can be explained by the fact that the *midreshei halakha* are seeking to legislate for Israel in this work and not for *benei Noah*.

---

16 A fetus from an eight month gestation was not considered viable. Even if it was born alive and remains alive, it is not considered a full person with legal status *nefesh adam* until it has survived for one month. See ET s.v. *ben shemoneh*. This certainly reinforces the idea that a fetus in utero does not have the status of *nefesh adam*.

17 The translation is based chiefly on Jacob Z. Lauterbach, *Mekhilta de-Rabbi Ishmael*, Philadelphia: JPS, 1935, vol. 3 pp. 64-65. I have updated the language and used the text from the Horovitz-Rabin edition. The midrash also clarifies that the word *yeledeha* includes any pregnancy even a singleton. The continuation brings the opinion of Rabbi Yehuda haNasi (the Patriarch) that *nefesh tahat nefesh* refers to monetary compensation. This probably reflects the lack of political power of the Jews under Roman rule.

18 Horowitz- Rabin (eds.), *Mekhilta deRashbi* chapter 21.

Philo, under Greek influence and the reading of the Septuagint, does consider causing a miscarriage manslaughter if not murder.

> But if anyone has a contest with a woman who is pregnant, and strike her a blow on her belly, and she miscarried, if the child which was conceived within her is still unfashioned and unformed, he shall be punished by a fine, both for the assault which he committed and also because he has prevented nature, who was fashioning and preparing that most excellent of creatures, a human being, from bringing him into existence. But if the child which was conceived had assumed a distinct shape in all its parts, having received all its proper connected and distinctive qualities, he shall die; for such a creature as that is a man, whom he has slain while still in the workshop of nature… (*De Specialibus Legibus* iii. 108-109)[19]

Josephus has what is considered the standard position in the land of Israel, monetary compensation only, although there is some rhetoric about interfering with creation: "He that kicks a woman with child, so that the woman miscarry, let him pay a fine in money, as the judges shall determine, as having diminished the multitude by the destruction of what was in her womb."[20]

The standard source for abortion is Ohalot 7:6: "A woman who is having difficult labor, they cut up the fetus in her womb and extract it limb by limb because her life has precedence over its life but if the majority of its body has emerged, they may not touch him for we do not push aside one life for another."[21] This Mishnah very clearly states the bottom line: the mother's life has precedence over the fetus until the majority of the fetus is born. If we look

19 See *The Works of Philo* (new updated edition, translated by C.D. Yonge), Peabody, Hendrickson Publishers, 1993, p. 605 quoted from Schiff p. 17.

20 *Antiquities of the Jews*, IV, 8, 33. Quoted from David Feldman, ibid. p. 259 and in n. 42, Feldman refers to Josephus, *Contra Apion*, II, 24 where he considers abortion and infanticide akin to murder. This may be a moral rather than legal stance.

21 A very close parallel to this mishnah is found in tYevamot 9:5. It adds that it is permissible to perform this operation even on the Sabbath but if the fetus' head was born, even on the second day [of labor] which Lieberman understands to be a weekday, its status becomes that of a person (*nefesh*). See Saul Lieberman, *Tosefta Kifshuta*, Part IV Order Nashim, New York: JTSA, 1967 p. 88. Lieberman also states that the sages knew that such a surgical procedure was extremely dangerous but that sometimes the woman was saved.

at the reality of this situation, it is likely that we are dealing with full-term birth, the most extreme form of feticide/abortion. All Jewish positions, even the most stringent, accept that feticide/abortion is not homicide. Questions arising from this Mishnah include the level of obligation to cut up the fetus, the extent of the danger to the mother — only her life or her health, the safety of her limbs, or other physical damage, or her sanity and well-being, whether the danger is immediate or in the future, who decides and what if there are objections on the part of the mother or the father.[22] It is generally considered that there are two positions on why it is possible to cut up the fetus. Rashi holds that until the head with the majority of the body had been born the fetus does not come into the category of *nefesh*, a soul or a person and hence has no legal personhood. Rambam, on the other hand, considered the fetus "like a *rodef*", the one pursuing someone who can be killed in order to protect the person he is pursuing. The difficulty with defining the fetus as a pursuer is that if the fetus is indeed a pursuer why does its status change when the head or the majority of the body is born? There is more than one answer to this difficulty: the birthing woman is being pursued by heaven at that point (bSanhedrin 72b apparently by Rav Hisda); or that we do not know who is pursuing whom (yShabbat 14:4, 14d by Rabbi Yose bei Rabbi Bun in the name of Rav Hisda and in yAvoda Zara 2:2, 40d by Rabbi Yose bei Rabbi Bun in the name of Rabbi Levi).[23] In reality there are a few situations in which the head of the fetus was born and the rest could not emerge or be pulled out, for instance if the shoulders were stuck in

22 Avraham Steinberg, "*Induced Abortion According to Jewish Law*," J*ournal of Halacha and Contemporary Society* 1 (1), Spring 1981, 29-52. Steinberg's language indicates his theological stance against abortion by claiming that the case attributed to Rabbi Yishmael is an instance of criminal abortion, that a *ben Noah* is liable to capital punishment for abortion, is normative Jewish law (p. 34). Moreover, he naïvely accepts Weiss' claim in *Dor Dor veDoshav*, New York and Berlin, vol. 2, p. 23 that "apparently, murder of fetuses has never existed in Jewish society during any period," (p. 36 n. 18) when we have ample legal literature which allows abortion. This is not to claim that abortion was a preferred action only that given its extensive practice in talmudic times, it is unlikely that Jews never practiced it.

23 Maimonides (*Hilkhot Rotzeah*_1:9) uses the phrase "and that that is the nature of the world," to describe the conflict between choosing the mother's life or the fetus' life after the majority of the body or head has been born.

the pelvis (shoulder dystocia), or if the majority of the body was born but the head was stuck in the pelvis (head entrapment).[24]

There is a general problem of how to understand the use of the participle in rabbinic texts. Ohalot 7:6 has מחתכין את הוולד which may be translated "they cut up the fetus" but may be understood either as an obligation to do so, "they [must] cut up the fetus" or as permission to do so, "they [may] cut up the fetus.[25] There are those who read these positions for leniency — that is, in all cases the fetus is not a *nefesh* so if there is a reason to abort there is no prohibition. Or alternatively, in the case of a *rodef*, there is an absolute obligation to cut up the fetus when the woman's life is endangered and in other situations where the woman's life may not be at stake, it is permitted to abort. Generally Rambam has not been read in that manner but two convincing studies one by Ernest J. Weinrib and the other by Daniel Schiff do read him in that manner.[26] Because Rambam opens *Hilkhot Rotzeah* 1:9 by emphasizing the prohibition to have mercy on a pursuer (הרי זו מצות לא תעשה שלא לחוס על הרודף), it seems that Weinrib and Schiff understand him correctly. The other tendency is to read Ohalot 7:6 for stringency — that is, a fetus may not be a complete *nefesh* but it has some element of personhood which would prohibit abortion except in limited situations, chiefly danger to the mother and only in a situation where the mother's life is endangered may the fetus be cut up.

Another source in the abortion corpus is bArakhin 7a: "A woman who goes out to be executed, we do not wait until she gives birth. If she is in labor, we wait until she gives birth." According to this mishnah (Arakhin 1:4), the fetus has no independent personhood from its mother, hence murder could never be applied to abortion. One may even ask if any ruling whatsoever can

---

24 I am grateful to Dr. Irving Brown for clarifying this issue and to Marlene Sagada, the midwife who demonstrated these situations on anatomic models.

25 This is exactly the same problem the commentators had with the *baraita* on "three women use a contraceptive absorbent (*mokh*)": some commentators interpret it that these three women *must* use it, meaning that other women may use it; other commentators interpret it to mean that these three women *may* use it, meaning that other women are not permitted to use a contraceptive absorbent.

26 This was Weinrib's interpretation in a seminar in Jewish Law at the Faculty of Law at the University of Toronto. See Schiff, ibid. pp. 59-61 where he points out the inconsistencies in Rambam's *rodef* argument.

be applied to a non-*nefesh*. Only if she is sitting on the birthing stool, that is, at the pushing stage, before the decision was made for execution do we delay the execution. The *sugya* claims that at this stage the fetus is "uprooted" and becomes a separate body from its mother. This claim, however, does not override Ohalot 7:6. It merely suggests that there is an additional stage of separation from the mother. Delaying the fulfillment of a punishment is considered an additional punishment which is why there is a strong push not to delay the mother's execution. The talmudic discussion goes on to say that the first stone for her execution should be cast at the pregnant belly in order to kill the fetus so that the woman's modesty will be preserved by not giving birth during the execution or immediately afterward.[27] This probably reflects the Stoic concept that the fetus is a "limb of its mother."[28] If that is the case, the fetus has no legal personhood and if she so chose to wound herself by aborting it would not be prohibited. This *sugya* continues stating that if a woman died on the birth stool, the Sabbath may be desecrated in order to bring a knife to save a fetus by removing it surgically post-mortem. This follows the principle that one may transgress the Sabbath in order to keep many more subsequent Sabbaths.

Two rabbinic sources relate to an embryo in the first forty days after conception as "mere water".[29] mNiddah 3:7 states that a woman who "aborts on the fortieth day does not suspect a fetus," i.e. that she was pregnant. bYevamot 69b states that the daughter of a priest who was married to a non-priest, making her ineligible to eat *terumah*, is permitted to eat *terumah* for the first forty days after she becomes a widow (presuming she has no children with

27 This reflects the understanding that the fetus may be responsible for initiating its own birth and that the fetus may survive for a short period of time after the mother's death. If the birth occurs during the woman's execution, she has no way to preserve her modesty and the birth and the resulting impurity will be visible adding to her humiliation.

28 See Schiff, ibid., pp. 15-20 and notes 63-67, 32-33 and notes 22-29. bYevamot 78a supports this idea because if a pregnant woman converts to Judaism, her ritual immersion suffices for the fetus as well and no additional conversion process is necessary for the child once it is born. This could, however, be understood that the immersion made the mother Jewish and a Jewish woman who gives birth imparts her Jewishness to the fetus even if it was conceived prior to her conversion.

29 *Halakhot Gedolot*, a geonic work, *Hilkhot Yom HaKippurim* 26 hold that the laws of *piquah nefesh* hold even for a fetus/embryo of less than forty days conception, Schiff, ibid., p. 48, n. 86. This is an extreme position as very early gestations cannot be saved even in the 21st century.

the non-priest) because any conception would be considered merely water for the first forty days.

A number of talmudic discussions reflect the unwillingness of certain sages to classify severely deformed and nonviable products of conception as human (yNiddah 3:4, 50d and bNiddah 23a, 24a, mBekhorot 8:1, mKeritot 1: 3-5). Consequently, in reference to some aspects of birth (such as birth impurity, obligation of the birth sacrifice, or days of the "blood of purity"), the product of conception was not considered human nor was the act of giving birth considered birth. This certainly creates the possibility that these products of conception, some of which can now be identified prenatally, may be aborted without any halakhic objection.[30]

As we can see, there has not been a totally uniform position about abortion/feticide in the talmudic sources, though there has been considerable room for leniency. Daniel Schiff[31] analyzed the positions of the *Rishonim* and *Aḥaronim* on the issue of abortion: Rashi's use of the non-*nefesh* argument (which was often interpreted leniently, i.e., even in non fatal situation abortion could be permitted); Rambam's use of the contradictory pursuer *rodef* argument (in which the fetus suddenly stops being a *rodef* when its head is born); the implications of his use of the odd term "like a pursuer" *ke-rodef*; the divergent positions in Tosefot (where Tos. Sanhedrin 57b *s.v. leka* and Tos. Hullin 33a *s.v. ehad* understand that abortion is prohibited to Jews but perhaps not punishable while Tos. Niddah 44b *s.v. ihu* states that it is permitted to kill a fetus); and the opinions of various *Aharonim* on how to interpret Rashi and Rambam. He concludes:

> When looked at collectively, it can be said that the *Rishonim* and *Ahronim* had navigated a centrist course: they had put in place a hitherto unspecified prohibition on Jewish abortion, but they had also provided extensive opposition to the notion that abortion was murder, they had preserved abortion to save the mother's life, and — within the contours of the Rashi-Maimonidean dialectic

30 See Tirzah Meacham (leBeit Yoreh), "Rabbi Yannai Shrieked: You Have Purified the Birthing Woman!" (Hebrew) *Te'uda*, vol. 13, 1997 pp. 67-77. This article discusses the legal status of the embryo/fetus at various stages of gestation.

31 See Schiff, ibid., pp. 58-84.

— they had kept open the potential for, and at times had even permitted abortion in non-life-saving circumstances. Their prohibition, then, can be regarded, as neither absolute nor inflexible. (p. 94)

Schiff[32] also quotes Daniel Sinclair who states that the Tosefot would seek to prohibit abortion because such a prohibition was a generally accepted notion, and they were possibly "influenced by the methods applied in the analysis of Roman and Canon Law by the Medieval French jurists, who tended to disregard the original historical sense of the texts under analysis in order to reach the desired end." This idea of external influence has had major impact on the modern abortion debate. Just prior to mid-twentieth century several individual *poskim* such as Shneur Zalman, Yehiel Epstein, Yosef Chaim Al-Chakam, Ben Zion Ouziel, and Chaim Ozer Grodzinsky had lenient rulings while Mose Schick and Chaim Soloveitchik had more stringent stances.[33]

The modern abortion debate created embarrassment for certain rabbinic figures because of the Jewish leniency in allowing abortion.[34] Issar Yehuda Unterman, then Ashkenazi chief rabbi of Israel applied the terminology "appurtenance to murder" to abortion even if the woman were dangerously ill. This response was the result of a question by a woman exposed to rubella shortly after conception. The conception was less than forty days ("merely water"), but Unterman applying a stringent understanding of the *rodef* principle and following the idea that the language of Tos. Niddah 44b is imprecise forbade abortion.[35] He also took into account the future of the fetus. It should be noted that the pro-natal stance of the State of Israel had major impact on abortion policy. Post-Holocaust pressure to rebuild the Jewish people, however, could not compete with the economic realities in the new state.[36] Moshe

32 See Schiff, ibid., p. 65 quoting Daniel Sinclair, "The Legal Basis for the Prohibition on Abortion in Jewish Law", *Israel Law Review* 15(1), 1980, p. 120.

33 See Schiff, ibid., pp. 95-130.

34 It is likely that the loss of so many Jewish children in the Holocaust and the fact that the Jewish people have not returned to their pre-war population is an additional factor in the condemnation of abortion.

35 See, I. Y. Unterman, "BeInyan Piquaḥ Nefesh she Ubar", *Noam* 4, 1963, pp. 1-11.

36 Saturday nights became the preferred time for under the table abortions which were relatively safe because they were performed by physicians. It is likely that Unterman was attempting to

Yonah Zweig of Antwerp responded similarly to the situation where a Belgian woman was acquitted for infanticide of her thalidomide damaged child and extended his moral abhorrence to the case of abortion where the mother took thalidomide.[37] He swerved Rashi's non-*nefesh* argument to mean that only in a life-threatening situation would abortion be permitted. He claimed that the *rodef* argument is to compel the destruction of the fetus if the mother or father did not want to do so, but *piquah nefesh* for the mother is a biblical concept. An unusual aspect of Zweig's responsum demonstrates his embarrassment. He not only brought the views of Belgian physicians and jurists who objected to abortion but also included the papal view forbidding abortion in the case of congenital (or teratological) defects.[38] He claimed that this causes *hillul hashem* as it could not be kept secret and no other nation should be holier than Israel. Only by interpreting the sources in the most stringent manner could he prevent what he considered the embarrassment of the people of Israel. Jakobovits[39] is slightly more moderate in his presentation of the topic but strongly condemns it on moral grounds. Jacobovits firmly holds that deformity of the fetus has no role in the decision about abortion but that if the pregnancy continued to have "debilitating effects (whether psychologically or otherwise) on the mother as to present a hazard to her life, "however remote such a danger may be",[40] abortion may be contemplated. For him, abortion without strong grounds constitutes a crime.

---

bring at least Orthodox Jews under control in this area by taking an extreme stance. Even his reference to abortions as "a type of murder" (ibid., p. 9) would have negative resonance after the murder of six million Jews .

37 See M. Y. Zweig, "'Al Hapala Melakhutit", *Noam* 7, 1964, pp. 36-56.

38 Presumably that is his reference in "*gam hakemura vehao'med berosh*." (p. 56)

39 Immanuel Jakobovits, *Jewish Medical Ethics: A Comparative and Historical Study of the Jewish Religious Attitude to Medicine and Its Practice*, New York: Bloch Publishing Company, 1959, pp. 170-192. His language is weighted, for example, "the artificial termination of a pregnancy is strongly condemned on moral grounds," (p. 190). Jakobovits in his article, "Jewish Views on Abortion," in *Jewish Bioethics*, (eds. F. Rosner and J.D. Bleich) New York: Sanhedrin Press, 1979 refers to abortion as a "grave offense, although not murder" (p. 121).

40 I. Jakobovits, "Recent Halakhic Periodical Literature", *Tradition*, vol. 5 (2), 1963, p. 270.

Eliezer Waldenberg, despite his lenient decisions in reference to abortion for the health of the mother, potential fetal abnormalities and Tay Sachs,[41] does argue that one should refrain from abortion unless there are compelling reasons lest Israel should be less holy than surrounding nations which have legislated against abortion.

Moshe Feinstein, incensed with Waldenberg's leniency concerning the abortion of a Tay-Sach's fetus wrote a position paper on Waldenberg's responsum.[42] In it he states:

> I have written all this because of the great outbreak of licentious behaviour, in that the governments of many countries have allowed the killing of fetuses, among them the political leaders of The State of Israel and countless fetuses have already been killed. Hence, at this time, there is a need to make a fence for the Torah, and not to undermine this most serious prohibition against murder.

Most modern scholars writing in English have taken the strongest interpretation of Rambam[43] to prohibit abortion except in life-threatening circumstances and those who rely on English references in Jewish law accept those opinions.[44]

Feinstein and Arusi rely in part on the problem with the Noahide laws to prohibit abortion. Feinstein argues that since the prohibition on Jewish

41 See the discussion in Schiff, ibid., 157-169, especially 163. Waldenberg described great need on the part of the mother is a compelling reason for abortion and expressed a preference that if abortion were necessary it be done in the first forty days but extended that to three months ("the time in which the pregnancy could be recognized [mNiddah 1:4]) and finally in the case of Tay-Sachs to the limit of viability, seven months.

42 M. Feinstein, *Iggerot Moshe*, New-York, 1961 on Chosen Mishpat vol II no. 69. A full and excellent analysis is found in Schiff, ibid.

43 For example, J. D. Bleich, "Abortion in Halakhic Literature", in Contemporary Halakhic Problems, Vol 1,, New York: Ktav Publishing House Inc., 1997. F. Rosner, *Modern Medicine and Jewish Ethics*, New York: Yeshiva University Press, 1986; D. Novak, "A Jewish View of Abortion", in *Law and Theology in Judaism*, New York: Ktav Publishing House, 1974; I. Jakobovits, *Jewish Medical Ethics*, 1959, and *Review of Recent Halakhic Periodical Literature*, 1963.

44 For example, J. Noonan, "An Almost Absolute Value in History", in *The Morality of Abortion: Legal and Historical Perspectives*, Cambridge, MA: Harvard University Press, 1970.

abortion is based on the the Noahide law which is derived from the prohibition of murder, then the prohibition of Jewish abortion must also be based in the prohibition of murder. Their embarrassment prevented these modern rabbis from a true legal analysis of the strange midrash attributed to R. Yishmael forbidding abortion as part of the Noahide prohibition of homicide. Moreover they could not hold that Jewish law may be entirely independent of other religions formulations of law. Rather they interpreted Noahide laws as a stage of Jewish law, to be kept by Jews even though different laws (e.g. mOhalot 7:6, bArakhin 7a, mNiddah 3:6-7) had been formulated as part of Oral law. That is, Judaism has an articulated position on abortion in the talmudic sources which is lenient, giving control over their bodies to women.

The rhetoric of these rabbis creates its own embarrassment which deserves expression. We do not say that a man who has a heart attack should not have medical treatment because he is "being pursued by heaven." Nor do we claim that that is simply "the way of the world." Attempts to ignore or to regulate other aspects of the abortion controversy which do not include women's voices are illegitimate and dehumanizing. Why did the abortion responsa not include Yehudit's question to her spouse R' Hiya (bYevamot 65a) whether women were obligated in procreation? His answer gave her control over her body. The "drug of sterility" was as likely an abortifacient as a contraceptive. When only a few of the modern *poskim* take into account what might constitute "great need" or "great suffering" for women, one wonders whether the rabbis should be asked questions of such halakhic import. J. Emden's question,[45] "who would permit abortion without reason" is the question which must be asked. The decision to carry a pregnancy to fruition includes the health and well-being of the woman, existing children, stability of the marital relationship, health of the fetus, and yes, economic reasons. When the decision is not between fewer luxuries and another child, but rather the issue is the ability to support, raise and educate a child while keeping all other family dynamics functioning positively, the question becomes one which sometimes only the potential mother can ask. Pregnancy

45 Jacob Emden, *Hegahot Yaavetz* to Niddah 44b.

and childbirth can be life-threatening and health-threatening situations for a woman. The theology which includes women's voices is the only theology about which we will not be embarrassed.[46]

46 When the rubella epidemic hit Israel in 1978-79, every woman who claimed exposure was given rabbinic permission to abort. Why? The social welfare and medical systems could not handle the influx of several hundred or a few thousand severely damaged infants. The financial repercussions were impossible for the social — welfare state to handle and the potential destabilization of families dealing with such influence was too great to risk. Behind some of the Jewish abortion rhetoric is the demographic reality that we have not returned to our pre-Holocaust population. This pro-natal stance has impact on women and though it is desirable to increase Jewish population — that is a separate issue. There is also a political agenda in the theology of the *posqim* about who stays in control of the religious courts, who makes halakhic decisions and the position of women in Judaism. In the case of abortion, the theology of many of the *posqim* led them to misuse the Noahide laws and their impact on Jewish law. To be intellectually honest we must keep agendas separate lest we embarrass ourselves.

"SUCH THINGS HAVE NEVER BEEN HEARD OF": JEWISH INTELLECTUALS AND HASIDIC MIRACLES

Justin Jaron Lewis (University of Manitoba)

"As everyone knows, the main ingredients of Chassidic tales are *tzaddikim* and miracles."[1]

Among the first non-Hasidic Jewish intellectuals to pay close attention to the Hasidic movement were the Eastern European *maskilim*, advocates of enlightenment and rationalism, who denounced and ridiculed Hasidic belief in magic and miracle.[2] Even sympathetic observers among the *maskilim* and their intellectual heirs, Jewish writers and historians of the early twentieth century, remained convinced that Hasidic miracle stories were false, the product of fraud and superstition. This intellectual climate seems to have affected even traditional Jews within, or close to, Hasidic circles.

By the late twentieth century, however, the intellectual climate had changed. Jewish writers and historians today are far from the scepticism of earlier generations and some have forthrightly affirmed the reality of Hasidic miracle-working. This paper offers a sketch of this paradigmatic process of embarrassment and re-embracement.

Rabbi Israel Berger of Bucharest, a Hasid and Kabbalist, published his hagiographical compilation *Eser Orot* in 1907. It is part of a four-volume collection of teachings and tales of Hasidic masters connected with Berger's family

1 Brawer, *Something from Nothing* (a booklet on Hasidic thought by an author associated with Habad-Lubavitch), 81.

2 This paper will not distinguish between "miracles" and "magic" in the Hasidic context. Though some scholarship on Hasidism does make such a distinction ("Miracles are not the same as magic" — Lamm, *Religious Thought of Hasidism*, 418 n. 15) it strikes me as theological rather than historical.

tree, under the collective title *Zekhut Yisrael,* which has been reprinted often in Hasidic communities, into the twenty-first century. [3]

These volumes can be seen as part of the Hasidic project of resistance to modernity.[4] Eastern European Jewry was in a time of upheaval and transition as Berger wrote. His hagiographical books are family chronicles in a time of generational strife; they are focused on the past, in a time of intense hopes and fears for the future; all their narratives claim factual truth, in a time of burgeoning Jewish creativity in literary fiction; they are written not in the nascent modern Hebrew but in rabbinic Hebrew mixed with Yiddish, a literary dialect hardly accessible beyond the religious Ashkenazi context. Collaborative works which constantly refer to their sources in oral tradition, earlier texts, and correspondence with other rabbis, Berger's books present themselves as products of a trans-historical religious culture that excludes the growing number of Jewish religious liberals or secularists.

In this anti-modernist context, it is surprising that *Eser Orot* includes a long introduction acknowledging and addressing readers' doubts about the "signs and wonders" (*otot umoftim)* which fill the book. Berger emphasizes that he is not addressing the scepticism of heretics or non-observant Jews, only that of "kosher souls who wonder at these matters in all innocence". First among these areas of doubt is "the reality of the wonders and awe-inspiring deeds that are told of our Rabbis (whose souls are in Eden), which are supernatural and beyond the limits of the order of Creation; [the doubters] think that such things have never been heard of."[5]

Berger's books are intended for an audience of learned men. They are written in rabbinic Hebrew rather than the Yiddish vernacular, printed in Rashi script rather than the easier-to-read square script or "big letters", and prefaced with approbations by rabbis. His response to the doubts he cites involves page after page of citations from the Babylonian and Jerusalem Talmuds. His in-

3 Berger's hagiographical works are a major subject of my book *Imagining Holiness* (McGill-Queen's University Press, 2009).

4 See Ira Robinson, "Hasidic Historiography and Jewish Modernity."

5 Berger, *Eser Orot*, beginning of *Petihta Rabata* and author's footnote there.

troduction thus testifies to a sense of embarrassment about Hasidic miracles among Jewish intellectuals steeped in traditional piety.[6]

Berger's acknowledgment of such embarrassment appeared after nearly a century of attacks on Hasidic gullibility by less sympathetic intellectuals. At least since the publication of the first book of Hasidic tales, *Shivhei HaBesht* (Praises of the Baal Shem Tov) in 1814, opponents of Hasidism had been ridiculing and bitterly denouncing miracle stories.[7] For *maskilim*, in particular, Hasidic belief in the wonder-working powers of the Rebbes was a leitmotif of anti-Hasidic polemic.[8]

Thus, Joseph Perl (1773-1889), whose satire *Megaleh Temirin*, which has been called "the first Hebrew novel",[9] was provoked by *Shivhei HaBesht* and the tales of Rebbe Nahman of Breslov, mocked miracle stories throughout his work. As Immanuel Etkes notes,

> Underlying Perl's satire is the assumption that no one — at least, among his enlightened readers — doubts the ridiculous and contemptible nature of magic in general and of the belief in the magical powers of the Hasidic leaders in particular. Hence the mere description of various instances of this belief among the Hasidim should suffice to provoke derision and revulsion.[10]

---

6 There are many Hasidic sources which indicate embarrassment about the telling of miracle stories, especially critiques of particular books deemed to be exaggerated or distorted. See Assaf, *The Regal Way,* 24-25. This is different from scepticism about the very possibility of such miracles (at least in our times) such as Berger is acknowledging.

7 Moshe Rosman, "Shivhei ha-Besht: document historique, ouvrage de propagande ou programme théologique?", 22-23, argues that the popularity of Shivhei HaBesht declined precipitately after its initial appearance, because mitnagdim, *maskilim* and even non-Jews were scoffing at its miracle stories, as well as its depiction of the Baal Shem Tov as other than a Talmudic scholar.

8 Immanuel Etkes has analyzed the importance of this theme in Haskalah literature and its role in buttressing the enlightened self-image of *maskilim*: "Magic and Miracle Workers in the Literature of the Haskalah", in *The Besht*, 259-271. For further examples see Gloria Wiederkehr-Pollack, *Eliezer Zweifel,* especially 146 (on Isaac Erter, 1791-1851), 158 and 160 (on Isaac Baer Levinsohn, 1788-1860), and the anthology of maskilic descriptions of Hasidism in Wodziński, *Haskalah and Hasidism*, 259-263, 279-280.

9 See Dov Taylor's annotated translation *Joseph Perl's Revealer of Secrets: The First Hebrew Novel.*

10 Etkes, *The Besht*, 261.

This firm assumption — that Hasidic miracle stories were lies propagated among superstitious followers by unscrupulous Rebbes — was sometimes expressed by *maskilim* in ways that can still shock a reader with any sympathy for Hasidism. Thus, Jakub Tugendhold (1794-1871) presented the government of Lublin Province with the following report on the Trisker Maggid, Abraham Twersky (1806-1889), a highly respected figure in Hasidic memory and one of the ancestors of the important Chernobyl dynasty:

> I can in all conscience report that Abraham Tweryskier is one of those roguish fanatics who, pretending to work wonders, take advantage of the credulousness of unenlightened persons of the Mo[saic] fai[th] and inveigle contributions out of them.[11]

The creative and thoughtful philosopher of Judaism, Nahman Krokhmal (1785-1840) wrote as follows about the beloved Rebbe Levi Isaac of Berdichev:[12]

> The scoundrel and sinner of Berdichev sits and narrates stories to his congregation... [T]hey stand trembling: "How many fortresses did he conquer today with his prayer, and how many worlds are subject to him!"

Even a later maskil distinguished by his unusual sympathy for Hasidism, who has been called "the forgotten father of modern scholarship on Hasidism",[13] Eliezer Zweifel (1815-1888), "criticizes the Hasidic rage for fabricated wonder tales — 'matters that are totally incomprehensible and which never even occurred to the founders of Hasidism.'"[14]

While by the time Rabbi Israel Berger was writing, "a decisive trend [had been] established in Hebrew literature, beginning in the 1890s, in favor of the positive evaluation of Hasidism which had begun among the later *maskilim*",[15] Hasidic belief in miracles remained a matter of embarrassment. This was

11 Wodziński, *Haskalah and Hasidism*, 287.

12 Krokhmal, *Moreh Nevukhei Hazman* 217, trans. in Wiederkehr-Pollack, *Eliezer Zweifel*, 151.

13 Wiederkehr-Pollack, "Eliezer Zvi Hacohen Zweifel: Forgotten Father of Modern Scholarship on Hasidism".

14 Zweifel, *Shalom al Yisrael* I:1:28, as cited in Wiederkehr-Pollack, *Eliezer Zweifel*, 212-213.

15 Jacobson, *Modern Midrash*, 19.

the case even among the several non-traditional Eastern European Jewish authors who were publishing retellings of Hasidic tales contemporaneously with Berger and his traditionalist colleagues: Micha Yosef Berdyczewski (*Sefer hasidim*, 1900), Yehuda Steinberg (*Sippurei hasidim* and *Sihot hasidim*, both 1904), and I.L. Peretz (*Khsidish*, 1901).[16] By presenting their tales as fiction or as quaint folklore, these authors distanced their projects from those of Hasidic compilers like Berger, who believed in the factuality of his stories, and distanced themselves from any belief in their contents.

The best known of these reworkings of Hasidic lore are probably those of Peretz. His Hasidic tales, written with an agenda "of transforming a negative perception of Hasidism into a positive one by seeing beyond the outer shabby appearance of Hasidism to the reality of its inner contents",[17] introduce miracles only through a complex web of heightened folksiness and literary irony. There is never any hint that the author believes in them, even if the narrator does; they are part of "the outer shabby appearance of Hasidism." The best-known of these tales, *Oyb nisht nokh hekher* ("If Not Higher"), succeeds in mocking Hasidic belief in miracles — the rebbe's putative ascents into heaven when he "disappears" before the Days of Awe — even as it celebrates Hasidic ethics — the rebbe's anonymous charitable visits to the poor, the real cause of his "disappearance."

Martin Buber, the great historian and popularizer of Hasidism in Western Europe and beyond, published his first work in this field in 1906.[18] In his major compilation of reworked Hasidic narratives, *Tales of the Hasidim,* stories with a supernatural element are inevitably introduced with "es wird erzählt" ("it is told"), as an indication of the author's own disbelief. Scholars have drawn attention to the extent to which Buber downplayed miracles altogether in his volumes on Hasidic tales and teachings. This was noted by Gershom Scholem

16 See Jacobson, "Neo-Hasidic Tales", in *Modern Midrash*, 17-43. Peretz wrote other neo-Hasidic tales not included in this compilation, such as *"Droshe-geshank (a mayse fun bal-shem)"* and *"Der bal-shem firt oys a shidekh"*, both included in the collection *Geshikhtn un stsenes.*

17 Jacobson, *Modern Midrash*, 30.

18 *Die Geschichten des Rabbi Nachman.*

in his critique of Buber's approach to Hasidism,[19] and has been demonstrated by Steven T. Katz in a thorough study of Buber's treatment of the Baal Shem Tov: "When we compare Buber's anti-kabbalistic... anti-magical... Besht to the image of the Besht that emerges from the original sources... there is little doubt that Buber's presentation is eccentric."[20]

In this intellectual climate, it is not surprising that embarrassment about Hasidic miracle tales had penetrated the traditional Jewish community as well, as registered by Israel Berger. This embarrassment remained the norm for decades. Thus, Louis I. Newman's *Hasidic Anthology*, first published in 1934 and often reprinted, though a celebration of Hasidic "lore and wisdom",[21] calmly maintains the maskilic assumption that there are no real miracles. Newman takes the liberty of ascribing this outlook to the best of the Rebbes themselves, of whom he speaks, typically for the scholarship of this time, as figures of the past. "The more learned Hasidic Rabbis cared little for miracles, and explained the true facts when among their own group. They permitted, however, the circulation of tales of wonder-working among the common people in the belief that thereby they might become attached to an ethical life."[22]

Historians of Hasidism maintained similar attitudes. Etkes has noted the ongoing influence of maskilic ideas about Hasidism and magic on the historiographical work of Heinrich Graetz (1817-1891),[23] Saul Israel Hurwitz (1861-1927),[24] Samuel Abba Horodezky (1871-1957),[25] and "Simon Dubnow (1860-1941) who laid the foundations for the critical historical treatment of Hasidism".[26] Dubnow saw miracle tales as integral to the strength and growth of Hasidism — and, without any qualification, as false:

19 Scholem charges that Buber neglects "the magical element" of Hasidism: "Martin Buber's Interpretation of Hasidism," 230. See Etkes, *The Besht*, 269.

20 Steven Katz, "Martin Buber's Misuse of Hasidic Sources," pp. 25-39 in *Post-Holocaust Dialogues*, 37.

21 Newman, *Hasidic Anthology*, title page.

22 Newman, *Hasidic Anthology*, 261.

23 Etkes, *The Besht*, 265-266.

24 Etkes, *The Besht*, 267-268.

25 Etkes, *The Besht*, 266-267.

26 Etkes, *The Besht*, 268.

> Granted... Chassidism used the phantasms and superstitions of the legends and wondrous stories, and particularly the cult of the miraculous 'Zaddikim' who mediated between God and man... Yet, just this... enabled Chassidism to capture the greatest number of people, to revolutionize the souls profoundly and to revitalize their minds with new hope.[27]

> By such nursery tales the Chassidim managed to calm down the excited masses [in times of persecution]. The... overcoming of reality by fantasy, even in the area of political life, was the main source of strength of the new movement.[28]

Yet, like Berger's works, most of the collections of Hasidic tales published in traditional circles from his time till the present day stubbornly persist in celebrating the miracles of the Rebbes.[29] This insistence on miracle — even in the face of embarrassment among learned and pious readers — can be seen as part of the Hasidic project, often conscious and deliberate, of resistance to modernity. These conflicting approaches played a part in the disconnection between non-traditionalist Jewish intellectuals, even those positively inclined towards Hasidism, and Hasidim themselves, well into the twentieth century.

The later twentieth century, however, saw the beginnings of a re-embracement of miracles by non-Hasidic Jewish intellectuals. Gershom Scholem, the great scholar of Kabbalah, took a significant step in this direction in his article on the Hasidic sources on the life of the Baal Shem Tov, published in 1960:

> Where is the boundary which separates the imaginary virtues from the real (even if para-normal) ones in a certain person? — this is far from clear. Yet I must say outright that in my humble opinion not only would the history of religion greatly benefit by an investigation of supra-normal, or para-psychological, visions, but that even the conventional use of the terms "imagination", "suggestion", and "auto-suggestion" does not convey the whole truth of the matter, and to the extent that it explains anything does not explain it fully... It would seem that the interaction between the charismatic person and the public, while at

27 Dubnow, *A History of Hasidism*, vol. I p. 13.

28 Dubnow, *A History of Hasidism*, vol. 2 pp. 2-3 (ch. 5 par. 27).

29 The major work on the literary history and themes of Hasidic hagiography, Gedaliah Nigal's *The Hasidic Tale*, is now available in English translation (Littman, 2008).

> times it gives rise to what are called miracles, is of a nature more complex than is commonly supposed.[30]

Though in context he is dealing primarily with visions, Scholem's statement has broader implications. As Etkes notes, "Scholem… is challenging the rationalist perspective, according to which every instance of the phenomenon of the supernatural is treated as a product of the imaginations of the ignorant."[131]

One of the points at issue between Scholem and his disciple and critic Moshe Idel has been Idel's call for greater attention to experiential aspects of Jewish mysticism, critiquing Scholem's textual emphasis.[32] In the context of this experiential emphasis, it is not surprising that Idel takes a positive stance toward magic and miracle. This is indicated even by the title of his major work on Hasidism, *Hasidism Between Ecstasy and Magic* (1995). In Idel's words,

> Although the activity of the Besht has been analyzed on several planes by scholars… it is strange that their academic analyses give no detailed account of magic… [T]he following discussion gravitates around the theory of magic… [T]he details of his practical magic, his use of clairvoyance, amulets, and healings, are beyond the scope of this work. [But their] omission should be understood neither as a rejection of the Besht's involvement in practical magic nor as an assumption that this is not an important domain of investigation.[33]

In more recent work on Hasidism, the kind of scepticism toward miracles that was taken for granted in earlier scholarship becomes difficult to find. Thus, while Dan Ben-Amos and Jerome Mintz in their annotated translation of *Shivhei HaBesht*, *In Praise of the Baal Shem Tov*, published in 1970, still assumed a contrast between "the mythical and realistic levels" of tales which "contain both supernatural and realistic elements,"[34] no such dichotomy can be found in the penetrating critical examination of *Shivhei HaBesht* in Moshe Rosman's *Founder of Hasidism* (1996). Rosman notes the historical problems in

30 Scholem, "*Demuto hahistorit shel R. Yisrael Baal Shem Tov*", as cited in Etkes, *The Besht*, 211.

31 Etkes, *The Besht*, 211.

32 See Idel, *Kabbalah*, 25-29.

33 Idel, *Hasidism*, 75.

34 Ben-Amos and Mintz, *In Praise of the Ba'al Shem Tov*, xxiii.

relying on a text permeated with legendary motifs and shaped by the agendas of its editors, but neither in this discussion[35] nor in his reconstruction of the Baal Shem Tov's career[36] does he treat supernatural elements as *ipso facto* unreliable. In summarizing his own conclusions about the historical Baal Shem Tov, Rosman writes, with no overt expression of scepticism,

> the Besht… was expert in amulets, exorcisms, and other techniques of shamanesque magical defense… Bringing the privileged information he gained during his soul's ascents to the attention of those who did not have such experiences was a means of involving them in the secrets of the supernatural realm.[37]

David Assaf's biography of Rebbe Israel of Ruzhin, *The Regal Way* (Hebrew 1997, translation 2002), similarly lacks any expression of scepticism about miracles even when this might be expected.[38] Further, Assaf harshly criticizes the value judgments of earlier scholars in this area:

> For some researchers of Hasidism, the performance of miracles has become a kind of touchstone: if zaddikim are "wonder-workers," they are automatically categorized as "practical" or "popular" (euphemisms here for hallucinatory, fraudulent, or primitive); if they question wonder-working, they may be considered expressions of rational, intellectual trends in Hasidism…. [Such categorizations] are outcomes of simplistic reasoning and generalization.[39]

Noteworthy is Assaf's implicit distancing of his own views from those of scholars who assume that miracles are "hallucinatory" or "fraudulent".

As with Idel's book on Hasidism, the title of Immanuel Etkes' biographical study of the Baal Shem Tov, *The Besht: Magician, Mystic, and Leader* (Hebrew 2000, translation 2005), indicates the author's positive outlook toward magic

35 Rosman, *Founder of Hasidism,* 143-155.

36 Rosman, *Founder of Hasidism,* "A Person of His Time", 173-186.

37 Rosman, *Founder of Hasidism,* 180-181.

38 E.g. in his discussion of the use of Hasidic tales as historical sources (23-27) or the Rebbe of Ruzhin's own reserved attitude toward miracles (261-264).

39 Assaf, *The Regal Way*, 261.

and miracle. In this important study, Etkes goes as far as anything yet published in the scholarly realm in affirming the historical reality of such wonders:

> Should we lend credence to claims that the Besht healed the sick and exorcised dybbuks and cleared demons out of houses?… And what about his performances in the Upper Worlds and the powers of seeing and hearing from afar? Is the critical scholar to believe in all of those too? Well, why not?[40]

Etkes continues:

> There is no doubt that the Besht himself believed he had such powers. This fact is clearly indicated by his letters. Nor is there any doubt that the Besht's associates and admirers believed in these powers as well. Consequently… the "wonders and miracles" of the sorts we have been listing are ensconced in the form of life within which the Besht lived and in the cultural and social reality of those who surrounded him. Given that this is the case, the miraculous elements in the tales of *Shivhei Habesht* are not only to be considered a reality the veracity of which the historian is permitted to acknowledge, but one that he is in fact required to recognize…
>
> For his part, the historian must ask of himself and of the sources available to him, What was it about the Besht that so fascinated the people surrounding him? And the conclusion one is forced to is: this was an effect, among other things, of the marvelous powers he was graced with.[41]

Alan Brill's significant article "The Spiritual Worlds of a Master of Awe" (2001) focuses on "the magical elements of a single work, the *Degel Mahaneh Ephraim*, whose author Rabbi Moses Hayyim Ephraim of Sudylkow… is a representative example of the wonder-working *zaddik*."[42] Brill strongly affirms the reality of at least one category of Hasidic miracle, that of physical healing by spiritual means. In his section on "Shamanistic Ascents and Faith Healing," he writes,

40 Etkes, *The Besht*, 243.

41 Etkes, *The Besht*, 243.

42 Brill, "The Spiritual World of a Master of Awe", 28.

> These healing abilities have generally been relegated, in twentieth century academic scholarship, to the realm of magic and superstition, meaning that they were false, primitive, or deceptive. A more tolerant and less condescending view of these matters has led to a more balanced view of these as literary records of folklore and oral tales. They were and are primarily stories, based on set genres and motifs... Currently, scholars are willing to consider [such] healing an actual diagnostic and healing process employing altered states of consciousness.[43]

The current scholars Brill cites, however, as well as the nineteenth-century predecessors of this affirming view whom he adduces, such as William James, are not dealing with Hasidic rebbes or other Jewish healers. Brill's view, like Etkes', is striking in the context of scholarship on Hasidism.

More recent work by other scholars, however, while not going as far as Etkes' and Brill's outright affirmation of the historical reality of miracles, remains at a vast distance from the scepticism of earlier generations of scholars and *maskilim*.

A journalistic study of Habad-Lubavitch, Sue Fishkoff's *The Rebbe's Army* (2003) expresses openness to the reality of Rebbe Menachem Mendel Schneerson's supernatural powers as celebrated in stories told by his Hasidim and admirers:

> The stories go on and on... Certainly, many of the miracle tales involve the creative interpretation of vague statements made by the Rebbe, statements that might have been taken several ways. But the sheer number of such "miraculous" interventions and predictions suggests to many people, including non-Lubavitchers, that Schneerson had tremendous insight, at the very least, and *perhaps something more.*[44]

An outstanding example of recent scholarship on Hasidism, combining the approaches of intellectual and social history, Glenn Dynner's study of Hasidism in Poland, *Men of Silk* (2006), takes a nuanced approach to the matter of miracles:

43 Brill, "The Spiritual World of a Master of Awe", 42.

44 Fishkoff, *The Rebbe's Army*, 83 (emphasis added).

> Polish zaddikim... seem in many cases to have sold magical services that they believed they could really render... If credulous petitioners had not conceived children, regained their health, prospered in business ventures, and felt empowered despite their unemancipated status, a zaddik's popularity could not have been sustained. When it comes to the potency of hope, faith, and a sensation of empowerment, the historian must withhold judgment. At the same time, perhaps we ought to be open to the possibility that deception did occur.[45]

Dynner's formulation is striking. He stops short of actually acknowledging a supernatural element in Hasidic miracles, and there is a note of scepticism in his reference to petitioners as "credulous" even while acknowledging that their petitions were often fulfilled. In stating, however, that "the historian must withhold judgment", he places the realm of miracles outside the domain of scientific investigation.[46] Dynner's line of thought is similar to that of Etkes with regard to the Baal Shem Tov: Rebbes believed in their own miracle-working power, Hasidim believed in their miracles and saw themselves as helped by them, and historians are not in a position to contradict this consensus.

Dynner goes on to use his most hesitant wording — "perhaps we ought to be open to the possibility" — regarding any actual faking of miracles. That is, the very possibility that was obvious to maskilic critics, that Hasidic miracles were fraudulent, is treated by the contemporary scholar as inherently unlikely.

Thus one of the barriers between Jewish intellectuals and Hasidim appears to be disappearing. This development arises from the contemporary intellectual situation, in which the authority of rationalism has been weakened. Sadly, this does not appear to be due to any increase in miracles in the world. Rather, it has much to do with a catastrophe during which miracles were notably absent: the Nazi Holocaust. "The seminal thinkers of postmodernism... have each insisted that the Holocaust marks a break in the trajectory of the West,

45 Dynner, *Men of Silk*, 194.

46 Earlier, Dynner does briefly endorse a psychological reading of dybbuk possession in the course of a long discussion of this phenomenon and Hasidic Rebbes' approaches to it: "Demonic possession was a socially acceptable way to express anxiety among unmarried women and pre-Bar Mitzvah boys" (142).

one which impels us to rethink the implications of the project of modernity."[47] As Moshe Idel spells this out with regard to Hasidism,

> The "warm" cosmology of Hasidism... was confronted with one of the reverberations of the "cold" scientific approach...: Nazism. The results are well known. They raise the problem of what is finally the more dangerous, magical lore that cares and is responsible, though the object of this care is a small community, or... a scientific-technological approach that is apparently more powerful but, at the same time, radically hostile to other human beings. When comparing the two worldviews, scholars must take the historical repercussions into consideration.[48]

In an intellectual climate where rationalism and attempts to maintain a single truth are tarred with the brush of Nazism, and in which truth is newly understood as plural and unstable, stubborn scepticism about non-rational phenomena has itself become embarrassing to the academic scholar.

On the other hand, the Hasidic movement's allegiance to its own truth continues unabated. "They're unswerving... They have the right answer and they're passionate about it."[49] The ambitious project of resistance to modernity continues. Dramatic miracle tales are told of contemporary Rebbes,[50] and collections of Hasidic tales continue to be printed and reprinted for readers who believe in them.[51]

In this ambiguous context, the postmodern scholar meets the anti-modern Hasid in (re)embracing the possibility of miracles.

47 Milchman and Rosenberg, *Postmodernism and the Holocaust*, 2.

48 Idel, *Hasidism*, 221.

49 Characterization of Chabad-Lubavitch by Conservative rabbi Jerome Epstein, cited in Fishkoff, *The Rebbe's Army*, 126.

50 See, for example, the stories of the Tosher Rebbe of Boisbriand, Québec, on William Shaffir's website, http://www.kiryastash.ca/tasher_rebbe.html.

51 A recent example available in English is the two-volume *Wonders and Miracles: Stories of the Lubavitcher Rebbe*. See Fishkoff, *The Rebbe's Army*, 82-83. Israel Berger's own compilations were reprinted in new, embellished editions in 2000.

WORKS CITED

Assaf, David. *The Regal Way: The Life and Times of Rabbi Israel of Ruzhin*. Stanford, California: Stanford University Press, 2002.

Ben-Amos, Dan, and Jerome R. Mintz, eds. *In Praise of the Ba'al Shem Tov* [English translation of *Shivhei HaBesht*]. New York: Schocken: 1984.

Berger, Israel. *Zekhut Yisrael: Eser Orot*. Pietrkow: Abraham Joseph Kleyman/ Enoch Henekh Falman, 5667/1907.

— . *Zekhut Yisrael* (2 vols.), ed. Hayim Joseph Waldman. Manchester: Torah MiTziyon (printed in Israel), 2000.

Buber, Martin. *Die Erzählungen der Chassidim*. Zürich: Manesse Verlag, 1949.

— . *Die Geschichten des Rabbi Nachman*. Frankfurt am Main: Rütter & Loenig, 1906.

— . *Tales of the Hasidim* [English version of *Die Erzählungen*]. Trans. Olga Marx. New York: Schocken, 1991.

Brawer, Yaakov. *Something from Nothing*. Montreal: TAV Seminary, n.d. (1990?)

Brill, Alan. "The Spiritual World of a Master of Awe: Divine Vitality, Theosis, and Healing in the *Degel Mahaneh Ephraim*." *Jewish Studies Quarterly* 8 (2001), 27-65.

Dynner, Glenn. *Men of Silk: The Hasidic Conquest of Polish Jewish Society*. Oxford University Press, 2006.

Etkes, Immanuel, trans. Saadya Sternberg. *The Besht: Magician, Mystic, and Leader*. Waltham, Massachusetts: Brandeis University Press, 2005.

Fishkoff, Sue. *The Rebbe's Army: Inside the World of Chabad-Lubavitch*. New York: Schocken, 2003.

Idel, Moshe. *Hasidism: Between Ecstasy and Magic*. Albany: State University of New York Press, 1995.

— . *Kabbalah: New Perspectives*. New Haven: Yale University Press, 1988.

Jacobson, David C. *Modern Midrash: The Retelling of Traditional Jewish Narratives by Twentieth Century Hebrew Writers*. Albany: State University of New York Press, 1987.

Katz, Steven T. *Post-Holocaust Dialogues: Critical Studies in Modern Jewish Thought*. New York: NYU Press, 1983.

Lamm, Norman. *The Religious Thought of Hasidism: Text and Commentary*. New York: Yeshiva University Press, 1999.

Lewis, Justin Jaron. *Imagining Holiness*. McGill-Queen's University Press, 2009.

Milchman, Alan and Alan Rosenberg, eds. *Postmodernism and the Holocaust*. Atlanta, Georgia: Rodopi, 1998.

Newman, Louis I. and Samuel Spitz. *The Hasidic Anthology: Tales and Teachings of the Hasidim*. Northvale, New Jersey: Jason Aronson, 1987 (reprint of 1934 edition).

Nigal, Gedalyah. *The Hasidic Tale*. Oxford: Littman Library of Jewish Civilization, 2008.

Peretz, I.L. *Khsidish*. Volume 5 in *Ale Verk fun Yud Lamed Perets*. Wilno: B. Kleckina, n.d. (1920s?)

— . *Geshikhtn un stsenes*. Volume 15 in *Ale Verk fun Yud Lamed Perets*. Wilno: B. Kleckina, n.d.

Robinson, Ira. "Hasidic Historiography and Jewish Modernity." In Carlebach et al., *Jewish History and Jewish Memory* (1998), 405-412.

Rosman, Moshe. *Founder of Hasidism: A Quest for the Historical Ba'al Shem Tov*. Berkeley: University of California Press, 1996.

— . "Shivhei ha-Besht: document historique, ouvrage de propaganda ou programme théologique?" *Les cahiers du Judaïsme* 8 (2000), 17-26.

Scholem, Gershom. *"Demuto hahistorit shel R. Yisrael Baal Shem Tov"*, *Molad* 18 (1960), 335-356.

— . "Martin Buber's Interpretation of Hasidism." *Commentary* 32 (1961), 305-316.

Shaffir, William. *Kiryas Tash* (website), www.kiryastash.ca.

Taylor, Dov, ed. and trans. *Joseph Perl's Revealer of Secrets: The First Hebrew Novel.* Boulder, Colorado: Westview Press,1997.

Wiederkehr-Pollack, Gloria. "Eliezer Zvi Hacohen Zweifel: Forgotten Father of Modern Scholarship on Hasidism", *Proceedings of the American Academy for Jewish Research*, Vol. 49 (1982), 87-115.

— . *Eliezer Zweifel and the Intellectual Defense of Hasidism.* Hoboken, NJ: Ktav, 1995.

Wodziński, Marcin, trans. Sarah Cozens and Agnieszka Mirowska. *Haskalah and Hasidism in the Kingdom of Poland: A History of Conflict.* Oxford: the Littman Library of Jewish Civilization, 2005.

"CHOSENNESS"

Edward Elkin

Perhaps no traditional Jewish theological notion makes contemporary Jews more uncomfortable than the idea of the Chosen People. While other discomfiting aspects of biblical theology such as the centrality of animal sacrifice can be fairly easily bracketed because they are so obviously archaic, and others such as the image of God as warrior can be fairly easily ignored because they do not feature prominently in the liturgy, the idea of chosenness suffuses the prayer life of the contemporary Jew. Even Jews who do not participate regularly in the life of the synagogue are likely to be familiar with the Torah blessing, the Friday night *Kiddush*, the *Aleinu* prayer and *Havdalah* — all of which highlight prominently the theme of Israel as having a special relationship with God, different from all the other peoples of the earth.

The traditional idea of chosenness has become quite controversial in many Jewish circles in the modern period for several different reasons. First, Jews have historically suffered terribly at the hands of peoples who thought themselves superior, so there is a sensitivity to systems of thought which seem to promote the privileging of one ethnic group over another. Second, some of the hatred that has been directed against Jews over the generations has been linked to the resentment felt by members of other groups concerning the idea of the Chosen People. Third, the modern western multicultural ideal valorizes differences among groups, but abhors intimations of superiority by those groups. In response to these objections, and others, the modern world has witnessed attempts to excise the vocabulary of chosenness from Jewish liturgy, and the idea from Jewish theology. But we have also seen attempts to defend, reinterpret, or reclaim this vocabulary and the theological notion behind it. This essay will touch on some of these efforts to deal with the problem of chosenness in the contemporary world.

The Scriptural basis for the idea of chosenness stems from two key places in the Torah. The first source is found in the book of Genesis, ch.12. Prior to ch.12, God is described as being in relationship with humanity as a whole. In the generation of Adam, Eve, and their descendants who begin to populate the world, there are no religious distinctions made among different groups within the human family. Similarly, in the generation of Noah, the violence and corruption that lead to God's decision to bring the terrible destruction of the Flood is said to characterize all of humanity. Only Noah and his family are saved, but they are not identified with a particular ethnic or religious group.

It is only in the time of Abraham that God determines to institute a special relationship, a covenant, with one particular man. God speaks directly to Abram and says, "I will make of you a great nation, and I will bless you. I will make your name great, and you shall be a blessing. I will bless those who bless you and curse those who curse you, and all the families of the earth shall bless themselves by you" (Gen.12:2). In what specific way will the "greatness" of this new nation be demonstrated? God promises Abram, and his son and grandson in turn, that the covenant promises will include both progeny in great numbers, and a land — the land known then as Canaan. (Gen.13:14-17; cf.Gen.26:3-5, 28:13-14). Thus we see that the foundation for the idea of chosenness is laid in the Torah's description of the special covenant God made with Abraham, the man Jews consider their founding father.

The second pertinent biblical source is Ex.19:5-6. In this passage, as Abraham's descendants, now grown into a people known as Israel and newly released from their Egyptian bondage, prepare to receive the revelation of the Decalogue, God tells them, "Now then, if you will obey Me faithfully, and keep My covenant, you shall be My treasured possession among all the peoples. Indeed all the earth is Mine, but you shall be to Me a kingdom of priests and a holy nation." Here, the idea of God's special relationship with the people of Israel is very explicit. An important element, however, is introduced into the concept of the covenant that had not hitherto been seen in the stories of the Patriarchs: the promise is conditional. Israel's status as *am sgula* is valid only *if* they obey God faithfully. Although this passage does not spell out the consequences of disobedience, the implication is that absent their obedience, their election as God's favoured nation is null and void. The rest of the Bible, however, does not take this extreme position. The children of Israel are lambasted again and again for their insubordination, and their suffering is directly attributable to their sins. The covenant between God and the people, however, is never utterly abrogated; the possibility for renewal is ever-present. Their standing as a "kingdom of priests" vis-à-vis the other nations is firmly established.

The Scriptural passages above provide the basis for later Jewish liturgical developments around the theme of chosenness. Four examples will suffice. First is the Torah blessing. Being called to recite this blessing is the most important ritual honour a Jew can receive, and it is one which emphasizes chosenness: "Blessed are You, Lord our God, King of the Universe, who has chosen us from all the peoples and has given us the Torah. Blessed are You O Lord Giver of the Torah." Out of all the peoples of the earth, God chose our people as the recipients of the Torah.

The second example is similar and is found in the Friday night *Kiddush* in which a Jew claims to be sanctified above all nations: "For You have chosen us and made us holy from among all the nations, and in Your love and graciousness You have bestowed upon us, Sabbath Your holiness. Blessed are You, Lord our God, King of the Universe, Who has made the Sabbath holy.

The third example is the *Aleinu* prayer. Originally appearing in the liturgy of the High Holidays, the *Aleinu* subsequently came to be featured in the liturgy of every service of the year, three times a day. It is generally a high point near the end of the service, when congregants join together to sing the catchy melody. What do they sing? "It is our duty to praise the Master of all, to exalt the Creator of the universe, who has not made us like the nations of the world and has not placed us like the families of the earth, who has not designed our destiny to be like theirs, nor our lot like that of all their multitude." The emphasis here is on the difference between us and them. We are not like the rest of the peoples of the earth; they have their destiny — but we, who know and bow down to the one true God, have our own, separate, destiny.

A final example among many in Jewish liturgy comes from Havdalah, the ritual which is performed at the conclusion of the Sabbath each week. Havdalah means separation or distinction, and the liturgy of Havdalah sets out a series of distinctions as the Sabbath comes to a close. We are told that God distinguishes between sacred and profane, between light and darkness, between the seventh day of rest and the other six days of work, and — between the people of Israel and the other nations of the world. In this Havdalah blessing it is difficult to miss the message that the Jews fall on the sacred/light/Shabbat side of the equation, while the rest of the nations of the world fall on the profane/darkness/six workdays side. These are the distinctions which we reflect on traditionally as we bid farewell to the Sabbath each week.

As mentioned earlier, many Jews in the contemporary world have been very troubled by their encounters with the biblical texts depicting chosenness as well as the liturgical texts which they are asked to recite on important occasions which reinforce this notion. Some scholars, rabbis, and liturgists have sought to address their discomfort by eliminating references to chosenness from Jewish prayer. Perhaps the most famous proponent of this view was Mordecai Kaplan, a professor at the Jewish Theological Seminary for many decades who founded the Reconstructionist movement in Judaism, at least partially so that there would be a place in the Jewish world to put his theological ideas into practice. Kaplan wrote in 1948 that "The idea of Israel as the Chosen People must…be understood as belonging to a thought-world which we no longer inhabit. It fits in with a set of ideas that were congruous and rational enough in their day. But it can no longer help us to understand relations, or to orient ourselves to conditions as they exist today. The very notion that a people can for all time be the elect of God implies an epic or dramatic conception of history, a history predetermined in form and aim. Nowadays for any people to call itself "chosen" is to be guilty of self-infatuation."[1]

Kaplan says we can understand why the ancestors of today's Jews might have been drawn to the idea of the Chosen People in their time, but this idea is clearly an anachronism today. We cannot afford to either be, or be perceived as, self-infatuated in the contemporary world. Today's world, in contrast to that of our ancestors, has accepted the Jews as equals. We are citizens of our countries, and we do not face legal disabilities because of our faith. We cannot continue, therefore, to erect barriers from our side between ourselves and our neighbours. Chosenness is a theological idea which has outlived its usefulness, and should therefore be discarded. The liturgy of the Reconstructionist move-

1 Mordecai Kaplan, *The Making of the American Jew*, p. 119 and p.211.

ment, therefore, in each of the examples set forth above — Torah blessing, kiddush, Alenu, and Havdalah — has altered the prayers in such a way as to take away the vocabulary of chosenness.[2] Any choosing that happens in Kaplan's view happens on the human side of the equation, when individuals make the choice to affirm their membership in the Jewish community.

Eugene Borowitz rejects Kaplan's sociological approach to Judaism, because it leaves us without any compelling reason to maintain Jewish particularity in the contemporary world. He sees our relationship with God as being about more than just the needs and responses of a particular generation at a particular moment in historical time. But he is also hesitant to use the vocabulary of chosenness: "I believe we must supplement human choosing with God's own action if we are to explain to ourselves our fundamental commitment to the continuity of the people of Israel. Yet I believe the traditional view that God 'chose us from among all peoples and gave us the Torah' clashes too much with our sense of history and reality for us to reaffirm it."[3] Borowitz prefers the metaphor of Covenant to the metaphor of chosenness as a way to describe Israel's continuing uniqueness. He is particularly uncomfortable with the passive nature of the chosenness metaphor,[4] rooted as it is in the Abraham narrative in which God, for no apparent reason and with no apparent expectations of anything in return, chose Abraham to found this new people. He is much more comfortable with the Exodus narrative of conditional covenant, in which the people's choices significantly (but not exclusively) determine the nature of their relationship with God. We note, however, that he sees both chosenness and covenant as metaphors. This metaphoric reading is a far cry from premodern characterizations of the unique relationship between God and Israel as being quite literal and concrete.

Although discomfort with the idea of Chosenness has been widespread, the idea is still very present in Jewish life through the liturgy in all Jewish movements other than the Reconstructionist and even the Reconstructionist liturgy hasn't eliminated it completely. Two scholars have recently attempted to

2 See for example, *Siddur Kol HaNeshama,* The Reconstructionist Press, 1994, pp.399, 445, 525.

3 *Renewing the Covenant: A Theology for the Post-Modern Jew.* Philadelphia: JPS, 1991, p.211.

4 Ibid., p.201.

explain the idea of Chosenness in a way that will allow contemporary Jews to talk about it and use it without feeling awkward or ashamed. Meir Soloveitchik approaches the subject by outlining what he sees as the distinction between Jewish and Christian views of divine love.[5] Basing his work on the ideas of the Swedish theologian Anders Nygren, Soloveitchik claims that in Christianity, the way God loves is utterly different from the way human beings love. God does not love because of a particular qualities possessed by the object of that love; God loves despite our specific qualities. God's love is utterly unmotivated. This contrasts with human love, which happens when we encounter qualities and characteristics in particular people that we find love-worthy.

Although Christians have historically seen their understanding of God as superior to what they perceive as the more primitive and tribal Jewish view, Soloveitchik accepts this distinction between the Christian and Jewish concepts of divine love and embraces it. In the Jewish view, he says, the way God loves is not so different from the way human beings love. Just like human beings, God is drawn to particular qualities and characteristics that make a particular people worthy of being loved. God's love in Judaism is not abstract, as a universal love would necessarily have to be. Rather, it is very concrete and specific — directed at the descendants of one particular man whom God favoured, Abraham. The validation of God's preferential love in Judaism leads to validation of the institution of the family as the next logical step. Familial ties are by definition preferential. We do not love anonymous people who live across town in the same way as we love members of our family. God's love operates the same way, and the centrality of the family unit in Jewish life is thus reaffirmed.

Soloveitchik does make an important concession to modern sensibilities in his analysis. He says that while God's love may be preferential, God's *justice* is universal. Using the people of Sodom as his primary example, Soloveitchik says that all are judged according to their merits. This includes the rewards of the afterlife, which are open to Gentiles as well as to Jews.

However, it is God's love which is central to Soloveitchik's argument. It is our sense that God loves the Jewish people in a special way that has sustained us through some difficult times: "The dedication of generations of Jews to

5 "God's Beloved: A Defense of Chosenness" Azure, Winter 2005.

Jewish law was not out of a blind sense of duty, but out of a firm belief that these laws were the expression of the Creator's special love for the Jewish people, and their betrayal would be a betrayal of that love. It is this belief, perhaps above all else, which sustained Jewish communities through the hardships of exile, persecution, and pogrom. And it may still."

Soloveitchik's defense of chosenness seeks to put the minds of contemporary Jews at ease as they think about chosenness. The fairness concern is addressed by his conviction that God's justice is in fact equal, even if God's love is not. And the preferential love that God displays toward us because we are descendants of Abraham is legitimate, because without it God would be too remote, distant, and abstract for people in our time who are looking to religion for a sense of warmth and intimacy. Soloveitchik's God is close, and comprehensible because He is, in many ways, like us.

Joel S. Kaminsky also defends the idea of Chosenness in his work Yet I Loved Jacob: Reclaiming the Biblical Concept of Election.[6] Kaminsky cites many stories in the Book of Genesis as displaying God's penchant for playing favourites. Cain and Abel, Ishmael and Isaac, Jacob and Esau — all these stories reflect God's choice of one brother over another. Kaminsky lays particular stress on the story of Joseph and his brothers. Joseph is favoured both by his father, and by God. His father manifests his special love for Joseph over his brothers by giving him the coat of many colours. God manifests His special love for Joseph by bestowing on him physical beauty, as well as the ability to interpret dreams. Initially, it appears as if these examples of favouritism are going to end in disaster. The resentment felt by Joseph's brothers leads to his being sold down to Egypt, and his father's heart is broken when he believes Joseph is dead. Yet in the end, these events lead to Joseph's ascent to the position of vizier over all the land of Egypt. Encountering his brothers years later, Joseph does not appear to have learned the lesson that favouritism is bad; he himself displays it with regard to his full brother Benjamin, both before and after he reveals his identity to them.[7] In this way, Kaminsky shows that the lesson of the story is *not* that choosing favourites is necessarily bad. God's choice of

6 Nashville: Abingdon Press, 2007.

7 Gen.43:44, Gen.45:22.

Joseph over the brothers not only benefited him eventually, *but also benefited them*. If not for Jacob's and God's preferential love for Joseph, the brothers and their families would have starved.

The choice, or election, of Joseph finally served everyone's needs. Chosenness is not raw ethnocentrism, Kaminsky says.[8] Like Soloveitchik, he believes that the idea of universal, equal love is generic and not terribly intimate. Chosenness reflects a belief that God lovingly and mercifully interacts with the world. What saves chosenness in the contemporary context for Kaminsky is the distinction between what he calls the "non-elect" and the "anti-elect". The latter are people who are viewed as so evil or dangerous that warfare against them may include a call for their annihilation.[9] Kaminsky recognizes this anti-Canaanite and anti-Amalekite polemic as problematic, but he does not see it as central to the idea of Chosenness. Much more central is what Kaminsky calls the "non-elect."[10] These are people who are neither part of the Israelite nation nor are they evil like the anti-elect. Many biblical passages reflect a concern that members of the non-elect be treated with compassion and kindness. Indeed, Kaminsky says, it is the very notion that Jews are the elect which propels them to treat the non-elect with the compassion which befits God's treasured people. In this way, as in the Joseph story, the non-chosen benefits from God's choice of the chosen.

Like Soloveitchik, Kaminsky cannot imagine the Jewish community sustaining itself in the absence of the idea of election. In fact, he notes that Christianity has appropriated the idea of chosenness for itself and could also not survive without it: "Jewish and Christian believers need to continue to wrestle with the idea of election in all its fullness rather than surrender to the temptation to empty it of its theological power by downplaying its particularistic dimensions or, worse yet, attempting to banish it from the larger theological landscape (the latter being an exercise in futility in my opinion). One must measure the loss that would be sustained by discarding such a central idea — central to both Judaism and Christianity — against the gain to be had by

8 Kaminsky, p.193.

9 Ibid., p.111.

10 Ibid., p.121.

embracing it."[11] That gain is the very perpetuation of the faith in the face of all the blandishments of the outside world. Even if we wanted to get rid of this idea, as Kaplan did, that aspiration is futile — because chosenness is embedded so deeply in our tradition. Removing it is like a surgeon removing a vital organ — what happens? The patient dies.

In her poem *El Hanun*, the Yiddish poet Kadya Molodowsky writes "O God of Mercy/ for the time being/choose another people. We are tired of death, tired of corpses/We have no more prayers. For the time being/ choose another people." These words reflect the double-edged sword that has often been part of the Jewish experience of chosenness. Like the poet, many Jews in the modern world have wanted to eliminate this idea from Jewish theology and Jewish self-perception. Whatever else we can say about the relationship between suffering and chosenness, that connection certainly obviates the notion that chosenness means that the elect receive special privileges. As Abel, Isaac, Jacob, and Joseph all found out, being chosen can lead to terrible suffering. Molodowsky picks up on this theme, and wants nothing of it, at least "for the time being".

If chosenness does not mean rewards, then what does it mean? Traditionally, it means that the one chosen bears special responsibilities. There are obligations which the members of "God's treasured people" have to bear, commandments they have to perform which no one else is obligated to perform. We might not want those responsibilities, and we certainly do not want the suffering that seems to go along with the status. How we can best square the circle of being chosen in the context of a modern, western, multi-cultural society is a major Jewish theological challenge in today's world. The Scriptural and liturgical texts emphasizing chosenness make us uncomfortable. They are part of our inheritance as Jews, however, so we must continue to mine them for insights, and together develop an approach to them that with which we can live.

11 Ibid., p.195.

DURÉE, DEVEKUTH, & RE-EMBRACING THE GODLOVER: INVOLUTION[1] OF UNIO MYSTICA VIA COLLOCATIVE HOMOSEXU*EL*ITY

Aubrey L. Glazer

בָּרוּךְ אַתָּה עוֹזְבֵנוּ אֲדֹנָי אֱלֹהֵינוּ

לֹא מֶלֶךְ הָעוֹלָם בְּקַשָּׁתֵנוּ

בִּתְפִלָּתֵנוּ שֶׁתְּחַיֵּנוּ

וּתְקַיְּמֵנוּ

וּתְבִיאֵנוּ

לֹא

לַזְּמָן

הַזֶּה.[2]

1 *In*volution as opposed to *e*volution implies that the process of spiritual growth is an internal process. In this sense, the following investigation takes leave of Art Green's most recent and comprehensive theological reflections on evolution. His ambitious and unique project is to reconcile the reigning scientific truths we are resigned to, like evolution, with a committed religious life of the spirit. His contribution will have many implications for Jewish theology for years to come and thus warrants a more sustained reflection and critique. While I agree that with Green's insightful rendering of a spiritual journey whereby one is called out to with the words of Genesis, Where are You? or *Ayekah* as an opportunity for each being to respond in stretching the human mind forward, the human into awareness and the human deed into redemption, it seems that there is still much that remains frozen at an earlier stage of evolution. See Art Green, "Jewish God-Talk: An Evolutionist Approach," *Arthur Cohen Lecture Series*, Yale University (*forthcoming*). The present investigation seeks to explore ecstatic spiritual evolution as internal process of eros, specifically how homo-eroticism rather than hetero-eroticism points to a neglected strand of experience and expression within Jewish mysticism. Both Idel and Wolfson have critiqued Scholem's blindspots in this regard. Scholem sidestepped ecstatic Kabbalah from his research after a certain point according to Idel. This involution is a necessary corrective, as implied by Wolfson's scholarship, to a system of theosophic mysticism that continues to perpetuate the ascendancy of the masculine over the feminine. I am grateful to Art Green for sharing an earlier draft of his lecture, "Jewish God-Talk: An Evolutionist Approach," with me and continually engaging in discourse arising from it together.

2 Binyamin Shvili, *Milon hadash shel yissurim,* p. 62.

1.0 WHEN TIME DISSOLVES INTO THE REAL: EMBARRASSMENT & THE RE-EMBRACE OF *DEVEKUTH*

Time, so elusive in its eternality, remains a guiding force in our journey through life. It is all the more elusive in that most systems for measuring time are not about eternality whatsoever but focus on what is fleeting. Consider the difficulty in breaking the hold of such a powerful image like the hourglass upon our view of time. With the power in acknowledgment of reaching לִזְמַן הַזֶּה *this time*, no other time seems possible but this moment. Yet this opening poem challenges even this moment as being truly singular. By wandering into the realm of לֹא לִזְמַן הַזֶּה *not this time,* rather than burning its reader through its mystical illumination, the poem risks being burned by rationalists who cannot read it. The questions implied by the poem seem beyond the rational: Can a time other than this moment ever really be noticed, or even be blessed? Perhaps this predilection for the illusion of time's construct is a vestige of those early sea voyageurs seeking to cross all the earth's meridians by merely relying upon the hourglass and magnetic compass to navigate their journey. Turning the ship's hourglasses would allow for the completion of the ship's log, and in so doing tell the story of its journey. The need to journey by turning over one's time through it remains a thoroughly human preoccupation. The fleeting reality of human existence escapes no one, especially those who set off perennially on life's journey of the spirit to seek all of its meridians, like the poet and the mystic.

For many such a journey is fraught with peril. For not all readers, or scholars for that matter, are poetically inclined. Let us begin this journey with such a moment not of this time, that marked esoteric wisdom's entry into the realm of critical study remains pristine to this day. Since the Enlightenment and its introduction of *Wissenschaft des Judentums*, but especially after the *Shoah*, the embarrassment over the intersection of esoteric and critical knowledge has only increased. It is a twofold embarrassment: on the hand, the mystic is embarrassed by the scholar's utter disconnection from the experience undergirding the subject under investigation; on the other hand, the scholar is embarrassed by the mystic's immersion in an experience beyond the scope of rational investigation. The aspirant and practitioner of kabbalah — known as a *mekkubal* — harbors skepticism of scholars like Gershom Scholem, a secular Jew who had received his esoteric knowledge as a university discipline. Yet on one occasion when Scholem crossed the line by inviting a *mekkubal*, Rabbi Abraham Chen, to visit a kabbalah seminar for his university students, the mystic is said to have remarked:

> A scholar of mysticism is like an accountant:
> He may know where all the treasure is,
> but he is not free to use it.

The embarrassment of the *mekkubal* as practitioner is over the detachment of the scholar from the true meaning of what s/he studies, yet notice how this embarrassment is subtly couched in the language of parable. The nature of the mystic‘s embarrassment is subtle in that it remains a question whether s/he must set out to re-embrace what may have otherwise been lost in the process. But by contrast, as the other side of embarrassment shall now reveal, the embarrassment of the scholar for the mystic‘s immersion in the irrational is simple casuistry. Yet this casuistry may indeed be the mark of a deeper wound in need of re-embracing what is otherwise lost through the neglect of embarrassment.

Recall the moment of this time still wounded by the deranged words of brilliant Lithuanian Talmudist, Saul Lieberman as he introduced the exiled scholar, Gershom Scholem, for a lecture on kabbalah at the hallmark institution of *Wissenschaft des Judentums*, the Jewish Theological Seminary of America. How fitting that the most elaborate recounting of this scenario is through the imaginative novelist, Cynthia Ozick. That a novelist, rather than a disciple of Lieberman or Scholem or even a JTS student for that matter recovers this embarrassment stands as a mark of the far-reaching nature of this embarrassment:

> It may have been in the early nineteen-forties (there are no living witnesses, and no one of the current generation is certain just when) that Scholem was invited to New York to deliver a lecture on Kabbalah at the Jewish Theological Seminary. He was introduced by Saul Lieberman, a leading Talmudic eminence, and thereby an adherent of Jewish rationalism.

> "Nonsense is nonsense," Professor Lieberman pronounced, "but the history of nonsense is scholarship." Whether Scholem responded to this now legendary maxim is not known. But the immensity, and the passion, of his scholarship intimates that he did not include visionary symbolism among the artifacts of nonsense.[3]

As apocryphal stories go, there are always alternate versions. It is equally fitting that the alternate version to this apocryphal story makes a much more pointed swipe at the academic study of Jewish mysticism by having Lieberman utter instead:

> If Jewish Mysticism is nothing but nonsense,
> then the history of Jewish mysticism
> is the history of nonsense!

Students at the Seminary, according to the apocryphal story, seem to have been pushing for a course in which they could begin the critical study of kabbalistic texts. Lieberman flatly refused, claiming "It is forbidden to have a course in nonsense. But the history of nonsense, that is scholarship!" The deeper irony being that as a student at the Seminary some fifty years later, I recall how much that apocryphal story still concatenated through the walls, even though Jewish mysticism was now being regularly taught with a dedicated professor.

To any arch-rationalist scholar, the mystical experience would logically appear to be beyond the realm of scholarship. But in those timely words of introduction, Lieberman staked his claim for what he thought should constitute the proper bounds of critical scholarship — writing *about* the experience rather than entering *the experience itself.* The embarrassment over the nature of the mystical experience as well as entering into any experience *per se* could never have been more lucidly articulated. If one possible way of defining mysticism centers around the experience itself, that definition would necessitate some form of *unio mystica*, that is, a mystical union or merging experience

3 Cynthia Ozick, "The Heretic: The mythic passions of Gershom Scholem," *New Yorker* 09-02-2002.

with God or the Other. But the study of Jewish mysticism has forever been delimited by Scholem's early devaluation of *devekuth* in his pioneering study, *Major Trends in Jewish Mysticism*, which seems to have been fueled by an overriding embarrassment:

> ...it is only in extremely rare cases that ecstasy signifies actual union with God, in which the human individuality abandons itself to the rapture of complete submersion in the divine stream. Even in this ecstatic frame of mind, the Jewish mystic almost invariably retains a sense of the distance between the Creator and His creature...he does not regard it as constituting anything so extravagant as identity of Creator and creature.[4]

Embarrassment surrounds that loss of distance with any dissolution of individual identity into the pool of ultimate unity. Even in his later period, Scholem remained cautious and openly skeptical about the possibility of complete union and identity loss of the individual within the divine stream as constituting an authentic Jewish mystical experience. The embarrassment is even more pronounced in the context of his later writing, that is within the pronounced universalist setting of the Eranos lectures:[5]

> The Jewish mystics used the term *devekuth* to denote this ultimate aim. The term, meaning literally "cleaving" or "adhering" to God...The necessity to compromise with medieval Jewish theology dictated terminology, not the act itself, which may or may not include a state of mystical union.[6]

4 Gershom Scholem, *Major Trends in Jewish Mysticism*, Schocken Books, New York 1947, pp. 122-123. See also Moshe Idel, Studies in Ecstatic Kabbalah, SUNY Press, New York, ff. 11, p. 21.

5 By 1961, Scholem was one of five members of the so-called guardian committee of *Eranos*. This group met regularly at a chateau in Ascona, Switzerland, beginning in 1933. See Steven M. Wasserstrom, *Religion after Religion: Gershom Scholem, Mircea Eliade, and Henry Corbin at Eranos*, Princeton University Press, New Jersey 1999.

6 Scholem, "Mysticism and Society," *Diogenes, Eranos Lectures,* vol. 58 (1967), p. 16. See also Idel, *Studies in Ecstatic Kabbalah*, SUNY Press, New York 1988, ff. 11, p. 21, where Idel challenges Scholem's assumption that the ambiguous term *devekuth* was dictated by the need to compromise with Jewish theology as completely unsupported by evidence in Abraham Abulafia, Isaac ben Yed'ayah and Abraham Shalom.

A re-embrace of *devekuth* as a truly unitive experience in Jewish mysticism has been argued by Scholem's disciple, Moshe Idel. In a thorough re-examination of the neglected sources in ecstatic kabbalah, Idel comes to prove, *contra* Scholem's embarrassment, that indeed there are "philosophical texts which openly speak about the possibility of total union with God."[7] The following study begins the process of necessary retrieval in the philosophical sources to then reveal the poetic path in Hebrew poetry that re-embraces *unio mystica* as a genuine sign of contemporary mysticism.

1.1 WHY EMBARRASSMENT & RE-EMBRACEMENT MATTER: SETTING OFF ON THE POETIC JOURNEY

As an aspiring poet, the import of Hebrew poetry's renaissance became apparent to me the first time I set off to sea in academia. Amidst my studies of French poetry at University of Toronto, especially intoxicated with Baudelaire and Rimbaud, I crossed the great divide into the Department of Near and Middle Eastern Studies, daring to take a course on Hebrew poetry with Professor Fox. I still recall that moment of radical amazement when I realized Rimbaud's usage of *tohu-bohu* in *Un Saison en Infer* originated in Hebrew. Unbeknownst to me, I would not be abandoning everything that drew me to French poetry and thinking, everything from Rimbaud's <<*Bateau Ivre*>> to Barthes' *Camera Lucida*. This mastermind before me in our Hebrew poetry seminar managed to allow all thinking to penetrate into the discourse before us. I mention Rimbaud and Barthes as the baggage I took with me upon my journey, recalling how Fox embraced these alchemical seekers with open arms and an even more open mind into his seminar. For over a decade after that first excursion with Fox, no matter where I was or what I was studying, I would set off seeking another meridian with him upon what seemed like a perennially new journey in Hebrew poetry. While we seemed to always be journeying in familiar waters — that intoxicating ingression and egression of Bialik — each new reading brought with it *novellae* never imagined. Fox's

7 Idel, *Studies in Ecstatic Kabbalah*, ff. 11, p. 21. Compare with Idel's later reflections on *unio mystica* via love and intellection, again from Abulafia in *Sefer 'Or ha-Sekhel*, see Idel, *Kabalah and Eros*, Yale University Press, New Haven 2005, p. 79.

love for poetry and his gift for reading it knows no bounds. That is why at some point in every seminar, he would take the trouble to re-embrace Ezra Pound's astounding edits to T.S. Eliot's, "The Wasteland." Here we discovered that even great poets were embarrassed or embarrassing (in the case of Eliot's and Pound's virulent anti-semitism), but with a discerning reader, could ultimately be *re-embraced.* Fox's facilitation of this ongoing revelation — with such humility and humor — is what lead me to ultimately re-embrace Hebrew Hermeneutics as my own path of scholarship through his guidance over the years. That ongoing study culminated at my Ph.D. defense along with Harold Bloom and Art Green. I am convinced Fox truly opened my eyes and my soul to every powerful ingression in Hebrew poetry— even those I apparently discovered on my own he already foresaw. Just like that renowned Yerushalmi passage which claims that all *novellae* in Torah up to and including this very moment between teacher and student were revealed to Moses at Sinai, so too were any discoveries in Hebrew poetry or *novellae* to be *re-embraced* into Jewish Thinking with Fox.

Not only does Fox teach and write poetry, but he also fosters friendships with Israel's up-and-coming voices in poetry. If I was not being introduced to new poets at Fox's Sabbath table in Toronto, then surely we would meet at his renowned Love Poetry Reading for *Tu B'Av* in Jerusalem. For as a godlover, Fox's love for scholarship can only be out-shined by his love for humanity. His love for *novellae* in every form of Torah — including the primordial Torah of Hebrew Poetry — is the singlemost important contribution Fox continues to make in his prolific Oral Torah to an entire generation of scholars. None who come to know Fox, as friend and as teacher, can escape his eternal *re-embrace.* There is almost no rupture between experience and poetry in his presence.

So now wending out of a moment of this time in returning to our opening poem — akin in form to the top half of a broken hourglass — one may indeed succumb to the reality that time is elusive, even while the poem breaks hold of this very symbol. This opening poem by Hebrew poet, Binyamin Shvili is an intentional misreading of an ancient prayer about time — the archetypal Hebrew hourglass. The blessing known as the *She'heḫaiyanu* has been read through the centuries as a marker of time and new experiences formed in the following language: *Blessed are You, Master of the Universe, who has enlivened us, sustained us, and brought us to this moment.* Daring to write against the hourglass view of time, Shvili's brilliant misreading seeks to unravel this temporal entanglement. By breaking out of the hourglass view of time and the apparent fullness of its measure, there is another view of temporality expressed:

Blessed are You, our Abandoner, Lord our God
Not Master of the Universe, our petitions
within our prayers that you should enliven us
that you should sustain us
that you should bring us
not
to this
time.

With these few grains of sand about to escape the broken hourglass into the journey of existence, Shvili dares to imagine the emptiness of time. The poet's misreading of the ancient Hebrew marker of time, the *She'hehaiyanu*, is iconoclastic to the core of the human experience of time. If existence cannot truly be captured and recorded through time, then what happens to this moment that is now escaping? How will it ever be known? The poet challenges, in merely eight lines, any preconceived notion of time, eternity and its unity along the journey of existence. Amidst all the pain it brings in its wake, the poet is committed to setting off upon a new course to journey through the experience of existence open to the emptiness of time. Through this pain of separation, the poet yearns to return to the unity of primal experience. Through Binyamin Shvili's re-embrace of homo-erotic poetics, our present reading seeks to uncover how an eternal season of intoxication makes the experience of *unio mystico* possible.

1.2 BEYOND THE ILLUSION OF TIME: SABBATICAL UNION SHATTERING THE ILLUSION OF TIME

While time may be a co-ordinate or a dimension, the grand illusion persists that time still seems to flow[8] — why? Elucidating the mysterious flux could reveal the nature of the human self. Without a real understanding of the flow of time (or its illusion), we will not know who we are, where we are going or what part we are playing in the great cosmic drama.[9] As much as this myth of time's flux may be a cerebral process from the perspective of physics, the journey of the soul persists through a variety of images, with the flux of its seasons remaining a recurrent one from the perspective of poetics. How might this perennial poetic journey through seasons, intoxicated with an eternality of heaven and hell, shed light on that crucial aspect of the human self — the soul?

Through this experiential dimension of time's flux in relation to an other it can open one to the profundity of existence. Such a profundity lies in its infinitude. But human finitude limits an ongoing connection with the infinite. Yet by delving into the depth each moment brings, the seeming passage of time invites an awareness of the infinitude pregnant within each moment. Such an infinitude encompasses past and future within the fullness of the present. The seasons of love and its loss open every human to the possibility of tasting the aroma of infinity within the finitude of existence. Many consider this quest for reunion and immersion in timeless love to be the *telos* of the mystical experience. Often this quest finds a home in the Sabbath, a moment where Shvili also sees the eros of time otherwise:

8 Paul Davies, *About Time: Einstein's Unfinished Revolution*, Simon & Schuster, New York 1995, pp. 252-255:
The flow of time has no significance in the logically fixed patterns demanded by deterministic theory, time being a mere co-ordinate. In a theory with indeterminacy, however, the passage of time transforms the statistical expectations into real events.

9 P. Davies, *About Time*, p. 278:
Attempts to explain the flow of time using physics, rather than trying to define it away using philosophy, are probably the most exciting contemporary developments in the study of time. Elucidating the mysterious flux would, more than anything else, help unravel the deepest of all scientific enigmas — the nature of the human self. Until we have a firm understanding of the flow of time, or incontrovertible evidence that it is indeed an illusion, then we will not know who we are, or what part we are playing in the great cosmic drama.

בְּ	in
קָרוֹב	time
יָבוֹא	Sabbath shall
שַׁבָּת	come
כְּמוֹ	like
מֶלֶךְ	a king
לֹא	not
כְּמוֹ	like
מַלְכָּה	a queen
לָבוּשׁ	garbed in
שְׁחֹ	bl
רִים	ack
בְּחֶרֶב	with a sword
פִּיפִ	dou-
יּוֹת	ble-bladed
יְקַצֵּר	which shall shorten
אֶת	the
הַכְּאֵב	pain
וְגַם אֶת	and the
הַגַּעְגּוּעִים[10]	longings.

Tearing into the holiness of time the poet sees the coming of the Sabbath. Shvili exposes the longing at the core of this irruption of eternality into temporality, of infinitude into the finite. The week begins and ends, but Sabbath is, as Heschel puts it, eternity uttering a moment. This narrowing of the eternal into the temporal is a painful moment. "Let the pious exult in glory: let them sing hymns even on their beds with the high praises of God in their throats and a double-bladed sword in their hands…" This double-edged sword of the Psalmist (149: 6) extrapolates from the bed into life. There is no place devoid of the presence of eros. But the other side of the phallic blade for Shvili is the homo-erotic. This perspective within eros allows for the true fluidity of the Sabbath to come to the fore. Just as in Alkabetz's sixteenth century liturgical

10 Binyamin Shvili, *Milon hadash shel yissurim*, p. 52.

poem, *Lecha Dodi* that welcomes the reunion of the lover with the beloved where gender is constantly in motion, so too Shvili invites a relationship with the other side of queen through king. The flux between queen [מַלְכָּה] and king [מֶלֶךְ] is the matter of a single letter [ה]. This more restrained alchemy shall serve for now as a taste of how poetry allows this irruption of eternality into temporality. The *be*longing that comes from such intense longing is quenched through the unique experience of time that is cleaving. To more fully understand the importance of Shvili's poetic contribution to the unspoken Jewish experience of *unio mystica*,[11] it is necessary to now review a brief history of *Hitdavekuth.*

1.3 A BRIEF HISTORY OF *HITDAVEKUTH:*

1.31 BIBLICAL PERSPECTIVES

The possibility of drawing near to the transcendent in the imminent within one's life could be said to begin in the Hebrew Bible. The expression *hitdavekuth,* or more commonly *devekuth,* originates with the root of the verb *DVK* as is known often in Deuteronomy (4: 4, 10:20, 11:22, 13:5, 30:20) in reference to God. Getting closer to the divine that is a "devouring fire" (Deuteronomy 4: 24) requires a delimitation on how close is possible without getting completely consumed. It is described in various ways as clinging, cleaving, keeping close, being loyal or affectionate.[12] Yet already in Psalm 63 there is a proximity of body and soul within the experience of cleaving whereby com-

11 Despite the vast genres available within Jewish literature, there does not seem to be much space for direct confessional or biographical accounts of the mystical experience as is the case within other religious and spiritual paths. Notwithstanding exceptions, most notably, the still unpublished prayer diaries of the Nazir (a.k.a. David Cohen, the disciple of Rav Kook). These prayer diaries (which apparently are in limited circulation amidst a closed circle of Kook's disciples) are unique in that they are said to be daily accounts of the Nazir's prayer life and its mystical import. Another exception are the journal entries of Hillel Zeitlin in Warsaw before the war. These dated entries bespeak a life of spiritual quietism that is being stirred up by the dissolution of Wiemar Germany. As the destruction encroaches, Zeitlin's tone becomes more and more prophetic, see Hillel Zeitlin, *'Al Gevul Shenei 'Olamot*, Yavneh, Tel Aviv 1965.

12 Brown, Drivers & Briggs, s.v. *DVK, A Hebrew and English Lexicon of Old Testament*, Clarendon Press, Oxford 1906, pp. 179-180.

plete dissolution of self is almost possible and perceptible, "My soul thirsts for you, my body longs for you…My soul is attached to You…" (Psalm 63: 2, 9). What Deuteronomy presents as a soul connection, Psalm 63 sees as equally ensouled and embodied.

There remain a few enigmatic scriptural narratives that suggest *hitdavekuth* experiences:

(1). Jacob encountering a sacred site (Genesis 28: 10-16);

(2). Jacob wrestling the angelic being (Genesis 32: 23-33);[13]

(3). Moses, Nadav, Avihu and the seventy elders ecstatic atop the mountain (Exodus 24: 9-11);

(4). The immolation scene of Nadav and Avihu (Leviticus 10: 1-7);

(5). Zipporah's divine encounter with the Bridegroom of Blood (Exodus 4: 24-26).

Each scenario suggests the danger of clinging, cleaving, and keeping close to the divine. The Nadav and Avihu immolation scene comes closest to describing a *hitdavekuth* experience, especially in God's poetic response to their father Aaron through Moses in the third verse:

בִּקְרֹבַי אֶקָּדֵשׁ וְעַל פְּנֵי כָל הָעָם אֶכָּבֵד

Through those close to Me I shall be hallowed
And gain glory before all the people

While the meaning of this cryptic poem remains elusive,[14] the vestiges of experiences such as these are curious in both their elliptic retelling as well as

13 וַיֵּאָבֵק in v. 25 is generally translated as "he wrestled" which echoes with resonances of וַיִּדְבַּק "he cleaved." Such an assonance or *lucis a non lucendo* did not escape the eyes of some Medieval commentators, but the embarrassment remained.

14 *The Five Books of Moses: A Translation with Commentary*, W. W. Norton & Company, New York 2004, tr. Robert Alter, p. 580, ff. 3:

their utter absence of any *hitdavekuth* language. Often the unsaid is a sign of latent embarrassment.

1.32 ALEXANDRIAN PERSPECTIVE

It is then in Alexandria around the first century (ca. 20 BCE - 50 CE) that Philo provides a number of ways to expand this biblical notion of *devekuth*. One only need to reconsider the ritual of the Therapeutae described in *De Vita Contemplativa* with its two separate lines of men and women chanting and dancing together. As the chanting intensifies, these separate lines merge, "forming a single choir…an harmonious consent, music in the truest sense." Immersed in this "piety" as Philo describes it, "…they continue till dawn, drunk with this drunkenness in which there is no shame…more alert and wakeful than when they came to the banquet, they stand with their faces and whole body turned to the east…"[15] It is in this alert and wakeful union that the group unifies into the experience of *eudaimonia* or "the summit of felicity."[16] It is even possible that the act of contemplating the truths of scripture allows Philo himself to merge with the divine. Elsewhere, in contemplating the meaning of the Cherubim, after exhausting all rational interpretations, Philo writes: "But there is a higher thought than these. It comes from a voice in my own soul, which oftentimes is god-possessed and divines where it does not know."[17] This inner voice that has merged with his external persona as philosopher is what allows him to write that God unites the attributes of goodness, sovereignty and reason through the symbol of the Cherubim and the flaming turning sword. Only through a *unio mystica* — a mystical merging of inner and outer voices — is there, for Philo, a possibility of discovering truth in Scripture.

"The meaning of this cryptic one-line poem is not entirely transparent…"

15 Philo, *De Vita Contemplativa*, ed. J. Henderson, Loeb Classic Library, Harvard University Press, Cambridge 2001, XI: 83-98, pp. 164-169.

16 Philo, *IX: De Vita Contemplativa*, XI: 98, p. 169.

17 Philo, *IX: De Cherubim*, IX: 27-30, pp. 24-27.

1.33 RABBINIC DELIMITATION

Through the Rabbinic period there appears to be a shift away from the possibility of a wholly ecstatic experience in body and soul as alluded to in its precursor of the Hebrew Bible, especially in the Psalms. The shift in the Rabbinic period rather is towards a deeper focus on ethically delimiting the practice of this experience as evinced in expressions like *lehitdabek b'midotav.*[18] This imitation of the divine or *imitatio dei* becomes an acceptable avenue through which it is still possible to draw closer to the divine through the social encounter between humans rather than being consumed in merging with the divine. Fueled in part by an anti-Christian polemic, the Rabbis are concerned with clarifying the divide between human and divine concerns experience. Imitating divine attributes in one's behavior is more palatable than merging with the source of these attributes, lest a blurring of the boundaries between divine and human take place in this mystical merging.[19]

1.34 ECSTATIC KABBALAH & SUFISM

A fascinating intracultural exchange between Jewish mystical pietism and Islamic Sufism really began in earnest with the pioneering work of Bahya ibn Paquda. The scholarly trends in reading this Sufi treatise, *Duties of the Heart* (ca. 1080) is replete with embarrassment. Regarding Bahya's *devekuth,* it was Vadja who first commented on how Bahya stops just short of complete union, as Lobel recently points out, by "maintaining a respectful distance rather than an intimation of real union."[20] Although Vadja's reading of *Duties* stresses the ultimate distance that remains, the *raison d'être* of Bahya's path to loving God

18 For example, bSotah 14a, 42b; bGittin 56b, 60 a; bKetubot 111b; Genesis Rabbah s.59, etc. Michael Sokoloff, s.v. *DVK, A Dictionary of Jewish Palestinian Aramaic,* Bar Ilan University Press, Israel 1990, pp. 138a-138b. Ibid, s.v. *DVK, A Dictionary of Jewish Babylonian Aramaic,* pp. 312b-313a.

19 Ephraim E. Urbach, *The Sages: Their Concepts and Beliefs,* Second edition, 2 volumes, Magnes Press, Hebrew University, Jerusalem Hebrew edition, 1986, pp. 413, 426 [Henceforth, Urbach, *The Sages*].

20 George Vajda, *La Théologie ascétique,* Impremerie Nationale, Paris 1947, pp. 131-137. Diana Lobel, *A Sufi-Jewish Dialogue: Philosophy and Mysticism in Bahya Ibn Paquda's Duties of the Heart,* University of Pennsylvannia Press, Philadelphia 2007, p. 239.

remains "so as to attach to his supernal light" [*kedi she'tidabek b'oro ha'elyon*]. Whether connecting to the emanation of light is not quite synonymous with the source itself as Vajda and Fenton attempt to argue, this compelling vision of the unitive ecstatic experience cannot be denied.

Yet the remarkably rigorous recent scholarship of Lobel comes closest to re-embracing the possibility of complete *unio mystica*. She points out the embarrassment from the side of Jewish scholarship, especially evident in Blumenthal's sharp distinction between "intellectualist mysticism" [*ittisal*] and "nonintellectual identification" [*ittihad*].[21] Using this sharp distinction, fueled by an agenda of embarrassment, Sufi mysticism is then classified as nonintellectual as compared Jewish mysticism. Lobel passionately dispels this embarrassment when she writes:

> Thus we cannot differentiate sharply between intellectualist mysticism and Sufi mysticism on the basis of their *telos*: both describe a union with God that transcends reason. What differentiates the two is the way they describe God and how this colors their understanding of the path to the divine.[22]

Once the false dichotomy between intellectual mysticism and philosophical mysticism is dispelled, Lobel is able to explore the true nature of Bahya's mystical quietism even further. She portrays this mystical inclination as beginning with an "overwhelming sense of fear, shame and awe before the divine presence" that gradually "...gives way to love companionship, and a kind of intersubjectivity, if not union."[23]

1.35 MEDIEVAL PERSPECTIVES: MAIMONIDES

It is in the Medieval period that both *Devekuth* and by analogy *Hitdavekuth,* come to preoccupy philosophers, thinkers and poets. *Devekuth* denotes an interlacing and connecting that is either spiritual or ethical.[24] For philosophers,

21 Lobel, *A Sufi-Jewish Dialogue*, p. 22.

22 Lobel, *A Sufi-Jewish Dialogue*, p. 23.

23 Lobel, *A Sufi-Jewish Dialogue*, p. 232.

24 Jacob Klatzkin, s.v. *Devekuth, Thesauraus Philosophicus Lingua Hebraica et Veteris et Recentioris*, Vol. 1, Eschkol, Berlin 1928.

this interlacing occurs primarily in the realm of the individual and one's quest to unite with the Active Intellect. While this expression of *Devekuth* occurs a few times in the philosophical opus of Maimonides, *Guide for the Perplexed* II:29, it is extended by analogy to *Hitdavekuth* in the *Guide* II: 45.[25] Most important is the usage of *Hitdavekuth* to describe the prophet who does not remain constantly connected in this state with the source of prophecy yet manages to prophesy nonetheless. This resurfaces by implication only near the close of the *Guide* III: 53. It is only possible for the philosopher-king to remain in the ideal state of elevated consciousness by intense focus on the attributes of Compassion [*Hesed*], Law [*Mishpat*] and Justice [*Tzedek*]. Through this process the individual then undergoes self transformation [*le'hashleem nafeshekha*] into a Pious One [*Hasid*], a Judge [*Shofet*], and a Righteous One [*Tzadiq*]. That process would seem to be a kind of *imitatio dei* that reiterates a reliance upon reading this experience as *hitdavekuth b'midotav* or cleaving to those attributes.

1.36 THE MAIMONIDEAN TURN: READING ECSTATIC UNION IN *THE GUIDE*

Each generation after Moses ibn Maimon seems to plunge further into the mystical possibilities intrinsic to what is unsaid in the *Guide*. Abraham ibn Maimon, according to Paul Fenton's reconstruction,[26] comes nearest to approaching the possibility of *ittiṣal* as union but stops short. Seeing their work as the next level of expansion upon the *Guide*, Obadyah (b. 1228) and David (b. 1335) ibn Maimon, begin the process of nuanced misreading within the realm of *Hitdavekuth*. Obadyah ibn Maimon's *Al-Maqala al-Ḫawḏiyya* or *Treatise of the Pool* distinguishes a number of experiential inner modes within the variety of experiences that could encompass *Hitdavekuth*. What is of interest to our exploration in *The Treatise of the Pool* is *ittiṣal* as union.[27] David ibn Maimon's

25 See the super-commentary on the *Guide's* usage of *Hitdavekuth* by Gersonides, *Wars of the Lord*, V: 24.

26 Paul Fenton, "En marge du *Kitâb Kifâyat al-Abidîn/La provision suffisante des serviteurs* de rabbi Abraham ben Moïse Maïmonide," *Revue des Etudes Juives* 150, 3-4 (1991), pp. 385-405.

27 Obadyah ibn Abraham ibn Moses Maimon, *Treatise of the Pool*: *Al-Maqala al-Ḫawḏiyya*, tr. Paul Fenton, Octagon Press, London 1981, p. 112, (25b). [Henceforth, Maimon, *Treatise of the*

al-Murṣid ila t-tafarrud wal-murfid ila t-tagarrud or *The Guide and Director of Detachment*, by contrast, speaks of true love as *taṣabbuh* or complete assimilation in God.[28] These dramatic shifts into the diverse experiences of ecstatic union within the divine may reach a pinnacle of sorts within these two treatises that have been all but forgotten from the study of Jewish mysticism.

1.37 FROM ECSTATIC KABBALAH TO LURIANIC KABBALAH

Between the thirteenth and the sixteenth century an interesting development takes place. There is a significant reworking of *devekuth* in ecstatic Kabbalah within parts of Spain and especially in Italy. Through a preparatory cycle, the balanced aspirant is able to concentrate upon the ten *Sefirot* or attributes intrinsic to human consciousness. It is only by means of concentrating upon this central connection, as Idel notes, that one is able to "collect or to capture the emanation flowing from the supernal *Sefirot*."[29] This direct contact, however, is not with the *Sefirot* but only by means of their emmantion.

Hitdavekuth is also seen as part of a larger discipline that cultivates a path unto itself. In Hayyim Vital's *Sha'arei Kedushah* there is an outline presented of this midway point along the path to *hitdavekuth*. It is worthwhile to consider this mapping of *hitdavekuth* so as to contextualize the practice:

התדבקות	[*hitdavekuth*]	Merging
השתוות	[*hishtavuth*]	Equanimity
התבודדות	[*hitboddeduth*]	Seclusion
רוח הקדש	[*ruah haqodesh*]	Holy Spirit
נבואה	[*nevuah*]	Prophecy[30]

Pool]. Consideration and comparison is also worthy of "bond" [*wuṣla*] (25b) and "ceaseless contemplation" [*muraqaba*] as (26a), see Maimon, *Treatise of the Pool*, pp. 112-114.

28 David ibn Abraham ibn Moses Maimon, "L'amour véritable," Ch. XXIV, *Le Guide du Détachement*, tr. Paul Fenton, *Deux Traités de Mystique Juive*, Éditions Verdier, Paris 1987, p. 288.

29 Moshe Idel, *Hasidism: Between Hasidism and Magic*, SUNY Press, New York 1995, p. 231. Idem, "*Hitbodedut* as Concentration in Ecstatic Kabbalah," *Studies in Ecstatic Kabbalah*, SUNY Press, New York 1988, pp. 103-170.

30 Hayyim Vital, Sha'arei Kedushah, 2: 5, vol. 4, Ahavat Shalom, Jerusalem, 5768, p. 9.

Already upon first reading it is unclear whether this is a linear or circular process. But gleaning from anecdotes that surround this list, it seems as though there is, in part, an initiatory cycle taking place. Unity is seen as a prerequisite to entering into a state of equanimity. Only then can true seclusion take place. What is of great practical import here is the primary role of merging into unity consciousness so as to facilitate the revelation of the holy spirit, setting the stage for the renewal of prophecy.

1.38 ON THE HASIDIC VARIETIES OF *DEVEKUT* AS TOUCHING THE DIVINE

The possibility of touching the divine through *devekut* in Hasidism is not a matter for speculation or embarrassment but a reality for the adept. Three models of *devekut* have been recently reiterated succinctly by the *Yam ha-Hokhmah.*[31] These models are drawn from a small sample of seekers surrounding the founder of Hasidism, the *Ba'al Shem Tov*, simply known as the BeSH"T. These three models should suffice our present needs in establishing degrees of practice of *devekut* in the face of all its ensuing embarrassment:

(1). **Filling all worlds [*Memale kol 'almin*]:** When the BeSH"T (1698-1760) went into his renowned *'aliyat-haneshama* or soul-ascension, his level of *devekut* was said to be beyond that of the prophets. In this state, the BeSH"T was completely free from all corporeality, like someone fainting, whose faculties of perception have been utterly numbed. All bodily perceptions were no longer perceptible in this state for the BeSH"T. Even so, he was still able to answer those posing him questions while in this state. The BeSH"T prayed before ascending to truly fill the upper and lower worlds in all their fullness that he remain connected to the lower world.

(2). **Encircling all worlds [*Sovev kol 'almin*]:** The *Alter Rebbe* or R. Schneur Zalman of Liadi (1745-1812) was said to enter into a deep state of *devekut*

31 See *"Ma'amar Kedusha Meshuleshet," Sefer Yam haHokhmah, Machon Yam haHokhmah,* Jerusalem 2008, pp. 551-640, esp. pp. 608-612. While beyond the scope of this investigation, the insights of the *Yam haHokhmah* are being explored in greater depth and wider correlations to Hebrew poetry in a monograph, entitled, *Touching God [forthcoming]*

by interiorizing the experience. No exterior signs of movement or sounds were present. This state of *devekut* was in the condition of *penimiyut ha'lev* or the inner depth of the heart. But when he heard someone crying, the *Alter Rebbe* was able to come out of his state to respond to the lower world concerns before him.

(3). **Enrapturing Ascent Into the Essence of Without End from Itself [*'Atzmut ain sof b'etzem mitzad atzmo*]:** The *Mittler Rebbe* or R. DovBer of Lubavitch (1773-1827) was said to enter into a state of *devekut* so deep that his attendants could transport him from one place to the next without him so much as flinching. This state of *devekut* was in the condition of *penimiyut ha'moah* or the inner depth of the mind. So when he heard someone crying, he was unable to come out of this state.

The deepest level of embarrassment, especially for *Mitnagdim*,[32] surrounding any experience of *devekut,* comes with the audacious claim of the *Mittler Rebbe* where union is possible with the very essence of the infinite from within its own self. While hagiographic claims to this degree of utter union dance onto the precipice of heresy in normative rabbinic circles, the Hasidic perspective remains unphased. For the seeker and the adept, the purpose of Judaism is to know the Limitless in every aspect of one's life, without restrictions.

1.39 THE AFTER-LIFE OF EMBARRASSMENT ON *HITDAVEKUT*: SCHOLARSHIP SINCE SCHOLEM

Yet most of this history of *Hitdavekuth* rather than its experience was transmitted through the eyes of scholarship, due in no small part to the afterlife of pioneering contributions by Gershom Scholem. Seeing that it is with Scholem that the academic study of Jewish mysticism begins in earnest as a dedicated

32 Such embarrassment of the *Mitnagdim* stemmed from their highly pessimistic view of the human's spiritual capacities. The etiology of this view was mainly as a "result of the enduring exile and ensuing decline of the generations, the unalterable condition of the contemporary Jew was one of severe religious and cognitive limitations. Given his circumscribed capacities for theosophical insight, it was not only pretentious but also harmful for man to try to exceed his natural, limited condition," Allan Nadler, *The Faith of the Mithnagdim: Rabbinic Responses to Hasidic Rapture*, The Johns Hopkins University Press, Baltimore 1997, pp. 47-48.

discipline, we might become aware of the framework within which *Hitdavekut* has been presented to the scholarly world and moreover why it has remained a *verboten* expression of the spiritual life ever since. It is significant then to consider the impact that the academic retransmission of these traditions has had upon contemporary expressions of Jewish mysticism, especially in Hebrew culture.

In his landmark essay on delimiting the case of *unio mystica* in Jewish Mysticism, "*Devekut* or Communion with God," as our opening reflections evinced, Scholem sees this mystical experience in its evolutionary framework. In commenting on the experience of *unio mystica* in the writings of Azkiri and Luria, Scholem attempts to historically trace the development of *devekut* only to be crystallized in its final stage through a messianically sublimated form of hasidic thought.[33] Yet as Idel has remarked, after *Major Trends*, Scholem's interest in ecstatic Kabbalah radically diminished.[34] In its stead, Scholem proffered a theory of theosophic myth and symbolism as the broad picture of Kabbalah which discounts the evolution of the ecstatic and the messianic as distinct moments within Jewish mystical experiences.[35] Given comments Scholem has offered elsewhere on the possibility of Jewish mysticism in our time, it seems that his historical analysis is filled with skepticism and perhaps explains his neglect and disdain for the ecstatic strain within Kabbalah. This skepticism allows for hasidic thought to have crystallized a sublimated messianic shard within a popularized *devekuth* that has served to propel what was once a folk religion into a mass religious movement. Though Scholem also speculates on how contemporary poets embody the intuitive kabbalah of tomorrow, he never goes so far as to search for traces of mystical experience within contemporary Hebrew poetry. Scholem's contribution sets the scholarly stage for an historical engagement with the experience of *unio mystica* that severely limits the

33 Gershom Scholem, "*Devekut*, or Communion with God," *The Messianic Idea in Judaism*, Shocken Publications, New York 1971, pp. 203-227

34 Moshe Idel, "The Contribution of Abraham Abulafia's Kabbalah to the Understanding of Jewish Mysticism," in *Gershom Scholem's Major Trends in Jewish Mysticism 50 Years After: Proceedings of the Sixth International Conference on the History of Jewish Mysticism*, ed. P. Schäfer, J. Dan, J. C. B. Mohr (Paul Siebeck), Tübingen 1987,p. 120. [Henceforth, Idel, *Abulafia's Kabbalah to the Understanding of Jewish Mysticism*]

35 Idel, *Abulafia's Kabbalah to the Understanding of Jewish Mysticism*, p. 123.

possibility of its occurrence, if at all, suggesting it no longer is a realistic or authentic quest in the devolution of contemporary Jewish mysticism.

Despite Scholem's shortcomings, one of his disciples, Joseph Weiss nuances the limits of experience intrinsic to *unio mystica* in his research on the Kalisker.[36] A proponent of the Tiberean school of hasidism, R. Abraham Kalisker (d. 1810) outlines the steps towards *devekuth* after the Magid of Mezeritzch. The first step in attaining *ayin* is not ecstatic but social humility and so it seems to evades all ecstatic implications.[37] The principal Weiss introduces in reading *devekuth* this way is one of reciprocal humility that is conducive to peace in human relationships. *Devekuth* is then seen as one's emotional relationship with God, not active but passive, and commensurate with one's *devekuth* is the exercise of providence towards that person. This correlation of *devekuth* and *hashgahah* is quite unique.[38] When in *katnut* or constricted consciousness, *devekuth* with a neighbour is ideal. *Devekuth* with one's fellow leads back to the same security as *devekuth* with God.[39] This type of transpersonal *unio mystica* known as *dibbuk haverim,* seems as if, for all practical purposes, *devekuth* with one's fellow has replaced *devekuth* with God.[40] The emotional integration within a small but concrete group (*dibbuk haverim*) is longed for rather than within the vague, sociologically abstract entity of Israel (*klal yisrael*). This *devekuth* of *dibbuk haverim* provides its members with a profound sense of belonging that may have otherwise escaped the lone seeker of *unio mystica.*[41]

In an attempt to be much more extensive in scope than his precursors, Pachter articulates and analyzes the elements of *devekuth* as they emerge from the sixteenth century written records of Safed mystics.[42] To undertake

---

36 Joseph Weiss, "R. Abraham Kalisker's Concept of Communion with God and Men," in *Studies in Eastern European Jewish Mysticism*, ed. David Goldstein, The Littman Library of Jewish Civilization, New York 1986 , pp. 155-169. [Henceforth, Weiss, *Kalisker's Concept of Communion*].

37 Weiss, *Kalisker's Concept of Communion,* pp.156-7.

38 Ibid, *Kalisker's Concept of Communion,* p. 158.

39 Ibid, *Kalisker's Concept of Communion,* p. 160.

40 Ibid, *Kalisker's Concept of Communion,* p. 164.

41 Ibid, *Kalisker's Concept of Communion,* p. 167.

42 Mordechai Pachter, "The Concept of *Devekut* in the Homiletical Ethical Writings of 16th Century Safed," in Studies in Medieval Jewish History and Literature, Vol. II, ed. Isadore Twersky,

this analysis, Pachter turns to the writings of Alkabez, Gallico and Alshech to expose how *devekuth* is one's attachment to Torah in opposition to human knowledge.[43] Its continuity from Medieval thought is that through this intellectual activity (of conjunction with the active intellect) one may attain immortality.[44] Much of what unites the experience of these mystics is the shared intention that the ultimate purpose of human reason is a reunion with its origin.[45] What Pachter adds to the conversation after Scholem about *devekuth* is the importance of the *a priori* factor of identity. The shared assumption of many Safedian mystics was that the basic identity of the soul is bound up with Torah and with God. With this assumption of self-knowledge of the soul, there is the possibility of a reciprocal influence that can then take place in a state of *unio mystica* between the soul and Torah.[46]

With the more recent reappraisal of hasidism in general, and its spiritual practices in particular, the contributions of Wolfson and Pierkaz further nuance our understanding of *devekuth* in mystical literature. In Wolfson's analysis of *devekuth*,[47] a two-tierd system of *devekuth* is proposed. Cleaving to God in hasidic sources is either: (a) a vertical one, which entails the metaphor of ascent and descent, and/or (b) a horizontal one, which entails the metaphor of traversing from place to place. Wolfson argues that the vertical and hortizontal metaphors operate simultaneously in the realm of experience. In Pierkaz's analysis of *devekuth*,[48] he is careful to admit that this concept is actually never

---

Harvard University Press, Cambridge 1984, pp. 171-230. See also ibid, "*Devequt* in Sixteenth Century Safed," *Roots of Faith and Devequt: Studies in the History of Kabbalistic Ideas*, Sources and Studies in the Literature of Jewish Mysticism, vol. 10, Cherub Press, 2004, pp. 235-316 [Henceforth, Pachter, *Devekut* in Homiletical Ethical].

43 Pachter, *Devekut* in Homiletical Ethical, p. 172.

44 Ibid, *Devekut* in Homiletical Ethical, p. 173.

45 Ibid, *Devekut* in Homiletical Ethical, p. 175.

46 Ibid, *Devekut* in Homiletical Ethical, pp. 178-9.

47 Elliot R. Wolfson, "Walking as a Sacred Duty: Theological Transformation of Social Reality in Early Hasidism," in *Hasidism Reappraised*, ed. Ada Rapoport-Albert, Littman Library of Jewish Civilization, London 1997, pp. 180-207, esp. p. 182.

48 Mendel Pierkaz, "Hasidism as a Socio-religious Movement on the Evidence of *Devekut*," in *Hasidism Reappraised*, ed. Ada Rapoport-Albert, Littman Library of Jewish Civilization, London 1997, pp. 225-248 [Henceforth, Pierkaz, *Hasidism as a Socio-religious Movement*].

categorically defined in either hasidic literature or in earlier kabbalistic musar works. This ambiguity brings a richness of meanings in its wake: sometimes *devekuth* is identical with *kavanoth*; sometimes it is cleaving to God; sometimes it is a personal experience of God or attributes beyond normative religion; and sometimes it is simply another name for faith or piety. Further complicating matters is the yiddish *dreykes*, which means feeling, emotion, outpouring of soul, devotion, inner arousal, a bond.[49] The lack of need to locate and limit this signifier is in itself revealing. Despite such a plethora of meanings, these categories can encompass the following three phenomena: 1. *devekuth* which involves leading a solitary existence cut off from the life of community; 2. *devekuth* as a platform for social action; 3. *devekuth* which is reverential in character.[50]

Despite these important reappraisals, it is really in Idel's continuous revisioning[51] of the Scholemean dismissal of *devekuth* as a mystical ideal (including extreme forms of *unio mystica*)[52] that a phenomenology of unitive language in Jewish mysticism once again becomes possible. What Idel suggests in tracing *devekuth* from Lurianic Kabbalah through to Hasidism is not another etiological equation of historical reactionism. Rather he notes the remarkable retreat in Lurianic Kabbalah from the emphasis of *devekuth* in Zoharic Kabbalah,[53] especially in light of how much it becomes re-emphasized in Hasidism. The central preoccupation and practice of *devekuth* in Hasidism is one of choice rather than reaction to Lurianism or Sabbeteanism.[54]

Even within Lurianic Kabbalah, the diverse articulations of *devekuth* bespeak what Idel calls a "coexistence of different models that explain the nature and the locus of *devekuth*." It is crucial to note through this coexistence how the ecstatic model can posit the "transcendental realm as the place where the human and the

49 Pierkaz, *Hasidism as a Socio-religious Movement*, p. 229.

50 Ibid, *Hasidism as a Socio-religious Movement*, pp. 234-236.

51 Moshe Idel, *Absorbing Perfections: Kabbalah and Interpretation,* Yale University Press, New Haven 1988, pp. 193-194, 302-304.

52 Idel, *Kabbalah: New Perspectives*, Yale University Press, New Haven 1988, ch. 3-4.

53 Ibid, *Hasidism: Between Ecstasy and Magic,* SUNY Press, New York, 1995, p. 13 [Henceforth, Idel, *Hasidism: Between Ecstasy and Magic*].

54 Ibid, *Hasidism: Between Ecstasy and Magic,* p. 13.

divine meet, while the magical model proposes the mundane realm as the place that the divine will is attracted in order to meet the human."[55] This shifting economy of *devekuth* explains in part its afterlife that is so central to Hasidism.

By seriously reconsidering the ecstatic element within kabbalah and then in Hasidism, in a landmark comparative study on *unio mystica*, Idel has nuanced the distinction between universalization [*devekuth*] and integration [*hitkalleluth*]. Building upon the Maimonidean quandary of an ambiguous Active Intellect, Idel shows how Abulafia presents a theory of cleaving to this Intellect that is universalization [*devekuth*], whereby one becomes universal while remaining an individual.[56] This is then compared with integration [*hitkalleluth*] of some elements into a more comprehensive entity or that it comprises a plurality of components.[57] Universalization [*devekuth*] then is part of a larger process that may lead to integration [*hitkalleluth*], as already apparent in Geronese kabbalistic sources. This process leads to an adorning that points to the "penetration of the soul in the inner part of the light rather than adhering to its external facet."[58] Universalization of the soul is more anthropocentric as a process that transforms the soul while it "has no vital impact on the divine," whereas integration combines the individual experience along with the transformation of the divine.[59] It is this experience of self-inclusion of the mystic in the divine realm that requires a reorientation of *devekuth*, from the ecstatic element within Kabbalah and then onwards into early Hasidism. It is the highest aspect of the human form then that is already part of the divine such that revelation is an encounter with it.[60] Given that Hasidism remains the most contemporary instantiation of *devekuth* as the main ideal of spirituality, it serves as a crucial link to its most contemporary iteration in Hebrew poetry to be discussed shortly.

---

55 Ibid, *Hasidism: Between Ecstasy and Magic*, p. 88.

56 Ibid, "Universalization and Integration: Two Conceptions of Mystical Union in Jewish Mysticism," in *Mystical Union in Judaism, Christianity, and Islam:An Ecumenical Dialogue*, ed. M. Idel & B. McGinn, Continuum Press, New York 1989, p. 31 [Henceforth, Idel, *Universalization and Integration*].

57 Ibid, *Universalization and Integration*, p. 35.

58 Ibid, *Universalization and Integration*, p. 36.

59 Ibid, *Universalization and Integration*, pp. 51-52.

60 Ibid, *Universalization and Integration*, p. 36.

1.4 UNRAVELING OF A *HITDAVEKUTH* FOOTNOTE: SWINGING BETWEEN CRESCAS AND BERGSON

A footnote in the history of medieval philosophy, however, suggests a forgotten component of this entire brief history of *Hitdavekuth*. In revising a translation of H. A. Wolfson's on Crescas, W. Z. Harvey notes that *Hitdavekuth* is more accurately rendered as continuity, continuousness or continuum which yields *durée*.[61] In this seemingly obscure footnote to the history of Jewish philosophy, Harvey is actually creating a crucial bridge. His offering attempts to bridge the limns of medieval thought with modern thinking. It is in this regard that Harvey overcomes the general embarrassment medievalists have with the modern period by bringing Crescas into conversation with Bergson's *durée*.

Durée, or duration rather than being an objective mathematical unit for Bergson, is but the subjective perception of space-time. The conventions of scientific practice were incompatible with lived experience. In his 1889 "Essay on the Immediate Data of Consciousness," Bergson argued that experience viewed as a succession of separate, thing-like states is no less an abstraction from lived consciousness than time as measured by the hands of a clock. Both are fundamentally spatial. Lived consciousness, on the other hand, is a spatiotemporal continuum, a mutual penetration, a solidarity, an intimate organization of elements. Such elements are representative of others and neither is distinguished from nor isolated by abstracting thought. What Bergson's *durée* introduces into the phenomenology of time is a deeper awareness that begins from lived consciousness.

The conditions of such a lived consciousness have radically changed since Bergson. So it is in the margins of this correlation, however, that W. Z. Harvey's thinking positions some of the unexpected problems facing twenty-first century Jewish philosophy.[62] With the challenges of a post-*Shoah* thinking di-

61 Warren Zev Harvey, "The term "*hitdabbekut*" in Crescas' definition of time," *Jewish Quarterly Review* 71: 1 (1980), pp. 46-47.

62 Warren Zev Harvey, "New and unexpected problems facing 21st-century Jewish philosophy," *Studia Judaica* 11-12 (2004), p. 187:
"Indeed 21st-Century Jewish Philosophy is faced with new and unexpected problems: (1) It has to rethink the meaning of the Diaspora for Jewish civilization, and find ways to strengthen it. (2) It has to reformulate an economic and political philosophy that will point

minishing Diaspora, an Israel not yet egalitarian, and the need to relearn our relation to time and otherness through language, this causes language itself to become radically altered.

This seismic shift for twenty-first century Jewish thinking described by Harvey finds a new window from this very reading of Crescaen *Hitdavekuth* as Bergsonian *durée*. That gesture of re-embracing a lost medieval moment in the contemporary quagmire of thinking is then able to open further into the contemporary embarrassment encountered in the writings of Emmanuel Lévinas. In establishing early on an ethics as first philosophy through the intrinsic relation between time and the other,[63] Lévinas fleshes out the very lived consciousness implied by *durée*. Even though Lévinasian thinking still shudders from the embarrassment rendered by deBeauvoir's earliest critique of the feminine as mystery and other,[64] attempts have been made recently at rebuilding and re-embracing that missing reciprocity of the feminine by way of his phenomenology of maternity.[65] By re-embracing the embarrassment sur-

---

the way to a just and egalitarian society in the State of Israel, and to help turn the State of Israel in to a land flowing with milk and honey, where Jews from all over the world want to live — and to make it a light unto the nations, *or la-goyim*. (3) And it has to learn Arabic, or rather re-learn it.

Most intriguing of these problems is the linguistic site of thinking. Harvey also sees that Hebrew in turn will be enriched by its contact with Arabic. This has implications for the Hebrew poetry of Shvili and others we are currently exploring, especially being written in Jerusalem."

63 Emmanuel Lévinas, *Temps et L'Autre*, PUF, Paris 1948.

64 Simone de Beauvoir, *Le deuxième sexe*, vol. 1, Gallimard, Paris (1949), 1976, pp. 15-16, ff.1: "Je suppose que M. Lévinas n'oublie pas que la femme est aussi pour soi conscience. Mais il est frappant qu'il adopte délibérément un point de vue d'homme sans signaler la réciprocité du sujet et de l'objet. Quand il écrit que la femme est mystère, il sous-entend qu'elle est mystère pour l'homme. Si bien que cette description qui se veut objectvie est en fait une affirmation du privilège masculin."

The counter-critique against gender neutralization notwithstanding, de Beauvoir's critique remains visionary in its initial embarrassment. For the 1973 counter-critique of Freddy Raphaël, see Mopsik, pp. 6-7, ff. 6:

"Identity of roles is not the real way of achieving this equality. [...] The objective is to denounce [...] the policy of gender neutralization supported by Simone de Beauvoir and which translates a powerlessness to accept difference [...]. Preserving the masculine/feminine difference is a way of combating the growing blandness not in sensation but in meaning of the couple".

65 Hanoch Ben Pazi, "Rebuilding the Feminine in Lévinas' Talmudic Readings," Journal of Jewish Thought and Philosophy, Volume 12, Number 3, 2003, pp. 1-32.

rounding the Lévinasian reading of eros and the feminine, Ben Pazi and Cohen[66] have attempted to reposition the role of eros within ethics. What remains a *desideratum*, however, is a queering extrapolation of Lévinasian ethics into the realm of homo-eroticism. It is this concern with ethics that contributes to the ensuing analysis of time in erotic relation between godlovers.

1.5 UNSAID *HITDAVEKUTH:* THE EVOLUTION OF READING HOMOSEXUALITY

The tension between truly loving another soul of the same sex and its apparent prohibition in the exoteric reading of Scripture confounds many readers and lovers. Still one does not even have to venture into the orchards of the esoteric to experience the eros between lovers in the *Song of Songs,* between Jonathan and David, between oneself and a companion, to realize that such eros permeates existence. Yet with a narrative as strong as the homo-erotic covenant between Jonathan and David barely used by mystics in their exegesis, the power of such *unio mystica* remains marginalized. While mystics through the ages have been nourished by the homo-eroticism implicit in their exploration of exoteric text for its esoteric root, it is poetry that allows for unbound expression of this homo-eroticism as experience. The highly eroticized metaphysical system of Kabbalists lent itself to supererogatory and hypernomian behavior on the inside while carrying a minimally traditional, if not entirely nomian life on the outside.[67]

Theorists and thinkers exploring gender tend to fall into one of two camps, either essentialist or constructivist. The essentialist sees sexuality as an intrinsic reflection of gender that can be anchored relative to the essence of one's being. Thus essentialists will argue for homosexuality as being a malady that

66 Richard A. Cohen, *Elevations: The Height of the Good in Lévinas and Rosenzweig*, University of Chicago Press, Chicago 1994, pp. 195-223, esp. the ninth chapter, "The Metaphysics of Gender."

67 Shaul Magid, "The Sin of Being/Becoming a Woman: Male Homosexuality and the Castration Complex: Leviticus 18:22 and 20:13, *From Metaphysics to Midrash: Myth, History and the Interpretation of Scripture in Lurianic Kabbalah,*" Indiana University Press (*forthcoming*), Bloomington 2008, pp. 111-143. Henceforth, Magid, *From Metaphysics to Midrash*. I thank Magid for sharing numerous versions of this article before publication.

can be cured, claiming that one's essential nature as a male for instance is to be heterosexual. The constructivist sees gender as a fluid construct that is played out in various cultural scenarios. Thus constructivists will argue for homosexuality as an expression of movement where no signifier is fixed, or that after Lacan, that the phallus is always shifting in its site of making meaning. Immobility or motion typify these approaches, but neither really reflect a third reality — the mystical experience. Despite the veil esotericism pierces, the desire does not subside — it only intensifies.

It is from this history of deep embarrassment regarding the evolution of sexuality and gender, — especially after Foucault's Greco-eclipse of Judaism's *ars erotica*[68] — that Fox's research re-embraces a new way of seeing homosexuality from a Hebrew perspective. To say that Fox's approach in his *Chapter on the Evolution of Sexuality in Judaism* or *Perek be'toldot ha'min be'yisreal*[69] is merely *halakhic* misses the point. Although a student of Urbach, the great systematizer of *The Sages,*[70] Fox's *Hitdavekuth* allows him to remain unafraid of the truth that lies beyond the systematization of exoteric versus esoteric textuality. Despite his deep reverence for the Talmudic know-how of his teacher, Fox has remained committed to this search for truth, even when it estranged him from the Hegelian systematization of Urbach. Part of that estrangement was a function of a divide that Fox dared to cross-over. That divide compartmentalized critical study from the lived life of ritual in which such thinking is instantiated.[71] For too long, the divide between *halakhah* and *aggadah* has breeded a coercive insularity and a de-poeticization of Jewish life.

As one delves deeper into Fox's *Perek* it becomes clear that this is not merely a *Wissenschaftlich historico-halakhic* investigation along the lines of Urbach's *The Sages.* While Fox does not claim this to be a missing chapter, it remains a curiousity that such a definitive work like Urbach's *The Sages* only marginally

68 Michel Foucault, *Histoire de la Sexualité* (1976), 3 tomes, Gallimard, Paris 1994; *idem, The History of Sexuality*, 3 vols, Vintage Books, New York 1990.

69 Harry Fox, *Perek be'toldot ha'min b'yisreal: Mishkav zakhur* (manuscript: 2005) [Henceforth, Fox, *Perek*].

70 Urbach, *The Sages.*

71 Urbach would not cross the line between scholarship and ritual life, evinced by his painful refusal to be a part of Fox's pioneering traditional-egalitarian wedding at Hebrew University, Jerusalem in the 1970's.

addresses the rabbinic attitudes towards sexuality and gender. In the course of the chapter on "the Human Being," Urbach briefly explores[72] the Amoraic *mis*reading of scriptural descriptions of human creation. Urbach focuses on the influence of Greek and Iranian mythology upon the Sages' etiology of the human condition. In drawing comparisons with other local myths of androgyny, Urbach sees the Amoraic project as one of demythologization.[73] But beyond demythologization there is nothing terribly constructive about this Amoraic project. Urbach does nuance his exploration near the chapter's close by reiterating just how far the Sages' etiology of the human condition seeks a separation between God and human. Contemporaneous to this Jewish demythologization, Gnosticism envisions human wholeness contingent upon the knowledge of the transcendence of Primeval Adam — "a treasure trove within which are contained the gods, the worlds and the times."[74] Through this important cross-cultural comparison, Urbach paints the classicly stoic picture of the Sages, one wherein this etiology of "Adam distinguishes between God and the created world, and through this distinction realizes divine sovereignity and providence."[75] As laudable as Urbach's project of systematizing the variegated Amoraic *aggadot* may be, it reveals a deep embarrassment over any possibility of alignment between Creator and creation,[76] over any modicum of *unio mystica* which was part of the spiritual path of the Sages' religion.

Fox, by contrast, is unafraid of such embarrassment and doubts the possibility of such systematization. In the wake of Bialik, Fox continues following the poet's clarion call that sometimes "a single detail of *Halakhah* fleshes out on us a whole world of *Aggadah* which lies hidden in it."[77] So Fox plummets the depths of *halakhah*'s four cubits to reveal and re-embrace a deeper poetic

72 Urbach, *The Sages*, pp. 200-204 are dedicated to this exploration within the larger chapter, pp. 190-226.

73 Urbach, *The Sages*, p. 201.

74 Urbach, *The Sages*, p. 223.

75 Urbach, *The Sages*, p. 226.

76 Urbach, *The Sages*, pp. 223-224.

77 Hayyim Nahman Bialik, "*Halakhah* and *Aggadah* (1916)," in *Revealment and Concealment*, Ibis Editions, Jerusalem 2000, p. 56. See Fox, *Perek*, p. 4, where he refers to Bialik's essay, "*Revealment and Concealment*".

moment. Fox reveals how a history of reading delimits תועבה [*toeivah*] from its beginnings as something disgusting to transform into the paradigmatic abomination. From the Essene's Dead Sea document called, *The Damascus Covenant*[78] to R. Feinstein's halakhic epistles known as *Iggeret Moshe*,[79] Fox is laying bare — in true Bialikian style — a process that moves תועבה from being delimited to categorical abstraction, while revealing how the poetic resonances of משכב זכור are then lost through generations of embarrassment.

Fox cannot remain silent to Bialik's burning rhetorical question, "Shall we return,then, to the *Shulhan Aruch*?" for the poet is already calling for a return "to their inner reality of meaning [that] is capable of extension and enlargement to cover the whole range of related phenomena, whether earlier or later than the Talmud."[80] Clearly the Hegelian humanism of Urbach did not allow for the "extension and enlargement" of inner meaning to reach the outer contemporary world. Nearly Nietzschean in his passion, Fox's by-path remains Bialikian, committed to the search for how ineffable truths become manifest in a life lived poetically. It is in the life poetically lived that one discovers the intimate correlation between *halakhah* and *aggadah,* as Bialik reflects:

> Let there be given us moulds in which we can mint our fluid and unformed [desire] into solid coin that will endure. We long for something concrete.
> Let us learn to demand more action than speech in the business of life, more *Halakhah* than *Aggadah* in the field of literature.
> We bend our backs. Where is the iron yoke? Why comes not the strong hand and the outstretched arm?[81]

In his re-embrace of homosexuality, Fox shows how within the narrow four cubits of *halakhah* there remains an interdependence between *halakhah* and *aggadah*.[82] Moreover there is a deeper calling out between the lines of this rigorous research, namely to uncover the pathmarks of a lived life of think-

78 Fox, *Perek*, pp. 20-22.

79 Fox, *Perek*, pp. 4-5.

80 Bialik, "*Halakhah* and *Aggadah* (1916)," p. 81.

81 Ibid, "*Halakhah* and *Aggadah* (1916)," p. 87.

82 Ibid, "*Halakhah* and *Aggadah* (1916)," p. 71.

ing, as Bialik proclaimed: "To each age its own *Aggadah*; to each *Aggadah* its own *Halakhah*."[83] Although Fox's *Perek* seems to only be focused on liberating the insular reading of *Halakah* by re-embracing its identity in *Aggadah*, echoing Bialik:

> We are speaking not of this or that particular *halakah* or *aggadah*. Our concern is with *Halakhah* in general — with *Halakhah* as a concrete and definite form of actual life, of a life which is not in the clouds, which does not depend on vague feeling and beautiful phrases alone, but has physical reality and physical beauty. *Halakhah* in that sense, I assert, is but the inevitable continuation and sequel of *Aggadah*.[84]

By re-embracing Bialik's poetic path, notwithstanding the embarrassment of Urbach, Fox is boldly revealing a critical shift. This shift peels open the possibility of re-embracing the factors behind תועבה as a delimitated phenomenological moment rather than a categorical abstraction of evil. Poetic resonances of משכב זכור otherwise lost are also revealed as they point towards the present re-embracement of התדבקות . And so Fox's *Perek* is pivotal in pointing a generation towards the unrealized renaissance of Hebrew culture.

1.6 *HITDAVEKUTH:* THE UNFOLDING OF HOMO-EROTICISM WITHIN HOMOSEXUALITY

While one of the first attempts at addressing the role of eros in Kabbalah was proffered by Yehudah Liebes in his "Zohar and Eros,"[85] it is in the later rejoinders to its revisionism by Wolfson that embarrassment begins truly setting in. This embarrassment comes from the lucid unfolding of homosexuality by way of homo-eroticism, most brilliantly articulated in the prolific and highly misunderstood work of Elliot R. Wolfson spanning over a decade.[86] With

83 Ibid, "*Halakhah* and *Aggadah* (1916)," p. 81.

84 Ibid, "*Halakhah* and *Aggadah* (1916)," p. 81.

85 Yehudah Liebes, "Zohar and Eros," *Alpayyim* 9 (1994), pp. 67-115.

86 Elliot R. Wolfson, *Circle in the Square: Studies in The Use of Gender in Kabbalistic Symbolism*, SUNY Press, New York 1995, esp. pp. 107-110, 112, 148 n., 196-197n., 221n., 223n., 226n., 227n.

Wolfson's recent contributions to the correlations of mysticism and homoeroticism, his revelatory scholarship needs to be re-embraced for opening the academic discourse in Jewish circles surrounding gender to reach new levels of nuance. What rejoinders to Liebes' *locus classicus* evince is a deep embarrassment over homosexuality and an overall inability to nuance any distinction between sex and gender. While Wolfson has gone to great lengths to nuance the discourse, much of the academic response to the phallocentrism of theosophic kabbalah has languished in embarrassment. The embarrassment stems from Wolfson's painstakingly nuanced reading that sought to show how "...homoerotic relations can be depicted theosophically in heteroxsexual terms,"[87] or more recently that "corresponding to the crossing of gender identities is a shift in the tenor of erotic experience from heterosexual to homoerotic..."[88] This embarrassment has, however, led to some re-embracement by other scholars after Wolfson.

Within the year following Wolfson's groundbreaking American studies published as *Circle in the Square*, a critical response came forth from Israel by Avraham Elqayyam in *Tarbiz*. This remarkable study, entitled, "To know the Messiah: The Dialectics of the Sexual Discourse in the Messianic Thought of Natan of Gaza,"[89] nuances a much misunderstood moment in the history of Jewish mysticism and re-embraces its embarrassment. Although Scholem already boldly attempted to re-embrace Sabbetai Tzevi through his monumental biography and publication of Sabbetean studies, Elqayyam seems better positioned to re-embrace the experiential element of the Sabbetean perspective. By explaining how Natan of Gaza's messianism rallied against Christian *Agape* and Neo-Platonic *Eros*, Elqayyam reveals a missing moment and nuance of *devekut*. "Redemption through sexuality becomes possible once it is conceived of as an eternal-sexual-spiritual touch between the Believer and

87 Elliot R. Wolfson, *Through a Speculum That Shines: Vision and Imagination in Medieva lJewish Mysticism*, Princeton University Press, New Jersey 1994, pp. 369-372, esp. p. 372.

88 Elliot R. Wolfson, *Language, Eros, Being: Kabbalistic Hermeneutics and Poetic Imagination*, Fordham University Press, New York 2005, esp. pp. 311-312, 322, 331-332, 337-338, 366- 368, 370 etc. [Henceforth, Wolfson, *Language, Eros, Being*].

89 Avraham Elqayyam, "To know the Messiah: The Dialectics of the Sexual Discourse in the Messianic Thought of Nathan of Gaza," *Tarbiz* 65 (1996) pp. 637-690, esp. 669-670. For the critique of Wolfson, see n.107, p. 665 [Henceforth, Elqayyam, *To know the Messiah*].

the incarnation of the Shekhina (Sabbetai Tzevi)."[90] The ultimate *coincidentia oppositorium* that occurs between Christian *Agape* and Neo-Platonic *Eros* or *Ahavat Hesed* and *Ahava Raba* lead to a new synthesis of redemption. What once was either disinterest or interest in one's love with God now reveals an urgent connection of a different order. The neglect has been not in connecting the godlover and god, rather it has been between the godlover and the messiah. By turning to the immanent manifestation of the *Shekhina* rather than hoping for a reach to the transcendent, a shift is taking place. By way of this very heretical *devekut* comes redemption.

Idel's recent attempt at continuing the exploration of this question is found in his study, *Kabbalah and Eros.*[91] Idel seeks to distinguish by Platonic categories the following three axiologies: *Agape, Eros,* and *Sex.*[92] While *Agape* is distinterested love devoid of libidnal urge and *Eros* is a complex of ontological constructs either corporeal or spiritual, *Sex* is not necessarily a consummation of the two former axiologies. Idel also sees a downplay by the Kabbalist in being influenced by the Aristophanean Symposium that has two missing halves of bodies provide an etiology of both *hetero*- and *homo*-erotic relations. By claiming "the halakhic propensity of many of the Kabbalists also prevented them from engaging in the full implications of Aristophane's discourse," Idel's axiological system falls short. Even if the influence of Aristophanes seems to be swerved, it is difficult to support this kind of generalization that *halakhah* eclipses the mystic from such speculation. Sources seem to support the exact opposite as being true — this likely is another case of surprising embarrassment on Idel's part to confronting such sources. In questioning Wolfson's reading of the multi-layered theosophical narratives uniformly as "the zoharic authorship," Idel is opening historically motivated models to consider.[93] In so doing, Idel offers a possible re-embrace of this embarrassment through five models of theoeroticism:

(1). Dyadic Structures (union of divine male and female);

90 Elqayyam, *To know the Messiah*, p. 669.

91 Moshe Idel, *Kabbalah and Eros*, Yale University Press, New Haven 2005, pp. 7, 64, 128, 233 [Henceforth, Idel, *Kabbalah and Eros*].

92 Idel, *Kabbalah and Eros*, p. 7.

93 Ibid, *Kabbalah and Eros*, pp. 128-129. See Abrams, *A Light of Her Own*, pp.11-12.

(2). First Triadic Model (one masculine power and two feminine powers on high);

(3) Second Triadic Model (two masculine powers and one feminine power on high);

(4) Model of Male with Oscillating Spouse (shiftng role of divine wife and concubine);

(5) Integrating Model (integration of female attribute within the male one).[94]

These models are meant to further nuance the discourse begun by Liebes and Wolfson, with Idel's re-embrace of the original embarrassment seen by the latter's contribution incorporated and accepted as the fifth model.

More recently, the re-embrace continues with a notable study by Abrams that attempts to evaluate recent contributions to Gender Studies and Kabbalah. Continuing down a feminist road travelled by Wolfson, Abrams chooses to apply the feminist insights of Judith Butler's "Lesbian phallus"[95] rather than Luce Irigaray's "Speculum"[96] to reading the feminine sphere of *Shekhina*. In his study, "A Light of Her Own — Minor Kabbalistic Traditions on the Ontology of the Divine Feminine,"[97] Abrams attempts to re-embrace the embarrassment over the theosophic myth as masculine. While Abrams maintains "a deeply rooted conviction to the importance of the history of ideas and the historical-philological inquiry into written texts," his recent focus explores the "meaning of isolated traditions for their psychological value and maps them on to the scale of their importance for key questions to discussions about gender."[98]

94 Ibid, *Kabbalah and Eros*, pp. 132-133.

95 Daniel Abrams, *The Female Body of God in Kabbalistic Literature: Embodied Forms of Love and Sexuality in the Divine Feminine*, Jerusalem 2004 [Hebrew].

96 Elliot R. Wolfson, *Through a Speculum that Shines: Vision and Imagination in Medieval Jewish Mysticism*, Princeton 1994.

97 Daniel Abrams, "A Light of Her Own — Minor Kabbalistic Traditions on the Ontology of the Divine Feminine," *Kabbalah: Journal for the Study of Jewish Mystical Texts* 15 (2006), pp. 7-29 [Henceforth, Abrams, *A Light of Her Own*].

98 Abrams, *A Light of Her Own*, p. 12.

Despite the patriarchal origins of its authorship, Abrams wants to avoid over-determining the meaning produced by these literary efforts:

> Kabbalistic male subjectivity seeks union and completion which only the feminine can provide and so looks with envy at what he lacks and what she offers and possesses. This is a critical point which forms the bedrock of my feminist reappraisal of the feminine in Kabbalah. The feminine is so envied for what she can provide, that the kabbalist fears the feminine, and envies what she has. This positive valence is flipped around so that the tension in the male mind of the kabbalist concerning the necessary and intermittent separation from her transforms this desire and envy into a demonization of the feminine. This might explain how the feminine is revered and loved in union and cast so negatively in separation. If we can see through this veil, I believe, that ultimately Kabbalistic texts are obsessed not with the masculinity of their authors, but with the feminine other, which becomes the focus of their spiritual, and presumably, emotional life.[99]

What Abrams' reappraisal does for the project of feminist readings in Kabbalah is to re-orient the yearning for union as positive rather than focusing on the lack as negative. This shift brings to the fore the underlying desire behind the theosophic text towards a state of re-union. This singular focus redresses the negative reading of the ontological and functional place of the feminine in union with the masculine.

Rather than beginning from a place of embarrassment of homo-eroticism, the French scholarship of the late Charles Mopsik seeks to re-embrace a "functional symbolic strategy" that might normalize forms of modern social behavior inculcated by traditionally inflexible religious institutions. In contrast to Wolfson's readings of homo-eroticism in confraternal settings as constituting the face of the *Shekhinah* — a deep embarrassment amongst critiques like Green and Liebes — Mopsik's writing calls for a constructive response of embrace. Although Wolfson's and Mopsik's contention that if gender is located not in the body but in the soul, then heterosexual and homosexual yearning is a legitimate

99 Abrams, *A Light of Her Own*, p. 29.

possibility for the kabbalists to embrace, it is unclear whether Mopsik intentionally ignores what Wolfson sees as the androcentric and misogynist bias of gender construction.[100] Wolfson and Mopsik proffer two different ways of dealing with this insight that legitimates the mystic's embrace of homoerotic yearning.

For Wolfson —

> ...the myth of the divine androgyne in kabbalistic sources...is yet another expression of socially dominant androcentricism. Salvation comes about through the containment of the feminine in the masculine, the neutralization of female power. Suffering the suffering of this axiom is a first step on the path to redeeming an ancient wisdom, tiredly waiting to be liberated from the confinement of its own textual embodiment.[101]

Even after over a decade of revealing this concealed truth, Wolfson's scholarship is hesitant to catalyze any more redemption of this ancient wisdom than necessary. If Wolfson's recent reflections on law and morality in kabbalistic mysticism are any indication, part of what makes change so longsuffering is the difference of ethical imperatives:

> As opposed to an ethical imperative that is based on affirmation of the individual moral will, the kabbalistic precept is ground in its radical negation. In confronting the effacement of God by facing that which cannot be faced, negation constitutes affirmation, and affirmation negation.[102]

Traversing along the Jewish mystical path necessitates a double suffering until a messianic liberation can free kabbalah of its socially dominant androcentricism.

For Mopsik —

100 Wolfson, *Language, Eros, Being*, p. 449, n. 137.

101 Ibid, *Language, Eros, Being*, p. 390.

102 Ibid, *Venturing Beyond: Law & Morality in Kabbalistic Mysticism*, Oxford University Press, New York 2005, p. 316.

> ...the writings which have come down to us from the mystics of Safed in the sixteenth century open up a certain theoretical possibility for the religious recognition of marriage between people of the same sex, multiparentality, co-parentality, and homoparentality. We simply need to extend the reasoning behind the Lurianic doctrine and enlarge the societal and legal aspects to integrate the physical consequences of the sexual mismatch between body and soul into new directions for thought.[103]

What is remarkable about Mopsik's posthumous writings is how courageously they set out to re-embrace the contemporary void of a "functional symbolic strategy," despite the aforementioned caveats. The scholarly re-embrace advocated by Mopsik must in his eyes combine in-depth historical analysis with contemporary sociology. The "functional symbolic strategy" he seeks to replenish comes by drawing "a direct lesson from these classic texts and apply them to modern reality."[104] So profound is Mopsik's direction in re-embracing the "functional symbolic strategy" nuances of homosexuality that any lingering embarrassment over heterosexual union is *de facto* alleviated. His re-embrace returns the whole quest of *unio mystica* — whether hetero- or homo-erotic — to "its pre-ontological proximity" towards original and final unity.[105]

1.7 HOMO-EROTICISM OF COLLOCATIVE HOMOSEX*UE*LITY: REVEALING THE JOURNEY OF THE GODLOVER

Desire is not *about* union, desire is union. A shift takes place when we move from secondary scholastic sources that analyze and speculate about the

103 Charles Mopsik, *Sex of the Soul: The Vicissitudes of Sexual Difference in Kabbalah,* Cherub Press, Los Angeles 2005, p. 49, esp. pp. 5, 6, 8, 11, 39 [Henceforth, Mopsik, *Sex of the Soul*].

104 Mopsik, *Sex of the Soul,* p. 51.

105 Ibid, *Sex of the Soul,* p. 146:
"...the place and support of this union is in...the mystic's body itself,... but their bonding, the in-between where they meet, a place that properly belongs neither to one nor to the other. Neither matter nor substance, but where both find their original unity which is also their final unity, not a unity of reabsorption, but a unity of expansion, the result of the inner tension towards exteriority which is metamorphosed into a supplement, into an increase of interiority. A triumphant interiority which brings about the revelation or the turning back of exteriority, which manifests its pre-ontological proximity."

mystical experience of *devekut*, towards poetic sources that are records of that experience itself. This intense mystical desire for *unio mystica* — towards original and final unity — finds the strongest reading in Jerusalemite poet, Binyamin Shvili (b. 1956). While the ecstatic poetry of Pinhas Sadeh (1929-1994) has much to contribute to the inner evolution or *in*volution of a contemporary mystical lexicon in Hebrew, it is Shvili whose erotic poetry is of another experiential level altogether. It knows no bounds and in a singular voice is able to break down all barriers between self and other in the face of universal desire.[106] I argue that Shvili's desire for ecstatic mystical union through homo-eroticism is reflected powerfully through his collocations in language. What is so unique about these homo-erotic collocations is that there has not been such a powerful and poetic expression since moments in the Hebrew Bible, the Babylonian Talmud and Medieval wine poems from the Golden Age in Spain. But Shvili's poems reveal remarkable journeys in search of authentic erotic union that traverse all boundaries between heterosexual and homosexual. The power of this poetic vision articulated in Hebrew takes leave where earlier sources and even contemporary sources remain incomplete.[107] What may have begun with

106 Jill Amuel, "*Yesh gam ahavah ahairet*," *Dimui Journal* no. 10, Jerusalem 1995, pp. 26-29, 81.

107 Recent reflections on GLBT spirituality in the Jewish world have begun to appear but remain in a very early stage of development. One of the earliest self-reflections remains *Twice Blessed* which attempted to articulate a sense of gay pride through participation in the Jewish community before Queer Theory really emerged in the academic and activist circles in the 1990's. See Christie Balka, *Twice blessed: on being lesbian or gay and Jewish*, Beacon Press, Boston 1989. Reflecting on the need to write LGBT life into visibility from the vantage point of thirteen years hindsight, Balka and Rose recontextualize the contributions of *Twice Blessed*. This pioneering document served to reveal the in/visibility and portray "the authentic lives of lesbian and gay men while remaining accessible to liberal/moderate heterosexual Jews." See Avi Rose and Christie Balka, "Creating our Histories: A Look Back at Twice Blessed," in *Queer Jews*, ed. David Shneer & Caryn Aviv, Routledge, New York 2002, pp. 16-22. Another reflection on the search for Queer Jewish spirituality tends to be consumed with its transition from pagan to proto-Jewish sex rituals as the entry into a spiritual awakening, see Jill Nagle, "Queer Naked Seder and Other Newish Jewish Traditions," *Queer Jews*, ed. David Shneer & Caryn Aviv, Routledge, New York 2002, pp. 73-76.
The discourse continues to develop, and this is apparent amongst Israeli Lesbians as well, see Tracy Moore, *Lesbiyot: Israeli lesbians talk about sexuality, feminism, Judaism and their lives*, London, Cassell 1995. By contrast, there is a focus on personal narratives of homosexuals in Israeli society as recounted within a more secular realm albeit embedded in the heart of a

alchemical fascination realizes the pinnacle of its freedom for Shvili's poetry in its experience of collocative homo-eroticism.

It is in Shvili's cycle, homosexuEL [הוֹמוֹסֶקְסוּאֵל], that his collocative homo-erotic poetry is strongest. By collocative language or *zeruf 'otiyot,* the mystical

deeply religious Hebrew culture, see *Independence park: the lives of gay men in Israel,* ed. Amir Sumaka'i Fink, and Jacob Press, Stanford University Press, California 1999.
More recently from a *halakhic* and *aggadic* perspective, Rabbi Steve Greenberg has begun to explore how homosexual relations can be re-read as sacred, namely "homospirituality," see Rabbi Steven Greenberg, *Wrestling with God and Men: Homosexuality in the Jewish Tradition*, University of Wisconsin Press, Madison 2005. Greenberg's research serves as a comprehensive index of next directions for the discourse on homosexuality, deeply grounded within the Jewish textual tradition, building upon his fourfold exploration of Sacred Texts, Evidence, Rationales and Conversations.
Finally Jay Michaelson's recent contributions must be considered as critic, activist and poet. His most recent review on Allen Ginsberg's genius as a homosexual mystic-poet makes scant reference to mystical experience *per se*. While of interest that Ginsberg names his 1948 auditory hallucination of William Blake a "mystical experience" that inspired him to become a poet for real, it is not clear that American Jewish poetry has the spiritual power to significantly transform homospirituality through a collocative language, see Jay Michaelson,"Portrait of a the Artist As a Nice Jewish Boy," Review of *The Book of Martyrdom and Artifice: First Journals and Poems 1937-1952, Forward*, Arts & Culture: July 13, 2007, B3. From a transdenominational perspective, there is Michaelson's *Nehirim: A Spiritual Initiative for GLBT Jews* (www.nehirim.org), an independent organization devoted to transdenominational, queer spirituality. *Nehirim*'s purpose is to "... create spiritual community for GLBT Jews, integrating the wisdom of the Jewish tradition, the unique perspectives of sexual minorities, and an experiential relationship with the Divine."
Finally in addition to *Nehirim,* Michaelson's recent collection of homoerotic mystical love poems, *Another Word for Sky* (Lethe Press, 2007), reflect a possible trajectory of return to deeper literacy within traditional texts and its growing lexicon that may contribute to this burgeoning *in*volution of homospirituality. In one such poem, called "It says 'woman came out of the man' and I am putting her back," Michaelson writes of the unitive experience:

god i love you and so i am putting her back
into me
by becoming her
and accepting him
and accepting you
and becoming him
and loving him
and loving you
it says woman came out of the man
and i am putting her back

The afterlife of this first collection of poetry will be telling. While Michaelson is often compared to Ginsberg, it is not clear just how strong an influence this new poetic voice will command, especially one that is not originating in Hebrew.

praxis which Bialik already recalled in *Gilui veKissui beLashon* (1917) is given an afterlife. While reviewing Bialik's profoundly mystical philosophy of language there, Yadin suggests *zeruf 'otiyot* should be translated not as a transmutation but as a collocation of letters. In so experimenting with the form of the journey itself, Shvili conveys the rocking motion of a boat. By setting off on this journey into the unknown depths, the poet and the reader both experience the *to and fro* motion of being at sea. As a traveler, Shvili embarks on this journey towards unitive consciousness in Hebrew poetry. It is this beloved traveler who reveals through homosexuality how the nature of Jewish mysticism can never be the same for it never was quite as had been imagined.

*

אֲנִי הַנּוֹסֵעַ הַמְאֹהָב	I am the beloved traveler
וְהַמִּתְקַדֵּם אֵין	and advancing no
לִי צֹרֶךְ בְּשַׁלְשְׁלָאוֹת	need for chains
מַשָּׂאִי בְּשָׂרִי הַדָּל	my journey my meagre flesh
וְהָעֲצָמוֹת כִּי אֲנִי הָאֱמֶת	and my bones for I am the truth
שֶׁל כָּל הַהַתְחָלוֹת	of all beginnings
לִי הַכֹּל רְאִי לַיֹּפִי שֶׁל	to me all is a mirror to the beauty of
הָאֶחָד לְהַגִּיעַ לַזֶּרַע	the One to reach the flow
שֶׁל הַטִּפָּה בְּיַמּוֹ חָפַצְתִּי	of the drop in its ocean is all I desired
אֲנִי הַנּוֹסֵעַ הַמְאֹהָב	I am the beloved traveler
וְהַמִּתְקַדֵּם גַּרְעִין אֲנִי בַּחַמָּה	and advancing I am a nucleus in the sun
הַבּוֹעֶרֶת בְּיֹפִי רִקּוּדָה	that is burning in the beauty of her dance
אֶל תּוֹךְ הָרֶחֶם שֶׁל	into the womb of
הָאֶחָד[108]	the One

This journey toward unification "into the womb of/the One," toward the ensouled body, is what arouses the apparent division here between each realm. As reflected in the distancing and tearing away of each strophe, so too the body often has a way of getting away from the soul. Although a unidimesional reality has been escaped, the robust experience of collocation also gives way to

108 Benjamin Shvili, *Shirai HaTayar HaGadol, III: HaZman Shel HaMetaylim*, Schoken Books, Tel Aviv 1999, p. 61 [Henceforth, Shvili, *Shirai HaTayar HaGadol*].

castration, wherein "homosexual" loses any further articulation and remains simply "sexy." A more robust sexuality is missing here as there are no letters available to map out any union with god or lover. This leg of the journey allows for a rediscovery of embodied desire necessary for the vitality of the soul.

הוֹמוֹסֶקְסִי	HOMOSEXY
הַגּוּף שֶׁלִּי רוֹצֶה	My body desires
לְזַלֵּל וְלִסְבֹּא	gluttony and satiation
אַחַר כָּךְ הוּא רוֹצֶה לִישׁוֹן	afterwards it desires sleep
הַגּוּף שֶׁלִּי רוֹצֶה	My body desires
לִכְלוּךְ וְזֻהֲמָה	filth and pollution
אַחַר כָּךְ הוּא רוֹצֶה לְעַנּוֹת אֶת הַנְּשָׁמָה	afterwards it desires answering the soul
אֲנִי אוֹמֵר לוֹ	I tell it
גּוּף סוֹפְךָ לָמוּת	body, your end is to die
אֲנִי אוֹמֵר לוֹ	I tell it
גּוּף אַתָּה בַּקֶּבֶר תֵּרָקֵב	you'll rot in the grave
אֲבָל הַגּוּף	But my body
עוֹנֶה לִי	answers me
בְּכָל זֹאת	even so
אֲנִי רוֹצֶה[109]	I desire

It is no coincidence that what opens section four of the poetry cycle, *Songs of the Great Tourist*, is a series entitled, *HomosexuEL*. The form of this poem reflects the *to and fro* movement of an ocean journey, perhaps by boat. Following this beloved traveler, the reader enters into the undulating ocean of love, so that in nearing the poem's end this traveler has shifted position. The movement is towards the One, towards ultimate unity. The opening journey of the beloved within this series is a spiritual one in search of the divine presence manifest in homosexuality. Shvili utilizes his poetics of collocation most frequently in this series, beginning the journey with the subtlest of vowel collocations. To the casual reader, homosexuEL is homosexual, but to the attuned reader, homosexuEL [הוֹמוֹסֶקְסוּאֵל] is not homosexual [הוֹמוֹסֶקְסוּאָל]. The difference of one vowel ([אֵ]

109 Ibid, *Shirai HaTayar Hagadol,* p.69

as opposed to [אָ]) shifts the meaning in a profound way, all the while appearing to be the same word at a glance. While the form of the word undergoes a most minute shift, its content undergoes a radical one. This poetic cycle embarks upon a search for God or the primordial Isra El [אֵל] while wandering through homosexual identity. This collocation of homosexuality and homospirituality is unique to Hebrew poetry being written in Jerusalem.

בַּגֶּשֶׁם הָרַב הַיּוֹרֵד עַכְשָׁו הוֹ יְדִידִי הַמְאֹהַב	O beloved friend in the abundant rain that now falls
עַל מִטָּתִי אֶשְׁכַּב אֶשְׁאַל עַל אֱלֹהַי וֵאלֹהָיו	I'll lay upon my bed I'll interrogate after his god and mine
הַמַּסְתִּיר פָּנָיו אֶכְאַב אֶדְאַב אֶת שְׂמִיכָתִי אֶסְחַב	that hides his face I'll suffer I'll undergo I'll drag my blanket
וּבְמִטָּתִי בְּדִמְיוֹנִי עַל אֱלֹהַי אֶשְׁכַּב[110]	I'll lay in my bed in my imagining my god

A journey begins in separation. The god of each lover is alone, separate as these lovers join in union. Their conjoining allows each one to discover the spirit of their ensouled bodies even while their spiritual connections remain as "my god and his god" [אֱלֹהַי וֵאלֹהָיו]. But as the journey toward utter union unfolds, any final separation between gods and lovers must dissolve. It is in bed that the lover interrogates after his own god as well as his lover's. No domain can remain separate in this quest for ultimate union. One god appears hidden while the other is revealed. If *my* god within the poem is revealed and *his* god is hidden, then the ecstasy experienced in union becomes the site of revelation of the other's god. The ecstatic experience melds one ensouled body into the other and in so doing, collocates lovers and gods, in body and in language.

A most brilliant example of this collocative homosexuality is found in the following poem that continues the journey of this cycle:

סַע לְאָן שֶׁתִּסַּע אֱלֹהֲבִי	Journey to where you shall journey mygodlover
אַחֲרֶיךָ אֶרְדֹּף	I'll chase after you

110 Shvili, *Shirai HaTayar HaGadol*, p. 47.

כְּמוֹ כּוֹכָב נוֹדֵד בְּבִטְנְךָ	as a lone star in your belly
סַע לְאָן שֶׁתִּסַּע אֱלֹהֲבִי	Journey to where you shall journey mygodlover
אֲנִי בְּךָ וְאַתָּה בִּי[111]	I'm in you and you're in me

This ecstatic poem conveys the depth of the journey for the ensouled body. The lover continually seeks reunion with the beloved. But the nature of the reunion is already troped as collocative. Collocation is a linguistic device whereby two separate words meld into one. In this case the two separate and distinct words "my god" [אֱלֹהַי] and "my lover" [אֲהֻבִי] melt through their union into "mygodlover" [אֱלֹהֲבִי]. This act of collocation is not a practice relegated merely to the mystics, but Hebrew poets like Bialik turned to it frequently.

In another poem from this cycle, a liberated *homosexbird* is revealed as Shvili collocates the word homosexual with bird obliquely referencing the Yiddish *feigele* as connoting the homosexual. By collocating this transmigrating symbol of the soul through the migratory pattern of birds, an even deeper evocation of the flight into erotic freedom becomes possible.[112]

הוֹמוֹסֶקְצִפּוֹר	**HOMOSEXBIRD**
לְאָן אֲנִי שַׁיָּךְ הַאִם אֲנִי תַּיָּר אוֹ שֶׁאֲנִי שָׁבוּי תְּנוּ	Where do I belong, am I a tourist or hostage let
לִי לָשׁוּב אֶל הָרֵאשִׁית וּלְהַסְבִּיר אֶת הָעַצְבוּת	me return to the beginning and explain my sorrow
שֶׁמְּצִיאוּת הִיא הַתְּפִלָּה שֶׁל צַיָּדִים שֶׁנִּכְנְסָה	that reality is the prayer of hunters who have entered
אֶל הַשָּׂדֶה	into the field
פִּתּוּי וּמַלְכּוֹדוֹת וְדַחְלִילִים הִסְתִּירוּ אֶת עַצְמָם	temptations, traps and scarecrows hide themselves
בַּעֲרֵמוֹת שֶׁל שִׂמְחָתִי	in the heaps of my happiness
אֲנִי הָיִיתִי פַּעַם לַהֲקָה שֶׁל צִפּוֹרִים הַצַּיָּדִים רָאוּ	I was once a flock of birds, the hunters saw

111 Shvili, *Shirai HaTayar HaGadol*, p. 51.

112 Compare with Shaul Magid's "The Sin of Being/Becoming a Woman: Male Homosexuality and the Castration Complex: Leviticus 18:22 and 20:13," in light of contemporary appropriations by Shvili of a Muslim homo-eroticism into his Hebrew poetry (*Shirai Gaguim l'Mecca*) that normalizes homosexuality through this "other" eros. Like the Sufis who contemplated the male wine servant, here birds are the object of contemplation and transformation. Specifically male birds find themselves in theological conversation with female birds, or the poet envisions himself returning to his origin flying in a school of birds — much of his poetics then plays with the migratory notion of desire. Considering Shvili's noted and self-professed Sufi and Sabbetean influence, these collocative exercises chart a new path back into Jewish mystical praxis within Hebrew poetry.

אוֹתִי וְהֵם קָרְאוּ	me and cried out to
לִי	me
בְּקוֹלוֹת כָּל כָּךְ מוֹשְׁכִים שֶׁבָּאתִי אֲלֵיהֶם וְאָז	with such seductive voices that I came out to them
רָאִיתִי אֶת עַצְמִי	and then I saw myself
בְּלוּלָאוֹת	in the loops
עַל צַוָּארִי לָזוּז נִסִּיתִי אַךְ כְּכָל שֶׁנֶּאֱבַקְתִּי	around my neck I tried to move even as I was strangled
נִתְהַדְּקוּ הַחֲבָלִים	the ropes tightened
וְלָחֲצוּ	and they beat
אוֹתִי	me
הֵכַנְתִּי אֶת עַצְמִי לָמוּת טָבַעְתִּי בְּיִסּוּרִים	I prepared myself to die, I drowned in afflictions
שָׁחַכְתִּי מֶה הָיִיתִי לְפָנִים	I've forgotten what I was before
אֲנִי הָיִיתִי פַּעַם לַהֲקָה שֶׁל צִפּוֹרִים[113].	I was once a flock of birds.

In the course of flying through ancient memories, the poet recalls his true freedom embodied in the symbol of the bird. The transmigration of souls, so often associated with the bird (especially in Sufi poetry),[114] suits the poet upon this journey, from affliction to love. It is the experience of eros bound to a flock or a group — often referred to as *dibbuk haverim* or a unified group — that moves in a unified motion. What binds each bird together is nothing more than the instinct to fly and be free together. Their flight is all the stronger as it takes place together, losing any distinct notion of individual identity. This unification of the group into a whole gives the impression of a larger organism or macrocosm that is revitalized by the microcosm. Such a shifting between worlds and perspectives is once again embodied by the two separate and distinct words "homosexual" [הוֹמוֹסֶקְסוּאָל] and "bird" [צִפּוֹר] as they each melt through their union into "homosexbird" [הוֹמוֹסֶקְצִפּוֹר]. This act of collocation is a mystical marker for the soul's journey, as it returns from its exile into the secret circle of a deeper self:

שִׁירֵי גָּלוּת אִדְּרָא	*EXILIC POEMS OF THE SECRET CIRCLE
אַתְּ צִפּוֹר הָעוֹמֶדֶת עַל גֶּדֶר תַּיִל	You are a bird perched on barbed-wire fence
בֵּין אֶרֶץ מַיִם וְשָׁמַיִם	between earth water and heavens

113 Shvili, *Shirai HaTayar HaGadol*, p. 68.

114 For example, see the twelfth century *locus classicus*, Farid al-Din Attar, *The Conference of the Birds*, tr. A. Darbandi, D. Davis, Penguin Classics 1984.

אֲנִי אָבוּד יוֹתֵר מִמֵּךְ	I am more lost than you
טוּרֵי הַמַּיִם שֶׁבַּיָּם זוֹרְמִים	Pillars of water in the sea flow
אֶל מוֹלַדְתִּי	towards my homeland
בָּאִים לְבַשֵּׂר לָךְ אֲהוּבָתִי	they bring you news of my love
אֶת	of
גָּלוּתִי	my exile
חוֹמוֹת הַשִּׂמְחָה	Walls of happiness
מַקִּיפוֹת אוֹתִי בְּאִדְּרָא	encircle me in the secret circle
שֶׁל	of
עַצְבוּת	sadness
מֵחַלּוֹן חַדְרִי רַק חֶלְקַת יָם קְטַנָּה	Only a fragment of sea from my room's window
נוֹשֶׁבֶת בֵּין עַרְבַּיִם בְּצִלְלֵי	blowing at eventide through shadowed
שֶׁמֶשׁ אֲדֻמִּים	crimson sun
וּמִלִּבִּי נִשְׁקֶפֶת הוֹי חֶמְדַּת יָמִים	& revealing from my heart O delight of days
אַתְּ יְרוּשָׁלַיִם.	you are Jerusalem

In witnessing the act of being perched between heaven and earth for the bird, the soul knows the journey before it. Through *dibbuk haverim* or group union by way of the secret circle or *idra*, the poet is able to overcome the sadness of singularity by enabling an opening of the heart that is Jerusalem. Moving from the fragmentary vision of the window to the heart of Jerusalem, the poet soars from depression to ecstasy, merging in flight with heaven and earth. This journey into the primordial sea undergirding terrestrial Jerusalem leads to a dissolution of self into the "pillars of water in the sea flow/into my nativity." Such a freedom of flight from the confines of a single dimensional perspective is what allows the imagination to soar. The next flight of the poem is guided still by the bird, however, this time traversing *eros* into *thanatos*, from love to the realm of death.

הוֹמוֹסֶקְסוּמֵת	**HOMOSEXUDEATH**
כָּךְ כִּמְעַט בְּסוֹף הַסּוֹף לְיַד הַחוֹף כְּשֶׁהַשְּׁפָחִים	So it was, almost at the end's end, along the coast with

בִּמְעוּפָם דוֹאִים	the seagulls soaring in their flight
טוֹבֵעַ בְּעַצְבוּת הִבַּטְתִּי מֵחַלּוֹן חַדְרִי וְרָאִיתִים	Sinking in depression I glanced out of my window &
פּוֹשְׁטִים יָדַיִם הָאֶחָד אֶל הַשֵּׁנִי	I saw them extending hands one to the other
נָחֲתוּ לָהֶם שְׁנֵי צִפּוֹרִים זָכָר וּנְקֵבָה הַזָּכָר	Two birds, male and female, descended to them,
שָׁקֵט עָמַד עַל הֶעָפָר וְהַנְּקֵבָה	The quiet male stood upon the earth, & the female
קָפְצָה וְצִפְצְפָה וּבִשְׂפַת הַצִּפּוֹרִים שָׁמַעְתִּי	Hopped and chirped. I heard bird language
הַצִּפּוֹר אוֹמֵר לַצִּפּוֹרָה כַּמָּה מִלִּים עַל מָוֶת	the bird saying to her a few words about death
"וּפּוֹלוֹס לֹא קָם הוּא רַק נָשַׁף בְּקֹצֶר נְשִׁימָה לְיָדוֹ	"And Paul did not arise, he only exhaled a short breath,
עָמַד תִּימוֹתְיוֹס מַנִּיחַ עַל מֵצַח פּוֹלוֹס שְׁתֵּי יָדָיו	at his side, Timothy laid his hands on Paul's brow
עָמַד שָׁם בֵּין כֻּלָּם גַּם טִיטוּס וְנִזְכַּר אֵיךְ	There in their midst Titus stood and recalled
בָּאִגֶּרֶת שֶׁשָּׁלַח אֵלָיו צִוָּה	how in the epistle he sent instructing him to
לִכְרֵיתֵי לֵךְ אֶל אִי הָעַקְשָׁנִים חוֹשֵׁב לוֹ טִיטוּס אָכֵן	walk to Crete the isle of stiff-necks, thinks
לֹא כָּל דָּבָר יָדַעְתִּי הַמּוֹרֶה עַל כֵּן אָנוּ מֵתִים	Titus, since I did not know that everything teaches
וּפְלֵימוֹן מְלֵא הַבָּשָׂר וְהַפָּנִים הַדְּשֵׁנוֹת מִתְפַּלֵּל	why we die, & Phlaimon potbellied, with his full
לוֹ כָּל אוֹתָהּ שָׁעָה שֶׁפּוֹלוֹס	face praying all the while as Paul
גָּסַס לוּ יְהִי לוֹ לַצַּדִּיק הַזֶּה שֶׁכָּל חַיָּיו	expired if only he would be his saint all his life
נִטְרַד בַּהֲפָצַת דְּבָרָיו שֶׁל הַנִּרְדָּם	preoccupied with disseminating the sleeper's words
לוּ יְהִי לוֹ בֵּית מָלוֹן זְמַנִּי לְנִרְדָּמִים	if only he had a temporary hotel for sleepers
וְכָךְ עִם עֶרֶב רַד נִשְׁאַרְנוּ עֵירֻמִּים לְעוֹלָמוֹ	& so with eventide falling we remained naked,
הָלַךְ לוֹ הַמּוֹרֶה כַּאֲדוֹנוֹ	off he went to his world, the teacher like lord
עַכְשָׁו הוּא מְצַיֵּץ וְשָׁר חָפְשִׁי שִׁירָה	now he chirps & freely sings a song
לְלֹא מִקְצָב לְלֹא כְּלָלִים לֹא	without rhythm without rules not
מְגֻיֶּסֶת בְּלִי שִׁרְיוֹן וּבְלִי מַדִּים".	conscripted without armor & without uniform."
עָף לוֹ הַצִּפּוֹר לְקָאף וְאַחֲרָיו הַצִּפּוֹרָה	The bird flew to him at Kaff & after him she
בְּקַפְסָלִי לְיַד חוֹרָה עִיר בִּירָה שֶׁל קִיתֶרָה	in my capsule beside *Chora*, the capital of
הִקְשַׁבְתִּי לַסִּפּוּר שֶׁל הַצִּפּוֹר לַצִּפּוֹרָה[115]	*Kiterah* I listened to the story of the bird to the bird

115 Shvili, *Shirai HaTayar HaGadol*, p. 66.

In re-embracing the apostle Timothy's account of mystical transmission received from Paul, the poet overcomes the embarrassment that much of Hebrew poetry has with the New Testament. The first level of embarrassment is on a linguistic level, namely, that the scriptures transmitted are by and large Greek rather than Hebrew. But Shvili's re-embrace, much like that of Pinhas Sadeh, is a gesture of re-writing scripture as poetry as much as it is a re-embracing. By contextualizing a communal *unio mystica* within this New Testament setting, Shvili is listening with newly attuned ears of the heart. The collocation of two separate and distinct words "homosexual" [הוֹמוֹסֶקְצֻאָל] and "bird" [צִפּוֹר] as they each melt through their union into "homosexubird" [הוֹמוֹסֶקְצִפּוֹר] find their rest in death [הוֹמוֹסֶקְסוּמֶת]. The *eros* soaring so free, already lucid in some of Bialik's bird poems,[116] is also the mark of *thanatos*, that impending death on the underside of that very freedom of the bird's flight. Why does the poet bring an impure bird[117] into this domain of prohibition as his guide for the flight into freedom? In a highly Sabbatean key for the poet,[118] it is by way of the impure moving through the law that redemption takes place.

1.8 RE-EMBRACING *UNIO MYSTICA*: JOURNEYING BY WAY OF THE GODLOVER

Much remains to be learned and integrated from the new perspectives of ancient days of re-embracement after Fox, especially re-embracing homo-erotic *unio mystica*. Despite the influence of over a jubilee of Scholem's embarrassment, a re-embracement of *unio mystica* remains slow in coming. While it appears that the devotional world has become less embarrassed by

116 For example, see H. N. Bialik's bird poems: *'El haTzippor, Tavas Zehavi Perah Lo, Hachnisani Tahat Kenafeikh, Shirah Yetomah, Bein Nahar Perat uNahar Hidekel*; compare with Pinhas Sadeh's reading of these transformational bird poems, see Pinhas Sadeh, *Tavas Zehavi*, Mivhar Shirai Bialik, Dvir-Schocken, Israel 1985, pp. 175-185.

117 The seagull figures as part of a list of biblically impure birds, see Leviticus 11: 16.

118 See the Sabbetean cycle that figures prominently into Shvili's larger *œuvre*, Shvili, *Yeled Me'if Afifon b'meah ha-sheva esra, Shirai HaTayar HaGadol*, pp. 89-104. Compare with Glazer, *Contemporary Hebrew Mystical Poetry: How It Redeems Jewish Thinking*, Edwin Mellen Press, New York 2009, pp. 173-242.

utter union with the essence of the Creator,[119] the road of the godlover remains in the offing. If a by-path between the scholarly and the devotional worlds is to be discovered and experienced, then clearly Shvili's poetics needs to be heeded.

What Shvili's poetics of homosexuELity reveals with such prowess, *contra* Scholemean embarrassment thinking, is how very much human individuality abandons itself to the rapture of complete submersion in the divine stream. How fitting then that concatenations of this rapture of submersion are echoing with greater frequency and power in the devotional Hebrew culture of Israel.[120] In this ecstatic frame of mind, both Jewish mystic and Hebrew poet release any sense of the distance between the Creator and creature.[121] The embarrassment that once surrounded that loss of distance with any dissolution of individual identity into the pool of ultimate unity is being shed. As the cautious skepticism about the possibility of complete union into original and final unity within the divine stream is egresses away, a new wave of ingression reveals the constellation of another authentic Jewish mystical experience. Yet only the poets — the true godlovers — are daring enough to fully embrace the journey, revealing the ultimate unity of לא לַזְמָן הַזֶּה *not this time* already לַזְמָן הַזֶּה within *this time*.[122]

---

119 See "*Devekuth b'Aztmut ha'Boreh*," *Sefer Yam haHokhmah, Machon Yam haHokhmah*, Jerusalem 2007, pp. 651-656; ibid, "*Ma'amar Kedusha Meshuleshet*," *Sefer Yam haHokhmah, Machon Yam haHokhmah*, Jerusalem 2008, pp. 551-640.

120 See "*Devekuth b'Aztmut ha'Boreh*, *idem* pp. 652b-653a, where the anonymous author offers a unique re-reading of Lurianic Kabbalah that explicates the reality of complete *unio mystica*. The devotional shifts between the personnae of Leah and Rachel exemplify the polarity between complete and partial *devekuth*. Whereas the luminosity of Rachel is revealed in exteriority, the luminosity of Leah is concealed in its interiority. In moments of devotional life, especially during prayer, where luminosity appears to be eclipsed, it is through the persona of Leah that a deeper connection is possible. This moment of eclipse through interiority is what gives the aspirant merit to feel the essence of the King [להרגיש בבח' עצמות המלך]. and to touch a deeper *jouissance* in the divine essence beyond all rational perception and ideation [עד שזוכה להתענג על עצמות אלוקותו ית"ש למעלה מכל השגה ורעיון].

121 Gershom Scholem, *Major Trends in Jewish Mysticism*, Schocken Books, New York 1947, pp. 122-123. See also Moshe Idel, *Studies in Ecstatic Kabbalah*, SUNY Press, New York, ff. 11, p. 21.

122 I recently shared such a unitive experience with Fox during a phone call from Jerusalem to New York on *Tisha B'Av*. Fox expressed true wonder at how he could be calling from Jerusalem at the end of *Tisha B'Av* there, while here in New York *Tisha B'Av* was still unraveling.

How was it possible that within his experience of the redemptive afterglow of לִזְמַן הַזֶּה within *this time,* that the peak of destruction, לֹא לִזְמַן הַזֶּה *not this time,* could simultaneously be experienced in its unraveling?

ENVIRONMENTAL EMBARRASSMENT: GENESIS 1:26-28 VS. GENESIS 2:15

Tanhum Yoreh (York University)

In 1967, Lynn White Jr. published an essay in *Science* under the title of "The Historical Roots of Our Ecological Crisis." In his essay he accuses the Judeo-Christian tradition of being the source of the world's environmental ills. He claims that this tradition began as a result of Genesis 1:26-28, which granted humans dominion over the rest of creation. Tikva Frymer-Kensky claims that Lynn White has been refuted hundreds of times on different grounds.[1] Ellen Bernstein affirms that "[m]any environmentalists and theologians are still haggling over White's thesis even after hundreds of articles and books have tackled the topic over the last thirty years."[2] Jeremy Benstein states that:

> [r]egarding the immediate responses to White, in that first decade there were a handful of rabbis and scholars who took up the cudgels to defend the honor of Israel. Robert Gordis, Eric Freudenstein, Norman Lamm, and others wrote persuasively about the environmental values of biblical and rabbinic Judaism.[3]

Neal Joseph Loevinger sums up the line of such arguments concisely:

> Extracting a few isolated verses from the Bible and interpreting them as representative of the "Judeo-Christian tradition" do little justice to a complex and

1 Tikva Frymer-Kensky, "Ecology in a Biblical Perspective." ***Torah of the Earth: Exploring 4,000 Years of Ecology in Jewish Thought, Vol. 1.*** Arthur Waskow (ed.). Woodstock, Vermont, Jewish Lights Publishing, 2000, pp. 55-69.

2 Ellen Bernstein, ***The Splendor of Creation: A Biblical Ecology***. Cleveland, Ohio,The Pilgrim Press, 2005, pp. 110-111.

3 Jeremy Benstein, ***The Way Into Judaism and the Environment***. Woodstock, Vermont, Jewish Lights Publishing, 2006, p. 25.

important issue and may tell more about the bias of the writer than about the verses in question.[4]

Christian scholars also came out in droves to refute White and other scholars who subscribed to what Cameron Wybrow calls "The Mastery Hypothesis." Wybrow then goes on to dismiss this hypothesis as being the product of both a misreading of the bible, as well as a misunderstanding of Paganism.[5] It must be noted, however, that it was White's prerogative to interpret scripture as he pleased, as these texts in general, and Genesis 1:28 in particular lend themselves to multiple interpretations, as can be seen in the commentary tradition.

It is no surprise that when White searched through history to discover the origins of Western ideologies he found himself looking in the Hebrew bible, the foundation text of all Western civilization. As a devout Christian, there is no doubt that White was embarrassed with his tradition. So embarrassed, that he called for a wide-scale change in his own religion, or the development of a new one, a statement that for some could be considered bordering on blasphemy. Lynn White's cry was for a change in values that would allow humanity to live in harmony with the rest of the world. It is often forgotten that White was an environmentalist. He was embarrassed with the morals that he saw as having guided his tradition throughout the course of its history.

White's dictum was adopted by some in the environmental movement, while others rushed to defend the bible in light of his accusations. As Manfred Gerstenfeld mentions, most of the literature on Judaism and the environment was apologetic in nature and was more a response to White than a real exploration into the field.[6] It is only due to the persistence of the ecological crisis of which White spoke, as well as a new generation of environmentalists, more specifically Jewish environmentalists, that the area is being approached not as a response to White, but for its own sake. There is now an attempt to

4 Neal Joseph Loevinger, "(Mis)reading Genesis: A Response to Environmentalist Critiques of Judaism," ***Ecology and the Jewish Spirit: Where Nature and the Sacred Meet***. Ellen Bernstein (ed.). Woodstock, Vermont, Jewish Lights Publishing, 1998, p. 34.

5 Cameron Wybrow, ***The Bible, Baconianism, and Mastery over Nature: The Old Testament and its Modern Misreading***. New York, Peter Lang Publishing Inc., 1991.

6 Manfred Gerstenfeld, ***Judaism, Environmentalism and the Environment: Mapping and Analysis***. Jerusalem, The Jerusalem Institute for Israel Studies, Rubin Mass Ltd., 1998, p. 56.

truly understand how the Jewish tradition has approached these issues and to offer some guidance as to the direction tradition should go in light of this new knowledge.

It is curious to note the obsession with Lynn White Jr. in scholarship on religion and the environment, and more specifically Judaism and the environment. His essay was indeed seminal, as it has been called by Cohen (1989), Benstein (2006) and others, having produced many responses over the past few decades. Indeed, White has been vilified and refuted throughout the years but he has also received numerous accolades for his work and his views were adopted by many in the larger environmental community.[7]

To engage in refuting White's argument, regardless of what new insights one may bring to the table in doing so, is apologetic. More recent scholarship has pointed to the apologetic response in the past (Gerstenfeld, 1998 and Benstein, 2006), but ironically, it too has not been able to transcend this trend. While current scholarship may indeed delve deeper into understanding the connection of Judaism to environmental issues, it has not been able to abandon White's legacy nor the discourse set by him. More to the point, however, is that even though the analysis of recent scholarship is more complex than in the past it remains obsessed with Lynn White Jr.

Yaffe, in his introduction to an important edited volume of compiled essays on the topic of Judaism and environment states that:

> [t]he following readings supply considerable counterevidence against the claims of White... and others to the effect that, given its ongoing deference to Genesis 1:28, Judaism is environmentally indifferent or worse... Assuming that White... would not fault his historicism, as seems to be the case, Cohen can proceed in confidence to embarrass them for overlooking the considerable body of evidence during the period between biblical and modern times which fails to support, and even goes against, their contentions.[8]

7 Jeremy Benstein, ***The Way Into Judaism and the Environment***. Woodstock, Vermont, Jewish Lights Publishing, 2006, p. 16.

8 Martin D. Yaffe, "Introduction," ***Judaism and Environmental Ethics: A Reader***. Martin D. Yaffe (ed.). New York, Lexington Books, 2001, pp. 9-11.

It is curious that Yaffe maintains the obsession with White even 30 years after it initially began, and even claims that Cohen "embarrasses" White with his own analysis. Although Cohen identifies some of the more potent commentaries relating to dominion, he dismisses them too light-handedly, which will be demonstrated in this essay.

One could, of course, argue that because his paper was so fruitful and is still brought up in contemporary dialogue, that it is at present impossible to discuss the field of Judaism and environment without mentioning White's impact on the existing scholarship. To this one might answer that if the field is moving into a stage of development beyond those first footsteps inspired by White which are littered with apologetics, then White must be divorced from the dialogue altogether. The fact that Cohen states in his introduction that his work on Genesis 1:28 yields a conclusion in which "the ecologically oriented thesis of Lynn White and others can now be laid to rest" illustrates that on some level and to some degree his work is coming as a response to White's accusations.[9] Gerstenfeld, after bringing up White in the first chapter of his book mentions in his conclusion that "Lynn White's accusations with regard to the relation between environmental degradation and the Judeo-Christian tradition should be reassessed from an integrated Jewish perspective."[10] He then goes on to show why, in his opinion, White was wrong. Benstein, in the first chapter of his book claims that "[t]here are more commonalities between ecological and religious thought than first meet the eye, which might just be the ultimate response to White's critique."[11] Why does White need such a response? The moment White comes into the picture it becomes difficult to divorce such scholarship from the long list of previous scholarship that has been classified as apologetic.

Why does any of this matter? Who cares if the scholarship takes on an apologetic or polemic tone or neither? Does the message that the author wanted

9 Jeremy Cohen, ***Be Fertile and Increase, Fill the Earth and Master It: The Ancient and Medieval Career of a Biblical Text***. Ithaca, New York, Cornell University Press, 1989, p. 5.

10 Manfred Gerstenfeld, ***Judaism, Environmentalism and the Environment: Mapping and Analysis***. Jerusalem, The Jerusalem Institute for Israel Studies, Rubin Mass Ltd., 1998, pp. 228-229.

11 Jeremy Benstein, ***The Way Into Judaism and the Environment***. Woodstock, Vermont, Jewish Lights Publishing, 2006, p. 20.

to convey get across? Since the answer to the last question in most cases is yes, why should its analysis under this lens be of any interest? To answer these questions, it is important to understand that such apologetic responses are a scholarly way of conveying embarrassment with the initial argument. It is clear that the respondents to White are embarrassed with his position. They are embarrassed to the degree that they found it necessary to publicly defend the environmental legacy of the bible in light of the aforementioned accusations in the form of scholarship. This embarrassment comes as little surprise; the more we know about the environmental consequences of human behavior, the more dire White's accusations. In essence White's claim was that the bible destroyed or is destroying the environment. This constitutes an embarrassing claim to say the least, considering just how many people in the world revere the biblical legacy.

The irony of it all is that the scholarship White's essay inspired, as apologetic in nature as it was, has and continues to answer his call to "...find a new religion, or rethink our old one [Christianity]."[12]

From Lynn White's rant, as it were, a new way of looking at Judaism and the Jewish experience in regard to the environment has emerged. A large part of this new experience is through environmentally oriented learning sessions at traditional houses of learning or sometimes altogether new places as well. Others have taken to going out into nature on weekend getaways, which include things like bike rides, nature hikes, local and organic food for meals, and a few spiritually oriented talks along the way.[13] It is of interest to point out that it was a Presbyterian Christian who started this dialogue amongst Jews. This too could be considered an embarrassment for some from the perspective that Jewish leaders should have had greater environmental awareness on the basis of their own traditions if such indeed exist.

12 Lynn White Jr., "The Historical Roots of Our Ecological Crisis," ***Science***. Vol. 155, 1967, p. 1207.

13 For example: The Eco Activist Beit Midrash: www.shlomoyeshiva.org/eco, The Coalition on the Environment and Jewish Life: www.coejl.org, Aish HaTora: http://www.aish.com/tubshvat/tubshvatinterests/Judaism_and_the_Environment.asp,
www.Hazon.org, The Teva Learning Center: www.tevacenter.org, Adam VaAdamah: www.av-a.org, and others

The Jewish tradition is well endowed with a "dominionist" approach in its exegesis of Genesis 1:28. The long list of medieval commentary on this verse indicates just how fruitful the verse is conceptually. Cohen analyzed the first part of the verse, be fruitful and multiply throughout its entire tradition histories. His work, however, does not do justice to the dominionist reading of the verse. Cohen states:

> My research on the career of Gen. 1:28 has yielded three kinds of conclusions. First, with regard to Gen. 1:28 itself, the ecologically oriented thesis of Lynn White and others can now be laid to rest. Rarely, if ever, did premodern Jews and Christians construe this verse as a license for the selfish exploitation of the environment. Although most readers of Genesis casually assumed that God had fashioned the physical world for the benefit of human beings, Gen. 1:28 evoked relatively little concern with the issue of dominion over nature. One might, of course, find that other biblical texts did evince such concern, but in the exegesis of Gen. 1:28 other issues so eclipsed the matter of dominion that the little attention it receives in this book might appear to be unfair or perhaps altogether unnecessary. Yet the imbalance accurately reflects the data and itself comprises a significant result of this book.[14]

It is important to point out Cohen's misnomer, as the vast majority of rabbinical sources would have agreed with White's analysis of the verse. The majority of interpretations support just such a dominionist reading of the text. Some have even interpreted the verse as having a strong dominionist theme. Saadiah Gaon (882-942 C.E., born in Egypt, but moved to Babylonia where he became the leader of Babylonian Jewry)[15] is one such exegete who has quite a strong and elaborate list of what dominion over other living things includes. It is worth bringing forth the rather lengthy quote to illustrate the point:

> Now the benefit of all these, I mean animal, crawler, and beast, in medicine is immeasurable [as] for example the benefit of their fats, biles, and bones. From their wool, fur, and hair — something to cover oneself with for protection from

14 Jeremy Cohen, ***Be Fertile and Increase, Fill the Earth and Master It: The Ancient and Medieval Career of a Biblical Text***. Ithaca, New York, Cornell University Press, 1989, p. 5.

15 ***Encyclopedia Judaica,*** Volume 14, Column 544. Entry: Saadiah Gaon.

chill for these [materials] return to the body mists coming up from its pores. From the elephant teeth, bones, ivory [may be made] as is described of Solomon: "And Solomon made a large chair of ivory." (II Chron. 9:17) And even the lowliest of things like the beetle may be used to fumigate congealed blood until one puts a spider web or *shiq'nam* on wounds and fats of vipers and snakes as an antidote to absorb whatever poison one's body may have There are much more [uses] that I shall not mention here…"Ruling" includes the [use of] equipment by which man may gain dominion over the animals. Over some of them [he has dominion] with mines and hobbles and over others with cords and reins and yet others with pits and collar, hunting equipment and *adbaan*. Others are with cages and towers and the like until God teaches {man} everything [about this]…[Ruling over] "Fish" includes [the use of] tactics in hunting fish from the bowels of the sea and rivers, preparing those permissible [for eating] with cooking utensils so that {one} can eat it, taking pearls from the shell, benefiting from the parts of the skin and bones that one prepares, and whatever applies to this…It adds "the sea" in order to include man's dominion over the water in this so that he can take it out from the bowels of the Earth and raise it out until it is visible with buckets or basins or pressing or pushing machines. Likewise he dams in rivers in order to transfer from one side to the other and uses it for turning grindstones and mills. As when it says elsewhere: "And many of those who pass on his ways." (Ps. 8:9) It alludes to making boats and ships to pass in them from side to side. He too makes large *Daramin* which hold thousands of men to cross the widths of the sea and in a place where there are stones they make vehicles of papyrus in which to travel so that they do not break. Like Isaiah explained: "And in vessels of papyrus." (Is. 18:2)…"[Ruling over] the birds" accords the [various] tactics to hunt birds that fly in the air and to make them work for us until they [actually are used to] hunt each other. The benefit from them is [also] to prepare food for {man's} sustenance and herbs for his medicines and the like…It adds "the sky" to include this {man's} ability to know the celestial spheres, their structure and composition. Also to forge copper in a shape, to construct the astrolabe for [investigating] the descent and the ascent [of the stars] and to make the various equipment so that one be able to calculate hours and their parts…By [ruling over] "animals" God gave {man} the power of leading, the power to make use of every one of them, to

> eat their meat that is fit for eating by means of various preparations and the kinds of various foods, to be healed by whatever healing potential it has, to ride on those fit for this like mules, and to know all their sustenance and how they sustain…"And in the entire Earth" alludes to God's giving him the wisdom [to know] how to build houses, fortresses, and castles and to plow the Earth with various seeds and plants. Also how to extract gold and so with silver and bronze and copper from mines; how to make vessels and ornaments in crafts, and also how to make equipment for farm work like ropes and the plow and making carpentry equipment like saws and axes; [making] equipment for sewing clothes like pants, like weaver's beam, and [making] writing utensils like pens and inks and the like as it says of Bezalel: "And I completed in him the knowledge of all the crafts and the carving stone to arrange," (Ex. 31:3-4) and "In the heart of the rest of the wise men I have placed wisdom." (Ex. 31:6) I have been brief and have not cited proofs from the verses for each one of these. In the statement of "all the crawlers" it refers to giving the understanding to man [of how] to capture bees in their hives so that they make honey for him and surround it some…[16,17,18]

It is curious that Saadiah Gaon is singled out by Cohen (1989) and quoted by Benstein (2006), but afterwards dismissed. While Cohen sees him as an anomaly in terms of his elaborate description of what having dominion entailed, it is important to remember that this tenth century figure was the greatest Jewish thinker of his time, a good indicator that his opinions were followed by many and were well known. He cannot merely be dismissed out of hand such as occurs in Cohen's essay when he states: "Although the gaon of

16 Saadiah Gaon, ***Rabbi Saadiah Gaon's Commentary on the Book of Creation***. Michael Linetzky (ed. and trans.), Northvale, New Jersey, Jason Aronson Inc., pp. 106, 113-115.

17 When cross-referencing Linetzky's English translation with Tzuker's authoritative Hebrew translation of Saadiah Gaon's *Tafsir*, the translation holds up relatively well. Rav Saadiah Gaon, ***Peirushei Rav Saadiah Gaon LeBereishit***. Moshe Tzuker (ed.). Israel, Daf-Chen Press, 1984, pp. 250, 258-259.

18 It should be noted that in Saadiah Gaon's Book, *HaEmunot VeHadeot*, he does mention in reference to Genesis 1:28 that God gave humans the choice between good and evil, and commanded them to choose good. While this does not take away from his dominionist position, it does make it clear to the reader that Saadiah Gaon was an advocate of dominion and not destruction.

Sura was the first in a series of Jewish exegetes to redress the traditional rabbinic neglect of that blessing, his extensive comments remained the colloquial exception that proves the rule."[19]

The tradition that Saadiah started, is an anomaly for Cohen not because of his strong dominion stance, but rather because he elaborated on dominion and not on the fertility edicts of Genesis 1:28, the subject of his book. It is quite possible that a didactic tradition based on a stronger dominion of humans over nature developed as a result. *Encyclopedia Judaica* refers to him as an important leader of Babylonian Jewry and calls him the greatest scholar and author of the gaonic period. They write that: "Saadiah was one of the creators of rabbinic literature if not the actual pioneer in this field, and the first to write 'books' in the modern sense of the word." Since most manuscripts of his works have been lost, his actual teachings have been difficult to compile, but Yehuda Ratzabi has sifted through the glosses of other important commentators who have attributed certain teachings to Saadiah using formulas such as "the gaon said" or "the gaon taught" in his compiled commentary of the Gaon on Exodus.[20] A quick look through the book gives the reader the impression of the significant quantity and quality of the scholars influenced by him.

Conversely, Benstein does not go so far as to make this claim. He concedes that: "[t]here is no linguistic way to get around the central terms here. They cannot be reinterpreted to align with twenty-first-century environmental sensibilities."[21] He goes on to explain the undisputable meanings of the words *KaVaSh* and *RaDaH* commonly translated as "master" or "conquer" and "dominate" or "subdue"[22] respectively. Benstein even singles out Nahmanides' interpretation of the verse "as referring to the relationship between master and slave."[23]

19 Jeremy Cohen, ***Be Fertile and Increase, Fill the Earth and Master It: The Ancient and Medieval Career of a Biblical Text***. Ithaca, New York, Cornell University Press, 1989, p. 187.

20 For example, Saadiah Gaon, ***Rav Saadya's Commentary on Exodus***. Yehuda Ratzaby (ed. and trans.), Jerusalem, Mossad HaRav Kook, 1998.

21 Jeremy Benstein, ***The Way Into Judaism and the Environment***. Woodstock, Vermont, Jewish Lights Publishing, 2006, p. 42.

22 The definition of *RaDaH* as subdue is my own, not Benstein's.

23 Jeremy Benstein, ***The Way Into Judaism and the Environment***. Woodstock, Vermont, Jewish Lights Publishing, 2006, p. 43.

Benstein, however, dismisses the "dominionist" reading as well. He states:

> But the easy, superficial, and *therefore mistaken*[24] reading would be one in which Genesis 1 is stereotyped as the environmentally "bad" chapter, and Genesis 2 as the "good" one — that reads 1:28 as the root of all ecological evil, effectively counterbalanced only by 2:15, the mission to "work and to guard" the Garden. A closer look at the specifics of the texts shows why this simplistic dichotomous reading is misguided.[25]

Just because the verse has been interpreted in a literal, non-environmental way must it be mistaken? It is difficult to argue with this type of logic. Interestingly, Israel Rozenson also sees a balancing element in Nahmanides' gloss — a prohibition to make any large scale changes to creation. It takes a creative reader, however, to find such meaning in the text.[26] Nahum Rakover, however, realizing the difficulties with Nahmanides' gloss brings a modern gloss by Rabbi Abraham Isaac HaCohen Kook (1865-1935, Latvia and Israel)[27] on Genesis 1:28, who interprets the verse in a much more benevolent manner to the rest of creation.[28]

Even though the following views have been dismissed as not being deep enough to be correct, these medieval scholars clearly demonstrate a strong "dominionist" reading of the text. For example, one of the scholars who often quoted Saadiah and was obviously highly influenced by him was Nahmanides (Ramban) (1194-1270 C.E., Spain and later on Israel).[29] Nahmanides, like the Gaon, had a very clear idea of what dominion entails: "He gave them power and governance on the earth to do as they pleased with livestock and insects and all things that crawl in the dust; and to build, to uproot plants to mine copper from

24 Emphasis is my own.

25 Jeremy Benstein, ***The Way Into Judaism and the Environment***. Woodstock, Vermont, Jewish Lights Publishing, 2006, p. 43.

26 Israel Rozenson, ***VeHineh Tov Meod***. Jerusalem, Yeshivat Beit Orot, 2001, p. 29.

27 ***Encyclopaedia Judaica***, Volume 10, Column 1182. s.v. Abraham Isaac Kook.

28 Nahum Rakover, ***Eikhut HaSviva: Hebetim Ra'ayoniyim UMishpatiyim BeMekorot HaYehudiyim***. Jerusalem, Moreshet HaMishpat BeYisrael, 1993, p. 14.

29 ***Encyclopaedia Judaica***, Volume 12, Column 774. s.v. Nahmanides.

the earth's mountains, and the like."[30,31] Rozenson claims that Nahmanides has reservations about human mastery over nature and dominion does not preclude large-scale changes to creation. It is difficult to accept this interpretation, however, as the image that Nahmanides' gloss evokes in the readers' minds is very strongly associated with the much later industrial revolution of the nineteenth century, which signifies the very essence of human exploitation of nature.

The following depiction by *Encyclopedia Judaica* illustrates clearly just how important Nahmanides *was*:

> ...Nahmanides' commentary became very popular and has been widely drawn upon by later commentators. Supercommentaries have been written upon it and Kabbalistic treatises have been composed on its Kabbalistic allusions...The commentary of Nahmanides is more than a mere commentary...Nahmanides' halakhic works rank among the masterpieces of rabbinic literature and some of them have become classics...Nahmanides' halakhic writings had a decisive influence on the entire history of subsequent rabbinic literature...In the course of time Nahmanides became such an authority that other author's works were wrongly attributed to him...[32]

It is clear that Nahmanides' glosses cannot be taken lightly. While Cohen admits that "some of Saadya's successors, including Moses Nahmanides and Ovadiah Sforno, also referred to the mechanical devices whereby humans subdued the animals and the earth in their own behalf, as they commented on Gen. 1:28," his reservation is that "most medieval Jewish discussion of the superior human status and its cosmological ramifications ensued without reference to our verse."[33]

While Cohen claims that commentaries belonging to rabbis as Judah HaLevi, David Kimhi, and Isaac Abarbanel are seen "as confirming human superiority

---

30 Rabbi Moses ben Nahman, ***Peirushei HaTorah LeRabbeinu Moshe ben Nahman***. Haim Dov Chavel (ed.), Jerusalem, Mossad HaRav Kook, 1976, p. 28.

31 All translations are my own unless otherwise noted.

32 ***Encyclopedia Judaica***, Column 778.

33 Jeremy Cohen, ***Be Fertile and Increase, Fill the Earth and Master It: The Ancient and Medieval Career of a Biblical Text***. Ithaca, New York, Cornell University Press, 1989, pp. 186-187.

more than as circumscribing human dominion,"[34] this distinction is feeble at best. Human superiority is precisely what allows us to have dominion. Though the list is by no means exhaustive, what follows is a list of other exegetes who have expressed a dominionist theme in their glosses to Genesis 1:26-1:28.

Rabbi Shlomo Yitzhaki (Rashi) (11th century, Northern France)[35] — Genesis 1:26:

> **And they shall have dominion over the fish of the sea**: there is a *double entendre*, one meaning is the word dominion, and the other is descent. If the person is found worthy, he has dominion over the animals, and if not, he becomes lower than the animals and they rule over him."[36]

Rabbi David Kimhi (~1160-1265 Southern France)[37] — Genesis 1:28:

> "...and the simple meaning of the verse is that humans shall rule over the creations of the earth and shall conquer them so as to be under their [human] authority."[38]

Rabbeinu Avraham ben HaRambam (1186-1237, Egypt)[39] — Genesis 1:28:

> ...the second blessing given in the verse is that of dominion, which is hinted at... ***VeKivshuha***: (according to the simple meaning)...which is derived from Jeremiah...[where it is written:]"and he conquered them and made them into slaves.[40,41]

---

34 Ibid. p. 187.

35 ***Encyclopaedia Judaica***, Volume 13, Column 1558. s.v. Rashi.

36 Rabbi Shlomo Yitzhaki, ***Peirushei Rashi al HaTorah***. Haim Dov Chavel (ed.), Jerusalem, Mossad HaRav Kook, 1982, p. 8.

37 ***Encyclopaedia of Great Men in Israel,*** Volume Two, Columns 419-420. s.v. Rabbi David Kimhi (Radak).

38 Rabbi David Kimhi, ***Peirushei Rabbi David Kimhi al HaTorah***, 2nd edition. Moshe Kamlher (ed.), Jerusalem, Mossad HaRav Kook, 1975, p. 22.

39 ***Encyclopaedia Judaica***, Volume 2, Column 150. s.v. Abraham ben Moses ben Maimon.

40 Rabbi Avraham ben HaRambam, ***Peirush Rabbeinu Avraham ben HaRambam Z"L al Bereishit VeShemot***, Saleiman David Sasson (ed.). London, L. Honig and Sons Ltd., 1959, p. 12.

41 It should be noted that Maimonides, in his *Guide to the Perplexed*, stated that it is not the purpose of man to subdue the rest of creation, but rather it is his nature to do so. Rabbi Moses ben Maimon

Rabbi Isaac Abarbanel (1437-1508, Portugal, Spain and Italy)[42] — Genesis 1:26-28:

> ...the Holy One blessed is He wanted the creation of the world in order to subdue the lowly earth and show the dominion of God in the land, and that the man is an officer, a policeman, a governor over the earth from the hand of God and therefore must subdue all the other lowly creatures, because it demonstrates his advantage and intelligence over them and from this advantage he will rule over them.[43]

Rabbi Isaac Caro (~1440-1518, Spain, Portugal and Turkey)[44] — Genesis 1:28:

> ...if God had not made it their nature [to subdue them], then man would not have dominion over them and not be able to control them, because there are animals of a stronger composition than man, such as the lion, the bear, and the leopard/tiger [but in the end man has dominion]."[45]

Later on, in the Noah narrative, Caro reinforces his views on the relationship between humans and nature:

> "...you will rule over them, to hunt them and enslave them and accomplish your labors through them."[46]

Rabbi Avraham Saba (~15th-16th centuries, Spain, Portugal and North Africa)[47] — Genesis 1:26:

(Maimonides), ***Moreh Nevuhim LeRabbeinu Moshe ben Maimon***, Volume Two, 3,13. Michael Schwartz (trans.), David Tzeri (ed.). Jerusalem, Tel-Aviv University Press, 2002, p. 464.

42 ***Encyclopaedia of Great Men in Israel***, Volume Three, Columns 896-897. s.v. Don Yitzhak (ben Rabbi Yehuda) Abarbanel.

43 Rabbi Isaac Abarbanel, ***Peirush al HaTorah — Bereishit***, Jerusalem, Bnei Arbael Publishing, 1964, p. 70.

44 Rabbi Isaac Caro, ***Toledot Yizhak***, Jerusalem, Makor Publishing Ltd., 1978, introduction.

45 *Ibid.* p. 11.

46 *Ibid.* p. 29.

47 ***Encyclopaedia of Great Men in Israel***, Volume One, Columns 81-82. s.v. Rabbi Avraham (ben Rabbi Yaakov) Saba.

...after all of creation was made for him, and he is the intention with the initial thought [of creation], it is fitting that he shall rule [have dominion] over all things, and this is what is meant with "and you shall have dominion over the fish of the sea" and all the other things that were mentioned above.[48]

Rabbi Ovadiah Sforno (~1470-1550 C.E., Italy).[49] — Genesis 1:28:

"***VeKivshuha*** - ...and prevent the animals from entering your domain, and you will rule them...and subdue them with your nets to make them surrender [להכניעם] to your work."[50]

Rabbi Shlomo Ephraim (*Keli Yakar*) (~16th century-1619, Prague)[51] — Genesis 1:26:

"...these are three species which man has the power to rule, each one more than its friend...if man is worthy then he rules them...not only the land animals, but also the birds, and not only the birds which he can see, but also the fish [which he cannot see]."[52]

Though the list of commentaries have by no means been exhausted, it is most likely to yield even more "dominionist" commentaries on the text. The rabbis quoted in this paper, however, are sufficient to observe the way in which the text has been understood throughout a long period of history. They are clearly "dominionist". Furthermore, there are streams within the hermeneutic tradition that are even more extreme in terms of their "domionist" stance: Saadiah Gaon (as seen above), Nahmanides, Rabbi Abraham son of Maimonides, Rabbi Isaac Caro and Rabbi Ovadiah Sforno.

Nahmanides, in addition to his elaborate description of the way in which humans have dominion over the rest of creations on Earth, uses the words

48 Rabbi Avraham Saba, ***Tzror HaMor***, Tel-Aviv, Offset Brody-Katz Publishing, 1975, p. 4.

49 ***Encyclopaedia Judaica***, Volume 14, Column 1209. s.v. Sforno, Ovadiah ben Jacob.

50 Rabbi Ovadiah Sforno, ***Beiur HaSforno al HaTorah***. Zeev Gotleib (ed.), Jerusalem, Mossad HaRav Kook, 1980, p. 16.

51 ***Encyclopaedia of Great Men in Israel***, Volume Four, Columns 1272-1273. s.v. Rabbi Shlomo Ephraim (ben Rabbi Aharon) Ish Luntshitz.

52 Rabbi Shlomo Efraim, ***Keli Yakar — Miqraot Gedolot***, Aharon Samet (ed.), Jerusalem, Mahon HaMaor, 1990, p. 43.

ימשלו בחזקה, which means that humans will have a **strong** dominion over the rest of creation. He also uses a master/slave analogy, calling the language of ***rediya*** as the rule of the master over the slave.[53]

Rabbi Abraham son of Maimonides (Rambam) uses slave imagery from Jeremiah in his comments about the relationship between humanity and creation — ויכבשום לעבדים. The use of slave imagery is particularly potent as it runs deep in the collective memory of Jews.[54]

Rabbi Isaac Caro, in one of his glosses to the Noah narrative uses the words — להשתעבד בהם when referring to the relationship between humans and the natural world.[55] Once again it can be seen that master/slave terminology is being used.

Rabbi Ovadiah Sforno used the words להכניעם לעבודתם, which means that they (i.e. the rest of creation) will surrender to their (i.e. human) works.[56]

It must be stated, however, that to the best of my knowledge nowhere in the Jewish exegetical tradition for Genesis 1:26-28 or anywhere else is there authorization for wanton destruction of nature. The same, unfortunately, cannot be said for everyone speaking on behalf of the Christian tradition. Some fundamentalist rightwing Christian groups such as "Wise Use" have, unfortunately, taken the understanding of these verses to an extreme, and have even gone so far as making statements such as "God gave us these things to use. After the last tree is felled, Christ will come back."[57] Though this statement is extreme and uncommon, it only illustrates a view which believes in expedit-

---

53 Rabbi Moses ben Nahman, ***Peirushei HaTorah LeRabbeinu Moshe ben Nahman***. Haim Dov Chavel (ed.), Jerusalem, Mossad HaRav Kook, 1976, p. 28.

54 Rabbi Avraham ben HaRambam, ***Peirush Rabbeinu Avraham ben HaRambam Z"L al Bereishit VeShemot***, Saleiman David Sasson (ed.). London, L. Honig and Sons Ltd., 1959, p. 12.

55 Rabbi Isaac Caro, ***Toledot Yizhak***, Jerusalem, Makor Publishing Ltd., 1978, p. 29.

56 Rabbi Ovadiah Sforno, ***Beiur HaSforno al HaTorah***. Zeev Gotleib (ed.), Jerusalem, Mossad HaRav Kook, 1980, p. 16.

57 This statement was made by James Watt in Austin Miles, ***Setting the Captives Free: Victims of the Church Tell Their Stories***. Amherst, New York, Prometheus Books, 1990, p. 229. Found in Stephenie Hendricks, ***Divine Destruction: Wise Use, Dominion Theology, and the Making of American Environmental Policy***. Hoboken, New Jersey, Melville House Publishing, 2005, p. 49.

ing the trend for environmental destruction which has existed at least as early as the Industrial Revolution.[58]

David Ehrenfeld and Philip J. Bentley argue that the concept of dominion has simply been misunderstood, and that "[t]here is no evidence that we are aware of that these verses of Genesis were ever interpreted by the Rabbis as a license for environmental exploitation."[59] Clearly, if they had read Nahmanides or Saadiah Gaon, they would not be able to make such a statement. Aloys Hüttermann, would agree with such an analysis, and claims that in order to find the concept of stewardship in Genesis 1:28, one need not look further than Rashi's gloss on the verse.[60] Hüttermann argues that Rashi's gloss, which states that while man has the mandate to dominate, he still must show himself worthy of it or else man himself will be dominated, is very environmental, and any other interpretations of the verse are incorrect. Rashi's gloss could be translated: "if man is worthy then he exploits nature, and if man is unworthy, then nature exploits him."[61] There is no reason to believe that nature exploiting man is environmental, but the text does perhaps allow for such an understanding, when considering natural balances. If one were to use a more popular approach to understanding Genesis 1:26-28, one could end up with the same conclusion as Ellen Bernstein. She states that:

> The blessing of mastery over the earth calls us to exercise compassion and wisdom in our relationship with nature so that the creation will keep on creating for future generations. We use nature every day in every thing we do; nature provides our food, shelter, clothing, energy, electricity, coal, gas. "Mastering"

58 I do not wish to imply that James Watt is by any means the sole representative of Christianity's position on these matters, as this would be patently false. What is important to note here is that groups such as "Wise Use" have enough advocates so as to significantly influence and weaken environmental policy in the U.S.A.

59 David Ehrenfeld and Philip J. Bentley, "Judaism and the Practice of Stewardship," ***Torah of the Earth: Exploring 4,000 Years of Ecology in Jewish Thought, Vol. 1.*** Arthur Waskow (ed.). Woodstock, Vermont, Jewish Lights Publishing, 2000, p. 147.

60 Aloys Hüttermann, ***The Ecological Message of the Torah: Knowledge, Concepts, and Laws which Made Survival in a Land of "Milk and Honey" Possible.*** Atlanta, Georgia, Scholars Press, 1999, pp. 15-18.

61 Rabbi Shlomo Yitzhaki, ***Peirushei Rashi al HaTorah.*** Haim Dov Chavel (ed.), Jerusalem, Mossad HaRav Kook, 1982, p. 8.

> nature involves determining how much land and which animals should be designated for human use and the development of civilization, and what should remain untouched.[62]

Lenn E. Goodman also clearly advocates a stewardship understanding of the blessing of dominion: "...the Jewish tradition has clearly and articulately understood the biblical theme in terms of stewardship."[63]

Nevertheless, it is painstakingly clear that the tradition histories of Genesis 1:26-28 is dominionist. The overwhelming majority of exegetes who have related to the dominion aspect of the verses in their glosses have supported a strong dominionist reading.

BAVLI TRACTATE SANHEDRIN

There is considerable difficulty understanding exactly what the Hebrew word *lirdot* (root RDH) means. It has been commonly translated into English as subdue. This translation is quite accurate. It is reflected by the rabbis own interpretation of Genesis 1:28. There is without a doubt a strong theme of dominion in the medieval glosses. The rabbis in the Talmud, however, seem to be confused over what exactly was meant by the verb RDH.

Benstein states that:

> ...a close reading of the verses reveals the surprising fact that whatever else dominion of the animal kingdom may have meant when the text was originally promulgated, it did not include eating animals...Although no ban on eating meat is explicitly stated here...the affirmation of those things that are permitted fare makes the limitation clear (*Sanhedrin* 59b). And as the next verse attests [Genesis 1:30], this was true of all living things: there was no carnivory in Creation as originally conceived. This condition also implied a deeper affinity or fellowship between humans and other animals than what

62 Ellen Bernstein, ***The Splendor of Creation: A Biblical Ecology***. Cleveland, Ohio, The Pilgrim Press, 2005, p. 114.

63 Lenn E. Goodman, "Respect for Nature in the Jewish Tradition," ***Judaism and Ecology: Created World and Revealed Word***. Hava Tirosh-Samuelson (ed.). Cambridge, Massachusetts, Harvard University Press, 2002, p. 252.

> might be otherwise inferred from the verses on subjugation: here, all humans and animals were on the same side of the knife and fork (and tooth and claw).[64]

While he later on writes that the situation changed after the Deluge, he emphasizes that this was not the initial purpose of creation. This view is widely supported by the rabbinical tradition, and is elaborated upon as early as the Talmud in Bavli Tractate *Sanhedrin*. Even though Rav Yehuda (~ 260 C.E.)[65] in the name of Rav specifically states that there was a prohibition to eat meat at this time, it would have been more correct to state that there was a prohibition to kill animals. This can be seen from Rabbi Yehuda son of Teima's (~ 175 C.E.?)[66] homily (also found in b. *Sanhedrin* 59b) stating that the Ministering Angels (*Malakhei HaSharet*) grilled meats and poured wine for the first human. His argument/homily is reconciled with a statement that the meats being grilled came from heaven, and that no animals were actually killed.

It is clear, however, from the accounts in b. *Sanhedrin* that the rabbis did not have an easy time understanding what might have been meant by the Divine command of having dominion over other living creatures if that command did not also allow for humans to eat/kill these animals.[67] In order to reconcile this issue with their vegetarian reading of the text, they had to come up with far-fetched homilies in order to demonstrate that there are more ways to have dominion over animals than simply eating them. For example, Rehava claimed that men can use fish driven chariots, and Rava son of Rav Huna claims that snakes could have been used by men to bring them precious stones had they not been cursed.[68] Clearly, these stories are not more than mere fanciful folklore. It is curious then that Benstein uses the word "fact" in his acceptance of

---

64 Jeremy Benstein, ***The Way Into Judaism and the Environment***. Woodstock, Vermont, Jewish Lights Publishing, 2006, pp. 44-45.

65 H. L. Strack and G. Stemberger, ***Introduction to the Talmud and Midrash***. Markus Bockmuehl (trans.). Minneapolis, Minnesota, Fortress Press, p. 13.

66 *Ibid.* p. 89.

67 It should be noted that Dietary Laws (*Kashrut*) would not have been an issue at this point, as none existed, and therefore, it should come as no surprise that even though some *Kashrut* issues are brought forward in this passage, they do not pertain to the issue at hand.

68 Babylonian Talmud, *Tractate Sanhedrin*, 59b.

the exegetical tradition of antediluvian vegetarianism. Does he mean that, as a rule, we are to accept homiletics as fact?

What makes the matter even more interesting is that this is one of the passages upon which Saadiah Gaon based his extensive commentary of human dominion over creation. While trying to find justifications for a "vegetarian" reading of scripture, the rabbis of the Talmud ended up elaborating on the ways in which dominion is played out. In other words, the solace that Benstein finds in rabbinical assertions of pre-Deluge vegetarianism is precisely what disturbs him and others regarding some medieval commentaries' interpretation of a strong human dominion over nature. Moreover, it should be stated that as far as the tradition of a strong dominionist reading of the text is concerned, it is not a tradition that only began with Saadiah Gaon, but rather it appeared hundreds of years prior to him in the Talmud. Its appearance in the Talmud, the written version of Jewish oral law, means that likely, the strong dominionist reading of the text has always been a part of Jewish tradition.

GENESIS 2:15

Modern environmentalists have tried to demonstrate that the parallel or second story of creation found in chapter two of Genesis balances out the dominion oriented message found in the first chapter. Eilon Schwartz calls it the "contradictory or complementary command" to Genesis 1:26-28.[69] This section presents a list of both classic and modern exegesis on Genesis 2:15.

MODERN

Ehrenfeld and Bentley claim that Genesis 2:15 has

> ...always been assumed to have a bearing on how the dominion [from Genesis 1:26-28] was to be exercised. In other words, although the "dominion"

69 Eilon Schwartz, "Mastery and Stewardship, Wonder and Connectedness: A Typology of Relations to Nature in Jewish Text and Tradition," ***Judaism and Ecology: Created World and Revealed Word.*** Hava Tirosh-Samuelson (ed.). Cambridge, Massachusetts, Harvard University Press, 2002, p. 94.

phrases of Genesis could have been interpreted in the harsh, exploitative way that some critics suggest, they were never in fact interpreted that way within the Rabbinic tradition.[70]

Similarly, Moshe Zemer claims that Genesis 2:15 "...has served as a guideline throughout the ages."[71] Jonathan Helfand reinforces such a reading by stating that Genesis 2:15 makes it "...apparent that man was not given a license to destroy at will."[72] Norman Lamm even goes so far as to describe Genesis 2:15 as "...a model for ecological health."[73] Daniel Hillel states that Genesis 2:15 shows that "...humanity was not given the license to rule over the environment and use it for its own purposes alone, but — quite the contrary — was charged with the responsibility to nurture and to protect God's creation..."[74] Shirley Wurst claims that "[t]he concept [*leshomera*] denotes careful and close observation — this is attentive and protective tending."[75] Daniel B. Fink contends that "[o]nly here [Genesis 2:15] do we learn what our mastery of the earth and our dominion over the animals actually entails. Genesis 2 defines the mandate set forth in Genesis 1."[76] Shalom Rosenberg

70 David Ehrenfeld and Philip J. Bentley, "Judaism and the Practice of Stewardship," ***Torah of the Earth: Exploring 4,000 Years of Ecology in Jewish Thought, Vol. 1.*** Arthur Waskow (ed.). Woodstock, Vermont, Jewish Lights Publishing, 2000, p. 147.

71 Moshe Zemer, "Ecology as a mitzvah," ***The Environment in Jewish Law: Essays and Responsa.*** Walter Jacob and Moshe Zemer (eds.), New York, Bergahn Books, 2003, p. 24.

72 Jonathan Helfand, "The Earth Is the Lord's: Judaism and Environmental Ethics," ***Torah of the Earth: Exploring 4,000 Years of Ecology in Jewish Thought, Vol. 1.*** Arthur Waskow (ed.). Woodstock, Vermont, Jewish Lights Publishing, 2000, p. 130.

73 Norman Lamm, "Ecology in Jewish Law and Theology," ***Torah of the Earth: Exploring 4,000 Years of Ecology in Jewish Thought, Vol. 1.*** Arthur Waskow (ed.). Woodstock, Vermont, Jewish Lights Publishing, 2000, p. 126.

74 Daniel Hillel, ***The Natural History of the Bible: An Environmental Exploration of the Hebrew Scriptures.*** New York, Columbia University Press, 2006, pp. 242-243.

75 Shirley Wurst, "'Beloved, Come Back to Me': Ground's Theme Song in Genesis 3?" ***The Earth Story in Genesis.*** Norman C. Habel and Shirley Wurst (eds.), Sheffield, England, Sheffield Academic Press, 2000, p. 90.

76 Daniel B. Fink, "Creation, Covenant and Ecology," ***Judaism and Ecology: A Hadassah Study Guide.*** New York, Hadassah the Women's Zionist Organization of America and Shomrei Adamah, 1993, p. 24.

would agree, and he writes that "[w]e are commanded, *le-'ovdah u-leshomrah*, namely, to develop the earth and protect it."[77]

Interestingly, Walter Jacob concedes that Genesis 2:15 is limited to the Garden of Eden, which is indeed the *peshat* (literal meaning) of the verse, but this does not prevent him from claiming that it is actually Genesis 1:28-29 "...that describes how God gave the natural world into the care of human beings."[78] Like Hüttermann, Jacob finds a message of stewardship within the dominion verse. They are joined by Donald B. Sharp who claims that "...[humankind] was to exercise stewardship (*radah, kabaŝ*) over all of the other living creatures and the earth itself...Humankind's role as the steward of creation encompassed all of God's creative work."[79] The common understanding of Genesis 2:15 by modern environmentalists, though, goes beyond the *peshat*. Evan Eisenberg writes that "[t]hese tasks [*le'ovda and leshomera*] were not just for our brief tenure in Eden, but for the whole span of our stay on earth."[80] Though most modern environmental commentaries on Genesis 2:15 do not make this statement in such explicit terms as Eisenberg, it is clear that most subscribe to this understanding of the text.

Martin Palmer even claims that "[i]n the Judaeo-Christian tradition at its best, humanity is seen as being a steward to God."[81] Unfortunately, he does not go on to substantiate his claims. Later on in his book, Palmer uses the classic juxtaposition of Genesis 1:26-28 and 2:15 claiming that "...the core of Jewish belief about this is that God gave humanity authority over nature. And this

77 Shalom Rosenberg, "Concepts of Torah and Nature in Jewish Thought," ***Judaism and Ecology: Created World and Revealed Word***. Hava Tirosh-Samuelson (ed.). Cambridge, Massachusetts, Harvard University Press, 2002, p. 220.

78 Walter Jacob, "Eco-Judaism — Does it Exist?" ***The Environment in Jewish Law: Essays and Responsa***. Walter Jacob and Moshe Zemer (eds.), New York, Bergahn Books, 2003, p. 9.

79 Donald B. Sharp, "A Biblical Foundation for an Environmental Theology: A New Perspective on Genesis 1:26-28 and 6:11-13," ***Science et Esprit***. Vol. 47, 1995, p. 306.

80 Evan Eisenberg, "The Ecology of Eden," ***Judaism and Ecology: Created World and Revealed Word***. Hava Tirosh-Samuelson (ed.). Cambridge, Massachusetts, Harvard University Press, 2002, p. 49.

81 Martin Palmer, ***Genesis or Nemesis: Belief, Meaning and Ecology***. London, England, Dryad Press Limited, 1988, p. 26.

brings with it responsibilities."[82] Jeremy Benstein even offers an interpretation of the verse to be "sustainable development."[83] Certainly such interpretations are in line with the environmental movement, sustainable development being one of its great slogans, but are they congruent with the tradition histories of the verse? The only person to raise considerable interest was Eric Rosenblum. He claimed that "[s]ome commentators even hold that this commandment [Genesis 1:28] is superseded entirely by the instructions in the following chapter to till and keep (*le-avdah ul-shamrah*) [*sic*] the Garden of Eden."[84] It turns out, however, that his source was Michael Lerner, who brings forth no tradition commentaries, but rather states that:

> There are some in the ecology movement who have misread the Torah and believe that the Jewish tradition calls for the conquest or domination of nature. This is false. Torah calls on us to work with it and to protect it, *le'avdoe ule'shomroe* [*sic*].[85]

While it was a slight disappointment that no traditional commentaries were quoted, it comes as little surprise. Lerner is yet another clear example of a modern environmental interpretation of Genesis 2:15.

Although more the anomaly than the rule, there do appear to be a number of sources which indicate some level of environmental awareness in the interpretive tradition histories of Genesis 2:15.

CLASSIC

Rabbi David ben Amram (*Midrash HaGadol*) (13th century, Aden, Yemen):[86]

---

82 *Ibid.* p. 134.

83 Jeremy Benstein, ***The Way Into Judaism and the Environment***. Woodstock, Vermont, Jewish Lights Publishing, 2006, p. 49.

84 Eric Rosenblum, "Is Gaia Jewish?" ***Judaism and Environmental Ethics: A Reader***. Martin D. Yaffe (ed.). New York, Lexington Books, 2001, p. 189.

85 Michael Lerner, ***Jewish Renewal: A Path to Healing and Transformation***. New York, G. P. Putnam's Sons, 1994, p. 328.

86 Rabbi David ben Amram, ***Midrash HaGadol: Sefer Bereishit***, Mordechai Margaliot (ed.). Jerusalem, Mossad HaRav Kook, p. 10.

> *LeOvda ULeShomera*: "And what was the need for work and preservation, for there was everything until man was created? Rather, to work in Torah and keep her commandments..."[87]

It is not the homiletic conclusion that is of interest in *Midrash HaGadol*, but the question that precedes it. The message of the midrash is once humans come into the picture, there is indeed a need to preserve the earth. While it certainly is not the author's central message, it indicates an awareness of the impact humanity has on Earth's resources.[88]

Rabbi Isaac Abarbanel:

> "...and the Holy Blessed One took the human and created him from meager dust and placed him in the Garden of Eden to till it and watch over it, and not be master and patron over it."[89]

Abarbanel interprets Genesis 2:15 as an indicator that humans indeed do not have the final say over creation, as one might have thought from the reading of Genesis 1:28. Instead, he sees the position of humanity, at least in the context of the Garden of Eden as being a guardian of creation. Understanding Abarbanel's commentary in the context of a comparative reading of the two verses, one can see that Abarbanel has a weak domionist stance.

Rabbi Abraham son of Rambam:

> "*LeShomera*: I wish I knew (*LeShomera*) from whom, from the animals who do not speak, or from himself..."[90]

This is a curious interpretation by the son of the Rambam. He exhibits a relatively high degree of environmental awareness, insofar as he knows that human tendency is to foul up the earth. In other words, it can be understood from his statement that he is aware that the Garden of Eden needs to be protected

---

87 *Ibid.* p. 83.

88 When tested against the references in the critical edition of *Midrash HaGadol*, it is clear that the environmental aspect of Rabbi David ben Amram's gloss is his own.

89 Rabbi Isaac Abarbanel, ***Peirush al HaTorah — Bereishit***, Jerusalem, Bnei Arbael Publishing, 1964, p. 93.

90 Rabbi Avraham ben HaRambam, ***Peirush Rabbeinu Avraham ben HaRambam Z"L al Bereishit VeShemot***, Saleiman David Sasson (ed.). London, L. Honig and Sons Ltd., 1959, p. 38.

from humans. The way he approaches the text is particularly enlightening for the modern environmental reader, as there is a strong indication that he, too, was struggling to understand whether or not the meaning of the text did indeed refer to human impact on the environment. Whereas today's environmentalist might not hesitate to attribute such a meaning to the text, the son of Rambam is somewhat more cautious. He only wishes he knew, but does have some idea that the verse may indeed be referring to the impact of humans on the environment. He, however, shows restraint in terms of making a final judgment on the verse's meaning. His inconclusiveness is more likely the product of erudite hesitation as opposed to true ignorance.

Pesikta Zutarta (late 11th century, Bulgaria)[91]:

> "Is not the word "garden" (*gan*) masculine? Rather, to till and to tend (*LeOvda ULeShomera* [which are feminine]) refers to the earth of the garden [which is also feminine]."[92]

By asking a grammatical question, *Pesikta Zutarta* addresses the matter from a new angle. His question is valid and his conclusion ends up allowing for a more environmentally oriented reading of the text. He concludes that the verse must be referring to something feminine, and the most logical answer would be "*adama*" or earth, gendered feminine in Hebrew as oppose to the masculine gendered "*gan*". This results in a more environmentally oriented reading, because it means there is now a call to preserve not only the garden but also the earth itself.

Rabbi Bahya Ibn Paquda (~10th-11th Century, Spain)[93]:

> God placed man in the garden of Eden to till and to tend, and to use the rest of the animals for his benefit, and his food, and the building of empires, and the preparation of food, and to use women for procreative purposes. Then he will

---

91 ***Encyclopaedia of Great Men in Israel***, Volume Two, Column 565. s.v. Rabbeinu Tuvia ben Rabbi Eliezer.

92 Rabbeinu Tuvia ben Rabbi Eliezer, ***Midrash Lekah Tov HaMehuneh Pesikta Zutarta al Hamisha Humshei Torah***. Shlomo Baber (ed.). Israel, Books Export Enterprises Ltd., (1900's), p. 20.

93 ***Encyclopaedia of Great Men in Israel***, Volume One, Columns 259-260. s.v. Rabbeinu Bahya (ben Rabbi Yosef) Ibn Paquda.

receive merit for his intentions in the name of God in his heart and thoughts, whether he achieved his goals or not.[94]

Ibn Paquda illustrates that it is even possible to read Genesis 2:15 as reinforcing the concept of dominion. Though his interpretation seems to be anomalous, it goes head to head with the stewardship readings of the verse. While it is clear that the modern interpretations of the verse are eisegesis *par excellence*, Ibn Paquda's gloss demonstrates that the tradition histories of the verse can go either way.

As is evident, there is but little tradition of environmental interpretation for Genesis 2:15. Finding the above sources required sifting through dozens of others. It is difficult to argue that there is a tradition of interpreting the verse in an environmental light. Nevertheless, it draws attention to the above commentaries, and begs for a deeper reading of their works. The most common interpretations, however, were mostly homilies. *LeOvda ULeShomera* was interpreted as observing the Sabbath and ritual sacrifices.[95] While this *midrash* was originally found in *Bereishit Rabah*, it has been borrowed extensively and the Sabbath is sometimes replaced with the Torah and its commandments.

It is impossible to deny that Genesis 1:28 has rich tradition histories of humanity having a strong dominion over nature. Genesis 2:15, though, does not boast the strong environmental reading that modern environmentalists have claimed. That is not to say that Genesis 2:15 has not received ample attention over the course of history. As mentioned above, the tradition has focused on references to observing the commandments and studying the Talmud or Torah. The evidence points to the environmental understanding of Genesis 2:15 to be largely the work of eisegesis. One could argue that the lack of an environmental hermeneutic to this verse is an embarrassment, and that this is what inspired the modern environmental reading of the verse.

94 Rabbi Bahya Ibn Paquda, ***Sefer Hovot HaLevavot.*** Yosef Kapah (ed. and trans.). Jerusalem, Akiva Yosef Publishers, 1973, p. 207. (HaSha'ar HaRevi'i, Sha'ar HaBitahon, Pereq Gimel). Ibn Paquda's misogynist stance is indicative of the rabbinic view of women, and does not come as a surprise.

95 ***Midrash Bereshit Rabba.*** J. Theodor and Chanoch Albeck (ed.). Jerusalem, Wahrman Books, 1965, p.149.

The Jewish tradition appears to be rich in environmental messages. This is obvious to the modern environmental reader. While it would seem that White was correct in his understanding of Genesis 1:28 or at least consistent with a predominant perception of it, it has been pointed out multiple times that his arguments were too narrowly defined. There is much more to the Jewish and Christian traditions than this one verse. Ilana Stein discusses Genesis 1:28 side by side with Genesis 2:15.[96] Stein is far from being alone in what is becoming a classic comparison. For instance, Mark G. Brett claims that Genesis 2:15 "...effectively revers[es] the vocation to rule and to subdue the earth."[97] This is an indication that it has become the norm to compare these two elements within the creation narratives.

It is now apparent, though, that a simple juxtaposition of the parallel stories of creation will not suffice to win a historical environmental battle or debate. As a result, this paper comes to three conclusions. The first is that Lynn White Jr. must be divorced from the Jewish environmental discourse. While he can certainly be considered a catalyst to the field as a whole, the responses that he has elicited have been on the whole (though not exclusively) ideologically motivated, replete with embarrassment, and as a result, are left with ample room for deconstruction. Once White Jr. is cut out, the text and traditions can be approached in a more academic manner. For example, Jeremy Benstein's book titled *The Way into Judaism and the Environment*, devotes large sections of his book to discussing the impact of White on Jewish environmental scholarship and analyzing his arguments. This paper, however, aims to point out that the way into Judaism and the environment is not through Lynn White Jr.

The second conclusion is that historically, there are other narratives that are much more forthright in their environmental message. This is not to take away from the modern readings of the Genesis 2:15, but rather to point the readers to other sources that have a much richer tradition of being interpreted environmentally, such as *Bal Tashhit* (Do not destroy). This has been done in

96 Ilana Stein, "*Le'ovda Uleshomra: Judaism and the Environmental Ethic*," Yitzchak Breitowitz (ed.). in ***Compendium of Sources in Halacha and the Environment*** 5766, Ora Sheinson and Shai Spetgang (eds.), Jerusalem, Canfei Nesharim Publication, 2005, pp. 16-17.

97 Mark G. Brett, "Earthing the Human in Genesis 1-3," ***The Earth Story in Genesis***. Norman C. Habel and Shirley Wurst (eds.), Sheffield, England, Sheffield Academic Press, 2000, p. 80.

the past,[98] but the analysis has been mostly superficial and popular. It detracts from the Jewish environmental cause to remain caught up in popular arguments without the substantiation of an in-depth investigation.

Finally, modern environmentalists should be lauded for rekindling and re-embracing the hermeneutic tradition of Genesis 2:15 and providing the world with a new and perhaps more correct understanding of this verse for our time. This should not, however, fall prey to hermeneutic paralysis because of embarrassment, rather what is truly needed is a genuine in-depth critical analysis of the Jewish texts and traditions in light of environmental knowledge.

BIBLIOGRAPHY

Babylonian Talmud, ***Tractate Sanhedrin***, 59b.

Benstein, Jeremy. ***The Way Into Judaism and the Environment.*** Woodstock, Vermont, Jewish Lights Publishing, 2006, pp. 1-53.

Bernstein, Ellen. ***The Splendor of Creation: A Biblical Ecology***. Cleveland, Ohio, The Pilgrim Press, 2005, pp. 91-121.

Brett, Mark G. "Earthing the Human in Genesis 1-3," ***The Earth Story in Genesis***.

Norman C. Habel and Shirley Wurst (eds.), Sheffield, England, Sheffield Academic Press, 2000, pp. 73-86.

Cohen, Jeremy. ***Be Fertile and Increase, Fill the Earth and Master It: The Ancient and Medieval Career of a Biblical Text***. Ithaca, New York, Cornell University Press, 1989, pp. 1-18, 183-187.

98 See for example ***Judaism and Ecology: A Hadassah Study Guide***. New York, Hadassah the Women's Zionist Organization of America and Shomrei Adamah,1993.

Ehrenfeld, David and Philip J. Bentley. "Judaism and the Practice of Stewardship," ***Torah of the Earth: Exploring 4,000 Years of Ecology in Jewish Thought, Vol. 1.*** Arthur Waskow (ed.). Woodstock, Vermont, Jewish Lights Publishing, 2000, pp. 141-156.

Eisenberg, Evan. "The Ecology of Eden," ***Judaism and Ecology: Created World and Revealed Word.*** Hava Tirosh-Samuelson (ed.). Cambridge, Massachusetts, Harvard University Press, 2002, pp. 27-59.

Fink, Daniel B. "Creation, Covenant and Ecology," ***Judaism and Ecology: A Hadassah Study Guide.*** New York, Hadassah the Women's Zionist Organization of America and Shomrei Adamah, 1993, pp. 20-33.

Frymer-Kensky, Tikva. "Ecology in a Biblical Perspective." ***Torah of the Earth: Exploring 4,000 Years of Ecology in Jewish Thought, Vol. 1.*** Arthur Waskow (ed.). Woodstock, Vermont, Jewish Lights Publishing, 2000, pp. 55-69.

Gerstenfeld, Manfred. ***Judaism, Environmentalism and the Environment: Mapping and Analysis.*** Jerusalem, The Jerusalem Institute for Israel Studies, Rubin Mass Ltd., 1998.

Goodman, Lenn E. "Respect for Nature in the Jewish Tradition," ***Judaism and Ecology: Created World and Revealed Word.*** Hava Tirosh-Samuelson (ed.). Cambridge, Massachusetts, Harvard University Press, 2002, pp. 227-259.

Helfand, Jonathan. "The Earth Is the Lord's: Judaism and Environmental Ethics," ***Torah of the Earth: Exploring 4,000 Years of Ecology in Jewish Thought, Vol. 1.*** Arthur Waskow (ed.). Woodstock, Vermont, Jewish Lights Publishing, 2000, pp. 127-140.

Hillel, Daniel. ***The Natural History of the Bible: An Environmental Exploration of the Hebrew Scriptures.*** New York, Columbia University Press, 2006, pp. 242-243.

Hüttermann, Aloys. ***The Ecological Message of the Torah: Knowledge, Concepts, and Laws which Made Survival in a Land of "Milk and Honey" Possible***. Atlanta, Georgia, Scholars Press, 1999, pp. 7-22.

Jacob, Walter. "Eco-Judaism — Does it Exist?" ***The Environment in Jewish Law: Essays and Responsa***. Walter Jacob and Moshe Zemer (eds.), New York, Bergahn Books, 2003, pp. 1-23.

Lamm, Norman. "Ecology in Jewish Law and Theology," ***Torah of the Earth: Exploring 4,000 Years of Ecology in Jewish Thought, Vol. 1.*** Arthur Waskow (ed.). Woodstock, Vermont, Jewish Lights Publishing, 2000, pp. 103-126.

Lerner, Michael. ***Jewish Renewal: A Path to Healing and Transformation***. New York, G. P. Putnam's Sons, 1994, p. 328.

Loevinger, Neal Joseph. "(Mis)reading Genesis: A Response to Environmentalist Critiques of Judaism," ***Ecology and the Jewish Spirit: Where Nature and the Sacred Meet***. Ellen Bernstein (ed.). Woodstock, Vermont, Jewish Lights Publishing, 1998, pp. 32-40.

Margaliot, Mordechai (ed.). ***Encyclopaedia of Great Men in Israel***, Tel-Aviv, Yavneh Publishing House Ltd., 1973.

Miles, Austin. ***Setting the Captives Free: Victims of the Church Tell Their Stories***. Amherst, New York, Prometheus Books, 1990, p. 229. Found in Stephenie Hendricks, ***Divine Destruction: Wise Use, Dominion Theology, and the Making of American Environmental Policy***. Hoboken, New Jersey, Melville House Publishing, 2005.

Palmer, Martin. ***Genesis or Nemesis: Belief, Meaning and Ecology***. London, England, Dryad Press Limited, 1988, pp. 24-26, 133-138.

Rakover, Nahum. ***Eikhut HaSviva: Hebetim Ra'ayoniyim UMishpatiyim BeMekorot HaYehudiyim***. Jerusalem, Moreshet HaMishpat BeYisrael, 1993, pp. 13-19.

Rosenberg, Shalom. "Concepts of Torah and Nature in Jewish Thought," ***Judaism and Ecology: Created World and Revealed Word.*** Hava Tirosh-Samuelson (ed.). Cambridge, Massachusetts, Harvard University Press, 2002, pp. 189-225.

Rosenblum, Eric. "Is Gaia Jewish?" ***Judaism and Environmental Ethics: A Reader***. Martin D. Yaffe (ed.). New York, Lexington Books, 2001, pp. 183-205.

Roth, Cecil (ed.). ***Encyclopaedia Judaica***, Jerusalem, Keter Publishing House, 3rd edition, 1974.

Rozenson, Israel. ***VeHineh Tov Meod.*** Jerusalem, Yeshivat Beit Orot, 2001, p. 29.

Schwartz, Eilon. "Mastery and Stewardship, Wonder and Connectedness: A Typology of Relations to Nature in Jewish Text and Tradition," ***Judaism and Ecology: Created World and Revealed Word.*** Hava Tirosh-Samuelson (ed.). Cambridge, Massachusetts, Harvard University Press, 2002, pp. 93-106.

Sharp, Donald B. "A Biblical Foundation for an Environmental Theology: A New Perspective on Genesis 1:26-28 and 6:11-13," ***Science et Esprit***. Vol. 47, 1995, pp. 305-313.

Stein, Ilana. "*Le'ovda Uleshomra: Judaism and the Environmental Ethic,*" Yitzchak

Breitowitz (ed.). in ***Compendium of Sources in Halacha and the Environment*** 5766, Ora Sheinson and Shai Spetgang (eds.), Jerusalem, Canfei Nesharim Publication, 2005, pp. 16-20.

Strack, H. L. and G. Stemberger, ***Introduction to the Talmud and Midrash.*** Markus Bockmuehl (trans.). Minneapolis, Minnesota, Fortress Press, pp. 13, 89.

White Jr., Lynn. "The Historical Roots of Our Ecological Crisis," ***Science.*** Vol. 155, 1967, pp. 1203-1207.

Wurst, Shirley. "'Beloved, Come Back to Me': Ground's Theme Song in Genesis 3?" ***The Earth Story in Genesis.*** Norman C. Habel and Shirley Wurst (eds.), Sheffield, England, Sheffield Academic Press, 2000, pp. 87-104.

Wybrow, Cameron. ***The Bible, Baconianism, and Mastery over Nature: The Old Testament and its Modern Misreading.*** New York, Peter Lang Publishing Inc., 1991, pp. 3-35, 197-207.

Yaffe, Martin D. "Introduction," ***Judaism and Environmental Ethics: A Reader.*** Martin D. Yaffe (ed.). New York, Lexington Books, 2001, pp. 1-70.

Zemer, Moshe. "Ecology as a mitzvah," ***The Environment in Jewish Law: Essays and Responsa.*** Walter Jacob and Moshe Zemer (eds.), New York, Bergahn Books, 2003, p. 24-33.

CLASSIC BIBLICAL COMMENTARIES

Midrash Bereshit Rabba. J. Theodor and Chanoch Albeck (ed.). Jerusalem, Wahrman Books, 1965, p. 149.

Rabbi Isaac Abarbanel, ***Peirush al HaTorah — Bereishit***, Jerusalem, Bnei Arbael Publishing, 1964, p. 93.

Rabbi David ben Amram, ***Midrash HaGadol: Sefer Bereishit***, Mordechai Margaliot (ed.). Jerusalem, Mossad HaRav Kook, p. 83.

Rabbi Isaac Caro, ***Toledot Yizhak***, Jerusalem, Makor Publishing Ltd., 1978, p. 11.

Rabbi Shlomo Efraim, ***Keli Yakar — Miqraot Gedolot***, Aharon Samet (ed.), Jerusalem, Mahon HaMaor, 1990, p. 43.

Rabbeinu Tuvia ben Rabbi Eliezer, ***Midrash Lekah Tov HaMehuneh Pesikta Zutarta al Hamisha Humshei Torah.*** Shlomo Baber (ed.). Israel, Books Export Enterprises Ltd., (1900's), p. 20.

Rabbi David Kimhi, ***Peirushei Rabbi David Kimhi al HaTorah***, 2nd edition. Moshe Kamlher (ed.), Jerusalem, Mossad HaRav Kook, 1975, p. 22.

Rabbi Moses ben Maimon (Maimonides), ***Moreh Nevuhim LeRabbeinu Moshe ben Maimon***, Volume Two. Michael Schwartz (trans.), David Tzeri (ed.). Jerusalem, Tel-Aviv University Press, 2002, p. 464.

Rabbi Moses ben Nahman, ***Peirushei HaTorah LeRabbeinu Moshe ben Nahman.*** Haim Dov Chavel (ed.), Jerusalem, Mossad HaRav Kook, 1976, p. 28.

Rabbi Bahya Ibn Paquda, ***Sefer Hovot HaLevavot.*** Yosef Kapah (ed. and trans.). Jerusalem, Akiva Yosef Publishers, 1973, p. 207. (HaSha'ar HaRevi'i, Sha'ar HaBitahon, Pereq Gimel).

Rabbi Avraham ben HaRambam, ***Peirush Rabbeinu Avraham ben HaRambam Z"L al Bereishit VeShemot***, Saleiman David Sasson (ed.). London, L. Honig and Sons Ltd., 1959, p. 12.

Saadiah Gaon, ***Rav Saadya's Commentary on Exodus.*** Yehuda Ratzaby (ed. and trans.), Jerusalem, Mossad HaRav Kook, 1998.

Rav Saadiah Gaon, ***Peirushei Rav Saadiah Gaon LeBereishit***. Moshe Tzuker (ed.). Israel, Daf-Chen Press, 1984, pp. 250, 258-259.

Saadiah Gaon, ***Rabbi Saadiah Gaon's Commentary on the Book of Creation***. Michael Linetzky (ed. and trans.), Northvale, New Jersey, Jason Aronson Inc., pp. 106, 113-115.

Rabbi Avraham Saba, ***Tzror HaMor***, Tel-Aviv, Offset Brody-Katz Publishing, 1975, p. 4.

Rabbi Ovadiah Sforno, ***Beiur HaSforno al HaTorah***. Zeev Gotleib (ed.), Jerusalem, Mossad HaRav Kook, 1980, p. 16.

Rabbi Shlomo Yitzhaki, ***Peirushei Rashi al HaTorah***. Haim Dov Chavel (ed.), Jerusalem, Mossad HaRav Kook, 1982, p. 8.

WEBSITES

Adam VaAdamah: www.av-a.org

Aish HaTora: http://www.aish.com/tubshvat/tubshvatinterests/Judaism_and_the_Environment.asp

The Coalition on the Environment and Jewish Life: www.coejl.org

The Eco Activist Beit Midrash: www.shlomoyeshiva.org/eco

Hazon: www.Hazon.org

The Teva Learning Center: www.tevacenter.org

VIXENS DISTURBING VINEYARDS: WHY FOX'S EMBRACEMENT OF SCRIPTURES CAN BE EMBARRASSING

Afterword by Aubrey Glazer

I recall vividly how embarrassed I was after having agreed to respond to a panel of esteemed scholars (some of whom were my teachers) at a recent panel on *Embarrassment of Scriptures* at the American Academy of Religion in Chicago. So why all the embarrassment? After all we were in a pleasant hotel and not dropped off into some seedy motel that might figure into the renowned local play like David Mamet's *Sexual Perversity in Chicago*! In trying to unravel the looming embarrassment in that moment, straddling Freud and Maimonides, I hope to share an afterword to this wonderful and long overdue *Festschrift*, dedicated to my dear friend and teacher, Harry Fox (*leBeit Yoreh*).

So why all that embarrassment quelling up in Chicago? To begin with, who really wants to act as the respondent to such an embarrassing situation — there were moments during many of the papers presented, outstanding as they were, where I must admit that I was dreaming! Contrary to what some might think, this does not mean being caught unawares in a *reverie*, rather dreaming is actually a sign of real insight being shared by those gathered. There were indeed a few moments where I was out of the conference room while in an *isthmus*, that nexus somewhere between imagination and reality! After all, having just passed by the fabled guru of religion, J. Z. Smith in the hallways I was reminded of his clarion call to all students of religion, that "...there is no data for religion. Religion is solely the creation of the scholar's study. It is created for the scholar's analytic purposes by his imaginative acts of comparison and generalization. Religion has no independent existence apart from the academy."[1] I remember my reaction to first hearing about this take on religion while a student at the Jewish Theological Seminary of America. I was at once liberated and embarrassed. Liberated, in realizing that we are more than co-authors but creators of a given religious construct within a community; and embarrassed, in thinking how much time I had spent pontificating about whether revelation was a 50/50 split between the divine/human matrix or something else altogether!

So despite any misgivings, I had still agreed to come to that panel as long as I was permitted to wear an extra layer of clothing. Why? To obviate any ensuing "paralysis". Of course, even on a panel at the American Academy of Religion in Chicago, it quickly became clear that we could neither escape the embarrassment of [Fox,] Freud nor Maimonides.

Everyone recalls that classic case of paralysis from Freud's embarrassment over his own dream in a letter he penned to Wilhelem Fliess of 1897. In that *locus classicus* for psychoanalytic thinking, Freud recounts going up a staircase wearing very few clothes and upon encountering a women, he then felt "glued to the spot…paralyzed!" What concerns us is how Freud then returns to the initial embarrassment of this dream when interpretation time comes in 1900, only to become part of the classic, *Interpretation of Dreams.* Just as the anxiety dream of falling is only one form of descent dreams, so these nakedness dreams are only one form of embarrassment dreams.[2] Freud read his own dream of nakedness as fulfilling an exhibitionistic wish identical in everyone. Any critical thinker — whether a psychoanalyst or scholar of religion — should be poised to question how a particular dream moves from being typical to becoming universal. And most importantly, such *Sexualwissenschaft* should never reduce the imaginal to the sexual, but see how the sexual is also an activity of the imagination, that indeed "the sexual is a way the soul speaks."[3] Such embarrassment can be a reaction to the dreamer's impulses or

1 See J.Z. Smith, *Imagining Religion: From Babylon to Jonestown*, The University of Chicago Press, Chicago, p. xi

2 See Leon J. Saul, "Embarrassment Dreams of Nakedness," *The International Journal of Psychoanalysis*, 1966.

3 See James Hillman, "Sexualwissenschaft," The Myth of Analysis, Northwestern University, Illinois, 1972, p. 141

it can be a response to external situations. Now we are better poised to understand Fox's reading strategy that begins with primal embarrassment — that inwardly felt emotion outwardly directed. Rather than undergoing Freudian displacement and substitutions, Fox is suggesting a re-embracement. Why is this move so crucial?

The volume before you is testimony to the urgency of re-embracing scriptures in the contemporary moment. On the one hand, it is urgent because religion today (even if only a creation of the academy) is being eclipsed, as the godlessness of the village atheists tops the best-seller lists. Feasibly, if a culture is continuously turning to Dawkins, Hitchens & Harris (not actually a law firm, no these are indeed the village atheists!) for its truths on religion, then we will soon be living in a deeply impoverished state. Not merely because "holy names are lacking" as the poet Hölderlin once decried, but a deeper disconnection seems to be operative in a culture turning to secularism and politics as its new religion.

On the other hand, when I say urgent, it really is a matter of life and death, seeing how the Sages already warned that embarrassing anyone publicly is akin to murder. So to begin with, we should all be embarrassed by the pleasure of re-embracement — regardless of how brilliant — as a kind of death. But it is precisely that death which rebirths the reading of Scriptures that is so exciting, dare I say, urgent in our time.

On that AAR panel, we had the pleasure of hearing from diverse scholars all engaged in a re-embracement of scriptures. That panel, as well as these authors, are trailblazing in their collective awe of tradition combined with critical thinking. What became apparent both to those gathered to hear that panel as well as with a few of the authors included in this volume, is that despite a courageous balancing act, embarrassment becomes just too embarrassing. For certain scholars, admitting that embarrassment is the driving force behind their critical scholarship becomes tantamount to unfair critique, which results in apologetics. Apologetics, once in vogue, especially for Medievals, seems to be undergoing a re-embrace of its own within a specific niche of the scholarly world. Scholars may indeed find themselves too bound by *doxa* in their private practice of religion to be able to fully critique religion in the academy (a few notable and courageous exceptions in this volume merit mention, like

Yaakov Elman and Dov Friedberg). But regarding those scholars who cannot manage the balance, *what can I say?*

I am utterly embarrassed by their embarrassment.

But in the spirit of Fox's *ahavat hinam*, his hallmark senseless, poet*hi*cal love,[4] we have sought to re-embrace these fallen moments (despite the apologetics) in the service of higher scholarship. But let there be no misunderstanding on this point — embarrassment and re-embracement are by no means a dogma, rather these reading strategies remain a cornerstone of any viable religion.

Not having any desire whatsoever to embarrass a beloved friend and teacher, but feeling a need to inspire further re-embracement, Fox should be lauded for his years of inspiring us all to take that primal embarrassment — that inwardly felt emotion outwardly directed — into this project of re-embracement. While Harold Bloom swerves and avoids issues of embarrassment, going directly to the jugular of anxiety in his brilliant mapping of influence,[5] we need to pause and appreciate the masterful revelation of Fox. More than merely peeking through the latticework of contemporary literary criticism and being content with Freudian anxiety, Fox dares to strip away at the palimpsest of canons with his own hands, peeling back to the vast corpus of rabbinic literature to contemporary Hebrew poetry as Scripture(s). Anyone who has studied with master teachers, like Fox and Meacham, knows intimately that moment of insight as being nothing short of revelatory. Many scholars can attest to this reality (as embarrassing as it might seem to some).

Let us then reflect for a moment about the embarrassment and re-embracement so deeply embedded in revelation itself.

How unique could this revelation be if as the *midrash* claims, Torah was shopped around to other nations, rejected by all, except Israel? What kind of chosenness is that? It seems to evoke less of a theology of chosenness as "My treasured possession" (*'am segulah*)[6] and more akin to Israeli poet, Aharon

4 See Harry Fox, Preface: Poet*hi*cs: How Every Poet is a Jew, " *How Hebrew Poetry Thinks*, Edward Mellen Press (forthcoming 2009).

5 See Harold Bloom, *The Anxiety of Influence: A Theory of Poetry*, Oxford University Press 1997.

6 For example, see Ex. 19: 5, Deut. 7:6, 14:2, 26:18, etc.

Shabbetai's poetics of neglect as "disgusting people" (*'am megula*). Or think of the embarrassment surrounding Ezekiel's neo-revelations, so steeped in their mystical shapings of the godhead, that the Sages must downgrade its power — recall that even a handmaiden at the Reed Sea saw more than Ezekiel in his height of envisioning!

Re-embrace can then take place in all its glorious belatedness by a Hasidic master like *Hiddushai ha-Rim*,[7] who sees every last human being, regardless of status, to have been included on the special moment of revelation with intention. There is nothing to be embarrassed about in the list preceding the covenant ceremony in Exodus or Deuteronomy — or is there? What begins in the Elohistic authorship of Exodus 19 as a revelation open to all men and women is quickly misunderstood by Moses. Preparing for the theophany through abstinence does not preclude both genders from receiving Torah, even though the Sages have to later explain scripture[8] as referring to *men* ("the children of Israel") as well as *women* ("the House of Jacob")! Yet the Moses of scripture already seems to confuse the invitation by adding the prohibition "do not go near a woman,"[9] just as he did at the waters of *Meribah*[10] — taking too many liberties with the divine word.

Adding insult to injury, the Deuteronomistic authorship seeks to ameliorate the perceived exclusivity of the earlier revelation, so now the scope reaches to even menial laborers, from "wood-chopper and water-drawer".[11] It is indeed embarrassing to those scholars who like to read the content of revelation solely as a particularistic form of covenant paralleling a vassal treaty, whereby a king protects his treasured subjects. Who could possibly see the uniqueness of revelation if it includes even these rabble rousers?

So for a brilliant re-embrace of the *Hiddushai ha-Rim* to be possible, this later Hasidic misreading needs to be embarrassed by an earlier embarrassment (from E to Dtr) so that the presence of "wood-chopper and water-drawer" at revelation completely inverts the notion of social status. The embarrassment

7 R. Isaac Meir Rothenberg (1799-1866).

8 Ex. 19: 3.

9 Ex. 19:15.

10 Num. 20.

11 Deut. 29: 10.

over status is now re-embraced in the height of *mis*reading as subtle typologies, i.e. "wood-choppers" are the iconoclasts like Abraham or the Kotsker Rebbe[12] who discovered God in the burning/illumining tower or *bira ha'doleket*[13]now need a canon that expands with their discoveries; whereas the "water-drawers" are the traditionalists like Ezra or Harold Bloom, who seek to keep every drop of tradition in the bucket to limit the canon by staying within the realm of safe, strong readers.

If revelation were not in need of re-embracement, then surely there is a need for that central vixen of the biblical narrative so often seen as the paragon of redemption — King David. David's endless faults, however, beyond being whitewashed by the rabbis, lead down a strange and dangerous road of re-embracement through the vineyards of mystical literature, culminating in the fallen messianism of "David the son of Jesse, higher than the kings of the earth, who was raised up on high, above all blessing and praise… the celestial lion and stag, Sabbetai S̱evi."[14] So even amidst re-embracement, further checks and balances are necessary, as Fox already mentioned regarding the first line of embarrassment.[15]

In closing by way of closing this glorious volume, let me express a heartfelt thanks to my diligent co-editors (Miryam Segal, Tzemah Yoreh and Justin Jaron Lewis) as well as extending our gratitude to all the students, disciples and colleagues of Harry that have shared and now dedicated the fruits of their scholarly labors with that wily fox in the vineyard. The palimpsest of voices collected in this *Festschrift* are all vixens by virtue of *validating* and *violating* the vineyards of their beloved scriptures, in the eyes of all those who care about religion today (I daresay, even Maimonides would be vindicated). *Validated,*

12 R. Menahem Mendel of Kotsk (1787-1859).

13 I re-embrace A. J. Heschel's own embarrassing regarding his own inconsistent translation of *bira ha'doleket* at the opening and closing of his masterpiece, *God in Search of Man: A Philosophy of Judaism*, New York 1955.

14 See Gershom Scholem, *Sabbetai S̱evi: The Mystical Messiah*, tr. R. J. Z. Werblowsky, Bollingen Series, Princeton University Press , New Jersey 1973, p. 601.

15 We should note further that Fox has already addressed the issue of checks and balances between ethics and poetics for years, most recently in his introduction to my forthcoming volume, entitled, *How Hebrew Poetry Works*, where he lays out what's at stake in his words on Poet*h*ics, see above, n. 3.

in that embarrassment should be avoided at all costs between human beings, whether great or small. *Violated,* in that embarrassment must be pursued at all costs between humans and the divine.[16]

One final remark that may sound like a call to onto-theology, but wait... If I have learned anything from Harry's tremendous influence upon a generation of scholars and their works contained herein (especially Yoreh's provocation in "The So-Called Rape of Dina"), I am convinced there needs to be more consideration to another layer of embarrassment — divine embarrassment. What Yoreh has uncovered as J's "Theology of Mercy," points to a whole other layer of research yet to be completed. Namely, the reality that these texts are more than the product of a divine inspiration of humanly authors, but the breath of a living God. The myriad of theologies and theosophies that need to be recovered and reborn remain an urgent project. I daresay it is urgent — a matter of life and death — in that the warning about public embarrassment as akin to murder, bespeaks a certain death of God that needs a rebirthing at this hour. We should all be embarrassed by the pleasure of re-embracement — regardless of how brilliant — unless there is a real rebirthing taking place.

16 Maimonides, *Mishneh Torah, Hilchot Deot* 6: 8.

העתקה עברית של רִסאלת אלחאתִמי: השוואה בין אמרות המיוחסות לאריסטו לבין בתי שיר למֻתַנַבִּי

(קמברידג׳, ט״ש, ערבית, 45.2)[1]

יוסף טובי, אוניברסיטת חיפה

א. השירה הערבית בקרב היהודים בימי הביניים

הפתיחות לתרבות הסובבת היתה אחת מאבני היסוד של החברה היהודית בארצות האסלאם מאז המאה העשירית, בעיקר מכוח מפעלו העצום של רב סעדיה גאון (882–942). רב סעדיה לא רק התיר לרעיונות ודרכי חשיבה מן התרבות הערבית־המוסלמית ומן התרבות היוונית בלבושה הערבי להיכנס אל התרבות היהודית, אלא אף אימץ את הלשון הערבית, אמנם בכתיבתה באותיות עב־ריות, להוות לשון היצירה העיקרית של חכמי היהודים בארצות האסלאם. אף תרגם את המקרא (או רובו) לערבית ופירש חלקים רבים ממנו בלשון זו. כמובן לא כאן המקום לסכם את מפעלו העצום ולעמוד על מלוא משמעותו – אף ספק אם כבר הגיעה השעה לכך מבחינת התקדמות המחקר[2] – אך יש לציין שהיה זה לאחר מאות שנים רבות שבה שקעה התרבות היהודית בתוך עצמה, כמוכח מספרות התלמוד וההלכה ומן הפיוט הארץ ישראלי הקדום. בתקופה זו איבד המקרא את חשיבותו כיצירה ספרותית ולשונית ושימש בעיקר מקור להלכה ולמדרשי נחמה לעם ישראל הנשלט בארצו על ידי הביזנטים הנוצרים. אכן, אחת מאבני היסוד של האסכולה התרבותית החדשה מבית מדרשו של רב סעדיה היא השינוי המכריע ביחס אל המקרא. על כל צעד ושעל בפירושי רב סעדיה למקרא מתגלה הגישה החדשה הרואה בו יצירה ספרותית שיש לדון בה ולדון אותה גם על פי אמות מידה

1 תודתי נתונה לעובדי ספריית בית המדרש לרבנים בניו יורק וספריית אוניברסיטת קולומביה וכן לחתני אראל שביל, תלמיד מחקר באוניברסיטה זו, שלא חסכו כל מאמץ להשיג בעבורי את כל הספרים וכתבי העת שנדרשו לי למאמר זה. עוד נתונה תודתי למר ג׳לאל עבד אלגני מן החוג לשפה וספרות ערבית באוניברסיטת חיפה, שעבר על המאמר והעיר הערותיו המועילות והחשובות; ולתלמידי באוניברסיטת חיפה מר כ׳אלד זרעיני שהגיה את הטקסט הערבי.

2 החיבור המקיף היחיד על מפעלו התורני, הספרותי, התרבותי והרוחני של רב סעדיה הוא מלפני קרוב לתשעים שנה (מלטר 1921). מובן שמאז נתחדשו דברים רבים על רב סעדיה; אף על פי כן, עדיין לא באו לידי מיצוים.

לשוניות ואסתטיות–ספרותיות. עיקרון יסודי זה לא משו ממנו חכמי ימי הביניים בארצות האסלאם ומכוחו נתחדשו פרשנות המקרא, חקר הלשון העברית, שירת החול העברית ואף שירת הקודש בספרד ונעשו גולת הכותרת של היצירה היהודית בימי הביניים. עיקרון זה של שינוי ערכין כלפי טקסטים מסורתיים בתולדות ישראל, כבר עמד עליו כידוע בעל היובל פרופ׳ צבי פוקס ואף טבע את המונחים embarrassment ו–re-embracement.

יש לחזור ולהדגיש, כי כל תחומי היצירה הנ״ל נעשו מתוך זיקה הדוקה ביותר של התרבות הערבית ואל התרבויות האחרות שהוטמעו בתוכה, ובראש כולן תרבות יוון. להלן נדון בעניין אחד בלבד, בזיקה שבין השירה העברית לשירה הערבית בימי הביניים, על סמך תעודה ספרותית חשובה שנמצאה בגניזת קהיר. זיקה זו היא מן המפורסמות שאינם צריכים ראיה וכבר הוכיחו חוקרים רבים כי המשוררים היהודים הכירו היטב את השירה הערבית ואת ספרות הביקורת שנכתבה עליה בימי הביניים וכי אין להבין את השירה העברית בלא להזקיקה אל השירה הערבית.[3] מסתמא, יכלו רוב המשוררים היהודים בספרד, לפחות בני התקופה האנדלוסית (בערך 950–1140), ובמידה מסוימת גם בצפון אפריקה ובארצות המזרח, לקרוא את הספרות הערבית במקורה הערבי, כלומר כשהיא כתובה באותיות ערביות. עדויות לא מעטות לכך נשמרו בגניזת קהיר, שבה מצויים דפים רבים הכתובים ערבית ועניינם ספרות יפה, בייחוד שירה, בכלל כך מן הדיואנים של המשורר הגאהלי טַרַפַה (מת 569?) ושל המשורר הידוע מֻתַנַבִּי, שעוד נעסוק בו רבות להלן. כן נשמרו שרידי שירים ערביים שכתבו יהודים בשבח השליט צלאח אלדין במצרים (1163–1193) ואף שירי אהבה (גזליאת) אנונימיים.[4] חלק גדול מן העדויות להכרת השירה הערבית עולות מן השירה עצמה: קליטת מוטיבים הידועים היטב מן השירה הערבית בשירה העברית; תרגומי שירים ערביים או יצירות ערביות אחרות לעברית; וכמובן, כתיבת שירים בערבית על ידי משוררים יהודים.[5] על אלה יש להוסיף שיבוץ בתי שיר ערביים בספרות הערבית־היהודית לסוגיה (לשון, פרשנות המקרא, מוסר ופילוסופיה וביקורת השירה).[6]

לצד אלו יש עדויות מסוג אחר, שנשמרו בדרך כלל בכתבי הגניזה בכמות לא מעטה, אך המחקר לא נתן דעתו עליהם במידה הראויה. המכוון הוא להעתקה מאותיות ערביות לאותיות עבריות של שירה ערבית או של חיבורי ביקורת על השירה הערבית. מטבע הדברים נעשו העתקות אלו בעבור מי שהכירו את הלשון הערבית היטב, אך התקשו בקריאתה באותיות ערביות. הנחה זו עולה יפה עם העובדה הידועה, כי למן ימי הביניים ועד הזמן החדש כתבו היהודים את ספרותם הערבית

3 ספרות המחקר בשאלה זו עשירה ומגוונת למדי, אף כי רחוקה היא מאוד מלהיות ממצה. לדיון כולל על חקר הזיקה בין השירה העברית לבין השירה הערבית בימי הביניים ראו טובי תש״ס, עמ׳ 11–32.

4 ראו קאן 1986.

5 עד היום לא נתפרסם מחקר מקיף בנושא זה ואף לא רשימה ביבליוגרפית של המחקרים הרבים עליו. להלן ציונים בודדים לגבי כל אחד מסוגי העדויות הנמנים בִּפְנִים: קליטת מוטיבים ערביים – לוין תשנ״ה; תרגומי שירה ערבית – רצהבי תש״ל; כתיבת שירים ערביים – שטרן 1963; סדן תשנ״ה; רצהבי תשנ״ה; עוד ראו טובי תש״ס.

6 בתי השיר הערביים בספרות הערבית־היהודית הביניימית כונסו על ידי ואמורים לראות אור בשיתוף דר׳ עבד אלרחמן מרעי.

באותיות עבריות, בשומרם על מסורת זו עוד מן התקופה הקדם־אסלאמית,[7] ואולי אף בהשפעת האיסור הפורמלי לפחות שהטילו שליטי האסלאם על היהודים להשתמש באותיות ערביות.[8] אכן, מכתבי הגניזה עולה, כי לא היתה אחידות במידת הקִרבה של השכבות החברתיות היהודיות השונות לספרות הערבית הכתובה.[9] עדויות רבות מסוג זה נצטברו בידי במהלך עבודתי בספרות הערבית־היהודית באוספי הגניזה השונים באנגליה, בארה"ב וברוסיה ומהן אביא בזה עדות אחת, יחידה במינה, של העתקה לאותיות עבריות של חיבור ערבי שעניינו ביקורת השירה. בחיבור זה נקשר שם מחברו – חאתִמי, מחשובי המבקרים של השירה הערבית במאה העשירית, עם מי ששִירָתו נידונה בחיבור – מֻתַנַבִּי, בן זמנו הנחשב כגדול המשוררים הערבים (915–965).

ב. חאתִמי מבקר השירה הערבית

אַבּוּ עלי מחמד אלחאתִמי, מבקר השירה הערבית המפורסם בן המאה העשירית (931–998), נודע בספרות ישראל מספרו של משה אבן עזרא כִּתאב אלמֻחאצַרה ואלמֻדֹאכַרה, המזכירו במבוא לספרו זה לצד פואטיקנים חשובים של השירה הערבית בימי הביניים: קדאמה בן גִ'עפר, עבד אללה בן אלמֻעתַז, אבן רשיק ואבן קֻתַיבה. אכן, חאתִמי נחשב לאחד מפורצי הדרך בחקר הפואטיקה הערבית במחצית השנייה במאה העשירית בנוטלו חלק חשוב בפולמוס על שירת מֻתַנַבִּי.[10] שניים מחיבורים קצרים, מכלל חיבוריו המרובים של חאתמי שרובם אבדו ולא הגיעו לידינו, סובבים על שירת מֻתַנַבִּי:

(1) אלרִסאלה אלמוּצִׂחה פי דִכְּר סַרִקאת אַבִּי אלטַּיִּב אלמֻתַנַבִּי וסאקִט שִעְרִה, גַּבְּהַת אלאַדַבּ: מֻנאטֹאראת אַבִּי עלי אלחאתמִי לְאַבִּי אלטַּיִּב (=האיגרת המבהירה בעניין גניבות אַבִּי אלטַּיִּב

7 ראו טובי תשס"ו.

8 בכתאב אלעהד המסדיר מעמד הנוצרים והיהודים בכִּליפות המוסלמית והמיוחס לכִּליף עֻמר השני (717–720) נכלל סעיף האוסר על היהודים לקרוא בקוראן, להשתמש באותיות ערביות ולכנות עצמם בכינויים ערביים. ראו דינור תרפ"ו, עמ' 14.

9 ראו סקליר תשנ"ח, עמ' 117–119; בלאו 2002, עמ' 351. עוד ראו גויטיין תשכ"ב, עמ' נז, פְּסָקוֹ של רב האיי המתיר ללמד לתינוקות כתב ערבי בבית הכנסת. אולם לדבריו, ילדי היהודים בספרד התחנכו מקטנותם, ממש כמו ילדי המוסלמים, לקרוא ולכתוב בלשון הערבית, דבר שלא היה אופייני ליהודי ארצות האסלאם האחרות. עוד השוו דבריו הנרגשים של יהודה אבן תבון בצוואתו לבנו שמואל: "גם כתיבת הערבי שהחלות ללמוד אותו היום שבע שנים ועוד הייתי מפייס אותך עליה ולא רצית לעולם שמוע אלי. ואתה יודע כי הגדולים שבעמינו לא הגיעו אל הגדולה והמעלות הרמות כי אם בכתיבת הערבי" וכו'; "בני קבל עליך [...] לקרוא בכל שבת הסדר ערבי כי יועיל לך במלות הספרים הערביים ובהעתקה אם תרצה להעתיק". שטיינשניידר תר"ב, עמ' 4, 6–7. הפיזור במקור. 'הסדר ערבי' – בוודאי כוונתו לפרשת השבוע עם תפסיר רב סעדיה לתורה. העתקה – תרגום. אכן, שמואל אבן תיבון עסק בתרגום ספרים מערבית־יהודית לעברית, כגון ס' הכוזרי ליהודה הלוי. עוד ראו שם, להלן, עמ' 13, על הצורך להתאמן בכתיבה ערבית נאה.

10 על חאתמי וחיבורו חִליהֹ אלמֻחאצַרה ועל זיקת ספר הפואטיקה של משה אבן עזרא לחיבור זה ראו טובי, חאתִמי ואבן עזרא.

אלמֻתַנַבִּי ו[החלק] משירתו הירוד בערכו, פני הספרות: עיוני אַבִּי עלי אלחאתִמִי ב[שירת] אַבִּי אלטַיִּב).

(2) אלרִסאלה אלחאתִמיה (=איגרת חאתִמי).

החיבור הראשון כתוב במגמת ביקורת קשה על שירת מֻתַנַבִּי, על בסיס מפגש פנים אל פנים של המבקר והמשורר בבגדאד. אך על פי אחד מנוסחי החיבור ('הנוסח הקצר') הסתיים המפגש בפיוס בין חאתמִי לבין מֻתַנַבִּי לאחר שהמבקר הכיר במעלות המשורר ובעקבות כך החליט לכתוב רִסאלה אחרת, היא אלרִסאלה אלחאתמִיה.[11] שריד מהֶעתֵקה של איגרת זו באותיות עבריות, שנשמר בגניזת קהיר, מהווה נשוא מאמר זה.

ג. המשורר הערבי מֻתַנַבִּי ונוכחותו בתרבות היהודית בימי הביניים

אַבּוּ טַיִּב אחמד בן אלחסן, הידוע יותר בכינויו אלמֻתַנַבִּי (המתנבא) הוא אולי המשורר הערבי שנוכחותו בשירה העברית בספרד ובספרות הערבית־היהודית בימי הביניים גדולה יותר מזו של משורר ערבי אחר כלשהו. בספרו כתאב אלמחאצ̇רה ואלמד̇אכרה הביא ממנו משה אבן עזרא אחת עשרה פעמים (ראו להלן), יותר מכל משורר ערבי אחר,[12] וכינהו בדרך כלל 'אלשאער' (המשורר). אך פעמיים הקדים למובאותיו את המשפט: "כמא קאל אלאול" (כמו שאמר הקדמון).[13] כבר העלה המחקר, כי השפעת מֻתַנַבִּי על שמואל הנגיד היתה רבה בשירי המלחמה וההתפארות.[14] מכלל כארבע מאות מובאות מן השירה הערבית שליקטתי מתוך הספרות הערבית־היהודית בימי הביניים, שלושים ואחת הן משירי מֻתַנַבִּי.[15] אף יש עדות על קשר ישיר בינו לבין יהודי בשם אבן מַלְך, מאנשי תדמור שהתגורר בדמשק. יהודי זה, ממקורבי כאפור אלאכ̇שידי שליט מצרים, ביקש ממֻתַנַבִּי לכתוב שירי שבח בעבור מלכו, אך נענה בשלילה.[16] בכלל נראה, שדעת מֻתַנַבִּי על היהודים היתה רחוקה מלהיות חיובית, שכן לפחות בשני מקומות בשיריו כתב עליהם במגמה שלילית:

ما مقامي بارض نخلة الا   كمقام المسيح بين اليهود

---

11 ראו בונבקר 1984, עמ' 19.

12 אמנם בראון (תש"ג, עמ' 202), רשם שלושה עשר בתים שהביא אבן עזרא בספרו מן המשורר הערבי אבו תמאם בעשרה אזכורים ואלו מֻתַנַבִּי רשם תשעה אזכורים בלבד (עמ' 202), אך נעלמו ממנו שני אזכורים המובאים בנספח דלהלן.

13 אבן עזרא תשל"ה, עמ' 90, 110.

14 על שירי המלחמה ראו חייט 1966; לוין תשכ"ח, עמ' 348–363; שיפרס 1994, עמ' 231–241. על שירי ההתפארות ראו טובי תש"ס, עמ' 219–234.

15 ראו לעיל, הערה 6. בתי שיר אלו יובאו בנספח בסוף המאמר.

16 סיפור זה מובא על ידי אבו אלעלא אלמערי בראש פירושו על השירים שכתב מֻתַנַבִּי לכבוד כאפור. ראו מתנבי 1986, ד, עמ' 13. להעתקת הסיפור באותיות עבריות ולדיון קצר בו ראו גולדציהר 1870.

אין ישיבתי בארץ נכלה אלא   כישיבת ה'מסיח' בקרב היהודים[17]

בשיר זה, שמֻתַנַבִּי אמרו בימי נעוריו, כלשון הכתובת שמעליו (وقال ايضا في صباه), התלונן על יחסם העוין של תושבי נַכְּלָה כלפיו, עיירה סמוכה לבַּעַלְבֵּךּ בבקעת הלבנון, כפי שהיהודים היו עוינים ליֵשו. בשיר אחר מֻתַנַבִּי כינה אויביו לאות בוז בשם 'יהודים', שעדותם נגד מוסלמים אינה מתקבלת בבתי הדין השרעיים על פי חוקי האפליה הנוהגים נגדם בארצות האסלאם:[18]

فلا تسمعن من الكاشحين   ولا تعبان محك اليهود

אל תאזין לנוצרים השוטמים   אל תיתן לבך להתנצחויות היהודים[19]

ובשיר אחר דימה מֻתַנַבִּי את ישיבתו עם אנשים מסוימים כישיבה בקרב כופרים בגיהינום בס־מיכות ליהודים, בהנחה ברורה כי ככופרים, זה המקום הראוי להם:

لصوص اطاعوا ابا مرة   بترك الركوع وترك السجود

كاني قرنت بهم في الجحـ   يم ارى كل يوم وجوه اليهود

גנבים העובדים את אבּוּ מֻרה[20]   בזניחת הכריעות ובזניחת ההשתחוויות[21]

כאלו חֻבַרתי אליהם בגי־   הינום, אראה כל יום את פני היהודים[22]

הבוז כלפי היהודים בגלל שפלות מוצאם בעיני המוסלמים עולה גם בבית שיר אחר שבו הוא מכנה את אויבו כינוי 'בן יהודי':

اليس عجيبا ان بين بني اب   لنجل يهودي تدب العقارب

לא ייפלא כי בין בני אב   מזרע יהודי יזחלו העקרבים[23]

אין להסיק מכל ההתבטאויות הללו נגד היהודים כי מֻתַנַבִּי עָיֵן אותם במיוחד, ונראה כי השתמש במטבעות לשון ובאמונות מקובלות בקרב המוסלמים.

ההערכה הגדולה כלפי מֻתַנַבִּי כמשורר אינה מתבססת על הערכים הפרוזודיים והרטוריים של שירתו אלא על תכניה הרעיוניים. בכלל, ובניגוד לרוב המשוררים הערביים האחרים שהִרבו לכ־תוב שירי שבח חנפניים לשליטיהם תמורת בצע כסף, וכך נעשתה שירתם שירה מגויסת שאיבדה במידה רבה את ערכה הספרותי המהותי, הרי מֻתַנַבִּי היה משורר עצמאי והחשיב עצמו יותר מכל

17 מֻתַנַבִּי 1938, ב, עמ' 52, הבית השמונה עשר בשיר كم قتيل كما قتلت شهيد. והשוו היינריקס 1990, עמ' 236. משורר ערבי אחר שהונה את היהודים על יחסם השלילי לישו הוא מוסא בן יחיא בהראן (תימן, המאה הט"ז), ואפשר כתב דבריו בהשפעת בית השיר של מֻתַנַבִּי: لو كنت في ايام عيسى لما / اظهرت البهت عليه اليهود (=אילו הייתי בימי ישו, לא באו עליו היהודים בדברי כזב). ראו גאנם 1972, עמ' 78.

18 עדויות רבות מימי הביניים ומן הזמן החדש בספרות הערבית הכתובה ובשיח המדובר, בייחוד בפתגם, לשימוש בכינוי 'יהודי' כביטוי של בוז.

19 מֻתַנַבִּי 1938, ב, עמ' 81, הבית העשרים ושישה בשיר שכתב מבית הסוהר אל השליט, ايا خدد الله ورد الخدود.

20 כינוי לשטן.

21 המקובלות באסלאם בעבודת אללה.

22 מֻתַנַבִּי 1986, א, עמ' 197–198, הבתים העשרים ושלושה והעשרים וארבעה בשיר ايا خدد الله ورد الخدود. שני הבתים אינם מצויים בכל המקורות ולא הובאו במהדורת מֻתַנַבִּי 1938.

23 מֻתַנַבִּי 1938, א, עמ' 124, הבית התשיעי בשיר لاي صروف الدهر فيه نعايب.

אלו שהיללם בשירתו. לא בכדי נתכנה 'מֻתַנַבִּי' על שום שביקש להוכיח כי הוא יכול לכתוב בסגנון הקוראן, כשהוא מערער על אחד מעקרונות האמונה המוסלמית – אִעג'אז אלקֻראַאן, כלומר שהוא כתוב בלשון שאין שום בן תמותה יכול לכתוב כמוה.[24]

בשל נטייתו הפילוסופית, ניסח מֻתַנַבִּי רבים מבתי השיר שלו בניסוח הגותי־כוללני על דרך האמ־צעי הרטורי הידוע בשם 'סנטנציה', כלומר אפוריזמים בהתבטאות על־מקומית ועל־זמנית המנתקת את העניין מן ההקשר הייחודי־האישי של המשורר ומעבירה אותו אל המישור הכללי־האוניברסלי. אמת, מאמרי חכמה בשירה הערבית ידועים עוד מן השירה הג'אהִלית הקדם־אסלאמית, אולם ביצירת מֻתַנַבִּי הגיע מֵמד זה של השירה לידי פיתוח מיוחד שכמוהו לא נמצא ביצירת משורר ערבי אחר כלשהו. אכן, חובבי השירה הערבית ומבקריה, בימי הביניים ובזמן החדש, הרבו לחשוף את צִדָּהּ הרעיוני של יצירת מֻתַנַבִּי. כך נוצרה סוגה ספרותית מיוחדת שעניינה ליקוט מאמרי החכמה של מֻתַנַבִּי מתוך שירתו ודיון נרחב בהם. המפורסם בהם הוא הלקט של אסמאעיל בן עַבּאד שנודע בכינויו אלצאחִב (995/6–937/8), הווזיר של פכ'ר אלדולה אלבֻּוַיְהִי שנודע גם בשל חיבתו הרבה ולמעורבותו בענייני השירה והספרות בכלל.[25] יש להוסיף, כי גם בפירוש שירי מֻתַנַבִּי המיוחס לאבּו אלבַּקא אלעֻכְּבַּרי (מת 1219) הובאו מקבילות רבות לבתי השיר של המשורר מדברי אריסטו, המכונה בסתם 'אלחַכִּים', כמקובל בספרות הערבית באותם ימים. מקבילות אלו שאולות מן האיגרת של חאתִמי.[26] מבקרי השירה הערבית נתנו כמובן דעתם לעניין זה וכללוהו בספרי הרטוריקה שלהם, כגון חֻסֵין אלמַרְצַפִי (1810 לערך–1890), ששימש מורה ללשון הערבית ולספרותה בבתי ספר גבוהים שונים בקהיר, ושהקדיש פרק ארוך לנושא זה בספר הלימוד שלו לשירה הערבית: "ארסאל אלמת'ל ואלכלאם אלג'אמע" [=המשלת המשל והדי־בור הכולל]. הוא פתח דיונו בקביעה שהשימוש במשל מצוי כבר בדברי מֻחמד בקוראן ובדברי חכמי האסלאם הראשונים וחתם בכך שהשימוש באמצעי זה מהווה קישוט לשירה. לאחר מכן שילב בדבריו במלואו את הלקט של אלצאחִב הכולל מאתיים ותשעים ותשעה בתי שיר, ורק בסוף הדיון הביא בתי שיר מעטים ביחס משל משוררים ערביים מתקופת הג'אהִלִיה ומתקופת האסלאם.[27] גם בספרות הרטו־ריקה העברית מצא לו אמצעי זה דיון מיוחד, בכתאב אלמחאצ'רה של משה אבן עזרא.[28]

---

24 היינריקס 1990; שהיד 2004, עמ' 192. יש המסבירים כי כונה בשם זה לפי שבאחד משיריו השווה זָרוּתו בין בני עמו כזָרוּת צאלִח, הנביא הקדם אסלאמי, בקרב עמו תַמוּד. ראו למשל היינריקס 1990, עמ' 126; סלים במבוא לצאחב 1992, עמ' 9.

25 ראו צאחִב 1992; לביקורת ספרותית של אלצאחִב על שירת מֻתַנַבִּי ראו צאחִב 1974. בלקט של אלצאחִב במהדורת סלים מאתיים וחמישים ושניים בתי שיר, אולם נראה שבכתבי יד אחרים מספר בתי השיר היה שונה. ראו למשל בלקט של מרצפי 1991, ב, הכולל מאתיים ותשעה בתי שיר. ללקטים של מאמרי חכמה משירת מֻתַנַבִּי ולדיונים בפילוסופיה שלו מן המאה העשרים ראו כ'ואג'א 1982 (השוואה בין החכמה בשירת מֻתַנַבִּי לבין החכמה בשירת אבו אלעלא אלמערי); סלאמה 1981 (על ההשוואה בין מֻתַנַבִּי לבין אריסטו בעמ' 49–71); עלאם 1972; צאחִב 1992; רצ'א חש"ד. הלקט של רצ'א, ככל הנראה מראשית שנות השמונים במאה העשרים, כולל 285 בתי שיר והוגש על ידי המחבר כמנחת שי לבניו.

26 מחבר הפירוש היה בן דורו הצעיר של עֻכְּבַּרִי. ראו בונבקר 1984, עמ' 19–20, על פי סזגין 1967, ב, עמ' 495. מקבילות אלו צוינו בהערות לבתי השיר דלהלן.

27 מרצפי 1991, ב, עמ' 108–129.

28 אבן עזרא תשל"ה, עמ' 284–297. גם ב'עֲמָדה' פרק מיוחד לעניין זה, אבן רשיק 1988, עמ' 479–488: 'באב אלמת'ל אלסאיר' (שער המשל הנהוג). לדיון בעניין זה ובהשפעת אבן רשיק על אבן עזרא ראו דנה תשמ"ג, עמ' 175–178.

ג. אלרִסאלה אלחאתִמיה והֶעתֵּקהּ באותיות עבריות

אלרִסאלה אלחאתִמיה נדפסה פעמיים במהדורות ערביות מסורתיות בתוך קובצי ספרות ערבית, בתרגום לגרמנית בלוויית צילום אחד מכתבי היד ובמהדורה מדעית של המקור הערבי.[29] מספר בתי השיר של מֻתַנַבִּי משתנה מכתב יד אחד למשנהו, כמאה לערך. במחקר המודרני מתעוררת שאלת האותנטיות של האיגרת וייחוסה לחאתִמי מטעמים שונים: (א) היא אינה כלולה ברשימת חיבורי חאתִמי שהביאו בתולדות חייו כמה מחברים ערביים מימי הביניים, כגון יאקות, קִפְטי וסֻיוּטי; (ב) דברי השבח למֻתַנַבִּי בהקדמת האיגרת בנוסחיה השונים עומדים בסתירה חריפה לדברי הביקורת הקשים שהטיח בו חאתִמי ברסאלה אלמוצִׁחה; (ג) מספר בתי השיר ששולבו בחיבור שונים מכתב יד אחד משנהו ולא תמיד משכנעת ההשוואה בין מאמר החכמה של אריסטו לבין בית השיר של מֻתַנַבִּי, דבר המעורר ספק בשייכותם לחיבור המקורי.[30] מכל מקום, הדעה הרווחת היא שאין בכוח הספקות הנ"ל כדי לשלול את האותנטיות של האיגרת ואת ייחוסה לחאתִמי.

רסאלת אלחאתִמי שונה באופיה מן הלקט של אלצאחִב לפי שמגמתה אינה חד־משמעית, דהיינו פרסום נטייתו הפילוסופית של מֻתַנַבִּי.[31] חאתִמי לא הסתפק בליקוט גרידא של בתי שיר למֻתַנַבִּי המהווים מאמרי חכמה, אלא – כאמור – הִשְׁוָם למאמרי חכמה המיוחסים לאריסטו.[32] השאלה העומדת בפני החוקר היא אפוא מה היתה מגמת חאתִמי במעשה ההשוואה: האם להוכיח כי מֻתַנַבִּי הושפע מאריסטו או להוכיח את עליונות מֻתַנַבִּי המשורר על פני אריסטו הפילוסוף בניסוח רעיון החכמה?[33] אגב דרכנו נאמר, כי לדעת מחברים ערבים אחרים בימי הביניים, כגון אבן טַבאטַבא אלעַלַוִי (מת 933) ואבן קַיִּם אלגַ'וְזִיַּה (מת 1350) השפיעו חכמי יוון, ובראשם אריסטו, על המשוררים הערבים, ובכללם אבו אלעַתאהִיה מראשוני משוררי ההגות בשירה הערבית.[34] אמנם מן ההקדמה לאיגרת

29 התרגום הגרמני על ידי רֶשֶׁר 1926 והמקור הערבי על ידי בֵּסתאני 1931. לפירוט כתבי היד של החיבור, למובאות ממנו בספרות הערבית בימי הביניים ולמהדורות הנדפסות השונות ראו בונבקר 1984, עמ' 19–26.

30 ראו בונבקר 1984, עמ' 19–20, 26–27, 29; בונבקר 2004, עמ' 362; עבאס 1993, עמ' 235–237.

31 בונבקר (1984, עמ' 27, הערה 90) כותב, שכצפוי, כלל אלצאחִב בחיבורו רבים מבתי השיר של מֻתַנַבִּי המובאים באיגרת חאתִמי, אך אין כל ראיה לזיקה ישירה בין שני החיבורים.

32 כבר עמדו חוקרים שונים על כך שייחוס המאמרים לאריסטו מופרך בדרך כלל. ראו למשל עבאס 1993, עמ' 237–239. עבאס מראה יפה, כי המאמרים המיוחסים באיגרת חאתִמי לאריסטו היו מאוצר החכמה הנפוצה בקרב המחברים הערבים במאה העשירית ואף יש שהם מיוחסים לחכמים אחרים, כגון אפלטון ודיוגנס. נאה קביעתו, כי חאתִמי האמין שמאמרים אלו אמנם אריסטו אמרם. מאמרי חכמה רבים משל אריסטו כלל חֻנַין בן אסחאק (מת 873) בחיבורו 'אדאב אלפלאספה' שיהודה אלחריזי תרגמוֹ לעברית בשם 'מוסרי הפילוסופים'. ראו חנין תקס"ז. עוד ראו טובי תש"ס, עמ' 283–299, על 'הפואטיקה' של אריסטו בספרות הערבית־היהודית בימי הביניים.

33 לדעת עבאס 1993, עמ' 236, קביעתו המוקדמת של חאתִמי בחִלְיַהּ אלמֻחאצׂרה, כי מן הראוי שמשורר יטול רעיונות ממי שקדמוהו, היא שהביאתהו לערוך את ההשוואה הרעיונית בין מֻתַנַבִּי לאריסטו.

34 על דעות מבקרי השירה הערבית במאה העשירית בעניין השפעת היוונים על ביקורת השירה הערבית ראו עבאס 1993, עמ' 174–243; והשוו בונבקר 1984, עמ' 27.

עולה, כי המניע להשוואה זו הוא הרצון להוכיח את יתרון המשורר על פני הפילוסוף;[35] והדבר עולה בקנה אחד עם הנוסח הקצר של אלרסאלה אלמוצִ'חה, שלפיו הכיר חאתִמי במעלותיו הספרותיות של מֻתַנַבִּי וביקש להוכיח זאת באלרִסאלה אלחאתמִיה. על כל פנים, יש המגלים ברִסאלה מגמה סטירית מתוחכמת שנועדה לבקר את מֻתַנַבִּי על כך ש'גנב' מוטיבים רעיוניים ממי שקדמוהו, יהא זה אריסטו או משוררים ערבים; וראיה לדבר, שחאתִמי הביא תחילה את מאמר החכמה המיוחס לא־ריסטו ורק אחריו הביא את בית השיר של מֻתַנַבִּי.[36] כידוע, פרשת ה'גניבות' ('סַרִקאת') של מֻתַנַבִּי היא מן המפורסמות בביקורת השירה הערבית במאה העשירית ובמאה הי"א ורבים היו מבקריו על גניבות אלו.[37] מכל מקום, המגמה השולטת במחקר הערבי המודרני היא אפולוגטית וכוונתה להו־כיח כי מקור רעיונותיו ההגותיים של מֻתַנַבִּי אינם בדברי אריסטו או בספרות החכמה היוונית אלא במסורת הערבית ובדת האסלאם.[38]

כנזכר לעיל, הועתקה רִסאלה זו במקורה הערבי באותיות עבריות ושריד ממנה ובו שני דפים בלבד שאינם רצופים, נשמר בגניזת קהיר, עתה באוסף אוניברסיטת קמברידג' (ט"ש, ערבית 45.2). בשריד זה כלולה רוב ההקדמה וכן כשישה עשר ממאמרי אריסטו ומבתי השיר של מֻתַנַבִּי. אין כל ספק, שההעתקה נעשתה בעבור יהודים שאמנם הכירו היטב את הלשון הערבית, אך מצד אחר לא יכלו לקרוא באופן חופשי ספרות ערבית באותיות הערביות. תופעה זו אופיינית למדי לחברה היהו־דית בארצות האסלאם בימי הביניים. אף יש להניח שנעשתה לצורך יהודים שעניינם היה בספרות המוסר וההגות הערבית בסוגותיה השונות ולא בעבור מי שעניינם היה דווקא השירה הערבית, כגון משוררים יהודים שכתבו שירה ערבית בהשפעת השירה הערבית. אלו, לפחות בתקופה הקלַסית של השירה העברית באנדלוסיה (950–1140 לערך), בוודאי ידעו לקרוא היטב את השירה הערבית באו־תיותיה הערביות, שכן אחרת לא נוכל להבין כיצד נמשכה עליהם השפעה זו. זאת לפי שלמעֵט שירים ערביים מעטים או שרידי מקאמות ערביות מועתקות באותיות עבריות,[39] לא מצינו באוספי הגניזה העתקות דיואנים למשוררים ערבים באותיות עבריות. בין כך ובין כך, שריד זה מהווה עדות נוספת לפתיחותן של קהילות היהודים בארצות האסלאם אל התרבות הערבית ואל העניין שמצאו בה.

ולמעלה מכך: עיון במובאות משירי מֻתַנַבִּי בספרות הערבית־היהודית מעלה בבירור, כי לא תמיד – ואולי בדרך כלל – לא דיואן מֻתַנַבִּי שימש מקור למובאות אלו אלא איגרת חאתִמי שהיתה ידועה היטב בקרב היהודים בהעתקתה לאותיות עבריות. ראיה לדבר בכך ששני בתי השיר של מֻתַנַבִּי

---

35 לנוסח ההקדמה ראו בסתאני 1931, עמ' 22–23. בתרגום הגרמני של רשר 1926 ובכתב היד המצולם שם אין זכר להקדמה. לדיון מפורט בנוסחי ההקדמה השונים בכתבי היד ובמהדורות הנדפסות ראו בונבקר 1984, עמ' 27–36. ההקדמה נכללה בנוסח הערבי־היהודי, אך לא נשמרה אלא בחלקה. ראו להלן בסמוך.

36 ראו דרך משל מבארך 1980, ב, עמ' 141–142.

37 ראו דרך משל עמידי 1961.

38 ראו נופל [1987], עמ' 143–164, הדוחה בפירוש את דעת מבארך בעניין זה (לעיל, הערה 36). עוד ראו סלאמה 1981, עמ' 49–71; עלאם 1972, עמ' 8–9, 61; עבאס 1993, עמ' 239.

39 כגון מקאמות אלחרירי ויצירות ספרותיות ערביות בפרוזה חרוזה שמגמתן פילוסופית מוסרית, וכן שירי עגבים ושירי זימה מן התקופה המאוחרת של הגניזה (המאה הי"ד־הט"ו). העתקות אלו ראויות לדיון מיוחד שאין מקומו בזה.

שהביא יוסף אבן עקנין בפירושו על שיר השירים, 'אנכשאף אלאסראר וטֻהור אלאנואר', מצויים באיגרת חאתִמי ולפני כל אחד מהם בא מאמר החכמה של אריסטו, ממש כפי שהוא מצוי באיגרת זו.[40] עוד יש לציין, כי חמש מובאות אחרות משירי מֻתַנַבִּי בספרות הערבית־היהודית בימי הביניים בחיבורי אבן גבירול, בחיי אבן פקודה, משה אבן עזרא ויהודה הלוי, כלולות באיגרת חאתִמי.[41] מכאן עולה, שהאיגרת שימשה מקור לא רק לבתי השיר של מֻתַנַבִּי אלא גם למאמרי החכמה של אריסטו. קביעה זו עולה יפה עם מסקנת דן בקר באשר למובאות מן הקוראן והחדית' ובתי השיר הערביים שמביא יצחק אבן ברון כעדויות ('שַוַאהִד') בספרו כתאב אלמואזנה. על פי בדיקת בקר, רוב המובאות הללו מצויות במילונים שמהם העתיק אבן ברון ומכאן ברור שלא שאב ישירות מן המקורות הערביים הראשוניים אלא מן המקורות המשניים.[42]

על פי העיקרון שעמדנו עליו בפתיחת המאמר בדבר ה־embarrassment לעומת ה־re-embracement נוכל לומר, כי מאז המאה הט"ו חלה התרחקות גדולה בקרב הקהילות היהו־דיות בארצות האסלאם מן הספרות הערבית־היהודית שפניה היו אל עבר התרבות הכללית והסתגרות מחודשת בענייני הלכה ואסכטולוגיה כשהשפעת המיסטיקה הקבלית הולכת ומתחזקת. קרוב לוודאי כי התרחקות זו נבעה גם מן ההידרדרות החדה שחלה בתרבות העל הערבית־המוסלמית בפני עצמה. המגעים בין התרבות היהודית לבין תרבות הסביבה הצטמצמו למישור העממי בלבד ובמקביל לכך ניטשה כמעט לחלוטין היצירה היהודית מימי הביניים, הן שירת החול והן הספרות הערבית־היהודית, ואין צריך לומר הספרות הערבית המוסלמית (embarrassment). אמת, עד היום לא חלה התקר־בות מחודשת (re-embracement) בין התרבות העברית־היהודית לבין התרבות הערבית, בעיקר משום שזו עדיין לא התאוששה ורחוקה היא מהשגיה בימי הביניים. לעומת כן, עצם הפתיחות כלפי התרבויות הסובבות ניכר היטב בתרבות העברית־היהודית מאז יצירתו הספרותית של ר' משה חיים לוצאטו בסוף המאה הי"ח וההשכלה במהלך המאה המאה הי"ט.

העתקת אלרִסאלה אלחאתִמיה באותיות עבריות[43]

ההעתקה שלפנינו משובשת בכמה מקומות. על פי אופי השיבושים נראה שמקורם בקושי שעמד בפני המעתיק מן האותיות הערביות אל האותיות העבריות, אם בשל טיבו הגרוע של המקור שהיה לפניו או בשל הדמיון בין האותיות הערביות ומיעוט שליטתו בערבית.[44] מכל מקום, ברור שמקור

40 ראו להלן בנספח מובאות בתי השיר של מֻתַנַבִּי בספרות הערבית־היהודית, סי' 23–24.

41 ראו בנספח הנ"ל, סי' 1, 2, 9, 10, 21.

42 בקר תשס"ה, עמ' 75–76.

43 חלקה הראשון של ההקדמה חסר בכתב היד הערבי־היהודי (להלן: כ"י) והשלמתיו בזה על פי הנוסח שהדפיס בֶּסתאני 1931, עמ' 22–23. כאמור, השתבש מעתיק הטקסט הערבי אל הטקסט הערבי־היהודי בקריאת המלים. כאן הבאתי את הנוסח המתוקן על פי המהדורה הנדפסת, אבל ציינתי בהערות את הקריאות המוטעות. התרגום על פי הנוסח המתוקן.

44 שיבושים אלו צוינו להלן בהערות לטקסט.

השיבושים אינו בהעתקה שנייה או שלישית של החיבור אלא כבר בהעתקה המקורית הראשונה שנעשתה מן האותיות הערביות אל האותיות העבריות. הכתיבה העברית עצמה מהודרת למדי וחבל שלא שרד מן ההעתקה אלא חלק קטן בלבד. להלן נביא את ההעתקה בהשלמות על פי מהדורת בֻּסתאני 1931.[45] על פי השוואת נוסח ההעתקה באותיות עבריות לשינויי הנוסח שהביא בֻּסתאני במהדורתו, כולל סדר אמרות החכמה של אריסטו ובתי השיר של מֻתַנַבִּי, נראה שההעתקה העברית שווה כמעט תמיד לנוסח מהדורת הדפוס השני, קונסטנטינופול 1302 להגִ'רה (1884).[46]

[קאל אלאמאם אבו עלי מחמד בן אלחסן בן אלמט̇פר
אלכאתב אללגוי אלמערוף באלחאתמי רחמה אללה:
אמא בעד פאן אחק מא אחתכמת אליה נפוס אולי אלנט̇ר
ואנקאדת אליה אראא אהל אלפכר וג̇לת אלשבהה ענה בנט̇ר
אלמתצפחין ואמצ̇ת בה עזאימהא קלוב אלמעתברין אלעדל
פאנה שיח אלעקל ונסיג̇ אלנהי וצפו אלפהם ועדיל ען אלהוי
ואלד̇י בעת̇ני עלי תצניף הד̇ה אלאלפאט̇ אלמנטקיה ואלאראא
אלפלספיה אלד̇י אכ̇ד̇הא אבו אלטיב אחמד אבן אלחסן אלמתנבי]
[1א] [מנאפרה̈ כ̇]צומ[י פיה ל]מא ראית מן נפור [ע]קולהם
[ענה ותצגירהם ל]קדרה[47] וקד ת̇בת ענד ד̇וי אלעקל
[ואלתמייז] אן אלאנסאן אנמא פצ̇ל עלי סאיר אלחיואן
[באלע]קל אלמתנאול[48] בה עלם מא גאב ען אלחואס ות̇בת
[אן א]לנט̇ר אלפכרי פי אל[נפס] מפצח עמא תנאול[49] [על]מה
אלעקל וצחת בה[50] כ̇לאבה̈[51] ללנפס[52] והו עלי צ̇רבין צ̇רב מנה
מנט̇ור אלאלפאט̇ מת̇בות אלמעאני תתצרף[53] אלנפס פי

---

45 השינויים לעומת נוסח בֻּסתאני (ב) צויינו רק אם לא נמצא כמותם באחד המקורות שהשתמש בהם.

46 האיגרת האחת עשרה בתוך הקובץ التحفة البهية والطرفة الشهية. מהדורה זו נדירה ביותר, בדומה לראשונה (בירות 1868). בידי צילום ממנה על פי העותק בספריית הרוַרד. בֻּסתאני מסמן את השינויים על פיה באות ق. בהערות לטקסט הפניתי למספר האמרה ובית השיר על פי בֻּסתאני 1931.

47 כ"י: [ל]אקדארהם.

48 הנון בין השיטין מעל לתיבה.

49 כ"י: יתאול. המעתיק קרא את התיבה تناول: يتاول.

50 תיבה זו אינה בכ"י.

51 כ"י: גלא רקה. המעתיק קרא את התיבה خلابة כשתי מלים: جلا رقة.

52 כ"י: אלנפס. המעתיק קרא את התיבה للنفس: النفس.

53 כ"י: בתצרף. המעתיק קרא את התיבה تتصرف: بتصرف.

אגׄתלאבה[54] מן חיתׄ יסנח[55] וצׄרב מנה מנטׄום מוגׄז מפהום פוגׄדנא[56] אבו אלטייב אחמד בן אלחסין[57] קד אתא פי שערה באגראץׄ פלספיהׄ ומעאן מנטיקייהׄ[58] פאן כאן דׄלך מנה ען פחץ ונטׄר ובחתׄ פקד אגרק פי דרס אלעלום ואן יכן דׄלך מנה עלי סביל אלאתפאק פקד זאד עלי אלפלאספהׄ באל[איגׄאז ואלב]לאגהׄ ואלאלפאטׄ אלערביהׄ והו פי אלחאלתין עלי גאיהׄ מן אלפצׄל וסביל נהאיהׄ מן [1ב] אלנבל וקד אורדת[59] מן דׄלך [מ]א יסת[דל] בה עלי [פצׄלה פי] נפסה ופצׄל עלמה ואדבה ואגראקה [פי טלב אלחכמהׄ ממא אתי פי שערה] ובאללה אלתופיק[60]

תרגום

[אמר האִמאם אבו עלי מחמד בן אלחסן בן אלמטַּפר, הסופר, הבלשן, הידוע בשם אלחאתמי, ירחמהו האל: הנה הדבר הנכון ביותר שפנו למשפטו נפשות בעלי העיון ונשמעו לו דעות אנשי המחשבה ונסתלק הספק ממנו בעיון המדקדקים בדבר וחתמו בו את נחישותם לִבּוֹת המתבוננים הוא היושר. והוא מתינות השכל ורקמת הזהירות וזַכּוּת ההבנה והסתלקות מן היצר. ואשר עוררני לחיבור דברי ההגיון והדעות הפילוסופיות הללו שאבו אלטיב אבן אלחסן אלמתנבי אימצם] [1א] הוא סלידת בעלי דבבי ממנו, לפי שראיתי ששכלם סולד ממנו וכי הם ממעיטים ביכולתו. וכבר נתברר לבעלי השכל וההבחנה, כי אמנם מותר האדם מבעלי החיים האחרים בשכל, שחכמה מושגת בו, דבר הנעדר מן החוש. ונתברר כי העיון הרעיוני בנפש מגלה את אשר תושג ידיעתו על ידי השכל ויושג בו שכנוע הלב. והוא משני סוגים: הסוג האחד שמלותיו פרודות [פרוזה] ועניניו נכוחים שהנפש נוהגת

54 כ"י: א[ג]תלא. המעתיק קרא את התיבה اجتلابه: اجتلا.

55 כ"י: תסנח. המעתיק קרא את התיבה يسنح: تسنح.

56 כ"י: פוגׄדנא. המעתיק קרא את התיבה ووجدنا: فوجدنا.

57 ב נוסף כאן: المتنبي.

58 תיבה זו כתובה בין השיטין מעל לתיבה אחרת שתחתיה שנמחקה במשיכת קולמוס.

59 האלף בין השיטין מעל לתיבה.

60 ב: والله تعالى الموفق للصواب [=והאל יתעלה הוא הקולע אל האמת].

בהבאתו ככל העולה על רוחה; וסוג אחר חרוז, אמור בקיצור וברור.
ומצאנו כי כבר הביא אבו אלטיב אחמד בן אלחסין
בשירתו כוונות פילוסופיות ורעיונות הגיוניים. זה
נעשה על ידו מתוך בחינה ועיון וחקירה וכבר שקע בלימוד
המדעים. ואף שעשה זאת על דרך ההתאמה, הרי כבר עלה
על הפילוסופים בקיצור וביפי הלשון והמלים הערביות
ובשני העניינים הרי הוא בתכלית המעלה ובעל דרך השלמות
[1ב] באצילות. וכבר הבאתי בזה מה שמורה על מעלת
נפשו ומעלת חכמתו והשכלתו ושקיעתו בדרישת החכמה כפי שבא בשירתו
וההצלחה מן האל

1. קאל ארסטאטאליס[61]

אד֗א כאנת אלשהוה [פו]ק אלקדרה כאן הלאך אלג֗סם דון
בלוג אלשהוה
אם היתה התאוה למעלה מן היכולת, יהיה כליון הגוף בלא
השגת התאוה
ק[אל אלמ]תנבי[62]
אד֗א כאנת אלנפוס כבאר / תעבת פי מראדהא אלאג֗סאם:
אם היו הנפשות גדולות / ייעפו ברצונותיהן הגופים

2. קאל[63] רסטאלס[64]

רום נקל אלטבאע מן[65] דוי אלאטמאע שדיד אלאמתנאע
השאיפה לשנות את טבעם של החמדנים בלתי אפשרית ביותר

61 בסתאני 1931, עמ' 24, סי' 1. ברקוקי הביאו בפירושו בשם עֻכּבַּרִי, מֻתַנַבִּי 1938, ד, עמ' 83, הערה 1. אך בהמשך הביא עֻכּבַּרִי את דברי המדקדק הערבי אלוַקיע, בן זמנו של חאתִמי (מת 1003), המכחיש כי מֻתַנַבִּי לקח בית שיר זה מאריסטו והטוען כי המשורר הושפע ממשורר ערבי קדום בשם עֻבַּיד אללה בן טאהִר וממשוררים אחרים; וראו בונבקר 1984, עמ' 20.

62 הבית השישי בשיר اين ازمعت ايهذا الهمام, מֻתַנַבִּי 1938, ד, עמ' 83. בית השיר מובא גם בכתאב אלאצלאח לאבן גבירול (1902, עמ' 40): وقيل فيه شعر: وإذا كانت النفوس كبارا / تعبت من مرادها الأجسام; תרגום נח בראון (אבן גבירול תשי"א, עמ' 92): ונאמר בו שיר: ואם תהיינה הנפשות גדולות / ייעפו הגופים מרצונותיהן. עוד השוו אבן פקודה 1912, עמ' 231; שמחוני תרפ"ו, עמ' 107 (במשקל): ואם שגבו נפשות וגדולות הן / הלא אז ייגעו גופים במשאלם; אבן פקודה תשל"ג (מהדורת קאפח), עמ' רנג: וכאשר יהיו הנפשות גדולות ייגעו במילוי רצונם הגופות. שמחוני זיהה את מֻתַנַבִּי מחבר בית השיר הערבי, שהוא היחיד שהביא אבן פקודה בספרו זה. יצוין שיהודה אבן תיבון, מתרגמו הראשון של חובות הלבבות לעברית, השמיט את בית השיר וכמובן לא תרגמו. הביאוהו גם צאחִב 1992, עמ' 114, סי' 39; רצ֗א 1980, עמ' 77.

63 בסתאני 1931, עמ' 24, סי' 2. אמרה זו של אריסטו ובית השיר של מֻתַנַבִּי שלאחריה מובאים בשול הימני לאורך העמוד.

64 המעתיק קיצר שמו של אריסטו בערבית: אריסטוטאליס, וכן להלן.

65 ב: عن.

קאל אלמתנבי[66]

יראד מן[67] אלקלב נסיאנכם / ותאבא אלטבאע עלי אלנאקל

שכחתכם מתבקשת מן הלב / אבל הטבעים אינם נענים לַמְשַׁנֶּה

3. קאל[68] רסטאלס

נפוס אלחיואן אגראצ̇א[69] לחואדת̇ אלזמאן

נפשות בעלי החיים מקרים למאורעות הזמן

קאל אלמותנבי[70]

אד̇א אעתאד אלפתא כ̇וץ̇ אלמנאיא / פאהון מא ימר בה אלוחול:

אם התרגל הגבר לעמוד מול המוות / הרי יקל עליו לעבור ברפש

4. קאל[71] רסטאלס

אד̇א תג̇רדת אללטאיף מן אלשכוך אכתסת[72] אלצורה רונקא.

אם הוסרו משחקי הלשון מן הספקות תעטה הצורה יפעה

קאל אלמותנבי[73]

אד̇א כ̇לעת עלי ערץ̇[74] [לה חל]לא / וג̇דתהא [מנה][75]פי אבהא מן אלחלל:

אם העטיתי את הכבוד בגדי פאר / מצאתים עליו הבגדים ההדורים ביותר

---

66 כ״י בטעות: אלמצתבי. הבית השני בשיר الام طماعية العاذل, מֻתַנַבִּי 1938, ג, עמ׳ 186.

67 הביאו גם צאחִב 1992, עמ׳ 79, סי׳ 14.

68 בֻסתאני 1931, עמ׳ 25, סי׳ 4. אמרת אריסטו מובאת שם בהערה, על פי מהדורת אנטון בולאד, בירות 1868. אמרת אריסטו אינה מתאימה לבית השיר של מֻתַנַבִּי, ובֻסתאני קובע בצדק, כי נפלה טעות במהדורה זו, ומסתמא כך היה בכתב היד שהיה לנגד המהדיר אנטון בולאד, כלומר המעתיק דילג על בית השיר התואם של מֻתַנַבִּי ועל אמרת אריסטו הבאה לאחריו וזיווג בין אמרת אריסטו לבין בית שיר של מֻתַנַבִּי שאינם תואמים. יש להניח, שטעות זו התגלגלה גם לכתב היד הערבי שהיה לנגד מעתיק כ״י.

69 כ״י: אעראצ̇א. המעתיק קרא את התיבה اغراض: اعراضا.

70 צ״ל: אלמתנבי, וכן להלן. הבית התשיעי בשיר رويدك ايها الملك الجليل, מֻתַנַבִּי 1938, ג, עמ׳ 167. הביאו גם רצ̇א 1980, עמ׳ 55.

71 בֻסתאני 1931, עמ׳ 25, סי׳ 3.

72 כ״י: כסת. המעתיק קרא את התיבה اكتست: كست.

73 הבית השמונה עשר בשיר اعلى الممالك ما يبنى على الاسل, מֻתַנַבִּי 1938, ג, עמ׳ 205.

74 בכתב היד שני הקווים מתחת לתיבה לציון התנוין ביחסת ה־جرّ הערבית.

75 תיבה זו אינה בכ״י ואף במהדורה הנדפסת הובאה על פי כ״י ק.

5. קאל[76] רסטאל[ס][77]

אלאלפאט̇ אלמנטקיה[78] מצ̇רה בד̇וי אלג̇הל לנבו אחסאסהם ען
אדראכהא:[79]
הביטויים ההגיוניים מזיקים לאנשים הנבערים בגלל סלידת תפישתם מהשגתם
[קאל אלמותנבי[80]
25 **בד̇י אלגבאוה מן אנשאדהא צ̇רר / כמא תצ̇ר ריאח אלורד באלג̇על:]**
האוויל אשר ישיר אותם[81] הם נזק / כפי שניחוח הוורד מזיק לחיפושית

[2א] 6. [ק]אל[82] ארסטאלס[83]

[כרור אלאיאם אחל]אם וגד̇אוהא אלאם ואסקאם:[84]
חליפות הימים חלומות ומזונם ייסורים וחליים
קאל אלמתנבי[85]
הון עלי בצר מא שק מנט̇רה / פאנמא יקט̇את אלעין כאלחלם:
המעט להביט במה שקשה לראותו / שכן יקיצות העין הן כחלום

7. קאל[86] רסטאלס[87]

6 **אלחיואן כלה מנקלב וליס מן אלסיאסה שכוי בעץ̇ לבעץ̇.**
בעלי החיים כולם מתהפכים ואין זה מן החכמה להתלונן איש על רעהו

---

76 בֶסתאני 1931, עמ' 27, סי' 7.

77 ברקוקי הביאו בפירושו בשם עֻכּבַּרִי, מֻתַנַבִּי 1938, ג, עמ' 206, הערה 1.

78 כ"י: אלמנטיקיה.

79 האלף לאחר הריש בין השיטין. הנוסח 'אדראכהא' על פי כ"י ق, ובנוסח הפנים ב־ב: دركها. כאן חסרים כמה דפים בכ"י; וראו בהערה הבאה.

80 הבית התשעה עשר בשיר اعلا الممالك ما يبنى على الاسل, מֻתַנַבִּי 1938, ג, עמ' 206. הביאו גם צאחִב 1992, עמ' 81, סי' 18. בית השיר אינו בכ"י לפי שחסרים כאן כמה דפים. בית השיר הושלם על פי ב.

81 הערת בֶסתאני: הכינוי החבור מכוון לשירי השבח שכתב המשורר.

82 בסתאני 1931, עמ' 65, סי' 84.

83 ברקוקי הביאו בפירושו בשם עֻכּבַּרִי, מֻתַנַבִּי 1938, ד, עמ' 372, הערה 4.

84 ב: אסקאם ואלאם, אבל באחד מכתבי היד הערביים כמו בכ"י.

85 הבית השלושים ושניים בשיר حتام نحن نساري النجم في الظلم, מֻתַנַבִּי 1938, ד, עמ' 372.

86 בסתאני 1931, עמ' 66, סימן 66 .

87 ברקוקי הביאו בפירושו בשם עֻכּבַּרִי, מֻתַנַבִּי 1938, ד, עמ' 373, הערה 2, המתייחסת לבית השיר הסמוך לאחר בית השיר שלפנינו.

קאל אל[מת]נב[י][88]

[ו]לא תשכון[89] אלי כ̇לק פתשמתה / [שכ]וי אלג̇ריח אלי אלגרבאן ואלרכ̇ם:

אל תתלונן בפני הבריות ותביאם לשמחה לאיד / תלונת הפצוע בפני העורבים והרחמות

8. קאל[90] רסטאלס[91]

אלנפס אלשריפה תרא אלמות בקא לדרך אלנפס אמאכן אלבקא והד̇ה

חאל[92] יעג̇ז [אלכלק][93] ען רכובהא.[94]

הנפש הנעלה רואה את המוות הישארות להשגת הנפש את מקומות ההישארות וזה

מצב שנבצר מן הבריות להסתגל אליו

קאל אלמתנבי[95]

סבחאן כ̇אלק נפסי כיף לד̇תהא / פימא אלנפוס תראה גאיה אלאלם

השבח לבורא נפשי, הנאת ערבותה / במה שהנפשות רואות את תכלית הסבל

9. קאל[96] רסטאלס

מן כאן גד̇אוה אלאמאני מאת דון בלוג אמאלה[97] ומראדה

אשר היה מזונו שאיפות ימות בלא שישיג תקוותיו ומבוקשו

קאל אלמתנבי[98]

יעללנא[99] הד̇א אלזמאן בד̇א אלועד / ויכ̇דע[100] עמא פי ידיה מן אלנקד

הזמן מסיח דעתנו בהבטחה זו / ומוליך שולל במה שמזומן בידיו

88 הבית השלושים ושלושה בשיר حتام نحن نساري النجم في الظلم, מֻתַנַבִּי 1938, ד, עמ' 373. הביאו גם רצ̇א 1980, עמ' 92.

89 כך בנוסח שהדפיס רשר.

90 בסתאני 1931, עמ' 66, סי' 86.

91 ברקוקי הביאו בפירושו בשם עֻכְּבַּרִי, מֻתַנַבִּי 1938, ד, עמ' 373, הערה 4.

92 כ"י: חאלה; ואין נפקא מינה לעניין המשמעות.

93 תיבה זו השמיטה המעתיק.

94 כ"י בטעות: רכובהמא.

95 הבית השלושים ושישה בשיר حتام نحن نساري النجم في الظلم, מֻתַנַבִּי 1938, ד, עמ' 373. הביאו גם עלאם 1972, עמ' 54.

96 בסתאני 1931, עמ' 72, סי' 98.

97 ב: ליתא.

98 הבית השלושים ושלושה בשיר نسيت وما انسى عتابا على الصد, מֻתַנַבִּי 1938, ב, עמ' 205.

99 כ"י: תעללנא. המעתיק קרא את התיבה يعللنا: تعللنا.

100 כ"י: ותג̇דע. המעתיק קרא את התיבה ويخدع: وتجدع.

10. קאל[101] רסטאלס[102]

אדֹא כאן [צלאח][103] סקם אלנפס [באל]גֹ[הל] כאן אלמות להא שפא מברי לא גירה

אילו היה [תיקון] חולי הנפש בנבערות היה המוות בעבורה מַרְפֵּא מחלים ואין זולתו

[קאל אלמת]נבי[104]

קד אסתשפית מן [דאא בדאא / ואקת]ל מא אע[לך מ]א שפאכא:

אם ביקשת להירפא ממחלה במחלה / הרי מה שריפאך, ממיתך יותר ממה שהחליאך

11. [קאל[105] רסטאלס]

חלול אלפנא[106] פי עט]ים אלאמור כחלולה] פי צגירהא[107]

חֲלוּת החידלון בחשוב שבעניינים כחֲלוּתו בפְּחוּת שבהם

[קאל[108] אלמתנבי

פטעם אלמות פי אמר חקיר [נ"א: صغير] / כטעם אלמות פי אמר עט̇ים:]

טעם המוות בעניין בזוי / כטעם המוות בעניין חשוב

[2ב] 12. קאל[109] רסטאלס[110]

מן לם יקדר עלי פעל אלפצ̇איל פלתכן פצ̇אילה [תרך אל]רד̇איל

מי שאינו יכול לעשות מעשים טובים יהו מעשיו הטובים נטישת המעשים הרעים

קאל אלמתנבי[111]

---

101 בסתאני 1931, עמ' 67, סי' 87.

102 ברקוקי הביאו בפירושו בשם עֻכְּבַּרִי, מֻתַנַבִּי 1938, ג, עמ' 156, הערה 1.

103 תיבה זו ליתא בכ"י וכן לא בכמה מקורות אחרים.

104 הבית התשעה עשר בשיר فدًا لك من يقصر عن مداكا, מֻתַנַבִּי 1938, ג, עמ' 156.

105 בסתאני 1931, עמ' 59, סי' 71.

106 כ"י: אלפתא. המעתיק קרא את התיבה الفتاء: الفنا.

107 כ"י: חקידהא. המעתיק קרא את התיבה صغيرها: حقيدها.

108 הבית השני בשיר اذا غامرت في شرف مروم, מֻתַנַבִּי 1938, ד, עמ' 310. משום מה לא הביא בזה המעתיק את בית השיר המקביל לאמרה המיוחסת לאריסטו והשלמתי על פי ב.

109 בֻסתאני 1931, עמ' 68, סי' 90, בשינויים קטנים וכן על פי כ"י ק.

110 ברקוקי הביאו בפירושו בשם עֻכְּבַּרִי, מֻתַנַבִּי 1938, ג, עמ' 506, הערה 2.

111 הבית הארבעים וחמישה בשיר لا خيل عندك تهديها ولا مال, מֻתַנַבִּי שם, שם. הביאוהו גם צאחִב 1992, עמ' 95, סי' 55; רצ̇א 1980, עמ' 69.

אנא לפי[112] זמן תרך אלקביח בה / מן אכת'ר אלנאס אחסאן ואג'מאל:[113]

אכן אנו [חיים] בזמן שבו המתרחק מן הרע / נחשב לטוב שבאנשים שמעשיהם נאים וטובים

13. קאל[114] רסטאלס

תכ'ליד אלד[כר] פי אלכתב עמר לא יביד והו [פי] כל יום ג'דיד[115]

הנצחת הזיכרון בספרים היא חיים שלא יחדלו והם בכל יום חדשים

קאל אלמתנבי[116]

[ד'כר] אלפתא עמרה אלת'אני[117] וחא[ג'תה / מ]א קאתה[118] ופצ'ול אלעיש אשגאל:[119]

זכרון הגבר – חייו השניים,[120] וצרכיו – / מה שיזינהו, ומעלות החיים – עיסוקים

14. קאל[121] רסטאלס

אעג'ז אלעג'זה מן קדר אן יזיל אלעג'ז ען נפסה פלם יפעל

תכלית חוסר האונים מי שיכול לסלק את חוסר האונים מעצמו ואינו עושה [זאת]

קאל אלמתנבי[122]

ולם אר פי עיוב אלנאס שיא / כנקץ אלקאדרין עלא אלתמאם

לא ראיתי דבר במומי האנשים / כחסרון היכולים [להגיע] אל השלמות

112 כ"י: אתלפי. המעתיק קרא את שתי התיבות انا لفي כתיבה אחת: اتلفي.

113 כ"י: אחסאנא ואג'מאלא, והוא טעות המעתיק שהחליף את התנוין ביחסת הנומינטיב (רַפע, הנושא) לתנוין ביחסת האקוזטיב (נַצב, המושא).

114 בֶסתאני 1931, עמ' 69, סי' 91, בשינויים קטנים וכן על פי כ"י ق.

115 בנדפס הוסיף את המלים 'והו פי כל יום ג'דיד' על פי כ"י ق.

116 הבית הארבעים ושישה בשיר הנ"ל, שם, שם. מערי (מתנבי 1986, ד, עמ' 550) מציין שבית שיר זה הוא משל; וכן הביאו גם רצ'א 1980, עמ' 96.

117 כ"י: אלבאקי. המעתיק קרא את התיבה الثاني: الباقي.

118 כ"י כנראה: חאתה. המעתיק קרא את התיבה قاته: حاته.

119 כ"י: אשגאלא, והוא טעות המעתיק. ראו לעיל, הערה 112.

120 הביאו גם אבו בַּכְּר אבן טֻפַיל בספרו 'הנהגת המתבודד', פרק ד: ועל כן אמר המשורר: "זכרון הדבר ימותיו השניים". ראו דוקס תרי"ג, עמ' 54.

121 בֶסתאני 1931, עמ' 69, סי' 92.

122 הבית השישה עשר בשיר ملومكما يجل عن الملام, מֻתַנַבִּי 1938, ד, עמ' 348. הביאוהו גם צאחִב 1992, עמ' 126, סי' 70; רצ'א 1980, עמ' 91; עלאם 1972, עמ' 9.

15. קאל[123] רסטאלס[124]

אסתבצאר אלעקלא צ̇ד לתמני אלג̇האל[125] ואלחאל[126] אלתי יבכי מנהא
15 אלעאקל יחסדה עליהא[127] אלג̇אהל:
בינת הנבונים ניגוד לתשוקת הנבערים והנסיבות שהנבון בוכה בגינן, יקנא בו הנבער בגינן
קאל אלמתנבי[128]
מא ד̇א לקית מן אלדניא ואעג̇בהא / אני למא אנא באך מנה מחסוד
מה מצאת בעולם, והמופלא שבו / שאשר אני בוכה עליו, מקנאים בו

16. קאל[129] רסטאלס[130]

לא [גנא למן מלכה] אלטמ[ע ואסתולת עליה] אלאמאני:
אין עושר לאשר היתה החמדנות בעליו והשתלטו עליו התשוקות
קאל [אלמתנבי] [131]
21 אמ[סית] ארוח מת̇[ר כ̇אזנא וידא / אנא אל]גני ואמואלי אלמועיד:
נעשיתי האמיד ביותר, אוצֵר הון ובעל יכולת / אני העשיר ורכושי ההבטחות

---

123 בֶּסתאני 1931, עמ' 64, סי' 82.

124 ברקוקי הביאו בפירושו בשם עֻכּבַּרִי, מֻתַנַבִּי 1938, ב, עמ' 170, הערה 1; והשוו עלאם 1972.

125 המלים 'אסתבצאר אלעקלא צ̇ד לתמני אלג̇האל' נוספו בנדפס על פי כ"י ק.

126 אלג̇האל ואלחאל – כ"י: אלג̇הלא פאלחאלה.

127 כ"י: עליהא יחסדה.

128 הבית התשיעי בשיר عيد بأية حال عدت يا عيد, מֻתַנַבִּי 1938, ב, עמ' 170. הביאוהו גם צאחִב 1992, עמ' 58, סי' 28; עלאם 1972, עמ' 56.

129 בֶּסתאני 1931, עמ' 65, סי' 83 ק.

130 ברקוקי הביאו בפירושו בשם עֻכּבַּרִי, שם, עמ' 171, סוף הערה 2 (מן העמוד הקודם).

131 הבית העשירי בשיר הנ"ל, שם, עמ' 170.

נספח:

בתי שיר משל מֻתַנַבִּי בשירה העברית ובספרות הערבית־היהודית בימי הביניים[132]

1 שלמה אבן גבירול, אצלאח אלאכֿלאק (תיקון מידות הנפש), והובא גם באיגרת חאתִמי ובלקט צאחִב:[133]

ואדֿא כאנת אלנפוס כבארא   תעבת מן מראדהא אלאגֿסאם

ואם תהיינה הנפשות גדולות   ייעפו הגופים מרצונותיהן

2 בחיי אבן פקודה, אלהדאיה אלי פראיץֿ אלקלוב (חובות הלבבות) מביא אותו בית:[134]

ואדֿא כאנת אלנפוס כבארא   תעבת מן מראדהא אלאגֿסאם

ואם שגבו נפשות וגדולות הן   הלא אז ייגעו גופים במשאלם

3 יהודה אבן בלעם, פירוש ישעיהו ג,ב:[135]

אלראי מקדם עלי אלשגֿאעה כקול שאער אלערב:

אלראי קבל שגֿאעה אלשגֿעאן   הו אול והי אלמחל אלתֿאני

פאדֿא המא אגֿתמעא לנפס מרה   בלגת מן אלעליא כל מכאן

התבונה עדיפה על האומץ כדברי המשורר הערבי:

התבונה קודמת לאומצו של אמיץ   זו ראשונה וזה במקום השני

אך אם יתקבצו פעם בנפש אחת   תשיג כל מעמד עילאי

4 יצחק אבן ברון, כתאב אלמואזנה (ספר ההשוואה), מביא את הבית הראשון מן השניים הקודמים:[136]

132 בתי השיר יובאו על פי סדר כרונולוגי של החיבורים, תחילה במקור הערבי ואחריו התרגום העברי של המהדירים החדשים, לעתים בשינויים קלים.

133 מקור – אבן גבירול 1902, עמ' 40; תרגום – אבן גבירול תשי"א, עמ' 92; מֻתַנַבִּי 1938, ד, עמ' 83; בֶּסתאני 1931, עמ' 24, סי' 1 (בהעתקה הערבית־היהודית, לעיל, סי' 1); צאחב 1992, עמ' 114, סי' 39.

134 מקור – אבן פקודה 1912, עמ' 231; תרגום – שמחוני תרפ"ו, עמ' 107. יהודה אבן תבון, מתרגם חובות הלבבות בימי הביניים, השמיט את בית השיר, וכך נהג גם בבית שיר ערבי אחר בכתאב אללֻּמַע (ספר הרקמה) ליונה אבן ג'נאח. ראו טובי תש"ס, עמ' 65, הערה 1.

135 הבית הראשון והשני בשיר الراي قبل شجاعة الشجعان, מֻתַנַבִּי 1938, ד, עמ' 389. מקור ותרגום – דרנבורג 1892, עמ' 25; אבן בלעם תשנ"ב, עמ' 35 (ג2).

136 מקור ותרגום אנגלי – וכטר 1964, עמ' 142, הערה 111.

קאל [=אמר] אבו אלטיב:[137]

אלראי קבל שג'אעה אלשג'עאן	הו אול והי אלמחל אלת'אני

5 **הנ"ל, שם:**[138]

אמר אבו אלטיב:

יסתכת'רון אביאת נאמת בהא	**לא תחסד עלי אן ינאם אלאסד**
יתפלאו איך חיברתי שירים לתפארת	**אל תקנאו באריה כשישאג**

6 **משה אבן עזרא, כתאב אלמחאצ'רה ואלמד'אכרה (ספר העיונים והדיונים):**[139]

[לאן ג'אד שער אלחסין פאנמא	**תג'יד אלעטאיא] ואללהא יפתח אללהא**
[לפי שטובה היא שירת אלחסין והרי היא	*משפיעה מתנות]* **והדורון יפתח את הגרון**

7 **הנ"ל, שם:**[140]

אתי אלזמאן בנוה פי שביבתה	**פסרהם ואתינאה עלא אלהרם**
באו בניו אל הזמן בנעוריו	**וישמחם ובאנו אנו אליו לעת זקנה**

8 **הנ"ל, שם:**[141]

[אעז מכאן פי אלדני סרג' סאבח]	**וכ'יר ג'ליס פי אלזמאן כתאב**
[המקום הנכבד בתבל – אוכף סוס שוטף]	**והטוב בחברים בעולם – הספר**

9 **הנ"ל, שם:**[142]

ואבעד מן נאדאך מן לא תג'יבה	**ואגיט' מן עאדאך מן לא תשאכל**
הרחוק בקוראיך הוא אשר לא תענהו	**והכעוס בשונאיך – אשר לא תדמה לו**

137 אַבּוּ אלטַּיִּב הוא הכינוי המקובל בספרות הערבית למֻתַנַבִּי.

138 הבית הראשון בשיר يستعظمون ابياتا نامت بها, מֻתַנַבִּי **1938**, ב, עמ' **106**. מקור – **קוקובצב תש"ל, עמ' 169**; מקור ותרגום אנגלי – **וכטר 1964, עמ' 142, הערה 111**. המעתיק קרא את התיבה: يستعظمون – يستكثرون.

139 בית השיר אינו כלול בדיואנים הנדפסים של שירי מֻתַנַבִּי. מקור ותרגום – **אבן עזרא תשל"ה, עמ' 90–91**. אבן עזרא מביא רק את שלוש המלים האחרונות בסוגר.

140 הבית האחרון בשיר حتام نحت نساري النجم في الظلم, מֻתַנַבִּי **1938**, ד, עמ' **374**. מקור ותרגום – **אבן עזרא תשל"ה, עמ' 90–91**. המלים 'פי שביבתה פסרהם' הושמטו במהדורת הלקין, על פי נוסח הפְּנים של כתב היד של מחאצ'רה, ועל פיו גם נדפס 'פי' במקום 'עלא'. אבל הבית בשלמותו ובנוסחו המדויק נמצא בשולי כ"י. ראו **בראון תש"ג, עמ' 130–131**.

141 הבית השמונה עשר בשיר منى كن لي ان البياض خضاب, מֻתַנַבִּי **1938**, א, עמ' **222**. מקור ותרגום – **אבן עזרא תשל"ה, עמ' 108–109; צאחִב 1992, עמ' 43, סי' 36**. אבן עזרא הביא רק את סוגר השיר.

142 הבית העשרים ושבעה בשיר دروع لملك الروم هاذى الرسائل, מֻתַנַבִּי **1938**, ג, עמ' **295**. מקור ותרגום – **אבן עזרא תשל"ה, עמ' 110–111**. בית השיר כלול גם באיגרת חאתמי, **בֶּסתאני 1931, עמ' 35, סי' 21** ובלקט **צאחִב 1992, עמ' 43, סי' 36**.

10 הנ"ל, שם:[143]

פליס אלתטבע כאלטבע ולא אלתכחל פי אלעין כאלכחל. פקד קיל: מבאינה אלמתכלף[144] לל־מטבוע כמבאינה אלחק ללבאטל.

שכן אין ההתראות־כטבע טבע ולא ההתכחלות בעין כחל. וכן נאמר: החִלוק בין המתיימר ובין הטבוע כחלוק בין האמת ובין השקר.

המשפט 'ולא אלתכחל פי אלעין כאלכחל' שאול מסוגר בבית שיר של מֻתַנַבִּי, בשינוי קטן,[145] ואלו המשפט 'מבאינה [...] ללבאטל' הוא מאמר חכמה המיוחס לאריסטו.

11 הנ"ל, שם:

סהאד לאג̇פאן ושמס לנאט̇ר — וסקם לאבדאן ומסך לנאשק

נדודים לעפעפים ושמש למביט — ומחלה לגופים ומור למריח

12 הנ"ל, שם:[146]

ללסבי מא נכחו וללקתל מא ולדו — ואלנהב מא ג̇מעו ואלנאר מא זרעו

לשבי אשר נשאו ולהרג אשר ילדו — ולבז אשר אספו ולאש אשר זרעו

13 הנ"ל, שם:[147]

ומא קלת ללבדר אנת אללג̇ין — ומא קלת ללשמס אנת אלד̇הב

ולא אמרתי לסהר אתה הכסף — ולא אמרתי לשמש אתה הזהב

---

143 מקור ותרגום – אבן עזרא תשל"ה, עמ' 136–139.

144 בנדפס 'אלתכלף' (ההתקשטות), וכן אבן עקנין (להלן, סי' 26) ובאיגרת חאתִמי. הנוסח 'אלמתכלף' (המתקשט) יותר מתאים מבחינת העניין – השוואת המתקשט לטבוע ולא השוואת ההתקשטות לטבוע.

145 סוגר הבית הארבעים ושלושה בשיר اجاب دمعي وما الداعي سوى طلل, מֻתַנַבִּי 1938, ג, עמ' 261. התיבה הראשונה בסוגר בדיואן מֻתַנַבִּי היא ليس. והשוו צאחִב 1993, סי' 28, עמ' 85. המאמר ובית השיר כלולים באיגרת חאתִמי, בֶּסתאני 1931, עמ' 32, סי' 17. והשוו להלן, סי' 25.

146 הבית השלושה עשר בשיר غيري باكثر هذا الناس بخدع, מֻתַנַבִּי 1938, ב, עמ' 398. מקור ותרגום – אבן עזרא תשל"ה, עמ' 246–247.

147 הבית השישי בשיר فهمت الكتاب ابر الكتب, מֻתַנַבִּי 1938, א, עמ' 112. מקור ותרגום – אבן עזרא תשל"ה, עמ' 260–261. בנדפס 'אללג̇ען' במקום 'אללג̇ין' (اللجعن — اللجين), והוא שיבוש כפי שכבר ציין בראון תש"ג, עמ' 195, סי' 54, אך הלקין לא חש לכך.

14 הנ"ל, שם:[148]

לכל אמריא מן דהרה מא תעודא   ועאדאת סיף אלדולה אלטען פי אלעדא
לכל איש מֻנָּה מזמנו מה שהורגל בו   והרגלי סיף אלדולה לדקור אויב בחרבו

15 הנ"ל שם:[149]

עדוך מד֗מום בכל לסאן   ולו כאן מן אעדאיך אלקמראן
כל הלשונות יגנו אויביך   ולו היו השמש והירח אויביך

16 הנ"ל, שם:[150]

וקד וג֗דת מג֗אל אלקול ד֗א סעה   פאן וג֗דת לסאנא קאילא פקל
כבר מצאת מקום נרחב לדיבור   ואם תמצא לשונך שָׁרָה, שיר!

17 הנ"ל, שם 153:[151]

בפרע יעיד אלליל ואלצבח ניר   ווג֗ה יעיד אלצבח ואלליל מט֗לם
בשֵׂער ישיב את הליל והבוקר מאיר   ופנים ישיבו את הבוקר והליל מחשיך

18 הנ"ל, שם:[152]

[אד֗ כנת תרצ֗י באן יעטו אלג֗זי בד֗לוא   מנהא רצ֗אך] ומן ללעור באלחול
אם תיאות שיתנו כופר יחרפו נפשם   עליה לרצונך כייחול העיוורים לפזילה

19 הנ"ל, שם 172:[153]

בעידה מא בין אלג֗פון כאנמא   עקדתם אעאלי כל הדב בחאג֗ב
רחוקים הם העפעפַּיִם זה מזה כאילו   קשרתם עליוני כל ריס בגבה

148 הבית הראשון בשיר لكل امرىء من دهره ما تعودا, מֻתַנַבִּי 1938, ב, עמ' 3. מקור ותרגום – אבן עזרא תשל"ה, עמ' 274–275. בנדפס 'אמר' במקום 'אמריא' (امر — امرىء).

149 הבית הראשון בשיר عدوك مذموم بكل لسان, מֻתַנַבִּי 1938, ד, עמ' 472. מקור ותרגום – אבן עזרא תשל"ה, עמ' 274–275. בנדפס 'באללסאן' במקום 'בכל לסאן' (باللسان — بكل لسان)

150 הבית העשרים וחמישה בשיר اجاب دمعي وما الداعي سوى طلل, מֻתַנַבִּי 1938, ג, עמ' 254. מקור ותרגום – אבן עזרא תשל"ה, עמ' 280–281. בנדפס 'מכאן' במקום 'מג֗אל' (مكان — مجال).

151 הבית השישי בשיר نرى عظما بالبين والصاد اعظم, מֻתַנַבִּי 1938, ד, עמ' 259. פנטון 1997, עמ' 409.

152 הבית השלושים וארבעה בשיר اجاب دمعي وما الداعي سوى طلل, מֻתַנַבִּי 1938, ג, עמ' 257. פנטון 1997, עמ' 410. אבן עזרא הביא רק את שלוש המלים האחרונות בבית.

153 הבית השלישי בשיר اعيدوا صباحي فهو عند الكواعب, מֻתַנַבִּי 1938, א, עמ' 170. פנטון 1997, עמ' 410. בנדפס 'ג֗פן' במקום 'הדב' (جفن — هدب)

20 יהודה הלוי, כתאב אלרד ואלדליל פי נצר אלדין אלדליל (הכוזרי):[154]

קאל: אנא אלגריק פמא כ֗ופי מן אלבלל

אמר: אני הטובע ואיני חושש מן הרטיבות

על פי בית שיר לְמֻתַנַבִּי, שהובא גם באיגרת חאתִמי ובלקט צאחִב:[155]

والهجر اقتل لي مما اراقبه	انا الغريق فما خوفي من البلل
הפירוד ממיתני יותר מִצִּפִּייתי לבואו	אני הטובע ואינני מפחד להירטב

21 יהודה הלוי, דיואן:[156]

יוֹם שְׁעֲשַׁעְתִּיהוּ עֲלֵי בִרְכַּי	וַיַּרְא תְּמוּנָתוֹ בְאִישׁוֹנַי
נִשַּׁק שְׁתֵּי עֵינַי מְתַעְתֵּעַ	אֶת תָּאֳרוֹ נָשַׁק וְלֹא עֵינַי

שיר קצר זה הוא תרגום שני בתים מתוך שיר ארוך של מֻתַנַבִּי, כפי שכבר עמדו על כך החוקרים:[157]

شامية طالما خلوت بها	تبصر في ناظري محياها
فقبلت ناظري تغالطني	وإنما قبلت به فاها
[שפחה] סורית בכל עת שנתייחדתי עמה	ראתה בתוך עיני פניה
אז נשקה עיני ורימתני	ולא נשקה בה אלא את פיה!

22 נתנאל בן פיומי, בסתאן אלעקול (=גן השכלים):[158]

ומן עג֗ב אלדהר עלי אלמרא אן ירא	עדו לה מן מא מצאדקתה בדי
ומפלאי החיים על האדם בראותו	אויבו יוצא מבין ידידיו

154 זיהוי בית השיר ותרגומו – יהודה הלוי תשל"ג, עמ' קכח. למקור הערבי, בלא זיהוי בית השיר לְמֻתַנַבִּי, ראו יהודה הלוי 1887 (מהדורת הירשפלד), עמ' 189; יהודה הלוי תשל"ז (מהדורת בנעט־בן־שמאי), עמ' 121; יהודה הלוי תשנ"ז (מהדורת קאפח), עמ' קכב.

155 הבית השישי בשיר اجاب دمعي وما الداعي سوى طلل, מֻתַנַבִּי 1938, ג, עמ' 247; בֻּסתאני 1931, עמ' 30, סי' 14; צאחִב 1992, עמ' 83, סי' 23.

156 יהודה הלוי תרנ"ו/ז, עמ' 16.

157 הבתים השלישי והרביעי בשיר اوه بديل من قولي واها, מֻתַנַבִּי 1938, ד, עמ' 513.

158 מקור ותרגום – נתנאל תשמ"ד, עמ' צה–צו.

נוסח אחר בדיואן מֻתַנַבִּי:[159]

ومن نكد الدنيا على الحر ان يرى عدوا له ما من صداقته بد

ומייסורי האדם האציל בתבל כי יראה אויב שאין מנוס מלהתיידד אתו

23 שמואל בן עלי, אגרות:[160]

וכמא לכ֗צה אבו אלטיב אלמתנבי פי קולה:

ואן פארקתני אמטארה פאכת֗ר גדראנהא מא נצ֗ב

וכמו שהביעו בקיצור אבו אלטיב אלמתנבי בשירו:

אף כי חדלו ממני גשמיו הנה לא יבשו רוב נחליו

24 יהודה אבן עקנין, אנכשאף אלאסראר וט֗הור אלאנואר (התגלות הסודות והופעת המאורות):[161]
כקול ארסטו אלאלפאט֗ אלמנטקיה צ֗ארה בד֗וי אלג֗הל לאנהא מעדיה תודי בהם אלי מא יהלכ־הם. וקאל אלמתנבי:

בד֗י אלגבאוה מן אנשאדהא צ֗רר כמא תצ֗ר ריאח אלורד באלג֗על

כמאמר אריסטו: המלות ההגיוניות מזיקות לבעלי הבערות מפני שהם מַעֲבְרוֹת שיוליכו אותם אל מה שישמידם. אמר מתנבי:

נזק בשירה לחסר הלב כאשר יזיק ריח השושנה לחיפושית

159 הבית השמיני בשיר اقل فعالي بله اكثره مجد, מֻתַנַבִּי 1938, ב, עמ' 107.

160 הבית השמונה עשר בשיר فهمت الكتاب ابر الكتب, מֻתַנַבִּי 1938, א, עמ' 115. מקור ותרגום – שמואל בן עלי תש"ל, עמ' 73.

161 הבית התשעה עשר בשיר اعلى الممالك ما يبني على الاسل, מֻתַנַבִּי 1938, ג, עמ' 206. מקור ותרגום – אבן עקנין תש"ל, עמ' 140–141; בית השיר – צאחִב 1992, סי' 18, עמ' 81. בנדפס 'ריאחה' במקום 'ריאח' (رياحة — رياح). המאמר ובית השיר כלולים באיגרת חאתִמי, בֶּסתאני 1931, עמ' 27, סי' 7. מאמר אריסטו באיגרת חאתִמי שונה בחלקו השני, לאחר המלה 'אלג֗הל': لبنو احساسهم عن دركها.

25 הנ"ל, שם:[162]

וכמא קאל ארסטו והדֹא נצה. מבאינה אלמתכלף[163] ללמטבוע כמבאינה אלחק ללבאטל. ונטֹאם הדֹא אלמתנבי פי קולה:

לאן חלמך חלם לא תכלפה ליס אלתכחל באלעינין כאלכחל

וכמו שאמר ארסטו וזה לשונו: ההבדל שבין המתקשט לטבוע כהבדל שבין האמת לשקר. וחרז זאת מתנבי בשירתו:

כי אורך אפך לא אורך רוח עדיתו לא ככוחל התכחלות העיניים

26 אלעזר הבבלי, פרקים בתורת השיר:[164]

בדת קמרא ומאלת כֹוט באן ופאחת ענברא ורנת גזאלא

הופיעה – סהר, התנועעה – ענף עבות הפיצה ענבר ונראתה צבייה

27 הנ"ל, שם:[165]

נהבת מן אלאעמאר מא לו חויתה להנית אלדניא באנך כֹאלד

גזלת חיים, אשר לו חיית אותם היה העולם מתברך בהיותך נצחי

28 הנ"ל, דיואן:[166]

ללמתנבי ערביא אקלבה עבראנייא

ביאץ̇ וגֹה יריך אלשמס חאלכה ודר לפטֹ יריך אלדר מכֹשלבא

חרוז ערבי למתנבי אתרגמנו לעברית

צְבִי לוֹ אוֹת בְּעַפְעַפָּיו וּמוֹפֵת בְּעַד לֶחְיוֹ וּבָהּ דָּמִים נְקִיִּים

162 סוגר הבית הארבעים ושלושה בשיר اجاب دمعي وما الداعي سوى طلل, מֻתַנַבִּי 1938, ג, עמ' 261; ראו לעיל, סי' 10. מקור ותרגום – אבן עקנין תש"ל, עמ' 438–430; בית השיר – צאהִב 1992, עמ' 85, סי' 28; המאמר ובית השיר כלולים באיגרת חאתִמי, בֶּסתאני 1931, עמ' 32, סי' 17. בנדפס 'לא' במקום 'לאן' (لا — لان).

163 בנדפס 'אלתכלף' וראו לעיל, הערה 145.

164 הבית העשירי בשיר بقائي شاء ليس هم ارتحالا, מֻתַנַבִּי 1938, ג, עמ' 423. מקור ותרגום – אלעזר הבבלי תשס"א, עמ' 137–134.

165 הבית השלושים ושבעה בשיר عواذل ذات الخال في حواسد, מֻתַנַבִּי 1938, א, עמ' 316. מקור ותרגום – אלעזר הבבלי תשס"א, עמ' 149–146.

166 הבית החמישה עשר בשיר دمع جرى فقضى في الربع ما وجبا, מֻתַנַבִּי 1938, א, עמ' 130. מקור ותרגום – אלעזר הבבלי תרצ"ה, עמ' מז.

הֲדָרוֹ יַרְאֲךָ יוֹמָם וְלַיְלָה	וְעֵינוֹ תַּרְאֲךָ מָוֶת וְחַיִּים

29 יהודה אלחריזי, תחכמוני:[167]

מִזִּיו מְאוֹרוֹ יֶחֱזוּ עִוְרִים וְשִׂפְ-	תוֹת אִלְּמִים טוּב נָאֳמִי תַּבַּעְנָה

עיבוד בית מפורסם של מֻתַנַבִּי:[168]

انا الذي نظر الاعمى الى ادبي	واسمعت كلماتي من به صمم

אני האיש אשר הביט העיוור לשירי	והשמעתי נאומי לכל החֵרשים

30 אברהם גבישון, עומר השכחה:[169]

ומשוררי הערב זכרו בזה בתים והם אלו:

אדֿא אנת אכרמת אלכרים מלכתה	ואן אנת אכרמת אללאים תמרדא

וצֿע אלנדא פי מוצֿע אלסיף באלעלא	מצֿר כוצֿע אלסיף פי מוצֿע אלנדא

והעתקתים ללשוננו הקדום:

בכבדך נדיב יכבדך אכן	בכבדך נבל ישלם לך קלון

מקום קלון כבוד יהי מזיק כאשר	מקום כבוד קלון כקוצים וכסילון

167 אלחריזי תשי"א, עמ' 122.

168 הבית החמישה עשר בשיר واحر قلباه ممن قلبه شبم, מֻתַנַבִּי 1938, ד, עמ' 108; והשוו מרעי תשנ"ח, עמ' 188.

169 הבתים העשרים ותשעה והשלושים בשיר لكل امرىء من دهره ما تعودا , מֻתַנַבִּי 1938, ב, עמ' 13. מקור ותרגום – גבישון תק"ח, דף צג,ב. בנדפס נפלו טעויות רבות מחמת אי־ידיעת הלשון הערבית: "אדֿא אנת אכרמת אלכרים מלכתא / ואדֿא אנת אכרמת אל לאים תמרדא // ווצֿע אלאדֿא פי מוצֿע אלכאס ללפתי / מצֿר כואצֿתו אלכאס פי מוצֿע אלנדא".

ביבליוגרפיה

אבן בלעם תשנ"ב	יהודה אבן בלעם, פירוש לספר ישעיהו. מהדורת משה גושן־גוטשטיין ומערבי פרץ. רמת גן
אבן גבירול תשי"א	שלמה אבן גבירול, ספר תקון מדות הנפש. מהדורת נח בראון. תל אביב
אבן גבירול 1902	Shlomo Ibn Gabirol, *The Improvement of the Moral Qualities.* Ed. Stephen S. Wise. New York
אבן עזרא תשל"ה	ספר העיונים והדיונים. מהדורת א"ש הלקין. ירושלים
אבן עקנין תשכ"ד	יוסף אבן עקנין, התגלות הסודות והופעת המאורות. מהדורת א"ש הלקין. ירושלים
אבן פקודה 1912	Bachja Ibn Paquda, *Al-Hidāja Ila Farā'iḍ, al-Qulūb*. Ed. A.S. Yahuda. Leiden
אבן פקודה תשל"ג	בחיי אבן פקודה, ספר תורת חובות הלבבות, מקור ותרגום. מהדורת יוסף קאפח. ירושלים
אבן רשיק 1988	ابن ر شيق, العمدة في محاسن الشعر وادابه. تحقيق محمد قرقزان. جزآن. بيروت
אלחריזי תשי"א	יהודה אלחריזי, ספר תחכמוני. מהדורת יהודה טופורובסקי. ירושלים
אלעזר הבבלי תרצ"ה	אלעזר הבבלי, דיואן. מהדורת חיים בראדי. ירושלים
אלעזר הבבלי תשס"א	-- , פרקים בתורת השיר. מהדורת יוסף יהלום. ירושלים
בונבקר 1984	Seeger A.Bonebakker, *Ḥātimī and His Encounter with Mutanabbī: A Biographical Sketch.* Amsterdam

בונבקר 2004 --, Ḥātimī, Abū Ꜥ̓Alí Muḥammad B. Al-Ḥasan B. Al-Muẓaffar. *EI* XII, pp. 360–363

בלאו 2002 Yehoshua Blau, Hebrew versus Other Languages of the Traditional Medieval Jewish Society. *JSAI* 27, pp. 348–355

בֻּסתאני 1931 فؤاد افرام البستاني. الرسالة الحاتمية فيما وافق المتنبي في شعره كلام ارسطو في الحكمة للامام ابي علي محمد بن الحسن بن المظفر البغدادي الحاتمي. بيروت [נדפס תחילה בהמשכים בכתב העת المشرق באותה שנה, עמ' 273–280, 348–355, 461–464, 623–632, 759–768, 921–934]

בקר תשס"ה דן בקר, מקורות ערביים של 'ספר ההשוואה בין העברית והערבית' ליצחק בן ברון. תל אביב

בראון תש"ג נח בראון, בתי־השיר הערביים ב"כתאב אלמחאצ̇רה ואלמד̇כרה". תרביץ יד, עמ' 136–139, 191–203

גאנם 1972 Muhammad A. Ghānim, Verse Used in Sanꜥānī Songs. *Al-Abhath*. 25, pp. 17–326

גבישון תק"ח אברהם בן יעקב גבישון, עומר השכחה, פירוש משלי, ליוורנו תק"ח (ד"צ עם מבוא מאת מאת שמואל סירא, ירושלים תשל"ג)

גויטיין תשכ"ב שלמה דב גויטיין, סדרי חינוך בימי הגאונים ובית הרמב"ם – מקורות חדשים מן הגניזה. ירושלים

גולדציהר 1870 Ignaz Goldziher, Mutanabbi und ein Jude. *Hebräische Bibliographie* 10, pp. 59–60 (=Ignaz Goldziher, *Gesammelte Schriften*, 1967, Band I, p. 1)

דוקס תרי"ג יהודה ליב דוקס, זכרון המשוררים בספרי חכמי ישראל. בתוך ספרו: נחל קדומים, חוברת ראשונה, עמ' 41–54. הנובר

דינור תרפ"ו בן-ציון דינור, ישראל בגולה, כרך ראשון, ספר ראשון. ירושלים

דנה תשמ״ג	יוסף דנה, הפואטיקה של השירה העברית בספרד בימי הביניים על פי ר׳ משה אבן עזרא ומקורותיה. ירושלים-תל אביב
דרנבורג 1892	Joseph Derenbourg, *Gloses d'Abou Zakariya Ben Bilam*. Paris
היינריקס 1990	Wolfhart Heinrichs, The Meaning of Mutanabbī. In: James L. Kugel, *Poetry and Prophecy*, pp. 121–139, 231–239. Ithaca
וכטר 1964	Pinchas Wechter, *Ibn Baruns's Arabic Works on Hebrew Grammar and Lexicography*. Philadelphia
חייט 1966	שמעון חייט, שירי המלחמה של ר׳ שמואל הנגיד והשוואתם לשירי המלחמה של אלמותנבי. מפגש ב, עמ׳ 201–192.
חנין תקס״ז	חנין בן אסחאק, מוסרי הפלוסופים [בתרגום יהודה אלחריזי]. בתוך: גורן נכון: תקון מדות הנפש להחכם ר׳ שלמה בן יודא גבירול ז״ל עם ספר מוסרי הפלוסופים וספר התפוח לאריסטוטליס. לינוויל
טובי תש״ס	יוסף טובי, קירוב ודחייה – יחסי השירה העברית והשירה הערבית בימי הביניים. חיפה
טובי תשס״ו	--, הספרות הערבית־היהודית והגניזה. אוניברסיטת תל אביב [בדפוס]
טובי, חאתִמי ואבן עזרא	--, עיונים ראשונים בחִלְיַה אלמֻחאצַרה לאבּו עלי מֻחמד אלחאתִמי: המקור ׳האבוד׳ של משה אבן עזרא בכִּתאב אלמֻחאצַרה ואלמֻדַאכַּרה [בדפוס]
יהודה הלוי 1887	יהודה הלוי, כתאב אלחגֹה ואלדליל פי נצר אלדין אלדליל. מהדורת הרטויג הירשפלד. לייפציג
יהודה הלוי תרנ״ו/ז	--, דיואן, ספר שני, שירי החול. מהדורת חיים בראדי. ברלין
יהודה הלוי תשל״ג	--, ספר הכוזרי. מהדורת יהודה אבן שמואל. ירושלים

יהודה הלוי תשל"ז	--, כתאב אלרד ואלדליל פי אלדין אלדליל (ספר המענה והראיה על אודות הדת המושפלה). מהדורת ד"צ בנעט וחגי בן־שמאי. ירושלים
יהודה הלוי תשנ"ז	--, ספר הכוזרי. מהדורת יוסף קאפח. ירושלים
כ'ואג'א 1982	زهدي صبري الخواجا. موازنة بين الحكمة في شعر المتنبي والحكمة في شعر ابي العلاء المعري. الرياض
לוין תשכ"ח	ישראל לוין, שירי המלחמה של שמואל הנגיד על רקע שירת הגיבורים הערבית העתיקה. הספרות 1, עמ' 343–367
לוין תשנ"ה	--, מעיל תשבץ – הסוגים השונים של שירת החול העברית בספרד . כרכים א–ג. תל אביב
מבארך 1980	زكي مبارك. النثر الفني في القرن الرابع. ٤ اجزاء. بيروت [כתיבת הספר נסתיימה בינואר 1934, כמצוין בסוף פתיחת המחבר, חלק א, עמ' 16]
מלטר 1921	Henry Malter, *Saadia Gaon, His Life and Works*. Philadelphia
מרעי תשנ"ח	עבד אלרחמן מרעי, השפעת מקאמות אלחרירי על מקאמות אלחריזי. עבודת דוקטור, אוניברסיטת בר־אילן. רמת גן
מרצפי 1991	حسين المرصفي. الوسيلة الادبية الى العلوم العربية. جزآن. تحقيق عبد العزيز الدسوقي. القاهرة
מֻתַנַבִּי 1938	عبد الرحمن البرقوقي. شرح ديوان المتنبي. ٤ اجزاء. [القاهرة][2]
מֻתַנַבִּי 1986	ابو العلاء المعري. "معجز احمد". شرح ديوان ابي الطيب المتنبي. تحقيق عبد المجيد دياب. ٤ اجزاء. [القاهرة]
נַופל [1987]	نبيل رشاد نوفل. ابو علي الحاتمي — افكاره النقدية وتطبيعاته. الاسكندرية

נתנאל תשמ"ד נתנאל בן פיומי, בסתאן אלעקול (גן השכלים). מהדורת יוסף קאפח. תל אביב2

סדן תשנ"ה יוסף סדן, ר' יהודה אלחריזי כצומת תרבותי. פעמים 68, עמ' 16–67.

סזגין 1967 Fuat Sezgin, *Geschichte des arabischen Schrifttums*. Leiden

סלאמה 1981 يسري محمد سلامة الحكمة في شعر المتنبي. الاسكندرية

סקליר תשנ"ח דוד סקליר, ר' דוד בן סעדיה אלגר וחיבורו אלחאוי. בתוך: יהושע בלאו, חגי בן־שמאי, מ"ע פרידמן ויואל קרמר (עורכים), מפגשים בתרבות הערבית-היהודית של ימי הביניים (תעודה יד), עמ' 103–123. תל אביב

עבאס 1993 احسان عباس، تاريخ النقد الادبي عند العرب، نقد الشعر من القرن الثاني حتى القرن الثامن الهجري. عمان. מהדורה חדשה מורחבת ומוגהת

עלאם 1972 محمد مهدي علام، فلسفة المتنبي من شعره. [القاهرة]

עמידי 1961 محمد بن احمد العميدي، الابانة عن سرقات المتنبي. تحقيق ابراهيم الدمشقي الدسوقي البساطي. القاهرة

פנטון 1997 Paul B. Fenton, *Philosophie et exégèse dans Le Jardin de la Methaphore de Moise Ibn Ezra (philosophe et poete andalou duXII^e^ siècle)*. Leiden

צאחב 1974 Al-Ṣaḥib ibn ʿAbbās, *Al Kashf ʿAn Masa̱wi Al Mutanabbi*. pp. 1-28. Tr. A.Wormhoudt. William Penn College

צאחב 1992 الصاحب بن عباد، امثال ابي الطيب المتنبي. تحقيق محمد ابراهيم سليم. القاهرة

קאן 1986 Geoffrey Khan, The Arabic manuscripts in the Genizah – Part Two, *Genizah Fragments* 11

קוקובצב תש"ל פאול קוקובצב, מספרי הבלשנות העברית בימי הביניים. ירושלים [ד"צ]

רצֹא חש"ד — علي رضا ، المتنبي — حكمه وامثاله. حلب

רצהבי תש"ל — יהודה רצהבי, פתיחה מתורגמת בשיר־פירוד לר' יהודה הלוי. בקורת ופרשנות 1, עמ' 46–50

רצהבי תשנ"ה — שירה ערבית בפי יהודים באנדלוסיה. בתוך: ראובן צור וטובה רוזן (עורכים), קובץ מחקרים בספרות העברית לדורותיה – ספר ישראל לוין, א, עמ' 329–350. תל אביב

רֶשֶר 1926 — O. Rescher, Die *Risālat el-Hātimijje*: Ein vergleich von Versen des Motenabbi mit Aussprüchen von Aristoteles, *Islamica* 2, pp. 439–473

שהיד 2004 — Irfan Shahid, The *Sūra* of the Poets, Qur'ān XXVI: Final Conclusions. *Journal of Arabic Literature* 35, pp. 175–220

שטיינשניידר תר"ב — משה שטיינשניידר, ויבא יעקב אל העין [...] צוואת ר' יהודה אבן תבון [...]. ברלין

שטרן 1963 — S.M. Stern, Arabic Poems by Spanish-Hebrew Poets. בתוך: משה לזר (עורך), מחקרים בתרבות המערב מוקדשים לזכרו של חירם פרי, עמ' 254–263. ירושלים

שיפרס 1994 — Arie Schippers, *The Hebrew Poetry and the Arabic Literary Tradition – Arabic Themes in Hebrew Andalusian Poetry*. Leiden

שמואל בן עלי תש"ל — שמואל בן עלי, אגרות. מהדורת שמחה אסף. ירושלים[2]

שמחוני תרפ"ו — יעקב נפתלי שמחוני, ספר 'חובת הלבבות' במקורו הערבי. העתיד ו, עמ' 85–110

אשת יפת תואר בספרי ובפרשנות הקדומה

יועם יורה (אוניברסיטת טורונטו)

המסגרת החוקתית

פרשת אשת יפת תואר (דברים כ׳ 11) מופיעה במסגרת חוקי המלחמה של ספר דברים. הקש־רה המיידי הוא הקריאה לשלום (דברים כ׳ 10-20) ופרשת החלל (כ״א 1-9) לפניה, וחוקי האישה האהובה והשנואה (כ״א 15-17) ובן סורר ומורה (כ״א 18-21) מיד אחריה.

חשיבות המסגרת החוקתית להבנת הטקסט

ציון המסגרת הטקסטואלית ראויה לציון מפני שהמפרשים לדורותיהם מייחסים חשיבות לסמיכות פרשיות בכלל ובמיוחד במקרה זה. ישנן שתי דרכים בסיסיות ומנוגדות להתייחס לסוגיית סמיכות הפרשיות במקרא. האחת היא להתייחס לכל חוק כאל יחידה אטומית ולא קשורה לסביבתה, והשנייה היא לייחס חשיבות פרשנית לסמיכות הפרשיות אף במקרה שהפרשיות שונות מאד. פרשת אשת יפת תואר פותחת במילים: ״כי תצא למלחמה״. בניגוד למשמעותה הרווחת בעברית המודרנית, המילית ״כי״ מופיעה פעמים רבות במקרא כפתיחת משפט או עניין (ובמיוחד בניסוחי חוק). אף פה נראה שהמילית ״כי״ פותחת עניין חדש שאינו קשור מיידית לסוגייה הקודמת (פרשת החלל).

אם מנתחים את פרשת אשת יפת תואר בניתוק מסביבתה אזי נראה כאילו התורה מאפשרת בקלילות רבה אינוס אישה שבוייה מכיוון שהחוק לא מפרש באיזה סוג של מלחמה, ולכן הפירוש הסתמי של המקראות הוא שמדובר בכל סוגי המלחמות. הבנת המקראות באופן זה סותר את חוקי המלחמה בפרשיות הסמוכות (אך אם כל חוק הוא אטומי בפני עצמו אין בזה בעיה). חוקי המלחמה בפרק כ׳ מבדילים בין שני סוגי מלחמה, מלחמה נגד שבעת העממים שבמקרה זה חייבים להמית את כולם, ומלחמה נגד ערים רחוקות שאינם חלק משבעת העממים, שדינם שונה. המפרשים (רש״י לדוגמא) מכנים את שני סוגי המלחמה – מלחמת מצווה ומלחמת רשות. אף במקרה של מלחמת רשות אין לכאורה שבויים, שכן פשט הכתובים: ״והיו לך למס ועבדוך״ מתייחס למעמד העיר ולא למעמד האנשים שבתוכה, היינו העיר הופכת להיות וואסאלית של ממלכת ישראל, מסתמא תושבי

העיר אינם הופכים לשבויים. אך ניתן לכאורה לתרץ שמדובר במקרה של מלחמת רשות שהעיר לא נכנעה לישראל והיו צריכים להילחם עליה, ובעת הלחימה ייתכנו מקרים של שבויים ושבויות.

אם מנתחים את פרשת אשת יפת תואר כחלק ממסגרת חוקתית מקיפה יותר (ואת המילית "כי" כמקשרת – ואכן יש לציין שחלק גדול מן החוקים במסגרת חוקתית זו פותחים במילית "כי") ומני־חים שהחוק הנדון מתיישב עם שאר חוקי המלחמה, אזי אשת יפת תואר היא שבוייה במלחמת רשות (על אף האמור למעלה לגבי המעמד הוואסלי של העיר). התורה מניחה שמנהג החיילים במלחמה אינו זהה למנהגם בחיי היום-יום ושאם התורה מתירה להרוג אזי קשה לאסור אינוס ומעשי אלימות פחות חמורים. בהתחשב בכך התורה מנסה ליצור חוק שייטיב עם האישה השבוייה – האישה לא יכולה להימכר לעבדות והאיש חייב לקחת אותה לתוך ביתו ולשמור עליה.

אם מייחסים חשיבות לסמיכות הפרשיות מעבר למסגרת הכללית של חוקי מלחמה (זוהי דרך המדרש, אך לפעמים סדר הפרשיות הוא הפירוש הראשון לטקסט) התורה מרחיקה לכת אף יותר ומזהירה שאם חייל נושא אישה בדרך זו הדבר עתיד לגרום בעיות עתידיות, יריבות בין נשים (חוק האישה האהובה והאישה השנואה) ואף בן סורר ומורה שלא ישמע לאביו או לאימו בגלל הסביבה שבה הוא גדל (אביו אנס את אמו).

אשת יפת תואר בפרשנות היהודית הקדומה

א.פילון האלכסנדרוני

פילון האלכסנדרוני בפירושו לפרשה זו (Philo, De Virtutides, XXII, 110-115) מייחס חשיבות לסמיכות הפרשיות אך הוא מתעלם לגמרי מעניין האונס ומהעובדה שהמלחמה היא יוזמת עם ישראל, וטוען בדוחק שמדובר במלחמת הגנה. כמו כן פילון טוען "שכל החוקים הללו ראויים לשבח", ובמגמה זו הוא מתרגם את המילה עיניתה, שמשמעותה לפי רוב החוקרים קשור באונס, במילה פחות טעונה. פילון משבח את התנהגות החייל המציל את האישה מן השבי שלדידו גרוע ממוות, הוא (החייל) נותן לה זמן להצטער על אובדן משפחתה, ומפרש את איסור מכירתה לעבדות כערבון לביטחונה האישי. לפי פילון פרשת האישה האהובה והשנואה קשור לחוק הנדון, ומשמש כעין נימוק לצורך לערוב לביטחונה האישי של האישה השבוייה, שכן כל מצב שישנן שתי נשים עלול להוביל למריבות ותככים.

ב. יוסף בן מתתיהו

לעומתו יוסף בן מתתיהו (Antiquities IV, 257-259) לא מייחס חשיבת לסמיכות הפרשיות, שכן הוא פוסח על רוב חוקי המלחמה, ובדיונו, חוק הייבום מופיע ליד פרשת אשת יפת תואר ול־אחר מכן הוא מדלג לפרשת בן סורר ומורה. יוסף בן מתיתיהו מתייחס לבעיית העבר של האישה,

ייתכן שאשת יפת תואר היא אשת איש, והיאך החייל לוקח אותה לאישה? לפי יוספוס האיש לא שוכב עם האישה מיד אלא מחכה שלושים יום, הוא מתעלם מן האונס לגמרי, ומסביר שאין זה מן הראוי להתחתן מיד ולעסוק בשמחת החתונה, אלא שיש לתת לה זמן להתאבל. יוספוס לא מנמק כלל וכלל את עניין שחרורה לחופשי.

ייתכן כמובן שיוספוס ופילון לא מתביישים מהחוק שנותן לאדם רשות לאנוס אישה שבוייה מפני שבעולמם ברי הוא שהאישה תרצה להזדווג לחייל ששייך לצד המנצחים.

עיקר ניתוחינו יתמקד בפירוש לפרשת אשת יפת תואר על פי מדרש ההלכה, ספרי דברים.

ג. ספרי דברים (מהדורת פינקלשטיין)

פיסקא ריא

כי תצא למלחמה, במלחמת הרשות הכתוב מדבר. על איביך, כנגד אויביך, ונתנו ה' אלהיך בידך, אם עשית כל האמור בענין סוף שה' אלהיך נותנו בידך. ושבית שביו, לרבות כנענים שבתוכה.

וראית בשביה, בשעת שביה. אשת, ואף על פי שהיא אשת איש. יפת תואר, אין לי אלא בזמן שהיא נאה מנין אפילו היא כעורה תלמוד לומר וחשקת בה אף על פי שאינה יפת תואר. ולקחת לך לאשה, שלא תאמר הרי זו לאבה הרי זו לאחי.

כי תצא למלחמה – "במלחמת רשות הכתוב מדבר".

ניתוח: מדרש ההלכה מצמצם את משמעות הכתוב וטוען שמדובר רק במלחמת רשות מפני שבמלחמת חובה (נגד שבעת העממים) המחוקק המקראי מצווה: "לא תחיה כל נשמה", ואם כן אין אפשרות של שבוייה יפת תואר.

הבדלי נוסח: חלק מכתבי היד מוסיפים את המילים "על אויבך" (המשך הפסוק) אך מפני שהספרי מתייחס למילים אלו לחוד, לדעתי המילים גם עומדות לחוד.

על אויביך – "כנגד אויביך".

ניתוח: הספרי שואל על כפל הדברים, הרי אם אתה יוצא למלחמה ברי הוא שאתה נלחם נגד אויביך. לפי פרוש תולדות אדם שכנראה התבייש מכך שבני ישראל יוצאים למלחמה יזומה, מדובר במלחמת הגנה.

הבדלי נוסח: כתב יד רומי גורס איביך בכתיב חסר כמו נוסח המסורה.

ונתנו ה' אלוהיך בידך – "אם עשית כל האמור בעניין סוף שה' אלוהיך נותנו בידך"

ניתוח – לפי בעל הטורים "כל האמור" מתייחס לפרשת העגלה הערופה, אם אתה מקיים את מצוות העגלה הערופה אחרי שנמצא חלל לא מזוהה אז תנצח במלחמה.

הבדלי נוסח – מדרש הגדול גורס "נותנן" במקום "נותנו", כנראה מדובר בטעות סופרים עקב הדימיון בין "ו" ל "נ" סופית.

ושבית שביו – "לרבות הכנענים אשר בתוכה"

ניתוח – המילים "שבית שביו" באות ללמד אותנו שהכנענים שחיים בגבולות הארץ יוצאים מן הכלל של "לא תהיה כל נשמה" אם הם מתיהדים. בבלי סוטה ל"ה: יש מחלוקת בתוספות לגבי הכנענים בארץ ישראל שמתיהדים למשל, רחב הזונה.

וראית בשביה – "בשעת השבייה"

ניתוח – ממעט את הזמן לאחר הכיבוש (פסודו ראב"ד); דין אשת יפת תואר אינו תקף אלא בעת המלחמה כשהאישה נמצאת בשבי (רבינו הלל ס"ד.).

אשת – "ואף על פי שהיא אשת איש"

ניתוח – לפי רבינו הלל אם האישה רוצה להתגייר הם יכולים להתחתן מיד, גיור מבטל את נישואיה הקודמים, ולכן מדובר על מצב שהאשה אינה רוצה להתגייר. פנקלשטיין טוען שלפני רבינו הלל הייתה הוספה, "כשאינה רוצה להתגייר הכתוב מדבר", אך יכול להיות שרבינו הלל הסתמך על הבבלי לפירושו.

יפת תואר – "אין לי אלא בזמן שהיא נאה מנין אפילו היא כעורה? תלמוד לומר **וחשקת בה** אף על פי שאינה יפת התואר."

ניתוח – מדרשי ההלכה שואלים, **האם האישה יכולה להיות מכוערת או אם יש הכרח שהיא תהיה יפה.** המילים וחשקת בה מרמזות שקריטריון החשק הוא יותר חשוב מיופי האישה, ואם אתה חושק באישה היא לא צריכה להיות יפה בכדי שדין אשת יפת תואר יחול. פסוידו ראב"ד טוען שהמילה "בה" מלמד שדין אשת יפת תואר חל רק על אישה אחת ואסור לקחת שתי נשים יפות תואר; "בה – ולא בחברתה".

הבדלי נוסח – המילה "אפילו" מופיעה בכתבי יד **אמהג** והמילים "אף על פי" מופיעים בכתבי יד **בטלד**, מדובר בהבדל סגנוני בלבד (וכמוהו הבדלים אחרים).

ולקחת לך לאשה – "שלא תאמר הרי זו לאבה הרי זו לאחי."

ניתוח - פסוידו ראב"ד מבהיר שהשבי הוא לא מרכול, ושאסור לקחת אישה אלא לעצמו. גם במדרש תנאים הכתוב מבהיר שהאיש לא יכול לקחת שתי נשים אחת לו ואחת לבנו/אביו.

פיסקא ריב

והבאתה אל תוך ביתך, ולא לבית אחר. וגלחה את ראשה ועשתה את צפרניה, רבי אליעזר אומר תקוץ רבי עקיבה אומר תגדל אמר רבי אליעזר נאמרה עשיה בראש ונאמרה עשיה בצפרנים מה עשיה האמורה בראש העברה אף עשיה האמורה בצפרנים העברה רבי עקיבה אומר נאמרה עשיה בראש ונאמרה עשיה בצפרנים מה עשיה האמורה בראש ניוול אף עשיה האמורה בצפרנים ניוול וראיה לדברי רבי אליעזר ומפיבושת בן שאול ירד לקראת המלך לא עשה רגליו ולא עשה שפמו.

והבאתה אל תוך ביתך – "ולא לבית אחר"

ניתוח – אתה צריך להביא אותה אל תוך ביתך כדי שתראה אותה בכיעורה. בבלי קידושין כב ע"א מפרש פסוקית זו כמגן על האישה בפני האונס הראשוני בזמן המלחמה (מלמד שלא ילחצנה במלחמה), סביר להניח שהתלמוד בוש ונסוג מפשט הפסוק שמניח אונס ראשוני בשדה הקרב.

וגלחה את ראשה ועשתה את ציפורניה – "רבי אליעזר אומר תקצוץ, רבי עקיבה אומר תגדל" [יש כאן מחלוקת לגבי משמעות המילה עשתה]. אמר רבי אליעזר נאמר עשיה בראש ונאמרה עשיה בצפרנים, מה העשיה האמורה בראש העברה, אף עשיה האמורה בצפורנים העברה" [רבי אליעזר משוה בין עשית הראש והציפורניים, וטוען שמשום שעשייה בראש משמעותה לגזום אף לגבי צפרניים משמעותה לגזום]. רבי עקיבה אומר נאמרה עשיה בראש ונאמרה עשיה בצפורנים מה העשיה האמורה בראש ניוול אף עשייה האמורה בציפורנים ניוול וראיה לדברי רבי אליעזר: "ומפיבשת בן שאול ירד לקראת המלך ולא עשה רגליו ולא עשה שפמו" (שמ"ב י"ט 25) [הראיה היא לדברי רבי אליעזר לדברי הספרי, אך באותה מידה היא יכולה להיות ראיה לדברי רבי עקיבה].

הבדלי נוסח – בכתבי היד **בלד** מוסיפים ראייה לדברי רבי עקיבה, כנראה המקור להוספה זו היא מדרש תנאים אשר שם כתוב: ולרבי עקיבה אעפ"י שאין ראייה לדבר זכר לדבר כמה שנ' [דניאל ד' 30]: "עד כי שעריה כנשרין רבא וטפרוהי כציפרין". מכאן תולדות אדם מסיק שגידול שער הוא ניוול. אסמכתא זו גם

אינה מספקת, הרי לציפורים אין שיער וייתכן שציפור בלי נוצותיו גם יהיה מכוער. הרעיון המנחה של רבי אליעזר ורבי עקיבה הוא כיעורה של האישה, הם חלוקים לגבי הביטוי הפיזי של הכיעור.

פיסקא ריג

> והסירה את שמלת שביה מעליה, מלמד שמעביר ממנה בגדים נאים ומלבישה בגדי אלמנות שהגוים ארורים הם בנותיהם מתקשטות במלחמה בשביל להזנות אחרים אחריהן. וישבה בביתך, בבית שמשתמש בו נתקל בה ונכנס נתקל בה ויוצא דומה לקרויה ורואה בניוולה. ובכתה את אביה ואת אמה ירח ימים, אביה ואמה ממש דברי רבי אליעזר רבי עקיבה אומר אין אביה ואמה אלא עבודה זרה שנאמר אומרים לעץ אבי אתה. ירח ימים, שלשים יום. דבר אחר ירח אחד ימים שנים הרי שלשה חדשים כדי בגדי נויה שהיו עליה וחמדה ותיקון הוולד כדברי רבי עקיבה בין זרע ראשון לזרע שני רבי אליעזר אומר ירח ימים כמשמעו וכל כך למה שתהא בת ישראל שמחה וזו בוכה בת ישראל מתקשטת וזו מתנוולת. ואחר כן תבא אליה ובעלת, הא אם לא עשה בה את כל המעשים האלו ובא עליה הרי זו בעילת זנות.
>
> ואחר כן תבוא אליה ובעלתה, אין לך בה אלא מצות בעילה. והיתה לך לאשה, כענין שנאמר שארה כסותה ועונתה לא יגרע.

והסירה את שמלת שביה מעליה – "מלמד שמעביר ממנה בגדים נאים ומלבישה בגדי אלמנות שהגוים ארורים הם, בנותיהם מתקשטות במלחמה בשביל להזנות אחרים אחריהן"

ניתוח – היינו מניחים מלכתחילה שבזמן המלחמה בגדי הנשים אינם נאים במיוחד, מדוע אם כן צריך להפשיטה? מדרש ההלכה מסביר שהנשים היו מתגנדרות לקראת הקרב בכדי להסית את ליבם של החיילים הישראלים. היינו האישה אשמה בכך שהיא נאנסת על ידי החיילים הישראלים ולא החייל הישראלי שאונס. יוספוס טוען שהאישה מסירה את בגדי השבי ולובשת בגדי אבלות. רבי עקיבא טוען שהאישה מתלבשת בבגדים מכוערים על מנת לכער את עצמה, וראו להלן.

וישבה בביתך – "בבית שמשתמש בו נתקל בה ונכנס נתקל בה ויוצא, דומה לקרויה ורואה בניוולה."

ניתוח – רצוי שהאיש יראה את האשה בכיעורה, כדי שישנה את דעתו או להעמיד את חשקו של האיש במבחן, האם הוא עדיין חפץ באישה לאחר שהוא רואה אותה בנוולה.

ובכתה את אביה ואת אמה ירח ימים – "אביה ואמה ממש דברי רבי אליעזר. רבי עקיבה אומר אין אביה ואמה אלה עבודה זרה שנאמר: "אומרים לעץ אבי אתה" (ירמיהו ב' 27).

ניתוח – רבי עקיבה מוסיף מרכיב דתי להתאבלותה של אשת יפת התואר; ייתכן בכדי להכשיר אותה כגרת צדק. הפשט כמובן הוא כדברי רבי אליעזר (וכך גם פילון ויסופוס).

הבדלי נוסח – בבבלי יבמות מ"ח ע"ב כתוב עבודת כוכבים במקום עבודה זרה. עוד שינויים קלים בין כתבי היד הם לדוגמה: "דברי רבי אליעזר", במקום "רבי אליעזר אומר".

ירח ימים – "שלושים יום [ובכתב קטן]. דבר אחר ירח אחד ימים שניים – הרי שלושה חודשים כדי בגדי נויה שהיו עליה ותיקון הוולד כדברי רבי עקיבה בין זרע ראשון לזרע שני. רבי אליעזר אומר ירח ימים כמשמעו וכל כך למה שתהא בת ישראל שמחה וזו בוכה, בת ישראל מתקשטת וזו מתנוולת."

הבדלי נוסח – בכתבי יד **אמו** המילים בכתב קטן חסרות, וכן במדרש תנאים, חסר הקטע: מ"דבר אחר", עד "כמשמעו" . בכתבי יד **בלטזפ** המילים נמצאות. פינקלשטיין טוען שקטע זה (בכתב קטן) "אינו מעיקר הספרי".

[ממשיך בכתב קטן] **ואחר כן תבא אליה ובעלת** – "הא אם לא עשה בה את כל המעשים האלו ובא עליה הרי זו בעילת זנות"

ניתוח – אם האיש אינו נוקט בפעולות הנ"ל, הנישואין אינן תופסים, ובעילתו אינה משמעותית מבחינת החוק.

הבדלי נוסח – בכתבי יד **רבאהט** כתוב "ואחר כן" ובכתבי יד הגרסה המוטעית **למט2** "ואחר כך".

[ממשיך בכתב יד רגיל] **ואחר כן תבא אליה ובעלת** – "אין לך בה אלא מצוות בעילה"

ניתוח – לפי תולדות אדם והרמב"ן ביאה היא הדרך היחידה שבה האישה השבוייה "נקנית". הרמב"ם טוען שאפשר לקנותה גם בכסף ובשטר.

והיתה לך לאשה – "כענין שנאמר 'שארה כסותה ועונתה לא יגרע' (שמות כ"א 10).

ניתוח – המדרש מדגיש שכול המחויבויות של איש יהודי כלפי אישתו עדיין בתוקף.

הבדלי נוסח – מדרש תנאים מוסיף שאם האישה מתגיירת מרצונה מיד, לא צריך לחכות שלושים יום ואפשר להינשא מיד.

פיסקא ריד

והיה אם לא חפצת בה, הכתוב מבשרך שאתה עתיד לשנאותה. ושלחת לנפשה, ולא לבית אלהיה. ושלחתה בגט כדברי רבי יונתן ואם היתה חולה ימתין לה עד שתבריא קל וחומר לבנות ישראל שהן קדושות וטהורות. ומכור לא תמכרנה בכסף, אין לי אלא שלא ימכרנה בכסף מנין שלא יתננה במתנה ולא יעשה בה טובה תלמוד לומר ומכור לא תמכרנה בכסף. לא תתעמר בה, שלא תשתמש בה. דבר אחר לא תתעמר בה כדברי רבי יונתן. דבר אחר הרי זו אזהרה לבית דין.

תחת אשר עניתה, אפילו לאחר מעשה יחידי.

והיה אם לא חפצת בה – "הכתוב מבשרך שאתה עתיד לשנאותה."

ניתוח – הספרי רומז שהנישואין בין השובה לשבוייה אינם רצויים, היינו הספרי מתבייש מהחוק ורומז לא להתנהג כך. ייתכן שזוהי זיקה לחוק שתי הנשים, האהובה והשנואה.

הבדלי נוסח – בכתב יד ר כתוב "לשמחה" וזה כנראה טעות מכיוון שהדבר נוגד את המשמעות הפשוטה של הפסוק.

ושלחתה לנפשה – "ולא לבית אלוהיה. [ובכתב קטן] ושלחתה בגט כדברי רבי יונתן, ואם היתה חולה ימתין לה עד שתבריא, קל וחומר לבנות ישראל שהן קדושות וטהורות."

ניתוח – רמב"ן מפרש שאע"פ שהשובה אינו מתחתן עם השבוייה היא לא חוזרת לסטטוס הקודם שלה כנכרית. במדרש הגדול נוסף הקטע הבא: "מלמד שאם לא רצת להתגייר לאחר שלושים יום מגלגל עליה כל שנים עשר חודש, לא רצת מקבלת שבע מצוות שנצטוו בהן בני נח, לא רצת לקבל אחר שני עשר חודש הורגין אותה".

ומכור לא תמכרנה בכסף [בכתב גדול] – "אין לי אלא שלא ימכרנה בכסף, מנין שלא יתננה במתנה? ולא יעשה בה טובה? תלמוד לומר 'ומכור לא תמכרנה בכסף'.

ניתוח – הספרי מרחיב את האיסור המקראי ואוסר על כל מקח וממכר של האישה השבוייה.

ולא תתעמר בה – "שלא תשתמש בה [ובכתב קטן]. דבר אחר לא תתעמר בה כדברי רבי יונתן. דבר אחר הרי זו אזהרה לבית דין".

ניתוח – על פי הרמב"ן הכוונה כאן שלא תשתמש בה כשפחה. דברי רבי יונתן נמצאים במדרש תנאים ושם נאמר: " 'לא תתעמר בה תחת אשר עיניתה', ולא תתעמר בה – אחר כל המעשים הכתוב מדבר, אתה אומר אחר כל המעשים הכת' מדבר או אינו אלא לאחר הבעילה, אלא אם אמרת כך הרי היא אשתו לכל דבר הא[מה], ת"ל לא תתעמר בה תחת אשר עיניתה אחר כל המעשים הכתוב מדבר, דברי ר' יאשיה. ר' יונתן אומר אחר הבעילה הכת' מדבר או אינו אחרי כל המעשים..."; רבי יונתן אומר שאסור להתעמר בה אחרי הבעילה הראשונה ולא רק אחרי כל התהליך. הספרי מוסיף שהאזהרה של "לא תתעמר בה" יכול להיות הפנייה לבית הדין שישגיח על המצב, כי אחרת האיש עלול להתעמר בה (ולדברי תולדות אדם, אף מועד לכך).

הבדלי נוסח – פינקלשטיין טוען שהקטע בכתב קטן הוא הוספה מגיליון ולא מעיקר הסיפרי, וכן ניכר שהספרי מצטט את רבי יונתן שכתוב באופן שלם במדרש תנאים.

תחת אשר עניתה – "אפילו לאחר מעשה יחידי"

ניתוח – לאחר האונס החד פעמי אסור לך להשתמש באישה לרעה.

סיכום

בסיכום זה נעסוק רק במימד אחד של פירוש הספרי והיא בושתו לנוכח החוק המקראי. מימד זה מתבטא כמעט בכל דבור מתחיל. ראשית כל הספרי מדגיש שמדובר במלחמת הגנה (כך גם יוספוס), היינו עם ישראל לא יזמו את המלחמה, וכך לקיחת שבויים (ובייחוד אשה יפת תואר) אינו מצטייר כמעשה ביזה. הספרי ממליץ נגד לקיחת אישה שבוייה מפני שלדבריו הדבר עלול לגרום לבעיות בעתיד. זהו עוד ביטוי לבושה והניסיון להתרחק מפשוטו של מקרא שאינו מתייחס למעשה באופן שלילי. אם בכל זאת לקח החייל את האישה, הספרי מדגיש את כל המחויבויות של אותו השובה כלפי שבויותו, מעל ומעבר מה שכתוב או מובן מן החוק המקראי. למשל אחר האונס החד פעמי של האישה אסור לך להשתמש בה לרעה, עליך להתייחס אליה כאל אשתך לכל דבר עם כל הזכויות השמורות לאישה יהודייה. אי נוחות זו ניכרת אף יותר אצל מפרשי הספרי ביניהם תולדות אדם, פסוידו ראב"ד ורבינו הלל.

"...וקצתה את כפה לא תחוס עינך" (דברים כה, יב)

אריה סטריקובסקי, מכון פרדס

עונש חמור זה של כריתת כף ידה של האישה המצילה המצוטט בכותרת המאמר מקבל משנה תוקף כשקוראים אנו את הפסוק בהקשרו:

> כי יהיה ריב בין אנשים ... ארבעים יכנו לא יסיף! פן יסיף להכתו ונקלה אחיך לעיניך.
>
> לא תחסם שור בדישו.
>
> כי ישבו אחים יחדו ...ואם לא יחפץ האיש לקחת את יבמתו ...ונגשה יבמתו אליו לעיני הזקנים וחלצה נעלו מעל רגלו וירקה בפניו וענתה ואמרה: ככה יעשה לאיש אשר לא יבנה את בית אחיו...
>
> כי ינצו אנשים יחדו איש ואחיו וקרבה אשת האחד להציל את אישה מיד מכהו ושלחה ידה והחזיקה במבשיו, וקצתה את כפה לא תחוס עינך (כה א-יב).

אחרי שהתורה מגבילה את עונש הרשע כדי למנוע "ונקלה אחיך לעיניך" מרחמת על השור, היא מצווה, את היבמה לבזות את היבם על שאינו מקים שם לבעלה, באה התורה בעונש חסר תקדים על אישה שבאה להציל את בעלה: וקצות את כפה, לא תחוס עיניך!

ננסה להאיר פרשה זו מהאספקלריות של חז"ל, מחקר המקרא והמשפט ההשוואתי, לאחר מכן נקרא מחדש את הפרשנים המסורתיים וניעזר בהם לגשר בין האספקלריות הללו.

נפתח בחז"ל:

עקב הכלל "השווה הכתוב אישה לאיש לכל דינים שבתורה"[1] דרשו חכמים את הפסוק הזה גם על גברים המביישים ודיבר הכתוב בהווה [כמו "מכשפה לא תחיה"]. בעקבות המצווה של "הצלת נפשות" קבעו

1 ב"ק טו ע"א. הכלל מבוסס על מדרש פסוקים, עיינו שם.

חז"ל שאם האישה אינה יכולה להציל בדרך אחרת אין מענישים אותה[2] ובעקבות הכלל "עין תחת עין - ממון", אין בית הדין קוצץ כף-יד אלא מחייב ממון.

מובא בספרי דברים רצב-רצג:

...אנשים- איש עם אישה מניין? ת"ל : יחדו – מכל מקום.

וקרבה אשת האחד ולא אשת שליח בית דין.

...אף כל דבר שיש בו סכנת נפשות הרי הוא בוקצת את כפה.

וקצתה את כפה, מלמד שאתה חייב להצילה בכפה. מנין שאם אין אתה יכול להציל אותה בכפה הצילה בנפשה, תלמוד לומר לא תחוס עינך.

רבי יהודה אומר: ...לא תחס עינך האמור כאן – ממון.[3]

התלמודים במסכת בבא קמא בבבלי (כח ע"א) ובירושלמי (פ"ח ה"ג), דרשו פסוק זה כרבי יהודה, כמקור לנזקי בושת ולפי זה, כתבה התורה "אישה" כי הבושת גדולה באישה מאשר באיש. בספרי דברים (רצב, רצג) דורש התנא קמא פסוק זה על דין "רודף" כשהיא מסכנת את הגבר וגם כאן דין האיש כדין האישה. בבבא קמא, כאשר היא מביישת, בית הדין הוא שמחייבה ממון ובספרי, כאשר היא "רודפת", כל אדם נקרא לקוץ את כפה כדי להציל את המותקף.

שני התרחישים הם בעייתיים. התרחיש הראשון שעוסק בבושת[4] גרידא ובתשלום קנס אינו תואם את ההכרזה: "לא תחוס עיניך!"; התרחיש השני, העוסק בהצלה מרודפת, אינו מבהיר, למה דווקא רודפת ולא רודף?

נראה לי שבפרשת דרכים זו נפרדת הפרשנות ההלכתית מפרשנות הפשט והמדרש. בעוד שפ־רשנות הפשט והמדרש תרה אחרי פשר המקראות וסממנים ספרותיים, הרי שהפרשנות ההלכתית מציגה לעצמה מטלות מעשיות. בנידון דידן הפרשנות ההלכתית זקוקה לפרשה זו כמקור למכלול של דיני בושת ולהצלה מרודף. כל סטייה ממטלה זו הייתה מקעקעת את הלימוד. מה עוד שמבחינה הלכתית, אין כל ייחודיות בפגיעה באשכים ודינה ככל נזקי גוף.

---

2 ב"ק כח ע"א. כ"כ חז"ל התירו לאחוז במבושים הן לשליח בית דין והן לאשתו המסייעת לבעלה (ירושלמי ב"ק פ"ח ה"ג).

3 ר' יעקב מקלנברג ב'הכתב והקבלה' וכן ר' ברוך אפשטיין ב'תורה תמימה' מנמקים פירוש זה בשימוש במילה 'וקצות' שעניינה קיצבה ולא במילה 'וקצצת'.

4 בספר המצוות לאוים רצג, רצז מעתיק רמב"ם את מקורותיו מהספרי.

שיטת אבן עזרא

ראב"ע מציע פירוש ייחודי:

כי ינצו – היפך [׳כי] ישבו אחים יחדו׳...

במבושיו – ביציו, מגזרת בושה, והוא עזות מצח לגלות דבר הנסתר שהוא ערווה. גם הוא מקום מסוכן.

וקצות את כפה, כמו ׳עין תחת עין׳ (שמות כא:כד) .

אם לא תפדה כפה - תקוץ.

לא תחוס עינך - אם הייתה ענייה.

לפי ראב"ע מדובר בעונש של בית דין, וקיימים שני תרחישים: אישה עשירה תשלם ממון; אישה ענייה - ידה תקוצץ. פירושו נוח מבחינת מבנה הפרשה, אך בעייתי מבחינה מוסרית.

מסתבר שראב"ע מציע למזג את הפשט המילולי: ׳וקצותה׳ – ממש, עם פרשנות חז"ל: ׳וקצותה׳ – ממון.

יש לעיין מהי כוונת ראב"ע בהשוואה "כמו עין תחת עין", האם כוונתו שאף ב"וקצותה את כפה" העונש הוא ממוני, או שמא יש כאן רמז שאף ב"עין תחת עין" יש להבחין בין עשיר שישלם לעני שעינו תיעקר. ייתכן שראב"ע שאב פרשנות זו מהסוגיה בבבא קמא:

תניא רבי אליעזר אומר: עין תחת עין - ממש. ׳ממש׳ סלקא דעתך?

... אלא אמר רב אשי: לומר שאין שמין אותו ב[עינו של] ניזק אלא ב[עינו של] מזיק (ב"ק, פד ע"ב).

בא ראב"ע ומפשר בין דברי רבי אליעזר המקוריים לבין פרשנות רב אשי: באישה ענייה, עין תחת עין ממש; באישה שיכולה לשלם, דמי כופר עבור העין.

בפירושו הארוך לשמות כא כד, מציע ראב"ע את סברת רב אשי ש׳עין תחת עין׳ אינו אלא כופר עבור העין, מבלי לציין את האפשרות שפעמים מדובר ב׳עין תחת עין׳ ממש.

כיצד נוכל להסביר את ההבדלים?

לכשנתבונן נמצא שבפירוש על שמות, ראב"ע מביא את הוויכוח בין רב סעדיה גאון, שהגן על פרשנות חז"ל, לבן זוטא, ושם הוא לא רצה להיות בצד של בן זוטא. מה עוד שבסוגיה בבבא קמא כל גדולי החכמים מנמקים את השיטה ש׳עין תחת עין - ממון׳ כעמדה מוסכמת של התורה שבעל פה ולא היה לראב"ע סיבה להוציא עצמו ממסורת חז"ל. מה שאין כן בסוגית ׳וקצותה את כפה׳, שם אין הסכמה שמדובר בקציצה ממונית, והראיה, שבספרי מדובר בקציצת יד על ידי מציל. כאן, הרחק מהזרקורים, יישם ראב"ע פרשנות זו על עונש מטעם בית הדין.

שיטת רמב״ם

רמב״ם פותר את הבעיות הללו על ידי שילוב שני התרחישים[5]: בהלכות חובל פ״א ט-י הוא לומד מפסוקינו דיני בושת ובהלכות רוצח פ״א הוא לומד מהם דיני רודף:

נפתח בהלכות רוצח פרק א׳:

(ה) רוצח שהרג בזדון אין ממיתין אותו העדים ולא הרואים אותו עד שיבוא לבית דין וידינוהו למיתה...
(ו) במה דברים אמורים בשעבר ועשה העוון שחייב עליו מיתת בית דין.

אבל הרודף אחר חבירו להרגו אפילו היה הרודף קטן הרי כל ישראל מצווין להציל הנרדף מיד הרודף ואפילו בנפשו של רודף:

(ז) כיצד אם הזהירוהו והרי הוא רודף אחריו אע״פ שלא קיבל עליו התראה כיון שעדיין הוא רודף הרי זה נהרג ואם יכולים להצילו באבר מאיברי הרודף ... עושין ואם אינן יכולין לכוין ולא להצילו אלא אם כן הרגוהו לרודף הרי אלו הורגין אותו ואע״פ שעדיין לא הרג שנאמר (דברים כ״ה י״ב) ״וקצותה את כפה לא תחוס עינך״.

(ח) אחד מבושיו ואחד כל דבר שיש בו סכנת נפשות אחד האיש שאחז את האשה ענין הכתוב שכל החו־שב להכות חבירו הכייה הממיתה אותו מצילין את הנרדף בכפו של רודף ואם אינן יכולין מצילין אותו אף בנפשו שנאמר: לא תחוס עינך.

רמב״ם מרחיב את היקף מצוות ההצלה וקובע אותה כצו מוסרי שאין למעלה ממנו:

(י) אחד הרודף אחר חבירו להרגו או רודף אחר נערה מאורסה לאונסה .

(טו) הרואה רודף אחר חבירו להרגו או אחר ערוה לבועלה ויכול להציל ולא הציל הרי זה ביטל מצות עשה שהיא וקצותה את כפה ועבר על שני לאוין על לא תחוס עינך ועל לא תעמוד על דם רעך:

(טז) אע״פ שאין לוקין על לאוין אלו מפני שאין בהן מעשה חמורים הם שכל המאבד נפש אחת מישראל כאילו אבד כל העולם כולו וכל המקיים נפש אחת מישראל כאילו קיים כל העולם כולו.

נעבור להלכות חובל ומזיק פרק א׳:

(א) החובל בחבירו חייב לשלם לו חמשה דברים נזק וצער ורפוי ושבת ובושת.

5 זאת למרות העובדה שבספרי מובאות דעותיהם של תנא קמא ורבי יהודה כדעות מנוגדות.

״...וקצתה את כפה לא תחוס עינך״ (דברים כה, יב)

... זה שנאמר בחובל בחבירו ומזיקו ״לא תחוס עינך״ שלא תחוס בתשלומין שמא תאמר עני הוא זה ושלא בכוונה חבל בו ארחמנו, לכך נאמר ״לא תחוס עינך״.

(ט) ומניין שהוא חייב בבושת בפני עצמה שהרי נאמר (דברים כ״ה י״א) ״ושלחה ידה והחזיקה במבושיו וקצותה את כפה״. בכלל דין זה קנס המבייש.

(י) אינו חייב על הבושת עד שיהיה מתכוין שנ׳ ״ושלחה ידה״.

רמב״ם קורא את פסוקינו בשתי דרכים: לפי הפשט המילולי: קציצת כף היד, ולפי הפירוש התלמודי: קציצה ממונית.

לפי הפירוש הראשון הוא קורא:

וקרבה אשת האחד להציל את אישה מיד מכהו ושלחה ידה [ל]...מבשיו, וקצתה את כפה [ממש] לא תחוס עינך.

לפי הפירוש השני הוא קורא:

וקרבה אשת האחד להציל את אישה מיד מכהו ושלחה ידה והחזיקה במבשיו, וקצתה את כפה [בממון].

את התרחיש הראשון משלים רמב״ם עם סוף הפסוק: ״...לא תחוס עינך״, שבדלית ברירה הורגים כדי להציל. את החיוב המוסרי של הצלה לומד רמב״ם מהכתוב ״לא תעמוד על דם רעך״.

כל עוד האישה לא בצעה את זממה, כל אחד נקרא לעצור בידה אף על ידי הריגתה, כיון שחבלה, נכנס לתמונה בית הדין והעונש היא ממוני בלבד. מדבריו בהלכות חובל ומזיק הלכה ט: ״בכלל דבר זה קנס המבייש״, משמע שהמשמעות הראשונית של הפסוק היא זאת המובאת בהלכות רוצח היינו שמדובר בכריתת כף היד[6].

מבנים ספרותיים

לפי הפשט המילולי של מחקר המקרא לפנינו שלוש פרשיות: ריב בין אנשים, יבם המתנכר ליבמתו ו״כי ינצו אנשים״. שלושתן מתחילות בפתיחה דומה: ״כי ... ״, בשלושתן יש מתח בין אנשים או אחים ובשלושתן יש עונש. בראשונה ובשנייה העונש מוגבל ובשלישית כשהאישה נוקטת באמצעי דרקוני, מופעל העונש החמור: ״וקצות את כפה לא תחוס עיניך״.

המקרה השלישי שואב מקודמיו. דומה שלפנינו פירמידה הפוכה ששני העונשים הראשונים מטרימים ומכינים להענשת האישה. מהגנה על כבוד המוכה: ״פן...ונקלה אחיך לעיניך״, עוברים להגנה על כבוד הגבר, ומהענשת יבם המסרב להקים שם לאחיו על ידי פגיעה בכבודו באמצעות

6 עמד על כך רש״ר הירש.

חליצה ויריקה. אנו עוברים להענשת החצופה שסיכנה את יכולתו של המותקף להקים זרע. אישה זו תיענש באופן מחמיר מקודמיה. לא נחוס עליה!

בפרשנות ההלכתית של חז"ל, המבנה הספרותי הזה אינו קיים. בפרשה הראשונה, כשיש ריב בין אנשים, אין עונש מלקות,[7] ובפרשה השלישית, כשהאישה באמת מצילה את בעלה – אין היא נענשת כלל. לפי התנא קמא בספרי, הדנה כ'רודפת', האירוע שלה מנותק מקודמיו. בניגוד לשני האירועים הקודמים שבהם היה בית הדין מעורב; הרי אצלה מתקיים דין "וקצות" על ידי מציל-מתנדב ולא על ידי בית הדין. לפי התלמודים, שם היא נענשת על ידי בית הדין בתשלום קנס, עונשה קל משל קודמיה וקשה להבין את ההתראה "לא תחוס עיניך".

הפרשנים המסורתיים תורמים, בדרכים שונות, ליצירת מבנים ספרותיים. לפי רמב"ם, הפרשה השלישית עוסקת הן בשעת ניסיון התקיפה, כשחיוב ההצלה מהאישה ה"רודפת", מוטל על כל אדם והן לאחר מעשה, כשבית הדין מחייבה בתשלום. בדרך זו נשמרת הזיקה לפרשיות הקודמות הדנות בעונשים הנעשים על ידי בית-דין: הלקאת עבריין וטקס החליצה, והן במעשה ביוש הנעשה על ידי היבמה: חליצת נעל ויריקה. לפי התרחיש שמדובר ברודפת, קיימת בפרשה הענשה הדרגתית: הלקאת הרשע על ידי בית דין, עובר לביוש היבם על ידי היבמה במסגרת בית דין ומכאן לעונש ה"רודפת" הנעשה על ידי מציל מהחוץ. לפי התרחיש שמדובר לאחר מעשה, ועונשה ממוני, קיים ניגוד בינה ליבמה, כדברי ספורנו: היבמה מביישת על פי בית דין ובעידודם והחצופה שביישה על דעת עצמה, תיענש.

אברבנאל מקשר את פרשתנו לדין ייבום. בשניהם קיים עונש על השחתת הזרע. פרשתנו רצף וניגוד: רצף - לפרשה הראשונה 'כי יריבון אנשים' , שם העונש מלקות, וכאן, קציצת יד עם אפשרות לכופר; ניגוד, לפרשת ייבום. שם, 'כי ישבו אחים' וכאן, 'כי ינצו אנשים'.

שני פרשנים מקשרים ומנגדים את הריב שבתחילת הפרשה לריב השני. רבי משה אלשייך עושה זאת במישרין ואלו רמב"ן בעקיפין. רבי משה אלשייך[8] מנגד את הריב הראשון שהובא להכרעת בית הדין לריב השני שלא הובא לדיינים, ובסופו של דבר התלקח עקב התערבות האישה. לפי התרחיש שלו האישה התערבה ללא כל צורך[9]. בתחילה רק כדי להציל את בעלה, ההתערבות הביאה את היריב להתאזר בהכאותיו ואז היא שלחה ידה למבושיו. הלקח הוא שאין להתערב בריב אלא על מנת להפריד בין הנצים ולהרגיעם.

מתוך נימוקים הלכתיים, מפרש רמב"ן שהפרשה הראשונה עוסקת בהכאה קלה שאין בה שווה פרוטה שעונשה 40 מלקות. באמצעות פירושו נוצרת זיקה רציפה בין הפרשה הראשונה שבה מוטל עונש חמור על מכה קלה לפרשה השלישית שבה מוטל עונש כבד על האישה שביישה.

בעוד שהפרשנים שראינו מקשרים את הפרשה לקודמותיה הרי שד"ל מקשרה לפרשיות שלאחריה.

---

7 על כך עומד ר' שמעון שקופ.

8 תורת משה על התורה.

9 כך גם אברבנאל ומלבים.

"...וקצתה את כפה לא תחוס עינך" (דברים כה, יב)

היא עשתה ברמייה... ותשלם דמי כפה שהייתה ראויה להיקצץ...והנה אחרי שדיבר על מעשה רמייה זה , הזכיר רמייה אחרת שהיא אבן ואבן איפה ואיפה. ולחזק שנאת הרמייה הזכיר עניין עמלק, שעשה בעקבה ויזנב בך כל הנחשלים אחריך".

נוסיף ונאמר, לפי פרשנות חז"ל, המבדילים בין הצלת אמת להצלת כזב, תובן סמיכות הפרשיות לפרשה הבאה המבחינה בין מאזני צדק למאזני כזב, והאוסרת להחזיק "בכיסך אבן ואבן איפה ואי־פה". מקונוויל מקשר כיס זה לכיס האשכים. הקשר זה מאפשר לקשר את האישה התוקפנית לסוחר הרמאי. היא פגעה בכיס האשכים והוא בכיס האבנים."

דילמה פרשני: הצלה או "הצלה"

לפי ההלכה קיימים שני מצבים קוטביים: האישה נידונת כמצילה או כרודפת. איך לשלב זאת עם פשט המקראות המענישים את האישה המצילה? שד"ל פותר את הבעיה כשהוא מכנה את מעשה האישה כהצלת רמייה. דומה שהוא שם את הביטוי "להציל את אישה" במרכאות: אל תקרי הצלה אלא "הצלה". רלב"ג לעומת זאת מגלה הבנה לחוש הצדק ולהצטדקות הפנימית של העבריינית. לדבריו, מצילים מן האישה הרודפת אע"פ "שהיה לה קצת התנצלות לפי מה שיחשוב הרודף". בניגוד לשניהם, רבנו בחיי אינו מפקפק בכוונותיה הכנות של האישה. האישה אומנם ניסתה להציל ולכן אנו מענישים אותה בקנס כספי בלבד. רבנו בחיי לא טרח ליישב את פירושו עם ההלכה שפוטרת את האישה כאשר לא הייתה יכולה להציל באופן אחר. מסתבר שרבנו בחיי כתב כפרשן: זהו פשוטו של מקרא על הדיאלקטיקה הכרוכה בו, היא מצילה ובכול זאת נענשת. דומה שרבנו בחיי אומר: אם תבקשו ממני לנסח את דבריי בשפה הלכתית, אסייג ואומר: האישה שאומנם הצילה את בעלה, אך יכלה לברור באמצעים, חצתה את הקו הדק, המבדיל בין מצילה למשחיתה, ותיענש בקנס כספי. לפי פירושו, נוכל למצוא זיקה מקורית בין תחילת הפרשה, כשדינו של הרשע מוגבל לארבעים מלקות, לסופה, כאשר דינה של האישה מוגבל לענישה כספית.

הרי לך שלוש התייחסויות למעשה ההצלה: הצלת רמייה, הצטדקות עצמית והצלת אמת.

משפט משווה

בחוקי אשור התיכונה סעיף 8 מובא:

אם אישה שיחתה אשך איש במריבה, יקצצו אחת מאצבעותיה; ואם חבש הרופא את האשך, אך האשך השני נוגע אף הוא, או אם שיחתה גם את האשך השני במריבה, את שני /שתי [שדיה /עיניה] יעקרו.[10]

10 תרגום מילולי מובא על ידי חנה גוירצמן: עונשי גוף, באשור... עבודת דוקטורט, אוניברסיטת בר-אילן תשנ"ט. עמ' 262

לפנינו מקרה של אישה התופסת במבושי הגבר והעונש הוא כריתת אצבעותיה ואם נפגעו שני האשכים - העונש הוא חמור בהרבה.

במבט ראשון יש מקום להשוואה בין חוק התורה לחוק האשורי. אך לכשנקרא את החוק האשורי במלואו נמצא שאינו מרשה לאישה להגן על עצמה על ידי אחיזה במבושים. עקב נחיתותה הגופנית של האישה, נמנעת ממנה הזכות להגנה עצמית.

חנה גוירצמן מתלבטת האם החוק מפלה הפלייה שוביניסטית או יש בו הפלייה מעמדית כשה-אישה משתייכת למעמד נמוך ממעמד הגבר. הפלייה מעין זו היתה קיימת בתחומים שונים במשפט האשורי. לדוגמה, דינה של שיפחה מניקה שהואשמה בהנקת תינוק נוסף, ללא הסכמת מעסיקיה הוא בכריתת פטמותיה. בכלל החוק האשורי דוגל בעיקרון של lex talionis [מידה כנגד מידה] באופן עקבי ואכזרי.

הניגוד הגמור בין דין התורה ובין החוק האשורי ברור לפי חז"ל, אך גם לפי פשוטו המחקרי של המקרא המפליל רק את האישה המתערבת בריב לא לה, קיים ניגוד בין החוק האשורי לחוק התורה.

סיכום

בפרשה זו של "וקצות את כפה" קיימים ניגודים בין הפשט המקובל במחקר המקרא ובין הפ-רשנות ההלכתית של חז"ל. מתוך המודעות לניגודים אלו קראנו את הפרשנים המסורתיים ולמדנו כיצד הם הציעו אפשרויות לאיחוי הניגודים ולבניית מבנים ספרותיים. כמו כן עמדנו על השוני בין חוק התורה ובין המשפט האשורי.

אם נשווה את המתודה של חז"ל לזו של מחקר המקרא נמצא שחוקרי המקרא רואים את הפרשה בהקשרה המיידי ואילו חז"ל, בהקשרו של המקרא כולו על תורת המוסר הגלומה בו.

תודתי לחברים שהעירו והאירו על המאמר: שלמה רוזנר, ד"ר עמנואל בן נאה, הרב דני רוזנטל, פרופ' יעקב בלידשטיין, פרופ' אד גרינשטיין, ג'ודי קליצנר, נעימה נובצקי, ד"ר ברוך פלדשטרן ור' דניאל רוט. ישלם ה' פועלם.

מאמר זה הוקרא בכנס "ההלכה והפילוסופיה של ההלכה: היבט רב תחומי", האוניברסיטה העב-רית ומכון ון-ליר, ירושלים, טבת תשס"ה.

בין חכמים לציבור:
כיצד נוצרה ההלכה שבתורה שבעל פה

שמואל וחנה ספראי ז"ל וזאב ספראי, אוניברסיטת תל-אביב

פתח דבר

המשנה כמסמך הלכתי-משפטי[1]

לומדי המשנה לדורותיה רואים בה מסמך הלכתי-משפטי לכל דבר המנוסח בקפידה ובדייקנות. על כן מרבה התלמוד הבבלי לשאול על כל משפט ומשפט מה החידוש שבו, ולשם מה יש צורך בסדרה של דוגמאות, וכן שאלות נוספות. ברם המשנה במקורה אינה רק מסמך משפטי, וספק אם מותר לשאול שאלות אלו. המקרה הבודד הוא הגרעין ההלכתי. על כן יש צורך בהצגת מספר רב של דוגמאות, אף שהריבוי לעתים נראה כמיותר[2]. כידוע, לא אחת היוו שאלות אלו תשתית לסוגיות ארוכות שבהם שאלה הגמרא "פשיטא?", ומצאה צריכותה זו או אחרת. ברם גם בתלמוד הגישה אינה אחידה, ולא תמיד התלמוד שואל את השאלה. יתרה מזו, לפחות בחלק מהמקרים השאלות מטי־פוס זה הן סבוראיות ושובצו בתלמוד רק בשלב מאוחר של עריכתו. לעתים יותר משיש כאן קושי ותירוצו, יש כאן ניסיון של הסוגיה לקשר מספר רב של הלכות ידועות ללשון המשנה. שרשור זה הוא מעין "אסמכתא" המקשרת בין ההלכה לפסוק בתורה, או למשפט במשנה.

1 בידוע לתורה שבעל-פה שני מקצועות מרכזיים ההלכה והאגדה. חיבור זה עוסק רק בחלק ההלכתי, והוא חלק מתוך פירושנו למכלול המשנה בה החילונו ביחד עם אבינו שמואל ספראי ז"ל מורו ורבו של צבי מיודענו ומכובדנו. מסיבה זו אין הדיון עוסק במכלול ספרות האגדה התפתחותה ומקומה בחברה. דיון מקיף בכל מקצועות התורה שבעל פה מחייב גם לבחון את מכלול העולם התרבותי והספרותי בו חיו חכמים ולעסוק במהלכים משווים. אך בבואנו לעסוק בדיון ההלכתי גרידא נמצינו כמעט פטורים, שכן להיבט ההלכתי בהיקף המתגלה בספרות המשנה ומקבילותיה, אין אח וריע בספרות הנוצרית במאות הראשונות לספירה. ההשואה בין ספרות המשפט הרומי וספרות חכמים היא תחום המצריך דיון שונה במעט ומקומו לא בחיבורנו זה.

2 ראו, למשל, פירושו של גולדברג למשנה שבת פ"א מ"ב - מ"ד.

לעתים ההכפלה והחזרה נובעות משילוב של משניות קדומות מעריכות שונות.[3] אבל דומה שגם המשניות הקדומות עצמן חזרו על נושאים או הדגימו אותה הלכה במספר דוגמאות החוזרות על עצמן. נסתפק כאן בדוגמא אחת. משנת ביכורים פ"א מ"י מסכמת את אלו המביאים ביכורים וקוראים. כמעט כל שנאמר בה כבר מופיע במשניות הקודמות באותו פרק. פרק זה ערוך בצורה מסודרת ובעל הגיון ספרותי ברור. יש בו כותרת ובה שלוש סעיפים, ואחר כך מרחיבים בכל סעיף וסעיף. כולו עשוי מקשה אחת ברורה ומלוכדת. ואף על פי כן חוזרת המשנה על פרטים הנמצאים במשניות קודמות.

זאת ועוד; פרשנים חיפשו את ההיגיון שבהעמדת סדר המקרים במשנה, כאילו חייבת המשנה לסדר את הדוגמאות בסדר היררכי כלשהו. גם לכך לא מצאנו צידוק, ולא ניסינו למצוא סדר משפ־טי, אלא אם כן הוא סביר ואינו מאולץ. שכן איש המדע מוכן לפרש משנה כמו התלמוד הירושלמי בניגוד לתלמוד הבבלי, וכן להפך. הוא גם מוכן להציע, בהיסוס מה, ולאחר בדיקה ולימוד קפדני, לפרש משנה שלא לפי התלמודים. עד כאן אין חידוש בהצהרה זו, אם כי גם החוקרים שונים זה מזה ב'תעוזתם' או ב'חוצפתם'. עם זאת הצעת הפירוש הנראה בעינינו כסביר אינו סוף פסוק. עלי־נו לברר מה הניע את התלמוד או את התלמודים לפרש בדרך אחרת, בדרך שלדעתנו אינה הפשט המקורי של המשנה. הפירוש האמוראי איננו טעות, אלא תורה הוא ולימוד הוא צריך, גם אם לדעתנו אינו פשט המשנה. אין זה סתם שיבוש, אלא פירוש המבוסס על מציאות משתנה, או על תפישות משפטיות מפותחות ושיטתיות יותר.

כאמור שני התלמודים מבטאים גישה יותר פורמליסטית, המקרים השונים אוחדו וגובשו כללי הלכה. לאור כללים אלו הם מנסים להסביר את המשנה. גישה זו רווחת בתלמוד הבבלי יותר מאשר בירושלמי. יסודות ביקורתיים מצויים בספרות חז"ל בתלמודים ובספרות הפרשנית. המפרש האמו־ראי אינו חושש לקבוע שמשפט מסוים נאמר בהקשר אחר מזה שבו הוא מופיע לפנינו[4]. הירושלמי אינו מהסס לקבוע שמספר סיפורים היסטוריים על עימותים בין כיתתיים הם בעצם סיפור אחד[5]. פרשן מסורתי כר' שלמה עדני מציע בהיסוס מה פירושים המנוגדים לתלמוד[6]. ולא באנו אלא להו־סיף מעט למסורת מפוארת זו.

---

3 ראו, למשל, משנה, שבת פ"א מ"א; פי"ח מ"א; עירובין פ"י מי"א וכיוצא באלו רבים. בשאלה העקרונית של החובה לדקדק בלשון המשנה ראו שפיגל, דרך קצרה. תרומתו העיקרית היא ציטוט מדברי ראשונים הקובעים במפורש שלא תמיד יש לדקדק בלשון המשנה. ראו, למשל, פירוש המאירי לקידושין (מהדורת סופר), עמ' 8. כאמור פירוש שיטתי למשנה מראה שלעתים דקדקו אמוראים ופרשנים בלשון המשנה, אך לא תמיד נהגו כך.

4 ראו, למשל, משנה, עירובין פ"י מט"ו.

5 ראו משנה, יומא פ"א מ"ה, ועוד.

6 ראו משנה, שבת פ"א מ"ג, וכן יומא פ"ג מ"א; שביעית פ"ב מ"ו; מעשרות פ"ד מ"ד (שם גם הרמב"ם והר"ש פירשו כנגד הבבלי); מעשר שני פ"ד מ"ג ומ"ה. בעל מלאכת שלמה נשען במקרים אלו על רבי יוסף אשכנזי שאת חיבורו מכירים אנו רק מדברי בעל מלאכת שלמה. בכל המקרים הללו, ורבים אחרים מצניע החכם (ר' יוסף אשכנזי) את גישתו ותוקף את ר' עובדיה מברטנורא, ולא את הגמרא עצמה, וראו פירושינו המצוינים לעיל. בחרנו להביא דוגמאות מתוך כבשונה של הפרשנות עצמה, ולא מתוך הדיונים על "הפילוסופיה של הפרשנות". במקביל עסקו חכמים בשאלה העקרונית אם מותר לפרש משנה בניגוד לגמרא. רבים דחו אפשרות זו מכל וכל, אך היו גם ש"התירו" לחלוק על הגמרא אם אין מדובר על פסיקת הלכה. ראו אוצר הגאונים, לכתובות

הקדמה

השאלה כיצד נוצרה התורה שבעל פה מנסרת בעולמה של היהדות וימיה כימי התורה שבעל פה הידועים לנו. הדיון בנושא הושפע עמוקות מהצרכים האפולוגטיים. המשיבים ביקשו להסביר בכך כיצד יש לחכמים בלעדיות על הנגישות לתורה שבעל פה - הלגיטימציה לחדש מחד גיסא, והזכות הבלעדית לשלשול המסורת מאידך גיסא. מניעים אלו השפיעו כמובן על התיאורים הקדומים, אך לא הטיבו עם הדיוק ההיסטורי. זאת ועוד! התיאורים הקדומים אינם מהווים מקור היסטורי אמין מתוך החשש הטבעי שאירועים ותהליכים שהתחוללו בעבר הרחוק נשכחו, והמציאות בה תיפקד כל חכם, נראתה לו כקיימת מאז ומעולם.

החוקר בן זמננו ניגש, בדחילו ורחימו לשאלה זו, ומבין שיש להבחין בין שתי שאלות. האחת היא כיצד תיארו לעצמם חז״ל את ראשיתה של התורה שבעל פה, והשניה היא כיצד יש להעריך את שלבי הבראשית של התפתחות התורה שבעל פה, ומתי התרחשו שלבי בראשית אלו. השאלה הראשונה חשובה מאד לגופה, אך במסגרת זו לא נעסוק בה כשלעצמה, בהנחה שהתדמית העצמית של חז״ל בנושא היא בעיקרה בעלת חשיבות תיאולוגית, וממילא הציפיות למידע היסטורי מעטות, וכל עיוננו כאן נועד לשאלה האם ניתן להפיק מתיאור התדמית העצמית של חכמים, גם מסקנות היסטוריות.

כיצד תיארו חכמים את התפתחות התורה שבעל פה

מסורת ויצירה

משה קיבל תורה מסיני, ואיש לא הטיל ספק כי זו התורה שהיא בידנו. חכמים מודעים היו לפער הגדול שבין דברי התורה לבין מציאות חייהם ומציאות לימודם ותורתם. פער זה הוא ה׳תורה שבעל פה׳. בספרות חז״ל שתי גישות אידיאולוגיות: האחת מתארת לעצמה שמשה ירד מסיני עם התורה שבכתב והתורה שבעל פה וכל שלמדו וחידשו תלמידי הדורות כבר ניתן למשה מסיני. כפי שדרשו התנאים: ״דבר אל אהרן, יכול הדבר הזה שנאמר לאהרן ששמעו מפי הקב״ה אמרת אלה החקים והמשפטים וגו׳ (ויקרא כו מו) הא כל המצות הקלות והחמורות הזדונות והשגגות הכללים והפרטים הגופים והדקדוקים נאמרו למשה מסיני״ (ספרי זוטא ו כג, עמ׳ 742).

וכן אומר המדרש: ״... מקרא ומשנה ותלמוד ואגדה, ואפילו מה שתלמיד וותיק עתיד להורות לפני רבו, כבר נאמר למשה מסיני. הדא הוא דכתיב ׳יש דבר שיאמר ראה זה חדש הוא וחבירו משיבו כבר

צג ע״א (עמ׳ 310); הגהות הרא״ש, פסחים עד ע״א; חכמת שלמה סנהדרין נב ע״א, ועוד. ללקט מקורות המשקף גישות שונות ראו ח׳, בן מנחם ואחרים, *המחלוקת בהלכה*, ניו יורק תשנ״ב ,עמ׳ 206-218. ראו גם פירושו הנועז של המאירי למשנה, עירובין פ״ו מ״ה, שם מפרש הוא משנה בניגוד לבבלי, ומסביר שדברי ר׳ שמעון הועברו ממשנה אחרת (שם, פ״ד מ״ו) ושובצו שלא בהקשרם. עם כל זאת יש להדגיש כי מקרים אלו, של מחלוקת של פרשן מאוחר על הגמרא, נדירים ביותר, כך למשל במשנה, מעשר שני פ״א מ״ז מפרש הרמב״ם את משנה בניגוד לתלמוד, אך במשנה תורה הוא פוסק כתלמוד.

היה לעולמים״״.[7] או ״ואמר רבי לוי בר חמא אמר רבי שמעון בן לקיש: מאי דכתיב ״ואתנה לך את לחת האבן והתורה והמצוה אשר כתבתי להורתם״, לחות - אלו עשרת הדברות, תורה - זה מקרא, והמצוה - זו משנה, אשר כתבתי - אלו נביאים וכתובים, להרתם - זה תלמוד; מלמד שכולם נתנו למשה מסיני״ (בבלי, ברכות ה ע״א). כל המחלוקות שנתהוו במהלך הדורות נבעו מתלמידים שלא שימשו את רבותיהם כל צורכם (תוס׳, סנהדרין פ״ז ה״א; סוטה פי״ד ה״ט ומקבילות רבות). לעומת זאת מצינו במקורות חז״ל גם גישה אחרת המכירה בהתפתחות ההלכה ומודעת לכך שכל דור מוסיף משלו לבנין, ועולם ההלכה הוא בבחינת עץ הצומח וגדל ״[או אינן חסירין ולא יתירין? תלמוד לומר נטועים] מה נטיעה פרה ורבה, אף דברי תורה פרין ורבין״ (תוס׳, סוטה פ״ז הי״א ומקבילות רבות). ביטוי לכך יש באגדה על משה שאינו מבין דבר בבית מדרשו של ר׳ עקיבא, ואף על פי כן הכל נקרא על שמו ויו־נק מכוח תורתו של משה (בבלי, מנחות כט ע״ב). לכל גישה ניתן לגבב מספר רב של מקורות שונים המעידים בדרכם על מקומה המרכזי של השאלה בעולם המחשבה של חכמים.

כאמור ניתן לזהות שתי עמדות תיאולוגיות, אך לעתים דומה שחכמים לא ראו ביניהם סתירה, אלא האמינו ששני התיאורים משלימים זה את זה. חכמים נדרשים להיות כבור סוד שאינו מאבד טיפה, ומ־חויב לשמירה קפדנית על המסורת וממילא נמנע מחידוש, ובמקביל גם כמעין המתגבר יוצר ומתחדש תדיר. כזכור התיאור הראשון הוא דימויו של ר׳ אליעזר בן הורקנוס, והשני של ר׳ אלעזר בן ערך.[8]

לא נאריך כאן בעמדות העקרוניות, שכן השאלה הנידונה כאן איננה מה היא התיאולוגיה של החכמים אלא כיצד התנהלו בתי המדרש בפועל. דומה שקריאה ביקורתית מבחינה שר׳ אליעזר הוא אכן שמרן שאינו מרבה לחדש מה שלא שמע מרבותיו, אך גם הוא מחדש לא מעט, ואילו ר׳ יהושע מניח שאין בית מדרש ללא חידוש. ושני התיאורים הם שילוב של תכונות נפש אישיות של החכמים הבודדים עם המימד האידאי המוצהר בבית מדרשם.

עם כל זאת דומה שספרות חכמים מניחה ככלל שמה שהווה הוא בבחינת מה שהיה. כלומר הם מניחים שגדולי הדורות הקודמים ישבו ולמדו בחבורות ובבתי המדרש, כשם שהם לומדים ומלמ־דים. יעקב, משה, דוד או חזקיה מוצגים כחכמים לכל דבר, הפועלים בראש ובראשונה במישור של בית המדרש.

הכנסת הגדולה

המקורות המציגים את כל התורה שבעל פה כמי שניתנה למשה מסיני, מכירים בכך שהיו כמה מוסדות שהיו בעלי סמכות יצירה בנושאים אלו או אחרים. הנביאים נהנו כמובן מסמכות זאת, ולא־חר מכן אנשי הכנסת הגדולה. לאנשי הכנסת הגדולה מייחסים חידושן של הלכות מרכזיות. בהקשר דומה נזכרים מוסדות נוספים כ׳בית דין של יעבץ׳ (בבלי, יומא פ ע״א) שבהם לא נעסוק. כולם

---

7 ירו׳, מגילה פ״ד ה״א, עד ע״ד; פיאה פ״ב ה״ב, יז ע״א; חגיגה סוף פ״א עו ע״ד; ויקרא רבה כב א, עמ׳ תצז; שמות רבה י י ועוד.

8 ראו משנה, אבות פ״ב מ״ח. הפרשנות שבור סוד אינו מחדש היא פרשנותו של בעל אבות דרבי נתן נו״ב פי״ג, טז ע״ב. אך אפילו בעל אבות דרבי נתן מדגיש שם שגם ר׳ אליעזר בן הורקנוס חידש יותר ממה ששמע מפי רבו.

מעניקים למסורת ההלכה הוד קדומים ולגיטימציה, כלומר לכולם מימד אידיאי מובהק אך לצורך דיוננו השאלה המיוחדת למסורת על הכנסת הגדולה היא, האם היא משקפת זיכרון היסטורי כלשהו, המאפשר להעריך את טיבו ההיסטורי של המוסד.

במסכת אבות מייחסים להם שלוש מימרות "הוו מתונים בדין והעמידו תלמידים הרבה ועשו סייג לתורה" (אבות פ"א מ"א ומקבילות). מתינות בדין יאה תמיד. אך שתי המימרות האחרות הן תשתית ההלכה של חכמים. עשיית הסיג - ההרחקה ההלכתית מדבר עבירה, היא מפתח יוצר להלכות רבות וניתן לומר שהיא שינתה וממשיכה לשנות את פני עולם ההלכה לדורותיו. יתר על כן דומה שבמימרא זאת מתכוונים חכמים למגמה של ניסוח משפטי של הלכות – המהווה את לב ליבה של התורה שבעל פה. בדומה לו גם המשפט 'העמידו תלמידים הרבה' הוא לב ליבה של מצוות לימוד תורה, כפי שננתח זאת להלן. עוד מייחסים להם את שיטת הכללים והפרטים, ואף זה מרכיב מרכזי בשיטת מדרשי ההלכה של חכמים (ירו', שקלים פ"ה ה"ז, מח ע"ג)[9]. אם מייחסים לאנשי כנסת גדולה מימרות אלו כלומר חידושים מרכזיים מעולמה של ההלכה, הרי שיש בכך קביעה מרחיקת לכת, הליבה ההלכתית איננה הלכה מסיני אלא מסורת הכנסת הגדולה מראשית עולמם של חכמים. אמנם קדום וראשית המהלך אך חלק מן התורה שבעל פה.

בנוסף מסורות חכמים מייחסות לכנסת הגדולה החלטות בנושאים חשובים שאין להם כל בסיס במקרא; קביעת תפילות, ברכות, קדושות והבדלות (בבלי, ברכות לג ע"ב). קביעת התפילות חוזרת בסדרת מסורות בירושלמי ובבבלי, אמנם ניתן להידחק ולפרש שכוונת חכמים הייתה רק לקביעת הנוסח. כן מייחסים להם את קביעת ימי הפורים (בבלי, מגילה ב ע"א) ואת הקביעה שספר יחזקאל הוא חלק מן האסופה של כתבי המקרא (אבות דרבי נתן נו"ב פ"א, ב ע"א), וכן מייחסים להם גם סדרה קצרה של מדרשים.

כל אחת מהמסורות הללו בעייתית. על התקבלותו של ספר יחזקאל שומעים אנו במקבילות מסורות אחרות, הקובעות את המאורע לשלהי ימי הבית השני בלבד. גם ייסוד התפילות זוכה למסורות אחרות, המייחסות את התפילות לאבות עולם אחרים. אין צריך לומר שחוקרים מהססים לקבל מסורות אלו כעדות היסטורית. כך למשל ניטש ויכוח על זמנה של קביעת התפילה, אך אפילו המקדימים אינם מקדימים אותה לשלהי ימי הבית השני.[10] על כן דומה שאין טעם להתמקד בבירור מסורות אלו ופרטיהם, אלא לראות בהם מסורת עמומה ששיני הזמן אכלו בה, ונופך של השקפת עולם ניצוק בה. אך ניתן לסכם שמסורת חז"ל רואה בחבריו של אותו מוסד עלום את מניחי התשתית לשיטתה של ההלכה והתורה שבעל פה.[11]

---

9 לסיכום העדויות התלמודיות על אנשי הכנסת הגדולה ראו ח"ד, מנטל, *אנשי הכנסת הגדולה*, תל אביב תשמ"ג, עמ' 145-63.

10 ע', פליישר, לקדמוניות תפילת החובה בישראל, *תרביץ* נט (תש"ן), עמ' 441, וכנגדו ד', פלוסר, 'מקצת מעשי התורה' וברכת המינים, *תרביץ* סא (תשנ"ב), עמ' 374-333. מ"צ פוקס, "פולמוס סמוי בתפילה", בתוך ספר זיכרון לפרופסור פלק ז"ל, מאמרים במדעי היהדות ובשאלות השעה, עורכים רבקה הורוביץ, משה דוד הר, יוחנן דוד סילמן, מיכאל קורינאלדי, הוצאת מישרים, מכון שכטר למדעי היהדות, ירושלים תשס"ה, 164-123. מ"צ פוקס, תשובות לשני מהפכנים, *סיני* נז (תשנ"ד), עמ' קסד-קע.

11 מסורות אחרות מייחסות להם תיקונים בנוסח התנ"ך (תנח' בשלח טז טז; כי תשא יד). בעל אותיות דרבי עקיבא ומסורות אחרות מתורת הסוד ממקמות את אנשי הכנסת הגדולה לפני עזרא הסופר וזו כבר קביעה א-היסטורית, כדרכם של אנשי תורת הסוד.

מסכת אבות מונה את שושלת המסירה של תורה שבעל פה וממקמת את אנשי הכנסת הגדולה בין הנביאים לימי הזוגות. בעל אבות דרבי נתן מפרש שהכוונה לדורות שאחרי הנביאים חגי זכריה ומלאכי (אבות דרבי נתן נו"א פ"א, א ע"ב). מסורות אחרות מייחסות להם את כתיבתו של ספר נחמיה.[12] אם כן אין אחידות דעות בזמנו של המוסד[13]. מכל מקום שמעון הצדיק, שהיה כוהן גדול, מכונה "משיירי הכנסת הגדולה", כלומר נראה שהם מתארים את הכנסת הגדולה כמוסד שפועל עד ימי הכיבוש ההלניסטי.

כפי שהגדרנו ענייננו הוא רק בשאלה האם ניתן לראות בגרעין המסורות הללו זיכרון היסטורי, והאם ניתן לשחזר את טיבו של המוסד? והעלנו עד כה שלושה היבטים שונים. מצד אחד אין לצפות ממסורת חז"ל שנערכה רק במאה השניה לשמר זיכרון היסטורי מהמאות החמישית והרביעית מלפני הספירה. כמעט ואין בידנו מסורות אחרות אוטנטיות מתקופה זו ואפילו מימי המכבים (מאה שניה לפני הספירה) נותרו רק זיכרונות עמומים ביותר. ובנוסף ברור לחוקר שחכמים ערבו בתיאורי העבר שלהם את השקפת עולמם ושיבשו לא במעט את העובדות ההיסטוריות. מצד שני כמה נתונים מסייעים לטענה כי אכן לפנינו הד למוסד שפעל הלכה למעשה. במציאות של חכמים לא היה מוסד דומה שמשלשלי המסורת יכולים היו להעתיקו לתקופה הקדומה. יתר על כן מיקומו של המוסד כאילו פוגע בשושלת המסירה. כפי שראינו הם מייחסים לכנסת הגדולה את ייסודם ועיצובם של מרכיבי יסוד של עולמם. פעולות שהן לב ליבה של ההלכה, ואם כך הוא, הרי שלא כל התורה נמסרה למשה מסיני, וקשה להניח שמסורות על גוף ביניים בין עולם החכמים ותורה מסיני צמחו בבחינת יש מאין.

עד כאן תיאור התדמית העצמית של חז"ל, עדות לעיצוב הזכרון ההיסטורי שלהם כפי שרצו להציגו בפני הציבור. מעתה עלינו לנסות ולברר מה יודעים אנו על שלבי הבראשית של היווצרות התורה שבעל פה. לא נעסוק כאן במכלול השאלות, ונמנע מסקירת ספרות המחקר העשירה ונצמצם דברינו למספר הערות והיבטים שברצוננו להדגיש.

הכנסת הגדולה הרקע הריאלי

דומה שביכולתנו להתקדם צעד נוסף בבירור הפרשה. במקדשי העיר אורוך (Uruk – היא ארך המקראית) פעלה מועצה שנקראה 'כנישתו'. ה'כנישתו' הרגילה הייתה של שנים עשר חברים. והייתה גם 'כנישתו' אחרת, גדולה, שהיו בה כנראה כשבעים אנשים, אך לה אין כינוי מיוחד.[14]

12 ירו', ברכות סוף פ"א, ד ע"א; בראשית רבה ו ו, עמ' 45; לה ב, עמ' 328; שמות רבה כא ג; רות רבה ד ה; תנח' שמות ב; ומדרשים רבים נוספים.

13 בכמה מדרשים נקשרים אנשי הכנסת הגדולה עם תאריך הנס שנעשה בחודש שבט, והמן ידע על מאורע זה (אסתר רבה ז א; מדרש אבא גוריון ג). ופרט זה חסר באגדת אסתר פ"ג, עמ' טו.

14 Doty. L.T., *Cuneiform Archives From Hellinistic Uruk*, (Yale Dissertion), Yale 1977. עמ' 15-18; *In Het Seleucidische Rijk*, Amsterdam 1986 ובעיקר עמ' 70-74.

הכנישתו הייתה מועצה של המקדש שעסקה בענייני משפט אזרחי, של מכירות וקניות בשיפוט ואולי גם בחקיקה. מן הסתם עסקה גם בניהול הצד המשפטי-חוקי של המקדש, אך לכך אין ראיות. ה'כנישתו' מיוחדת בכך שיש בה שילוב של פשוטי עם ולפחות חלק מהחברים לא היו כוהנים.

שמו של המוסד, כמו שמותיהם של בעלי תפקיד אחרים באורוך בתקופה הסלבקית הם ממוצא ארמי ונראה שהמוסד שנוסד קודם לכן בימי ממלכת פרס (ואולי קודם) והמשיך לתפקד גם בראשית ימי השלטון ההלניסטי. העדות הראשונה לקיומו של המוסד היא אכן מימיו של כורש, והאחרונה מימי הסלבקים, והתעודות שבידנו מוכיחות כי הייתה זו מדיניות סלבקית עקבית לאמץ מסגרות שלטוניות קדומות וליצוק לתוכן תוכן הלניסטי.

על כן יש מקום להשערה שהכנסת הגדולה בדומה לאותה 'כנישתו' פעלה במקדש ירושלים. המוסד פעל בשלהי ימי שלטון פרס, ואולי אף קודם לכן. לפי הסבר זה הכנסת הגדולה הייתה מועצה של המקדש, בראשה עמד מן הסתם, הכוהן הגדול, כמו שמעון הצדיק בזמנו. ברוח זו פעל המוסד בתקופת שלטון פרס (לאו דווקא בראשית שלטון פרס), עד ראשית השלטון ההלניסטי, ואולי אף מעט קודם לכן.

ההצעה לקווי דמיון בין מקדש ירושלים והמקדש באורוך, ובערים סמוכות אינה רחוקה. בשתי הערים, כמו גם בבבל גופא, העיר כולה הייתה עיר-מקדש, והנהלת המקדש שימשה גם כהנהלה עירונית. שמות בעלי התפקידים במקדש בירושלים מופיעים גם בבבל. הגזבר בירושלים הוא הגנזברה הבבלי-ארמי, והסגן התלמודי הוא הסכנו, או סגנו הבבלי-ארמי. התואר אמרכל אינו מופיע בצורתו זו, אך כמה בעלי תפקידים במקדשי בבל או אורוך, נשאו את התואר מר- כמו מר ביתו, הממונה על הבית וכיוצא באלו. חנות המקדש נקראת מכורו, ואולי מכאן המילה אמרכל. כן מופיע במקורות הבבליים המונח 'קופה', לאוצר המקדש שאליו מביאים תרומות.[15] אחד הממונים במקדש הבבלי הוא ה'פקדו', שצורתו העברית היא פקיד.[16] על כן מתבקשת המסקנה שהמקדש של שלהי ימי הבית השני משמר את מערכת התפקידים מהמקדש בימי השלטון ההלניסטי או הפרסי. וכי מקדש ירושלים בתקופה זו התנהל במתכונת המקדשים בבבל או באורוך.

מבחינתו של דיון זה מתברר שאת ראשית המסורות על התורה שבעל פה מייחסים חכמים למועצה שפעלה במסגרת המקדש. בשושלת המסירה שבמסכת אבות מתעלמים חכמים ממקומם של הכוהנים. ברם כל העדויות מימי הבית השני מלמדות על תפקידם המרכזי של הכוהנים בלימוד התורה והוראתו, עד למהפכה הפרושית. העדות על הכנסת הגדולה כמועצת המקדש הולמת את ידיעותינו על מעמדם של הכוהנים כמורי ההלכה מחד גיסא ומאידך גיסא ה'כנישתו' הבבלית כללה גם לא כוהנים ומן הסתם זה גם מאפיין מובהק של הכנסת הגדולה שבירושלים. ניתן אפוא

---

15 Spek לעיל; McEwan, G.J.P., *Priest and Temple in Hellenistic Babylonia, Wiesbaden* 1981. לפקדו ראו, עמ' 27, לגנזברה ראו עמ' 34, לקופה ראו עמ' 152, ולמכורו היא החנות של המקדש ראו עמ' 33.

16 דברי הימים ב כד יא; לא יג. השאלה האם קווי הדמיון בין מקדש ירושלים למקדשי בבל מופיעים כבר בתקופת המקרא אינה בתחום דיוננו. המונח 'פקיד' למשל מופיע במקרא הרבה, אך ברוב האזכורים אין לו קשר ישיר דווקא למקדש, ברם בדברי הימים שנערך בימי שלטון פרס ה'פקיד' הוא ממונה במקדש. בספרות חז"ל נעלם תואר זה. 'סגן' מופיע במקרא בצורה סוכן, אך ללא קשר ישיר למקדש, ובספרות חז"ל הסגן פועל רק במקדש.

להעריך ששלבי הבראשית של עיצוב התורה שבעל פה קשורים לאותו מוסד של הכנסת הגדולה שפעל בימי שלטון פרס ובראשית התקופה ההלניסטית.

בניגוד לחוקרים אחרים איננו סבורים שהמסורות התלמודיות על אנשי הכנסת הגדולה משקפים זכרונות ריאליים של פעולתם. העדויות אגדיות וסותרות זו את זו. מצד שני איננו יכולים גם לקבל את הסבורים שכל מערך העדויות הוא דמיוני ואגדי. מסקנתנו היא שאכן קיים היה מוסד שכונה 'כנסת גדולה'. מוסד זה פעל בתקופה הפרסית ו\או ההלניסטית הקדומה והיה הגוף הראשון שקבע הלכות שלימים הפכו לתשתית התורה שבעל פה. עם זאת הזכרון הקולקטיבי של עם ישראל לא שימר פרטים מדויקים על פעילותו. לענייננו חשוב שחכמים מבינים שלא הם ייסדו את התורה שבעל פה, ומצד שני גם אינם טוענים לרצף בלתי מופרע מימי המקרא ועד ימיהם. הם מכירים בכך שהיה 'סוכן תיווך' שתיווך (והבדיל) בין תקופת המקרא ובין הפעילות בבית המדרש. אנו מעריכים שאכן היה קיים מוסד מעין זה, והוא אכן עסק בשיפוט וחקיקה, ונכללו בו כוהנים ומנהיגים שלא ממוצא כוהני. עם זאת עדיין אין בכך לקבוע שמוסד זה ניהל את דיוניו באותו אופן, ולפי אותם קווי מחשבה כמו בית המדרש של חכמים.

הסופרים

בניגוד לסנהדרין נזכר במקורות מוסד נוסף שאפילו חכמים עצמם לא ראו בו בהכרח מוסד קדום הלא הוא 'תקופת הסופרים'.

במסורת המשנה מצינו קבוצה נכבדה של משניות הבנויות על מספרים. לט אבות מלאכה (שבת פ"ז מ"ב), ארבע אבות נזיקין (בבא קמא פ"א מ"א), חמישה לא יתרומו (תרומות פ"א מ"א), חמי־שה עשר נשים (יבמות פ"א "א) וכיוצא באלו. אמוראים חשו כי שמדובר בקבוצת משניות בעלת ייחוד והציעו כי כל אלו נוסדו בידי ה'סופרים' קריא קבוצה קדומה של החכמים שפעלו אי שם בימי הכנסת הגדולה. ולמה נקראו סופרים? "שעשו את התורה ספורות ספורות" (ירו', שקלים פ"ב ה"ב, מח ע"ג). ואכן יש לראות בדברים עדות לשיטת העריכה ולכך שאמוראים הכירו אותה והכירו בייחודה, אך ספק אם ניתן ללמוד מהם על הכרונולוגיה של השיטה.[17] ניתוח של משנת תרומות, למשל, מצביע על כך שהפתיחה המספרית מאוחרת ומשנית לגוף הטקסט, הפתיחה למעשה חוזרת על מה שכתוב בהמשך המשנה "אין תרומתו תרומה". הווה אומר שהפתיחה המספרית מהווה תור־ספת לגוף המשנה.[18]

---

17 א"א, אורבך, הדרשה כיסוד ההלכה ובעית הסופרים, בתוך: *ספר היובל לג' שלום*, ירושלים תשי"ח, עמ' מ-נו. פיתח שיטה שלמה על תקופת הסופרים כתקופת היסוד של תורה שבעל פה. לא כאן המקום לפתח את הנושא, אך להערכתנו המינוח "סופרים" בספרות חז"ל כמתייחס לחכמי העבר רווי תפישות סטריאוטיפיות ואינו משקף זכרון היסטורי ריאלי.

18 בחלקו השני של המאמר נדון בשלבי העריכה ודומה שיש לשייך משניות מספריות למה שיכונה 'שלב ב'. כלומר: הפתיחה המספרית אופיינית למשניות שיש בהם רצף מובנה של דוגמאות ובשני המקרים שהבאנו (שבת פ"ז מ"ב; ותרומות פ"א מ"א) הפתיחה המספרית מן הסתם מאוחרת.

הפתיחה המספרית הייתה חשובה לקדמוננו, משום שהם זכרו את המשניות בעל פה ומספרים הם כלי עזר חשוב ביותר לזיכרון. ייתכן גם שהייתה פעם משנה קדומה שרבות ממשניותיה היו סדורות בצורה מספרית. או לחילופין שהייתה זו שיטת עריכה, אולי של בית מדרש מסוים, אך לאו דווקא שיטת עריכה קדומה. ואכן למשניות המספריות אופי מסכם של כלל ועל כן סביר יותר שזו שיטה מאוחרת יחסית בעריכת המשנה. לאחר שנעשה שימוש בכלל מספרי לא ויתרו חכמים על המניין, אף אם במהלך הדורות חלו בו שינויים. כך למשל חלו שינויים במניין של לט אבות מלאכה, אך הניסוח המספרי (לט אבות מלאכה) לא שונה.[19] הדוגמא הבולטת היא תפילת 'שמונה עשרה' המכונה כך היום, ובמקורות חכמים י"ח ברכות, זאת אף שבבבל הוכללו בתפילה תשעה עשר ברכות. הגמרא עצמה טורחת להסביר זאת, אך כפשוטו השם כבר הפך למותג ספרותי ואין להחליפו. וכן הסיכום שחמש נשים פסולות להעיד על קרובת משפחתם. במשנה מופיעה הרשימה ללא מנין (משנה, יבמות פט"ו מ"ד). הירושלמי מעיר בפשטות שבנוסף לחמש הנשים הנזכרות יש עוד נשים (ירו', טו ע"א) ובתלמוד הבבלי ברייתא "הכל נאמנין להעידה חוץ מחמש נשים, והבבלי מבין שחמש אלו דווקא, ומתלבט מדוע לא נזכרו נשים נוספות (בבלי, יבמות קיז ע"א).

וכן המניין "חמש עשרה נשים פוטרות צרותיהן" (משנה, יבמות פ"א מ"א) נותר, אף שיש המוסיפים דוגמאות נוספות (ירו', ב ע"ג). משנת זו ביבמות היא אליבא דבית הלל בלבד, שכן היא מניחה ש'צרת הבת' פטורה מיבום, ואילו בית שמאי סוברים ש'צרת הבת' אסורה ביבום (תוס', יבמות פ"א ה"ח-ה"י ומקבילות). הויכוח בין הבתים הוכרע רק באמצע דור יבנה (שם, ה"י ומקבילות). ברור אפוא שניסוח המשנה מאוחר למחלוקת בית שמאי ובית הלל. אילו היה כלל קדום וידוע, קשה להניח שבית שמאי היו מעוררים מחלוקת על כך.

אורבך[20] לעומת זאת קיבל את המדרש כמעט כפשוטו. אמנם אין הוא מקבל את קדמותן של המשניות האמורות, אך מקבל את התפישה שהייתה אי פעם תקופת סופרים שהיא תקופתם של חכמים ראשונים. עוד בטרם בירור יאמר שלהערכתנו אין כל חשיבות לכך אם חכמים ראשונים נקראו 'סופרים' או 'חכמים', חשוב כיצד פעלו, ושיטתו של אורבך אינה עוזרת להבהרת הפרשה. עוד יאמר שהיא כולה שייכת לשאלה כיצד תיארו חכמים לעצמם את היווסדות התורה שבעל פה, וכאמור השאלה בה אנו עוסקים היא שונה, מה ניתן להפיק כעדות היסטורית מתפישתם של חכמים.

המונח דברי סופרים נזכר רבות בספרות חז"ל. אלו הן הלכות שאינן מן התורה, וחכמים מודים שאין להן בסיס בדברי התורה. "השרתוע, והדוקרן, והמעדיר, והמלקוט של כובשין, שניטלה אחת משניהן ועשה של מתכת הרי אלו טמאין. על כולן אמר ר' יהושע דבר חדש חדשו הסופרים, ואין לי מה אשיב".[21] וכן מופיע המונח במקורות רבים נוספים.[22] האבחנה שהלכה פלונית היא מדברי

---

19 ראו דיוננו להלן.

20 א"א, אורבך, הערה 11 לעיל ; מנטל, (הערה 3 לעיל), עמ' 146-165. הספרות בנושא רבה עד למאד, והנושא מחייב דיון ארוך, ולא באנו אלא לחוות את דעתנו בנושא.

21 תוס', כלים בבא מציעא פ"ג הי"ד, עמ' 582; וכן תוס' טבול יום פ"ב הי"ד, עמ' 686.

22 כגון משנה, ידים פ"ג מ"ב; יבמות פ"ט מ"ג; תוס', פ"ב ה"ד; משנה, עורלה פ"ג מ"ט; תוס', דמאי פ"ב ה"ה; תענית פ"ב ה"ו; עדיות פ"א ה"א ומקבילות ומקורות נוספים.

סופרים אינה רק תיאורטית (היסטורית) אלא היא בסיס להקלה, מה שמדברי סופרים מותר להקל בספקו,[23] אך דווקא משום כך יש להקפיד עליו הקפדה יתירה. עד כאן אין כל אמירה על זמנם של הסופרים וטיבם המיוחד.

התלמודים חשו בטיבו המיוחד של המונח וביארוהו. לאמוראים הסברים שונים כאמור בירושל־מי: "ולמה נקראו סופרים? "שעשו את התורה ספורות ספורות" (ירו', שקלים פ"ב ה"ב, מח ע"ג). הבבלי מסביר: "'איה סופר'? שהיו סופרים כל אותיות שבתורה, 'איה שוקל'? שהיו שוקלים קלין וחמורין שבתורה. 'איה סופר את המגדלים'? שהיו שונין שלש מאות הלכות במגדל הפורח באויר" (חגיגה טו ע"ב). הסבר אחר הוא: "לפיכך נקראו ראשונים סופרים - שהיו סופרים כל האותיות שבתורה, שהיו אומרים: וא"ו ד"גחון", חציין של אותיות של ס"ת וכו'" (קידושין ל ע"א). ברור שיש כאן דרשות למינוח ותו לא. מכל מקום בדברי תנאים ובעצם גם בדברי אמוראים אין קביעה שהסופרים פעלו בעבר הרחוק בדווקא. מיחסים להם החלטות שונות, מהן קדומות, אך אין בכך תרומה לתיארוך ה'סופרים' או אף להגדרת טיבם המיוחד.

עם זאת הסופר הוא מונח מקראי, ובימי חז"ל משמש בעיקר לתיאור הלבלר (כותב הספרים) או המורה בבית הספר. ברם לעתים ניתן להבין ש'סופרים' הם גם סתם חכמים. כגון "שער חדש ששם חידשו סופרים את ההלכה" (ירו', עירובין פ"ה ה"א, כב ע"ג). וכן "אמר רבן גמליאל הניחו לי סופרים, ואומרה כמין חומר...",[24] וכן "תניא נמי הכי: שנים שאכלו - מצוה ליחלק. במה דברים אמורים" שהיו שניהם סופרים, אבל אחד סופר ואחד בור - סופר מברך ובור יוצא" (בבלי, חולין קו ע"א). אם כן לעיתים סופרים הוא מונח מקביל לחכמים.

את המינוח המדוקדק של 'דברי סופרים' יש להבין במישור שונה לחלוטין. חכמים עמלים למעט בחידושיהם ולהראות שפסקי דינם מעוגנים במקרא המקודש. הסיבות לכך ברורות ונהירות, ואף על פי כן הקורא הביקורתי מותיר לעצמו את הזכות להחליט מתי הלכה פלונית היא מדברי תורה, או בגדר פרשנות לתורה, ומתי היא בבחינת 'פרשנות יוצרת', חידוש שחידשו חכמים. המונח 'דברי סופרים' בא כאשר גם לחכמים ברור שהלכה פלונית אינה מדברי תורה, כגון טומאת הגוי, הכתובה, או הרחבה של המונח 'קרוב' לצורך איסורי נישואים וייבום. בהקשר זה המינוח הרווח הוא 'דברי סופרים', לעומת זאת המינוח המקביל 'דברי חכמים' כולל את כל דבריהם, אף כשהם מפרשים או מרחיבים את שנראה להם כדבר התורה.

כאמור הגדרת הלכה כ'דברי סופרים' מאפשרת להקל במקרה של ספק, ולפיכך ייתכן שבמקור־רו בא המינוח לאפשר הקלות אלו, ולתת להן מעמד לגיטימי.[25] היוצא מדברנו הוא שאף חז"ל לא התכוונו לומר שאי פעם בעבר הייתה 'תקופת הסופרים', אף אם רצו לתאר כך את ההסטוריה, הרי

23 תוס', נידה פ"ט הי"ד, עמ' 651; בבלי, תענית כח ע"א ועוד.

24 ספרי במדבר ח, עמ' 14, והשוו בבלי, סוטה טו ע"א.

25 את הצעד הראשון לבירור התופעה יש לזקוף לזכותו של דה פריס שהראה שבספרות התנאים ההבחנה בין דבר תורה לדברי חכמים (סופרים) אינה חתוכה ואינה משפטית, ורק בספרות האמוראים קיבלו שני המונחים הללו (דברי תורה לעומת דברי סופרים) משמעות משפטית ראו דה פריס, המושגים. גילת דן בנושא שנית וקיבל את מסקנתו תוך דיון מפורט בכמה דוגמאות נוספות ראו

שאין סיבה לקבל את הטענה שהתיאור של מעשי הסופרים הוא יותר ממיתוס הבא לתאר הכרעות הלכתיות קדומות. מכל מקום אין בדברי חז"ל טענה שהסופרים למדו או לימדו אחרת מהמקובל בבית המדרש התנאי. בדיון זה אנו מתמקדים בהתפתחות התוכנית של צורת הלימוד ואף אם נקבל את דברי אורבך וחוקרים קרובים כפשוטם, הדבר אינו מסייע בבירור שיטת הלימוד הקדומה.

כיצד התפתחה התורה שבעל פה

העדות המקראית

כידוע מתארת התורה את חוקי ההלכה שנמסרו למשה מסיני. כל העדויות שבידנו מלמדות שהלכה למעשה, בתקופת המקרא, שמירת המצוות לא רווחה בעם ישראל . לא רק שהיו תקופות ארוכות בהם העם מואשם באי ציות לדבר ה', אלא שאין הרבה עדויות המעידות על קיום שוטף של המצוות והדברים ידועים. לעומת כל זאת שומעים אנו מעט על מצוות (נוהגים) הקרובים להלכה, אך אינם זהים לה. הדוגמא הידועה ביותר הוא מעשה היבום והגאולה של רות. בתיאור במגילת רות נעשה שימוש במונחים המקראיים 'גאולה' 'להקים שם המת על נחלתו' (רות ד א-י),[26] ברם הגאולה אינה זהה לחובת הגאולה שבמקרא. יתר על כן מגילת רות מלמדת על נוהג למכור קרקעות בנוכחות כל זקני העיר, ועל נוהג קדום לבצע את המכירה באמצעות חליצת הנעל (רות ד ז). בתיאור מצוות היבום שבתורה מהווה חליצת הנעל קנין (דברים כה יט). כבר עורך המגילה יודע שצורת קנין זו בטלה, שכן הוא מדגיש: "וזאת <u>לפנים בישראל</u> על הגאולה ועל התמורה לקים כל דבר שלף איש נעלו ונתן לרעהו וזאת התעודה בישראל" (רות שם). אם כן בימיו כבר קנו באופן שונה. נראה אפוא שהתורה השתמשה בשיטת קנין ישנה ומסורתית. בזמן שנכתבה פרשת יבום כבר הנוהג לקנות בחליצה לא היה מקובל, אך התורה משתמשת בו כמרכיב במעמד הדתי של חליצה. מכאן רשאים אנו להסיק כי בצד מצוות התורה פעלה מערכת של נוהג מקומי. לצורך דיוננו אין זה משנה אם בזמן המתואר במגילת רות, בכלל נפוצים היו כבר חוקי התורה. מכל מקום אי אפשר שלא להעיר כי חלק מנוהגים המתוארים במגילת רות מופיעים יותר מאוחר כנוהג בחברה היהודית של תקופת המשנה הקדומה. כך למשל הנוהג הקדום בתקופת המשנה, היה למכור קרקעות בפני עשרה, ובכלל לצמצם במכירת קרקע שלא לאחד מבני המשפחה, כמשתמע ממגילת רות.[27]

גילת, מדאורייתא לדרבנן. להערכתנו בחלק מהמקרים הגדרת הלכה מסוימת ש'מדרבנן' או ' מדברי סופרים' באה לנמק הקלות בהלכה, ולעתים החמרה בהלכה כי יש להקפיד על דברי סופרים יותר מאשר על דברי תורה לבל יבואו לזלזל בהם.

26 אך לא נזכר המונח ייבום שהתורה מייחדת אותו לנישואי אחי המת (ע"צ, מלמד, לתרגום מגילת רות, *בר-אילן א* (תשכג) 190-194.

27 משנה, סנהדרין פ"א מ"ג המשנה עוסקת בפדיון הקדש קרקע, ולדעתנו בפדיון זה נשתמר הנוהג הקדום של מכירת הקרקעות. על ההגבלות הקדומות על מכירת קרקעות מחוץ לחוג המשפחה ראו גולאק, מקרקעין, עמ' 41-42. הד לנוהג למכור קרקעות

הוא הדין לתביעה המקראית מבני ישראל לפרוש מנשותיהן ערב מתן תורה. בתורה אין הסבר לדרישה זו. דיני אישות וטוהרה מופיעים בפרקים אחרים במקרא ובהם אין כל הד לאיסור כלשהו החל שלושה ימים לאחר קיום קשרי אישות. בכל דיני טוהרה אין משמעות לפרק הזמן של שלושה ימים, וניתן לטהר אדם לאחר יום או לאחר שבעה ימים, אבל לא נזכרת טוהרה מיוחדת לאחר שלושה ימים. בפרקי התורה האחרים לא מופיעה הגבלה על השתתפות הטמאים במעמדים ציבוריים. ואין זה מקרי שדוגמה זו נבחרה בדיוננו, כיון שנוהג (עממי?) מאוחר אימץ חלק ממגבלות אלו. למרות שזו טומאה קלה יחסית, היו שאסרו על לימוד והנחת תפילין לטמא בטומאת בעל קרי[28] ואסור לו בכלל לעסוק בקודש. הוא אפילו מנוע מלגעת במעשר למרות שהמעשר אינו דורש טהרה כלל. המשנה מניחה שהטמא רשאי לאכול, ולכל היותר הוטלו מגבלות על ברכת המזון או על הצטרפותו לזימון. אבל בירושלמי מתברר שהיו שהחמירו ולא אכלו עד שטבלו מטומאת בעל קרי. בירושלמי סיפור על אדם פשוט הרוצה לסכן עצמו ולטבול כדי שיוכל לאכול ולשתות. מהסיפור משמע שבעל קרי מנוע מלאכול בגלל טומאתו עצמה או בגלל שאינו יכול לברך. גם בספור זה משתמעת דבקות במצוות טהרה מקרי.

במקביל מצינו גם גישה שונה מקילה, שרווחה בבבל: העדות הברורה ביותר במעשה בר' יהודה בן בתירא: "מעשה באחד שעמד לקרות בתורה בנציבין. כיון שהגיע להזכרה התחיל מגמגם[29] בה. אמר לו רבי יהודה בן בתירה: פתח פיך ויאירו דבריך, שאין דברי תורה מקבלין טומאה. אמר רבי יעקב בר אחא: ונהגין תמן (שם [בבבל] נוהגים) כרבי יהודה בן בתירא בבעלי קריין ... ". (כר' יהודה בן בתירה בבעלי קרי) דתני: ר' יהודה אומר: אין דברי תורה מקבלין טומאה.[30] דומה שחשוב לציין בהקשר זה, שהחכם מתנגד לנוהג המקובל והגבלותיו, ואילו התלמיד סבור שמותר ללמוד, אך לא להזכיר את השם הקדוש.

בספורת המקראית אין הרבה עדויות לשמירת דיני טהרה, אך דווקא על שמירתה של מצווה זו אנו שומעים גם מדוד וגם מנעריו.[31] בתקופת המשנה והתלמוד, בחברה שונה לחלוטין, עמי הארץ

במעמד ציבורי יש במנהג הקצצה ראו ירו', קידושין פ"א ה"ה, ס ע"ג; רות רבה ד ז; בבלי, כתובות כח ע"ב. הירושלמי שם מתאר את מעמד הקצצה כמעשה הקנין עצמו.

28 משנה, ברכות פ"ד מ"ד-מ"ו; תוס', פ"ב הי"ג; ירו', ו ע"ג; וכן אומר הבבלי כ ע"ב; משנה, תרומות פ"א מ"ו; כלים פ"ו מ"ה. טומאת בעל קרי היא הטומאה הנגרמת לאדם מעצם קיום מעשה אישות.

29 כפשוטו 'מגמגם' משמעו שהקורא היסס האם להמשיך בקריאה ורצה להפסיק בכך. אבל בתלמוד הבבלי "אינו מפסיק ועולה אלא מגמגם וקורא. ר' מאיר אומר אין בעל קרי רשאי לקרוא בתורה יותר מג' פסוקים" (בבלי, כב ע"ב). אם כן קריאה בגמגום היא הפתרון לבעל קרי שמצא עצמו באמצע הקריאה. במשמעות המונח מגמגם נחלקו ראשונים. אין זה סביר שהכוונה למי שחוזר על חלקי מילים פעמים מספר (כמות שהמונח היום). פירוש זה מתאים למקומות אחרים בהם נזכר הגמגום, אך לא לסוגייתנו, וכי מה תועיל חזרה מעצבנת על הברות. נראה שהכוונה לקריאה בקול עמום בהבלעת עיצורים. כך למשל על הזב נאמר שהוא מגמגם (מדרש כסא שלמה, אוצר המדרשים, עמ' 528). לגמגם משמעו גם להתעכב, בניגוד ל"מיד" (מדרש תנאים לדברים ו, ז, עמ' 27), וראו עוד הביטוי לגמגם ב"ארוריא" (בקללות שבתורה), בבלי מגילה לא ע"ב; קוהלת רבה ח א, ומקבילות). אם כן הבבלי לשיטתו. הבבלי סבור שאין בעל קרי אסור מלברך, ואפילו התלמיד מחמיר רק בפרט משני, אך מסכים לעצם הדין.

30 ירו', ברכות פ"ו ה"ג, ו ע"ג; בבלי, ברכות כב ע"א.

31 שמואל א כ כו; כא ה-ו. יתר הפרטים שם אינם מתאימים לדיני התורה. לפי דין תורה רק כוהן רשאי לאכול מלחם קודש, ואם הוא לחם חול, לא חלים עליו חוקי טהרה. כמובן ששערי פירושים לא ננעלו.

לא הקפידו על מצוות הטהרה, אך על טהרה שלאחר יחסי אישות הקפידו דווקא בחומרה יתרה, כשם שכל הציבור נהג בכך. בתלמוד (ירו', ברכות פ"ו ה"ג, י ע"ג) מסופר על פלוני שרצה לטבול לאחר קיום יחסי אישות. ר' יוסי אוסר עליו משום שטבילה בלילה באותו מקום נחשבה לסכנה. האיש, שהיה החמר של ר' יוסי, מסביר שהוא נטמא מאשת איש שהיא נידה. ובכך הוא מסביר את רצונו העז לטבול. מבחינה הלכתית יש מקום לטבילה אחרי קיום יחסי אישות. אבל אין זה משנה אם האישה נשואה או לא. ר' יוסי מקבל את נימוקו של המהלך למרות שלחטא הניאוף הטבילה אינה מועילה.[32] הוא אמנם אוסר עליו לטבול, אך אינו אומר לו שאין לטבילתו ערך מיוחד. מכל מקום האיש טבל ונענש משמים. יש לשער שהמעשה ספרותי, אך דווקא משום כך הוא מייצג את עולם האמונה העממי. החמר אינו תלמיד חכם או חבר. אלו אינם מתוארים כבועלי אשת איש וני־דה. זהו עם הארץ שאינו מקפיד על חלק ממצוות שעונשם כרת, אך מוכן להסתכן כדי שלא יפסיד טבילה. וכן מסופר על פלוני שרצה להזקק לאשת איש, אך העדר מקווה לטבילה הרתיע אותו.[33] וכן משמע מהסיפור של ר' יוסי בר חלפתא. על תפוצתה של ההקפדה על המצווה ניתן ללמוד מדברי ההתנגדות של הנוצרים. בעל דידסקלה אפוסטולורום (מאה ב) מדגיש שאין צורך לטבול אחרי מגע עם אישה (פרק כו).

גם אם קשה להעריך עד כמה נשמרו הפרטים השונים של חוקי התורה בחיי המעשה, ברור שלצד החוקים הייתה מערכת נוהגים שהיא בבחינת תורה שבעל פה. זאת ועוד חוקי התורה עצמה דורשים הסברים. ברור שמי ששמר על החוקים פירש לעצמו מהי מלאכה שאסורה בשבת. בדברי הנביאים ביטוי לכמה הלכות בתחום זה, ויש בהם הרחבה של איסור מלאכה.[34] מחלקם אף ניתן להסיק שהנביא מתלונן נגד הנוהגים לעשות מלאכות אלו בשבת, וקשה לדעת אם יש כאן חידוש הלכתי של הנביאים, או אולי מאבק נגד המזלזלים בדינים המקובלים. כך או כך יש בפסוקים ביטוי למסורת הלכתית שאינה מקרא מפורש, בבחינת תורה שבעל פה.

אם כן כבר בתקופת המקרא חייבת הייתה להיות תורה שבעל פה כלשהי. בצד או במקביל לחוקי התורה היו נוהגים עממיים בתחום ההלכתי, נוהגים השייכים לעולם החוק המקראי, אך אינם זהים לו. דווקא לחוקים אלו יש המשכיות בנוהג העממי בחברה היהודית בתקופת המשנה והתלמוד, במקביל להלכה, אך לא בניגוד לה.[35] עם זאת לא ניתן להוכיח כי אותה תורה שבעל פה כפי שנהגה היא התורה שבעל פה המוכרת לנו מספרות חז"ל. אדרבה אופיה של תורה שבעל

32 לפי ההלכה הפורמלית אין גם טעם לטבול אחרי בעילת נידה, הרי הוא טמא שבעת ימים.

33 ירו', ברכות פ"ו ה"ג, ו ע"ג; ברכות כב ע"א. להלן נראה שדווקא בבבל לא הקפידו על חמרה זו של טומאת בעל קרי, ולפיכך סביר שזהו סיפור ארץ ישראלי. הסיפור מתחיל ב"מעשה באחד" זו פתיחה של ז'אנר סיפורי הבא לתאר, בדרך כלל, מעשה של אחד מפשוטי עם.

34 ביקור אצל הנביא בשבת (מלכים ב ד כב-כג) – בניגוד מסוים למסורת ההלכה האוסרת הליכה למרחק בשבת. החלפת משמרת במקדש בשבת (מלכים ב יא ד-יב). איסור מכירה בשבת כנוהג מקובל (עמוס ח ה-ו), וכחידוש הלכתי (נחמיה י לב; יג טו-כא). איסור הליכה בשבת [למרחק] (ישעיהו נח יג). נוהג לעלות לרגל למקדש בשבת (ישעיהו סו כג). נשיאת משא בשבת, אולי כחידוש הלכתי (ירמיהו יז כא-כב).

35 במקום אחר הוצע לראות בנהגים אלו נוהג עממי של חברה יראת שמים, שקיום ההלכה אינו מגביל את יראתה.

פה זו אינו הולם את העקרונות המכוננים של התורה שבעל פה של ימי בית שני (של כל הכ־תות). במקביל אין גם ספק שבחברה היהודית התפתחו נוהגים דתיים (הלכות) שאינם במקרא. איננו יכולים לקבוע אם אלו נוסדו בתקופת בית שני, או בימי בית ראשון, ואולי אף נהגו בימי המקרא הקדומים. כזה למשל הוא מוסד ה'מיאון'.[36] כבר בית שמאי ובית הלל חולקים בפרטיו (משנה, יבמות פי"ד מ"א). לשאלה מתי נוצר המוסד אין תשובה היסטורית, והיא ענין לבירור אידיאולוגי-תיאולוגי בלבד.

עקרונות היסוד של התורה שבעל פה

מעתה עלינו להגדיר מהם העקרונות המכוננים של התורה שבעל פה של הפרושים, זו המוכרת לנו מספרות חכמים.[37] מסורת חז"ל עצמה לא הגדירה את העקרונות המכוננים שלה. דומה שהיא מדגישה עקרון אחד, והוא קבלת עולם של חכמים. ברם אין בה הגדרה מה תוכנם של דברי חכמים. אך דומה שמן המקורות ניתן להצביע על עקרונות אלו:

א. מרכזיות ה'תורה' והעיסוק ההלכתי בה.

ב. קשר רצוף עם התורה שבכתב, תוך תודעה של השוני בין התורה להלכות חכמים.

ג. שמירה נורמטיבית של המצוות, פרטיהן ופרטי הפרטים. המצוות הופכות ממושג כולל למערכת פרטים מחייבים. כך למשל בתורה הגדרה כללית של מצוות מעשרות, ובתורה שבעל פה פרטים: מאיזה פירות מפרישים מעשר, מתי הפרשת המעשר היא רק מספק, באיזה שלב של הפרי מותר לעשר, מתי חייבים לעשר, מה סדרי ההפרשה, וכיוצא באלו. אם נקבע שיש להרים מעשרות לאחר 'גמר מלאכה' תדון המשנה מהו גמר מלאכה במקרים מיוחדים, מה דינה של סעודה בשדה, או בישול בשדה. מה דינו של מי שהרים מעשרות שלא לפי ההגדרות הקודמות ושאלות רבות כיוצא באלו.

ד. החלת העקרונות על פרטי היום יום. המצוות הכלליות כמו אהבת הריע, או זיכרון השבת מיתרגמות למערכת הלכתית נורמטיבית הכוללת פרטים רבים. מרכיב זה קרוב באופיו למרכיב הקודם.

ה. בניית מערכת משפטית הגיונית שיש בה כללים רבים, וכמובן גם חריגים. אלו הם הכל־לים והפרטים שנזכרו לעיל כתרומתם של אנשי הכנסת הגדולה. במסגרת זו יש טיפוח ועיסוק רב במקרים של התנגשויות בין מצוות (שבת ומקדש, מצוות יבום מול האיסור לשאת אשת אח בכל מקרה אחר וכיוצא באלו דוגמאות)

ו. עשיית סייג לתורה – הטלת מגבלות כדי שלא להתקרב לחשש איסור.

36 המיאון מבוסס על ההנחה שלאב זכות לקדש את בתו כשהיא קטנה, עם מותו יורשים האם והאחים הגדולים זכות זו. אבל קטנה שהתארסה (או נישאה) בתנאים אלו רשאית, בעת הגיעה לגיל בגרות ל'מאן' והיא כאלו לא נישאה מעולם. מערך הלכתי זה משקף מספר שלבים מחשבתיים. להלכות העיקריות ראו במשנה, יבמות פי"ג.

37 היחס בין הלכות הפרושים ומסורת חז"ל מחייב בירור לגופו.

ז. סמכותם של חכמים לפרש את המקרא, לחדש הלכות ולתקן תקנות חדשות. דומה שה־אבחנה בין סוגים הלכתיים אלו לא הייתה חשובה לחכמים.[38]

ח. חשיבות הלימוד כערך מכונן לעצמו וככלי לבירור ההלכות, ולשמירה עליהן.

ט. 'תרבות המחלוקת' ההלכות, לפחות כפי שהן מובאות בספרות ההלכה, שנויות לעתים רבות במחלוקת, וזאת במקביל להעמדתן כ'מסורת' קדומה. אין כל נסיון להציג את ההלכות כפרי ההתגלות מאל עליון, ואף אין דמות של 'מורה הצדק' או מנהיג כריסמטי כישו הנוצרי שהם דמויות מכוננות של ההלכה והנוהג, אך יש ייחוס של ההלכה לחכ־מים קדומים ומאוחרים.

י. התורה שבעל פה עוסקת בכל מכלול הנושאים, דיני מקדש וקורבנות, מצוות החגים, דיני ממונות, הלכות מוסר כהשבת אבידה וצדקה. בכך עוקבת התורה שבעל פה אחר התורה שבכתב, ומפתחת את הדברים בהרחבה רבה. אין לכך תקדים בעולם הקדום. בידינו ספרי חוק רבים, חלקם עוסקים רק בדיני מקדש, ואחרים רק בדיני ממונות, אך אין חיבורים המ־ציגים את כל המכלול כיחידה דתית נורמטיבית אחת.

יא. התורה שבעל פה עוסקת בכל מקצועות התורה. כולל אלו שלדברי חכמים אף פעם לא הגיעו לכלל מימוש (כגון דין בן סורר ומורה (משנה, סנהדרין פ"ח מ"א –מ"ה)). לעתים ההלכות מרובות והמקרא מועט (כגון דיני טהרה), ולעתים הלכות מעטות ועיקר ההלכות שנויות במקרא (דיני ערכין והקדשות). המשנה עצמה ערה למצב זה ומציינת אותו בהדגשה (משנה, חגיגה פ"א מ"ח; תוס' פ"א ה"ט; עירובין פ"ח (י"א) הכ"ג-הכ"ד).

יב. בתורה בעל פה הלכות הנסמכות לעתים על המדרש. עם זאת למרבית ההלכות אין מקור מקראי, ולו בדרך מדרש כלשהו ולכך נשוב להלן.

לכל העקרונות הללו אין ביטוי שיטתי בתורה, אם כי ניתן להבחין בניצנים שלהם בספרי עזרא ונחמיה ומעט יותר מכך בספר דברים ודברי הימים. בהם למשל, ביטוי ברור למרכזיות ה'תורה' אם כי במקביל לה מדגיש המחבר ערכים פולחניים אחרים כמקדש, כוהנים, ולוויים.[39]

כאמור כבר בתנ"ך ואפילו בתורה, רמזים לתורה שבעל פה, ברם כולם רחוקים ממהותה של התורה שבעל פה כפי שהוצגה לעיל. יש בהם פרט זה או אחר, אך אין בהם עדות למערכת ה'תורה שבעל פה'. אין בכך כדי לשלול את הטענה כי אכן כבר בימי ירמיה, למשל, הייתה הגדרה הלכתית-משפטית לאיסור המלאכה בשבת. אבל אין במקורות עדות לתפישה כזאת.

38 התלמוד הבבלי מתחיל לפתח את האבחנות בין תקנה\גזירה להלכה, ובין מנהג להלכה. אבחנות אלו שוכללו לכלל מערכת משפטית בידי הרמב"ם הלכות ממרים פ"ד. בספרות חז"ל כל האבחנות הללו אינן חדות ואינן תופשות מקום של ממש ראו למשל, ש', ספראי, הלכה למשה מסיני, היסטוריה או תיאולוגיה? זוסמן, י', רוזנטל, ד' (עורכים), מחקרי תלמוד, ירושלים, תש"ן, עמ', 38-11 (בימי הבית ובימי המשנה, עמ' 578-548).

39 י"א, זליגמן, ניצני מדרש בספר דברי הימים, תרביץ מט (1980), עמ' 32-14

אין בידנו מידע ישיר מתקופת היסוד של תורה שבעל פה. מן הראוי לזכור שכך המצב כמעט בכל תהליך חברתי בכלל ותהליך תרבותי בפרט אשר התרחשו בימי קדם. ייסודה של תורה שבעל פה לא היה, מן הסתם, אירוע פתאומי, אלא תהליך. מדרכם של תהליכים שהם מתפתחים אט אט במחשכים (שלבי 'ההסתרה') והופכים לגלויים רק בשלב מאוחר יחסית (שלב 'ההמראה'). רק בשלב עוד יותר מאוחר הופכים הסובבים להיות מודעים לתהליך. בדרך כלל הספרות ההיסטו־רית מבטאת את התהליך בשלב מאוחר עוד יותר, לאחר שחדר לתודעת הסביבה כולה (כולל אלו שאינם שותפים לתהליך). בשלב זה נוצרת ספרות פסוודו היסטורית המייצרת מיתוס של יסוד. לעתים קרובות המיתוס תולה את ראשיתו של התהליך באירוע טראומטי, נס או גילוי אלוהי. אין צריך לומר ששחזור זה של 'רגע היסוד' אינו ניתוח היסטורי, ואף אינו זיכרון, אלא ביטוי למי־תוס. למסגרת זו של עיצוב סיפורי הייסוד. שייכים מן הסתם סיפורי בראשית של חכמי הפרושים ראשיתו ועלייתו של הלל לנשיאות (תוס', פסחים פ"ד ה"יג ומקבילות) תחילתם של חכמים כהלל (בבלי, יומא לה ע"ב), ר' עקיבא (אדר"נ, נו"א פ"ו, עמ' 30-28 ומקבילה נו"ב פ"יב, עמ' 30-29), או ר' אליעזר בן הורקנוס (כנ"ל, עמ' 30- 31 ומקבילות בנו"ב פ"יג, עמ' 32-31). המיתוס כולל דמויות וארועים, מוצא נחות או גבוה, השוואות עם דמויות בראשית מן המקרא ומעולם החכמים (ספרי דברים שנז, עמ' 427-425), ומייחס לאישים השונים את עקרונות הלימוד בבחינת דמויות מופת. (משנה, אבות פ"א מ"א).[40]

ניתן לנסח סולם סכימתי לשלבי היסוד:

א. ההסתרה
ב. המראה
ג. מודעות עצמית
ד. פרסום
ה. התגבשות הספרות העצמית ועריכתה ברמה זו או אחרת (בכתב או בעל פה).
ו. עיצוב מיתוס הייסוד.

את דברי התורה שבעל פה אנו מכירים, באופן ממשי, מימי שמאי והלל ובעיקר מימיהם של תלמי־דיהם. בידנו גם מעט מימרות קדומות להם, אך מספרן קטן והולך ככל שהן קדומות יותר. מטיבם של דברים עדויות אלו הן לאחר שלב 'ההמראה'. הן משקפות מערכת מובנית ומוסדרת. העקרונות המכוננים של תורה שבעל פה נקבעו דורות קודם לכן. אין באפשרותנו להעריך כמה דורות קודם, אך בהתחשב במורכבות השלבים יש לקחת בחשבון דורות אחדים. לשם הבהרה נסתפק בשתי דוגמאות.

"אלו דברים שבין בית שמאי ובית הלל בסעודה. בית שמאי אומרים מברך על היום ואחר כך מברך על היין ובית הלל אומרים מברך על היין ואחר כך מברך על היום" (ברכות פ"ח מ"א). שני

40 ראו דיוננו לעיל על הכנסת הגדולה והסופרים.

הבתים מסכימים שבסעודת השבת יש לברך על שתית יין ויש לברך על יום השבת, כלומר שיש מעמד של 'קידוש'. עצם ההלכה שיש 'ברכות' מוכרת ומוסכמת וכפי שאמרנו לעיל יש שייחסו את החידוש לאנשי הכנסת הגדולה. שני הבתים מסכימים שהקידוש כולל לפחות שני מרכיבים: ברכה על יין וברכה על היום. שניהם גם מסכימים שיש חשיבות לסדר, ונחלקים מהו הסדר הנכון. במשנה ה' באותו פרק מחלוקת על סדר הברכות בהבדלה במוצאי שבת, ורשימת הנחות הבסיס שם ארוכה עוד יותר. חשוב להדגיש שבמשנה זו באים לידי ביטוי הן הצורך בכללים (הדבר בולט בטיעונים ה'משפטיים' והעקרוניים של שני הצדדים[41]), והן החשיבות שבפרטים. ושניהם כאחד ממרכיביה המרכזיים של תורה שבעל פה.

כדוגמא שניה ישמשו עבורנו דברי שמאי הזקן בעצמו "כל המחמץ, והמתבל, והמדמע בתרומה, ובערלה ובכלאי הכרם אסור, ובית שמאי אומרים אף מטמא. ובית הלל אומרים לעולם אינו מטמא עד שיהא בו כביצה. דוסתאי איש כפר יתמה היה מתלמידי בית שמאי, ואמר: שמעתי משמאי הזקן שאמר: לעולם אינו מטמא עד שיהא בו כביצה" (משנה, עורלה פ"ב מ"ד-מ"ה). במשפט זה מערכת מוסכמות. נסתפק באחת מהן. יש הסכמה שכדי שדבר יטמא יש צורך בכך שיהיה בכמות מסוימת, והמחלוקת היא מהי הכמות. שמאי אף מבחין בין מדמע, למשל, ומטמא. מכל מקום יש כאן בירור פרטני של דיני התערובת. דוגמאות נוספות יובאו להלן.[42]

נתמזל מזלה של תורה שבעל פה ובידנו מקור מקביל המאפשר לנו להעריך את השלבים שבהם יצירת התורה שבעל פה עדיין הייתה בצל, בשלב 'ההסתרה'. ספרות כתות מדבר יהודה נערכה במאה הראשונה לפני הספירה לערך. היא באה מחוגים שלא היו שותפים לתורה שבעל פה של חז"ל, אך הייתה להם תורה שבעל פה משלהם. אופייני הוא שחז"ל יודעים להגדיר שיש להם 'תורה שבעל פה' שאינה חלק מהקודקס המקראי (שלב ג' של המודעות העצמית), ואילו בספרות קומראן עדיין חסרה אבחנה זו.[43] אין בכך פלא שכן ספרות קומראן נחתמה כמאה וחמישים שנה לפני העדויות שבספרות חז"ל. עם זאת גם בתורה שבעל פה של כתות קומראן הגיעו לשלב ההמראה בו כתבו ספרים שיש בהם מאותה תורה שבעל פה, למדו ולימדו בפומבי מכתבים אלו.

התורה שבעל פה של כתות קומראן, אינה זהה לזו של חז"ל, ואף לא לזו של הפרושים. אבל ניכר שיש להן בסיס משותף: בסיס הבא לביטוי בנושאים משותפים, מונחים הלכתיים כגון 'פרת חטאת', 'הערב שמש', 'מוצקות', 'ידות כלים', 'טהרת הקודש' 'תערובת', 'ארץ ישראל' (במובן ההלכתי)',[44] התפישה שקיימים מעין שלוש מחנות, ומונחים נוספים כמו כן ניתן לאבחן שיתוף

41 השאלה האם הטיעונים המופיעים בתוספתא פ"ה הכ"ה ומקבילות הם מקוריים עדיין לא הוכרעה, אך למעשה אין סיבה להניח שהם אינם מקוריים.

42 המשנה האחרונה כרוכה בשאלות נוספות של מחלוקות בית הלל ובית שמאי ולא באנו לפרש את המשנה אלא להעמידה כדוגמא בלבד.

43 על כך: מ"ד, הר, הרצף שבשלשלת מסירת התורה: לבירור ההיסטוריוגראפיה המקראית בהגותם של חז"ל, *ציון* מד (תשלט) 56-43.

44 י', זוסמן, לחקר תולדות ההלכה ומגילות מדבר יהודה, בתוך: ברושי, מ', ואחרים (עורכים), *מגילות מדבר יהודה, ארבעים שנות מחקר*, ירושלים תשנ"ב, בעיקר עמ' 112; א', קימרון, מונחי ההלכה במגילות מדבר יהודה וחשיבותם לחקר תולדות

בתפישות בסיסיות. שתי הקבוצות שותפות לדעה שיש צורך בהבהרת הפרטים ולגבי שתיהן שמירת המצוות היא נורמטיבית.

את התפתחות התורה שבעל פה ניתן להציג בססכמה הבאה:

התורה שבעל פה הקדומה

תורת בני הכת | **תורת הפרושים**

ספרות חז"ל

בידנו קטעים מתורתם של בני הכת, ומעט מידע ניתן לשאוב מתוך ספרות חז"ל, באותם קטעים המשמרים את שלבי הבראשית.

התורה שבעל פה והמקדש

כאמור אחד העקרונות המכוננים הוא שלהלכה אופי 'נורמטיבי', ויש חשיבות עליונה לפרטים הטכניים הקובעים את כללי הביצוע. תפישה זו שונה מהתפישה של החוק הדתי הקדום, עם זאת היא הייתה רווחת בכל המקדשים הקדומים וכמובן גם במקדש בירושלים. על הכל היה מקובל שיש לדקדק בפרטי הביצוע של מעמדות הקודש במקדש. גם המקדש בירושלים התנהל לפי כללי טקס נוקשים שקבעו היכן יעמוד הפר הנשחט, באיזה כיוון ולהיכן יפנו פניו, באיזה כלי תוגש הקטורת וכמה כוהנים ישתתפו בתהלוכה בה מעלים את אברי הקורבנות שנשחטו. על כן יש מקום לשער שגם התפישה בדבר הצורך לקבוע את פרטי המצוות מקורם למעשה בהרחבה של נוהלי המקדש, והחלתם על כלל המצוות. זאת ועוד העדויות הראשונות לקריאת שמע, למשל, הן במקדש (משנה, תמיד פ"ה מ"א). כפי שראינו לעיל הכנסת הגדולה פעלה אולי במקדש, על כן מתבקשת ההצעה לראות במקדש את המוסד אשר יצר את האקלים והסביבה בה עוצבו הלכות תורה שבעל פה. אין גם ספק שאכן שומעים אנו על לימוד תורה במקדש ועל הגהת ספרים במקדש (ירו', שקלים פ"ה ה"א, מח ע"א ועוד), וכמובן שגם הסנהדרין שכנה במקדש.[45]

עם זאת דומה שיש לדחות הצעה זו. הכנסת הגדולה אמנם פעלה במקדש (לפי המשוער), אך ראינו שכנראה הרכבה כלל גם מי שאינם כוהנים. התורה שבעל פה אינה מותירה לכוהנים תפקיד ייחודי בעיצוב ההלכה, וקשה להניח כי כך היה מתנהל מוסד מקדשי. זאת ועוד התורה בעל פה מת־

ההלכה, בתוך: ברושי, מ', ואחרים (עורכים), *מגילות מדבר יהודה, ארבעים שנות מחקר*, ירושלים תשנ"ב, עמ' 138-128. ל', שיפמן, *הלכה, הליכה ומשיחיות בכת מדבר יהודה*, ירושלים 1993.

45 אין במחקר הסכמה על טיבו של מוסד זה, ועל הרכבו וסמכויותיו.

אפיינת במחלוקות הלכתיות, ריבוי יוצרים, וב'תרבות המחלוקת'. לו הייתה התורה שבעל פה נוצרת בחסות המקדש הייתה מתפתחת הכרעה מוסדית תדירה ומתגבשת הלכה אחידה. יש אף להניח שגם בפרטי ההלכות במקדש עצמו נפלו מחלוקות, אבל במוסד מתפקד בפועל צריך היה להגיע להכרעה, אחרת לא יוכל המקדש להתקיים כמוסד מלוכד ומלכד. אופיה של התורה שבעל פה הידועה לנו מלמד כי נוצרה בעיקרה דווקא מחוץ למקדש, ברחבי ישראל. עם זאת ייתכן שהשלבים הראשונים והקדומים, אלו שאותם אנו משערים ושעל קיומם איננו יודעים דבר, נוצרו במקדש. ואכן מסורת חכמים בדרכה משמרת רמזים עמומים לכך בייחסה לכהן הגדול יהושע בן גמלא את הקמתם של בתי הספר והלימוד ברחבי ישראל (בבלי, בבא בתרא כא ע"א)[46]

פרטים וכללים

שתי צורות להלכות של תורה שבעל פה. האחת שיטת המקרה, השיטה הקזואיסטית, והשניה שיטת הכללים.[47] במשנה עצמה ניתן למצוא ניסוח הלכה במספר אופנים:[48]

א. מקרה בודד – כגון: "המעלה פירות מן הגליל ליהודה, או עולה לירושלם,[49] אוכל מהם עד שהוא מגיע למקום שהוא הולך" (משנה, מעשרות פ"ב מ"ג) בדרך כלל המקרה הוא דוגמא למקרה הרגיל, ולעתים מקרה מיוחד, או מקרה העשוי להראות כמיוחד, אך חל עליו הדין הנוהג.

ב. סדרת פרטים כגון: "הקלין שבדמאי: השיתין, והרימין, והעוזרדין, ובנות שוח, ובנות שקמה, ונובלות התמרה, והגופנין" (משנה, דמאי פ"א מ"א). לעתים הסדרה אינה מאוזנת ונכללים בה פרטים שיש בינהם הבדל לענין אחר. כך למשל עיון במשנה זו מראה על כך שיש בה מינים הפטורים ממעשר גם כשהוא ודאי (שכן אינם בעלי ערך כספי), ויש הפטורים רק ממעשר שהוא ספק (דמאי).

ג. כלל פשוט כגון: "פירות שתרמן עד שלא נגמרה מלאכתן רבי אליעזר אוסר מלאכול מהם עראי וחכמים מתירין חוץ מכלכלת תאנים כלכלת תאנים שתרמה ר' שמעון מתיר וחכמים אוסרין" (משנה, מעשרות פ"ב מ"ד).

ד. סדרת כללים פשוטים כגון: "הדמאי: מערבין בו, ומשתתפין בו, ומברכים עליו, ומזמנין עליו, ומפרישין אותו ערום בין השמשות" (דמאי פ"א מ"ד).

---

46 על *משמעותה* של המסורת חולקים החוקרים והדיון חורג ממסגרת זו ראו ד', גודבלט, המקורות על ראשיתו של החינוך היהודי המאורגן בארץ-ישראל, *מחקרים בתולדות עם-ישראל וארץ-ישראל* 5 (תש"ם) 103-83. ז', ספראי, *הקהילה היהודית בארץ-ישראל בתקופת המשנה והתלמוד*, ירושלים תשנ"ה.

47 לאבחנה כללית זו ראו זילברג, כך דרכה.

48 הנחת העבודה היא שניסוחים שונים אלה מהוים גם שלבים כרונולוגיים. שלב א הקדום שבהם ושלב ה' האחרון, וכך גם ראו את הסכום והמסקנות בסוף המאמר.

49 הכתיב הקדום כמעט בכל עדי הנוסח של המשנה ובמקורות מקבילים (מטבעות, כתובות וכו') הוא 'ירושלם', ורק לעתים נדירות ביותר 'ירושלים' (עם י').

ה. כלל גדול ומורכב כגון: ״כלל אמרו במעשרות: כל שהוא אוכל, ונשמר, וגדוליו מן הארץ, חייב במעשרות. ועוד כלל אחר אמרו: כל שתחלתו אוכל, וסופו אוכל, אע״פ שהוא שומרו להוסיף אוכל, חייב קטן וגדול. וכל שאין תחלתו אוכל, אבל סופו אוכל. אינו חייב עד שיעשה אוכל״ (מעשרות פ״א מ״א).

כידוע משנה המשנה את סגנונה ועוברת ממקרה פשוט לכלל מורכב או פשוט, ולא תמיד ניתן לומר שאלו משניות המלוקטות ממקורות שונים. השאלה למה בחרו העורכים להציג את החומר בצורה מעורבת מחייבת עיון, אבל לא בכך נעסוק כאן. אנו משערים שכך היו ההלכות ערוכות במשניות הקדומות שעמדו לפני עורך המשנה, וכך נשמרת צורתן הקדומה של ההלכות, כלומר שאלו גרעיני מידע על הלימוד הקדום. מכל מקום ההלכות הקדומות מבטאות את רמת העיסוק בפרטים עליה כבר עמדנו.

אשר לעריכת המשנה כל מסכת מוקדשת לנושא מסויים. ברם הסידור רופף למדי. לעתים ניתן למצוא פרטים שלא במסגרת המשנה המיועדת להם. כך למשל ניתן למצוא כמה מהלכות שבת במסכת ביצה, או אפילו במסכת רחוקה, בהקשר מקרי כלשהו. גם סדר הפרטים בתוך המסכת אינו מובנה והדברים ידועים.[50]

במקביל למשנה בידנו קורפוס הלכתי אחר, הכולל חיבורים רבים שנמצא במערות מדבר יהודה, ואשר אנו מיחסים אותה לכתות קומרן. החיבורים ההלכתיים העיקריים הם: ה׳סרכים (׳ברית דמשק׳, ׳סרך היחד׳ ו׳סרך העדה׳), ו׳מגילת המקדש׳, כל אלו נכתבו כספרי קודש והלכה לבני הכת. וכן את ׳מקצת מעשי תורה׳ שנכתב ככתב הלכה פולמוסי. למכלול זה מן הראוי לצרף את ספר היובלים, הקרוב ברוחו לספרות קומראן, שהשתמר באסופת כתבי הקודש של הקהילה הנוצרית בשפת הגז. ספר היובלים הוא סיכום סיפורי התורה ויש בו קטעים הלכתיים. חיבורים הלכתיים נוספים נמצאו במערות, ומהם שרדו קטעים בלבד, וקשה לעמוד על שיטת העריכה שלהם.

ספרות קומראן שונה באופיה מהמשנה. גם בספרות קומראן סדרות של הלכות, וכמו המשנה היא ערוכה בסדר רופף. מגילת המקדש ערוכה כך שכל נושא הלכתי מצוי במרוכז בקטע רצוף, אבל אין סדר בין הנושאים השונים. בספר היובלים פרקים המכילים הלכות, סדר העלאת הנושאים הוא לפי סדר האירועים המקראיים, ובכל אירוע הלכה או סדרת הלכות באותו נושא. אבל בסופו של הספר סדרה של הלכות שבת והלכות פסח, שאולי אינן חלק אינטגרלי מהחיבור המקורי.[51] מגילות הסרכים מעלות סדרות הלכות, כל נושא מכיל סדרת פרטים, אין תופעה של פרט הנוגע להלכות שבת, למשל, שאיננו מצוי בתוך הריכוז של הלכות שבת. כנגד זה קשה להבין את סדר

50 פרשנים מסורתיים ובני זמננו מנסים למצוא סדר למשנה, ואף מבחינים בעריכה ספרותית, אך אין זה הסדר ההגיוני של הצגת הדברים, ודומה שקדמוננו לא ניסו כלל להציג את ההלכות בסדר המקובל כיום.

51 ל׳, רביד, הלכות שבת בספר היובלים נ 13-6, *תרביץ* סט (תש״ס), עמ׳ 168-161 לצורך דיוננו אין זה משנה האם הקטע הוא מדברי המחבר, או תוספת מעט מאוחרת יותר. דיון מפורט על השוואת הלכות קומרן לאלו של חכמים.

הפרטים בתוך הפרק העוסק בשבת. ולא ניכרת בניה שיטתית של הפרטים לפי סדר מסוים.[52] בכך דומה אפוא העריכה של ברית דמשק או סרך היחד למשנה. ברם ספרות קומראן מסודרת מעט יותר, וכל הפרטים בנושא מסוים (שבת או טהרה למשל) מרוכזים באותו רצף. לעומת זאת כמות החומר ההלכתי שבחיבורים הכיתתיים, והיקף החיבור כולו נופל בהרבה מהמשנה, וכך עורכי החיבורים הכיתתיים לא ניצבו לפני אותן בעיות מורכבות של ליקוט ועריכה, שעמם התמודד עורך המשנה. עד כאן באשר לעריכת החומר.

אשר לצורת הלימוד והצגת החומר - בספרות קומראן אין כללים מורכבים ואין גם מקרים בודדים או סדרות של מקרים אלא רק כללים פשוטים. כגון: " ששת ימים תעשה מלאכה וביום השביעי שבת לה' אלוהיכם לא תעשו בו כל מלאכה ובניכם ועבדיכם ואמהותיכם וכל בהמתכם וגריכם אשר בכם. והאיש אשר יעשה בו כל מלאכה יומת וכל איש אשר יחלל את היום הזה ואשר ישכב עם אישה ואשר ידבר דבר לעשות ולצאת בו לדרך וכל משא ומתן והשואב בו מים אשר לו הכין לו ביום השישי ואשר ישא כל משא להוציא מאהלו או מביתו ומת". (ספר היובלים פ"נ ז-ח) הכללים הגדולים (כגון "לא תעשו מלאכה") הם ציטוט של המקרא. רוב ההלכות הם כללים פשוטים (ישכב עם אשה, ידבר בו וכו'). אבל מצוי גם כלל ברמה גבוה יותר (כלל יותר מופשט) "אשר לא הכין לו" כלומר שכל מה שאינו מן המוכן אסור בשבת. לכלל זה נשוב להלן.

וכן בברית דמשק פ"י: "אל יעש איש ביום השישי מלאכה מן העת אשר יהיה גלגל השמש רחוק מן השער מלואו. כי הוא אשר אמר שמור את יום השבת לקדשו. וביום השבת אל ידבר איש דבר נבל ורק אל ישה ברעהו כל. אל ישפוט על הון ובצע. אל ידבר בדברי המלאכה והעבודה לעשות למשכים. אל יתהלך איש בשדה לעשות את עבודת חפצו השבת.[53] אל יתהלך חוץ לעירו על אלף באמה. אל יאכל איש ביום השבת כי אם המוכן ומן האובד בשדה..." גם כאן כללים פשוטים ומעט כללים ברמה גבוהה יותר כגון "אל יאכל איש ביום השבת כי אם מן המוכן", כלל זה שנזכר גם בספר היובלים, יחזור וידון להלן. בברית דמשק כבר ביטוי להקפדה על הפרטים. כך למשל נדונה השאלה מתי בדיוק נכנסת השבת, כולל 'תוספת שבת' המוכרת מהמקורות התלמודיים אם כי מהתקופה האמוראית בלבד. יש בברית דמשק גם מקרים פרטיים כגון: " אל ירם את ידו להכותה באגרוף", אגרוף כמוהו ככל מכה אחרת, והוא מקרה פרטי כדוגמא. וכן "אל ישא איש עליו סמנים לצאת ולביא [ולבוא] בשבת". סימנים דינם ככל משא אחר, ונתן הכתוב דוגמא מציאותית. אם כן זו דוגמא להלכה 'קזואיסטית' כמקובל בספרות חז"ל.

במידה וניתן להניח שההלכה מקומראן התקדמה במקביל להלכה התלמודית, הרי שהעדר כללים מורכבים (שלב ה') בספרות קומראן, מצביע על כך שבזמן שנערכה ספרות ההלכה הכיתתית, הגדירו כבר כללים פשוטים, אך טרם הגיעו לניסוח של כללים עקרוניים או של סדרות כללים. אזי ניתן להסיק שהדיון במקרים קדם לדיון בכללים, או לפחות לניסוח הכללים המורכבים והעקרוניים.

52 'מקצת מעשה תורה' הוא יצירה של ויכוח המעלה נושאים שונים ללא סדר הנראה לעין, אך הדבר מתבקש מטיבה כמעין מכתב של פולמוס.

53 המילה "השבת" עשויה להיות גם הפתיחה למשפט הבא.

זאת ועוד, אם אכן נכונה המסקנה הרי שבידנו כלי להערכת הכרונולוגיה של ההתפתחות הספרותית-משפטית של ההלכה. לאמור: במאה הראשונה לפני הספירה טרם התגבשו כללי הלכה עקרוניים כדוגמת הכלל בדיני מעשרות שציטטנו לעיל.

מעתה עלינו לברר מה ניתן להפיק מתוך ספרות חז"ל על היחס הכרונולוגי שבין העיסוק בכללים וניסוחם, לבין העיסוק בדוגמאות, וניסוחם. השאלה היא מה קדם למה, מהכלל נגזרו הדוגמאות, או שמן הדוגמאות נוסח הכלל.

עדויות לשלבים הקדומים של התפתחות הלכות תורה שבעל פה

קודם שנפנה לדיון בפרטי הדוגמאות יש לשרטט את הנחות העבודה, ואלו מורכבות משני היבטים התלויים זה בזה: מחד גיסא מערכת היחסים האפשרית בין הציבור שומר ההלכה ואנשי המקצוע קריא תלמידי החכמים המתדיינים ולומדים בבית המדרש. ומאידך גיסא מערכת היחסים האפשרית בין הכללים והפרטים הנידונים במשניות השונות.

א. ציבור ובית מדרש

לטענתנו תהליך ההתפתחות של תורה שבעל פה הוא שהציבור יזם את ההלכה, ובבתי המד־רש עסקו רק מאוחר יותר, בניסוחה ובעיצובה המשפטי. בתי המדרש הביאו את הדוגמאות השונות לכלל מערכת משפטית, אגב כך כמובן גם קבעו מחדש את ההלכה, ולא תמיד הילך בית המדרש אחרי הציבור. מאידך גיסא לעתים קרובות עמלו אנשי המקצוע (החכמים) בבית המדרש להכיל את כל הדוגמאות למערכת אחת.

הנחת העבודה שלנו היא שלעיצוב ההלכה מספר שלבים כרונולוגיים סכמתיים: ראשיתו בציבור הרחב המגבש נוהגים והלכה למעשה והמשכו בבירור המשפטי בבית המדרש. בשלב האחרון נוסחו ההכרעות ואלו הגיעו לידנו לאחר שלבי עריכה רבים. על השלבים הקדומים יכולים אנו ללמוד, רק משרידי העדויות כפי שהשתמרו בספרות שבידנו.

יש לזכור שהתפתחות ההלכה לא הייתה ליניארית. במקביל לתהליך היורודיפיקציה עלו גם ער־כים חדשים, שאולי נוצרו לראשונה בבית המדרש, אך גם הם היו חשופים לכל שלבי ההתפתחות. כך למשל רק בדורות התנאים המאוחרים התגבש הרעיון של ברכה על המצוות, לאחר שהרעיון התפשט בציבור נהגו ברכות שונות, ובבתי המדרש עיצבו נוסחים מקובלים.

כאמור עריכת המשנה והמקורות התנאיים שימרה את הניסוח של כל השלבים, אך בדרך כלל השלבים הראשונים טושטשו, ורק לעתים נותרו מהם שרידים בספרות המאוחרת. איננו יכולים להצביע על דוגמא אחת הכוללת את כל השלבים שהיצענו, אך נעלה כמה דוגמאות בולטות. כל אחת מהדוגמאות מדגימה חלק ממרכיביו של התהליך.

ב. כלל ופרט בספרות חז"ל

ניתן לטעון שהכללים הם פרי עיונם של אנשי מקצוע (תלמידי החכמים) הדנים בנושא באופן חופשי ועיוני. הם המנסחים של הכלל, והם גם משפרים את הניסוח בבוא הזמן. אנשי המקצוע איש איש בבית מדרשו ובעיתו דנים בכל כלל במקומו, ומציעים ניסוחים שונים, ובדור שלאחריו לאחר שנמסרו הניסוחים השונים, מעמתים אותם זה עם זה וחוזרים ומציעים ניסוח אחר. אחד ממרכיביו של קביעת הכלל הוא הניסוח של דברי התנאים. כך למשל כאשר מדובר בכלאים (כלאי זרעים) הרי שמנסחי הכלל יקבעו האם חשוב לדבר על גודל החלקה, אורכה ו\או רוחבה, האם חשוב לציין מרחק בין הגידולים השונים, או האם יש מרכיבים אחרים המשנים את ההלכה. מרכיבים אלו הם השפה ההלכתית וכדי לאפשר עיון והשוואה יש צורך באיחוד שפה הלכתית, כך שכל בעלי הדבר ינקטו באותה שפה ויתייחסו לאותם מרכיבים. הדוגמא אותה הבאנו אינה מקרית ונשוב אליה להלן. בבית המדרש של התורה שבעל פה מתחולל תהליך העיצוב המשפטי, בו מנוסחת ההלכה כחוק ובו גם הופכות האבחנות משפטיות ליותר ויותר מתוחכמות.

כנגד זה עשויה ההלכה גם להתפתח בסביבה שונה. בציבור הרחב שומרים על ההלכה בצורה פחות מודעת ומתוחכמת. הציבור אינו נזקק לניסוח המשפטי, אלא שומר את ההלכה לפי תפישתו. כך למשל גם אדם פשוט צריך להגדיר לעצמו מהי מלאכה האסורה בשבת. המקרא נתן מספר דוגמאות (חריש, קציר, אפיה והבערת אש) אך מה דינן של מלאכות פחות מובהקות. ברחוב נוצרה הסכמה על סדרת מלאכות מותרת, ועל סדרה אסורה. אבחנות אלו לא נוסחו בצורה משפטית אלא קזואיסטית.

ומכאן נדון בפרטי דוגמאות וננסה לעמוד על הרמזים המשוקעין בהן הנוגעים לתולדות ההלכה עיצובה וניסוחה.

המשנה קובעת: "רבי יוסי אומר כל הכלים הניטלין, חוץ מן המסר הגדול, ויתד של מחרישה. כל הכלים ניטלין לצורך ושלא לצורך, רבי נחמיה אומר אין ניטלין אלא לצורך" (שבת פי"ז מ"ד). כפשוטו טלטול שלא לצורך שנוי במחלוקת וטלטול לצורך מותר ובתנאי שלא יהיו אלו כלים גדו־לים, שאפילו לצורך אסור לטלטלם. ייתכן גם שאותם כלים גדולים ניטלים רק לצורך, וכל המשפט הראשון הוא אליבא דר' יוסי בלבד. המשניות הקודמות למשנה זו מנוסחות לשיטת ר' נחמיה "נוטל אדם קורנס לפצע בו את האגוזים, וקורדום לחתוך את הדבלה, מגירה לגרור בה את הגבינה, מגריפה לגרוף בה את הגרוגרות, את הרחת ואת המזלג לתת עליו לקטן, את הכוש ואת הכרכר לתחוב בו, מחט של יד ליטול בו את הקוץ, ושל סקאים לפתוח בו את הדלת" (שם מ"ב). כולן דוגמאות לטלטול לצורך. אם כן הצורך הוא כל צורך שהוא, אף שאינו הצורך המקורי של הכלי. מכאן שהניסוח של משנה ד' בעייתי, ושפתו ההלכתית שונה מן השפה בה נוקטת משנה ב'. במשנה ב' הגורם הקבוע הוא 'צורך', ולפחות לפי התלמודים והתוספתא[54] הכוונה ל'צורך' המקורי והיעודי של כלי, ומשנה ד', מפרשת את הצורך באופן שונה. התלמודים דנים בהתאמה בין משנה ב' למשנה ד' וזהו תהליך היורידיפיקציה עליו דברנו. תחושת אי ההתאמה קיימת גם אם ה'צורך' של משנה ד' הוא צורך כל־שהו, שאם כן משניות ב-ג הן רק לר' נחמיה, כך פירש הירושלמי למקום (טז ע"ב), אם כי אין זו דרכה של משנה להציע משניות סתמיות כאשר בהמשך יתברר שהן רק לדעה אחת.

בתוספתא עדות מובהקת לקיומם של שלבים הקודמים למשנה: "בראשונה היו אומרין שלשה כלים ניטלין בשבת"[55]: בראשונה היו אסורים כל הכלים שמשתמשים בהם למלאכות אסורות, כלים שדוגמתם נפרטו במשנה ב' והתירו להשתמש רק בשלושה כלים שמשתמשים בהם גם לאיסור והם כמפורט בברייתא: "מקצוע של דבילה וזומא לסטרון[56] וסכין קטנה שעל גבי שלחן. חזרו להיות מוסיפין והולכין עד שאמרו כל הכלים ניטלין בשבת". ובבבלי: "התירו וחזרו והתירו וחזרו והתירו עד שאמרו וכו'".[57]

מסתבר כי לפנים האיסור חל רק על כלים שמשתמשים בהם למלאכות אסורות או אף למלאכות האסורות כשלעצמן. כלים שאין חשש שישתמשו בהם למלאכות אסורות כגון קערות שולחנות שהיו

54 תוס', פי"ד (טו) ה"א; ירו', שבת פי"ז ה"ד, טז ע"ב; בבלי, קכז ע"ב-קכד ע"א; באותה הלכה בתוספתא שנוי פירוט לדברי רבי נחמיה: "ר' נחמיה אומ' אפילו טלית אפילו תרוד אין ניטלין אלא לצורך". ובבבלי שבת בסוגיה אחרת: "דתניא רבי נחמיה אומר אפילו תרווד ואפילו טלית ואפילו סכין אינן ניטלין אלא לצורך תשמישן" (בבלי, שבת קמו ע"א; עירובין לה ע"א). כלומר שתי מגבלות כאן, שנטילת הכלי תהיה לצורך מלאכה מותרת, ושהשימוש הרגיל בכלי הוא לצורך המותר בשבת.

55 תוס', פי"ד (טו) ה"א; בבלי, קכג ע"ב.

56 היא כף גדולה של מרק מעין התרוד אלא שבראשו השני היה מזלג להוציא את הבשר. ראו משנה, כלים פי"ג מ"ב ובפירוש הגאונים לטהרות, עמ' 29.

57 בבבלי שם: "אמר רבי חנינא בימי נחמיה בן חכליה נשנית משנה זו (שהחמירה ואמרה שאין נוטלים אלא שלושה כלים – רש"י) דכתיב בימים ההמה ראיתי ביהודה דורכים גיתות בשבת ומביאים הערימות" (נחמיה יג טו). אין זו מסורת על קדמותה של משנה זו אלא מעין אסמכתא והסבר מדוע החמירו ואסרו לפנים מליטול בשבת כל הכלים.

שמים לפני המסובים לסעודה וכיוצא באלו היו מותרים. בהמשך הדורות הלכו והתירו את הטלטול של כל הכלים. משנתנו השונה כל הכלים ניטלים בשבת היא לאחר שהותרו כל הכלים, "חוץ מן המסר הגדול ויתד של מחרישה" שהם שני כלי עבודה גדולים. מפרשי המשנה מסבירים איסור זה מפני שהם כלים שמקפיד עליהם שלא יתקלקלו ואין משתמשים בהם למלאכה אחרת. קרוב יותר לפרש שכלים אלו נשארו באיסורם כי הם גדולים במיוחד ואין משתמשים בהם אלא לאיסור וטלטולם נראה כמעשה הכנה ליציאה לעבודה. באותה הלכה בתוספתא נוספו כלים נוספים: "רבן שמעון בן גמליאל "אף האיגן[58] של ספינה" ו"רבי יוסה אומר אף צפורן גדולה", שהיא מוט ברזל גדול עקירת אבנים בתהליך הסיתות.[59] שני כלים אלו אין מקפידים עליהם כי אינם מתקלקלים. הם כלים גדולים וכבדים ואינם ניטלים אלא למלאכה האסורה בשבת.

מהמשך התוספתא שלא ציטטנו[60] עולה שדברי ר' נחמיה הם בשיטת בית שמאי, ור' יוסי בשיטת בית הלל.

ברור שההלכה בדבר טלטול חפצים ("מוקצה" בשפת ההלכה המאוחרת) עברה שינויים. יתר על כן ברור גם שההתפתחות לא הייתה אחידה מבחינה משפטית. המסורת ש'היו מתירין והולכים' אומרת שהתירו כלים מסוימים ללא שיטה משפטית אחידה. יתר על כן אין חובה לפרש ש"המתירין" הם חכמים וייתכן שהמסורת מרמזת דווקא על הכרעות בפועל של הציבור, שחכמים ניסו לאגדם למסגרת משפטית שיטתית. במקרה זה הכלל המשפטי שנקבע על ידי בית שמאי ובית הלל, נבנה על תקדימים שונים שסתרו זה את זה.

ספקות בגר

התלמוד הבבלי (חולין קלד ע"א) מונה שמונה 'ספקות בגר' שארבע מהן הוכרעו לאיסור, וארבע להיתר. המדובר במקרים בהם נפל ספק. כגון ספק אם החלה שהורמה מבצק מסוים, הורמה לאחר שהתגייר או לפני שהתגייר. קשה למצוא הגיון בחלוקה[61] ואין זאת אלא שכל מחלוקת הוכרעה לגופה, ללא הגיון משפטי עקיב. בית המדרש מסדיר אפוא את הדיונים המוכרים לו בנושא הנידון.

נשים במצוות עשה שהזמן גרמן

לכאורה נקבעה הלכה פסוקה שנשים פטורות ממצוות עשה שהזמן גרמן, וזהו כלל גדול ומורכב. אלא שמתברר שההכרעה אינה אחידה, יש בה יוצאים מהכלל רבים שלחלק מהם הסברים מצמצמים. כמו כן מתברר שתנאים קדומים לא הכירו את ההכרעה. ושוב דומה שכל עניין הוכרע לגופו,

58 הוא האוגן – העוגן.

59 צפורן היא מוט ברזל לקידוח חורים לחציבת אבנים, ולעקירת אבנים.

60 וכן תוס', ביצה פ"א הי"א, ירו', שבת למשנה טז ע"ב.

61 המפרשים ניסו למצוא קו אחיד הגיוני לחלוקה ראו למשל רש"י על אתר.

והכלל הוא סיכום מאוחר, מעין סימן ולא כלל היוצר הלכה.[62] אם כי בשלבים הבאים הוא הופך לכאורה לכלל המעצב הלכות אחרות.

הלכה כבית הלל

לכאורה נקבעה הכרעה אחידה כבית הלל, אבל בפועל מצינו משניות רבות שנסתמו כבית שמאי, ותנאים המהלכים בשיטתם. מסתבר שהכלל 'הלכה כבית הלל', לא נוסח בהכרח ככלל, וניתן לפרשו כסיכום מאוחר, לאחר תהליך ממושך בו הוכרעה כל הלכה לגופה (ואכן רוב ההלכות נקבעו כבית הלל)[63]. הכלל ההלכתי מיוחס לדור יבנה, אם כי בדור יבנה טרם נחשב לכלל מחייב וחכמים בולטים כר' אליעזר, ר' אלעזר בן ערך, ר' טרפון ורבן גמליאל בעצמו, נוהגים בהלכות מסוימות כבית שמאי. כלל הלכתי זה חריג משום שיש בו גם מרכיב מרכזי של פסיקה. לעומת כל זאת בספרות האמוראית ברור שהכלל מחייב, והאמוראים נדחקים לפרש משניות כבית הלל, אף כשניתן לפרשם בפשטות כבית שמאי.

מצוות התלויות בארץ

גם כאן במשנת קידושין נזכר הכלל, ואליו נוספו שלושה או ארבעה יוצאים מהכלל. "כל מצוה שהיא תלויה בארץ, אינה נוהגת אלא בארץ. ושאינה תלויה בארץ, נוהגת בין בארץ בין בחוצה לארץ, חוץ מן הערלה והכלאים, רבי אליעזר אומר אף מן החדש" (משנה, ערלה פ"ד מ"ט ומקבילות). בפועל מצינו מחלוקות וגישות נוספות שאינן נרמזות במשנה, ולמעשה על כל אחד מהיוצאים מהכלל מצינו גם מחלוקת.[64] ושוב קשה להבין מה הבסיס ההגיוני לכך שמצוות אלו יוצאות מהכלל. הסבר אפשרי ופשוט עשוי להיות שהפסיקה נעשתה בכל מקרה לגופו, והכלל מאוחר להן ותפקידו לסכם את התתרחשויות. בשלב הבא הוא גם הופך לכלל מעצב של הלכה.

מועד הפרשת חלה

משנת חלה דנה במועד הפרשת חלה. המשנה (חלה פ"ג מ"א) מהלכת לפי הדעה שזמן הרמת חלה הוא גלגול העיסה, כלומר תחילת עשיית הבצק. וזו שיטתו של ר' יוחנן בן נורי. ר' עקיבא אומר

62 ש', ספראי, מחויבותן של נשים במצוות במשנתם של תנאים, שטיינפלד, צ"א (עורך), *בר-אילן* כה-כו (תשנ"ה), עמ' 227-237.

63 ש', ספראי, ההכרעה כבית הלל, *בימי הבית ובימי המשנה*, א תשנ"ד, עמ' 382-405. במהלך פירושנו למשנה עמדנו על משניות רבות נוספות שנסתמו כבית שמאי.

64 א', שמש, עיון במצוות התלויות בארץ, *סידרא* טז (תש"ס), עמ' 151-177. במאמר זה מצוי רוב החומר, ואנו חולקים על פרטים בו, ולא כאן המקום להרחיב

שזמן חלה הוא סיום האפייה,[65] והתהוות הקרום (פ"ג מ"ו). רבי יהודה בן בתירה אומר משתעשה מקרצות" (תוס', פ"א הי"ב; ירו', נט ע"ד). בירושלמי דיעה נוספת על מועד הרמת החלה "רבי לעזר בשם רבי הושעיה משתעשה גבלולין גבלולין. מה ופליג?[66] כאן להלכה כאן לדבר תורה" (ירו', נט ע"א) זמן הרמת החלה הוא כשהבצק הפך לערימה עגולה מעין גבלול. על כך שואלת הגמרא האם הוא חולק על המשנה, ואומרת שמדין תורה יש להפריש מאוחר יותר (כדעת ר' עקיבא משיקרמו פניה), או כדעת ר' יהודה בן בתירא משתעשה מקרצות, אבל ההלכה דורשת להקדים את מועד ההפרשה ל"משתעשה גבלול". אפשר גם לפרש את הירושלמי אחרת. אבל יש להניח ש"ההלכה" תמיד מחמירה מדבר תורה ולא מקילה, על כן פירשנו כפי שפירשנו. אבל בפרק הקודם באים דברי ר' אליעזר, במשנה ד' הוא מתבטא כאילו זמן הרמת חלה הוא מהלחם המוכן, ובמשנה ח' מהעיסה. נמצאנו למדים שבראשית דור יבנה לא ייחסו חכמים חשיבות לשאלת הזמן המדויק של הרמת חלה, בסוף דור יבנה עולה מחלוקת בנושא, ובירושלמי נעשה נסיון לאחד את הדעות. זהו ביטוי תמצי־תי של תהליך היורידיפקציה. כמו משנה זו יש דוגמאות רבות. בדרך כלל המשנה הקדומה (התנא הקדום) מנוסחת באופן כללי, תנאים מאוחרים חלוקים בפרטים, ובמקרה שלפנינו אכן נשתמרה עדות טקסט מובהקת שהתנא הקודם (ר' אליעזר) אינו מייחס לפרטים חשיבות.

מעשרות בשנת שמיטה

במסורת חכמים נשתמרו מספר קטעים של דיונים בבית המדרש התנאי. עיון בדוגמאות מוכיח, כי בידי התנאים היו סדרה של תקדימים משפטיים, שלא תמיד היו אחידים. הם ניסו להתאים מקרה למקרה, והמחלוקת היא לאיזה מן התקדימים דומה המקרה הנדון. הקטע העוסק בדיני מעשרות מעיד על מבנה הלימוד, וגם על ערכים חברתיים שהיוו נר לרגלי חכמים.

"בו ביום אמרו עמון ומואב מה הן בשביעית? גזר ר' טרפון מעשר עני, וגזר ר' אלעזר בן עזריה מעשר שני. אמר רבי ישמעאל, אלעזר בן עזריה עליך ראיה ללמד שאתה מחמיר, שכל המחמיר עליו ראיה ללמד. אמר לו ר' אלעזר בן עזריה, ישמעאל אחי אני לא שניתי מסדר השנים טרפון אחי שינה, ועליו ראיה ללמד. השיב ר' טרפון: מצרים חוץ לארץ, עמון ומואב חוץ לארץ מה מצ־רים מעשר עני בשביעית אף עמון ומואב מעשר עני בשביעית. השיב ר' אלעזר בן עזריה בבל חוץ לארץ, עמון ומואב חוץ לארץ. מה בבל מעשר שני בשביעית אף עמון ומואב מעשר שני בשביעית. אמר ר' טרפון: מצרים שהיא קרובה עשאוה מעשר עני שיהיו עניי ישראל נסמכים עליה בשבי־עית אף עמון ומואב שהם קרובים נעשים מעשר עני שיהיו עניי ישראל נסמכים עליהם בשביעית. אמר לו ר' אלעזר בן עזריה הרי אתה כמהנן ממון ואין אתה אלא כמפסיד נפשות, קובע אתה את השמים מלהוריד טל ומטר שנאמר (מלאכי ג ח) היקבע אדם אלהים כי אתם קובעים אותי ואמרתם

65 ראו משנה, חלה פ"ג מ"ו. ממשנה, פסחים פ"ג מ"ג ניתן להסיק שגם ר' אליעזר מהלך בשיטה זו.

66 כלומר: האם זו מחלוקת?

במה קבענוך המעשר והתרומה. אמר רבי יהושע הריני כמשיב על טרפון אחי אבל לא לענין דבריו. מצרים מעשה חדש, ובבל מעשה ישן, והנדון שלפנינו מעשה חדש. ידון מעשה חדש ממעשה חדש ואל ידון מעשה חדש ממעשה ישן. מצרים מעשה זקנים ובבל מעשה נביאים והנדון שלפנינו מעשה זקנים. ידון מעשה זקנים ממעשה זקנים ואל ידון מעשה זקנים ממעשה נביאים. נמנו וגמרו עמון ומואב מעשרין מעשר עני בשביעית" (משנה, ידים פ"ד מ"ג).

לפי ההלכה עמון ומואב פטורים ממעשרות ומשביעית, ובכל הארץ פרות שביעית פטורים ממ־עשרות. ממשנתנו מסתבר שנהגו להפריש מעשרות בשנת שביעית בחוץ לארץ [אולי כחומרה אישית, אך כחומרה שעליה חלים פרטי ההלכות], מבנה זה כאמור אינו עולה בקנה אחד עם הדרך המשפטית הרגילה. מעבר לכך מסתבר שבמצרים הפרישו מעשר עני באותה שנה, ובבבל מעשר שני, כלומר במקומות שונים הוכרעה הכרעה שאינה אחידה. הדיון נסב סביב השאלה למי יש לדמות את עמון ומואב למצרים או לבבל. לכאורה, דין מצרים היה צריך להיות כדינה של בבל, ואת ההכרעות העקרוניות צריך היה לקבל בעת ההחלטה על בבל או על מצרים. בפועל נקבעו נהגים שונים ונוצרו תקדימים שונים. מעתה צריך היה להחליט לאיזה מהתקדימים דומה המקרה החדש. איננו יודעים, אם באי בית המדרש עסקו בשאלת המעשרות מבבל וממצרים. אדרבה דומה שרק הפעם הקדיש בית המדרש דיון מסודר לשאלה, והנהגים בעבר נקבעו בדרך אחרת, בנוהגם של הציבור ולא בבית המדרש.

דוגמאות נוספות של השוואת מקרים רווחות בבית המדרש התנאי, ובמידה פחות גם בבית המדרש האמוראי. כאן לא נעסוק בדרכי ההיגיון המשפטי התנאי שיש בו עירוב של היגיון משפטי של הדמיית מקרים עם ניתוח דרשני מעט של הפסוקים; לענייננו חשוב רק להראות שלפני ראשוני החכמים המוכרים לנו כבר ניצב שלל של תקדימים, שאינם בהכרח שיטתיים.

המשכת עבודה שהחלה בערב שבת

במסכת שבת סדרת מחלוקות של בית שמאי ובית הלל על עבודה האסורה בשבת שהחל לעשותה בערב שבת והתהליך נמשך באופן אוטומטי בשבת (פ"א מ"ו- ואילך). מהתוספתא (פ"א ה"כ-הכ"א) עולה ששני הבתים הכירו תקדימים שהיו מקובלים על הכל. האחד: "ושוין אלו ואלו שטוענים קורות בית הבד ועגולי הגת" (משנה, שבת פ"א מ"ט). והשניה ש"אין צולין בשר בצל וביצה אלא כדי שיצולו מבעוד יום. אין נותנין פת לתנור עם חשכה, ולא חררה על גבי גחלים, אלא כדי שיקרמו פניה מבעוד יום ..." (שם מ"י). לכאורה המחלוקת בין הבתים נסבה על הבחירה באיזו מההלכות יש לראות כתקדים.[67] לגופו של דבר לפחות ההלכה האחרונה עוסקת בנושא אחר של הטמנת אוכל בערב שבת ואכילה ממה שאינו מוכן בשבת (להלן), אבל בית שמאי אינם סבורים שגורם זה משמעותי, ועבורם זה המודל לאיסור של כל עבודה מתמשכת. פרשנים עמלו להסביר מדוע שני המקרים הללו מקובלים על הכל, ולמרות הנסיונות לא ניתנה לכך תשובה משכנעת. לשיטתנו התהליך ברור. השאלה בדבר רצף נמשך של עבודה התעוררה אי שם בשלהי ימי הבית השני. ראשיתה בציבור, והתגבשו שתי הכרעות שלא עלו בקנה משפטי אחד. לאחר מכן עברה השאלה לבית המדרש (או אולי הגיעה לבית המדרש), והפכה לשאלה איזו הלכה צריכה לשמש כתקדים מחייב, וכך הוכרעה סדרת הדוגמאות במשנה שם. כתוצאה מהליך זה הכלל הסופי המבוסס על התקדימים הפרטיים שקדמו להכרעה, אינו עקבי מבחינה משפטית ובכך גם נשתמר במשנה.

תהליך דומה מצינו במחלוקות רבות של שני הבתים. המחלוקת נסובה סביב העובדה שיש שני תקדימים סותרים וכל אחד מהבתים מאמץ לו תקדים אחר. אלא שברוב הפעמים המחלוקת היא מאיזה מקרה יש להקיש וללמוד, ואיזה מהם מתאים יותר לשאלה הנדונה. לעתים קרובות הלימוד נעשה באמצעות קל וחומר,[68] והמחלוקת היא הגיונית, מהו המקרה הקל ומה החמור. אבל במקרה שלנו המחלוקת היא איזה תקדים לאמץ.

הבאה מן הקציר

נחלקו אבות עולם מה דינה של אישה המעידה שבעלה נפטר, ואין לה ראיות מסייעות. "בית הלל אומרים לא שמענו אלא בבאה מן הקציר, ובאותה מדינה, וכמעשה שהיה. אמרו להן בית שמאי אחת הבאה מן הקציר, ואחת הבאה מן הזיתים, ואחת הבאה מן הבציר, ואחת הבאה ממדינה למדינה, לא דברו חכמים בקציר אלא בהווה" (משנה, יבמות פט"ו מ"ב; עדיות פ"א מי"ב). הדין המוסכם היה שמאמינים לאשה שיצאה עם בעלה לקציר וחזרה לבד כשהיא טוענת שבעלה נפטר. מנוסח המשנה עולה שראשית הדיון במעשה שהיה בפועל. המחלוקת נסבה על השאלה האם המעשה נותק כמקרה בודד או שהוא יכול לשמש דוגמא כללית. בית הלל מצמצמים את הדין לאותו מקרה, בית

67 במשנה מנוסחת ההסכמה כאילו אין בה מחלוקת אבל מהתוספתא עולה שאכן שתי הלכות אלו היו נקודות המוצא למחלוקת.

68 או למשל משנה, תרומות פ"ה מ"ד; ביצה פ"א מ"ו; תוס', תרומות פ"ו מ"ד; מעשר שני פ"י הי"א וכמוהן דוגמאות נוספות.

שמאי רואים בו דוגמא מקרית ומציאותית. אם כן איננו יודעים מי הכריע במעשה הראשון בפועל,[69] אך חכמים המשיכו ללמדו ולדון בו. אין זה מקרה שהתלמוד הירושלמי מכניס את דעת בית שמאי למסגרת הלכתית, ותולה את ההלכה בנסיבות מסייעות (ירו,' יבמות פ"טו ה"ב, יד ע"ד).

טומאת כלים

כדי להבין דוגמא זו עלינו להציע את משנת אהלות (פ"ו מ"א):[70]

אדם וכלים נעשין אהלים לטמא אבל לא לטהר כיצד ארבעה נושאין את הנרבד[71] **טומאה תחתיו** – הטומאה (המת עצמו שכן רק מת מטמא באוהל) מונחת על הרצפה, והמיטה מאהילה עליה **כלים שעל גביו** – המיטה (האלונקה) משמשת ברגע זה לנשיאת משאות **טמאין** – הכלי איננו משמש לאוהל כדי לטהר. אילו הייתה האלונקה אוהל הרי שהמת היה בתוך האוהל ומה שמעל גג האוהל היה טהור. אבל כלים אינם אוהל לטהר. **טומאה על גביו** – המת מונח על האלונקה **כלים שתחתיו טמאין** – האלונקה מהווה אוהל ומטמאת כל מה שמתחתיה. **ר' אליעזר מטהר** – לא נאמר מה נימוקו, ונראה שלדעת רבי אליעזר האלונקה נחשבת לאוהל. והטומאה 'נכלאת' באוהל. לפי הסבר זה רבי אליעזר חולק גם ברישא, ומיקל ביצירת אוהל. כלומר לדעתו כל מיטה באשר היא נידונה בבחינת אוהל.

בהמשך המשנה עוד שלושה מקרים דומים שההבדל ביניהם הוא מה מעמיד את הנרבד. ובהם לא נרחיב. בתוספתא תוספת הלכתית הפותחת פתח להבנת הנרווד והרקע ההלכתי כאחד. הקטעים שאינם במשנה הודגשו בקו "ארבעה שהיו נושאין את הנדבך (נדבד בכתב יד וינה) 1. ואין במוטות כעובי המרדיע טומאה תחתיה כלים שעל גביו טמאין טומאה על גביו כלים שתחתיו טמאין, ר' אליעזר מטהר .... (תוס', אהלות פ"ז ה"א, עמ' 306). התנאי החשוב בתוספתא הוא שאין במוטות האלונקה עובי מרדע. עובי מרדע הוא הגודל הקבוע בהלכה, פחות מזה אין הכלי נחשב לכלי והכוונה כמובן לכלים שיש להם צורת מוט ארוך, כגון אותו מרדע בו מדרבנים את הפרה. וכן שנינו: "כל המטלטלין מביאין את הטומאה בעובי המרדע, לא גדול ולא קטן אלא בינוני, איזה הוא בינוני כל שהקיפו

69 הבבלי, קטז ע"ב משחזר את המעשה ומסיים שבית דין שלחו ומצאו את גופת המת. אך דומה שזה שחזור ולא מסורת היסטורית. מן הראוי להעיר שבדרך כלל המחלוקת בין הבתים היא בטעמים הגיוניים ועקרוניים. המדובר באותם מקרים שבהם המשנה או התוספתא עצמה מביאה את הטעמים השונים. מחלוקת עקרונית (שיקולים הגיוניים) – משנה, יבמות פי"ג מ"א; פט"ו מ"ב; נזיר פ"ה מ"ג; גיטין פ"ד מ"ה ועוד הרבה. רק לעתים רחוקות הנימוק הוא מדרשי ואז כנראה שלא המדרש גרם לפער ההלכתי ראו למשל תוס', תרומות פ"ג הט"ז המעמידה את המחלוקת כאילו על מדרש, אך המחלוקת היא עקרונית והגיונית, האם אדם שהרים תרומה שלא לפי כל כללי ההלכה, האם תרומתו חלה, ויש בכך מחלוקת עקרונית בין בית שמאי ובית הלל ולא נרחיב בכך במסגרת זו.

70 מתוך פירושנו למשנה אוהלות (בהכנה). הטקסט לפי כ"י קופמן.

71 כך בכתב יד קופמן ורוב עידי הנוסח בדפוס הראשון, דפוס ווילנה ומפ 'נדבך' וביתר הנוסחים נרווד נדוד ונוסחאות דומות. בבירור הנוסח נעסוק בפירושנו למסכת אהלות – עת יזכנו החונן לאדם דעת להגיע למשנה ולפרשה. נסתפק בכך שנוסח התוספתא שנביא להלן מוכיח שהכוונה לנדבך' או נרוד שהיא מיטה המורכבת ממוטות ועליה סריגת חבלים ואשר נועדה בעיקר להובלת המת.

טפח" (משנה, כלים פי"ז מ"ח; תוס', כלים בבא מציעא פ"ו הי"ב, עמ' 585).[72] הלכה זו נמנית על המחלוקות שבהם הכריעו במעמד 'בו ביום', שבו גברו בית שמאי על בית הלל. הרשימה של הלכות בו ביום מצויה בתוספתא שבת ובמקבילות התלמודיות ...."בו ביום אמרו כל המטלטלין מביאין את הטומאה בעובי המרדע ונמנו ורבו בית שמיי על בית הלל" (תוס', שבת פ"א הי"ח, ירו', פ"א ה"ד, ג ע"ג; בבלי, יז ע"א). משתמע אפוא שזו הלכה כבית שמאי, ולא נמסר כלל מה סברו בית הלל.

משנה אחרת משלימה את התמונה: "כל המטלטלין מביאין את הטומאה כעובי המרדע. אמר רבי טרפון אקפח את בני שזו הלכה מקופחת, ששמע השומע וטעה. שהאיכר עובר והמרדע על כתפו והאהיל צדו אחד על הקבר וטמאוהו משום כלים המאהילים על המת. אמר רבי עקיבא אני אתקן שיהו דברי חכמים קיימין, שיהו כל המטלטלין מביאין את הטומאה על אדם הנושאן בעובי המרדע, ועל עצמן בכל שהן. ועל שאר אדם וכלים בפותח טפח" (משנה, אהלות פט"ז מ"א; בבלי, שבת טז ע"ב)

אם כן סתם משנה אהלות שונה את ההלכה הידועה. אבל רבי טרפון הידוע כממשיכם של בית שמאי טוען קשות נגד הלכה זו שהיא "הלכה מקופחת".[73] לדבריו היה מקרה שאדם שנשא מרדע בחוסר זהירות וקצה אחד שלו היה מעל קבר וטמאוהו משום שהמרדע נחשב לאוהל. אבל כנראה שכל כלי המאהיל על אוהל טמא ולא נצרך עובי של מרדע.

אותה מסורת חוזרת ביתר בירור בתוספתא ושם שלוש הלכות דומות: "כל המטלטלין מביאין את הטומאה בעובי המרדע - אמר ר' טרפון אקפח את בני שהלכה זו מקופחת. אינו יודע חוזיו של דבר מה הוא, אלא ששמע השומע וטעה. ומעשה באחד שהיה עובר ומרדע על כתיפיו והאהיל צידו אחד על הקבר וטמאוהו, משום שהאהיל על המת והשומע שמע וטעה (תוס', אהלות פט"ו הי"ב, עמ' 316). רבי עקיבא מציע עמדת בינים. עובי מרדע נצרך כדי לטמא אדם, וכדי לטמא כלים די בכל שהוא.

מבחינה הלכתית נראה שלפנינו מסורות סותרות. בתוספתא שבת בית שמאי הם דורשים עובי מרדע ולא נאמר מה עמדת בית הלל. אבל במשנת אהלות ובתוספתא ממשיכי בית שמאי אומרים שאדם טמא בעובי כלשהו, ורבי עקיבא מציע עמדת ביניים. המשנה הסתמית בכלים איננה מקבלת את הפשרה של רבי עקיבא, וודאי שלא את תרעומתו של רבי טרפון. לפנינו תופעה תדירה של חילוף מסורות בין בית שמאי ובית הלל. ואכן גם במשנתנו רבי אליעזר מטהר, משום שלדעתו הנרבד הוא אוהל גם לטהר, וזו עמדת רבי טרפון. כלומר שהמשנה מדברת כשמוטות אינן כעובי המרדע ובמקרה כזה לדעת בית הלל זהו אוהל חלקי (מטמא אבל לא מטהר) ולדעת רבי אליעזר (בית שמאי) זהו אוהל מלא המטהר ומטמא. אבל לוא היה במוטות עובי מרדע לדעת כולם היה האוהל מטמא ומטהר.

---

72 רוחבו שתי אצבעות לפי התוספתא שהבאנו ולמעשה היקפו 1.28 טפחים ולא דייקו חכמים במידותיהם.

73 אקפח את בני הוא ביטוי מובהק שרק רבי טרפון משתמש בו במקורות רבים. הביטוי 'שזו הלכה מקופחת' יחידאי להקשר זה.

נמצאנו למדים שהכלל במשנה "אדם וכלים נעשים אהלים לטמא אבל לא לטהר" איננו כלל כללי, אלא הסבר למקרים הפרטיים שבהמשך המשנה. קודם נשנו הפרטים ולאחר מכן ניתנה להם כותרת הלכתית בעלת אופי כאילו כללי.

הלכה זו התפתחה אפוא בצורה מעניינת במיוחד והשתמרו העדויות להתפתחות ההלכה והתפתחות ניסוחה.

1. אירע מעשה ונפסקה הלכה באותו מעשה – ההלכה נפסקה על ידי חכמים או על ידי הציבור.
2. השומע טעה והסיק שתנאי המעשה הם תנאי ההלכה העקרונית. שני השלבים הללו התחוללו אי שם בימי בית שני לפני השלב השלישי.
3. במעמד 'בו ביום' בשלהי ימי הבית השני נפסקה הלכה בנושא. פסק זה לא היה סוף הויכוח אלא תחילתו.
4. רבי טרפון מתנגד להלכה ותובע שכלים יטמאו בכל שהוא.
5. רבי עקיבא מציע עמדת ביניים.
6. סתם המשנה בכלים מציע את המסקנה (כמו 2) כהלכה כללית.
7. התנא במשנתנו מציע את ההלכה של 2 כהלכה השנויה במחלוקת במסגרת סדרת מקרים.
8. ניתנת כותרת לסדרת המקרים – כותרת המנוסחת כעקרון הלכתי, אף שאיננה מתאימה אלא למקרה מיוחד.

בנוסף לכך קיים חילוף מסורות בין בית שמאי ובית הלל. עוד מן הראוי להעיר שלעיל (פ"ה מ"א) מחמירים בית שמאי בטומאת אוהל. ארבעה אנשים הנושאים את המת נחשבים כאוהל לכל דבר ובית הלל מסכימים שהם אוהל אך בפחות חומרה. יתר על כן העמדה שבית שמאי מטמאים בכל שהוא מתאימה יותר לקו הפסיקה של בית שמאי (וליתר דיוק לזו של שמאי הזקן).[74]

זו דוגמא נוספת לכך שההלכה הקדומה נקבעה בראשיתה בסדרת הכרעות מקומיות לא שיטתיות. את השיטתיות של המערכת ההלכתית יש לייחס לחכמים מאוחרים. והמקרה שלפנינו מהווה דוגמא מובהקת לכך, תודות להערה משום ר' טרפון שהמסקנה ההלכתית השיטתית בטעות יסודה. אבל מסורת ההלכה דחקה למעשה את התנגדותו של רבי טרפון (בית שמאי).

בהמשך התוספתא שם עוד שני מקרים בהם "השומע שמע וטעה" כלומר שההלכה צמחה ממקרה והסקת המסקנה ההלכתית הייתה שגויה לדעתו של רבי יהודה (תלמידו של רבי טרפון). לא נעסוק כאן בבירור הרקע ההלכתי של קביעות אלו ובמסגרת זו נסתפק במסקנה שההלכה צמחה מתקדים, ובטענה שהתקדים לא הובן כהלכה. כלומר המעשה התקדימי ארע במקום אחד וההלכה העקרונית התפתחה במקום אחר לגמרי.

74 ראו עדיות פ"א מ"ז; אהלות פ"ב מ"א ומקבילות לרבי עקיבא מייחסת ההלכה שם עמדה הקרובה לקביעה שטומאה היא בכל שהו, וגם אצלנו הוא נוקט בעמדה שיש בה קבלה חלקית של עמדה זו. במקביל, במקורות אחרים, מיוחסת לרבי עקיבא עמדה אחרת לפיה חזר בו מקרבתו לפסיקת שמאי הזקן, ולא כאן המקום לברר שאלה זו.

צירוף בצק להפרשת חלה

בהקשר זה מצינו במשנה (משנה, חלה פ"ד מ"ג). הלכה המכילה מעין סתירה פנימית: נאמר בה שאם יש שני בצקים החייבים בחלה מאותו סוג, ובצק שלישי באמצע שאינו חייב בחלה הם אינם מצ־טרפים.[75] אבל אם הבצק האמצעי הוא כזה שכבר הורמה חלתו הוא מצרף ומצטרף. כבר ממבט ראשון קשה להבין מה בין בצק שאין מרימים ממנו חלה לבין בצק שכבר הורמה חלתו, הרי צריך היה לצפות לאותה הלכה בשני המקרים. בתוספתא מסופר במפורש שההלכה במשנה היא ההלכה הקדומה, ובשלב שני "הוסיפו עליהן" ושינו את ההלכה הקדומה. "קב מיכן וקב מיכן, וקב חדש באמצע. קב מיכן וקב מיכן, וקב שעורין באמצע, הרי אילו מצטרפין. הוסיפו עליהן קב מיכן וקב מיכן, וקב של אשה אחרת. קב מיכן וקב מיכן, וקב דבר שניטלה חלתו באמצע, הרי אילו מצטרפין. קב מיכן וקב מיכן, וקב הגוי באמצע. קב מיכן וקב מיכן, וקב תרומה באמצע אין מצטרפין" (תוס', חלה פ"ב ה"ב).

הווה אומר שההחלטה הייתה על המקרה הבודד מבלי לקבל החלטות שיטתיות, מאוחר יותר כשנעשה ניסיון לגבש מערכת החלטות עקיבה, לפיה עדיף לצרף מאשר ליצור במטבח אחד מער־כות שונות. נותרה הסתירה בין ההלכה הקדומה והמערכת המאוחרת בעינה. כלומר הרישא במשנה היא ההלכה הקדומה, והסיפא הוא פרי התוספת, שמגמתה ההלכתית שונה. בזכות התוספתא השת־מרו עקבות ההחלטות השונות, וכך נחשף לעיננו התהליך. במקרה זה ברור שההלכה נקבעה שלב אחר שלב, פרט אחר פרט, ובשלב הראשון לא נקבעה מדיניות אחידה. ההחלטה הייתה על המקרה הבודד מבלי לקבל החלטות שיטתיות. בשלב שני איחדו את ההחלטות במטרה לקדם מערכת שי־טתית, ונותרה בתוכה סתירה פנימית מסוימת. שערי פירושים לא ננעלו, וניתן להסביר סתירה זו באופנים אחרים.

מצינו דוגמאות רבות נוספות לטיפוס מעין זה של חוסר עקביות שיטתית במשנה, ובמהלך פירוש המשניות נשקול אפשרות פרשנית זו במקרים נוספים.[76] מסורת חכמים מייחסת מגמה משפטית זו במפורש לר' אליעזר 'השוה במידותיו' בהלכות קטינה (בבלי, יבמות קח ע"א) ובהלכות בדק הבית (ירו', שקלים פ"ד ה"ד, מ"ז ע"ד). מעבר לשיקול המיידי המטרה היא לבנות מערכת משפט קוהר־נטית גם אם לכאורה נוצרת סתירה פרטנית.

ערכים

המשנה (ערכין פ"ד מ"א) קובעת: "עני שהעריך את העשיר נותן ערך עני, ועשיר שהעריך את העני נותן ערך עשיר" המשנה שאחריה מוסיפה "אבל בקורבנות אינו כן הרי שאמר קורבנו שלמ־צורע זה עלי אם היה מצורע עני מביא קורבן עני עשיר מביא קורבן עשיר". אם כן קיים הבדל בין

75 'מצטרפין' כלומר ששניהם יחד מהווים בצק אחד שיש בו כמות מספקת להרמת בצק.

76 כך תרומות פ"ז מ"ה. ודוגמאות מורכבות מצינו במסכת כלאיים ולא נפרטן כאן. למסגרת זו יש להוסיף את האבחנות ההלכתיות והערכיות בין סריס לאיילונית (משנה יבמות פ"ח מ"ד-מ"ה ושינויים במקבילות).

קורבנות לערכין. על כך טוען רבי "רבי אומר אני אף בערכים כן וכי מפני מה עני שהעריך את העשיר נותן ערך עני שאין העשיר חייב כלום. אבל העשיר שאמר ערכי עלי ושמע העני ואמר מה שאמר זה עלי נותן ערך עשיר". כלומר גם בערכים יש לשלם לפי התעריף המוטל על מי שמעריכים אותו. כלומר ההבדל איננו בין ערכים לקורבנות אלא בצורת ההקדשה. במקרה של מצורע ובמקרה שהביא רבי מי שיצר את חובת התרומה הוא העשיר, וערכה נקבע לפי ערך המתנדב. העני קיבל עליו את ההתחייבות של השני ולכן עליו לשלם קורבן עשיר. אזי ההבדל איננו בין ערך לקורבן אלא שהמתנדב אמור להגדיר את גודל הקורבן. מי שנטל עליו את ההתנדבות (חובת התשלום) מקבל עליו לשלם את מה שחייב השני, ופרטי החובה נקבעים לפי החייב.

ניכר שרבי וחכמים מכירים את ההלכות הקדומות (שלושת התקדימים) ואינם חולקים בהם. הם יודעים שנותן ערך לפי יכולתו של הנותן, ובמצורע לפי יכולתו של החייב בקורבן. המחלוקת היא בניסוח הכלל ההלכתי המסכם את שני המקרים, אותו כלל שממנו יגזרו גם המקרים הבאים. במקרה שלנו מוצעים שני כללים מנוגדים שכל אחד מהם מכנס ומסביר את שני התקדימים שכבר מקובלים. אך רק רבי יודע להסביר את שלושת התקדימים וליצור כלל חדש מסכם.

מלאכות השבת, הכללים המספריים.

המשנה מונה לט אבות מלאכה האסורים בשבת, ותולה את הדבר במלאכות שנעשו במקדש. זה לכאורה כלל מורכב ורשימת פרטים נגזרת הימנו. קביעה זו שימשה נקודת מוצא לדיונים הלכתיים רבים, לחלוקה בין אבות מלאכה ותולדות, ולכאורה מה שלא נעשה במקדש, אינו בכלל המלאכות האסורות. המשנה עצמה מציגה את הרשימה ללא הקדמות "אבות מלאכות ארבעים חסר אחת: הזורע, והחורש ..." (משנה, שבת פ"ז מ"ב), אבל במשנה שקדמה לה "כלל גדול" ובו מדובר על "העושה מלאכות הרבה מעין מלאכה אחת" (משנה, שבת פ"ז מ"א), ולכאורה כבר הכלל תלוי ברשימה של המשנה הבאה, הקובעת מהי מלאכה, ומהי 'מעין מלאכה'. אם כן במשנה ריכוז דוגמאות (שלב ב), או אולי כלל הלכתי מורכב (שלב ד). מכל מקום המספר לט הוא ספרותי (ארבעים חסר אחת) ולכאורה הוא מעיד על גישה וניסוח ספרותיים של כלל הלכתי. ברם דומה שאין זו משמעות המשנה. כאמור[77] המספר לט מלאכות עצמו חשוד כספרותי וסכמתי. רושם זה מתחזק מעיון ברשימה. מתברר שבתלמודים יש החולקים על הגדרת מלאכה זו או אחרת. כך למשל התוספתא והירושלמי מוסיפים שהצבעים (בירושלים) היו עושים סחיטה מלאכה לעצמה.[78] הירושלמי הבין שהצבעים הם קבוצה למדנית, וברשימתם היו ארבעים אבות מלאכה. זו עדות מרתקת לקבוצת בעלי מלאכה שיש להם עמדה בתחום הלכתי מובהק. אמנם המשפט עצמו עשוי להתפרש בצורה מצומצמת יותר, שצבעי ירושלים הפכו את הסחיטה לאומנות מיוחדת, אך כאמור לא כך הבינו חכמי התלמוד את המשפט.[79] לשיטתו של התלמוד אכן הצבעים, הנמנים על ההמון הפשוט,

77 ראו דיוננו לעיל על הסופרים.

78 תוס', פ"ט הי"ח; ירו', פ"ז ה"ב, י ע"ג. בתוס' חסרה התיבה 'בירושלים'.

79 לאיסור סחיטה ראו להלן פכ"א מ"ג.

נוקטים בעמדה הלכתית מתוך כבוד לאומנותם. מכל מקום השינויים הללו לא פגמו במספר המלאכות. זאת ועוד הרשימה אינה מאוזנת. יש מלאכות שכל שלב בהם הוא מלאכה לעצמה כמו אפיה. ויש שכינוי אחד 'מכסה' שלבים רבים כמו הבונה הכולל בתוכו מלאכות הרבה. יתר על כן יש מלאכות האסורות בשבת שאינן ברשימה כמו המודד או אולי גם המאכיל בהמה ומטפל בה, המרפא וכיוצא באלו.

עדות לשלב הקדום יותר של הגדרת המלאכות יש כנראה בירושלמי לשבת פ"ד מ"א. המשנה אוסרת להטמין מאכל בחומרים מסוימים ולא ברור האם מדובר בערב שבת או בשבת עצמה. ככל הנראה הלכה זו סותרת את הנאמר בפרק ג' משנה א' ובפרק א' משנה ט'. ואכן בירושלמי (י ע"ד) מבואר שאין בכך איסור בישול, ומובאים שני נימוקים אחרים לאיסור הטמנה, "מפני ביטול בית המדרש", ונימוקו של רבי בא מפני החשד "שאם את אומר לו שהוא מותר, אף הוא אינו עושה אותן כל צורכו מבעוד יום... מה נפק מן ביניהן לטמון שלג וצונין ...". ובהמשך: "אסרו טמינה מפני כירה, אסרו כירה מפני טמינה, אסרו כירה שהבלה ממועט מפני כירה שהבלה מרובה וכו'" (שם, שם). אם כן המשפט האחרון אוסר הטמנה משום בישול, והיא דומה להסבר הבבלי. הרישא מציעה כיוון שונה לחלוטין, האיסור להשהות אוכל על כירה נובע משני חששות: החשש שמא ישהה אוכל על כירה הממשיכה לבשל, אך גם בגלל חשש הטמנה. הווה אומר שהחשש העיקרי הוא עצם העיסוק בהכנת הסעודה. חכמים רוצים שכל הכנת האוכל תסתיים לפני שבת, ובשבת יהיו פנויים לדברים אחרים (בית המדרש).

שני טעמים ניתנים לאיסור. האחד ביטול בית המדרש. התלמוד מניח שליל שבת הוא זמן לדרשה,[80] ולכן הם תובעים הפסקת עבודה עם כניסת השבת, כולל עבודות מותרות. טעם שני הוא הרצון שאדם לא ישהה את ההכנות לשבת עצמה, ולכן אסרו על עבודות השלמה בשבת, ואפילו עבודות מותרות. הירושלמי מעיר, שלפי ההסבר השני אין סיבה לאסור הטמנת צוננים לקירור; אבל בהמשך נקבע שאסור להטמין צונן בשלג. אם כן לדעת התלמוד הירושלמי "ביטול בית המדרש" הוא הנימוק העיקרי. הצד השווה שבשני התירוצים הוא רצונם של חכמים להפסיק את העיסוק בהכנות לסעודה עם כניסת השבת.[81] לאור הסבר זה יש להבין גם את המשנה המתירה להטמין במים חמים, או אולי אף לחמם אוכל מוכן (פ"כד מ"ב).

נימוק אחרון זה מתקשר לפרשה הלכתית מורכבת הרבה יותר, שכבר רמזנו לה. בספרות כת קומראן מופיע האיסור לאכול אוכל שלא הוכן.[82] בספרות חז"ל ביטוי מקביל מדויק: "ואין ניאותין ממנו לפי שאינו מן המוכן" (פ"ג מ"ו), "כל הכלים ניטלין בשבת... שאינן דומין לדלתות הבית לפי שאינן מן המוכן" (פי"ז מ"א), וכן במקבילות רבות.[83] לפי ההלכה של חז"ל מתרחב האיסור וכולל שימוש בחומר שאינו מוכן, ואפילו טלטולו נאסר. מאוחר יותר, בתקופת האמוראים, נטבע מונח מחודש "מוקצה". בראשיתו, במקורות התנאיים, ציין המונח חפץ שהוקצה לעבודה זרה, או אוכלים

80 באופן עקרוני איסור הטמנה הוא גם בהמשך יום השבת, ברם נראה שעיקר ההטמנה הייתה בערב שבת, כאשר האוכל החם הוסר מהתנור.

81 ברית דמשק, י 22; ספר היובלים ב כט; נ ט.

82 ברית דמשק, י 22.

83 משנה, שבת פכ"ד מ"א; ביצה פ"א מ"ב; פ"ג מ"ד; שם מ"ו. וכן מקורות נוספים כגון תוס', שבת פי"ד ה"ח; ביצה פ"ג הי"א.

שהוקצו לאכילה ועל כן חויבו במעשר.[84] בתלמודים משתמשים במונח זה כדי לציין את מה שאינו מוכן. במשמעות זו מופיע המונח בבבלי רבות, ולעתים נדירות גם בירושלמי.[85]

מבחינה משפטית ה"הכנה" קשה להגדרה, אין היא מצב פיזי אלא תובנה מחשבתית-נפשית. על כן המונח בעייתי מבחינה הלכתית, שקשה היה להגדירו באופן משפטי. ההלכה של חז"ל, כפי שהתפתחה במהלך הדורות היא משפטית ומחייבת הגדרות מדויקות, ו"הכנה" אינה מאפשרת הגדרה מדויקת. מחלוקות על הגדרת המונח הכנה מצויות בכמה משניות, למשל, בראש מסכת ביצה חולקים בית שמאי ובית הלל אם מותר לאכול ביצה שנולדה ביום טוב, ולפחות לפי חלק מההסברים המחלוקת היא על האיסור לאכול מזון שאינו מוכן. הלכה אחרת דנה אם מותר לאכול "נשרים" – פרי [תמר] שנשר – בשבת (פסחים פ"ד מ"ח). למשנה זו הוצעו מספר פירושים והפירוש הרמוז כאן הוא רק אחת מהאפשרויות להבנת המסורת הקדומה.

האיסור להטמין בשבת עשוי להיות תולדה של האיסור לאכול אוכל שאינו מוכן, שכן אוכל שיש להטמינו אינו נחשב למוכן; ואפשר שחז"ל גזרו על הטמנה כדי שלא יבוא לכדי אי הכנה. דומה שניתן להצביע על ההתפתחות המשפטית של איסור "מוכן". מלכתחילה נדרש שכל האוכל יהא מוכן (ספר היובלים, ההלכה של כת קומראן), ובשלב שני נקבע שכל אוכל שאינו מוכן אסור בטלטול – איסור זה נהג בסוף ימי הבית השני.[86] בשלב שלישי, האמוראי, הוגדר כל מה ש"אינו מוכן" בתור מה שאינו מיועד לשימוש בשבת [איסור "מוקצה" האמוראי]. הגדרה זו העתיקה את משמעותו של האיסור מאכילה לטלטול והרחיבה אותו על תחומים נוספים. ייתכן, שדווקא הרחבה זו היא שרוק־נה מעט את האיסור המקורי מתוכנו, הווה אומר: אוכל שבישולו לא הושלם, אך מתכוננים לאוכלו בשבת, אינו בבחינת "מוקצה", שהרי לא הוקצה ממחשבה, ולכן לכאורה מותר לטלטלו [ולאוכלו] בשבת. על כן נדרשו חכמים להדגיש פנים אחרות בטעמו של האיסור: כדי שיהיה אדם פנוי בערב שבת (ירושלמי), או גזרה שמא יחתה בגחלים ושמא יבשל בשבת (בבלי).

נראה אפוא, שבנושא זה רווחו מחלוקות ולמעשה שתי תפישות לפנינו. האחת משפטית ומדגישה את בעיית הבישול, איסור חיתוי בגחלים, חשש שמא ירתיח וכדומה. ואילו השנייה ערכית – יש להמעיט בעיסוקי החול, יש להשלים את כל ההכנות בערב השבת, כך שכל האוכל יהא מוכן והאדם יהיה פנוי ללימוד בבית המדרש. מכל מקום משנתנו האוסרת להטמין מחמירה בהרבה ממשנה י בפרק א של מסכת שבת שהתירה המשך בישול תבשיל, לפחות זה שרובו התבשל. נמצאנו למדים, שמערכת איסורי ההטמנה בפרקנו אינה רק משפטית. הוספת ההבל היא נימוק אחד, וחוברת לה הגזירה שמא יבוא לטמון

---

84 משנה, תמורה פ"ו מ"א; תוס', נזיר פ"ד ה"ט; מכות פ"ה ה"ד, עמ' 444; עבודה זרה פ"ב ה"א, עמ' 462; פ"ה ה"ט-ה"י, עמ' 469 , ועוד.

85 בבלי, שבת מג ע"א; מג ע"ב; מה ע"א; ביצה לו ע"א, ומקורות בבליים נוספים; ירו', ביצה פ"ד ה"א, סב ע"ב-ע"ג, ועוד. מהפך סמנטי שאינו משנה את המשמעות ההלכתית מצינו גם בנדרים. שם מצינו שתי לשונות נדר האומר 'אני אוכל' או לחילופין 'איני אוכל' ומן הדיונים מתברר שמדובר בלשון נדר זהה אם כי מנוסחת בשני ביטויים הפוכים.

86 משנה, שבת פי"ז מ"א; ביצה פ"א מ"ב. שתי ההלכות שבמשניות הללו קדומות מאוד, וראשיתן מימי הבית השני.

בדבר המוסיף הבל; ושני אלה הם הפנים המשפטיות של התביעה שאדם יסיים את ההכנות לשבת לפני בוא שבת מלכתא. תביעה זו חלה על כל הטמנה באשר היא, אף במה שאינו מוסיף הבל כלל.

הרשימה בשבת פרק ז' מבטאת את השלב המאוחר, חובת ההכנה (האיסור לאכול שלא מן המו־כן) נדחה, ואיננו מופיעה כלל, ובמקומו באה סדרת מלאכות אסורות.

הוא הדין לאיסור מודד, ולאיסור הפרת נדרים. שניהם אינם נכללים ברשימת המלאכות ושוב נובעים 'מעובדן דחול' (משנה, שבת פכ"ד מ"ה)[87] וגם כאן שניהם הותרו רק לצורך השבת. ושוב לפנינו איסור קדום, שכן דנים בו תנאים מראשית דור יבנה, כדבר ידוע ומוכר, אך אינו ברשימה במשנת לט אבות המלאכה. זאת ועוד! המשנה אינה מסבירה כלל את האיסור ומבחינתה הוא נתון וידוע, אלא רק את ההיתר למדוד, או להפר נדרים לצורך השבת. נמצאנו למדים שמלאכות אלו היו אסורות וידועות לכל, ולעומתם הרשימה הספרותית של מלאכות השבת אינה כוללת את כל המלאכות, ואלו נאסרו ללא כל קשר למלאכות המשכן. איסורי מלאכה בשבת עוצבו מכוח מגמות שונות בתובנת השבת, תחושת הקדושה, תחושת השבות בשבת, איסורי מלאכה המקראיים, תהליכים מורכבים של ארגון משפטי והשוואת מידות. כמו גם עיצוב ספרותי, ויצירת מיתוס קדומים.[88]

מועד ההתחייבות במעשרות

בספרות חז"ל דיונים רבים על השלב החקלאי בו פירות מתחייבים במעשר. השאלה כולה אופ־יינית לדרך החשיבה המיוחדת של חכמים. לחכמים היה חשוב לקבוע מתי בדיוק חלה חובת מעשרות והאם אכילת פירות לפני הבישול מחייבת במעשרות. אין צריך לומר שהשאלה כולה משקפת משק חקלאי במצוקה בו לעתים נזקקים לאכול פירות עוד לפני גמר בישולם. בספרות ההלכה שלוש זמנים: 'בתר חניטה' (הפרי חייב במעשרות מרגע שהפרי חנט), 'בתר לקיטה' ואחר הבאת שליש. בפועל נקבע שירקות בתר לקיטה, תבואה אחר הבאת שליש ונותרה מחלוקת על זמן חיוב פירות אילן.[89] במקביל במשנה רשימה ארוכה של פירות ומועד חיובם ולכל אחד זמן משלו המבטא את תחילת הפיכתו לאכיל (משנה, מעשרות פ"א מ"ב). בפועל מתברר שלאתרוג מועדים מיוחדים ובחלק מההלכות הוא דומה לאילן ובחלק לירק (משנה, מעשרות פ"ב מ"ו). בפועל מתברר שלרבי נחמיה עמדה שונה אבל העם נהגו בחרובים כר' נחמיה (ירו', שביעית פ"ה ה"א, לה ע"ד). קשה למצוא הסבר שיטתי שיש בו לכידות משפטית, ונראה שלכל עץ נקבעו נוהגים שונים. התלמוד הירושלמי מדגיש את ההבדל בין המנהג כר' נחמיה, ובין הלכה רגילה, אבל בפועל המנהג הוא ההלכה וההלכה היא המנהג.

87 ע' קוסמן, *לתולדות הקטגוריה של איסורי 'עובדין דחול'*, עבודת דוקטורט בשיכפול, אוניברסיטת בר אילן, רמת גן, תשנ"ג.

88 ראו גם דיוננו לעיל על תקופת הסופרים ומשניות המספרים.

89 ראו משנה, ביכורים פ"ב מ"ו לדיון ארוך ובו המקורות השונים ראו י', פליקס, חמישה עשר בשבט – הלכה ומציאות, ירושלמי שביעית ב, ירושלים תשמ"ט, עמ' 384-354.

כלאי זרעים (ירקות)

ההלכות של הרחקה בכלאי זרעים מסובכות עד למאד. המשניות העוסקות בהם אינן נוקטות בשפה אחידה, המחלוקות רבות, והלכות רבות נותרו עמומות והפרשנים נחלקו בביאורם. בפרק ג׳ של מסכת כלאים ניכרת אבחנה בין ירק בודד לבין שדה שלם, ולכל סוג של גידול הלכות משלו. סוגי הגידולים, לפי תפישת חז"ל, הם דגנים, ירקות ודילועים או אולי רק דלעות. ונוספו עליהן הל־כות מיוחדות לכמה גידולים כגון החרדל (פ"ב מ"ט), או דלעת יוונית (פ"ב מי"א).

השונות בפסקי ההלכה מתבטאת לא רק בהלכות אלא גם (ובעיקר) בשפה ההלכתית, וגם ההבדלים בין תבואה לבין ירקות לבין דילועים קשה להסבירם על רקע ריאלי (כמות מראית העין). משנה אחת (פ"ב מ"ו) מניחה שמותר לזרוע חלקות רבות ממינים שונים ובלבד שכל חלקה תהיה משמעותית, ובית שמאי ובית הלל חולקים בניסח ההגדרה מה צריך להיות הרוחב המינימלי. מכל מקום אין במ־שנה דיון לא באורך החלקות ולא ברוחב הנדרש ביניהם. וכן יוצא ממשנה ז׳ באותו פרק ממנה משמע שמותר לזרוע זרע אחר ובלבד שיהיה ברור שאין זו זריעה בערבוביה, קיימת מחלוקת ראשונים האם נדרש רווח בין המינים השונים.[90] מעבר לתירוצים אלו בולטת העובדה שמשנה אחת (פ"ב מ"ה) אינה מזכירה את המרחק בין המינים, משנה שניה אף היא אינה מזכירה מרחק, ומדברת רק במקרה מיוחד (ראש תור – פ"ב מ"ו), ובמשניות אחרות המרחק נדרש והוא נושא הדיון (פ"ב מ"ט). כלומר קיים קושי ספרותי מדוע מרכיב המרחק אינו נזכר במפורש כרגיל בספרות ההלכה.

במשניות אחרות מתירים לסמוך מינים ואין דרישה לחלקה ברוחב מינימלי ושוב קשה מדוע אין השפה ההלכתית אחידה, ומדוע מרכיב הרוחב נעדר. במשנה אחרת (פ"ב מי"א) העוסקת במי־נים שאינם תבואה מוגדרת החלקה לפי מידות שטח או אורך ושוב קשה מדוע השפה ההלכתית כה שונה. במשנה אחרת בפרק הבא (פ"ג מ"ג) נדרש שהשורה מהמין השני תהיה ארוכה ואילו רבי יהודה דורש שיהיה לה רוחב מסוים. דומה שתנא אחד אינו מתייחס לדרישות של תנא אחר (לא לחיוב ולא לשלילה), כאילו טרם עוצבה השפה ההלכתית.

משנה ט׳ באותו פרק (פ"ב) מתירה לזרוע במעורבב ובתנאי שיהיה מרחק מסוים בין המינים, ובה אין דרישה לאורך או לרוחב של החלקות של המינים השונים. אגב כך שומעים אנו שלחרדל דין שונה והוא נחשב לצמח 'משתלט' או 'מתפשט'. העקרון המנחה שונה, לא עוד מרחק בין המינים, או גבול ברור ביניהם, אלא החשש שהחרדל יתפשט לתוך השדה והשדה כולו יראה כמעורבב.

דוגמא אחרת היא משנה ד׳ בפרק ג׳ המאפשרת לזרוע מיני ירקות שונים ובתנאי שיהיו אלו שתי שורות אחת ליד השניה. הדרישה לשתי שורות דווקא אינה עולה במשניות שמנינו לעיל. משנה ו׳ באותו פרק מדברת אף היא על זריעת שורות של בצלים ודילועים ומעלה תביעות אחרות להרחקה. לפי אותם ראשונים התובעים הרחקה בין מינים שונים המשנה נמצאת במכלול הלכתי רגיל. אבל לפי הפירושים שאין צורך בהרחקה בין מינים קשה להבין מדוע כאן נדרשת הרחקה כה רבה.

---

90 רמב"ם והר"ש לכלאים פ"ב מ"א ופרשנים נוספים. לכל אחד מהצדדים משניות המסייעות לשיטתו, והרושם הוא שהמשנה פשוט אינה שלמה ואין בה את כל הפרטים הרלבנטיים לקביעת ההלכה.

רוב ההלכות העוסקות בכלאי זרעים מרוכזות בפרק ג׳ במסכת כלאים. הפרק, או נושא כלאי ירקות כולו, הוא אחד מהקשים שבכל המשנה. כמה מהמשניות העקרוניות סתומות ונפלו בהם לא רק מחלוקות תנאים ואמוראים בסיסיות, אלא גם הראשונים עמלו קשה לפצחם ולנסח את תורת כלאי זרעים ולא עלה בידם.[91] במיוחד קשות הן המשנה הראשונה והשביעית. דומה שלא קיים אף עקרון הלכתי שאין מחלוקת מהותית על טיבו, כגון כמה יש להרחיק מינים שונים זה מזה, ובאיזה מקרים מדברת כל משנה. אי ההבנה מהותית, ואין כאן רק בעיה של הבנת הנקרא אלא גם של התוכן וההנחות ההלכתיות שאינן שיטתיות ולא אחת אינן מבוססות.

הרושם הכללי הוא שהנושא עדיין לא הוגדר במערכת הלכתית שיטתית בתקופת התנאים. אמוראי בבל מיעטו לעסוק בו להוציא סוגיה אחת במסכת שבת (פה ע״א-פו ע״א), גם בסוגיה זו הלימוד עוסק רק בפרט אחד ואין בידנו משנה סדורה של ההלכה הבבלית. אמוראי ארץ ישראל עסקו כמובן בפרק אבל לא מצינו תשובה לשאלות הבסיסיות. המשניות אינן מנוסחות בחדות ובבהירות הרגילה, יש בהם החלפת מונחים (כגון משנה ו), וחוסר שלמות. נסתפק בשתי דוגמאות. הראשונה: *משנה ג* בפרק ג׳ מדברת על ערוב ירק בירק, ונוקטת מידות שונות. לא כתוב שם האם מידות אלו הם מידות שדה שמותר לזרוע בה ליד שדה אחר, או שאלו מידות השטח הפתוח הנדרש בין מיני ירקות שונים. זו מחלוקת ראשונים, אבל מעבר לכך המשנה מנוסחת בצורה לא ברורה. שלושה חכמים נחלקים האחד קובע רק מידת אורך, השני מידת אורך ורוחב ״מילואו״, שזה מינוח סתמי המעיד על כך שלמחבר היה המונח ברור, אך עבורנו הוא עמום ודורש פירוש. חכם שלישי נוקט רק במידת רוחב (פרסה), במינוח שבעצם אין לו אח ורע בספרות ורק בזכות הפרשנות האמוראית מבינים אנו מהו. דוגמא שניה היא *משנה א׳* המתירה לזרוע חמשה מיני ירקות בערוגה אחת. ברוח זו מהלכת גם משנה ה׳ באותו פרק המתירה לזרוע שני מינים באותה גומה. ברור שמי ששנה זו לא שנה זו, אבל הדעות קרובות. *משנה ב׳* מתירה לזרוע שלושה זרעונים אחד ליד השני, בתנאי שהם בתלם העמוק טפח. אבל חסרה בה דרישת העומק, וההיתר לזרוע חמישה מינים בערוגה אינו קשור לעומק טפח. הוא הדין במשנה ה׳ שאין בה אזכור לדרישה לעומק מוגדר. מעבר לסתירה בין המשניות תמוה הוא שאין הן נוקטות באותה ׳שפה הלכתית׳ העומק אינו נדרש אלא במשנה אחת, ובאחת מדובר בגומה ובשניה בערוגה. ואילו ביתר המשניות (ג׳, ד, ו׳) נדרשת הרחקה מסוימת בין ירקות ממינים שונים, והמשניות משתמשות באבחנות שונות[92] שאין להן רמז במשניות א׳, ב׳, ה׳. התלמודים דנים ביחס שביניהם, אך מעבר להצעת פתרון זה או אחר עצם הניסוח המעורפל נותר מוזר.

הרא״ש שהקדיש לפרקנו פירוש ארוך (בעקבות הר״ש) מנסח בתסכול: ״בתי כלאים החבאו ממני ונסתרו מעיני ונעלמו ממני עקרי יסודותיה היאך מותר לזרוע מיני זרעונים שהם כלאים בגומה

---

91 בין הנסיונות הקדומים יש להעיר על סדרת תשובות גאונים המרוכזות באוצר הגאונים לשבת, פה ע״ב. וכן מ׳, מרגליות, *הלכות ארץ ישראל מן הגניזה*, ירושלים תשל״ד, עמ׳ מו, המנסה לתאם בפשטות בין המשניות השונות, תוך התעלמות מהמחלוקות התנאיות.

92 כגון סוג הגידול, מספר השרות, מרחק בין המינים וכיוצא באלו.

אחת..."[93] בתשובת גאון אחד למשנה א' בפרקנו מסכם הגאון המשיב "כי חלוקים אלו (כך צ"ל) פתרוני קדמונים אשר נכונו בזאת השמועה. ואף על פי כי מי שחבט בה כמה חבטין ולא עלה בידו כלום. ואנו יש לנו בה קושיין בעיקרי חוקי כלאים שצריכים להיתרץ דבר דבר על מכונתו".[94]

אנו עומדים תמהים מול תופעה זו של דעות שונות ומשניות המנוסחות באופן כללי ואין בהם הסבר פנימי לסתירות בינן למשניות אחרות. כל זה תופעה בלתי רגילה בספרות ההלכתית-משפטית של חז"ל. הידע המעורפל שנמסר במשנה מלמד אולי על כך שהתחום ההלכתי של הלכות כלאי זרעים טרם הגיע להתפתחות משפטית כיתר תחומי ההלכה. ערפל הידע בפרק רק מבהיר את גדולתה של ספרות חז"ל ביתר התחומים.

אנו ננסה לתרום את חלקנו לברור המשנה בקצרה ונפנה לפירושי הפרשנים שביניהם מחלוקות כמעט על כל פרט. עם זאת מעבר לכל לפנינו תופעה משפטית וספרותית מיוחדת. לירקות דינים מיוחדים בתחומים הלכתיים שונים (מעשרות, ברכות וכיוצא באלו).[95] נראה שהירקות נכנסו ללוח המזון ולמערכת המשק החקלאי רק בתקופה ההלניסטית. זאת כנראה הסיבה למעמדם המעורער בספרות ההלכה. כפי שנראה בתקופה שהלכות התורה שבעל פה התגבשו טרם הפכו הירקות למרכיב מהותי בסל המזון, ועל כן טרם גובשו ההלכות העוסקות בהן. ההלכות הקדומות התגבשו, ועוצבו מבחינה משפטית וספרותית אי שם בסוף ימי בית שני, ובתקופה זו עדיין הדיון בירקות היה בשלבי הבראשית שלו. בדורות יבנה-אושה כאשר בכל התחומים ההלכתיים נעשתה עבודת העריכה של החומר הקודם, הלכות ירקות עדין היו בשלב היולי. שלב זה מתבטא במשנה. בכל התחומים ההלכתיים האחרים אנו מכירים את החומר ההלכתי רק לאחר גיבושו. רק פה ושם שומעים אנו על השלבים של "בראשונה", אבל בכל הנוגע לדיני ירקות המשנה חושפת את שלב טרום עריכתי. אנו מניחים ששלב כזה עבר על כל תחום אחר (שבת, יום טוב, טומאה וכיוצא באלו), אך בתחומים האחרים העריכה המאוחרת יישרה את הסתירות הפנימיות, ומההלכה הקדומה נותרו רק שרידים מעטים, אך בכלאי זרעים וירקות נותר העיבוד הראשוני של אותו מצב היולי. זו עשוייה להיות סיבה לעריכה הבלתי מליאה מחד גסא, לסתירות, לכפילויות ולשפה ההלכתית הבלתי אחידה מאידך גיסא.

מצב דומה קיים בהלכות טהרה. בכל פרק דיון בכמה מהפרמטרים אך מפרק לפרק משתנים נושאי הדיון והאבחנות שלפיהן ההלכה נקבעת. אין מדובר בסתירות, אלא במשניות שונות שכל אחת מהן מציגה 'סדר יום' הלכתי שונה במקצת. דומה שגם כאן לפנינו אפשרות להציץ לפניה של ההלכה הקדומה עוד בטרם עטתה את אדרת השיטתיות המשפטית. להערכתנו אין מקום ללכת בדרכם של ראשונים שניסו ל'אנוס' על המקורות ולעטותם מערכת משפטית עקבית ואחידה. לא בתוכן ובעיקר

---

93 פירוש הרא"ש, למשנה ד בפרק ג'.

94 ב"מ, לוין, *אוצר הגאונים*, חיפה, ירושלים, תרפ"ח-תש"ג, עמ' 88. משנה א' וקשייה גררו עוד מספר ביטויים לאוזלת היד של מפרשים קדמונים, ולא באנו למנות את כל הביטויים הציוריים הללו שבספרות הפרשנית.

95 חלק מהמקורות אסף ב', דה פריס, *תולדות ההלכה התלמודית*, תל אביב תשכ"ב עמ' 86-83. דה פריס עסק רק בדין מעשרות ולא במכלול הספקות הקשורים לדיני ירקות בכלל.

לא בניסות.[96] גם מסכת ערכין קשורה לנושא זה ויש להזכירה כמצב טרום עריכתי ואפילו מדרשי. וכן נגעים, בה אנו עוסקים כרגע.

השוואת המידות

תהליך היורודיפיקציה הנדון במאמר מכונה בספרות חז"ל 'השוואת המידות'. שיטה זו מיוחסת לר' אליעזר בן הורקנוס ועוררה התפעלות בין החכמים. "אמר ר' ישמעאל חזרתי על כל מדות חכמים ולא מצאתי אדם שמדתו שוה ...",[97] במשנה אחרת מעדיף ר' עקיבא את דברי ר' אליעזר על החולקים עליו, ושוב משום שרבי אליעזר השווה את מידתו (משנה, שקלים פ"ד מ"ז). הדיון ההלכתי שם מצביע על כמה מהטיעונים עליהם עמדנו. מתברר שר' יהושע וחכמים אחרים שחולקים עליו ביותר מתריסר מחלוקות לא 'השוו את מידותיהם', ולא חשו שיש בכך חולשה הלכתית. זאת ועוד רק בשלהי תקופת יבנה ראו חכמים ב'השוואת המידות' יתרון הלכתי. עד אז העדר תפישה סיסטמטית ושיטתית לא נחשב כחולשה כלל. אבל בשלהי דור יבנה הפכה האחידות ההלכתית לתנאי, ויותר מאוחר לאבן פינה בדרך החשיבה ההלכתית.

למרות השבחים שחולקו לר' אליעזר הרי שגם הוא לא השווה מידותיו באופן מלא. כך למשל הוא זה שקובע ש"אין מעשה קטנה כלום" (משנה, יבמות פי"ג מ"ב), כלומר של מעשה האירוסין בה אין לו כל משמעות. אבל בעניין אחר הוא קובע שאירוסיה תקפים ויש צורך ללמדה למאן (שם מ"ו). דומה שאמנם לדעתו המעשה לא מעשה, אבל בכל זאת הוא מחמיר ודורש מיאון כדי לא לעורר שאלות הלכתיות אחרות.

בספרות חז"ל דוגמאות נוספות לתהליך השוואת המידות. בספרות התנאית לא נקבע גיל לקיום מצוות: קטן חייב במצוות שאותם יכול הוא לקיים. התלמודים נקטו כאן כלל אחיד: בגיל 13 חייב הבן במצוות, והבת – בגיל 12.[98] החלתו של הכלל על המקורות התנאיים הביאה, כמובן, לפירושם בדרך דחוקה. הוא הדין במונחים ותפישות הלכתיות אחרות כגון כרמלית, צער בעלי חיים, פטור אבל אסור, ואחרים.[99]

96 וראו למשל אהלות פ"ב מ"ו ופ"ג מ"א-מ"ב. או הפרקים הראשונים של מסכת נגעים. דומה שליחידה זו יש לצרף את הפרקים האחרונים במשנה ערכין העוסקים בגאולת בתים ומשקפים מצב טרום עריכה ואולי רק מצב מדרש קדום.

97 תוס', יבמות פי"ג ה"ד ומקבילות. נראה שהשוואת המידות היא קו במחשבתו ההלכתית של ר' אליעזר כפי שהראה גילת, משנת ר' אליעזר, עמ' 80-74.

98 ראו למשל משנה, חגיגה פ"א מ"א; סוכה פ"ג מט"ו; יומא פ"ח מ"ד; שקלים פ"א מ"ג ועוד. י"ד, גילת, בן שלוש עשרה למצוות, *מחקרי תלמוד* א (תש"ן), עמ' 54-39.

99 'כרמלית' ו'פטור אבל אסור'. או הלכות המושג 'צער בעלי חיים' בשבת. וכאמור קטן איילונית וסריס ביבמות.

חזרת תינוקת ממאנת

הדוגמא האחרונה שנביא מדגימה את שני הטיעונים העיקריים אותם אנו מציעים: תהליך היורודיפקציה והשוואת המידות. השלב הראשון הוא במחלוקת בית שמאי האם קטנה הממאנת יכולה להנשא בשנית בקטנותה. הלכה זו עברה מספר שלבים: הרי היא כיתומה בחיי אביה (משנה, יבמות פ"יג מ"ו). אביה איבד את הזכות לקדשה, וכאילו היא בוגרת, ומצד שני עדיין אין לה סטטוס משפטי לקדש עצמה. עם זאת חכמי דור יבנה מניחים שייתכן שגרושה קטנה זו תחזור לבעלה ואפילו שתמאן בו (כלומר שמרצונה תפקיע את קדושיה השניים). כך אומרים ר' יהודה בן בבא (מזקני דור יבנה[100] - תוס', יבמות פי"ג ה"ה) ור' אליעזר (משנה, שם פ""ג מ"ו). אם כן בדור יבנה החזרת הגרושה הקטנה אפשרית למרות ההסתיגות המשפטית, סתם המשנה כנראה מאוחר יותר ובו ברור שכלל אי אפשר להחזיר גרושה קטנה. מאוחר יותר קובעים האמוראים את המתבקש מעצמו מבחינה משפטית. כלומר שאסור לקטנה שהתגרשה להנשא שנית ואסור לה גם לחזור לבעלה הראשון, הרי חזרה זו היא כנישואים "קידושיה וגירושיה תורה, חזרתה אינה תורה" (ירו', שם יג ע"ד).[101] הבבלי מנסח "אין חזרתה חזרה גמורה" (שם, קט ע"א). ההלכה הקדומה מתעלמת מהשאלה ההלכתית ומכך שחזרת הקטנה אין לה מעמד משפטי, וההלכה המאוחרת אינה יכולה לקבל התעלמות כזאת מסדרי הדין.

המנהג

המונח 'מנהג' מופיע תדיר בספרות חז"ל . בספרות הפסק והמחשבה ההלכתית בימי הביניים המנהג היה מושג הלכתי מגובש. מנהג הוא נוהל שאין לו שורשים חד משמעיים בספרות ההלכה, אך הוא מחייב. המנהג עשוי להיות מקומי, והייתה לגיטימציה מסוימת למנהגים מקומיים ולהבדלים בין מנהג מקום אחד לשני. לגיטימציה זו התהוותה בעיקר כאשר נפגשו בני קהילות שונות שלכל אחת מהם הייתה מסורת אבות מקודשת, אך שונה. חוקרים קיבלו אבחנה זו כפשוטה, וכך היא מופיעה בספרי מבוא.[102] עיון בפרק ד' של מסכת פסחים ובמשניות אחרות מוביל למסקנה אחרת. כנראה שבספרות התנאים, הגדרת המנהג בעייתית הרבה יותר. המנהגים עוסקים בכל תחומי החיים; ביחסים החברתיים, אך גם במצוות. למעשה אין בין הלכה למנהג ולא כלום. כך למשל המשנה קובעת שהיה מנהג לעשות מלאכה ערב פסח עד חצות, ומנהג שונה לחדול מעבודה כבר בהנץ החמה של ערב פסח (משנה, פסחים

100 מסורת אחת מספרת שמת לפני המרד, ואחרות מונו אותו בין ההרוגים בגזירות הדת שאחרי המרד.

101 'תורה' כאן משמעו 'הלכה'. בתלמוד הבבלי הבינו מונח זה בדרך שונה, כמו 'דבר תורה' בניגוד לדבר חכמים. כך גם הביטוי 'דאורייתא' בדברי חכמים הוא כל הלכה ברורה, ובספרות האמוראים השתמשו בו כתיאור הסטורי להבחין בין הנאמר בתורה (אף אם אינו כתוב בה במפורש), ובין חידושי חכמים. ראו ב', דה פריס, המושגים דאורייתא ודרבנן בהתפתחותם, בתוך: *תולדות ההלכה התלמודית*, תל-אביב, תשכ"ב, עמ' 95-69.

102 ב', דה פריס, *תולדות ההלכה התלמודית*, תל אביב תשכ"ב עמ' 168-157; א"א אורבך, *ההלכה מקורותיה והתפתחותה*, גבעתיים 1984, עמ' 33-27 ושם ספרות רבה נוספת. ראו למשל הלכות ממרים לרמב"ם, פ"ד ה"ב, ההקדמה לתשובות המאירי. לתיאור סיסטמתי ראו למשל מ', אלון, *מבוא למשפט עברי*, ירושלים תשמ"ח, עמ' 751-713.

פ"ד מ"א ומ"ה). אך הייתה זו גם מחלוקת הלכתית בין בית שמאי ובית הלל (שם, מ"ה). אכילת גדי מקולס בליל הסדר מופיעה כמנהג אפשרי ומותר (שם, מ"ד) ובמקורות אחרים שנוי הדבר במחלוקת חכמים.[103] המשנה מתארת את מנהגם של אנשי יריחו, מנהגים שחלק מהם נדחו על ידי חכמים. אבל לפחות חלק מהם שנויים במחלוקת הלכתית לכל דבר, כגון האם לתת פיאה מירק. מסתבר שאנשי יריחו נהגו כמו ההלכה הקדומה. הבבלי אומר במפורש ש"בראשונה היו נותנין פיאה ללפת ולכרוב, ר' יוסי אומר אף לקפלוט" (בבלי, פסחים נו ע"ב). התוספתא והתלמודים מעידים על אדם ששמו בן היני או בן "נבו היין" שבנו נתן פיאה משדה לפת,[104] והאב התנגד לכך לא משום שעינו הייתה צרה בעניים, אלא משום שחשש שהעניים יאכלו ירקות החייבים במעשר. לפיכך אילץ את העניים להחזיר את הפיאה, ונתן להם ירקות מעושרים משלו. נמצאנו למדים כי ההגבלה על נתינת פאה מחלק מהירקות לא הייתה ברורה. נראה שפעם נוספת מנהגם של אנשי יריחו לא היה רק מנהג מקומי, אלא הלכה קדומה שנדחתה מההלכה הקנונית. או להיפך היה זה מנהג מקומי שחדר לבית המדרש והפך לדעת מיעוט שנדחתה מהפסיקה והנוהג המקובל.[105] נראה שגם מנהגם לאכול מתחת הנשרים הוא עמדה הלכתית לכל דבר.[106] כן שומעים אנו על מנהג עממי שהוא למעשה פסיקה במחלוקת במשנה.[107] וכן ציטטנו לעיל את המנהג העממי לפסוק כר' נחמיה במעשר מחרובים, ושוב זהו מנהג שאינו אלא פסיקת הלכה.

אם כן ההבדל בין הלכה למנהג אינו במהות המעשה אלא בהתקבלותו. המנהג נפוץ בצבור, ושורשיו הלכתיים או חברתיים או בשילוב שבין השניים. ייתכן שמנהג הוא נוהג (דתי-הלכתי, דתי-חברתי או חברתי) שצמח ברחוב ולא בבית המדרש. עם זאת בשלב שני הוא התקבל בבית המדרש והפך להלכה. בדרך זו נהלך בפרוש המשניות בפרק ד' של מסכת פסחים, ולהערכתנו כמעט אין אפשרות לפרשנות שונה. כך יש לפרש גם חלק מהמנהגים האחרים אותם מזכירים המקורות.[108]

לעומת כל זאת התלמודים כבר הבינו שמנהג אינו הלכה, ועל כן התחבטו כיצד זה מופיע מנהג כאילו היה כהלכה רגילה. ההבחנות המאוחרות אילצו את התלמודים, ואת פרשני התלמוד, להידחק ולפרש את המשניות שלא כפשוטן. כפי שאמרנו לעיל אנו רואים במנהג את שורשיה של התורה שבעל פה. מנהגים נוצרו והפכו לתקדימים, ובשלב שני נידונו בבית המדרש והפכו לכללים הלכתיים.

---

103 ספראי ש' וז', *הגדה של פסח, הגדת חז"ל*, ירושלים תשנ"ח, עמ' 27-30.

104 תוס', פסחים פ"ג ה"כ; בבלי, פסחים נו ע"ב; ירו', שם פ"ד ה"ט, לא ע"ב.

105 הבבלי מדגיש שאנשי יריחו הסכימו עם הכלל שכל פרי ש"מכניסו לקיום" (נשמר במחסן) חייב במעשרות, וחלקו עם חכמים בשאלה אילו ירקות נכנסים לקיום. אם כן המחלוקת היא פנים הלכתית לכל דבר.

106 ובני יריחו נהגו כבית שמאי במשנה, ביצה פ"א מ"א. הצעה זו היא אחת האפשרויות לפירוש המשנה, ובתלמודים גם הצעות אחרות.

107 בבלי, ערובין סב ע"ב, המחלוקת היא במשנת עירובין פ"ו מ"א.

108 כגון המנהג לברך או שלא לברך על אמירת הלל ראו משנה, סוכה פ"ג מי"א; חילוף מנהגים נוסף שהוא מחלוקת הלכתית מהווה השאלה האם אבל מותר ברחיצה ראו משנה, ברכות פ"ב מ"ה; מעשרות פ"א מ"ד (ירו', שם מט ע"א).

כאמור אנו מניחים שהדיון בפרטים קדם לניסוח הכללים. הבאנו לכך מספר ראיות, אבל עדיין יש מקום לטעון לטעון שניסוח הכלל קדם, והפרטים נוספו רק מאוחר יותר. הטיעון המרכזי מבוסס לא על דוגמא זו או אחרת, אלא על ההגיון הפנימי, שהרי אם הכלל מוצק וברור לשם מה יש צורך בבירור הפרטים, ומדוע בדיון על הפרטים אין אזכור לכלל. ואכן בחלק מהמקרים יש בספרות הפניה אל הכלל. עוד טוענים אנו שספרות קומראן מוכיחה שבזמן עריכת הספרות הכתתית הוכרו רק הכללים הפשוטים ואין בה ניסוח של כללים מורכבים.

אנו טוענים אפוא שהכללים מאוחרים לפרטים, עם כל זאת איננו טוענים שכל הדיון הקזואיסטי קדום. בימי תנאים מאוחרים רווחה התפישה שיש ללמוד וללמד בצורה הקזואיסטית, אף כאשר הכללים כבר היו קיימים. קשה להכריע האם היה זה השיקול ה'חינוכי' - 'פדגוגי' שגרם להעדפת לימוד הפרטים, או שמא הייתה זו השמרנות שבלימוד. כך או כך היו חכמים שהטיפו ללמוד וללמד בשיטת המקרה הפרטי.

ברוב המקרים הכלל שבספרות חז"ל אינו סיכום מלא, ואינו יוצר את כל הפרטים, בזה דומה הכלל המשפטי לכלל דקדוקי. כלומר סיכום של רוב המקרים שאינו מתיימר לכלול את כולם, אלא את רובם. לדוגמה, הכללים של משנת מגילה "אין בין יום טוב לשבת אלא אוכל נפש בלבד", כלל שיש לו יוצאים מן הכלל ותוספות.[109] דוגמה מובהקת לכללים מסוג זה הוא הכלל שנשים "פטורות ממצוות עשה שהזמן גרמן", שכבר הזכרנו, ויש בו יוצאים רבים מן הכלל.[110] הוא הדין בכלל שהלכה כבית הלל.[111] לדעתנו, אבחנה זו נכונה לפחות על חלק גדול מהכללים בספרות התנאים.

האמוראים עצמם מגדירים את הכללים בצורה מעט רופפת. בשמו של ר' יונה נמסר "לית כללוי דרבי כללין",[112] כלומר שהכללים אינם מלאים ואי אפשר להסיק מהם מסקנות הלכתיות. כמעט לכל כלל שמצינו, יש גם יוצאים מן הכלל.[113] ברור אפוא שנקודת המוצא של החשיבה התנאית לא הייתה ניסוח הכלל, אלא רשימת המקרים שנידונו לגופם.

אנו סבורים אפוא שהפרטים (התקדימים) קדמו לכללים. עם זאת גם לאחר שהכללים נקבעו המשיכו להיווצר תקדימים נוספים והכלל הלך והשתכלל. הפרטים והכללים הם מעין ספירה של הפרטים המעצבים את הכלל, הכלל מעצב את הפרטים הבאים, אך הפרטים השונים 'דוחפים' לשיפור הכלל או אפילו לשינויו.

---

109 משנה, מגילה פ"א מ"ה.

110 ראו ש', ספראי, מחויבותן של נשים במצוות במשנתם של תנאים, שטיינפלד, צ"א (עורך), *בר-אילן* כה-כו (תשנ"ה), עמ' 227-237.

111 ש', ספראי, הלכה כבית הלל, *בימי הבית ובימי המשנה*, א (תשנ"ד), עמ' 382-405.

112 ירו', תרומות פ"א ה"ב, מ ע"ג; חגיגה פ"א ה"א, עה ע"ד; יבמות פ"ט ה"ג, י ע"א.

113 דוגמא מובהקת הם הכללים במגילה פ"א מ"ה-מי"א.

בספרות חז"ל עצמה מציגים את הכללים לא כיוצרי ההלכה אלא כדרך לסיכומה. "היה רבי מאיר[114] אומר לעולם הוי כונס דברי תורה כללים שאם אתה כונסם פרטים מייגעים אותך ואי אתה יודע מה לעשות, משל לאדם שהלך לקיסרי וצריך מאה זוז או מאתים זוז הוצאה. אם נוטלם פרט מייגעים אותו ואינו יודע מה לעשות, אבל מצרפם ועושה אותם סלעים ופורט ומוציא בכל מקום שירצה " (ספרי דברים שו, עמ' 833; מדרש תנאים לדברים לב ב, עמ' 581; ילקוט שמעוני לדברים תקמב, עמ' 816). אם כן הלימוד הנכון הוא של פרטים, אך מטעמים פדגוגיים יש ללמד כללים כדי שההלכה תיקלט ותובן.

ייתכן שבמדרש ניתן להבחין בשתי גישות ביחס אל הכללים והפרטים. "ר' ישמעאל אומר כללות נאמרו בסיני ופרטות באהל מועד, ורבי עקיבא אומר: כללות ופרטות נאמרו בסיני, ונשנו באהל מועד, ונשתלשו בערבות מואב" (בבלי חגיגה ו ע"א-ע"ב; סוטה לז ע"ב). אם כן הכללים והפרטים הם דבר ה', אבל ר' ישמעאל סובר שהכללים קודמים לפרטים ור' עקיבא חושב שנוצרו ונתנו באחת. במדרשים אחרים מודגש שמשה למד כללים בלבד: "וכי כל התורה למד משה כתיב בתורה (איוב יא) ארוכה מארץ מדה ורחבה מני ים ולארבעים יום למדה משה אלא כללים למדהו הקב"ה למשה, הוי ככלותו לדבר אתו (תנחומא כי תשא טז; שמות רבה מא ו). ברם דומה שאין כאן דיון על היחס בין הכלל פרט במובן בו אנו עוסקים, אלא המדרש עוסק בשאלה אחרת. המדרש מנסה להסביר כיצד יש מקום ליצירה עצמית למרות, מתן כל התורה בהר סיני, ולאחר נתינתה. אם התורה ניתנה כללים כללים, הרי שיש מקום רב לפרשן לפרש ולהסביר שאלה זו של היחס בין שלשול המסורת ליצירה העצמית העסיקה את חכמים, אך אינה במסגרת דיון זה.

מכל מקום מסורת חז"ל מייחסת לר' עקיבא את שיטת הלימוד של גיבוש הכללים: "למה רבי עקיבא דומה? לפועל שנטל קופתו ויצא לחוץ. מצא חטים מניח בה, מצא שעורים מניח בה, כוסמין מניח בה, עדשים מניח בה. כיון שנכנס לביתו מברר חטים בפני עצמן, שעורים בפני עצמן, פולין בפני עצמן, עדשים בפני עצמן. כך עשה ר' עקיבא ועשה כל התורה טבעות טבעות" (אבות דרבי נתן נו"א, יח, לד ע"א). אבל ר' עקיבא חוצב בסלע ועוקר הרים פרט אחרי פרט, וכן לומד שלוש מאות הלכות מכל קוץ של תורה. אם כן, הלימוד הוא פרטים פרטים, ורק לצורך ארגון החומר מעצבים כללים. ואכן חלק גדול מהכללים שבספרות חז"ל מיוחסים לר' עקיבא. כפי שראינו ר' עקיבא הוא שמהלל את מי שהשווה מידותיו. ושוב הכללים מצטיירים כשלב מאוחר יחסית בגיבוש תורה שבעל פה, ניסוח שחכמים לא ראו אותו כיצירה משפטית מחייבת, אלא כדרך לאיסוף וסידור בלבד.

מסקנות

לעיצוב ההלכה מספר שלבים כרונולוגיים סכמתיים:

א. קביעת נוהג ציבורי העוסק במקרים ספציפיים מעין תקדימים הלכתיים.

114 בחלק מעדי הנוסח ר' נחמיה.

ב. מקרים חדשים המתעוררים נקבעים בהתאם לתקדים המקומי תוך התחשבות מסוימת בתקדימי העבר, אך גם תוך סתירות אפשריות.

ג. דיון בבית המדרש על קביעת הכלל.

ד. שיפור הכלל, וניסוחו המשפטי.

ה. עיצוב השפה ההלכתית (קביעת התנאים שאליהם ההלכה צריכה להתייחס ובהם היא תלויה)

ו. תהליך עיצוב משפטי, תוך חדירה לפרטים נוספים ופרטי פרטים, וקביעתה של המערכת המשפטית (תהליך יורודיפיקציה של ההלכה).

ההלכה של קומראן מצויה אי שם בין שלב ג לשלב ד׳. והיא מוכיחה כי אכן שלבים אלו קדמו לשלבים המפותחים יותר מבחינה ספרותית.

השלבים הראשונים (א-ב) התחוללו מאז שניתנה התורה לעם ישראל. איננו יודעים מה הייתה עוצמת היצירה של תורה שבעל פה, כשם שאיננו יודעים מה הייתה עוצמת שמירת המצוות בימי התנ״ך. מכל מקום יש להניח שרק בציבור שומר מצוות מתגבשים נוהגים של ׳תורה שבעל פה׳. כאמור מסורת חז״ל רואה במוסד הכנסת הגדולה את ראשיתו של התהליך. הכנסת הגדולה הייתה מועצה של המקדש, ששותפו בה גם מי שאינם כוהנים, או על כל פנים אינם מראשי המקדש. עצם שיתופם מצביע על מגמה של התפשטות שמירת המצוות מחוץ למקדש ומעבר לשכבת הכוהנים (פקידי המקדש). בכנסת הגדולה נקבעו כללי היסוד ובעיקר עוצבה האסטרטגיה הדתית של שמירת מצוות נורמטיבית, ושל התפשטות לימוד התורה כערך מכונן. כאמור עצם שותפותו של הציבור במועצה כבר מבטא את התפישה שתלמוד תורה הוא מצווה החלה על כולם, והוא נחלת הכלל.

כבר בשלבי הבראשית, ולא יאוחר מימיהם של הזוגות החל תהליך היורודיפקציה, זהו תהליך מתמשך שמבחינה מסוימת טרם הסתיים עד היום. ההלכה של המשנה יותר משפטית מזו שלפניה, והתלמודים עמלו לעצב ולגבש עוד יותר את ההלכה כמשפט מסודר. כל התקדימים שאינם מתיישבים עם המערכת ההלכתית-משפטית הותאמו למערכת המשפטית, ורק לעיתים רחוקות נותרו תקדימים שלא הוכלו לתוך המערכת, או שספרות ההלכה שימרה את ההלכה הקדומה, ובזכותה יכולים אנו לעקוב אחר שלבי ההתפתחות ולאתר את אותה מגמה של יורודיפיקציה.

CPSIA information can be obtained at www.ICGtesting.com
Printed in the USA
BVOW03*0621071013

332944BV00005B/78/P